# UCLA Football Encyclopedia

SPENCER STUEVE

FOREWORD BY JOHNATHAN FRANKLIN

SPORTS PUBLISHING

Sports Publishing books may be purchased in bulk at special discounts for sales promotion, corporate gifts, fund-raising, or educational purposes. Special editions can also be created to specifications. For details, contact the Special Sales Department, Sports Publishing, 307 West 36th Street, 11th Floor, New York, NY 10018 or sportspubbooks@skyhorsepublishing.com.

Sports Publishing® is a registered trademark of Skyhorse Publishing, Inc.®, a Delaware corporation.

Visit our website at www.sportspubbooks.com.

10 9 8 7 6 5 4 3 2 1

Library of Congress Cataloging-in-Publication Data is available on file.

Cover design by Tom Lau
Cover photo credit Associated Press

ISBN: 978-1-68358-254-0
Ebook ISBN: 978-1-68358-255-7

Printed in Canada

This book is dedicated to the "Lot H Legends."

# Contents

# Foreword

As I reflect on my journey in life, it probably would not be as fascinating without taking a route that lasted four and a half years at the greatest university in the world, the University of California Los Angeles. I remember when I sat in a room with a group of then-strangers and now best friends, listening to Coach Karl Dorrell and DeWayne Walker talk about the philosophy, history, and vision for Bruins football. That was a special day during my sophomore year at Dorsey High School. I remember after freshman orientation, Rahim Moore turned, looked at me, and called me by my former nickname, "Hey Jetski, you sure you want to do this? If you do, I will. Let's come here and turn this place out and take it to the top." I looked at Rahim with a smile and said, "Hell yeah, let's be remembered for something." On that day, Rahim Moore, Datone Jones, Tony Dye, Damien Holmes, and I all committed to turning UCLA football into the program we knew it could be. There was something special about the group I bonded with that weekend. It was a group that didn't just want to play, we wanted to win. It was a decision that ultimately took me on an unexpected journey at UCLA, but also helped me launch a legacy that will never be forgotten.

After leaving an inner-city community of predominantly African Americans and Hispanics, notorious for its gang violence, drug related issues, and teen pregnancy, it would be a challenging transition for me attending UCLA as a freshman. It was the first time I would ever have an intellectual conversation with someone outside of the African American or Hispanic race. At first it was intimidating, uncomfortable, and discouraging. Through the social difficulties, demanding classroom responsibilities, and football, it was a tough freshman year. Football should've been my distraction from the off-field troubles, but after entering as a safety and moving to running back midsummer, football initially just brought another world of troubles.

Khalil Bell, Chane Moline, Christian Ramirez, Derrick Coleman, Raymond Carter, Aundre Dean, Milton Knox, Johnathan Franklin, and Craig Shepard—I'm not just naming running backs. I'm listing the names in order of the depth chart. One rep, no reps, one rep, no reps. That's exactly how my freshman summer camp went until I was told the disappointing news that I would be redshirting. I spent the majority of my freshman year wanting to transfer, and I made choices that put me in unfortunate positions socially and academically. However, the more I talked to my peers, the more I realized no one who redshirted was happy about it, so I figured that it was just the life of a freshman. On top of that, the whole coaching staff that recruited me was gone by the time we all got to campus (I'll save that piece for another day). Freshman year was challenging, but it was the year that actually lit the fire that kept me going throughout my years at UCLA, and in that fire was humility, purpose, and inspiration. This fire became an inferno the summer after my redshirt year.

Few people probably remember, but entering UCLA I wore number 8 (now retired by UCLA). It was my favorite number and the one I had worn all throughout high school. Entering my sophomore season, I received a call from a member of our UCLA coaching staff about a week before camp started. I believed the coach was calling just to check in. I was wrong. I answered the phone, feeling on top of the world, and what he said was, "Hey Jet, how's summer going? We have a big recruit coming to UCLA named Morrell Pressley and he wants to wear number 8, so what we have available for you to wear is 22, 23, 25, and 28. What number do you want to wear?" In my mind, this was definitely the moment that the UCLA coaching staff was telling me it was all over and I would never play at UCLA. I hesitated at first but finally said, "I'll take 23." After working hard all summer, the call from a coach saying I had to give my number to a freshman was a shot to my pride. I worked to just put it aside and focus on becoming a better player and teammate.

Entering camp, it was intimidating in the beginning. After being recruited as a safety and moving to running back, I was competing for a starting job with Ramirez, Coleman, Carter, Moline, Knox, Dean, and Shepard. The majority of these guys were the top running back recruits in the country and state coming out of high school. I was just a three-star-rated athlete who loved to play football. I sat there the year after redshirting and being seventh on the depth chart, and the first few weeks I was still only getting one to two reps per day. I was discouraged, but it all changed when I received a call from Russell Ellis, my mentor, after the second week of practice. He gave me words of encouragement, and I hung up the phone with the belief that I belonged on that practice field. I started to have positive self-talk. Before I knew it, I went from sixth to fifth to fourth, to the starter by the time the 2009 football season opened against San Diego State. It was a fun, humbling, and worthwhile journey.

My UCLA experience was nothing if not memorable: from scoring on my first-ever carry at UCLA, to losing my starting job to Derrick Coleman, then winning it back; being benched a few games, struggling with fumbling, then overcoming fumbling my senior year; from finding Christ to breaking and still holding four UCLA records and becoming a consistent captain; from almost being moved back to safety, to praying with teammates on the rooftop of Ackerman every day, sacrificing party nights and social events senior year to have the success I had that season; casual conversations on Bruin Walk with students, heading to Orlando for the college awards ceremony, holding an all-team Bible study; from losing the respect of teammates, to gaining it back; the bonfires before playing USC, having four different offensive coordinators, three different head coaches, four different starting quarterbacks; graduating with honors, having the whole dining hall one night chant my name; from beating USC, to watching Melvin Emesibe score his first touchdown; almost entering the draft my junior year, and having an internship with the mayor and with city hall—these are just a few of the things that made up this UCLA journey.

The most memorable moment for me through it all, though, would have to be meeting a janitor who changed my life and led me to Christ, becoming the all-time leading rusher in UCLA history, and learning to accept and converse with everyone, regardless of their nationality, economic background, religious affiliation, or culture. To have graduated, been drafted, and played for the Green Bay Packers, been injured, retired as a player, and worked within the organization, gone through depression, overcome it, moved on to Notre Dame, and now to be blessed with the opportunity to work for the Los Angeles Rams has been a journey that has taught me so much. I have learned how to take my experiences and make the best of them. I have a purpose. I have patience, faith, love, and joy. I would not be where I am now without the experiences and opportunities that I received at UCLA. It is truly a one-of-a-kind university, and the lessons that I learned there reach far beyond the football field. I will never forget my time in the blue and gold. I will never forget the roar of the crowd every time I ran through the Rose Bowl tunnel. I am confident that one day UCLA will reach the pinnacle of the college football world, and when it does, wherever I am, I'll be cheering.

Johnathan Franklin
"The Mayor"
UCLA running back 2008–2012

# CHAPTER 1
# Fred Cozens (1919)

Before there was Red Sanders, before there was Terry Donahue, and before there was Jim Mora, there was Fred Cozens. Before John Wooden, before Larry Brown, and before Jim Harrick, there was Fred Cozens. Before John Savage, there was Fred Cozens. Before he went on to a long, distinguished career as UCLA's Athletic Director, Fred Cozens was the first football, basketball, and baseball coach in UCLA history.

Cozens was a first-generation American, born in Portland, Oregon, to Frederick and Carrie Cozens on November 19, 1890. Fred was an intellectual who enjoyed studying and learning about physics, history, and biology. He received a Bachelor's degree from the University of California Berkeley, though records are not confirmed regarding the year (1915 or 1916). In 1918, he received a Master's degree from Cal, and in 1928, he was awarded a PhD from the University of Oregon.

After coaching freshman baseball at Cal his junior and senior seasons, Cozens moved south to a new school, a beautiful but as yet incomplete university whose campus location and school name would soon change. When Cozens left Cal, he landed at the University of California Southern Branch (soon to be renamed the University of California Los Angeles). Along with coaching football, basketball, and baseball, Cozens followed his first love—academics. Fred was an associate of Physical Education from 1919 to 1942. In the United States census of 1920, and again in 1930, Fred listed his occupation as an educator. Fred married Helen Kerron in 1916 and had two boys, Frederick Jr. and James.

Fred Cozens, 1919 (Southern Campus Collection)

Cozens would continue to educate in the classroom, but just as he did with the Cal freshman baseball team, he would educate on the field, as well. The popularity of basketball and football in 1919 was growing. In basketball, backboards were implemented in 1909 and open nylon nets were approved in 1912. The game was still in infancy, ever evolving. Fred Cozens was a successful basketball coach, though he was certainly not a strategic expert. In his two years as the Southern Branch basketball coach, Cozens compiled a 20–4 record and won the Southern California Intercollegiate Athletic Conference in 1921. Cozens also coached baseball—his favorite sport—at UCLA for five years and improved his record every year, twice winning the conference.

Yet despite Cozens's own interests in basketball and baseball, it was college football that took center stage on fall Saturdays. Yale and Princeton dominated the late 19th century, but Knute Rockne and the Notre Dame Fighting Irish, along with Fielding Yost at Michigan and Charley Daly at West Point, ushered in a new era. Fred Cozens ushered in a new era, as well, though what initially came out of it was far from the glamour of a program like Notre Dame. He only coached football at SBUC for one year, but he sent SBUC and their fans, both present and future, down a path of highs and lows, starting in the fall of 1919.

## 1919

The University of California Southern Branch officially opened September 15, 1919, and 18 days later the history of UCLA football began. The year 1919 has been documented as an up-and-down year for the United States. With World War I combat ending in November of 1918, and the Treaty of Versailles being signed in June of 1919, the world had turned the page on the most devastating war in history to that point. There were over thirty-seven million casualties in World War I, and most Americans were happy to see it come to an end. They were ready to move on and help build lives for themselves back home. Things were changing at home, however. Beloved former President Theodore Roosevelt died on January 6. The country mourned and longed for the days of Teddy in the White House. Woodrow Wilson was now president, and one of the lasting memories of his administration was the passing of the 18th amendment , which started the period of prohibition in the United States.

On campus, football was an afterthought, and the building of a winning program was seen as a very long-term goal that would not be attainable in the near future. Despite Fred Cozens's accomplishments as a teacher and baseball coach at Cal, he was not well versed in the Xs and Os of American football. In the Cubs' (nickname before the Bruins) first year they competed as an independent school, without a conference. There were only 12 players on the roster. They played eight games against high schools, JCs, and other freshman teams in the area. Home games were at Moore Field on Vermont Avenue, and the attendance for their first game was a mere 150.

On October 3, 1919, the University of California Southern Branch Cubs took the field for the first time. Despite Coach Cozens putting his team through ardent football practices and scrimmages in preparation for what he considered a grueling schedule, Manual Arts High School proved to be much too difficult of a challenge. Coach Cozens promised the SBUC students an exciting game and an excellent display of the art of football. Unfortunately, he was on the wrong side of the display. Opening kickoff was at 3:30 PST, and despite cancelling practice all week prior to the game because of rain, Coach Cozens felt his team was prepared and that the boxing workouts that he put his team through the week of the game would help them strike their opponent at

1919 Southern Branch (UCLA) team photo (Southern Campus Collection)

the line of scrimmage. Yet when the clock struck 3:30 and the ball was in the air, Cozens and his band of 12 were simply overmatched. The Manual Arts team, which was defending its Southern California High School Championship, whipped the Cubs by a final score of 74–0.

Cozens believed the problem with his team was not strategy, but rather lack of practice and conditioning. Despite having put his team through what he believed were difficult practices, Cozens felt he had to increase the players' workload. With only 12 players on the roster, he knew his team had to be more physically fit than any opponent on his schedule. With the next game three weeks away, Cozens vowed to get his players in shape. Despite the opening game's drubbing, Cozens knew his boys had fight in them and promised to take it out on Occidental College 21 days later. Meanwhile, two more games were added to the schedule. One week after losing handily to Manual Arts High School, the Cubs took the field again.

On October 10, the day after the final game of the infamous 1919 World Series, in which the White Sox threw the World Series vs. the Cincinnati Reds and eventually eight men were banned for life from baseball in what became known as the "Black Sox Scandal," Coach Cozens and the Cubs took the field for the second time. While Cozens and the Cubs fared better in their second game, against Hollywood High School, they lost 19–6, and the wait for the first win in school history would continue. The team did, however, score the first touchdown in SBUC history when Wayne Banning, a team captain, returned an interception 65 yards.

As the season continued, Coach Cozens grew more frustrated, but he remained outwardly optimistic. As an educator, Cozens found great joy in teaching others. This applied on the field, as well. The players were keenly aware of their place in history, and Cozens continually was forced to play multiple roles, not only teaching them the sport of football, which he himself didn't know very well, but also serving as a constant calming presence to the players.

After losing to Bakersfield College, the 0–3 Cubs had their first home game on October 24 and came away with their first victory. Cozens's boys beat the Occidental freshmen, 7–2, for the first win in school history, and followed that up with a win the following week, 7–0, vs. Los Angeles JC. Though the Cubs would go on to lose their final three games of the 1919 season and finish just 2–6, Fred Cozens and the 12-man roster would go down in UCLA history.

After the 1919 season, Cozens stepped down from his role as the football coach to focus his attention on the sports he knew best, basketball and baseball. Harry Trotter would be the next man to carry the torch for UCLA football.

The College Football Researchers Association named Harvard University the 1919 National Champions.

UCLA's first captain, Wayne Banning, 1919 (Southern Campus Collection)

# CHAPTER 2
# Harry Trotter (1920–1922)

Harry Elbert Trotter, nicknamed "Cap" when he was named team captain of his high school track team, was not a football man. He was a teacher. He was a track and field coach, the first ever in UCLA history, and following Cozens's resignation as the head football coach, Cap took the position in 1920. Despite the little success Cozens had on the field (the first two wins in school history), Cap was not able to build any momentum. He finished 2–13–1 in his UCLA football coaching career before deciding he had enough.

Cap was born in rural Kansas on October 18, 1890. Like most Kansas boys of the 19th century, Cap's life centered around his work on the farm. By the time he reached the University of California Southern Branch in 1919, he was ready to leave the farm behind. With the gold rush in the rear view mirror and the oil, agriculture, and entertainment industries in California growing rapidly, migration west jump-started once again.

At the turn of the century, California was booming and Cap was along for the ride. When he became the track and field coach in 1919, he had high hopes. Growing up, nothing had excited Cap more than the Summer Olympics, and with the 1916 Summer Olympics being cancelled due to World War I, Cap felt that 1920 would be better than ever. The track and field job at UCLA was a position that piqued his interest, despite its being a low profile, start-up school with only 250 students, not only because he was able to teach his passion, but because he dreamed of one day coaching an Olympian. Cap's dreams came true. He coached three Olympians, including the pride of his coaching career, Jimmy LuValle, to Olympic medals. Cap Trotter also coached Jackie Robinson to the 1940 NCAA broad jump championship. In 1946, after 27 years as the UCLA track and field coach, Cap Trotter retired and was replaced by a former UCLA track athlete, Ducky Drake, who competed under Coach Trotter and would eventually be inducted into the inaugural UCLA Athletics Hall of Fame class.

Harry Trotter, 1920 (Southern Campus Collection)

Cap Trotter's legacy was never that of a football coach. He did, however, pass the baton and was responsible for an important period in the growth of UCLA football, as 1920 marked the first year in which SBUC was a part

Old Southern Branch campus on Vermont Avenue (Southern Campus Collection)

of the Southern California Intercollegiate Athletic Conference. Nevertheless, on the field, the 1920 season appeared to be arguably the worst in UCLA history, setting a losing precedent matched only by the 1921 season.

## 1920

In 1920, SBUC was still dealing with a major personnel problem. Along with coaches who knew little about the intricacies of football strategy, the roster itself was very limited. The school only had freshman and sophomore classes. While the Southern California Intercollegiate Athletic Conference made a ruling that freshmen would be allowed to play on the varsity squad for conference games, SBUC did not play any, and thus the freshmen played on the freshman team and the varsity team was made up of only sophomores.

Despite the disadvantages, SBUC took the field for the first game of their second season on October 2, 1920, vs. Pomona College, the first conference game in school history. Pomona College, which went on to win the conference championship and finish the 1920 season undefeated, jumped out of the gate early and led the Cubs, 41–0, at halftime. While the score may suggest a thorough dismantling, the *Cub Californian* newspaper noted that SBUC had actually performed well. As a perennial powerhouse, Pomona College was expected to beat the Cubs convincingly, and while they did that in the first half, the second half told a different story. The Cubs played the Pomona College Sagehens to a second-half draw, so despite the 41–0 final score, there was reason for optimism.

The *Cub Californian* wrote: "At first comparison of the teams, it seemed the Cubs were far out-classed as to weight and experience. But before the game had progressed very far, the most inexperienced could see that the predictions of the dopesters were going astray and instead of walking on the Blue and Gold, as had been predicted, Pomona found they had a real team to reckon with."

The following week, the Cubs played their first home game of the year against Occidental College. While the offense still struggled and failed once again to put any points on the board, the defense improved and held Occidental, which would finish the season 3–2, to 21 points. The Cubs fell again and would have to wait three more weeks for their next chance to get in the win column.

On October 30, 1920, the SBUC Cubs played their third game of the year, against the University of Redlands. This game proved to be the best outing of the year for Cap Trotter's young squad. As had been the case in the previous outings against Pomona and Occidental Colleges, the Cubs started slowly and fell behind early. At the end of the first quarter, Redlands led, 7–0. The Cubs offense was able to move the ball well for the first time all season but failed to turn any of the team's early drives into points. Just before the half, SBUC had a punt blocked, and Redlands was able to punch in a touchdown from the 1-yard line to lead, 14–0. The third quarter saw much of the same. Redlands scored 14 points, and as the fourth quarter, started, it appeared the Cubs were headed for another disappointing loss. However, in the remaining quarter Cap Trotter was able to rally the troops. The Cubs scored 21 unanswered points on three touchdown receptions by Eddie Rossell. The Cubs would go on to lose the game, 28–21, but optimism abounded in the locker room. They had scored their first points of the year, and their defense was improving. Yet two weeks after the loss to the University of Redlands, SBUC was back at home for a matchup against Cal Tech, and the Cubs would go on to lose, 32–0, their third shutout in four games. Any momentum they thought they had after a stellar fourth quarter performance against Redlands was gone.

Just five days later, the Cubs would take the field

1920 team picture (Southern Campus Collection)

again, this time against Whittier College. November 18, 1920, has gone down as one of the most painful days in UCLA/SBUC football history. Tied for second in the Southern California Intercollegiate Athletic Conference, Whittier served the Cubs what remains the worst loss in school history, 103–0. The Bruins finished the 1920 season with a record of 0–5.

The College Football Researchers Association named the University of California Berkeley the 1920 National Champions.

## 1921

In 1921, hope sprang eternal. The Cubs were in their third year. They now had a larger pool of players to draw from, as the school had a junior class for the first time. Also for the first time, they had a head coach returning. Harry "Cap" Trotter looked to rebound from his first-year failures and turn the lessons learned in 1920 into success in 1921.

Part of the optimism entering the 1921 season was due to the schedule. On October 8, the Cubs would play their first game of the season against the University of Redlands, a home game on Moore Field, and would attempt to finish what they had started the previous season. In 1920, the Southern Branch compiled an 0–5 record, but their closest game of the year came against the University of Redlands. Despite losing the game, 28–21, the Cubs thoroughly outplayed their opponent in the second half and almost completed a historic comeback. SBUC scored 21 unanswered points in the fourth quarter but fell just short. In 1921, it was time for revenge.

Prior to the start of the 1921 season, the hope was that members of the SBUC football program would see a change in fortune, just as there was a change in the executive office of the United States with the inauguration of Warren G. Harding as the 29th president of the United States that year.

When toe hit ball and the opening kickoff was in the sky at Moore Field, it was no longer time to dream, but time to play. As things turned out, the University of Redlands would win the football game that day, 35–7. It was a disappointing start to the season for Cap Trotter and the Cubs, who believed 1921 would be the season they finally hit their stride. One week later, SBUC lost, 55–7, to Pomona College. They followed that up with a 35–0 loss to Occidental College two weeks later, and a 62–0 loss to Whittier College the following week. The last game of the year was on October 24, 1921, against the California Institute of Technology. Caltech's coach, Fox Stanton, the former star halfback at Drexel University, led the Beavers to a 27–0 victory. The Cubs had only scored 14 points all season and finished their second straight winless campaign. Cap Trotter was 0–10 over his two-year stretch as Cubs coach.

The College Football Researchers Association named the University of California Berkeley National Champions for the second consecutive year.

## 1922

Coming off back-to-back winless seasons, the Cubs weren't quite as optimistic in 1922 as they had been in the fall of 1921. Cap Trotter was 0–10. They had yet to win a conference game since joining the Southern California Intercollegiate Athletic Conference two years earlier. The Southern Branch Cubs had just finished what nearly a century later would still be seen as the two worst seasons in school history. Maybe the lowered expectations in 1922 would help.

On October 7, 1922, the Southern Branch Cubs defeated San Diego State College (later renamed San Diego State University). While little is remembered about the game other than small excerpts in school newspapers, the Southern Branch Cubs finally appeared to be a bit on the lucky side. Over their first three years, the Cubs played a very difficult schedule, against several teams in the Southern California Intercollegiate Athletic Conference who were well-established, West Coast powerhouses. San Diego State, on the other hand, was also a new school. When San Diego Normal School and San Diego Junior College merged in 1921, a new school was created, and a football program was born. In just its second year, Charles E. Peterson's San Diego State College could not handle the Cubs and were defeated, 24–6. Despite its transition to a four-year school, San Diego State was allowed to compete in the Southern California Junior College Conference, which it won in 1922. The Cubs had conference champion aspirations, as well.

The second game of the year was against the University of Redlands on October 14 at Moore Field. The previous two meetings between Redlands and the Southern Branch had been frustrating for the Cubs, but in 1922 the Cubs turned the table, defeating Redlands, 34–9, and boosting their season record to 2–0.

With renewed optimism, Coach Trotter and the Southern Branch Cubs would take the field four more times in 1922. The season was already a success with two wins in two games, which is two more than in the previous two years combined. On October 21, the Cubs took on Occidental College, and while they wound up losing the game, 14–7, the improvement was noticeable. With now a full squad from freshmen through seniors, the Cubs were finally on an even playing field (the previous two years, Occidental had outscored the Cubs, 56–0). Despite the defeat, the team walked away confident.

The only problem was that Whittier College was waiting in the wings, for a matchup on November 4. The Southern Branch Cubs would take the short train ride (some teams were travelling by bus, but not yet the Southern Branch) to Whittier with a possible conference championship on the line. The end result? A 6–6 tie. Despite not coming away victorious, the Cubs could consider the result a dramatic turnaround from the previous two years—which had seen Whittier romps of 103–0 and 62–0!

Nevertheless, the Cubs would lose the following two games, and the long wait for conference superiority would continue. The Southern Branch lost to Pomona College, 20–6, on November 18 and in an odd scheduling quirk lost to Caltech, 7–6, just three days later. The Southern Branch finished the season 2–3–1.

The College Football Researchers Association named Princeton University the 1922 National Champions.

Timmy Dodges running the ball against the Whittier Poets in 1922 (Southern Campus Collection)

# CHAPTER 3
# James J. Cline (1923–1924)

In 1923, the University of California Southern Branch football program underwent a change in management. The results under Coach Harry "Cap" Trotter were unquestionably disappointing in 1920 and 1921. By 1922, however, Southern Branch football appeared to be on the rise. They won two games in 1922, after back-to-back winless seasons. By 1923, Coach Trotter was out and Coach James J. Cline was the new man in charge.

Coach Cline, who was originally from Iowa, was a disciple of legendary University of California Berkeley coach Andy Smith. After successive leaders who didn't know the finer details of football strategy in Fred Cozens and Cap Trotter, Cline was seen as someone who could reverse that lack of strategic knowledge and win by outsmarting the opponent, much like his mentor at Berkeley had often done. The downside of hiring the football whiz was his youth and inexperience. Prior to accepting the head coaching job at Southern Branch, Cline had never coached before at any level. He was just twenty-four years old, but as a recent graduate of powerhouse Berkeley, he was used to winning. At the Southern Branch, he would have to be much more patient. While Coach Cline and his young, energetic staff worked the finer points of the game at the varsity level, Coach Cap Trotter was assigned to coach the freshman team, where his primary goal was to toughen up the players and teach them the value of teamwork.

[Insert photo: James Cline, 1923 (Southern Campus Collection)]

Before Coach Cline even got started in his inaugural season, he made a major change. With a growing student body who wanted to distance themselves from their University of California brethren to the north, the decision was made to change the nickname from "Cubs" to something else. Jimmie Cline decided to choose the more ferocious name of "Grizzlies." For the entirety of the 1923 season, the Southern Branch would still go by the name Cubs, but by 1924, the change was made official. How that change would impact the team's play had yet to be determined.

## 1923

Prior to the start of the 1923 football season, new head coach Jimmie Cline realized his team was lacking in terms of usable talent. The previous year, the Southern Branch had seen improvement, but many of the players from the 1922 squad had left the program. Coach Cline called for a total makeover and encouraged many young men, with or without prior playing experience, to try out for the 1923 team.

That year also marked the first for which Coach Cline decided to name team captains, personally choosing senior tackle Walter Wescott as the first. Guard Cece Hollingsworth, elected by the team, would also serve as captain. Other team leaders in 1923 included star defensive back/halfback Loran Peak, halfback Cap Haralson, left end George Bishop, quarterbacks Maury Parker and Tillie Parisi, and end Horace Bresee.

As of October 13, the season was officially underway with a game against San Diego State College. For the second year in a row, the Cubs came away victorious. San Diego State was a large team, but the Cubs had superior speed and athleticism. Cap Haralson would score both of the game's touchdowns, and the Cubs won, 12–0.

Loran Peak 1923 (Southern Campus Collection)

The following week, the Cubs took on Loyola College. While for the second week in a row the Cubs failed to show a strong offense, they also, once again, showed a dominant defense. Through two weeks, it seemed almost impossible for opponents to move the ball on the stingy Cubs defense, except via penalty, which is something that was becoming all too frequent for Coach Cline's liking. The Cubs scored the lone touchdown of the day and won the game, 6–0. SBUC was 2–0, and Coach Cline was looking like the right man for the job.

On October 27, things started to unravel for Cline's young team, though. The minor mistakes that his team was able to overcome in victories over San Diego State and Loyola College came back to bite the Cubs against Whittier College. While penalties were no longer an issue in the third game of the season, the Cubs beat themselves in other ways. The SBUC defense remained strong, not allowing a single point to the Whittier offense. However, the Poets were able to get on the board after intercepting a Loran Peak pass and returning it 70 yards for a touchdown. SBUC countered with a Cap Haralson touchdown. In the third quarter, Whittier was able to score once again on a blocked punt. SBUC bounced back again with another rushing touchdown. The difference in the final score came in the kicking game. SBUC did not have a reliable kicker, missing both of their extra-point drop kicks, and ultimately lost the game, 14–12.

Following the tough loss to Whittier College, the SBUC Cubs were soundly defeated, 27–6, by Pomona College. The defense had finally allowed the opponent into their end zone, and, unfortunately for Jimmie Cline and his Cubs, it would be a trend for the rest of the season. University of Redlands would defeat the Southern Branch, 12–6. Occidental College won, 20–6, and California Tech would defeat the Cubs, 59–6, in the final game of the year. In Coach Jimmie Cline's first year, the Cubs would finish 2–5 overall, and 0–5 in Conference play. Amazingly, the kicking problems continued for the duration of the year: the Cubs were not able to make one drop kick all season!

The College Football Researchers Association named University of Illinois the 1923 National Champions.

## 1924

In 1924, Coach Jimmie Cline was entering his second year as the head coach of the Southern Branch Grizzlies.

Prior to the season, Cece Hollingsworth was again named team captain, along with first-time captain Earle Gardner. Much like the 1923 season, the new campaign featured a solid defense, but the offense struggled mightily. On October 4, the Southern Branch Grizzlies and Loyola College played to a scoreless draw. The following week, the offense improved and was able to get the ball into the end zone two times, but it was not enough, and the Grizzlies lost, 14–13, to the University of La Verne. October 18, however, was the game for which everyone had been waiting—a rematch of the 1923 loss to Whittier College. In front of the largest crowd ever assembled at Whittier, the Grizzlies made many of the mistakes that doomed them the previous year. The offense struggled and was unable to get into the end zone. The Whittier Poets' lone score came on a fumble recovery in the end zone, and they won the game, 6–0.

A tricky, shifting offense employed by Occidental College proved too much to handle, and SBUC lost once again on October 25. The following week, the Grizzlies stood no chance against a powerful Pomona College squad and lost decisively, 50–7. The Grizzlies would then play a rare Tuesday game 10 days later against the University of Redlands. During this game, a battle of attrition, neither team had much offense, but both sported ferocious, hard-hitting defenses. Several injuries hampered the Grizzlies' ability to move the football, and neither team threatened to score throughout the game. At the end the scoreboard read, 0–0.

Still looking for their first win of the season, Coach Cline's Grizzlies would take on San Diego State just four days after the grueling bout with the University of Redlands. Again, the Grizzlies failed to come away victorious. After defeating the up-and-coming San Diego State program the previous two years, in 1924 the two teams played to a 13–13 tie. It was the Grizzlies' third tie of the season, and with just one week to play, their last chance at a win would come against the improving Caltech program a week later. The Grizzlies successfully moved the ball up and down the field all game against the Caltech Beavers. They smashed through the line like warriors, only to be stopped near the goal line time and again. Several fumbles and the all-too-familiar blocked punt doomed the Grizzlies. Following a blocked punt, the Beavers pounded the ball into the end zone from a short field and scored the game's only points. Ultimately, the Beavers defeated Southern Branch, 6–0, in the final game of the season, which the Grizzlies finished with a record of 0–5–3.

Elsewhere in college football, the Notre Dame Fighting Irish continued their dominant stretch under Head Coach Knute Rockne. In 1924, the accomplishments of Notre Dame were not symbolized by wins and losses alone, but by imagery, as well. The 1924 Notre Dame Fighting Irish would best be remembered by the nickname bestowed upon their backfield by Grantland Rice of the *New York Herald Tribune*: "The Four Horsemen." The four backs—Harry Stuhldreher, Don Miller, Jim Crowley, and Elmer Layden—were also known as Death, Destruction, Pestilence, and Famine. They would be immortalized in college football lore forever.

The College Football Researchers Association named the University of Notre Dame the National Champions.

# CHAPTER 4
# William Spaulding (1925–1938)

As it turned out, the Jimmie Cline era at the Southern Branch was brief. In 1925, SBUC would hire a new football coach, the fourth coach in just seven seasons. Following the eras of Fred Cozens and Harry Trotter, SBUC was in desperate need of someone with football knowledge. They got that in Jimmie Cline. What was lacking, however, was experience. Cline was young. He knew football, but he struggled with discipline. In 1925, the Southern Branch finally found a coach with knowledge, experience, and generalship. That man was William Spaulding.

UCLA Head Coach William Spaulding, 1928 (Southern Campus Collection)

William Henry Spaulding was born May 4, 1880. He was a Midwestern boy, born and raised in Wisconsin. Although basketball was his first true love, Spaulding had a deep passion for competition. Growing up, he played a number of sports and would continue to stay involved in multiple sports well into his coaching career. In 1902, Spaulding was off to college. By the time he was of college age, Spaulding realized that, although he had a thorough knowledge of multiple sports and could see himself coaching any of them in the future, his playing future was as a football player. In the fall of 1902, Spaulding left his Wisconsin home and was off to Crawfordsville, Indiana, where he would attend Wabash College. After playing on the freshman team in 1902, Spaulding was eligible for varsity the following year. He wasted no time and made his mark immediately. In 1903, Spaulding was a significant contributor to the varsity team.

In 1904, Spaulding was named a team captain. As a man interested in teaching the game, and already someone with an eye on a coaching career, this was a great honor. The 1904 Wabash College team was one to remember. Despite being much smaller physically than most opponents, Wabash used toughness, wit, and strategy to have a successful season. A local Indianapolis writer would nickname the 1904 team the "Little Giants." Much of the strategy employed by Coach Francis Cayou shaped the beliefs of Spaulding, and he would carry those lessons with him into his coaching career. In 1905, Spaulding's playing days came to an end. He was once again named team captain and closed his career with another successful season for Wabash College.

After one year away from the game, William Spaulding's coaching career began. In 1907, he accepted his first head coaching job at Western State Normal School (now known as Western Michigan University). He had a long tenure at Normal School and in his 15 years coaching compiled a 62–25–3 record. True to his beliefs, Spaulding proved he could coach more than one sport. In 1911, he became the baseball coach at Normal School and in 11 seasons compiled a 63–18–4 record. In 1913, he also took the job as the school basketball coach. In nine seasons, he had a 77–43 record.

In 1922, after his successful multisport stint at Western State Normal School, Spaulding was on the move. His success on the gridiron had been recognized, and he was now facing an entirely different challenge. He would be coaching in the Big 10 Conference, the preeminent conference in the nation at the time. William Spaulding coached at the University of Minnesota from 1922 to 1924. Despite a record of just 3–3–1 in his first season, there was a slight improvement over the 1921 campaign that finished with a 3–4 record. In 1923, however, William Spaulding left his mark. The Golden Gophers team finished with a 5–1–1 record, including wins over Iowa and Northwestern. In his final season at the University of Minnesota, Coach Spaulding did not fare as well. He finished with a 3–3–1 record and was westward bound, to the University of California Southern Branch.

Spaulding spent 14 years as the Southern Branch/UCLA head football coach and became the school's all-time leader in wins in his first year, 1925, an honor that he held over a span of 60 years, until 1985. William Spaulding was inducted into the Wabash College Athletic Hall of Fame in 1984 and the inaugural UCLA Athletics Hall of Fame class in 1984, as well. Spaulding died on October 12, 1966. The football practice field at UCLA is named Spaulding Field in his honor.

## 1925

With another new coach came new excitement. Prior to the start of the 1925 season, there was, as in most off-seasons, an abundance of optimism. The 1925 team was experienced. Senior captain and all-conference tackle Earle Gardner led the Grizzlies. Another prominent returning player was captain-elect Charles Hastings. Most important, however, was the experience of new Head Coach William Spaulding. After 18 years of college football head coaching experience, William Spaulding was set to take the SBUC Grizzlies to the next level. He made his mark right away.

The William Spaulding era kicked off on September 26, 1925, against San Diego State. Though blessed with a talented and experienced team, Coach Spaulding felt uneasy going into the season opener. Although backed by a bravado and self-confidence unmatched at the Southern Branch to that point, it was not up to the level that Coach Spaulding was accustomed to in his past coaching years. The excitement was nevertheless evident. Over 5,000 fans were in attendance at Moore Field, and for the first time a live bear was present as the mascot for the Grizzlies.

The game itself was a battle. Through three quarters the game remained scoreless, with San Diego State advancing the ball at will on the Grizzlies, only to stumble near the goal line. In the fourth quarter, the Grizzlies were finally able to break through and score the game's only touchdown on a short sweep to the right by Loran Peak. Jack Frost converted the extra point. The SDSU Aztecs would mount a long drive as time ticked off the clock but ultimately were stopped near the Grizzlies' goal line, and at the final gun the score was 7–0 Southern Branch. Coach Spaulding had won his first game.

The second game of the year proved to be another challenge, but once again the Grizzlies were up for it. A week after defeating San Diego State, SBUC took on the University of La Verne. The game was competitive throughout the first three quarters, with La Verne holding a 3–0 lead entering the fourth quarter. In the fourth, however, the Grizzlies remained composed and played possibly the best quarter of football to date in their brief history. Loran Peak scored early in the fourth quarter on a 7-yard plunge into the end zone. The extra point attempt was no good. Minutes later, the Grizzlies received the ball again following a punt and marched down the field to score again. The capper came on an off-tackle spurt to the left by Cy Wilson. After the successful extra point, the score was 13–3. The Grizzlies would have two more possessions in the fourth quarter, one of which ended in a field goal, and the next with the clock running out and the Grizzlies controlling the ball near the opponent's 10-yard line. The fourth-quarter dominance proved that Coach Spaulding had ushered in a new era, and the SBUC fans could not be more excited.

On October 10, SBUC continued the momentum with a dominant 26–0 victory over Pomona College in the first conference game of the year before a record crowd of over 8,500 spectators. The next two games against Whittier College and Occidental College proved to be two of the toughest challenges SBUC would face all year. With a 3–0 record, the Grizzlies had their eyes on the conference prize, but Whittier College had other plans. After an early score by Whittier, the Grizzlies struggled to gain any momentum. The defense was stout, but following the exit of Loran Peak due to multiple broken ribs, the offense sputtered, and SBUC was never able to get into the end zone. The final score was 7–0, Whittier. The Southern Branch bounced back, however, with a 9–0 victory over Occidental College the next week. A 28–0 defeat at the hands of St. Mary's College was followed by a 23–0 victory over the University of Redlands.

The 1925 Southern Branch Grizzlies were 5–2 with two games left on the schedule. The next test would come on November 14 against a team they had never played before, a nonconference foe, Stanford University, led by second-year Head Coach Glenn "Pop" Warner. With offensive leader Loran Peak still out with injured ribs, Coach Spaulding and the Grizzlies had hoped to play a low-scoring game and have a chance at the end against the much bigger, more powerful Stanford University. This was not the case, however. The Grizzlies' greatest scoring opportunity came in the first quarter. After receiving the ball at the 25-yard line, the Grizzlies marched 65 yards down the field, only to be stopped at the 10-yard line. They were not able to score the rest of the game. Stanford, on the other side, had no problem scoring. With the massive size differential, the Grizzlies were unable to stop Stanford throughout the game and wound up going down by the final score of 82–0. It was the second worst loss in school history. The following week, Coach Spaulding and the Southern Branch varsity football team regrouped, but were unable to get back into the winning column. The season finished with a 10–10 tie against Caltech. The Southern Branch Grizzlies finished the 1925 season with a 5–3–1 record, the first winning season in school history.

The College Football Researchers Association named the University of Alabama the National Champions.

## 1926

Coach William Spaulding's second campaign as the head coach of the University of California Southern Branch kicked off on September 25, 1926. Following the successful 1925 season, gone were the days of merely dreaming of a conference championship. The time for truly believing that conference superiority was an attainable goal had arrived.

By 1926, SBUC had developed enough depth that they could substitute with frequency, something that Coach Spaulding would do for the duration of his career. In 1926, the Grizzlies used fewer two-way players than they had ever used to that point and had the goal of always keeping fresh, strong bodies on the field at all times. This was evident in the first game of the year. The Grizzlies soundly defeated the Santa Barbara State Roadrunners by a score of 25–0. Two weeks after the Santa Barbara game, the Grizzlies would take on San Diego State. The Southern Branch had dominated San Diego State in recent years, and as the Aztecs continued to build a formidable program, they had a stated goal of catching up to the Grizzlies in skill, talent, coaching, and execution. In 1926, they were not yet there. The Grizzlies won by a score of 42–7. Quarterback Thomas Wilcox would lead the Grizzlies to a dominant offensive performance, and Bert Lambeck helped fuel a very strong defensive unit.

After a 2–0 start to the season, SBUC ran into a formidable opponent, the thorn in the Grizzlies' side: the Whittier College Poets. SBUC was outgained all day long. Two key fumbles ended drives for the Grizzlies, and the final score ended up 16–6, with the victory going to Whittier. On October 23, the Southern Branch would make history when a crucial conference matchup with a strong Pomona College team was played at the Los Angeles Memorial Coliseum. This would be the largest stadium SBUC had played in to date, holding a capacity of nearly 80,000, but on this October day there was a crowd of close to 12,000, a wave of support SBUC had rarely enjoyed. SBUC played its best game of the year that day. In the second quarter of a 7–0 game, in which the Sagehens had taken the early lead, Grizzlies star

Head Coach William Spaulding and Captain Charles Hastings in 1926 (Southern Campus Collection)

Bert LaBrucherie returned a kickoff 85 yards for a touchdown. It would be a sign of things to come for the small, yet brilliant LaBrucherie, and for the Grizzlies that day. The Grizzlies would go on to win the game, 27–7.

The team continued to show improvement the following two weeks. On November 6, the Grizzlies defeated Occidental College, 24–7, and on November 13, they defeated the University of Redlands by a score of 26–3. They were 5–1 on the season, and with two games left they controlled their own destiny. The Southern California Intercollegiate Athletic Conference crown was within sight.

A shifting offense by Caltech doomed the SBUC championship hopes on November 20. Caltech was able to confuse the SBUC defense on the first drive of the game and scored an early touchdown to take a 7–0 lead. It proved too much to handle for Coach Spaulding and his boys. After kicking a field goal, SBUC trailed 7–3 at the end of the first quarter. The defense adjusted and didn't allow Caltech to score again, but the offense flailed. After a long pass from Scribner Birlenback to Robert Henderson gave SBUC the ball at the 1-yard line, the offense wasn't able to capitalize and wound up losing a frustrating game, 7–3. The championship dreams weren't over, but they took a serious blow. The following week, SBUC played a nonconference game and faltered once again, losing to the Iowa State Cyclones by a score of 20–0. Pomona College, the team the Grizzlies soundly defeated in their head-to-head matchup, won the conference championship in a painful conclusion to the 1926 season. The Grizzlies finished the season with a 5–3 record. Despite having the top defense in the conference and a new star named LaBrucherie, the 1926 team felt like they underachieved.

While the results under William Spaulding had been much different from those of his successors, the results on the field were not the only change at the new, offshoot university. The team had consecutive winning seasons on the field and strived for change off it. They were tired of living in the shadows of the University of California Berkeley. While changes would come slow, and nothing was official until the

UCLA vs. Occidental, 1926 (Southern Campus Collection)

following year, the name "Southern Branch" was going out of style. Students preferred to be called the "University of California at Los Angeles," a name that would eventually stick.

The College Football Researchers Association named the University of Alabama the 1926 National Champions.

## 1927

Nineteen twenty-seven was a year of change. The nickname that was born in 1926 became reality in 1927. No longer was there a University of California Southern Branch. The new name was the University of California at Los Angeles (*at* would be removed in 1958). While some things changed, some remained the same. UCLA remained in the Southern California Intercollegiate Athletic Conference, and the team name remained the Grizzlies. As it turned out, both of these would change one year later.

As for the football team, William Spaulding was in his third year, and though the team improved significantly in his first two years, compiling winning seasons in both campaigns for the first time in school history, the ever-elusive conference crown was still out of reach. In 1927, the goal remained the same. It was time for the Grizzlies to take the next step and claim conference superiority.

With the bitter taste of 1926 came the motivated team of 1927, determined to not let the championship slip away once again. For the second consecutive season, the Grizzlies started with a game against Santa Barbara State College; and for the second consecutive season, the Grizzlies had a distinctive size advantage. Coach Spaulding's squad, led by a powerful running game and potent passing attack, marched down the field at will, scoring five touchdowns. The defense—the strength of the team during Coach Spaulding's tenure—was stout once again and didn't allow a single point. Earl Fields, Joe Fleming, and Bert LaBrucherie each scored on the ground, and UCLA came away victorious, 33–0, in the opener.

The following week, the Grizzlies would take on Fresno State College for the first time. The game was low-scoring throughout, and the Grizzlies' defense proved to be a stone wall protecting the goal line and preserving a shutout. In the second quarter, Fresno State was twice able to threaten the Grizzlies but on both occasions were stopped on downs inside the Grizzlies' 5-yard line. On offense, the Grizzlies struggled for much of the day. While star halfback Bert LaBrucherie continued to dominate on the field despite his diminutive stature, the Grizzlies could not cross the goal line. LaBrucherie, also a punter on the squad, proved valuable not only on offense, but by pinning the opponent deep in its own territory with his accurate, booming punts. Finally, in the second half, the Grizzlies were able to get on the scoreboard after a series of successful runs by LaBrucherie, Scribner Birlenbach, and captain-elect Joe Fleming. The capper of the drive came on a 52-yard burst to the end zone by Fleming. The Grizzlies won the game, 7–0, and were 2–0 on the season.

The third game of the year would come against the great Grizzlies foe, the Whittier Poets. Seven times in history had the Poets and the Grizzlies met, and seven times the Poets came away victorious. The eighth time, as it would turn out, would be the last time the two teams met as members of the same conference. If the Grizzlies were to challenge for the conference title, winning the Whittier game appeared to be of utmost importance. Whittier was led by the great Oak Pendleton, a star back who had in the past troubled UCLA and everyone else on the Poets' schedule. The battle was not only UCLA vs. Whittier, but Pendleton vs. LaBrucherie. On this day, however, the battle was one-sided. The UCLA Grizzlies played their best game in school history and thoroughly dismantled Whittier from start to finish. After one quarter, the battle of Pendleton and LaBrucherie would best be described as underwhelming. Neither man was able to break free and display his patented running style. The Grizzlies, however, were a much deeper team this year, and Joe Fleming, an underrated star himself, proved this in the first half. He scampered all over the field and crossed the goal line first on a 42-yard touchdown. The Grizzlies scored once again on a Scribner Birlenbach touchdown pass to Robert Henderson to give the Grizzlies a 12–0 lead. On the ensuing drive, Oak Pendleton would not be silenced, and he rumbled in for a short touchdown. The score was 12–6 at halftime. Following halftime, the Grizzlies' offense proceeded to gash the Poets' defense, and the Grizzlies' defense was able to keep Pendleton in check for the rest of the game. LaBrucherie eventually got in on the action and scored on a spec-

UCLA and Bert LaBrucherie came out on top over Oak Pendleton and the Whittier Poets, 1927 (Southern Campus Collection)

tacular run, in which he started to the left and cut back completely across the field, outracing the Poets' defense to the corner of the end zone on the right side. The Grizzlies would win the game, 25–6.

Following the triumph over Whittier College, the Grizzlies would continue the momentum by defeating Occidental College for the third time in a row at the Los Angeles Memorial Coliseum. Motivation was never an issue early in the season for the 1927 Grizzlies, and following the important triumph at the Coliseum, the Grizzlies were able to easily dispatch the University of Redlands on October 28 behind a dominant performance from LaBrucherie, including a 35-yard punt return for a touchdown.

The Grizzlies were 5–0 and riding high, but adversity finally hit when they took on Pomona College. The Grizzlies took the lead in the second quarter on a 48-yard run by Joe Fleming. The UCLA defense, however, was pushed around all game. Pomona College seemingly moved the ball at will and outgained the Grizzlies by a wide margin. Pomona could not score, however, and the game was 7–0 entering the fourth quarter. After a booming punt by LaBrucherie, the ball was set on the Pomona 33-yard line. Twelve plays and 67 yards later, the Sagehens pounded the ball into the end zone. The extra point was successful, and the final score was 7–7.

After a dismantling of Caltech, the UCLA Grizzlies would take on the University of Arizona Wildcats in a nonconference game on November 19. That afternoon, the Grizzlies were defeated in heartbreaking fashion. The game was tied at 13 with just 17 seconds to go. Arizona called a timeout and upon returning decided to attempt a game-winning field goal. The kick was good and the Grizzlies' undefeated season was over. The final score was 16–13 Arizona. The season concluded the following week, with Drake University soundly defeating the Grizzlies in a game once again played at the L.A. Coliseum. The final score was 25–6. The Grizzlies finished the season with a 6–2–1 record and were undefeated in conference play with a 4–0–1 record. However, due to a scheduling quirk, the Grizzlies were not named conference champions. Pomona College, which played one more conference game than the Grizzlies and boasted a 5–0–1 record, were instead named champions.

The College Football Researchers Association named Yale University the 1927 National Champions.

## 1928

Prior to the start of UCLA's 10th season, more changes impacted the football program. Coming off three successful seasons under Head Coach William Spaulding, UCLA was ready to up the competition. In 1928, UCLA joined the Pacific Coast Conference. The other member institutions were the University of California at Berkeley, the University of Idaho, the University of Montana, the University of Oregon, Oregon State University, the University of Southern California, Stanford University, the University of Washington, and Washington State University. A change in conference was not the only change, however. With the switch to the Pacific Coast Conference, UCLA could no longer call themselves the Grizzlies, since the University of Montana already claimed that name. The unofficial nickname of the team was then adopted, and the University of California at Los Angeles became the Bruins. Along with the conference change and the name change, the Bruins had a stadium change, as well. In 1926 and 1927, UCLA had played several games at the Los Angeles Memorial Coliseum. Starting in 1928, the Coliseum became the home of the Bruins for the next 54 seasons.

Coach Spaulding was aware of the challenges that switching to the Pacific Coast Conference would present the team. The seniors in 1928 had played on the freshman team in 1925, and the crushing 82–0 defeat handed to the varsity by Stanford that year is something they would never forget. Stanford was a strong team in 1925 and finished with a 4–1 conference record, but in second place in the standings behind the University of Washington. If the Bruins were to now win a conference championship, they would have to significantly improve their performance to match the size, skill, execution, and talent of their new Pacific Coast Conference partners. Stanford was not the only team to keep an eye on, however. The University of Southern California presented a natural rivalry for UCLA, as the schools were both located in Los Angeles and would share the Coliseum. Fans of both teams and students of both schools would interact almost daily. Howard Jones, who as a player won three national championships at Yale University and would later coach Yale to the 1909 National Championship, began coaching USC in 1925.

Heading into the 1928 season, there were many question marks for UCLA. The roster was talented, and had the Bruins still been in the Southern California Intercollegiate Athletic Conference, many believed it would finally be the season the team would bring home the conference crown. With the increase in competition, however, questions remained about the capabilities of Spaulding's men. Many believed the Bruins had the best defense in school history. A strong front line had been Coach Spaulding's calling card to that point. Line Coach Hugh McDonald had a plethora of talent and rotated them often. Marian French, Stan Gould, Gene Brown, Carl Brown, Ed Tendy, Don Jacobson, Harold Bishop, Bob Rasmus, and Jim Adkins were all stalwarts of the offensive and defensive lines. Established stars in the backfield Joe Fleming, Bert LaBrucherie, and Earl Fields were all returning starters. The team was also loaded with quality sophomores. The freshman team had steadily been improving over the years under the tutelage of former Varsity Coach Harry Trotter, and many were ready to contribute to the varsity program immediately upon eligibility.

For the third year in a row, the Bruins would open the season against nonconference foe Santa Barbara State College; and for the third year in a row, they would come away victorious—this time by the final score of 19–0. Earl Fields, Joe Fleming, and Clifton Simpson each scored touchdowns on the ground.

The following week, the Bruins would take on the University of Arizona Wildcats for the second time in school history. The first meeting, a year earlier, was a painful defeat in which the Wildcats escaped with a narrow victory. The frustration continued in 1928, when the Bruins dominated Arizona in every category except on the scoreboard. Early in the game the Bruins were driving, and Joe Fleming was nearing the goal line when he took a hard hit and fumbled. The ball was recovered by UCLA at the 5-yard line and dragged into the end zone. After the extra point, the Bruins took a 7–0 lead, but star Joe Fleming was hurt and would miss much of the season. Arizona tied the score in the third quarter, and despite driving the ball to the Arizona 2-yard line in the fourth, the Bruins were not able to score again and the game ended in a 7–7 tie. The final game before conference play was a week later and pitted UCLA against Caltech. The Bruins soundly defeated the Engineers, 32–0.

At last, the first conference game arrived. On October 13, the Bruins took on Stanford University. They had the opportunity to start conference play with a victory over the school that had crushed them in 1925, but it was not to be on this day. The Bruins lost, 45–7. Roughly 7,000 fans were in attendance at Stanford Stadium to witness Pop Warner and his strong team, led by halfback Buddy Forster, dismantle the Bruins from start to finish.

The Bruins took on Pomona College the following week and came away with a resounding 29–0 victory. UCLA had proven they could handle foes from their old conference, but could they compete against those in their new conference?

The Bruins' second conference game was against the Idaho Vandals, and to the surprise of many, including Coach Spaulding, the Vandals came out passing early and often. The Bruins were unable to stop the Vandals' passing attack and lost the game, 20–6. Washington State University also trounced the Bruins two weeks later in a snowy game played on a neutral site in Portland, Oregon. Roughly 2,500 pneumonia cases were reported from fans in attendance following the game, but the elements had no effect on Washington State. The final score was 38–0 Cougars.

After dismantling the University of La Verne, 65–0, in a nonconference match, the Bruins had one more chance to win a conference game on November 29 against the University of Oregon. Once again, the Bruins came up short. Despite the loss to the Webfooters, UCLA played their best conference game of the year. Each team tallied 12 first downs. Oregon scored two offensive touchdowns to the Bruins' one, as well as two touchdowns on interception returns of 95 and 60 yards, respectively. The final score of the game was 26–6. The Bruins would have to wait another year to win their first game in the Pacific Coast Conference. Coach Spaulding and his battered Bruins finished the year with an overall record of 4–4–1 but were 0–4 in conference play.

The College Football Researchers Association named Georgia Tech the 1928 National Champions.

## 1929

While 1927 and 1928 were years of change at the University of California at Los Angeles, 1929 was the year the location of the school changed, as well. Developers broke ground on a new campus in 1927, and by 1929 school was in session in the hills. The new campus, built in Westwood, was tucked in between Santa Monica, Beverly Hills, Century City, and Bel Air. Though small, it was a masterpiece. On March 18, 1929, the first class ever held on the new campus took place months before the official opening. Due to a small fire on the Vermont Avenue campus, Professor Hosmer Stone was given the honor of being the first professor to teach on the new campus when he was forced to move his Chemistry 1A class into the building now known as Haines Hall. Along with Haines Hall, the 1929 campus had only three other buildings. Royce Hall, which contains an auditorium that seats upwards of 1,800 students, was one of the original buildings. Powell Library and Kinsey Hall (now known as the Humanities building) were the other two buildings that were completed in 1929. Though a small campus at the time, still under construction, students were ecstatic about the new place they called their own. Completion of the campus, however, would be slowed in the coming years by economic depression, the depth of which the United States and the world had never before seen.

After four years, nearly half of the world's banks had failed and unemployment in the United States hovered around 30 percent. The pain was felt everywhere, even at UCLA. Many students who dreamed of getting an education were forced to leave school and to try to support their families. Schools nationwide were forced to make budgetary decisions. Fortunately for UCLA, the football program was not dropped and William Spaulding was retained.

UCLA opened the season on September 28, 1929, against the University of Southern California. It was the first meeting in what has become through all these intervening years a long-standing, fierce rivalry. Bert LaBrucherie and Joe Fleming had graduated, and the offense was a major question mark entering the 1929 season. Captain Carl Brown had proven his value the previous two seasons, but even though he didn't even play football while attending Santa Monica High School, he was now asked to do more. Brown was expected to lead the Bruins to the next level. He was expected to lead his team to their first conference victory since joining the Pacific Coast Conference. Captain-elect Eddy Solomon was tasked with replacing Joe Fleming. It proved to be a tough challenge. With a crowd of over 35,000 fans in attendance, the USC Trojans dismantled the Bruins on a chilly September afternoon. The Bruins were able to advance the ball into Trojans territory on the first drive of the game and score on a long touchdown run, but the play was called back due to a penalty. UCLA never threatened again. The defense, which had been strong under Coach Spaulding, stood no chance against the powerful Trojans offense. The final score on this day: 76–0. Despite the trouncing, great sportsmanship was shown throughout the game. This would not always be the case in the UCLA-USC rivalry.

Much as in the previous year, in 1929 there was a stark difference in results for the Bruins in conference games vs. nonconference games. The second game of the season was against nonconference foe Fresno State University. Led by the three-touchdown performance of Eddy Solomon, UCLA easily defeated the Bulldogs, 56–6. Another conference foe was on the horizon, though, and in just one short week Coach Spaulding and crew were tasked with taking on Stanford University. The game was eerily similar to the outcome of the USC game just two weeks earlier. The offense struggled again, and the defense was pounded into submission. The final score—Stanford 51, UCLA 0.

Two more nonconference games were on UCLA's schedule before they would have another chance to claim their first conference win in the PCC. On October 19, 1929, the Bruins easily dispatched

Caltech by a score of 31–0, and on October 26 the Bruins defeated Pomona College, 20–0. The following weeks would be difficult for the Bruins. Four days after the New York Stock Exchange collapsed, the Bruins took on the University of Oregon. For the third time in three conference games, the Bruins offense was unable to score, and Oregon won the game, 27–0. Bucking the trend of winning out of conference and losing in conference, the Bruins then fell to nonconference challenger St. Mary's College. The Gaels defense had yet to give up a touchdown all season. That did not change against the lowly Bruins offense. Despite reaching as far into Gaels territory as the 31-yard line (farther than Berkeley had managed to penetrate), the Bruins could never cross the goal line. The final score was 24–0. The Bruins were 3–4 on the season at that point, and in the last game of the year, the Bruins would face the Montana Grizzlies. It was the last chance for the Bruins to win a conference game.

It was Thanksgiving Day, 1929. The Bruins played their best game of the year. Halfbacks Howard Roberts and Charles Smith would come of age and perform at their best on this festive holiday afternoon. Eddy Solomon was electrifying. Coach Spaulding was in command. The question remained, would it be enough? On the first drive, it appeared the favored Montana Grizzlies would simply crush the Bruins like other conference opponents had done all season. They drove the ball quickly down the field to UCLA's 6-yard line. Penalties, however, stalled the drive, and eventually Montana turned the ball over on downs. Tied at zero going into the halftime break, the Bruins could sense their first opportunity for a conference win. In the third quarter, the Bruins came out firing on all cylinders. Eddy Solomon brought the 40,000+ spectators in attendance to their feet with a spectacular pass to Richard Mulhaupt, who then ran through, over, and around several defenders to cross the goal line. Solomon would add another score, and the Bruins won the game, 14–0. It was their first conference win since joining the Pacific Coast Conference. The UCLA Bruins would finish the season with an overall 4–4 record.

The College Football Researchers Association named the University of Notre Dame the 1929 National Champions

UCLA Captain Carl Brown, 1929 (Southern Campus Collection)

## 1930

By the fall of 1930, the United States had just suffered through the most brutal 12 months since the Civil War. The Great Depression brought the nation to its knees. President Herbert Hoover was in the second year of a tumultuous presidency, and optimism was waning. In Westwood, the UCLA Bruins were set to begin their third year in the Pacific Coast Conference. In the prior two years, they had won just one conference game. Nevertheless, optimism still abounded. With an increase in competition came an increase in stature, and if the Bruins could compete with the powerhouse programs of the PCC, they could dream of one day competing with powerhouse programs throughout the country. Coach William Spaulding had turned a floundering program into a perennial winner. Now, he was in his sixth season. In his third season, 1927, Coach Spaulding's Grizzlies had finished with a 6–2–1 overall record, and a 4–0–1 record in conference play. Now in his third season since joining the significantly higher-level PCC, it was time for another step up in performance.

After a 1929 season in which the offense

struggled to regain its 1928 form, Coach Spaulding would be reliant on several key returning players in 1930. Captain-elect Eddie Solomon, the younger brother of a University of California ballplayer, was Coach Spaulding's quarterback. The signal caller from nearby Venice was said to have the strongest arm of any quarterback Spaulding had coached to date. Other key contributors in 1930 included backfield mates Buddy Forster and Reuben Thoe. Maurice Goodstein and Ed Milum anchored the Bruins' offensive line. The roster was young and mostly inexperienced. The freshman squad in 1929 was perhaps the best in school history to that point and the future looked bright, but no one can ever predict the rate at which young players mature, and no one can say how sophomores will fare in battle for the first time when standing across the mighty players wearing Stanford and USC uniforms. That was Coach Spaulding's major question at the start of the season.

Eddie Solomon, UCLA Captain, 1930 (Southern Campus Collection)

On September 27, 1930, the season would open against the University of Southern California. For the second straight year, the Bruins were tasked with facing one of the toughest teams in the nation to start the season. With the question marks on offense, it was important not to let the Trojans get out of the gate early and take a lead that would be impossible to overcome. The start, however, did not go as planned. The opening kickoff was returned 67 yards by Marshall Duffield, and nine plays later the Trojans scored. On the Bruins' first drive, Howard Roberts fumbled, and the Trojans scored shortly thereafter. In the second quarter, the UCLA defense stiffened, but the offense and special teams continued to let down the team. After another fumble, USC's Orville Mohler scored on a short plunge over the goal line. Just before the half, things went from bad to worse. Mohler blocked a Bruins punt, picked it up, and raced into the end zone again. The Bruins were down four touchdowns at halftime. The Trojans would score three more times in the second half. The UCLA offense never could get it going. Despite improvements in the second half, and a passing game that came alive, the Bruins could never cross the goal line. The final score was 52–0.

Following the USC loss, the next three weeks were crucial if the Bruins were to have a winning season. If 1930 was to be anything like the prior season, despite losing in conference, the Bruins were fully capable of winning games out of conference. The three-game stretch in October was a chance for the Bruins to win games, build confidence, and work out the kinks before finishing the season with four consecutive conference games. Before a small crowd of just 7,000 fans (which had been considered a large crowd just a decade earlier), the Bruins took on Pomona-Pitzer on October 11. On this day, the Bruins played fine football. Coach Spaulding still had worries about his offense, however. The Bruins racked up only 273 yards, but the defense was able to hold the Sagehens to just 179. The Bruins' offense did not have a well-balanced attack. They could no longer rush the ball like they did with Joe Fleming and Bert LaBrucherie, but they could pass the ball better than any team Coach Spaulding had coached at UCLA. The Bruins were able to move the ball in part due to the receiving efforts of Leonard Wellendorf and Richard Mulhaupt. Robert Decker scored a touchdown, and Mulhaupt also rushed for one. The defense was only threatened one time. In the second quarter, the Sagehens were able to drive inside the Bruins 5-yard line but were stopped on 4th down for a loss after Wellendorf and Kerns Hampton knifed into the backfield to bring down the ball carrier. The Bruins would score one more time late in the game on a long interception return for a touchdown by Gordon Jones. UCLA won the game, 21–0.

Following the victory over Pomona-Pitzer, the Bruins took on Saint Mary's. On this day, UCLA was unable to stop the Gaels and lost, 21–6. The fourth game of the year was a contest with a foe very familiar to the Bruins. On this day, October 24, the Bruins soundly defeated Caltech by a score of 30–0. They were now 2–2 with four games to go. The meat of the conference schedule was ahead, and it was time for the Bruins to prove they belonged.

On Halloween, the Bruins were set to play Stanford University. In the previous two meetings, Stanford had carved through the Bruins' defense and stonewalled their offense repeatedly. Thirty-five thousand fans were in attendance at Stanford Stadium to see Pop Warner's squad battle William Spaulding's. Much like the USC game, the Bruins did not come out of the gates as well as they had hoped. Stanford marched the ball down the field and punched it in on a short run by William Simkins. Philip Moffatt had singlehandedly gotten Stanford in scoring position before Simkins finished off the drive. At the end of the first quarter, the score was 7–0. On offense, Buddy Forster and Robert Decker had success for UCLA but were unable to cross the goal line. At halftime, the score remained 7–0, still close enough so that William Spaulding and his men were within striking distance of the powerful Pop Warner-led team, and with just two excellent quarters they could accomplish what few thought possible. The third quarter turned out to be the most critical quarter of the season. But, as superstars often do, Harlow Rothert was there when his Stanford teammates needed him most. Rothert ran wild in the third quarter and scored two touchdowns. While the Bruins rebounded in the fourth quarter and held Stanford scoreless, the ineffectiveness of the Bruins offense once again turned out to be their downfall. The final score was 20–0 Stanford.

While the Bruins had shown improvement over both USC and Stanford from the year before, they were still on the losing side, and by 1930 moral victories were becoming tiresome. The next two games were once again frustrating showings. On November 8, the Bruins lost to the University of Oregon, 7–0, and on November 21, they lost to Oregon State University, 19–0. The offense had now been shut out four times in seven games. The last game of the year would come against the University of Idaho. On this Thanksgiving Day, the Bruins played their best game of the season. Senior captain Ed Solomon was responsible for two touchdowns, and Buddy Forster scored one. Reuben Thoe and Maurice Goodstein dominated on defense, much as they had all season long. The Bruins soundly defeated the Vandals by a score of 20–6. This win elevated the Bruins to a tie for 6th place in the PCC with the University of California Berkeley. The Bruins would finish the season 3–5, with a 1–4 record in conference play. It was the first losing season of Spaulding's coaching career at UCLA.

The College Football Researchers Association named the University of Alabama the 1930 National Champions.

## 1931

For the fans, players, and coaches hoping to start the 1931 season with a bang, they were surely disappointed on September 25, 1931. The season instead began with a thud. The Bruins kicked off the season not with the powerful Trojans of Southern Cal, but rather with Occidental College, an old Southern California Intercollegiate Athletic Conference rival. With a nonconference opponent, they had a more realistic shot at starting the season in the win column. Norman Duncan, known for his fancy attire, was now the team captain, and in 1931 he was tasked with helping the team bounce back from their first losing season under Coach William Spaulding. Len Wellendorf, Bob Decker, and Dick Mulhauft were all key contributors in 1930 on whom Coach Spaulding and the UCLA Bruins would be dependent in 1931. When the season began against Occidental, 1930 was a thing of the past, though it seemed that the same problem haunted the Bruins early in the season—the offense simply could not carry its weight. The score of the first game was 0–0. It was a disappointing tie, and one week later conference play began.

The first game of the conference season was against Washington State University. At the end of the third quarter, the score remained 0–0. The Bruins had played seven quarters so far that season and had neither allowed a point nor scored a single point. The fate of the Bruins' conference opener came down to one final quarter. Early in the fourth quarter, the Bruins made the single mistake that ultimately cost them the game. A poor center-quarterback exchange put the ball on the ground, and a Washington State defender pounced on it for the fumble recovery in Bruins territory. The Cougars quickly scored. They would tack on a last-minute touchdown, and the final score was 13–0.

The Bruins were 0–1–1 on the season. They still were searching for an offense, and the next big challenge came in the form of a nonconference game in Evanston, Illinois, against Northwestern University. The Northwestern Wildcats, led by Coach Dick Hanley, were a powerhouse program expected to compete for the National Championship. Entering the UCLA game, they were 1–0–1, having soundly defeated Nebraska in their first game of the year. In their second game they faced Notre Dame, which had a 20-game winning streak, but were breaking in a new coach themselves after Knute Rockne had suddenly died in a plane crash on March 31. As it turned out, the final score of that game was 0–0.

When Northwestern and UCLA met in Week 3, the script was once again all too predictable. The Bruins defense continued to play well, but the offense was stuck in the mud. The final score was Northwestern 19, UCLA 0. Coach Spaulding and the Bruins were close to turning the corner. Many believed the varsity Bruins already had a championship-caliber defense. Any semblance of offense could take the Bruins over the top. It had been 12 quarters, and the Bruins still hadn't scored a single point.

The offense was finally able to put it together on October 24 against Pomona-Pitzer. On this day, the Bruins smashed the Sagehens by a score of 46–0. The final score was not the story, however, but rather the way in which everything unfolded. It was utter domination. The Bruins racked up 703 total yards, while the Sagehens amassed just 81. With a 1–2–1 record, the outcome of the Bruins' season would rest on the final four games. The first nemesis was Stanford University. The mighty Stanford team and its coach, Pop Warner, had been a symbol of the Pacific Coast Conference in the mind of Coach William Spaulding. In order to prove that the Bruins belonged, they would have to eventually topple Stanford, as well as USC. The Bruins had improved each year but were yet to defeat Stanford. For the first time since joining the Pacific Coast Conference, the Bruins could taste victory over their new rival. Leonard Wellendorf and Lenny Bergdahl consistently marched the ball down field all game long. In the third quarter, after a long Wellendorf run, Robert Decker punched the ball across the goal line and the Bruins took a 6–0 lead over the Stanford Indians. The Bruins had the lead in the fourth quarter and were now counting on their strong defense to win the game. The bus ride home would, of course, be a much happier journey if the Bruins were to come away victorious. Stanford, however, would not go down without a fight. They quickly marched down the field and scored with relative ease. After missing the extra point, the game was tied and the Bruins offense had an opportunity to win. They failed again, however, and Stanford had one final chance. With just :09 to go, Stanford had the ball deep in UCLA territory. The game would come down to one final play. On the final play of the game, the Stanford offensive line surged, and there was little the defense could do. The final score was 12–6. The Bruins were heartbroken.

Despite the devastating loss, Coach Spaulding was able to rally the troops. Twelve days after the Stanford defeat, the Bruins took on Saint Mary's. The Gaels were eyeing the National Championship. A fierce aerial attack had helped Saint Mary's take down the University of Southern California Trojans earlier in the year by a score of 13–7. If the Gaels were able to defeat the Bruins and the final two opponents on their schedule, they were sure to garner National Champion consideration. The passing game, however, fell flat against the alert Bruins secondary. On the other end of the field, the Bruins were able to flip the script on the Gaels and throw the ball well themselves. Lenny Bergdahl had his best game of the season at quarterback. Bergdahl would throw two touchdowns, one to Bobby Decker and the next to Leonard Wallendorf. The Bruins won the game, 12–0, to end the Gaels' National Championship hopes. It was, to that point, the greatest win of Coach William Spaulding's career.

The next two games were of little interest to many at the time. The Bruins had proved that in 1931 they had possibly the best team in school history. While the Win-Loss-Tie record would not show the improvement, spectators noted the close scores with Stanford and Northwestern, and the great upset over Saint Mary's.

The final game was of historical interest, however. On November 21, the Bruins had fallen to the University of Oregon by a score of 13–6, despite having been considered by many to be the favorite. The final game was against the University of Florida Gators. Richard Mulhaupt played a fine game, and Joseph Keeble was said to have played his greatest game of the season. The Bruins won the game, 13–0, becoming the first western team to defeat an invading southern team in history. The Bruins finished the season with an overall 3–4–1 record and 0–3 conference record.

UCLA vs. Stanford, 1931 (Southern Campus Collection)

The College Football Researchers Association named the University of Southern California the 1931 National Champions.

## 1932

In 1932, football was growing nationwide, and William Spaulding was coaching an ever-improving team in Westwood. Nevertheless, baseball and boxing were still the most popular sports in America. Jack Sharkey became the Heavyweight Boxing Champion of the World after beating Max Schmeling in June, and the New York Yankees swept the Chicago Cubs in the World Series. The Yankees had a record nine future Hall of Famers on the roster, most notably Lou Gehrig and Babe Ruth. Closer to home, 1932 was an Olympic year, and Los Angeles was the host of the summer games.

1932 UCLA team photo (Southern Campus Collection)

The UCLA football season started on September 23 against a new opponent. For the first time in history, UCLA would take on the University of California at Davis. The captains for the 1932 season were Homer Oliver and Lee Coats. On this occasion, UC Davis stood no chance. Coach Spaulding displayed his usual confidence going into the 1932 season, but this team felt different. They truly were a conference contender. Following the defeat of UC Davis, the Bruins took on the Idaho Vandals in the conference opener. The results of this game, played under the lights and in a torrential downpour, provided a significant moment in UCLA history. The Bruins defeated Idaho by the score of 6–0 and for the first time in school history found themselves atop the PCC standings.

Two weeks after beating Idaho, UCLA was off to Oregon to face the Oregon Webfeet. The game was played in Portland at Multnomah Stadium, and UCLA struggled for much of the game. A serious leg injury took Haughton "Fat" Norfleet out of the game, and despite the most valiant of efforts from Homer Oliver and the defensive bunch, the Bruins fell behind in the third quarter on a 35-yard touchdown run by George Pepelnjak. With the clock ticking and 5:00 left to play in the fourth, the Bruins remained calm. "Papa" Joe Berry hauled in a

51-yard pass from Mike Frankovich, and two plays later Berry plunged into the end zone. The kick was missed, however, and the Bruins trailed, 7–6. As in the Stanford game the year before, this contest would end in classic fashion. The Bruins defense held, and the Webfeet were forced to punt. The Bruins had one last shot, with the ball at their own 7-yard line and :15 to go. The ball was snapped, and Frankovich dropped back into the muddy end zone. Ransom Livesay was streaking down the sideline. With everything he had, Frankovich released the ball, throwing it as far as he could, and hit Livesay in stride! The ball was caught, and Livesay sprinted down the sideline for the winning touchdown with no time left on the clock. The score was 12–7. The miracle in Portland made the Bruins 3–0 on the season.

Following the dramatic win against the University of Oregon, the Bruins easily dispatched Caltech by a score of 51–0 before facing the Stanford Indians. With each passing year, the Bruins had played closer and closer games against Stanford but had yet to defeat them. On October 29, 1932, that would change. This was the win that helped elevate UCLA to the next level. Despite falling behind early, the Bruins thoroughly outplayed the Indians in the second half. The game was close in the fourth quarter, with the Bruins leading by a score of 7–6, when Clayton "Dutch" Yearick blocked a punt and the Bruins recovered for a touchdown. The final score was 13–6. Coach William Spaulding had finally beaten Pop Warner, in what turned out to be their final meeting.

The Bruins were 5–0 with five games left to play. The back end of the schedule was daunting. If the Bruins wanted to win the PCC title, they would have to finish the season well. If they wanted to win the National Championship (something they had never even dreamed of until beating Stanford), they would have to finish flawlessly.

The sixth game of the season came on November 11, 1932, against Saint Mary's. The Gaels were sure to remember the upset of 1931, when the Bruins handed the Gaels the loss that ultimately cost them the National Championship. The Bruins got out of the gate early and took a 7–0 lead on a touchdown pass from Frankovich to Bobby Decker. The early offense, however, proved to be not enough. The Gaels regrouped and played a better brand of football than the Bruins the rest of the way. The final score was 14–7, with the Bruins suffering their first defeat of the season.

One week after the loss, the Bruins were tasked with playing the Montana Grizzlies, and in the Battle of the Bears, the Grizzlies proved no match for the Bruins. UCLA won, 32–0. With three weeks left in the season, the Bruins were 6–1, but still undefeated in conference play. The next opponent was conference foe Washington State University. This game was a battle in which any yardage gained was earned through force. UCLA outgained WSU in the first half but suffered a devastating injury when leading rusher Johnny Fletcher went down with a broken ankle. With 32 seconds left in a scoreless tie, John Eubank entered the game for the Cougars and attempted a 47-yard place kick. The ball had the distance and went straight through the uprights, for what was the longest successful kick in the entire country in 1932. The Bruins lost, 3–0.

The dreams of a conference championship were dashed the following week. After the brutal loss to WSU, the Bruins took on the University of Washington and were outclassed from start to finish. The final score was 19–0 UW. The season-ending game resulted in another defeat, this time at the hands of the revenge-minded University of Florida Gators. The Bruins made the long trip across the country and lost, 12–2. They finished the season with a 6–4 overall record and a 4–2 record in conference.

The College Football

UCLA vs. Oregon, 1932 (Southern Campus Collection)

Researchers Association named the University of Southern California the 1932 National Champions.

## 1933

The 1933 season included matchups against many familiar foes and several new ones. With the improvement of the squad finally evident on the scoreboard in 1932, Coach William Spaulding wanted to make sure his team didn't get complacent. The spring football season was treacherous. Spaulding pushed his men harder in 1933 than ever before. Captain Lee Coats was a centerpiece of the 1933 Bruins. Steady at center, Coats was a man who was not only gifted on the gridiron; he was a vocal leader as well, inspirational and self-motivated. Teammates often said that no man showed more pride than Lee Coats. Following the 1933 season, he would be honored for his efforts by being named the first All-American in UCLA football history.

The 1933 season would start with two nonconference opponents. The first game of the year was against Los Angeles Junior College on September 22. The Bruins handled business the way many anticipated they would. Now a known commodity on the West Coast, playing in a premier conference, the expectations were that William Spaulding's men would destroy inferior teams like L.A. J.C. They did just that. The final score was 34–0.

The following week, the Bruins were tested a bit more by San Diego State. After capturing a lead just 10 plays into the game, the offense stagnated. In the third quarter, SDSU was able to push the ball to the Bruins' 17-yard line. Four plays later, SDSU threw a pass into the end zone that found no receiver. They turned the ball over on downs. The Bruins then drove down the field and scored the game-clinching touchdown. UCLA defeated SDSU, 13–0, and conference play arrived.

Since joining the PCC, the most memorable of UCLA games would often come against the Stanford Indians. In 1932, the Bruins finally were able to defeat the Indians for the first time. In 1933, Stanford was a new team in the sense that legendary Head Coach Pop Warner had moved on, Coach Claude Thornhill was in his first year at the Farm, and expectations were very high. Despite the loss of Coach Warner, the Indians had a number of returning players. The defense was stacked, and the offense was led by quarterback Frank Alustiza. Many believed it was the Indians' year to win the PCC crown. Despite the low-scoring outcome and the closeness of the game, it was a one-sided affair. Stanford repeatedly drove the ball into Bruins territory, only to be stopped by the stalwarts of the Bruins defense: Sam Storey, Lee Coats, and Walter Muller. The Bruins were ultimately defeated on a drop kick off the toe of Stanford All-American guard Bill Corpus. The 3–0 defeat was a tough one to handle for UCLA, but the Bruins had to prepare for their next challenge, which was just a week away.

Chuck Cheshire runs the ball against Cal, 1933 (Southern Campus Collection)

Following the Stanford defeat, UCLA played a series of nonconference games against unfamiliar opponents. On October 6, the Bruins took on the University of Utah Redskins in a night game at the Coliseum. Despite a slow start, the Bruins were easily able to dismantle the Redskins by a score of 21–0. Mike Frankovich connected with Julian Smith for a touchdown, Ransom Livesay rushed for a touchdown, and Jack Caldwell intercepted a Utah pass and returned it for a touchdown. Next on the schedule was Loyola Marymount University. Billed as a tough matchup between two emerging western powers, the game was won by the Bruins by the score of 20–7.

The Bruins were 4–1 on the season, but just as in prior years, the back half of the schedule would be much tougher. On October 28, it was back to conference play. Coach Spaulding, Lee Coats, and the boys outplayed the Webfeet for the entirety of the ball game but struggled to get the ball into the end zone. They continued to batter Oregon all over the field and then struggle when it came time to put points on the board. The Webfeet themselves got on the scoreboard only once, when Anselmo Pozzo caught a pass while surrounded by multiple Bruins defenders. Down 7–0 in the fourth quarter, the Bruins offense came alive. After a long, sustained drive, the Bruins finally reached the end zone on a pass from Chuck Cheshire to Mike Frankovich. The Bruins were an extra point away from tying the game—until they weren't. It turned out that there was a flag on the field. Frankovich was ruled to have stepped out of bounds prior to catching the ball. The touchdown was nullified, and the Bruins lost, 7–0.

When the Bruins met the University of California Berkeley varsity squad on November 4, it represented a shift in attitude. No longer was UCLA to play second fiddle to their University of California counterparts up north, but they were now legitimate equals and demanded to be treated as such. It was the first game between the rivals ever played at the Coliseum, and though all promised to keep the rivalry friendly, it was the most important game on the calendar for all involved. On this day, defense reigned supreme. The UCLA defensive line, led by Fred Haslam and Verdi Boyer, stifled the Berkeley running game. Only twice were the Cal Bears able to cross into Bruins territory and only once reached as far as the Bruins 15-yard line. That drive stalled, however, and ended with the Bears turning the ball over on downs. The Bears were unable to score all day, but would the Bruins be able to capitalize? Could they score one time and come away victorious? The Bruins six times marched the ball into Cal territory but six times were denied. The closest they came to scoring came on an attempted drop kick from the 15-yard line by do-everything star Mike Frankovich. The kick missed by inches, and the game ended in a scoreless tie.

The Pacific Coast Conference was a grind. The Bruins were 4–0 out of conference, but 0–2–1 in conference in three close, hard-fought games, from none of which the Bruins came out victorious. On November 11, the Bruins were happy to see another non-conference opponent. A short trip to San Diego to face the San Diego Marines was just what the Bruins needed to get back in the win column. The game was much more difficult than expected, however, as the Marines fought until the very end. Down 14–0 in the fourth quarter, the Marines scored two touchdowns but failed on the second extra point, and the Bruins held on to win, 14–13. The following two weeks were difficult for the Bruins, as they achieved little to no success against the University of Washington and Saint Mary's. The once promising season was falling apart.

The last game of the year was against Washington State University on Thanksgiving Day. The only score for either team came on an interception return by Frankovich. He then converted the extra point himself, and the Bruins won, 7–0.

The 1933 season was much like the early history of UCLA football. While there was a measurable amount of success, there were also many moments of heartache. Expectations had been raised and so had the level of play. The Bruins finished the season with an overall 6–4–1 record.

The College Football Researchers Association named the University of Michigan the 1933 National Champions.

## 1934

After two years contributing to the varsity squad in the record books, Ransom Livesay was now a captain. Unlike the captain of the 1933 team, Lee Coats, Livesay was a quiet man who preferred to stay out of the spotlight, except of course when he was dominating opponents on Saturday afternoons. The 1934 season started off with two convincing

UCLA's version of the Four Horsemen—Livesay, Frankovich, Key, and Cheshire (Southern Campus Collection)

out-of-conference wins. The Bruins had proven in years past that they could start the season fast, and they had proven that they could dominate inferior opponents in nonconference games. This was again the case to start the '34 season. The Bruins easily defeated Pomona-Pitzer by a score of 14–0 and followed up their solid performance with an even better showing against San Diego State University. The Bruins moved to 2–0 after defeating the Aztecs, 20–0.

The rubber match in the Oregon series came on September 30. In 1932, the Bruins won the Miracle in Portland on a long 93-yard touchdown by Ransom Livesay on the last play of the game. In 1933, the University of Oregon varsity squad returned the favor, beating the Bruins in a thriller. Would more fireworks go off in 1934? The Bruins traveled nearly a thousand miles for the first conference game in Eugene. This game would set the tone for the rest of the season. If the Bruins were able to beat the Ducks, they would surely have a shot at bringing home the Pacific Coast Conference crown. Despite what appeared to all to be an important game, the '34 Bruins simply laid an egg. Fumbles, blocked punts, and interceptions were the theme. UCLA was thoroughly outplayed by a much better Oregon team on this day. The final score was 26–3 Oregon. UCLA was at a crossroads. The dreams of a conference championship that pushed the team through the offseason took a major hit. With seven games still on the schedule, the question presented itself—would UCLA bounce back?

The 1934 season was a roller coaster. Following the disappointing loss to Oregon, the second conference game came against the Montana Grizzlies. The Grizzlies were no match for the Bruins on this day. Led by Chuck Cheshire and his 93-yard touchdown run, UCLA defeated Montana by a score of 16–0. The second- and third-string players for the Bruins were able to gain valuable experience in the second half of a conference game.

The following week, the Bruins played the California Golden Bears. The previous year, the two teams had battled to a scoreless tie. In this game, the result was almost identical. The Bruins once again moved the ball up and down the field against the Golden Bears, only to stall in Cal territory. Chuck Cheshire, R.F. Key, and Ransom Livesay burst through the line for five yards per carry. Still, they couldn't get in the end zone. In the fourth quarter, the Berkeley offense finally came alive. On their only successful drive all game, the Golden Bears reached the Bruins' 18-yard line before Arleigh Williams place-kicked the ball right through the uprights. Another heartbreaker. Berkeley won the game, 3–0.

The roller coaster continued in the next two games, as well. After the brutal defeat at the hands of the Golden Bears, the Bruins trounced the University of California at Davis by a score of 49–0. Howard Haradon threw four touchdowns passes, one each to Sinclair Lott, Chuck Cheshire, Mike Frankovich, and R.F. Key.

The following week, the Stanford Indians marched into town. Unlike most of the meetings between the Bruins and Indians in the 1930s, this game was not even close. Stanford easily defeated the Bruins by the score of 27–0.

On November 12, UCLA took on friendly foe Saint Mary's. The nonconference rivals had become familiar with each other over the years. Despite being a prestigious program, Saint Mary's was unable to walk right through the Bruins. The 1934 game was like many before it—a hard-fought battle. The Gaels walked into the Coliseum sporting new jerseys. The flashy red, white, and blue caught the eyes of everyone in attendance. Unfortunately for the Gaels, they caught the eyes of the Bruins, as well. UCLA was able to easily stop the Gaels passing attack, never letting a Saint Mary's receiver break free. Only once did the Gaels threaten to score. In the second quarter, the Bruins defense was backed up near their own goal line. First and goal from the 3-yard line. Four times the Gaels tried to penetrate the goal line, and four times they were denied. Despite the Bruins offense never finding their rhythm, UCLA found a way to win. In the third quarter, after completing a short pass, a Saint Mary's receiver fumbled, and the ball was recovered and rushed into the end zone by a Bruins defender. The extra point was missed, but it mattered little. The final score was 6–0, and the Bruins were back in the win column.

On November 24, the Bruins would play their last conference game of the year. Behind a brilliant rushing performance by Chuck Cheshire and the steady passing of Mike Frankovich, the Bruins were able to defeat Oregon State University by a score of 25–7. Though the Bruins finished conference play with a 2–3 record, they still were assured of a winning season. With one game to go, the Bruins were 6–3 overall. While not relevant in the conference standings, the last game of the year against Loyola Marymount was very important in the record books. Three times previously, 1927, 1932, and 1933, the Bruins had won six games in a season. Never before had they won seven. On November 29, they had the opportunity to make school history.

After two quarters, the score was tied. Neither team had threatened to score, and when the second half began, the score was the same as at the kickoff, 0–0. While Frankovich and Livesay were the stars, it would take the entire roster, and especially the 10 graduating seniors, to put the Bruins over the top. LMU scored on the first drive of the second half, and the Bruins trailed, 6–0. With a struggling offense, even a mere six-point deficit can seem like a hole too deep to dig out of at times, but the Bruins of 1934 did not know how to quit. On the next drive, the Bruins answered right back. Chuck Cheshire threw a beautiful pass into the end zone that landed gracefully into the hands of the waiting Bruins receiver. The extra point try failed, and the score was tied, 6–6. The game could have easily ended in a 6–6 tie, but Cheshire would not be denied. On the last drive of the game, the last of the season, Cheshire did it all. He ran, passed, and willed his team into the end zone. The seventh win was official. The Bruins finished the season with a 7–3 record. While Coach Spaulding had turned the UCLA program from doormat to competitor, he still had one goal in mind. The ever-elusive conference championship was in his sights.

The College Football Researchers Association named the University of Minnesota the 1934 National Champions.

## 1935

Nineteen thirty-five was a special year. Coach William Spaulding was entering his eleventh season and believed he had his best team yet. As the popularity of college football grew, so did the media coverage. Fans were engaged from coast to coast, and not only were teams now known throughout the nation, but individuals prominent on the football field were becoming household names. The Downtown Athletic Club, which had a long history of love of sport, announced that following the 1935 season, a new individual award would be given to the best player in the nation. On December 9, the DAC Trophy was handed out for the first time. One year later, the name of the trophy was changed to the Heisman Trophy. The now famous trophy was modeled after Ed Smith, star of the 1934 New York University football team. The Heisman has stood the test of time, and no other individual award is as prestigious in all of sports.

If the Bruins were to achieve their dreams in 1935, they would have to do what they had yet to do since joining the PCC. They would have to dominate not only out of conference, but in conference. They had a brilliant record in nonconference games since joining the PCC, but when it came to conference play, the results never matched. With the help of Assistant Coaches Fred Oster, Edwin Horrell, and Al Strurtzenegger, Coach Spaulding and the varsity men hoped to finally claim the top spot. Though the expectations in Westwood were higher than ever before, not all was well in the world. The Depression raged on, and hope faded. College students dropped out in record numbers. Coach Spaulding barely had enough players on his roster to scrimmage full teams in practice. Despite lacking numbers, the season would go on. The Bruins, limited in bodies, still had a surplus of talent. The season would begin on September 28 against Utah State.

The first game of the year proved to be a preview of things to come. The Bruins routed the Utah State Aggies by a score of 39–0. Chuck Cheshire had already established himself as a star player, and in 1935 he took his game to another level. Don Ferguson, Bill Murphy, and Fred Funk all scored touchdowns in the opener. Following the dominant season opener, the Bruins took on Oregon State University. The game, played in Portland at Multnomah Stadium, was the first time the Bruins had played in Portland since the "miracle" against the University of Oregon in 1932. Immediately after kickoff, the Oregon State Beavers unleashed an aerial attack the likes of which the Bruins had never seen before. Coach Spaulding was expecting a heavy dose of running from the OSU backs, but when they came out passing, everyone was caught off guard. In just four minutes, OSU had driven down the field and scored. It was 7–0, and the Bruins had a fight on their hands. Much to the delight of the Bruins faithful, Cheshire and the offense then marched down the field 77 yards and countered with a touchdown, but the extra point was missed. Down

7–6 in the fourth quarter, the Bruins could see their dreams slipping away. It was just the second game of the season, but if the Bruins lost, it would be a tough task to win the conference. Just after the fourth quarter began, the Bruins capped a long drive with a short run into the end zone. On the ensuing OSU drive, UCLA's William Murphy intercepted a pass and returned it 52 yards for another TD. The final score was 20–7 Bruins.

Chuck Cheshire runs the ball against Cal, 1935 (Southern Campus Collection)

If the Bruins were to win the PCC in '35, their main competition appeared to be from Stanford and Cal. In the third game of the season, the Bruins had their first opportunity to make a statement. The team would travel to Palo Alto to take on the Stanford Indians. There was a noticeable difference on campus for this game, as the Westwood students seemed to have caught football fever. With Stanford next on the schedule, the student body chanted "On to Stanford" all week. The day before the game, nearly half of the student body migrated north to catch the big game. Stanford Stadium was filled with the blue of UCLA's blue and gold. In the first quarter, Stanford, the heavy favorites, looked like the dominant team they were said to be. Frank Alustiza intercepted a pass and advanced to the Bruins' 20-yard line. Two plays later, All-American halfback Bobby Grayson scored the game's first touchdown. The Bruins quickly bounced back. Still in the first quarter, after a punt pinned the Indians back, Robert "Bones" Hamilton of the Indians fumbled, and the ball was recovered by—who else but—Chuck Cheshire. Three plays later, Ted Key crossed the goal line. Unlike the Stanford attempt had been, UCLA's PAT was successful, and they took a 7–6 lead. Throughout the rest of the game, Stanford continued to push the ball into Bruins territory, only to be stopped. The Bruins thrashed through the Indians line but were also stopped. With one final chance, the Indians failed, turned the ball over on downs, and the Bruins had won the big game. They were 3–0 and in a prime position to take the PCC title.

On October 26, the Bruins handily defeated Oregon by a score of 33–6. The next test, however, would be against the other PCC championship contender, the California Golden Bears. The theme of Homecoming Week in Westwood was "Who's afraid of the big, bad bear? No one." While certainly Coach Spaulding and his players were fearless, the Golden Bears had an excellent team, and the game was of utmost importance. Coach Spaulding was said to have increased the practice load of his team all week, staying late at night preparing for the Bears. When it was time to put aside all the homecoming activities and play football, a record crowd of over eighty-five thousand filled the Coliseum. The game, however, did not live up to the hype, as the Bruins were soundly defeated in the biggest game of the year. Cal scored a touchdown early to take a 7–0 lead, and though the Bruins countered by forcing a safety in the second quarter, a blocked punt led to another Cal touchdown. The final score was 14–2. The Bruins were not out of the hunt in the PCC, but they would need Cal to falter, and they would need to win the rest of their own conference games.

Before that next conference game, the Bruins fell again. On November 9, Southern Methodist University traveled to Los Angeles and dismantled the Bruins by the score of 21–0. Six short days later, the Bruins would take on the University of Hawaii, defeating the Roaring Rainbows despite giving up a 102-yard kickoff return for a touchdown by Tommy Kaulukukui. The Bruins finished their three-game nonconference stretch with another matchup against Loyola Marymount. Despite being outplayed most of the afternoon, the Bruins won, 14–6. Cheshire and Fred Funk each scored for the Bruins.

With two games to go, the Bruins were 6–2. They no longer had to worry about the Golden Bears or the Stanford Indians. They had to focus on what was left on their schedule.

In the final conference game of the year, the Bruins took on the Idaho Vandals on December 7. In this incredibly important game, the Bruins dominated, but the scoreboard—which implied a deceptively close 12–6 UCLA victory—didn't reflect that. Just two weeks earlier, Stanford had beaten Cal. Both teams had finished the conference with one loss. After the Bruins defeated Idaho, all three teams—UCLA, Stanford, and Cal—were named co-champions.

For the first time in school history, the Bruins had won a conference title, and in finishing the season by dispatching Saint Mary's, they had won a school-record 8th game. The next goal would be to win the National Championship. The 1935 Bruins finished the season with an 8–2 overall record.

On December 9, the Downtown Athletic Club named Jay Berwanger of the University of Chicago the Downtown Athletic Club Trophy (Heisman) Winner.

The College Football Researchers Association named the University of Minnesota the 1935 National Champions.

The 1935 Bruins were co-PCC champions (Southern Campus Collection)

## 1936

Nineteen thirty-six was a year of change globally, as war clouds gathered over Europe.

In the college football world, there were significant historical events taking place in 1936, as well. The Seven Blocks of Granite gained great fame at Fordham University. The nickname came from Fordham publicist Tim Cohane and was used to describe the impenetrable defensive line. Most notable among the Seven Blocks was future Green Bay Packers legendary coach Vince Lombardi. Though deemed the least talented of the seven Blocks, Lombardi was the heart and soul of the unit, whose other members included future NFL Hall of Famer Alex Wojciechowicz, Al Babartsky, Nat Pierce, Ed Franco, Leo Paquin, and John Druze. Also of note in 1936, the Associated Press would for the first time release a college football ranking at the end of the season. For the next 62 years, the AP would be the premier college football poll in the nation.

As for the Bruins, the team now had a target squarely on its back. As cochampions of the PCC in 1935, they were no longer gunning for the top spot; they were themselves being hunted. Coach Spaulding was now in his 12th year, and if he were to keep the momentum and continue building the UCLA program, 1936 would be a critical season.

The 1936 season had appeared on paper to start with three easy games. With the Bruins breaking in a new quarterback, Coach Spaulding had seen this as a blessing. His players would be able to find their way before taking on the University of Washington in the fourth game of the year. Now, finding the balancing act between working out the kinks and still playing well enough to win football games was the great challenge facing his team in the fall of 1936. Some of the leadership responsibilities would fall on senior lineman Bob Barr and halfback Fred Funk. The first two games of the year were against Occidental College and Pomona-Pitzer. While the Bruins dominated both games on the scoreboard (winning 21–0 and 26–0, respectively), there were troubling signs for Coach Spaulding and the boys, as well.

Through two games, the Bruins' rushing offense and rushing defense performed well, but the passing offense and passing defense struggled mightily. The Bruins had a large team. Size was never an issue in 1936, but what the Bruins had in bulk they lacked in speed and agility. Though they outweighed the Tigers and Sagehens by over 20 pounds per man, the finesse game gave the Bruins problems.

After defeating the University of Montana in the conference opener the following week, 30–0, the Bruins would face the University of Washington in Week 4. By the time the Huskies showed up at the Coliseum on October 10, Coach Spaulding and staff had worked tirelessly on correcting the many issues in the passing game. Though the coaches felt they could work around the offensive passing deficiencies through sheer power, the defense was more worrisome. In the second quarter in particular, the Bruins' poor pass defense was exposed. The Huskies' offense, led by Bryon Haines, marched down the field as Fritz Waskowitz rushed to his left, only to lateral at the last second to Al Cruver, who ran 22 yards to daylight and into the end zone. In the fourth quarter, the Bruins still trailed, 7–0, when Merle Harris fumbled and Bud Douglas recovered for a Huskies touchdown. The University of Washington won the game, 14–0.

Despite the loss, the Bruins still had a chance at the PCC crown. In 1935, they had lost to California Berkeley but were still able to grab a share of the conference title. While the Washington loss was certainly disappointing, motivation was never an issue when the Bruins faced Cal, as they did one week after the UW loss. On October 17, the Bruins were once again able to make history. Playing in Berkeley Stadium, the Bruins brought their "A" game. Though the passing game had struggled to that point, Hal Hirshon played his best game in a Bruins uniform. In the second quarter, he dropped back and lofted a perfectly timed pass 33 yards into the end zone for the score. Bob Schroeder came down with the ball with no Golden Bears there to stop him. Billy Bob Williams added a field goal for the Bruins, and Hirshon and Schroeder connected once again for another score. The only points scored by Cal came on a short rushing touchdown by Floyd Blower. The final score was 17–6, the first Bruins victory over the University of California Berkeley Golden Bears in school history.

Halfway through the season, the Bruins sat at 4–1 and were still in contention for their second consecutive PCC crown. On October 24, the Bruins defeated the Oregon State Beavers, and on Halloween night they would take on the defending cochampion Stanford Indians. After defeating the Indians in '35, many called this the game of the year, not because of the result, but rather because of the expectations. It was Homecoming Week in Westwood, and as tradition had it, Homecoming was unsurprisingly festive. While the student body was able to enjoy the parade and bonfire, the Bruins' varsity football squad had a difficult task on their hands. If the results of the game were simply based on yardage gained and first downs attained, the Bruins would have fared much better than they did. Though they outgained Stanford in yardage and gained 14 first downs to Stanford's nine, the Bruins fell on the scoreboard. Stanford proved to be very opportunistic. Peter Zagar blocked a Fred Funk punt in the first quarter, and shortly after, Anthony Calvelli ran the ball into the end zone. The Bruins came back and in the third quarter scored on a 4-yard pass from Izzy Cantor to Charles Pike. As the game wore on, it became clear that the Pike score would be the Bruins' last success of the day. Stanford proceeded to score 13 unanswered points, and the Bruins fell, 19–6.

The Bruins were 5–2, and their chances of repeating as PCC champs had been dashed. With three games left, there was still cause for internal motivation. If the Bruins could come away with three more wins, they would tie the school record from the previous year with eight total for the season. The first victory came on November 7 against the University of Oregon. The Bruins offense struggled for much of the day, but the defense was superb and shut out the Ducks. Seven thousand spectators saw Cantor score the only touchdown of the day.

The next team on the schedule was Washington State University. With the University of Southern California just one week away, it was not the time to overlook an opponent, and Washington State was not the team to allow it. The Cougars easily dismantled the Bruins, 32–7. It was an embarrassing loss, and with one game to go against the rival Trojans, the Bruins would need to bounce back to finish '36 strong.

The 1936 Trojans presented a whole new problem for the Bruins. USC had won multiple National Championships in the decade, and though they would finish the '36 season with just a 4–2–3 record, the prestige and hype surrounding its program never dissipated. With 11 seniors playing their last collegiate game for UCLA, no better way could be imagined than going out with a victory over the Trojans. Prior to the game, there was talk of postponing or cancelling the affair because of continuous threats from each side to paint the other school's campus with rival colors. In the end, no such pranks occurred, and the game went on as scheduled. The game ended in a 7–7 tie. A new tradition was also born. As had been the custom at the time, the winner of the game would receive the game ball. However, on this particular occasion it was a tie and both sides wanted to take the ball, so it was decided that from then forward the winner of the game would take the 1936 ball as a trophy.

UCLA finished the season with a 6–3–1 record.

The Downtown Athletic Club named Larry Kelley of Yale University the 1936 Heisman Trophy Winner.

The Associated Press named the University of Minnesota the 1936 National Champions.

## 1937

In 1937, the Bruins got bit by the injury bug. Despite high expectations, the odds of returning to the top of the PCC standings took a hit when starting halfback Joe Kostopolisextcy broke his ankle in a preseason scrimmage. Joe's was just one of several injuries, and when the season kicked off in the fall, the Bruins would be seriously shorthanded. While Kostopolisextcy was lost for the season, a new man had arrived. Fresh from a successful stint the year prior on the freshman team, sophomore Kenny Washington was on the varsity and ready to make a name for himself. It was only a matter of time. Along with Kenny Washington, other prominent players on the 1937 team included William Williams, Hal Hirshon, Tex Harris, George Pfeiffer, Woody Strode, Johnny Ryland, Walt Schell, and Slats Wyrick.

Though not a prominent player while at UCLA, one member of the team who deserves special recognition is Francis Wai. Seventy-six years after his last game at UCLA, Wai would be inducted into the UCLA Athletics Hall of Fame. For two seasons, '37 and '38, Wai suited up for Coach Spaulding and his men. Several years later, Wai would suit up for the 24th Infantry Division of the United States Army. On December 7, 1941, Wai was stationed at Pearl Harbor when the United States came under attack. Though he survived Pearl Harbor, Wai's life would change. The United States was at war. During the Philippines campaign, Wai, now a captain in the United States Army, led an uncovered assault meant to draw Japanese fire and expose their position. Wai, who was killed during the courageous assault, was later awarded posthumously a Distinguished Service Cross and a Medal of Honor.

Before the war, however, before Wai was a hero, there was the 1937 football season, which kicked off on September 24. Led by Kenny Washington, the game was never in doubt. Several plays into the game, Bruins junior Johnny Baida intercepted an Oregon Webfoot pass. Two plays later, Washington ran for 57 yards and a touchdown. The Bruins never looked back. Dale Gilmore and Walt Schell played fine games, as well. Schell would score the second touchdown of the season, and the game quickly turned into a rout. Oregon would score two late touchdowns, but the Bruins easily won by a final score of 26–13.

The second game of the year would pit the UCLA Bruins vs. the Stanford Indians once again. The Bruins were favored on this afternoon in Palo Alto, and after a dominant opening week performance, many thought the meeting with the Indians could be similar. Stanford was 0–2 on the season, but hungry for their first win of 1937. While the Bruins may have looked good against the Webfeet, Stanford once again proved that football was a week-to-week sport and anything can happen at any given time. Jim Groves of Stanford scored early in the first quarter on an 11-yard run to give the Indians a 6–0 lead. In the second quarter, Groves once again led his team down the field and this time completed a 10-yard pass to Pete Fay for the second Indians touchdown. The Bruins offense, to the surprise of all in attendance, was never able to get on track. The only points the Bruins were able to muster came on a long interception return for a touchdown by Hal Hirshon. The Bruins lost the game, 12–7. Everyone was shocked, but the team was forced to regroup and hit the field again one week later.

Unfortunately for the Bruins, regrouping after the Stanford loss was easier said than done. After a Week 3 tie with Oregon State University, UCLA would go on to lose the next four games, including a 27–14 loss to top-ranked California. Facing the University of Washington on November 13, many of the players saw snow for the first time in their lives. When they took on Southern Methodist University, Kenny Washington ran for a touchdown, threw a touchdown, and intercepted a pass that he returned for a touchdown, though the interception return was called back due to a penalty. Mr. Washington, just a sophomore but on his way to becoming the greatest Bruin of all time, proved to be the lone bright spot during the midseason slump.

On November 27, the Bruins took the field against the University of Missouri Tigers in a nonconference battle. Riding a current four-game losing streak, facing a foe from the Big 6 Conference seemed like a daunting task, but despite their struggles throughout the season, the Bruins were up for the challenge. The star of the game was the Bruins defense. Entering the second half, the game remained scoreless. UCLA had threatened to score in the first, but their offense couldn't get on the board. On the other hand, the Bruins defense repeatedly pummeled the Tigers offense and gave the ball back to the Bruins offense. In the second half, the Bruins finally broke through. After scoring on a long drive to take the lead in the third quarter, UCLA scored once again, but this time in spectacular fashion. Early in the fourth quarter, Kenny Washington intercepted a pass in the flat and raced down the sideline. Seeing that the would-be tackler had an angle on him, Washington cut back, avoiding one man, and lateraled the ball in stride to John Ryland, who raced into the end zone. The Bruins took a 13–0 lead and never looked back.

Finally, on December 4, the season would come to an end, but not before one final clash, this one with the University of Southern California. The Trojans, predictably, got off to a quick start and grabbed an early lead. The score was 19–0 through three quarters, and it appeared the Bruins' season would end in defeat. In the fourth quarter, however, UCLA surged. Coach Spaulding, though criticized throughout the season for working his players too hard during the week only to have them fade on Saturdays, had a strong, well-conditioned team, while the much more talented Trojans, led by quarterback Grenville Landsell, faded. The Bruins scored two touchdowns in a minute and 26 seconds. Kenny Washington, to the surprise of no one, led the charge. Both touchdowns came on Washington passes, the second of which was the longest touchdown pass in college football that season. The 62-yard connection from Washington to Hirshon brought the Bruins within six points. Down 19–13, the Bruins were able to get the ball back in time for one final drive. Washington and the Bruins marched down the field to the Trojans' 15-yard line. There was time for one last play. Washington dropped back, looked to the end zone, couldn't find an open man, scrambled, and eventually threw a pass into the end zone that landed incomplete. It was a valiant comeback, but the Bruins lost the game, 19–13. UCLA would finish 1937 with a 2–6–1 record.

The Downtown Athletic Club named Clint Frank of Yale University the 1937 Heisman Trophy Winner.

The Associated Press named the University of Pittsburgh the 1937 National Champions.

Kenny Washington runs the ball against SMU, 1937 (Southern Campus Collection)

## 1938

Following a disappointing 1937, Coach Spaulding was challenged with turning the '38 squad into a winner. George Pfeiffer and Harold Hirshon were the 1938 cocaptains, and Kenny Washington was the star. After a scintillating sophomore campaign, the expectations for Washington's junior season were sky-high. The 1938 assistant coaches—Edwin Horrell, AJ Sturzenegger, Clifton Simpson, Ray Richards, Cecil Hollingsworth, and Wilber Johns—along with Head Coach William

Spaulding, would have the task of turning a talented roster that underachieved the previous year into men who could meet their potential and vie for the top spot in the PCC.

The opening game, which took place on September 23, was against the Iowa Hawkeyes of the Western Conference. In front of the largest opening game crowd in UCLA history, the Bruins easily defeated the Hawkeyes, 27–3. Woody Strode, Dale Gilmore, Merle Harris, and Jack Montgomery each scored a touchdown for the Bruins.

In the first PCC game of the year, UCLA would take on the Oregon Webfeet. Despite being dominated in yardage gained, the Bruins were in the game into the fourth quarter. Down 14–6, Kenny Washington strung together consecutive runs of 17 yards and 24 yards for a touchdown. Following both touchdowns, however, the Bruins failed to make the extra point. With under a minute to go, the Bruins had the ball, down two points. Charlie Fenenbock then busted through the line for 55 yards and a touchdown! The UCLA sideline went wild, but there was a flag on the play, which was brought back on a holding call, and the Bruins would go on to be defeated, 14–12.

In Week 3 against the Huskies, the only successful Washington that day went by the name Kenny. The UCLA star put the Bruins on his back and carried his underdog squad to a 13–0 win. Both touchdowns on the day were scored on Kenny Washington runs—one of which came from 30 yards out and the other from the 1-yard line. The fourth game of the year once again pit the Bruins against the rival Cal Golden Bears. California, which would ultimately finish tied for the PCC crown, proved to be too much for the Bruins and won by the score of 20–7. The left the Bruins 2–2 on the season, and, while they looked to be significantly improved over 1937, much remained to be proven before 1938 could be called a success.

Following the setback against Berkeley, the Bruins played two of their finest games of the season. On October 22, the Bruins easily defeated the highly publicized Idaho Vandals. Led by the great blocking of Johnny Ryland and the usual great running of Kenny Washington, the Bruins dominated from start to finish. The Vandals were only able to muster up 157 yards for the day. The Bruins gained 327 in the 33–0 win.

After the Vandals, old foe Stanford was next on the schedule. It was Homecoming Week, and the theme on campus was "Scalping Time in the Bruins Manner." Eleanor Flynn was named the Homecoming Queen. When the Bruins faced the Indians on the field, 37,000 were in attendance at the Coliseum to see the game. Coach William Spaulding was unavailable for the game due to sickness, so assistant Edwin Horrel took over the head duties. The game was not pretty. The Indians fumbled four times, and all four were recovered by the Bruins. Only once, however, were the Bruins able to capitalize. In the second quarter, Bus Sutherland plunged forward across the goal line. With just seconds to go in the fourth quarter, Stanford was able to drive the ball to the Bruins' 10-yard line but was unable to get off one final snap before the gun sounded, and the game was over. The Bruins won by the score of 6–0.

Following the Stanford game, it appeared to all observers that the 1938 team was one to be reckoned with. They continued their fine play the next week by traveling to Pullman, Washington, and defeating the Washington State Cougars, 21–0. Challenges lay ahead, though, as the Bruins were set to take on back-to-back ranked opponents. On November 12, the University of Wisconsin traveled from Madison to Los Angeles to take on the Bruins. The game was a frustrating affair for the home team. Despite outgaining the Badgers in yards and first downs, the Bruins continually tripped themselves up. A holding call brought back their lone first-half touchdown, and the offense sputtered in the opponent's territory. Trailing 14–0, the Bruins were able to get on the board late, but it wasn't enough. The No. 15 Wisconsin Badgers won the game, 14–7. Things would only get tougher for the Bruins the following week. Though the game was played at the L.A. Coliseum, the Bruins were the away team when they took on No. 14 USC. Sixty-five thousand spectators saw the Bruins take an early lead. Despite being underdogs, the Bruins came out inspired. Washington hit Strode on a bullet pass to the end zone. The Bruins were unable to keep the momentum on this day, though, as the Trojans were too strong. USC would go on to win the game handily by a score of 42–7.

The last game of the conference season for the Bruins came against Oregon State. The only OSU score came on an 84-yard kickoff return for a touchdown. Kenny Washington drove the Bruins down the field and scored a touchdown in the first half, but it wasn't enough. Both teams sputtered on offense, and the game ended in a 7–7 tie. For the first time in school history, however, the season did not end after the last regular season game. The Bruins were invited to their first bowl game, which actually ended up being two games. On December 26, the Bruins took on the Honolulu town team, comprised of alumni from various schools who were now residing on the big island, and UCLA won, 46–0. One week later, on January 2, 1939, the Bruins played in the Poi Bowl and easily defeated the University of Hawaii by a score of 32–7. The Bruins had played in, and won, their first bowl game in school history. UCLA finished the season with a 7–4–1 record.

The bounce-back season of 1938 would be the last on the sidelines for the great coach William Spaulding. For 14 seasons, Spaulding had roamed the sidelines. He had taken the Bruins from the Southern California Intercollegiate Athletic Conference to the Pacific Coast Conference and assumed responsibility for a losing program, which he turned into a winner. He was able to grab the school's first conference title and first bowl victory. Coach Spaulding's career coaching record was 145–83–15. At UCLA, his record was 72–51–8.

The Downtown Athletic Club named Davey O'Brien from Texas Christian University the 1938 Heisman Trophy Winner.

The Associated Press named Texas Christian University the 1938 National Champions.

In 1938, UCLA played in their first bowl game, the Pineapple Bowl. UCLA beat the University of Hawaii, 32–7. (Southern Campus Collection)

# CHAPTER 5
# Edwin Horrell (1939–1944)

When William Spaulding retired following the 1938 season, UCLA was at a crossroads. Under Spaulding's leadership, the program had grown and produced the first glimpses of success in Westwood. With the retirement of a popular and successful coach came a quick reality: UCLA would be hard-pressed to attract a top coach from around the country. They were still competing against the much more prestigious programs at the University of Southern California, Stanford University, and the University of California Berkeley.

On December 1, 1938, the UCLA Board of Directors named Edwin C. "Babe" Horrell—who had been the mastermind behind the UCLA offense—the fifth head football coach in UCLA history. Line Coach Ray Richards, who also coached under Spaulding, was retained, and Manual Arts High School coach James Blewett was hired, as well.

Edwin Horrell was born on September 29, 1902, in Jackson, Mississippi. While his time as coach at UCLA reached extreme heights, it also sank to some extreme lows. As an athlete himself, Horrell had rarely seen the lows. In high school, he lettered in five sports. Along with being a star football player, he also excelled in basketball, track, tennis, and swimming. He was an all-around athlete, but his heart never wavered from his favorite: Edwin "Babe" Horrell loved football. Following high school, Horrell headed west. In the fall of 1921, Babe enrolled at the University of California Berkeley and would play under legendary coach Andy Smith. Following a year on the freshman team, it was time for Horrell to make a name for himself on the powerful Berkeley Bears varsity squad. As a sophomore, Horrell won the starting center job right away and never relinquished it. In Horrell's three years as a varsity starter, the Cal Golden Bears went 26-0-3 and won two national championships (though in neither year did the most prominent poll, the College Football Researchers Association, name Cal the champion). In his senior year, Babe was named a team captain, and after his dominant season concluded, he was named to the All-America team. Cal coach Andy Smith would say of Horrell, "His ability and skill constitutes about 25 percent of our team." Opposing coaches knew the unique talent of Horrell as a player and upon his graduation were happy to see him go. St. Mary's coach Slip Madigan once said, "Horrell was about 50 percent of the psychological effect of the Bears. He could get his men together better than any football captain I ever saw. Andy Smith could have stood the loss of five good men better than the graduation of Horrell." Like every athlete, however, the need to walk away from the playing field and into a new stage of life was unavoidable. Horrell's accomplishments on the football field would be long-lasting. Following his coaching tenure at UCLA, Pasadena City College renamed its football field "Horrell Field." In 1969, he was named to the Honorable Mention All-Time Pacific Coast Conference team. Also in '69, Horrell was inducted into the College Football Hall of Fame. In 1987, he was inducted into the University of California Berkeley Athletic Hall of Fame.

For the first time in over a decade, Babe Horrell was out of football in 1925, but the time away would be short-lived. Professional football was an option for Horrell after graduation, but it didn't pay well and didn't come with the glitz and glam of college ball. He could move back home to Mississippi or he could stay in California. What he did know was that he wanted to stay involved in football in some way. In 1926, he got his chance. William Spaulding brought Horrell to the University of California at Los Angeles with the hope that the young, former All-American could help turn around the younger Bruins program. From 1926–1938, Babe Horrell faithfully served on Coach Spaulding's staff as an assistant coach. His primary duty was to remake the offense. Horrell's offensive scheme was known as the "Man-In-Motion" offense. The basic premise of his offense was the single wing with a wrinkle of confusion, one man going in motion on every single play. Rather than just plowing ahead, the Bruins relied on misdirection to slow the defense and, when the personnel was right, a passing game that would take deep shots and keep the defense honest. Coach Horrell was a bit of a revolutionary, adding small changes to an otherwise standard offense run throughout the country. As a young man, Horrell knew Xs and Os, but it took 13 seasons under coach Spaulding to prepare him for the next stage. In 1939, he was finally the head coach.

As it turned out, Babe Horrell was a wartime head coach, as the Japanese attacked Pearl Harbor and the United States entered World War II just after his third season. For the next three campaigns, unforeseen obstacles derailed many programs. Country was greater than football. The ups and downs that come with war also came to represent the UCLA football program under Babe. In Horrell's first year, the team went undefeated but set a unique record that stands today as the team with the most ties in one season. In 1942, his UCLA team became the first to beat USC. Also in '42, Horrell led the Bruins to their first Rose Bowl appearance in school history. Yet in his six years, Horrell only had two winning seasons. Despite this, his career was seen as a success. He coached the Bruins through a tumultuous time, and though Babe and the Bruins would part ways in 1945, Coach Horrell should be remembered for much more than being the man who coached Jackie Robinson, Kenny Washington, Bob Waterfield, and Burr Baldwin. He was one of the greatest players in college football in the 1920s and one of the early innovative offensive thinkers in UCLA history. Following his resignation in 1945, Horrell went into the produce business. On June 13, 1992, Babe died in his home in Beverly Hills after a 30-plus year battle with Parkinson's disease. Horrell had a son, Steve, and two daughters, Virginia Rookus and Winifred Cutting.

## 1939

Prior to the start of the 1939 football season, Edwin C. "Babe" Horrell was named the new UCLA football coach. Kenny Washington was now a senior, and with the disappointing season of '38 behind them, it was time to take advantage of Kenny's unique talent before it was too late.

Jackie Robinson, a recent transfer from Pasadena City College, enrolled at UCLA and joined the team. Years later, Robinson would make history as the first black player to ever play Major League Baseball. While at UCLA, he was one of four black football players. With Woody Strode, Kenny Washington, Ray Bartlett, and Jackie Robinson, the Bruins were the most integrated team in college football. While Jackie would later cement his place in history with the Brooklyn Dodgers, in '38 he cemented himself as the starting right halfback, and with him alongside Washington, the Bruins had their best backfield in school history. Jack Sommers was a quality left guard. Woody Strode held down the left end position, and Don McPherson was the starting right end. Ned Matthews was the man under center. Together with Head Coach Horrell, Ray Richards, Mike Chambers, Jim Blewett, Cece Hollingsworth, and Bus Sutherland did the coaching.

The first game of what ended up being a very memorable season kicked off on September 29, 1939, against Texas Christian University, the 1938 National Championship team led by Heisman Trophy winner Davey O'Brien. When TCU headed west for the opener of the '39 season, the Horned Frogs certainly expected their winning ways to continue. Though O'Brien, who along with the Heisman was also named the Maxwell Award and Walter Camp Award winner, had graduated and moved on to the Philadelphia Eagles, TCU was expected to continue their success without him. When TCU came to the Coliseum, they were surprised in more ways than one. Early in the game, the UCLA offense pulled off a trick play—the old hidden ball play—which netted a large gain and got the Bruins into TCU territory, though they wouldn't end up scoring on the drive. At halftime, the score was 0–0. The Horned Frogs had yet to find a suitable replacement for O'Brien and couldn't get their offense going. Kenny Washington and Jackie Robinson were both held in check in the first half for the Bruins. On the first drive of the second half, Bill Overlin and Kenny Washington softened the middle of the TCU defense by repeatedly pounding the ball and moving the chains. Jackie Robinson was able to rattle the defense with runs to the outside, showing a level of speed and athleticism for which TCU had not planned. Finally, the Bruins were able to punch the ball into the end zone. The extra point missed, and the Bruins led, 6–0. TCU's only serious scoring threat came in the fourth quarter. The Horned Frogs drove the ball to the Bruins' 1-yard line. Fourth and goal. Game on the line. The Bruins stopped the Frogs' attempted plunge up the middle! TCU turned the ball over on downs. On the next play, UCLA was stopped in the backfield for a safety. TCU would receive the ball again but were unable to do anything. UCLA pulled a major upset, 6–2, over the defending National Champions in Coach Horrell's first career head coaching game.

Ned Matthews leads the way for Kenny Washington against Texas Christian University, 1939 (Southern Campus Collection)

The Bruins were 1–0 entering conference play, with two consecutive away games coming up. In the first, UCLA took on the University of Washington Huskies. While UW was able to score an early touchdown on a fumble recovery returned to the end zone, UCLA was able to bounce back. Jackie Robinson returned a punt 65 yards in the third quarter to the 5-yard line, and Kenny Washington punched the ball into the end zone. UCLA scored once again in the fourth quarter on a Dale Gilmore interception return. The final score was 14–7 Bruins.

When the Bruins took on the Stanford Indians in Week 3, the theme of 1939 started to develop. Early in the game, Robinson gashed the Stanford defense and was repeatedly able to break off long gains, but the offense struggled to capitalize in Indians territory. In the second quarter, UCLA was finally able to capitalize as Overlin carried the ball 10 yards into the end zone. Though the Bruins took a 7–0 lead into halftime, they were in no way playing their best football. The offense was moving the ball, but the defense was being pushed back. It became clear that the team that would avoid mistakes in the second half and capitalize on their scoring chances would likely come out victorious. In the third quarter, the Bruins were able to do neither. On successive drives, the Bruins were forced to punt, and both punts ended in disaster. In the two punts combined, the net distance the ball traveled was only eight yards. Stanford would then use the short field to score. Entering the fourth quarter, UCLA trailed, 14–7. It appeared the Bruins were headed for defeat as Stanford drove the ball again. Momentum shifted, however, when Robinson intercepted a pass in Bruins territory with under 4:00 to go and retuned it all the way to the Stanford 8-yard line. Leo Cantor and Kenny Washington then ran the ball on successive plays, and the Bruins scored! Down 14–13, Robinson made the extra point, and the game finished in a 14–14 tie, just the first of the season.

Jackie Robinson, 1939 (Southern Campus Collection)

Following the tie against Stanford, the Bruins rattled off three consecutive wins. They easily dismantled the Montana Grizzlies, 20–6, behind a three-touchdown performance by Kenny Washington.

A week later, the Bruins defeated the University of Oregon by a score of 16–6. UCLA was outplayed in every way, but the scoreboard was all that mattered. Robinson scored both of the Bruins' touchdowns. On November 4, UCLA defeated the University of California in the Homecoming matchup. Eleanor Everett was the Homecoming Queen, and following the traditional Homecoming bonfire, the Bruins students were entertained in the gymnasium by Bob Hope. Without Robinson, who was nursing an injured knee, the Bruins fell behind early, 7–0 but came back to trounce the Bears. Kenny Washington did everything on this day, including running for a touchdown and throwing another touchdown to Woody Strode. UCLA won the game, 20–7, giving them a record of 5–0–1 on the season so far, and 4–0–1 in conference play.

Two weeks after the Homecoming game against Cal, UCLA was back home for a nonconference game against the No. 14 Santa Clara Broncos. The game was a physical battle from the get-go. There were only three significant scoring opportunities for either team throughout the entire game. In the second quarter, Santa Clara reached the Bruins 2-yard line but on fourth down were stopped. In the third quarter, the Broncos once again pushed the Bruins back to their goal line. This time, on fourth down with the ball on the 9-yard line the Broncos attempted a field goal but missed! The game was tied going into the fourth quarter. Finally, on the last drive of the game, the UCLA offense came alive. Leo Cantor and Kenny Washington pushed the ball deep into Broncos territory. With just five seconds left, the Bruins were called for a 15-yard penalty. The game would come down to one final play. Instead of going for the touchdown, the Bruins were now forced to rely on Jack Sommers to convert a 28-yard field goal for the win. As the ball hit Sommers's foot, it was immediately apparent to all that Sommers had popped it up. He had kicked too far under the ball and instead of the ball launching forward, it went up in the air. The kick was straight, however, and if it had the distance, it would go through the uprights and the Bruins would win. As the ball reached its peak and descended to the ground, it fell just short. The Bruins and Broncos would tie, 0–0, the second tie of the season for the Bruins.

One week later, the theme continued. UCLA and Oregon State would tie, 13–13. Remarkably, it was the third tie of the season for the Bruins. Down 13–0 in the fourth quarter, Cantor rushed for a touchdown and John Frawley missed the extra point. The next touchdown came on a Kenny Washington pass to Ned Matthews. This time, Frawley made the extra point to tie the game.

Five days later, UCLA defeated Washington State University, 24–7. Like many of the games already in the '39 season, it came down to the fourth quarter. Washington connected with Strode for a touchdown in the first half, but it wasn't enough as the Bruins entered the fourth trailing by a point. It was then that Robinson scored two touchdowns and the Bruins' reserves scored another late in the game. With one week to go, the Bruins were still undefeated.

Entering the final game of the year, the Bruins were 6–0–3 and No. 9 in the country, according to the Associated Press. The USC Trojans were 7–0–2 and ranked No. 3 in the country by the Associated Press. The winner of the game would win the Pacific Coast Conference and head to the Rose Bowl. In the first half, the Bruins moved the ball at will but twice fumbled in Trojans territory. USC had one serious scoring threat in the first half when they drove to the Bruins' 1-yard line. Trojan Grenville Landsell Jr. then fumbled as he was hit high by Ned Matthews and low by Robinson. Strode would recover in the end zone for a touchback. Entering the fourth quarter, the game was still tied, 0–0. One last scoring opportunity would present itself to the Bruins. All season long, UCLA had a flair for the dramatic, and once again the game would come down to the final minutes. On UCLA's final drive, senior leader Kenny Washington orchestrated a drive that put the ball at the Trojans' 2-yard line. The drive included five first downs, and now they sat just six feet away from defeating the Trojans and going to the Rose Bowl. On fourth down, the ball was snapped, the offensive line got pushed back, and the ball went nowhere! The Bruins were stopped. The score ended up 0–0—the fourth tie of the season for the Bruins, the most ever in college football to that point, and a record that still stands today. The Bruins finished the season with a 6–0–4 record. The following week, the conference would hold a vote to elect a Rose Bowl representative. USC was selected, and the Bruins' season was over.

The Downtown Athletic Club named Nile

Kinnick from the University of Iowa the 1939 Heisman Trophy Winner.

The Associated Press named Texas A&M University the 1939 National Champions.

## Kenny Washington

Kenny Washington is a UCLA legend, or at least he should be. While the memory of UCLA's first football superstar has faded away, his accomplishments live on forever. Kenneth Washington was born on August 31, 1919, in Los Angeles, California. He was raised in the Lincoln Heights neighborhood of Los Angeles, a community comprised mostly of Italian immigrants and poor working-class blacks. His parents were not involved much in his life; he was raised primarily by his grandmother and uncle Rocky. While his father played in the Negro baseball leagues, his uncle Rocky taught him toughness, and his grandmother taught him humility. Growing up, it was hard to be humble at times because he was such a dominant athlete. His junior year of high school, he led Lincoln to a championship in baseball. As a senior, he led the football team to a championship. He excelled in both sports. Decades later, his grandson, Kirk Washington, would say of his athletic exploits, "I heard a lot of tales about him, and I didn't believe it at first, but then you talk to people who saw him play and it was all true." His exploits didn't end in high school. In 1936, he enrolled at the University of California Los Angeles.

When Kenny Washington got to UCLA, there was still debate about which sport was his best. Like Jackie Robinson, a fellow Bruin who played multiple sports, Kenny was extremely talented in many things. At UCLA, he played football and baseball. In baseball, he was brilliant. In 1937, he hit .454, and in 1938 he hit .350. Former USC baseball coach Rod Dedeaux would say later that Washington was a much better player than Robinson, and statistics back him up. Prior to the integration of Major League Baseball in 1947 by Robinson, there was talk that Washington would be the man to do the job, but there was a stipulation. Brooklyn Dodgers Manager Leo Durocher approached Washington and asked him if baseball was something he would like to pursue professionally. He was, of course, interested, but when Durocher brought up the idea that Washington spend a year in Puerto Rico and try to pass himself off as a native Puerto Rican before joining the Dodgers, the discourse was over. Washington was no longer interested. In football, he was even better. After leading the freshman team in 1936, Washington joined the varsity in 1937, and for three seasons he was breathtaking. He was big. He was fast. He was elusive and hard to bring down. In his sophomore season, the Bruins won only two games. As a junior, they won seven. In 1939, Kenny Washington's last at UCLA, Jackie Robinson's first on the varsity, and Edwin Horrell's first as the head coach, UCLA went undefeated. Washington played 580 of the total 600 minutes on the season. He led the nation in scoring and was named the winner of the Douglas Fairbanks Trophy, awarded to the best player in America. He finished his career with 1,914 rushing yards, a UCLA record that stood for 34 years. When he came off the field for the final time, the Los Angeles Memorial Coliseum erupted in applause. All 80,000+ fans rose and cheered for the best player in UCLA history. Washington's teammate, Woody Strode, would later remark that the ovation was as though "the Pope of Rome had come out." Washington was a superstar. But he was black.

When Washington's collegiate career came to a close, one would surmise he had options about his athletic future. He could play football professionally. He could play baseball professionally. In the Jim Crow 1940s, however, this was not a real option. Kenny Washington went undrafted and in 1940 was looking for a job. Despite the best efforts of Chicago Bears coach George Halas to get the ban lifted that restricted black players from playing in the NFL, Halas failed. The idea was shot down, and Washington would have to take another route. Following graduation, he took a coaching job on Edwin Horrell's staff at UCLA, and for one season he coached the freshman squad. He joined the city's police department, as well, and for a short time was a uniformed officer. In 1941, his urge to compete as an athlete while he was still capable could not be contained, and when he got an opportunity, he gladly took it and put on the pads once again.

In 1941, Kenny Washington joined the Pacific Coast Professional Football League. Though the semipro league was considered a far cry from the real competition of the National Football League, Washington became a star and his celebrity continued to grow. Washington could run. He could catch.

He could even throw . . . with either hand! He was unstoppable, and impossible to ignore. After five seasons of semipro football with the Hollywood Bears and San Francisco Clippers, Washington got the break that would change the course of history. When the Cleveland Rams moved to Los Angeles in 1946 and the NFL lifted the ban on black players, there was immense pressure for the Rams to be the team to integrate the league. *Los Angeles Tribune* columnist Halley Harding, through newspaper columns, continually pressured the Rams to sign a black player. On March 21, 1946, the Rams signed Kenny Washington. Two weeks later, they signed fellow UCLA Bruin Woody Strode.

Kenny Washington, 1938 (Southern Campus Collection)

When Kenny Washington joined the Los Angeles Rams, he faced another challenge. His knees were shot. He had five surgeries, including one on each knee during the 1946 offseason. Though his body was starting to fail him, his incredible skill and determination were enough, if only for a short time. Despite dealing with racial prejudice throughout his career, Washington performed well. In opposing cities, he was often denied access to the same hotel where his teammates stayed. On the field, opponents would take cheap shots. In pileups, he would get his eyes poked, dirt rubbed in his face, and other dirty tricks. In his three-year NFL career, Washington averaged 6.1 yards per carry. His best season was 1947, in which he averaged 7.4 yards per carry. His 92-yard touchdown against the Chicago Bears in '47 is still a Rams record today.

Following the 1948 season, Kenny Washington's football career came to a close. When discussing Washington's professional career, one can only wonder "what if." If allowed to join the NFL in 1940, Washington may have become one of the best football players in history. If he had chosen to pursue a baseball career, he could have been a trailblazer in that sport, as well. Kenny Washington was a fantastic athlete whose legacy is all too often forgotten. He was a victim of the era in which he lived. Following his retirement from the NFL, Washington went back to work for the Los Angeles Police Department and worked honorably for the department for eight years. He was interested in politics and helped Richard Nixon campaign for the United States Senate in 1950. In 1956, he was recognized as one of the best college football players of all time and was inducted into the College Football Hall of Fame. Also in '56, his alma mater, UCLA, retired his number 13 jersey.

On June 24, 1971, Kenny Washington passed away from heart and lung problems at the age of 52. As football continued to gain popularity throughout the last century, Washington's family aimed to have his story told as often as Jackie Robinson's. Football is now the most popular sport in America. Kenny Washington is a major reason why. Since leaving UCLA in 1939, brilliant athletes have come and gone. Running backs have electrified fans for decades. Such players as Bert LaBrucherie and Mel Farr have left their marks on history. Others, including Gaston Green and Skip Hicks, have dashed past defenders and into the record books. Before there was Deshaun Foster, before there was Maurice Jones-Drew, there was Kenny Washington. Before there was Johnathan Franklin, before there was Paul Perkins, there was Kenny Washington. In 1939, Kenny Washington was the best player in America. In 1946, he made history. Kenny Washington is a Bruins legend.

## 1940

In 1940, the world was a mess, as war waged across Europe. After reaching a summit in 1939, UCLA would also find itself in a bit of a mess in 1940. Star Kenny Washington was gone due to graduation, and though no one expected one man to fill his void, UCLA coaches believed they had the roster to collectively replace the best player in team history. Ted Forbes and Ray Richards would be critical to the offense. Don McPherson was named a captain, though he missed significant time with a broken toe. Ned Matthews, a mobile quarterback and talented defensive back, was the other captain.

The season kicked off with a bang on September 29 against Southern Methodist University. Jackie Robinson took the opening kickoff 87 yards for a touchdown. Though the Bruins defense played valiantly in the first half, with no help from the offense they eventually tired. In the third quarter, SMU marched down the field with little resistance to the Bruins' 1-yard line. A series of short passes by quarterback Clement flummoxed the Bruins,, who were left with no answers. Finally, Johnny Clement kept it himself and scored from the one. "Presto" Johnson would add a field goal for the Mustangs, and the Bruins were never able to counter. UCLA lost the season opener, 9–6. While SMU would go on to complete a successful season, finishing No. 16 in the final AP Poll, the Bruins' misery was just beginning.

In Week 2, the opponent's name changed, but the results didn't. UCLA would lose to Santa Clara by the familiar score of 9–6. The Broncos would strike first early in the game, but the Bruins quickly responded with a touchdown of their own by Ned Matthews. Late in the fourth quarter, Santa Clara placekicker Jimmy Johnson nailed a 29-yard field goal, and the Bruins lost again. The last nonconference game of the year pit Texas A&M University against the Bruins at the Coliseum. Despite the best efforts of Robinson, Matthews, Leo Cantor, and Milt Smith, the Bruins fell for the third week in a row. In the fourth quarter, down 7–0, the Bruins had their best chance to reach the end zone. After driving to the Aggies' 12-yard line, on fourth down Smith stood alone in the end zone, but Cantor could not get enough on the throw, and the ball fell short of Smith's waiting arms. The Bruins were 0–3.

Three weeks after the disappointing nonconference season had ended, the Bruins looked up and were suddenly 0–6. After starting the season with three losses by a combined 13 points, the Bruins' next three losses were by a combined 15 points. Missing the superstar talent of Kenny Washington and the calming hand of Coach Spaulding, the Bruins continually lost close games. Statistics show the Bruins were much better than their record indicated, but history seldom cares about much other than the win-loss record. UCLA and Coach Horrell had four games left to play with any hope of writing a positive note in the history books.

After the six close defeats preceding their November 9 matchup with the University of Oregon, the Bruins simply got their butts handed to them. The Webfeet, led by Buck Berry, physically manhandled the Bruins. On a muddy day in Eugene, Robinson and Ted Forbes struggled. The offense was stuck in the mud. UCLA lost the game, 18–0, and the team was now 0–7.

The lone bright spot in an otherwise dark season came on November 8 against Washington State University. Jackie Robinson would have his most brilliant performance in a UCLA football uniform on this day. Trailing 20–6 in the second quarter, Robinson threw a touchdown to Art Anderson and followed that up by engineering a long drive that resulted in another touchdown on a circus catch by Robert Simpson from Matthews. At halftime, the score was 20–20. The offense had finally come alive, and if the defense performed in the second half as

Head Coach Babe Horrell, middle, along with Line Coach Ray Richards, left, and Backfield Coach Jim Blewett, right (Southern Campus Collection)

they had for much of the season, the Bruins could finally win a game. On the first drive of the third quarter, Robinson found a seam and ran 60 yards to the end zone. Touchdown Bruins! The Cougars were not shaken, however, and immediately came back to punch the ball into the end zone on a run by William Sewell. After missing the extra point, WSU trailed, 27–26. In the fourth quarter, Robinson would break free once more, this time for a 75-yard touchdown. The Bruins led, 34–26, and would hold on for their first victory of the season. Though the Bruins were 1–7, every victory is sweet, and the Bruins were proud to have finally gotten in the win column.

The season would end not with a mighty fight, but with more disappointment. After defeating WSU, the season was seemingly over for many involved. UCLA would lose to the University of Washington, 41–0, and to the University of Southern California, 28–12. Jackie Robinson would score the Bruins' only two touchdowns in the final two weeks in what were his final games at UCLA. In 2014, UCLA announced it would retire Jackie's number 42 in all sports. Along with the honor of having his number retired permanently, UCLA announced that 22 athletic and recreation facilities across campus would be named the Jackie Robinson Athletics and Recreation Complex. On every building, the number "42" is prominently shown. After all, before the Brooklyn Dodgers, before the MLB Hall of Fame, before his number was retired, Jackie was a Bruin.

The Downtown Athletic Club named Tom Harmon from the University of Michigan the 1940 Heisman Trophy Winner.

The Associated Press named the University of Minnesota the 1940 National Champions.

## Jackie Robinson

The man who would one day become a legend at the University of California Los Angeles, one of the best players in Major League Baseball, a businessman, and a Civil Rights leader was born on January 31, 1919, in Cairo, Georgia. Jack Roosevelt Robinson, whose grandfather was born a slave, and whose mother and father, Mallie and Jerry, were born into a still deeply divided America, accomplished what once seemed impossible. Jerry was a sharecropper, doing much of the same work his father did as a slave. Jerry worked the land of a white landowner and received half

Jackie Robinson runs the ball against USC in 1940 (Southern Campus Collection)

the profits from his work. This was a step up from the $12 per month that he earned for much of the early part of his life doing the same work. As Jerry was starting to accumulate saved income, his mind started to tempt him. Finally, when Jackie was just six months old, Jerry left. He told Jackie's mother he was going to visit his brother in Texas. He never returned. Seven months later, the Robinson family went west. After trying to regather and survive in Cairo, Mallie decided it was time for a change of scenery. She had a brother living in California, and they would live with him until they could get back on their feet and find a place of their own. Uncle Burton took in the struggling family, but Mallie did not want to stay for long. She found a job washing dishes and ironing clothing and moved into a new place. Her small salary was enough to put the family back in the right direction, but it was never easy. The meager salary allowed for no frivolous purchases. They could not afford to spend a single penny on what they didn't need. If not for the leftover food Mallie was able to bring home from work, the Robinson family would be forced to eat just two meals a day. Sometimes, leftovers were not enough. Mallie did not dream of a life where her children could enjoy the lavish lifestyle that rich parents could offer; rather, she simply dreamed of a life for her children in which they were educated and could provide a better life for her grandchildren.

When Jackie was young, he went to school with his older sister, Willa Mae. Even before he was old enough to enroll in school, he would come along with his sister and simply play in the sandbox all day. After one year of waiting for his big sister from the sandbox, Jackie was old enough to go to school himself. He was enthusiastic, but he would also face the harsh reality of racism directly for the first time. The family lived on Pepper Street in Pasadena, a neighborhood with few African Americans at the time. Jackie would later remember that, when he was eight years old, a young girl shouted at him, "Nigger, Nigger, Nigger!" as he was sweeping the sidewalk. From a young age, Jackie stood up for himself. He was a boy who spoke his mind and defended his beliefs. He learned at the time from his older brother that the insult that got under the skin of white people the most was "Cracker." After Jackie returned the racial jab, the father of the young girl came outside and confronted him. Though he had experienced racism in the past, ranging from neighbors calling the police because the Robinsons were said to be making too much noise when roller skating outside during the day, to neighbors signing a petition to have the family removed, Jackie specifically remembered this incident because it was the first time he would fight back. It became a life habit, one that he would have to break at one of the most important decision-making moments in his future.

As a child, Jackie was always busy. He had a paper route, he mowed lawns, he played sports, and he got in trouble. By Jackie's formative adolescent years, he was spending too much time with the Pepper Street Gang. In Jackie's autobiography, *I Never Had It Made*, he explains that, if not for two influential men, he may have led a life of delinquency instead of a life of purpose. A local mechanic, Carl Anderson, who had become an acquaintance of Jackie's and his mother's, pulled Jackie aside and warned about him the road he was headed down if he continued getting into trouble. Young boys often hear the message, but rarely can one man break through to teach the importance of their childhood decisions. Anderson was able to do this by speaking directly about Jackie's mother. Anderson knew that Jackie had a deep, unbreakable affection for his mother, and a bond that could withstand anything. He knew Jackie was protective and had pride in all she had done. By explaining that Jackie's actions had an impact on his mother, he got his message across. The other man who had the most valuable positive influence on Jackie's life at a young age was Reverend Karl Downs. Mallie made it a point to teach religion to her children, and Reverend Downs, being a young man himself, related to the Robinson family. Jackie would go on to say, "Reverend Downs was both stubborn and courageous." These two characteristics would become what Jackie Robinson is now known for. Downs made church fun. The Pepper Street Gang no longer appealed to him. He saw the bigger picture of life.

When he was growing up, sports became an outlet for Jackie. At John Muir High School, he earned varsity letters in football, baseball, basketball, and track. He was a star player, and he relished the responsibility of being known and being forced to perform for the fans who came specifically to see him. He was also a team player and tried his best to help his teammates improve, as well. After a successful high school career, Jackie was off to Pasadena City College. As a freshman, he suffered a setback in his football career before the season even started. In practice, Jackie fractured his ankle. When he made his way back on the field, he was once again dominant. Pasadena would win the five remaining games and follow up the next season with an 11–0 record. In track and field, he broke his brother's broad jump (now long jump) record with a leap of 25 feet 6 ½ inches. In baseball, he played shortstop and led the Pasadena team to a championship.

Jackie was heavily recruited out of Pasadena, and when it was time to make a decision about which university to transfer to, the choice was easy. Other schools seemed more interested in Jackie, but he wanted to stay close to home so his older brother, Frank, could see him play. This never came to be. After Jackie enrolled at UCLA, Frank died in a motorcycle accident. He never saw Jackie play in a Bruins uniform. Though extremely shaken by the tragedy, Jackie continued to thrive in athletics. He would become the first athlete in UCLA history to earn a varsity letter in four sports, just as he had done in high school football, baseball, basketball, and track. As it turned out, the sport he struggled with the most was baseball. In 1939, Jackie was one of four black players on the UCLA football team, along with Woody Strode, Ray Bartlett, and Kenny Washington, who would go on to break the color barrier in the NFL. In Jackie's two seasons on the Bruins football team, he was outstanding. Both seasons he led the nation in punt return average, and as of 2011, his 18.8 yards per punt return was fourth all time in NCAA history. As a senior, he led the Bruins in rushing, passing, total offense, scoring, and punt returns. In his two seasons on the UCLA basketball team, he led the Southern Division of the Pacific Coast Conference in scoring both times. In the spring, Robinson played two sports at once. Though he only competed one season in both baseball and track and field, he made a name for himself. In 1940, he won the NCAA title in the broad jump. Ironically, the only field he struggled on was the baseball field. In his lone season playing baseball for the Bruins, Jackie batted a porous .097. Though he struggled at the plate, fans came to see him. He was a slick fielder and an excellent base runner. His future appeared to be in football.

Following his career with the Bruins, Jackie Robinson signed a contract with the Honolulu Bears of the Pacific Coast Football League. The league was racially integrated, and Jackie was the sixth black man to play in the PCFL. The star of the league was his former UCLA teammate, Kenny Washington. In the second game of the season, Robinson and Washington faced off on opposing teams. The Honolulu Bears got off to a 10–3 lead behind the steady hand of Robinson at quarterback, but two late touchdown passes by Washington helped push the Hollywood Bears to victory. The two former teammates shook hands after the game and went on their separate ways. Both would make history. When the season ended in November, Jackie decided to head home. He arranged for a ship to take him back home to Los Angeles and left Honolulu on December 5, 1941. Jackie's football career—and the lives and careers of men throughout the country in many different occupations—came to an abrupt halt just two days later, when the Japanese bombed Pearl Harbor. In 1942, Jackie was drafted into the United States Army.

Jackie was playing poker on the ship when he heard the news of Pearl Harbor. He knew he would soon be fighting for his country. In May of '42, he was sent to Fort Riley, Kansas. In January 1943, he became a second lieutenant. As he would do throughout his life, Jackie fought for civil rights in the Army. After learning that only six or seven seats were assigned for black soldiers in the Fort Riley post theater, Jackie reached out to provost marshal Hafner and demanded this be fixed. Though his complaint was met with scorn, eventually the right was wronged. As a member of the 761st Tank Battalion in 1944, Jackie faced another controversy. After boarding a nearly empty bus and sitting in the front, he was ordered to move to the back. When he refused, the driver ordered the military police to arrive and arrest Jackie. He would be court-martialed, and though he was acquitted of all charges, Jackie missed the opportunity to deploy overseas, something he felt was a duty. His battalion would go on to become the first black tank unit to see combat action. He would not go with them. In November 1944, he was honorably discharged after two and a half years in the Army.

Following his military service, Jackie looked to get back into athletics, preferably football, but baseball now seemed like a better option. Prior to being discharged, he met a man named Alexander, who, prior to his service, had played professional baseball. The two spoke about his time with the Kansas City Monarchs, and Alexander told Jackie of the good money to be made in black baseball. The Monarchs were an all-black team playing in the Negro Leagues. Jackie wrote a letter to the Monarchs, and after checking him out in person, they invited him to a spring training tryout in Houston. The $400-per-month salary was far more than Jackie had ever earned in his life. Not only did Jackie make the team, but he hit. In 1945, he hit .387 with 5 home runs, 13 stolen bases, and 63 hits in just 47 games. He also caught the eye of a man who would not only change his life, but change baseball.

When Branch Rickey became the president of the Brooklyn Dodgers in 1943, he already had plans to integrate baseball. Thirty-three years earlier, when coaching at Ohio Wesleyan, Rickey demanded that a hotel that would not let one of his black players stay there provide the man with a bed or the entire team would leave. It was a bluff. He knew no other hotel would allow the player either, but after the hotel decided to give him a cot, which he could put in Rickey's room, he felt that he had won the battle. On the night in that room, Rickey spoke to his player, learned about his life, and watched him weep. Rickey knew that baseball was a way he could change the nation. Branch Rickey would launch an extensive talent search unbeknownst to the public for the black player who would lead the charge. In August of 1945, Dodgers Scout Clyde Sukeforth approached Jackie at Comiskey Park in Chicago and told him that the Dodgers were interested in learning more about him. A meeting with Rickey was arranged, and Robinson was off to Brooklyn to meet his future boss. Rickey was honest. He knew Robinson could play. He knew he was good enough to make his way to the major leagues and help the Dodgers bring home a World Series title. What he wanted to learn was about Jackie's attitude. He wanted a tough man. He knew it was a difficult task. He said to Jackie, "I know you're a good ballplayer. What I don't know is whether you have the guts." Rickey had Robinson transfixed, and also convinced he would do anything to play for the Dodgers, though it would be difficult to control his temper. Rickey said to him, "We can't fight our way through this, Robinson. We've got no army. There's virtually no one on our side. No owners, no umpires, very few newspapermen. And I'm afraid that many fans will be hostile. We'll be in a tough position. We can win only if we convince the world that I'm doing this because you're a great ballplayer and a fine gentleman." As Rickey explained to Robinson that it is a farce that a baseball box score is a democratic thing, it only matters what you do on the field, he laid out his dream. One day he hoped that it wouldn't matter who finished the game 2-for-3 with a double and a stolen base, but rather that he helped the team win. He continued, "It's all that ought to count, but it isn't. Maybe one of these days it will be all that counts. That is one of the reasons I've got you here, Robinson. If you're a good enough man, we can make this a start in the right direction, but let me tell you, it's going to take an awful lot of courage." As the meeting went on, Rickey tested Robinson. He threw subtle jabs at him, trying to break him down and show his temper. The line that Jackie would remember for the rest of his life came after Jackie asked, "Mr. Rickey, are you looking for a negro who is afraid to fight back?" Rickey replied, *"Robinson, I'm looking for a ballplayer with guts enough not to fight back."* The two left the meeting with an agreement. Though the contract would not be signed until two months later, Jackie would head to Montreal to play for the Dodgers' minor league affiliate and earn $600 per month with a $3,500 signing bonus.

After one season in Montreal, in which Jackie claimed the people treated him very well, Jackie broke the Major League Baseball color barrier. On April 9, 1947, just before an exhibition game, it was announced the Brooklyn Dodgers had picked up the contract of Jackie Robinson from the Montreal Royals. Six days later, Jackie would make his Major League Baseball debut, wearing number 42, and playing first base for the Brooklyn Dodgers against the Boston Braves. A total of 26,623 fans showed up at Ebbets Field to see the teams play, though many more would later claim to be there on that historic day. Jackie went 0-for-3, reached on an error, and scored a run. Jackie would endure racial incidents nearly everywhere he went. The Philadelphia Phillies were particularly vile. Screams of "Hey, nigger, why don't you go back to the cotton field where you belong?" poured out of the dugout. Players in St. Louis threatened to strike if Jackie was allowed to play. He received hate mail nearly every day. Teammates, including Pee Wee Reese, were allies on whom Robinson could depend, but other teammates, such as Hugh Casey, made the home locker room a place of discomfort. The first season was the hardest. Jackie was a proud man. He often thought that taking the abuse was a sign of weakness, but then he remembered the strength of character that Branch Rickey showed, and the deep belief that the only way to win them over was to not fight back. Jackie finished the 1947 season with a .297 batting average, 12 home runs, a league-best 29 stolen bases, and the Rookie of the Year award.

By 1948, Branch Rickey had a change of heart. He knew that Jackie had to find a balance between fighting back and holding back. From then on, he would allow Jackie to show emotion, to be more than just a figure. The racial tension continued for the rest of his career, but the respect for Jackie grew immensely. In 1949, Jackie won the batting title (.342) and Most Valuable Player award in the National League. In 1955, the Dodgers won the World Series. After the 1956 season, Jackie was traded from the Dodgers to the rival New York Giants. Instead of playing for the team he grew to hate, Jackie retired. Over 10 seasons, he had a .311 batting average, stole 197 bases, and hit 137 home runs. In his first year of eligibility, 1962, Jackie was inducted into the Major League Baseball Hall of Fame, breaking another color barrier, this time in Cooperstown. On June 4, 1972, the Los Angeles Dodgers retired Jackie Robinson's number 42. In 1987, Major League Baseball renamed both Rookie of the Year Awards the "Jackie Robinson

Award." Ten years later, the number 42 was retired throughout Major League Baseball. In 2007, Major League Baseball opened up the number 42 for all players to wear on April 15, now Jackie Robinson Day. Over 200 players participated, and since 2009 all uniformed MLB personnel have worn number 42 on Jackie Robinson Day. The baseball stadium at UCLA, opened in 1981, is named after Jackie and contains a large statue of the former UCLA legend. On November 22, 2014, it was announced that the number 42 would be retired campus-wide at UCLA, and no player would again wear that number in any sport after the three current players wearing it moved on.

Following his athletic career, Jackie continued to stay busy. In 1957, he was named the vice president of Chock Full O'Nuts. Though he was glad to work for William Black at Chock Full O'Nuts, he had one stipulation. He would not miss any opportunity to advance the lives of black people. Mr. Black was very gracious and flexible when it came to Jackie's other interests. In 1957, Roy Wilkins asked Jackie if he would chair the freedom drive for the NAACP. He graciously accepted. In 1964, he helped found the Freedom National Bank in Harlem, a neighborhood bank geared to helping black people obtain loans that they qualified for but would nonetheless be denied by larger banks. He was interested in politics, as well. Jackie would call himself neither a Republican nor a Democrat. He worked for both sides and made it clear that he would side with whichever candidates would do the most to help the cause of black people. In 1960, he campaigned for Richard Nixon. In 1964, he worked on the Nelson Rockefeller campaign, and when Rockefeller dropped out, Robinson switched allegiances to the Democratic Party because he felt he could not morally support Barry Goldwater. Though he went back to work for Rockefeller in '66, he supported Democratic candidate Hubert Humphrey for President in 1968. Jackie would be an influential Civil Rights speaker for the rest of his life. He regularly interacted with both Malcolm X and Martin Luther King Jr. He had differences with both but was always willing to learn and deeply appreciated the way they had dedicated their lives to helping the black cause.

On October 24, 1972, Jackie Robinson died. He was only 53 but had battled illness for years. Jackie was diabetic and had ongoing heart problems. He died of a heart attack in his Connecticut home and left behind a wife and two living children. Another child, his first, Jackie Jr., had died one year earlier in a car accident. Jackie Robinson changed America. He had the courage and strength to not fight back. He had the ability to perform under immense pressure. He was one of UCLA's greatest athletes and one of America's most influential men. On April 15, when every Major League Baseball player wears number 42, when children take pictures in front of his statue at Jackie Robinson Stadium, when we see the number 42 at every athletic facility on UCLA's campus, when we see all major sports in America integrated, we must remember Jackie Robinson. We must remember what he went through.

## 1941

On September 26, 1941, UCLA, fresh off a 1–9 season, was back on the field. The first game of the season pit the Bruins and the Washington State Cougars. Kenny Washington was gone after the 1939 season and Jackie Robinson after the 1940 season. Replacing Kenny proved to be impossible, and now replacing Jackie seemed like a daunting task, as well. After a year on the freshman squad, Burr Baldwin would now take over as the star player for the Bruins. Would it be enough to increase the season's win total? Time would tell. In the first game of the year, the Bruins would easily outgain the Cougars. Total yardage—Bruins 189, Cougars 91. Two interceptions thrown by the Bruins kept the game close. Despite losing the turnover battle by two, talented and tough defense prevailed, as UCLA won, 7–6.

The following three games fit in tidily with the script coach Horrell was writing in his UCLA tenure—the Bruins had moments of brilliance and moments of despair. In Week 2, UCLA would lose to the Stanford Indians, 33–0, and it could have been even worse. The Bruins fumbled an astounding seven times, losing three of them, and also threw an interception. In Week 3, UCLA defeated the Montana Grizzlies, 14–7. Though they outgained the Grizzlies by a wide margin, turnovers continued to be a problem. After the seven-fumble performance a week earlier, the Bruins somehow fumbled the ball an even more incredible 12 times against the Grizzlies, losing five of them. The roller coaster continued in Week 4, when the Bruins lost to the

Ted Forbes runs the ball against Florida, 1941 (Southern Campus Collection)

University of Washington, 14–7. The Bruins were 2–2 on the season.

On October 25, UCLA took on the No. 16 Oregon Webfeet. Through the first four games, the Bruins had won, alternately, every other game, and the trend would continue against Oregon in what ended up being the best game the Bruins played all season. Ted Forbes, a back weighing only 153 pounds, performed admirably and led the Bruins on offense. UCLA was able to cut down on their fumbling problem, though they still lost two, but accumulated massive chunks of yardage on the ground. UCLA rushed for 235 yards and defeated Oregon, 14–7. It was the third game in a row that ended in a final score of 14–7, with the Bruins coming out on top two of the three contests.

The month of November had UCLA facing two conference foes and two nonconference opponents. UCLA lost to both California Berkeley and Oregon State University on successive weeks to start the month. Both teams thoroughly dominated the Bruins. The Bears won 27–7 and the Beavers 19–0. The Bruins were 3–4 when they took on Camp Haan, a Coast Artillery Antiaircraft Replacement Training Center, which had opened in January 1941. UCLA defeated the servicemen stationed at Camp Haan by a score of 29–0. On November 22, the Bruins took on old foe Santa Clara. For the third time in the last four games, UCLA was easily defeated. The Bruins finished with just 130 yards and four turnovers. With two games to play, UCLA was 4–5. Though the month of November treated UCLA poorly, coming off an earlier, miserable 1940 season, UCLA could still have a successful 1941 and finish with a winning record.

On December 6, 1941, UCLA took on the USC Trojans. The two rivals had played seven times before. In five of those games, the Trojans came away victorious. In the other two, 1936 and 1939, the Trojans and the Bruins played to a tie. Coming into the 1941 game, the storied Trojans program was just 2–6 for the season. The Bruins, at 4–5, knew they were very capable of beating Troy for the first time in school history. Leo Cantor had possibly his best game of the year, and Ted Forbes also played well. On the defensive side of the ball, UCLA did well stopping the run. USC, however, threw the ball for 138 yards, more than doubling the Bruins' passing output. Thanks to a strong ground game, UCLA controlled the ball for much of the game. In the end, the yardage was almost identical. USC totaled 246 yards and the Bruins 250 yards. UCLA would play its only clean game of the year in the turnover department. After the season-long struggles protecting the ball, UCLA didn't have a single turnover in this matchup. USC scored one touchdown through the air and the Bruins one on the ground. For the third time in history, the rivalry game ended in a tie, 7–7, the same score as the 1936 affair.

On December 7, 1941, one day after the UCLA-

UCLA vs. USC on December 6, 1941, one day before Pearl Harbor was attacked (Southern Campus Collection)

USC battle, Japan attacked the United States in a relentless bombing of the U.S. Naval Base at Pearl Harbor. Two weeks after Pearl Harbor, the season resumed for the Bruins, but it was of little meaning to many. With the country now officially part of the war, many of the boys on the 1941 team would join the service themselves.

UCLA won the final game of the season, 30–27, over the University of Florida. After finishing 1–9 in 1940, the Bruins were 5–5–1 in 1941.

The Downtown Athletic Club named Bruce Smith from the University of Minnesota the 1941 Heisman Trophy Winner.

The Associated Press named the University of Minnesota the 1941 National Champions.

## 1942

By the time football season started in 1942, the war had escalated. While many young men had left college to join the armed forces, the ones who stayed home and played football had a season to look forward to. The 1942 team turned out to be one of the best in UCLA history. Coach Horrell, along with Assistant Coaches Ray Richards, Cece Hollingsworth, and trainer Ducky Drake, did their best to keep the team focused and healthy. Quarterback Bob Waterfield was a junior. He had contributed to the 1941 team, but in 1942, a star was born. Waterfield would complete 52 passes on the season for 1,095 yards. Both totals shattered the previous UCLA records. Milt Smith was Waterfield's primary target. Ken Snelling, Al Solari, Everett Riddle, and Vic Smith also were key contributors on offense. Burr Baldwin anchored both the offensive and defensive lines. The 1942 offense set a then-school record of 173 points scored.

On September 25, the season kicked off against Texas Christian University. The first quarter and a half was played rather evenly, with neither team threatening to score. Late in the second quarter, however, the Bruins found their stride. Waterfield would connect with Milt Smith for 38 yards, and on the next play another six. Snelling then rushed up the middle for two more yards. It was 3rd and 2 from the Horned Frogs' 7-yard line. On the next play, Snelling fumbled and the ball rolled forward. TCU would recover, and the teams went into the locker room at halftime tied, 0–0. Though the Frogs would receive the ball to start the third quarter, the Bruins would take over in a flash. On the first possession for TCU, Everett Riddle would intercept a pass and race to the Frogs' 10-yard line. Two plays later, Waterfield found Smith for a touchdown. The extra point attempt failed, and the Bruins led, 6–0. For the entirety of the game thus far, the Bruins' defense had been flawless. TCU was unable to mount any sort of drive that would threaten the Bruins until the fourth quarter. Beginning at their own 4-yard line, the Horned Frogs marched down the field, on and around the Bruins defense. On fourth and goal from the Bruins 4-yard line, the game was on the line. Quarterback Emery Nix rolled to the right. He then angled a pass to the front corner of the end zone to Don Ezell. Touchdown Horned Frogs! The extra point was successful, and the Bruins lost, 7–6.

One week after the opening game loss, the Bruins would take on Saint Mary's Preflight, a team made up of former college football greats now in the service and playing for the Navy. On the opening drive, the Bruins looked as if they had brought their "A" game. Within three plays, the ball was on the SMP 37-yard line. On the fourth play, however, Waterfield threw an interception to Bob de Lauer. Six plays later, Vic Bottari took the ball into the end zone. SMP scored three times in the game, and all three times missed the extra point. The former college standouts were physically too big and mature for the Bruins. UCLA would reach the end zone one time, and the final score was 18–7.

Though the Bruins were now 0–2, they were unfazed entering conference play. In the first conference game of the year, UCLA routed Oregon State University by a score of 30–7. The UCLA offensive line opened massive holes, enabling the backs to simply run through them all game long. Line Coach Ray Richards's bunch had physically dominated their opponent.

The following week saw much of the same. In Week 4, the Bruins headed north to take on the California Berkeley Golden Bears. The defensive line never allowed the Bears to impose their will, opening running holes and giving Waterfield time to throw the pigskin. On the opening drive, Waterfield hit Herb Weiner in stride down the sideline, and though the defender was draped all over him, Weiner dragged him in from the 12-yard line for a touchdown. Waterfield scored on a rushing touchdown in the third quarter and then connected with Burr Baldwin for another touchdown in the fourth. Memorial Stadium was quiet for much of the day. The Bruins left Berkeley with a 21–0 victory.

The consecutive decisive victories for the Bruins would not go unnoticed. On October 24, UCLA was ranked by the Associated Press for the first time that year. The No. 14 Bruins would face No. 9 Santa Clara in the next game at the Coliseum. In the first half, the Bruins were simply dominated. The Broncos' ground game could not be stopped. They churned out yardage in a fashion the Bruins hadn't seen in years. Along with a potent running game, they were also able to throw the ball. Quarterback Jesse Freitas helped balance out the offense by throwing for 155 yards. When the Broncos got near the goal line, however, they turned into a different team. Without a formidable kicker, they took chances they otherwise may not have taken. Repeatedly, the Broncos turned the ball over on downs in opponent territory. On the other side, the Bruins' offense was carrying an anchor. They couldn't move the ball at all. The closest they came in the first half was on a poor Broncos punt, capped by a 15-yard penalty. The Bruins had the ball at the Broncos' 25-yard line, but four plays later, they turned it over. At halftime, the score was still 0–0. In the second half, the Bruins released the anchor and sailed home to victory. The offense exploded out of the tunnel and took the ball 77 yards on 11 plays for the first score of the game. The Broncos bounced back, however, and Freitas took the ball into the end zone. Santa Clara missed the extra point, and the score was 7–6. With seconds remaining in the game, Santa Clara had the ball. Freitas dropped back, threw a pass, and was intercepted by Everett Riddle. He raced down the field. Touchdown Bruins. The final score was 14–6. The Bruins were 3–2 on the season and would now be ranked No. 11 in the country.

The following four weeks were critical for the Bruins. At 2–0 in conference play, the Bruins were in a fine position to run the table. They wouldn't play a ranked opponent until the Trojans in the final regular season game, but first came the challenge of the Indians, Webfoots, Huskies, and Vandals. In the first game of the stretch, the Bruins easily dismantled Stanford. The Indians would score on the first play of the game, recovering a Bruins fumble and racing to the end zone, but UCLA bounced back and won, 20–7. A week later, the Bruins quite literally slipped up. In a massive thunderstorm in Eugene, the Bruins would go to battle with the University of Oregon. UCLA started with a 72-yard kick return by Al Solari, but Waterfield was picked off on the next play. On the following Bruins drive, Solari had a long run to set up a scoring opportunity, but this time Snelling missed the short field goal. Five plays later, the Webfeet reached the end zone. UCLA would counter with a Waterfield touchdown, but the Webfeet scored again and won the game, 14–7. Two weeks later, UCLA beat the University of Washington, 14–10, and two weeks after that defeated the University of Idaho, 40–13.

Bob Waterfield, 1942 (Southern Campus Collection)

When No. 11 UCLA took on No. 14 USC on December 12, a Rose Bowl berth was on the line. For the second time in history, the rivalry matchup winner would head to the most prestigious bowl game in college football. In the previous meeting, a tie meant that there had been no winner—one of three ties in the history of the rivalry to that point. The other five matchups all resulted in USC victories. The Bruins would score first on this day. In the second quarter, after driving to the USC 20-yard line, Waterfield broke off a 14-yard run. Vic Smith then pounded ahead for four yards, and Snelling finished the job with a 2-yard touchdown plunge. The extra point was good, and the Bruins led, 7–0. In the third quarter, the Bruins came out firing on all cylinders. On the first drive, Waterfield found Baldwin for a long catch, and he rumbled through Trojans defenders to the end zone. Snelling converted the extra point and the Bruins led, 14–0. Though USC would score a touchdown in the fourth quarter, the Bruins maintained the lead. UCLA was going to the Rose Bowl! Students packed the streets of Gayley Avenue and partied all night. An impromptu parade marched down Westwood Boulevard. It was the greatest victory to date in UCLA's history.

The Bruins played in their first Rose Bowl game following the 1942 season. UCLA fan Joe Brown did his best to fire up the crowd, but the Bruins lost, 9–0, to the University of Georgia. (Southern Campus Collection)

On January 1, 1943, UCLA played in its first Rose Bowl game against the No. 5 University of Georgia Bulldogs. As it turned out, pregame festivities were more memorable than the first half of the game. At halftime, the score was 0–0, with neither team seriously threatening to score. In the third quarter, the Bulldogs marched down the field to the Bruins' 2-yard line. On the next play, Frankie Sinkwich fumbled, and the ball rolled to the 1-yard line. As players were pulled off the pile, it was revealed that UCLA's Herb Weiner had landed on the ball. The Bruins took over! After three plays, the Bruins were forced to punt. Waterfield stood in the back of the end zone to punt, and the rush came quick. As ball hit foot, Georgia was all over it and blocked the kick! It rolled through the end zone for a safety. After a Waterfield interception, Georgia marched the ball down the field for the game's only touchdown. The Bruins lost, 9–0.

The Downtown Athletic Club named Frank Sinkwich from the University of Georgia the 1942 Heisman Trophy Winner.

The Associated Press named Ohio State University the 1942 National Champions.

## 1943

Nineteen forty-three was Coach Babe Horrell's fifth season at UCLA, and once more he was in the front seat driving the Bruins bus down a bumpy road. He had twice reached heights unseen at UCLA. In his first season, 1939, UCLA went undefeated. In his second season, they went 1–9. In 1942, the Bruins won the Pacific Coast Conference and went to the Rose Bowl. In 1943, Coach Horrell was still looking for consistency. Though he was never able to get his Bruins squad to perform consistently from year to year, his teams were always entertaining. Nineteen forty-three was no exception.

Off the field, the war raged on. Yet, just as he did every other season during the war, Coach Horrell had a job to do. Though the nation focused on the fight for freedom, he needed to focus on football.

The season kicked off on September 25 against USC. On the UCLA side, the roster was less experienced than it had been in decades. Only five players had varsity experience, and half the players on the combined varsity/freshman rosters were straight out of high school. UCLA had been hit harder in '43 than in '42 by war attrition. All-PCC performer Herb Weiner was just one of many who had left school to serve the country.

Nevertheless, in '43, USC had a strong squad that would finish 8–2 on the season. Yet every time the Bruins took on the Trojans, it was more than just another game. In the first quarter of the 1943 matchup, UCLA played USC evenly. Neither team moved the ball very well, but UCLA kept up with the Trojans admirably. In the second quarter, it fell apart. The Bruins were physically dominated and went down by two scores at halftime. In the third quarter, it was much the same. USC scored on an 86-yard run by Eddie Saenz, and the game was all but over. UCLA mounted their most impressive drive of the game in the fourth quarter but were unable to score. USC won, 20–0.

In 1943, the Bruins would play three teams made up of former players serving at military bases. Following the loss to USC, the Bruins went on to lose to College of the Pacific in Week 2 and played March Field in Week 3. Entering that game, there was much hype about the March Field squad. The Flyers actually fielded two teams, both of which were very good, but the "A" team proved to be sensational. They would play other prominent football schools in '43, such as the University of Washington and the

University of Redlands, and would finish the season ranked No. 10 in the country by the Associated Press. Former Alabama player Jimmy Nelson and all-PCC performers Hank Norberg of Stanford and former Bruin Woody Strode were the leaders. UCLA surprisingly kept the game close early, but Nelson, Norberg, Strode, Jack Jacobs, and Joe Williams all proved to be too much, and the Bruins were soundly defeated by March Field, 47–7.

Three weeks into the season, the Bruins were 0–3, but the misery of losing would not come to an end anytime soon. Following the loss to March Field, the Bruins lost twice to the University of California Berkeley—once on October 16 at the Coliseum, and the second time at Memorial Stadium on November 13. Sandwiched between the two losses to Cal were games against two other military institutions. The first was against the San Diego Naval Training Station Blue Jackets. In the first half, the Bruins outplayed the Blue Jackets. Through a quarter and a half, the Bruins outgained the Jackets and appeared the more athletic team. Wasted first-half opportunities eventually came to bite the Bruins. The Jackets scored on the final play of the half and took a touchdown lead into the break. The Bruins should have been ahead but once again saw themselves in a familiar position . . . trailing. In the second half, it was all Navy. Running back Bill Cadenhead would lead the Jackets on offense, and the Bruins never got much going when in possession, ultimately suffering a 28–0 defeat. Though it was an honor to be on the field with some of the finest young men in the country, the Bruins were tired of losing. After facing the San Diego Naval Training Station, UCLA took on the Del Monte Preflight Horrelmen. UCLA would once again go down in defeat. The Horrelmen had six All-Americans on their team, and though UCLA's Johnny Roesch scored first, the Bruins never had a chance. Fordham's Len Eshmont crossed the goal line first for the Horrelmen, Paul Christman of Missouri threw a touchdown to Bowden Wyatt of Tennessee and ran another in himself, and Parker Hall of Mississippi broke off a long run for a score. UCLA went on to lose, 26–7.

On November 20, the Bruins played their eighth game of the season. Still winless, the Bruins would face Saint Mary's, which was 1–4 on the season and had fared no better than the Bruins against similar opponents. The Bruins felt that if they could stop the Gaels' best player, halfback Herman Wademeyer, a transfer out of Honolulu, they could win the game. UCLA's line was for once the physically dominant unit. The Bruins' backs were able to rush for over 300 yards, and the defense held Wademeyer in check for much of the game. Jack Boyd would score twice for the Bruins in the first half, and UCLA took a 13–0 lead into halftime. In the third quarter, the Gaels' Wademeyer left his mark. On a run near the left sideline, he lateraled the ball to a teammate, who scampered 15 yards to the end zone. With the score 13–6, pressure was back on the Bruins, who responded accordingly. UCLA would tack on another touchdown in the third quarter, the third of the day by Boyd. Neither team found the end zone in the fourth quarter, and the Bruins won their first game of the year by a score of 19–7.

UCLA would end the season in the same way they started it. The final game of the season pitted the Bruins against the Trojans for the second time. Though UCLA would lead at the half, 13–6, after scores by Don Borden and Dave Brown, the Trojans were too strong in the second half. The Victory Bell, which was not awarded to the winner of the season-opening game, was awarded to USC after the schedule's finale. UCLA would finish the season with a 1–8 record.

Merle Campbell, 1943 (Southern Campus Collection)]

The Downtown Athletic Club named Angelo Bertelli from the University of Notre Dame the 1943 Heisman Trophy Winner.

The Associated Press named the University of Notre Dame the 1943 National Champions.

## 1944

Nineteen forty-four was Coach Edwin "Babe" Horrell's sixth and final season at UCLA. He had coached an undefeated team and guided UCLA to the Rose Bowl. He also coached Bruins teams to two of the worst season records in the school's history. In 1944, the goal was to leave UCLA on an upward swing. After the disastrous one-win 1940 season, Coach Horrell had turned it around in '41 and won five games. Now, after the one-win '43 season, he had another daunting task. Could he improve the team? Could he still teach his players? Or were his winning days behind him?

For the second year in a row, UCLA football kicked off the season against rival USC. In '43, the Trojans had beaten the Bruins in both meetings and would look to continue the streak on September 23 of the new campaign. Though still relatively inexperienced and definitive underdogs to the Trojans once again, the Bruins of '44 were a special bunch. They had experienced the dreadful season of '43, and many young players had a coming of age, seeing the field when in other years they might have been relegated to the bench. The first half of the season opener started off much as many expected. USC jumped out to an early 13–0 lead, aided by a controversial pass interference call that gave the Trojans the ball at the Bruins' 1-yard line. USC pounded the ball into the end zone. The second USC touchdown came on an interception returned deep into Bruins territory, followed by another short rushing touchdown. Down at halftime, it would have been easy for UCLA to mentally check out and give up. Sixty thousand fans were in attendance, and few believed the Bruins could come back against Troy. It was 103 degrees that day at the Coliseum, and UCLA was physically weak compared to the bigger and stronger Trojans. What the Bruins lacked in size, however, they more than made up for in grit. If quitting was on the minds of the players, it never showed. The third quarter was scoreless, but the Bruins played with life. They moved the ball and kept the Trojans' offense quiet. Still down 13–0 with three minutes to go, the Bruins recovered a USC fumble near midfield. Bob Russell found himself in the right spot at the right time. A pass to Russell Tauscheck gained 16 yards on the first play. Johnny Roesch then ran the ball on four consecutive plays, the last resulting in a 3-yard touchdown. The Bruins were on the board. Hearts stopped as UCLA missed the extra point. The Bruins tried an onside kick, which failed, but though USC recovered, there was still time for the Bruins to get the ball back. After the Trojans were stopped on three consecutive plays, they were forced to punt. With 20 seconds remaining, the Bruins needed a miracle. Roesch fielded the ball at the Bruins' 20-yard line. After weaving through would-be tacklers, he broke through the line! If he could outrace the trailing Trojans to the end zone, he would score! 25! 20! 15! 10! 5! Touchdown! With no time remaining on the clock and down, 13–12, Coach Horrell chose to go for the tie. The extra point bounced off the crossbar and went through the uprights. This UCLA-USC game to open the 1944 season would end in a "miracle" last-second tie, 13–13.

As in the previous year, the Bruins' schedule was filled with games against military institutions. Following a heartbreaking 6–0 defeat to Cal in Week 2, the Bruins took on the San Diego Navy squad on October 7. In front of 5,000 Blue Jacket spectators, the Bruins almost repeated the script from the USC game. Entering the fourth quarter, the Bruins trailed, 14–0. Roesch would score the Bruins' first touchdown of the day early in the fourth, but the extra point failed. Minutes later, the Bruins were marching again, and Roesch once more smashed through the line and into the end zone. The two-point conversion failed. Down 14–12, the Bruins were in desperation mode. With the ball in possession in Blue Jackets territory and time for one last play, quarterback Bob Waterfield threw the ball into the end zone, and the pass was knocked down. UCLA fell just short of another spectacular comeback in a 14–12 loss.

The rest of the season was much like Coach Horrell's roller-coaster tenure at UCLA. The positive moments included beating Saint Mary's, 39–0, and Cal in the rematch, 7–0. Some of the negatives included losing to March Field, 35–13, and a final game rematch with USC, 40–13. Along with San Diego Navy and March Field, the Bruins played two other service

UCLA vs. March Field, 1944 (Southern Campus Collection)

teams, Saint Mary's Preflight and Alameda Coast Guard. The Bruins would split those games. On the season, the Bruins finished 4–5–1. After the dismal 1943 season, the most objective of observers would conclude that the '44 season was a success. Coach Horrell had repeatedly raised expectations, only to then lower them. Yet history rarely tells the full story of Edwin Horrell, a wartime coach, a mentor, and a leader of young men in a confusing time.

The Downtown Athletic Club named Les Horvath from Ohio State University the 1944 Heisman Trophy Winner.

The Associated Press named the United States Military Academy at West Point (Army) the 1944 National Champions.

# CHAPTER 6
# Bert LaBrucherie (1945–1948)

Bert LaBrucherie was born on January 19, 1905. From his earliest days, Bert was a football man. Though much of the country was fixated on the Bronx Bombers, Boston Red Sox, Philadelphia As, and New York Giants, Bert was a fan of the pigskin game. Many turned their attention to the power of Tommy Burns, Jack Johnson, Jack Dempsey, and Joe Louis in the ring. Bert loved the pounding of football between the tackles.

UCLA Head Coach Bert LaBrucherie, 1947 (Southern Campus Collection)

Nevertheless, the first NFL championship game, won by the Chicago Bears, would not be played until 1933, when Bert was twenty-eight years old. In the first half of the 20th century, fans were forced to follow the college game. Bert was no exception. In the fall of 1925, Bert would enroll at the University of California Southern Branch and play for Grizzlies Coach William Spaulding.

Despite being highly capable the minute he set foot on campus, Bert was forced to play his first year on the freshman team due to eligibility rules. Though Coach Spaulding could have used his talent, the acclimation process was key for Bert. As a freshman, not only did he dominate on the field, but he physically matured. As a sophomore, both Coach Spaulding and Bert knew that the team would need him. Nineteen twenty-five was just the seventh season in school history and Spaulding's first. The Southern Branch had been a perennial loser early in its history, but Spaulding brought them the key leadership and knowledge that was lacking. In Spaulding's first season, the Grizzlies finished with a 5–3–1 record, the first winning season in school history. In 1926, it was Bert's time to shine.

In the second game of Bert's sophomore year, he made his mark. Coach Spaulding frequently substituted players on both sides of the ball to keep them fresh. Many teams, including prior UCLA teams, would rely heavily on two-way players, but Spaulding knew that if his players, even those with lesser talent, were fresher, they could compete with anyone. Bert's first touchdown came against the Whittier Poets. Despite being undersized, Bert had speed not seen before in a Southern Branch back. On a kickoff in the second quarter, he fielded the ball at the 15-yard line, found a crease, and outraced everyone to the end zone. The 85-yard kickoff return was a sign of things to come. Not only did the Grizzlies win the game, but a large crowd was there to see it. For the first time in school history, SBUC played at their future home, the Los Angeles Memorial Coliseum. Though the stadium could seat roughly 80,000 spectators, 12,000 showed up to watch. It was the largest home attendance yet in school history. The Grizzlies finished Bert's sophomore season with a 5–3 record. He showed flashes of brilliance as a sophomore but as a junior would prove to be a superstar.

In 1927, SBUC became UCLA, and Bert became a leader. As a junior, much was expected of him, and he wouldn't dare let his teammates down. The Grizzlies would finish Bert's junior season with a 5–0–1 record, but because they played one fewer game than Pomona College, they would not be named conference champions. Bert and the Grizzlies came out of the gates fast in 1927. He would lead the team in rushing and score a touchdown in the first game against Santa Barbara College. In the second game of the season, Bert's running and booming punts helped the Bruins win a tough contest against Fresno State College. The defining moment of the season for the Grizzlies, and one of the moments that lives on in UCLA lore, came against the Whittier Poets. The game was dubbed "the battle of Oak Pendleton vs. Bert LaBrucherie." Oak was the halfback for Whittier, and, unlike Bert, he was a large man, hard to tackle. Bert was the shifty back who, despite his diminutive size, could seemingly do it all. At halftime, both Oak and Bert had been held in check. Neither had broken off their signature long runs, though Oak did score on a short touchdown in the first half. In the third quarter, the Bruins led, 12–6, when Bert received a handoff on a sweep to the right side. Racing toward the sideline, Bert saw a defender had the angle on him, and, in one swift move, he cut back to the left. He made several defenders miss and raced to the end zone. The spectacular run stamped the victory for the Grizzlies and solidified Bert's status as one of the best players in America.

Prior to Bert's senior season, more changes would occur. UCLA was no longer part of the Southern California Intercollegiate Athletic Conference but was now part of the Pacific Coast Conference. They were no longer the Grizzlies. They were now the Bruins. With their recent success under Coach Spaulding, the Bruins were now seen as formidable opponents and a welcome addition to a top-notch conference. With the increase in competition came an increase in uncertainty. Could the Bruins repeat their success of the previous three years? Could Bert LaBrucherie run wild against PCC defenses like he had against SCIAC defenses? They got their answer: though the Bruins would take a step back in 1928 as a team, nothing could stop the brilliance of LaBrucherie. After another dominant season, Bert LaBrucherie would go down as the greatest UCLA football player ever to that point. Though his playing career had come to a close, Bert's life in football was not over. It had barely begun.

After graduating from UCLA in 1929, LaBrucherie instantly went to work as a football coach. For six seasons, he was an assistant coach at Los Angeles High School. In 1935, Coach Bert received a promotion. Though football was something he loved, it was a job, and Bert had climbed the ladder. He was named the head coach at Los Angeles High School in 1935. For 10 seasons, Coach Bert did his best to emulate the leadership of Coach Spaulding. Bert was a professional in every sense of the word. He took many of his core strategic beliefs and combined them with discipline and a willingness to learn new things. He was a thinker, as well as an example to those around him. Coach Bert compiled a 67–10–2 record, and Los Angeles High School won seven "A" team titles. In 1945, he took another step up the ladder. This time, he returned to the school that he once represented—UCLA.

As the head coach of the Bruins from 1945 to 1948, Coach Bert achieved a 23–16 record. His best team was the 1946 squad. At the time he was hired, no one knew the future of football in America—nor the future of America, for that matter. World War II was winding down, and though many could see the writing on the wall, the geopolitical aftermath was largely uncertain. Coach Bert, like Coach Horrell before him, had to focus on his task: football. While Coach Horrell had fielded great teams, he also fielded atrocious teams. Coach Bert's task was to bring consistency. In 1945, he had his first opportunity. In 1947, he was on the cover of Wheaties. By 1949, he was looking for a new job. Following the '48 season, Bert could see that his future as UCLA head coach was nearing an end, and on December 13, Coach Bert and his entire staff resigned. When asked about his resignation, Bert said, "I saw the handwriting on the wall. That's all there was to it."

Following Coach Bert's four years as the head coach at his alma mater, he would remain in football for the majority of his life. From 1949 to 1967, coach Bert took on the seemingly impossible task of turning around the Caltech football program. Gone were the days when the Engineers could compete with the Bruins. Coach Bert once said that his players would line up on the wrong side, not know in which direction to go, and not fully understand the scoring system. Despite an seemingly impossible situation, Bert brought his signature professionalism to the job. Along with coaching football, he also coached cross country and track and field, where he had more success than on the gridiron. Coach Bert would finish his career at Caltech with a 42–137–2 record in football and a 107–105 record in track and field and cross country dual meets.

Bert LaBrucherie died on December 10, 1986, in Laguna Hills, California, following complications from heart surgery. Following Bert's death, the family requested that, instead of flowers, the public should donate to the UCLA Athletic Fund.

## 1945

On September 2, 1945, Japan formally surrendered to the Western Allies, ending World War II. That month would also mark the start of Bert LaBrucherie's tenure leading the Bruins on the field.

Along with Bert as head coach, Ray Richards, Cece Hollingsworth, and Shelby Calhoun helped coach the Bruins. The first game of the '45 season pitted the Bruins against the USC Trojans on September 21. In the crowd there was a general sense of optimism, given that the country had just defeated the greatest enemy ever known to the United States. UCLA fans hoped to start the season by defeating the greatest enemy known to the Bruins. More than 81,000 were in attendance to see the Bruins perform under their new coach. In the first quarter, they were not disappointed. UCLA held the strong Trojans team scoreless and had some success on offense, though they couldn't score. In the second quarter, UCLA broke the tie. Skip Rowland ran off right tackle for a 10-yard touchdown. USC came right back and scored themselves. At halftime, the difference was an extra point. UCLA had missed theirs, and USC successfully converted. It was 7–6 Trojans. Despite a strong defensive effort from UCLA's front line of Al Sparlis, Marion Childers, Tom Asher, and others, USC would score one more time. Verl Lillywhite of the Trojans scored in the second half, and the Bruins did not. The final score was USC 13, UCLA 6. Coach Bert's first win as the Bruins' coach would have to wait.

In Week 2, the Bruins took on the San Diego Navy. In previous years, the Bruins had struggled with military teams, which were much stronger and more physically capable of taking on the rigors of football. On this day, the Bruins were up for the task. Cal Rossi scored the first touchdown on a 34-yard scamper. "Crazy Legs," as he was known, had quite a day. He scored again in the second quarter on a lateral from Jack Porter and run of six yards. Porter then scored the final Bruins touchdown after Rossi and Skip Rowland helped by driving the ball deep into Sailors territory. San Diego Navy scored twice, but it would not be enough. Coach Bert won his first game as head coach by the score of 20–14.

UCLA would continue to play good football in the month of October. On October 5, UCLA defeated Pacific, 50–0, and a week later defeated Cal Berkeley, 13–0. After stumbling against Saint Mary's Preflight, the Bruins got back on track by defeating the University of Oregon, 12–0, on October 27. The Bruins finished the month 3–1 and faced the final three games on their schedule with a 4–2 record.

After a three-week layoff, the Bruins took the field against No. 5 Saint Mary's. On this day, UCLA outplayed the undefeated and untied Gaels from start to finish. The combination of Skip Rowland, Jack Boyd, Bob Hansen, and Russ Tauschek was too much for Ed Ryan and the Gaels. After scoring the first two touchdowns, the Bruins held on to win, 13–7.

The following week, the Bruins looked to continue their momentum but were caught in a downpour. Because they had already beaten the University of California handily early in the season, many thought the Bruins could do the same in Berkeley. When the Bruins arrived, they were not only battling the opponent, but the elements, as well. The only score on this day would come on a fluke play. UCLA was set to punt in Cal territory, hoping to pin the Bears back, when a poor snap forced the UCLA punter to pick the ball up off the ground and rush the punt. It was blocked by Dan Malmberg; the ball flew off in the air directly to the right, where it was caught in stride off one bounce by Joe Stuart, who raced down the sideline. Sensing he was about to be caught from behind, Stuart turned and lateraled to a teammate, who took it into the end zone. UCLA lost the game, 6–0.

With one game left, the Bruins were 5–3 and were set to take on the No. 16 USC Trojans for the second time that season. A large crowd of 103,657 fans packed the Los Angeles Memorial Coliseum to see the two rivals battle for city superiority. The weakened Bruins squad, which had dealt with several key injuries during the season, was battered in the first half. Instead of a competitive matchup, the fans witnessed one team playing out the final strings of the season and another gearing up for a Rose Bowl appearance. In the second half, Bert was able to rally his men. Though USC's 19–0 lead seemed insurmountable, the Bruins fought hard. Ernie Case threw a touchdown pass to Rowland, and the Bruins would score once again on a "Statue of Liberty" play. The final score was USC 26, UCLA 15. Coach Bert would finish his first season as the head coach with a 5–4 record.

The Downtown Athletic Club named Felix Anthony "Doc" Blanchard from the United States Military Academy at West Point (Army) the 1945 Heisman Trophy Winner.

The Associated Press named the United States Military Academy at West Point (Army) the 1945 National Champions.

## 1946

In 1946, the morale of the nation was high, and the hopes and dreams of the UCLA football team were still higher. Coach Bert LaBrucherie was starting his second season as the Bruins head coach. With the nucleus of the '45 team returning, the '46 team had dreams of the Rose Bowl. Coach Bert was a superb back in his playing days, and now his knowledge would be passed down. The '46 Bruins finished with the finest offense in the land. Would it be enough to win the PCC title?

Bert LaBrucherie, 1946 (Southern Campus Collection)

The season kicked off on September 28 against Oregon State University. In front of 40,203 spectators, the Bruins dominated. OSU had high expectations themselves coming into the '46 campaign, but those were soon lowered after the thrashing. Ernie Case connected with Cal Rossi for two touchdowns in the first half. Burr Baldwin blocked a punt, picked it up, and returned it for a touchdown. Gene Rowland rushed for a score from three yards out. Going into halftime, the game was all but over, and the second half was much of the same. UCLA would win the season-opening matchup, 50–7. The Bruins tallied up 599 yards on the day, and the 50-point performance was the largest total UCLA had scored in a game since joining the PCC.

Week 1 may have opened the eyes of the public to the strength of the Bruins, but Week 2 proved it wasn't a fluke. UCLA traveled to Seattle to take on the Washington Huskies. Forty-three thousand fans saw the Bruins ambush their opponent. Case connected with Rossi for a 61-yard score, Rossi then scored on an 8-yard run off left tackle, and Rowland scored on a 38-yard run—all in the first half. In the third quarter, the UCLA defense continued to stop the Huskies in their tracks, and after the Bruins forced a punt, Ernie Johnson returned it 76 yards to the Washington 10-yard line. On the next play, Case found Baldwin for a touchdown. Jack Myers and Johnson would each tack on touchdowns before Washington finally responded with two late scores. The final score was 39–13, UCLA.

Two weeks into the season, one thing was clear. The Bruins would contend for the PCC title, and possibly even the national title. On October 12, the No. 5 Bruins took on the No. 17 Stanford Indians and smashed them by a score of 26–6. The offense slowed a week later when the Bruins traveled to Berkeley, but coach Bert and his squad nonetheless escaped with a 13–6 victory. UCLA was 4–0 on the season, with all four wins coming in conference play. The next two games would be nonconference games against Santa Clara and Saint Mary's. Though the stakes weren't as high, the Bruins continued to shine. Against Santa Clara, Jerry Shipkey and Al Hoisch each scored touchdowns for the Bru-

1946 UCLA football team photo (Southern Campus Collection)

and Don Malmberg recovered and raced to the end zone. Just before halftime, USC scored a touchdown, as well. Both teams missed their extra point attempts, and the halftime score was 6–6. The third quarter was a slugfest. Both teams drove the ball into opponent territory, but neither was able to score. Early in the fourth quarter, UCLA was driving the ball into Trojans territory. The drive was capped on a quarterback sneak by Case. UCLA again missed the extra point, but it proved to mean little. Final score: UCLA 12, USC 6. The Bruins were 9–0 and Pacific Coast Conference champions! Before the Rose Bowl, UCLA had one game left on the schedule. The final regular season game was a nonconference battle against the University of Nebraska. UCLA defeated the Huskers, 18–0, to complete the undefeated (and untied) regular season.

ins, with Ernie Johnson adding three touchdowns of his own. The Bruins won easily, 33–7. Against Saint Mary's, UCLA scored three touchdowns in the first seven minutes and went on to win, 46–20, making the Bruins 6–0 on the season.

When conference play resumed, coach Bert was tasked with the increasingly difficult job of keeping his players focused. With success came expectations, but it also brought distractions. If the Bruins were to keep their PCC hopes alive, they had to take every opponent seriously. On November 9, UCLA took on the University of Oregon. The game was played in Portland in front of a packed house. Though the weather during the game was fairly decent, the field was soggy after a midweek storm. UCLA was unable to get its offense going in the first half, but the defense remained strong. At halftime, the game was scoreless. In the third quarter, the much-hyped UCLA offense broke free starting with their first offensive drive, when UCLA marched 52 yards to the end zone. The capper came on a 14-yard run by Rowland. The game was still tight in the fourth quarter. UCLA had a 7–0 lead with just minutes to go in the game. With the clock ticking down, Jack Brown smashed into the end zone and sealed the game for the Bruins. The final score was 14–0. UCLA had escaped again. The following week, UCLA would dismantle the Montana Grizzlies by a score of 61–7.

In one of the most important matchups between UCLA and USC, the fans saw a thriller. On November 23, the No. 10 USC Trojans took on the No. 4 UCLA Bruins. After winning the opening coin toss, UCLA decided to kick off. USC received the kick, and the battle was underway. UCLA got on the board first as Bill Chambers blocked a USC punt,

On January 1, 1947, the No. 4 UCLA Bruins took on the No. 5 Illinois Fighting Illini in the Rose Bowl. The Illini were 8–2, with their two losses coming early in the season to Indiana and Notre Dame. While UCLA boasted the most powerful offense in college football, Illinois was a balanced team with a strong offense and solid defense. The Bruins offense, which had averaged 30 points per game, had a challenge on its hands against a defense that only allowed 10 points per game. Though undefeated, UCLA had much to prove entering this final game. The three teams ranked ahead of them in the AP Poll (Army, Georgia, and Notre Dame) were all also undefeated, and though the final voting was done for both the AP poll and Coaches poll after the regular season, the Bruins had a chance to be named National Champions by any of the remaining polls. If the Bruins wanted to be voted National Champions, they would have to prove themselves worthy on the biggest stage. In the first quarter, the Bruins came out strong. UCLA marched the ball down the field and scored first, as Ernie Case crossed the goal line on a quarterback sneak. UCLA held the lead until the middle of the second quarter, when Illinois twice got on the scoreboard. UCLA's defense could not handle the combination of Buddy Young, Julie Rykovich, and Alex Agase. Though trailing at the half, the Bruins' never-say-die attitude was apparent until the very end. Al Hoisch took the opening kickoff three yards deep into the end zone and returned it 103 yards for a touchdown. It was the longest touchdown in Rose Bowl history to that point. It was not enough, however, and the underrated Illinois team thoroughly dominated the rest of the way. UCLA went on to lose the 1947 Rose Bowl game by a score of 45–14. In coach Bert's second season, UCLA had completed an undefeated (and untied) regular season. The Bruins beat USC and displayed the best offense in school history. They eyed a National Championship, and though they came up short in the Rose Bowl, things were looking up for the Bruins. If they were to consistently challenge the likes of Army, Notre Dame, and Michigan for national titles, they would have to consistently perform from year to year. In 1947, they would have the chance to prove if '46 had been a fluke, or if the Bruins were there to stay.

The Downtown Athletic Club named Glenn Davis from the United States Military Academy at West Point (Army) the 1946 Heisman Trophy Winner.

The Associated Press named the University of Notre Dame the 1946 National Champions.

## Burr Baldwin

Burr Baldwin was the first UCLA player to be named a consensus All-American. He was the first UCLA star player to leave school and join the Army during World War II. He was the first to do many things. He was the first in his family to attend college. He was the first to turn down the National Football League in favor of the All-America Football Conference. Burr Baldwin lived quite a life. It began and ended in Bakersfield, California.

Barrett "Burr" Browning Baldwin was born on June 13, 1922. He was a child of the Great Depression. When he was seven years old, the stock market crashed. Living in small-town Bakersfield, Burr's family struggled at times. Unbeknownst to Burr, life was not always easy. Growing up, he simply focused on sports. In the fall of 1936, Burr enrolled at Kern County Union High School (now Bakersfield High School) and thrived on the gridiron. In his junior season, the KCUHS Drillers went undefeated and won the 1939 Valley Championship. In 1940, as a senior, Burr was even better, but his Drillers team failed to repeat as champions, something that Burr would remember for the rest of his life. Though the season was over and his high school career came to a close, Burr Baldwin's football career was far from over. In 1940, he was off to UCLA to play under freshman football coach Kenny Washington.

Growing up, Baldwin had a love for country and sense of duty that many young men felt. He was an active reader, staying up to date on world events through local newspapers. He saw the rise of Nazi Germany in the 1930s and suspected the United States would soon join the war effort. On the football field, he thrived. After a successful freshman campaign, it was time for Baldwin to move to the varsity squad, and when he arrived on the big boy field in 1941, he was an immediate star. Though the 1941 Bruins would finish with a mediocre record, just 5–5–1, coach Babe Horrell saw promise and knew the following season could be special. They had tied crosstown rival USC, 7–7, in their annual meeting and beaten a strong Florida Gator opponent in the final game of the season.

The promise that coach Horrell may have felt going into the '42 season was unfulfilled early in the season. Things at UCLA, and for men like Baldwin nationwide, were not going well. The team was 0–2, but much more serious was that the sense of purpose was missing. The United States had suffered through Pearl Harbor 10 months earlier, and now willing and able young men were battling on the football field rather than in Europe or the Pacific with their fellow Americans. The season, however, would turn around for the Bruins, and the spirits of many of the athletes were raised. UCLA got its first win of the season on October 10, 1942, and would go on to win seven of the next eight games before taking on the USC Trojans. UCLA was ranked No. 11 in the country, and the Trojans were ranked No. 14. Like so many times to come, the big rivalry game had major implications. The winner would go to the Rose Bowl. UCLA went on to defeat the Trojans, thanks in large part to a 41-yard receiving touchdown by Baldwin from quarterback Bob Waterfield. On January 1, 1943, UCLA played in its first Rose Bowl. Though the Bruins would lose, 9–0, to the University of Georgia, Baldwin had helped take the team where they had never been before. Now it was time for him to go where he had never gone. It was time for him to join the war.

In 1943, Burr Baldwin joined the United States Army. For three years, he served his nation with honor, reaching the rank of captain. He served in Holland, France, Belgium, and Germany. According to his son, Michael, he served at the Battle of the Bulge. When the war ended, Burr came home. He had missed three seasons of college football but had no plans to return to a life in the States without the game he loved. He rejoined the UCLA football team in 1946 with one year of eligibility remaining. College football, in general, had struggled during the war. Teams were constantly decimated. Rosters were torn to pieces as young men decided they had a duty to fulfill. In 1946, the game was back. Rosters were loaded with talent and mature, adult men. They had seen the gruesome nature of war firsthand. Football was but a game. The Bruins of '46 were brilliant. Baldwin was again a superstar. As the Bruins rattled off win after win, fans came to understand that this season was special. Oregon State, Washington, Stanford—none stood a chance. Cal, Santa Clara, Saint Mary's—UCLA remained undefeated. Oregon and Montana were just stepping stones. On November 23, the undefeated Bruins took on the USC Trojans, the game once again deciding the conference title. Though the Trojans were able to slow the Bruins' brilliant offense, they weren't able to win. UCLA beat USC by a score of 13–6 and remained undefeated. After beating Nebraska in the final regular season game of the year, the Bruins went to the Rose Bowl, the second in a row for Baldwin, though separated by four years. UCLA had a chance to play for school history, and a chance to work their way into the national championship picture. For the second time, however, UCLA was denied. The University of Illinois beat the Bruins handily. Burr Baldwin's career was over. He was named a consensus All-American in '46 after leading the Bruins with 18 catches and 374 yards. He played in the college football All-Star game held in Hawaii and was drafted in the third round by the Green Bay Packers.

Baldwin turned down the Packers and instead chose a different path. For three seasons, he played with the Los Angeles Dons of the All-America Football Conference. He finished his professional career with 24 catches and 397 yards on offense and two interceptions on defense, before duty again called. When the United States entered the Korean War, Baldwin once again served his country. Captain Baldwin was never deployed overseas, but rather was called to teach ROTC at his alma mater, UCLA. Following the Korean War, Baldwin realized that his future was no longer in football. With a young wife and growing family, Baldwin took a job as an insurance agent. He worked in the insurance industry for over half a century before retiring. Burr Baldwin and his wife, Nancy, were married for 59 years before her death in 2006. They have two sons, Burr Jr. and Mike, as well as four grandchildren and four great-grandchildren. Burr was an avid lover of sports. He loved to golf. He loved to hunt. He loved his former high school and his former college, and they loved him back. Burr Baldwin was a 1969 inductee into the Bob Elias Kern County Hall of Fame, a member of the UCLA Athletics Hall of Fame, and an inaugural member of the Drillers Football Hall of Fame. He is one of 10 UCLA players to have his number retired (#38). In 2007, Burr Baldwin was diagnosed with cancer, and five months later, he died. Burr Baldwin was not only a UCLA legend; he was an American patriot.

## 1947

Following up the 1946 season with a successful 1947 campaign would be a difficult task. As teams win, expectations rise, and continuing to compete for titles can be a daunting challenge. Five head coaches came before Bert LaBrucherie, and each played an important part in the shaping of the Bruins' program. Fred Cozens was first. William Spaulding saw the most success. Edwin Horrell hit peaks not previously seen in UCLA football history. In 1947, it was up to coach Bert to demonstrate that he could take UCLA to the next level. It was up to him to prove that UCLA was now a true powerhouse program.

Though Burr Baldwin, an All-American from '46, was gone, the Bruins had strength in numbers in '47. Tom Fears, Mike Dimitro, and Bill Chambers were each named to the All-PCC team. Inspiration is gathered in many ways, but it is without question that some on the UCLA football team gathered inspiration from another Bruin: Jackie Robinson, the former UCLA four-sport star, integrated Major League Baseball in the spring. On April 15, Jackie made his major league debut against the Boston Braves at Ebbets Field in Brooklyn. Though he went 0-for-3 on the night, history was made. Jackie—the man who dazzled on the gridiron, dominated on the hardwood, soared through the air, and shined on the base paths—was a hero.

On September 26, the football season kicked off against the Iowa Hawkeyes. More than 90,000 fans flocked to the Coliseum to see the reigning PCC champs in the season opener. UCLA would start slow. At halftime, Iowa led, 7–0. But in the second half, the offense broke free and looked like the offense of '46. On the first drive of the half, UCLA marched downfield, and Benny Reiges tossed a touchdown pass to Tom Fears from two yards out. On the next drive, UCLA scored again. This time, it was Moose Myers who smashed into the end zone from the 2-yard line. In the fourth quarter, the Bruins would tack on 10 more points as Reiges knocked in a short field goal and Phil Tinsley scored a touchdown. The final score was UCLA 22, Iowa 7.

On October 4, UCLA would take on their second consecutive Big 9 opponent. The trip to Evanston, Illinois, proved to be a difficult one. Win or lose, it was evident early that the Bruins were in for a battle. The Northwestern Wildcats were a strong team. At halftime, UCLA led, 13–7. Northwestern had moved the ball well all half but struggled finding the end zone. UCLA scored twice in the second quarter, on touchdowns by Myers and Johnny Roesch. The halftime lead would not last long, however. On this day, special teams failed the Bruins. Northwestern's Frank Aschenbrenner took the opening kickoff of the second half all the way back for a touchdown. Four plays later, Northwestern returned a UCLA punt for a touchdown. In a matter of minutes, the lead was gone, and Northwestern was ahead, 20–13. Still in the third quarter, the Bruins responded. Myers and Carl Benton marched down the field, and Chuck Page battered into the end zone from three yards out. The wild momentum swings of the game were not over. On the final play of the third quarter, UCLA's Tom Fears broke through the Wildcats' line and blocked a punt, scooped it up himself, and raced 16 yards into the end zone. At the end of three quarters, the Bruins led, 26–20. If the Bruins could hold the fourth quarter lead, their regular-season winning streak would be intact. UCLA's defense had held up fairly well all game, only allowing one scoring drive. In the fourth, the Wildcats got on the scoreboard once again. Donald Farrar tossed a long touchdown to Julius Siegel for the game-tying touchdown. Extra points were never a given, but on this attempt, the ball sailed right through the uprights, and the Wildcats took a 27–26 lead. The Bruins couldn't answer, and the game was over.

Over the next four games, the Bruins proved to be an enigma. UCLA easily dismantled the University of Oregon on October 11 by a score of 24–7. Despite 130 yards from the Bruins in penalties, the Webfeet were no match on this day. UCLA climbed to No. 19 in the AP Poll. They then defeated Stanford, 39–6. Six different players reached the end zone for the Bruins. The next two games would define the Bruins' season. Though a nonconference game, the October 25 battle with SMU was a marquee matchup. The No. 12 Mustangs traveled to Los Angeles to take on the No. 16 Bruins. On this day, the much-feared Bruins offense was nonexistent. The UCLA defense performed admirably, but UCLA lost, 7–0. One week later, the result was almost identical. The No. 14

Skip Rowland returns a punt against Cal, 1947 (Southern Campus Collection)

California Golden Bears drove south and walked out of the Coliseum with a 6–0 win. The Bruins' offense had simply disappeared. With three games to play, UCLA had a disappointing 3–3 record.

On November 8, UCLA took on Oregon State University. The previous meeting between the two teams was fresh on the minds of all who had participated. UCLA had routed the Beavers, 50–7, one year earlier. In this game, UCLA was not quite able to repeat the domination of the prior year but had no problem coming away with a victory. Skip Rowland capped a 69-yard drive on the opening series for the Bruins with a 5-yard touchdown run. This was just a sign of things to come. UCLA was firing on all cylinders. The running game was effective all day, and the passing game contributed 12 completions on 19 attempts and 175 yards. The next opponent was the University of Washington. UCLA scored five touchdowns against the Huskies, one each by Rowland, Reiges, and Clements, and two touchdowns by Reisch. Chants from the crowd could be heard from the field, "Bring on Troy!"

UCLA was 5–3 on the season and No. 18 in the country when they took on the No. 4 USC Trojans. More than 102,000 fans showed up to support their respective teams at the Coliseum. The winner of the game would not only get the Victory Bell, but the PCC Crown as well and a berth in the Rose Bowl.

On the opening drive, UCLA appeared ready to play. With a series of short passes and successful runs, UCLA marched into Trojans territory but were eventually forced to punt after a series of negative plays. Much of the rest of the half was a punting battle. Finally, with four minutes to go, someone reached the end zone. Unfortunately for the Bruins, that man was USC's Jack Kirby. At halftime, the score was USC 6, UCLA 0. The second half had little action, with neither team threatening to score until the final minute. Down six with time winding down, UCLA had a chance to steal the victory. With 55 seconds to play, on 4th and 2 from inside the Trojans' 10-yard line, USC's Gordon Gray intercepted a pass from Ernie Johnson in the end zone. UCLA coach Bert LaBrucherie was convinced that the UCLA receiver had been interfered with, and over 50,000 fans in attendance agreed. But what mattered most was the opinion of the referees, and no flags were on the field. USC was headed to the Rose Bowl, and UCLA's season was over.

The Downtown Athletic Club named Johnny Lujack from the University of Notre Dame the 1947 Heisman Trophy Winner.

The Associated Press named the University of Notre Dame the 1947 National Champions.

## 1948

As it turned out, 1948 was a year of coming and going for UCLA athletics. After four seasons, Bert LaBrucherie would leave Westwood. He, like his predecessor, Edwin Horrell, had experienced ups and downs. While '48 would be coach Bert's last, another man was just beginning. The new basketball coach at UCLA was a thirty-seven-year-old Midwest boy named John Wooden.

It is appropriate to take a "time out" here, in this book about Bruins football, to say a few words about a man who will forever be a true legend in the annals of UCLA sports history—indeed, an American sports hero—even though he made his name not in football, but in the school's basketball program beginning during this period . . . not as a player, but as a coach.

John Wooden was born on October 14, 1910, in Hall, Indiana. At the age of eight, Wooden's family moved to a small farm town near Centerton, Indiana. The population of the town was just 86. Young John's father dreamed of a self-sufficient lifestyle on the farm, but in 1924 the Wooden family was forced to sell the farm and move to nearby Martinsville, where John's father would work in a local sanitarium. In Martinsville, John developed his love for basketball. In 1927, as a junior, he led Martinsville High School to the Indiana State Championship. It was the first of many successful seasons for John Wooden. Though Martinsville would lose the State Championship the following year, John was on to the next level, and it wasn't long before he was back to his winning ways. As a senior in college, Wooden would lead the Purdue Boilermakers

UCLA football players, 1947 (Southern Campus Collection)

to the 1932 National Championship. He was the first-ever three-time consensus All-American and was named the 1932 National Player of the Year. He was inducted into the Basketball Hall of Fame as a player in 1960. Following college, Wooden entered the coaching world. After pit stops coaching at Dayton High School and South Bend Central High School, Wooden joined the U.S. Navy during World War II. Following the war, Wooden briefly returned to coaching at the high school level at South Bend Central. In 1946, after a 218–42 record at the high school level, Wooden accepted his first college job. In his two seasons at Indiana State Teachers College, John Wooden and his team would twice win conference titles but both years turned down postseason invitations because black players were not allowed to play. It was clear at this point that John Wooden was a hot coaching commodity. In 1948, UCLA was not the only suitor looking to hire Wooden. Coach Wooden himself would once say, "I had hoped to take the job at the University of Minnesota, but a snowstorm knocked out television lines there and they didn't call me back at 6 p.m. as they had promised. UCLA called about fifteen minutes later and offered the job." It proved to be the greatest snowstorm in UCLA history. Wooden accepted the job and would go on to win 10 national championships at UCLA. He was six times named the College Basketball Coach of the Year. In 1973, he was inducted into the Basketball Hall of Fame as a coach. In 2000, *Sports Illustrated* named John Wooden as the Coach of the Century. In 2003, he was awarded the Presidential Medal of Freedom. In 2006, he was inducted into the inaugural class of the College Basketball Hall of Fame.

While UCLA had found its answer to the coaching question in basketball, Coach Bert LaBrucherie was playing out the final games of his career as the UCLA football coach. The season kicked off on September 18 against Washington State University. Though there were constant rumors in '48 of the Bruins' general apathy and unwillingness to play hard for coach Bert anymore, there were little, if any, signs of that in the season opener. After a long offseason, the Bruins' offense was unstoppable. Art Steffen, Ernie Johnson, Skip Rowland, Bill Duffy, and Rex Murphy each scored touchdowns for the Bruins. Steffen and Johnson each scored twice. The final score was 48–26. The LaBrucherie patented

Bill Clements, 1948 (Southern Campus Collection)

high scoring offense brought many cheers to the early season overreactors, but the defensive performance was troubling. What appeared to the casual fan as a great start to the season quickly proved to be false.

Following the season opening win against WSU, the Bruins lost four of their next five games. In Week 2, the offense was completely shut down by a far superior opponent, the Northwestern Wildcats. The final score was 19–0. UCLA would beat Idaho, 28–12, on October 2 and then go through a three-game stretch that coach Bert and the Bruins players would love to forget. UCLA took on the University of Washington in the fourth game of the season and lost by 21 points. The following week, Stanford beat them by 20 points, and one week later, Oregon State won by 28 points. UCLA's record was 2–4, and with four games to go, the season already looked like a disaster.

On October 30, UCLA traveled to Lincoln, Nebraska, to take on the Cornhuskers. The University of Nebraska beat UCLA in every statistical category except one. The Huskers outrushed the Bruins, 121–115, outpassed the Bruins, 219–164, and gained 15 first downs to the Bruins' eight. UCLA also had more penalties and penalty yardage. Each team turned the ball over twice. In the most important category, however, UCLA had the edge. On the scoreboard, it read UCLA 27, Nebraska 15. The Bruin defense was stingy in its own territory, and, despite being the inferior team all day, the Bruins escaped Lincoln with a win.

The final three games amounted to nothing more than a team ready for the offseason, and a coach playing out the final strings against a difficult schedule. In the eighth game of the year, the UCLA Bruins took on the No. 5 California Golden Bears. Despite playing very well in the first half and outgaining the Bears in total yardage on the day, the Bruins went down by a score of 28–13. Six days later, UCLA was back at the Coliseum to take on No. 15 Oregon. Clearly beaten down by the long season, the Bruins were simply outclassed from beginning to end. UCLA lost five fumbles on the day and only gained 61 yards through the air. Final score: 26–6 Oregon.

The Bruins finished the season against the University of Southern California. Though neither UCLA nor USC had anything to play for but city pride, the game was important to all involved. More than 90,000 fans packed the Coliseum to see the Bruins and the Trojans one last time in '48. The game was close throughout, but the nightmare season for the Bruins finally came to an end with another defeat. Art Steffen, Ernie Johnson, and Bob Watson all played well, but the Trojans would win the final game of the season, 20–13.

The Downtown Athletic Club named Doak Walker from Southern Methodist University the 1948 Heisman Trophy Winner.

The Associated Press named the University of Michigan the 1948 National Champions.

# CHAPTER 7
# Henry "Red" Sanders (1949–1957)

Henry Russell "Red" Sanders is considered by many the greatest football coach in UCLA history. Though John Wooden was hired one year prior to the arrival of Red in Westwood, the original nickname, the "Wizard of Westwood," was not assigned to Coach Wooden, but rather to Coach Sanders. When Coach Bert LaBrucherie left UCLA, the aim of the athletic administration was to find a coach who could compete with UCLA's natural rival, the USC Trojans. Not only did UCLA compete, they won. In coach Sanders's nine games against the Trojans, the Bruins won six times. Coach Sanders was an innovator. He was a motivator. He was intense and was always good for a classic quote. Like everyone else, coach Sanders was molded by his past. He had experimented and tweaked his game here and there. By the time he arrived in Westwood, coach Sanders was a master football mechanic; his job was to get the Bruins team to play like a finely tuned machine.

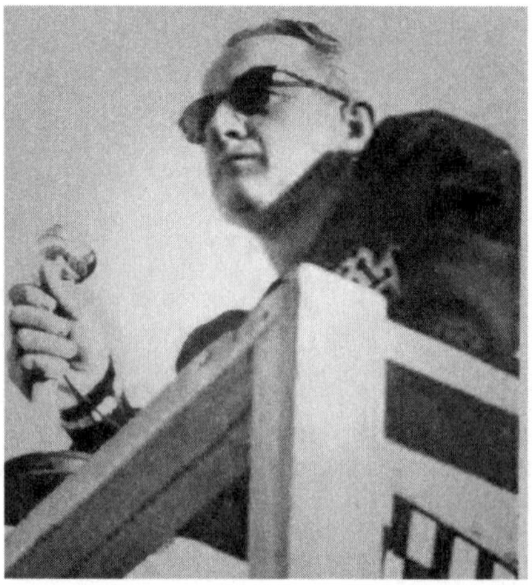

Head Coach Red Sanders, 1949 (Southern Campus Collection)

Henry "Red" Sanders was born in Asheville, North Carolina, on May 7, 1905. He was the only son of Ida Virginia Barr Sanders and Henry Edgar Sanders. From a young age, Red was taught to appreciate the importance of education. As a young boy, the Sanders family moved to Nashville, Tennessee, and Red attended Eastland School, Duncan College Preparatory School, and Central High School. Each step along the way, Red earned academic honors, and from a young age he was considered mature and motivated beyond the norm. After leaving Central High School, Red spent a brief time at Riverside Military Academy in Gainesville, Georgia, before enrolling at Vanderbilt University in the fall of 1923. While at Vanderbilt, Red was his typical active self. He was a member of the Alpha Tau Omega fraternity and a student leader. He played football and baseball, lettering four times in each and captaining the baseball team his senior year. Though he didn't have football skills as a player equal to those of Bert LaBrucherie, his predecessor at UCLA, coach Sanders was an incredible thinker. He played quarterback for Vanderbilt, and his coach, Dan McGugin, said of him, "Red Sanders has one of the best football minds I have ever known." Following graduation in 1927, Red was sure of one thing: he wanted to remain in sports. What he was unsure of was which sport. For three years, he was the backfield coach at Clemson College and played professional minor league baseball in the summers. Those summers included stints in Pensacola, Florida; Muskogee, Oklahoma; and Mobile, Alabama. Following the 1930 baseball season, Red made a decision. From then on, he would focus solely on football. He had developed a passion for football that far surpassed baseball, and he was dedicated to being the best coach he could be.

In 1931, Red got his first head coaching job at Columbia Military Academy in Tennessee. After his three-year stint with Columbia Military Academy, Red took a job at the Riverside Military Academy in Georgia, his alma mater, where he coached a young Tommy Prothro. Four years later, Red was on the move again; this time, he was headed to the college game. In Red's seven years as a prep coach, he compiled an excellent record of 55-4-2. The University of Florida saw the leader and brilliant football mind Red possessed and hired him as the freshman coach in 1938. After a year coaching freshmen in Gainesville, Red was on to Baton Rouge in 1939 to coach the backfield under Bernie Moore at Louisiana State University.

With the start of the 1940s came the beginning of a wild time in Red's life. After just one year at LSU, Red Sanders was offered the head coaching job at his alma mater, Vanderbilt University. Taking the position was a "no-brainer" for Red. After bouncing around from program to program working his way up the coaching ladder, he was ready to take what he had learned, implement his core philosophies, use his innovative ideas, and settle in to his Nashville home to build a winner. But it is often the case that what one wants one cannot fully receive due to circumstances beyond one's control.

Red's first season as a head coach would be the only losing season of his career. In 1940, the Commodores compiled a 3-6-1 record, with losses to LSU, Alabama, Tennessee, Princeton, Ole Miss, and Georgia Tech. Red could see instantly that he was no longer coaching prep football. Members of the Southeastern Conference were viable foes. Not only was he battling conference opponents, however, but poor luck. Following the second game of the year, a loss to Princeton, Red was hospitalized and immediately taken into surgery for an emergency appendectomy. The interim coach was a young Paul "Bear" Bryant. The man who would ultimately become known as one of the greatest college football coaches of all time coached one game for the Commodores, a 7–7 tie against the University of Kentucky. Red would be back the next week, but it wasn't until a year later, 1941, that his lessons paid off and the results were seen on the scoreboard.

In 1941, the Vanderbilt Commodores finished with an 8–2 record, a shocking turnaround to all who observed Southeastern Conference play. The things that coach Sanders implemented in 1941, which seemed "kooky" at the time, were now seen as brilliant one year later. Though coach Sanders come to be known as one of the great teachers of the "single wing" offense, he implemented different formations into his offense that had yet to be seen in high-level college football. His linemen would often line up with extra wide splits, and receivers would line up outside of the hashes. The quarterback was occasionally the only man in the backfield. These quirks of that day are now common, and though Red was a single wing coach until the day of his death, he was also an originator of the modern day spread offense. The spread punt formation was a staple of Red's special teams philosophy. Red also invented the squib kick as an alternative to kicking to dangerous return men or kicking out of bounds. His teams were known for a strong 4–4 defense that not only emphasized toughness at the line of scrimmage, but great team speed. In 1942, coach Sanders once again led Vanderbilt to a winning record, this time a 6–4 mark.

Though Sanders had a winning record in two of his first three seasons, all was not well in the world. After the United States entered World War II, Red put his football career on hold. Just before his thirty-eighth birthday, Red Sanders joined the United States Navy. For three years, Sanders served his country and rose to the rank of Lieutenant Commander in the Navy's preflight program at Pensacola, Florida. In 1946, he returned to Vanderbilt.

Following the war, coach Sanders had his work cut out for him. Without him barking the orders, the Vanderbilt football program had crumbled. In 1945, prior to his return, the team had a 3–6 record. In '46, Sanders hired an excellent assistant coaching staff that included the man he once coached in high school, Tommy Prothro. Over the next three years, Vanderbilt had a 19–10–1 record. The 1948 team is considered by many to have been the best Vanderbilt football team of all time to that point.

Though coach Sanders was happy at home, and his mission of building a national champion at his alma mater was not complete, he had earned respect and notoriety across the country, and the one suitor who was able to lure him away came from what seemed like a world away. At the end of the 1949 American Football Coaches Association convention, Wilbur Johns, the Athletic Director at the University of California at Los Angeles offered Red Sanders the head coaching position at UCLA. After speaking about the offer with his wife, Ann, whom he married while in the Navy, Coach Sanders decided the challenge was right for him, and he accepted the job at UCLA. Though Vanderbilt countered by offering him a lifetime contract, Red had given his word to Johns, and being a Southern gentleman, he could not turn back from his commitment. UCLA had won only three games the previous season, but when coach Sanders stepped foot in Westwood, the Golden Era for the Bruins began.

In nine seasons at UCLA, Red Sanders compiled a 66–19–1 record. His teams won the Pacific Coast Conference three times and were runners-up another four times. In 1954, UCLA finished the season ranked No. 1 in the country in the Coaches Poll, despite not playing in the Rose Bowl due to the newly implemented rule banning PCC teams from playing in the Rose Bowl in back-to-back years. If not for the rule, UCLA could very well have finished the season also ranked number one by the Associated Press. They would instead finish number two. He was named the 1954 National Coach of the Year by the National Collegiate Football Coaches Association and the Touchdown Club of Washington D.C. He was three times named National Coach of the Year at the *Los Angeles Times* National Sports Awards Dinner ('53, '54, '57). In 1996, he was inducted into the College Football Hall of Fame.

Red would ultimately fall victim to a tragic death while at the height of his coaching powers. In August 1958, Red and the Bruins were preparing for the start of a new season. The team had finished the previous season with an 8–2 record and were gearing up for another shot at the PCC crown and the national title. At 4:30 p.m. on August 14, 1958, shocking news hit radio and television sets everywhere. Red Sanders was dead. Complaining of the heat and humidity in his hotel room on Beverly Boulevard, Red had asked a friend of his, W.T. Grimes, to hand him a refreshment. When Grimes returned, he found a nonresponsive, shirtless Sanders lying on the floor motionless. When Grimes had walked out, Sanders grasped for air and clutched his chest, but there was nothing he could do as he succumbed to a massive heart attack. Though unknown at the time, it was later revealed that Red had an enlarged heart, nearly twice the size of what is considered normal. Scar tissue also indicated long-standing heart disease. His heart was a ticking time bomb, and when his time ran out, UCLA and the college football community lost one of the greatest coaches of all time at only 53 years of age.

When reminiscing about Coach Sanders, many people claimed to be acquaintances and many loved him, but few really knew him. He was cordial and polite to all, but inwardly shy. Though he displayed great public speaking ability, he was sensitive to the thoughts of others. He would let you in, but never close enough to understand his life. He was seen by some as an introvert, a man who couldn't share his life with others. But many more saw him as generous, a man who, despite insecurities, was a teacher until the very end. One sportswriter would say upon his death, "I have covered Red for nine years and I think I know him better than anyone else, but at the end of that time I don't think I knew him a lot better than the first time I met him."

Despite being one of the greatest coaches in college football history, Red Sanders is not often listed among his peers in the history of college football coaching. Had he not died in that hotel room, Red Sanders would likely forever be linked with the greats, such as Pop Warner, Bear Bryant, Woody Hayes, Joe Paterno, Bobby Bowden, Tom Osborne, Knute Rockne, Barry Switzer, Frank Leahy, Earl Blank, Fielding Yost, Urban Meyer, and Nick Saban.

*"Winning isn't everything. It's the only thing."—Red Sanders*

*"Beating 'SC is not a matter of life and death. It's much more important than that."—Red Sanders*

## 1949

Coming off a three-win season in 1948, and with a new coach at the helm in 1949, there were many question marks when the season finally kicked off. Could Red Sanders jump-start the program and take it to new heights like William Spaulding had two decades earlier? UCLA athletic director Wilbur Johns had made the decision to bring in a coach from across the country with experience coaching in an elite conference. He brought in a man who had success everywhere he went. Fans of the UCLA

Bruins were certainly optimistic about the future of the team. However, games are not won by splashy hires alone, but rather on the field, and Coach Sanders had his work cut out for him if he was to make the 1949 team a winner.

Before the season even kicked off, Sanders made one major change: the uniforms. Gone were the days of navy blue. The UCLA uniforms were now what Sanders called "powder keg blue." Not only did Sanders believe the uniforms looked better, but they also were easier to see on film and differentiated UCLA from Cal Berkeley. Five years later, Sanders would also be responsible for adding the famous "UCLA Stripe" and the Clarendon font to the uniform.

The first game of the Red Sanders era kicked off on September 16, 1949. When the Bruins took the field at the Coliseum against the Oregon State Beavers, they took with them everything they had learned from coach Sanders, as well as from new Assistant Coaches Tommy Harrison, Tommy Prothro, Mike Balitsaris, Jim Myers, and Tom Whitley. UCLA came out on fire. The single wing offense implemented by Coach Sanders was unstoppable. UCLA's offense amassed 327 yards on the ground, and the 4–4 defense forced six Beavers fumbles, five of which were recovered by the Bruins. Approximately 38,000 fans saw Ernie Johnson run and pass all over the field, including a dazzling 60-yard punt return for a touchdown. In the first test under the new coaching staff, the Bruins passed with flying colors. Final score: UCLA 35, Oregon State 13.

Howie Hanson running the ball against Cal, 1949 (Southern Campus Collection)

UCLA, a week later, looked like a different team. In Week 1, they had rushed the ball all over the field for 327 yards but against the Iowa Hawkeyes Bruins backs were able to only muster 88 yards on the ground. Iowa, the home team, was able to run all over the Bruins, rushing for 245 yards. Iowa also outgained the Bruins through the air with 202 yards to the Bruins' 187. Iowa had 24 first downs to the Bruins' nine. UCLA also had more penalties than the Hawkeyes. The key stat of the game, however, was turnovers. Iowa lost five fumbles and also threw three interceptions. UCLA only turned the ball over once, and, despite getting physically manhandled the entire game, UCLA won, 41–25.

After beating Oregon in Week 3, UCLA equaled the win total of the '48 campaign and were ranked No. 18. More than 5,000 Bruins fans traveled north to see their team take on the Stanford Indians, and what they saw was similar to the game against the Hawkeyes two weeks earlier. UCLA was outpassed and outrushed, but not outscored. Ernie Johnson reached the end zone twice for the Bruins, and that was all they needed. UCLA 14, Stanford 7. UCLA was 4–0, now ranked as No. 13, and once again dreaming of a Rose Bowl berth.

On October 15, UCLA's unblemished record was ended. UCLA was heavily favored against Santa Clara, but the Bruins' luck would finally run out. Despite outplaying the Broncos in the first half, the game was scoreless at intermission. In the second half, the script was flipped, and the Broncos simply dominated the Bruins. The Santa Clara ground game got on track in the third quarter and continued until the final whistle. UCLA could not stop Bronco Hal Haynes as he twice rumbled into the end zone, and when the game finally ended, he was near the goal line once again, ready to punch it in for the third time. UCLA lost, 14–0, and was 4–1 on the season.

After losing to Santa Clara, coach Sanders questioned how his team would respond. On October 22, the team took the fight to Pullman, Washington, to face the Washington State Cougars. Early in the game, it appeared the Bruins would not respond well at all to adversity. Before many fans could even settle into their seats, UCLA trailed, 14–0. UCLA would not lie down and surrender, however, and with ample time to make a comeback, they began to take over. Cliff Schroeder would play his best game of the season, and his second quarter touchdown evened the score at halftime, 14–14. In the third quarter, UCLA scored two touchdowns quickly, missing the extra point after one of them. Though the Cougars would score a late touchdown, it wasn't enough, and UCLA returned home from cold Pullman with a 27–20 win.

With a 5–1 record and three games to go, UCLA faced an immense challenge. The final two games of the season were against the University of Washington and the University of Southern California, but before them was the No. 5 University of California Golden Bears. There would be no upset on this day. Cal, led by quarterback Bob Celeri and Head Coach Lynn "Pappy" Waldorf, were simply the better team. UCLA kept the game close in the first half, but in the second half, they were unable to slow the Golden Bears. Sanders would say after the game, "We gave our best effort, but it wasn't enough." It was clear to him that the Bruins still had a ways to go, but he planned on getting them there.

In the ninth game, UCLA would display its finest offensive performance of the season. Sanders said, referring to his offensive line, "We hit harder than we have before." He was right. UCLA ran the ball for 340 yards and passed for another 166. The 506 total yards was a season high for the Bruins. Despite Ernie Johnson missing the game due to injury, the Bruins tallied 47 points. Senior Ray Nagle played the best game of his career, and Bob Wilkinson had a fine day receiving the ball. The defense wasn't as strong, allowing 26 points, but the Bruins won the game, and with one left to play they were 6–2.

Ernie Johnson leaps high to throw the ball against USC, 1949 (Southern Campus Collection)

Coach Red Sanders is famous to this day for saying, "Beating SC is not a matter of life or death. It is much more important than that." Though he would eventually dominate the rival Trojans, in his first year, that wasn't the case. USC beat the Bruins by a score of 21–7 and got to keep the Victory Bell. It wasn't long before coach Sanders decided he liked the bell better *blue.*

The Downtown Athletic Club named Leon Hart from the University of Notre Dame the 1949 Heisman Trophy Winner.

The Associated Press named the University of Notre Dame the 1949 National Champions.

## 1950

Ike Jones (22) and Werner Escher (26) lead the way as the Bruins enter, 1950 (Southern Campus Collection)

With the arrival of John Wooden in 1948 and Red Sanders in 1949, UCLA had two men who would become legends leading their two most important athletic programs for the foreseeable future. Another successful season was on the docket, but one game in 1950 gave rise to the legitimacy of the Bruins. The sleeping giant had awakened.

Despite a 6–3 record in '49 and a second place conference finish, the Bruins were predicted to finish near the bottom of the Pacific Coast Conference standings in '50. In coach Sanders's second season as the man in charge, UCLA was bit by the injury bug like no season in recent memory. Despite the bad luck, Coach Sanders reminded the team that luck is cyclical and bad luck only ruins the season of a team that lets luck control them. Instead, UCLA would prepare the same regardless of circumstance and would be ready to play every Saturday afternoon no matter who was in uniform and who was on the sidelines on crutches. On September 23, UCLA opened the season with a dominant victory over the University of Oregon, 28–0. UCLA gained 399 yards compared to the anemic Webfoot offense, which totaled only 105. Bob Wilkinson, expected to be a major contributor to the Bruins during the '50 campaign, scored his first touchdown of the season as the Bruins punched in one touchdown each quarter. UCLA's 4–4 defense completely shut down the opponents' offense.

The following week, UCLA proved that the performance in Week 1 was not a fluke, but something that fans should get used to. The Washington State Cougars traveled to Los Angeles feeling good about themselves after dismantling Utah State in Week 1 by a score of 46–6, but what they quickly learned was that the Bruins were not a pushover, but instead a team determined to turn the tables on the Cougars. Coach Sanders's single wing offense was unstoppable. Bob Moore, Ted Norleski, John Florence, and Joe Marvin led the ground game for the Bruins that accumulated over 400 yards rushing. Moore, equally capable through the air, threw for more than 150 yards. All told, the Bruins outgained the Cougars, 562–122. The final score was a UCLA win, 42–0.

While the United States was once again at war, this time in Korea, a different kind of battle took place on October 7, when the No. 13 Bruins traveled to Seattle to take on the No. 10 Washington Huskies. UCLA was 2–0 for the young season and had outscored opponents by a combined score of 70–0. UW was 2–0 and had outscored their opponents by a combined score of 61–20, including a win over the No. 18 Minnesota Golden Gophers. On this day, big plays haunted the Bruins. UCLA completed more passes for more yards. The running game struggled all day, and, despite the loss of All-American center and linebacker Donn Moomaw to injury, the Bruins were in the game the entire way. The Huskies fumbled six times, losing five of them, but also took advantage of gaps in the Bruin defense and broke off long gains throughout the game. In the end, the Bruins would lose by one point. Failing to make an extra point decided the outcome. The final score: 21–20, Washington over the Bruins. A week later, an injury-riddled and perhaps uninspired Bruins team lost again, this time 14–6 to Illinois.

After dropping two games in a row, it was the job of the master motivator, Red Sanders, to re-energize his team. The No. 6 Stanford Indians were coming to town and planned to deliver a third consecutive defeat to the Bruins. Despite his best efforts, Coach Sanders's Bruins were thoroughly outplayed on this day. It was a defensive battle, with the powerful Indians showing dominance over the weakened Bruins most of the way. UCLA only mustered 164 total yards, with—shockingly—only one first down! Stanford was not much better, however. They tallied only 286 yards. Coach Sanders played a field position game and relied on punting and an opportunistic offense to stay in the game. Stanford took more risks and were aggressive on fourth downs. Despite being the inferior team, smart, level-headed, strategic coaching prevailed. UCLA won, 21–7. When the Indians retreated back to the farm, their undefeated season was a thing of the past.

The next two games proved to be nothing more difficult than tasks on a checklist. On October 28, UCLA traveled to West Lafayette, Indiana, to take on the Purdue Boilermakers. Purdue came into the game with a 1–3 record, but their lone victory had come over the top-ranked Notre Dame Fighting Irish three weeks earlier. UCLA would easily defeat their nonconference foe, 20–6, on this day behind Ted Narleski's kickoff return for a touchdown, Joe Sabol's spectacular interception, and solid defensive performances by Cliff Livingston, Bruce MacLaughlan, and Francis Mandula. The next week, UCLA would return home and win again, this time defeating the Oregon State Beavers by a score of 20–13. With two games to go, UCLA was riding a three-game winning streak, but Cal and USC were the two remaining teams on the schedule, and the Bruins would have to perform their best to win the PCC title.

The most disappointing game of Coach Sanders's short tenure to that point was to be the eighth game of the season, against the California Golden Bears. The only thing Bruins fans could be proud of at the end of the day was the fine punting performance by Bob Moore. The UCLA defense was quite simply manhandled by the Bears. Though Cal was a strong performer, ranked No. 6 in the country, much was expected from the Bruins, and little was delivered. Cal outgained UCLA, 321–39, on the ground and the final score was 35–0 Bears. UCLA would have to regroup with one game left to play.

Howie Hanson, 1950 (Southern Campus Collection)

Despite the devastating loss to Cal Berkeley the week before, UCLA's 1950 season would be defined by what happened in the final game of the season. On November 25, UCLA took on the University of Southern California at the Los Angeles Coliseum. After the worst performance of the season defensively seven days earlier, this time the Bruins were inspired to play their best. USC rushed for only 30 yards and passed for only 49. The mere 79 yards the Bruins gave up shocked the crowd, which had expected to see two evenly matched teams. UCLA, on the other hand, rushed for 322 yards. Donn Moomaw was brilliant and opened up lanes for Bruins backs all day. UCLA scored on a fake punt early, in which Moore flipped a short pass to Howie Hansen, who, playing the best game of his career, weaved through defenders for the score. The redhead was ecstatic, and so were all the Bruins fans in attendance. UCLA continued to score and score and score, and the stunned Trojans could not respond. The final score was a UCLA shutout victory, 39–0. Coach Sanders, in his second game against USC, was victorious for the first time against the crosstown rival. In the massacre, UCLA handed USC Coach Jeff Craveth the worst loss of his career. The Bruins finished the season with a 6–3 overall record, 5–2 in conference play, 3rd place in the PCC. UCLA would not finish as low as 3rd place in the conference for another seven years.

The Downtown Athletic Club named Victor Felix Janowicz from Ohio State University the 1950 Heisman Trophy Winner.

The Associated Press named the University of Oklahoma the 1950 National Champions.

## 1951

Though the results were not completely clear from their win-loss record, the beginning of the UCLA Golden Era truly began in 1951. The team would play a tough schedule, including three teams ranked in the top 10 in the AP Poll and five ranked in the top 20. With the 1950 season ending on such a high note by trouncing USC 39–0, UCLA was now considered a dark horse contender for the Pacific Coast Conference crown. The season began on September 21 against the No. 6 Texas A&M Aggies. Raymond George was the coach at TAMU and in his first season was considered by many capable of taking the Aggies all the way to the National Championship and raising the trophy overhead. The Aggies were expected in '51 to have a strong ground game. UCLA was expected to have a strong defense. On this day, UCLA's defense bested the Aggies ground game, but it was the unexpected success that TAMU had through the air that made the difference. TAMU ran for only 124 yards but passed for 243. Teddy Narleski would score the first touchdown of the season for the Bruins, but UCLA lost its season opener, 21–14.

Don Stalwick, "The Masked Man," 1951 (Southern Campus Collection)

Things didn't get any easier in Week 2, when the Bruins traveled to Champaign, Illinois, to take on the No. 10 Fighting Illini. Though Paul Cameron was able to pound the ball for 164 yards on the ground for the Bruins, UCLA was unable to come away with the victory. Donn Moomaw and Hal Mitchell each saw limited action for the Bruins as the Fighting Illini won, 27–13. It was the third season in a row that UCLA lost to Illinois. The two teams would not meet again for six years, but coach Sanders never forgot the defeats handed to him at the hands of the Illini.

Despite the 0–2 start, the Bruins had one more nonconference opportunity to right the ship before heading into conference play. In Week 3, the Bruins did just that as they beat Santa Clara by a score of 44–7. Paul Cameron asserted himself and made it known that he was a star who would not fade. He was here to stay and leave his mark. Cameron threw for four touchdowns and ran for another two. The man known as the "Burbank Blazer" finished the day with 306 total yards. When conference play began the next week, the Burbank Blazer came ready to play, but success did not come so easy. UCLA traveled to Palo Alto to take on No. 19 Stanford. The UCLA defense did an admirable job in slowing down Stanford halfback Eric Southwood. Ike Jones, Cliff Livingston, and Cappy Smith each played well for the Bruins defense, but Gary Kerkorian and Robert Mathias of the Indians were too much. Final score: 21–7 Stanford.

UCLA was 1–3 on the season. With five games to go, Coach Sanders and company were in an uncomfortable position. The season was seen as a disappointment to that point, and the Bruins were left with two options. They could either play out the final handful of games and rev up the engines for '52, or they could make a push and finish '51 with a flurry. If they continued to lose, it would not be for lack of effort or preparation, but because of other circumstances. Red Sanders decided he did not plan on losing anytime soon. On October 20, UCLA took on the Oregon Webfeet. Whitney Arceneaux played a fine game for the Bruins on this day. UCLA pounded Oregon early, and sensing the victory well in their grasp, Coach Sanders chose to play Bruins backups much of the second half. The Bruins continued to move the ball, and after tacking on one final late score when the clock hit zero, UCLA had won, 41–0.

Don Foster, Chuck Fraychineaud, Don Stalwick, Ike Jones, Luther Keyes, and Julie Weisstein were all key parts of the Bruins team, and all played well against the No. 9 California Golden Bears, but Paul Cameron was once again UCLA's offensive star. Cameron accounted for 266 of the Bruins' 371 yards and was responsible for all three touchdowns the Bruins scored. Cal was never able to figure out the puzzle presented to them by the stifling Bruins defense, as UCLA won, 21–7. One week later, the Bruins extended their winning streak to three games with a 7–0 win over Oregon State. The game, played in Portland, Oregon, was not pretty, but the Bruins battled the Beavers in a rainstorm and came away victorious. Paul Cameron connected with Pete Doiley for an early score, and Werner Escher and the defense dominated. UCLA was now 3–1 in conference play. The Rose Bowl, which seemed like an impossible dream less than a month earlier, was back in play if the Bruins could finish the season strong.

On November 17, the Washington Huskies traveled to Los Angeles to take on the No. 18 UCLA Bruins. The game proved to be one of the most evenly contested games in many years for both teams. UCLA ran for 265 yards and passed for 87. Washington was a much more balanced team, running for 171 and passing for 174. UCLA edged out the Huskies in total yards gained by a mere seven yards. UCLA picked up 16 first downs, compared to the Huskies' 15. UCLA had just three penalties, but UW was called for only one. Each team fumbled once, with UCLA recovering theirs and UW losing theirs. Paul Cameron was his usual brilliant self, though this day mostly by rushing the ball. Don Stalwick, wearing a mask protecting his face after an injury, pounded his way up the middle all game. With seconds to go in the game, UCLA held the lead, 20–14, when Hugh McElhenny, the star player for the Huskies, skied into the air to make a miraculous catch near the goal line. After breaking several tackles, McElhenny drove his way into the end zone in the final seconds. UW would miss the extra point, and the game finished in a tie, 20–20. Coach Sanders was disappointed in the ending, knowing his team had an opportunity to win, only to blow it at the end, but he was relieved that UW's McElhenny was a senior and would not be back to torment him again.

The last game of the year, as was tradition, pitted the two rivals, the Bruins and the Trojans, against each other. Coach Red Sanders proved again that he was up to the challenge of taking on the Trojans. The UCLA defense, which had stunned all in attendance the previous year by holding USC to under 100 total yards and scoreless, was dominant once again. Dean Kirby repeatedly sacrificed his body by roughing it up with much bigger linemen and knifing past them into the backfield. He played a superb game against the Trojans. In big games, star players are often asked to perform at a higher level than even they are accustomed to. UCLA's star players answered the call with brilliance. The still-masked man, Don Stalwick, had his best game of the season and personally outgained the Trojans' yardage by his own performance. Stalwick scored the first touchdown of the game on a pass from Paul Cameron, who continued the fine play that Bruins fans had come to expect. Ike Jones added a touchdown, and the ever-reliable Donn Moomaw intercepted a pass and returned it the distance for another TD. Gayle Pace knocked in the extra point after each score, and the Bruins left the Coliseum with a 21–7 victory. It was the second year in a row UCLA had defeated the Trojans, and with Stalwick, Cameron, Jones, and Moomaw all coming back in '52, they all planned on doing it again.

The Downtown Athletic Club named Dick Kazmaier from Princeton University the 1951 Heisman Trophy Winner.

The Associated Press named the University of Tennessee the 1951 National Champions.

Whitney Arceneaux runs the ball against Oregon, 1951 (Southern Campus Collection)

## 1952

By 1952, the Korean War occupied the minds of most Americans. In November, Dwight Eisenhower was elected as the 34th President of the United States in a rout over Adlai Stevenson. Back in Los Angeles, coach Red Sanders was entering his fourth season. He had three successful winning seasons behind him, and in his fourth he dreamed of roses. Despite an overall inexperienced roster, his star players from the '51 squad returned. When the season kicked off, few could have predicted how it would end.

The No. 18-ranked Bruins' opponent in the season opener was the Oregon Webfeet. UCLA was without star halfback Paul Cameron due to injury, but with Ted Narleski replacing him, Coach Sanders was confident the offense wouldn't miss a beat. More troubling than the injury was the weather. It was 112 degrees at kickoff, and UCLA struggled early to find energy. After a scoreless first quarter, Oregon reached the end zone first on a 39-yard touchdown pass. Having fallen behind, the UCLA offense was able to remove the brutal conditions from the back of their minds and focus solely on execution. UCLA scored two touchdowns to retake the lead. Oregon, with one last chance to score late in the game, had the ball deep in Bruins territory. With minutes to go, Donn Moomaw intercepted an Oregon pass at the 10-yard line and clinched the victory for the Bruins. It was not a spectacular win, but a win nonetheless, and the Bruins could not wait to celebrate by jumping in a pool or heading to the beach to cool down.

After the Bruins' narrow escape in Week 1, the team found its groove and played all-around excellent football for the next three weeks. In the second game of the season, the Texas Christian University Horned Frogs traveled from Fort Worth to Los Angeles to have their No. 9 ranked squad, coached by Dutch Meyer, take on the Bruins. With Paul Cameron out for the second week in a row, Narleski, Ernie Stockert, and the rest of the Bruins offense did just enough to win again. The story, however, was not about the offense, but the defense. After the game, Red Sanders declared, "It's the best all-around defensive team I've had in four years of coaching at UCLA." This was high praise considering the fact that Sanders's UCLA teams had sported excellent defenses in each of his first three seasons. UCLA held TCU to 199 total yards, with just 38 of them coming on the ground. It was on to Seattle for the first Bruins away game of the year. The Huskies were no match. Coming into the game, many feared that UCLA could not stop the masterful quarterback for Washington, Don Heinrich. "The man with the arm" was considered by many to be the top quarterback in the country, a possible Heisman Trophy candidate. UCLA would not only prove they could stop him, they would expose him. Heinrich threw 42 passes for 204 yards, but five were intercepted. UCLA took advantage as Cappy Smith rushed for three touchdowns and Jack Ellena scored twice. When the game was over, the scoreboard read UCLA 32,Washington 7. When UCLA returned to the Coliseum one week later, they took on their second team from the state of Texas that season. The Rice Owls had come west with dreams of cracking the Bruin code and handing

UCLA its first loss of the season. For the second game in a row, the UCLA defense shined. Rice completed just two of 14 passes, and once again the UCLA defense intercepted five! Despite Paul Cameron missing his fourth game in a row, UCLA's offense scored 20 points and would win comfortably, as the Owls failed to light up the scoreboard even once.

After starting 4–0, UCLA was now a team to recognize on a national level. The next three games would be a major test for the Bruins, as all three opponents were ranked among the top 13 in the nation. But simply stating that the teams they faced were of high quality did not qualify UCLA as underdogs. The single wing offense was coming around, and the 4–4 defense was dominant. UCLA was the No. 10 team in America. On October 18, UCLA took on the Stanford Indians in the annual Homecoming game. The Bruins dominated the contest, despite the scoreboard indicating it as much more competitive. Paul Cameron was back in the lineup for the first time in the season and threw three touchdown passes. The defense, which had now become known for its unbelievable ability to force turnovers, did so once again, this time to the tune of nine turnovers. Stanford fumbled five times and threw four interceptions. The Indians only had one sustained drive for a score and also scored late on a deflected pass that caromed right into the receiver's hands while in stride. UCLA won the game by the score of 24–10, beating the defending PCC champions.

UCLA was 5–0, with a 3–0 record in the PCC, when they headed to Madison, Wisconsin, for the final nonconference game of the year against the University of Wisconsin Badgers. UCLA had moved up to No. 8 in the latest AP poll; their opponent was ranked No. 10. For the sixth consecutive game, the Bruins defense dominated. Terry Debay and Chuck Toud anchored the Bruins front eight, giving up only 193 yards on the day. The offense, however, struggled and gained only 187. The difference on the scoreboard came from nonoffensive touchdowns. UCLA scored on an interception return for a touchdown by Bill Stits and another on a 40-yard punt return touchdown by Joe Sabol, in which he snaked through the coverage team and into the end zone. UCLA knocked off the Big 10 champions and Rose Bowl participants by a score of 20–7.

The last of the three ranked teams that UCLA would play consecutively was the No. 11 California Golden Bears. On November 1, UCLA traveled to Berkeley and was able to do what they had done all year. UCLA dominated the Bears, 28–7, behind the usual strong defense and Paul Cameron, who was now hitting his stride and returning to his 1951 form after missing time because of injuries. Roughly 81,000 fans saw this Bruins victory, including 10,000 UCLA fans who had made the trip from Los Angeles. California coach Pappy Waldorf said of the Bruins after the game, "UCLA is the best-balanced football team that I have seen since coming to Cal, and that includes the bowl teams that we've met." UCLA was relieved to have made it through the tough stretch of the schedule unscathed, and following the win over the Golden Bears, they took on the unranked Oregon State Beavers, dismantling them, 57–0. That 57-point margin of victory was the largest win ever for the Bruins over a PCC team.

When the UCLA Bruins took on the USC Trojans on November 22, 1952, it was the biggest game in the history of the rivalry and the biggest game in the history of UCLA football to that point. UCLA had climbed to No. 3 in the latest AP rankings. USC was ranked No. 4. Both teams were 8–0, and though the Trojans had one game remaining in the regular season (they would lose to No. 7 Notre Dame), the winner of this rivalry battle would head to the Rose Bowl on January 1 to face Wisconsin, a team UCLA had already handily defeated. Ranked ahead of the Bruins were the Michigan State Spartans and the Georgia Tech Yellow Jackets. With the Spartans scheduled to play the lowly Marquette Golden Eagles and the Yellow Jackets scheduled to play Florida State, Georgia, and Sugar Bowl participant Ole Miss, the opportunity for either UCLA or USC to jump to the top of the polls was there. The winner would not only have to beat its crosstown rival, but would have to do so in impressive fashion. It was a tough task, but it was certainly possible.

The UCLA defense had allowed opponents to score 14 points just once and gave up on average of only a touch over five points per game on the season. USC, on the other hand, averaged nearly 25 points per game on offense. Something would have to give. UCLA got off to a fine start. In the first quarter, Paul Cameron and the Bruins offense marched down the field into Trojan territory but stalled near the end zone. UCLA was forced to settle for a field goal attempt, which Pete Dailey knocked through the uprights from 15 yards out. USC responded, however, on the following drive and, one play at a time, pushed the Bruins defense back until they were finally able to cross the goal line on a lateral from Al Carmichael to Jim Sears, who beat all defenders to the end zone. USC took the lead, 7–3. In the second quarter, the Bruins defense once again stepped up to the challenge and, after pushing USC back to their own goal line, broke free and forced a safety. UCLA kept the momentum going as Bill Stits scored the lone UCLA touchdown of the day to make the score 12–7. It was up to the defense to win the game. UCLA's offense had done just enough all season, and the dominant defense had suffocated opposing offenses. In the second half, USC scored one more time, and UCLA was never able to counter. The final score was 14–12, USC. The perfect season was over for the Bruins, and USC was on to the Rose Bowl. The loss would haunt coach Sanders, who firmly believed the '52 team was of championship caliber. On that fateful day, UCLA outgained USC, 199–168, they had ten first downs compared to USC's six, they had fewer penalties, and fewer turnovers. The difference came in UCLA's failure to execute inside USC territory. USC would go on to beat Wisconsin in the Rose Bowl, 7–0. Michigan State and Georgia Tech would each win out. UCLA would finish the season No. 6 in the final AP Poll and receive one first-place vote.

The Downtown Athletic Club named Billy Vessels from the University of Oklahoma the 1952 Heisman Trophy Winner.

The Associated Press named Michigan State University the 1952 National Champions.

## Donn Moomaw

Donn Moomaw has lived a fascinating life. Born September 3, 1931, in Santa Ana, California, Donn Moomaw has been an All-American football player. He has played football at the professional level. He has tried his hand at acting. He has been a Presbyterian Minister for over half a century. First, however, came his childhood. Like many kids of the day, Moomaw grew up around sports. That, however, was not his only love. Moomaw lived in a strict home. He was taught and practiced religion daily. From a young age, Moomaw set his dreams not singularly on athletic glory, but on the pulpit. After graduating from Santa Ana High School in 1949, Moomaw enrolled at UCLA, temporarily delaying his ministry plans in favor of football and further traditional education.

Donn Moomaw, 1952 (Southern Campus Collection)

When Moomaw arrived at UCLA, the team was in a state of flux. Well-liked head coach Bert Labrucherie was gone. New head coach Red Sanders had taken control, and though Moomaw would not be on Sanders's first Varsity team (he was forced to play a year on the freshman team), he knew UCLA had a bright future under coach Sanders. Donn Moomaw would have immense respect for his coach, and the feelings were mutual. Moomaw was a hard worker and a brilliant player. After a year on the freshman team, Moomaw was ready for the Varsity in 1950, and the team welcomed him with open arms. He was dominant from the very first time he set foot on the field. Donn was an All-American linebacker in 1950 and the team finished with a 6–3 record. In 1951, the team was 5–3–1 and Moomaw was snubbed for All-America honors. In '52, he would prove to be one of the nation's best players once again. After UCLA finished 8–1, losing only the last game of the season, to USC, and finishing No. 6 in the final Associated Press poll, Moomaw was named a consensus All-American. His punishing style was praised, and he was coveted by all, including professional teams. He was said to be "a ball hawk noted for his ability to diagnose play development." He was equally great in both pass coverage and run coverage. At the time of his graduation, his 11 interceptions tied an all-time UCLA record. He was big, 6'4" and 220 pounds, and ferocious when taking down a ball carrier. Moomaw was described as "strong, rangy, and agile to perfection. Like a submarine commander, Moomaw stalked enemy ball-carriers and downed them with torpedo-like tackling thrusts." Though the Los Angeles Rams drafted the National Lineman of the Year, as he was designated by the Associated Press and United Press International, Moomaw decided to play in Canada. His MVP performance at the North-South College All-Star Game put him on the map.

Donn Moomaw would only play three years of professional football. After one year with the Toronto Argonauts, he spent two years with the Ottawa Rough Riders before calling his football career quits and starting the life he had envisioned for himself decades earlier as a kid. Following his playing career, Moomaw attended Princeton Theological Seminary, where he received a Masters of Divinity Degree. In 1957, Moomaw was ordained a Presbyterian USA Pastor at First Presbyterian Church of Hollywood, where he served for seven years. For the next thirty years, Moomaw served as the senior pastor of the Bel Air Presbyterian Church of Los Angeles, where he met a young man finding his calling and climbing the political ladder, Ronald Reagan. When Reagan was inaugurated as the president of the United States in 1981, Moomaw was by his side and led a public prayer. Four years later, he did so again. Moomaw's career was not without controversy, however. In 1993, he was forced to resign after it was revealed that Moomaw had extramarital relations with women in his church. Following the scandal, many Presbyterian leaders praised the way Moomaw responded. He was forthright and contrite. He would say of the controversy, "Mistakes don't make or break us. If we are lucky, they simply reveal who we really are, what we're made of. Challenges will come, but if you treat them simply as tests of who you are, you'll come out of it not bitter and victimized, but smarter and stronger." Moomaw turned down opportunities to be a "celebrity pastor" at nondenominational churches, and in 1997 he was allowed to return to the pulpit. Donn Moomaw was a man of God and a Bruin. He was one of the first great players in UCLA history. He was a key part of the turnaround of the program under Red Sanders. Moomaw's number 80 is retired by UCLA, and he was inducted into both the UCLA Athletics Hall of Fame and the National Football Foundation Hall of Fame in 1973. The legacy of Donn Moomaw carries on each year at UCLA to this day. Following the annual game against rival USC, the "Donn D. Moomaw Award for Outstanding Defensive Player in USC Game" is given out. Moomaw may be a name that many Bruins fans have forgotten, but his legacy lives on. He was one of the greatest players in UCLA history, and his contribution to advancing the game under Red Sanders led UCLA to the greatest era in school history. He did not play on the 1954 UCLA National Championship team, but Donn Moomaw is as important a player as anyone who ever wore the Bruins blue and gold.

## 1953

In 1953, the war in Korea thankfully came to a close. On July 27, North and South Korea, though still divided, signed an agreement to stop fighting. In Westwood, Red Sanders never stopped wondering what had gone wrong against USC the prior season. UCLA was the better team but couldn't win the biggest game. The great thing about sports is that when one opportunity is blown, a chance to redeem it is only an offseason away. For Coach Sanders, though, it was a long offseason. When it came time for the 1953 campaign, Coach Sanders, along with players and staff, could hardly wait. The first victim was the Oregon State Beavers.

UCLA had defeated OSU in 1952 by a score of 57–0. An angry Bruins team in '53 did not bode well for the Beavers. UCLA started the season ranked as the No. 4 team in America. Primo Villanueva helped the Bruins once again thrash the visitors from up north by amassing 8.5 yards per carry. Paul Cameron gained over 5 yards per carry himself and also threw for three touchdowns. Sam Brown added speed to the Bruins offense and also threw a touchdown against the Beavers. UCLA's defense was again strong and held OSU scoreless. UCLA passed its first test of the season with an "A+" grade win. Final score: 41–0.

For the next three weeks, the Bruins of '53 looked eerily like the Bruins of '52. The offense was solid, yet not spectacular, and the Bruins defense was swarming and relentless. UCLA defeated the Kansas Jayhawks in Week 2, having no difficulty stopping the

Split T offense and the massive Jayhawks offensive linemen. In Week 3, UCLA struggled a bit with Oregon. Perhaps it was a tired team traveling to its first away game, or perhaps it was a worrisome sign for coach Sanders, but UCLA would not score until the fourth quarter against the Webfeet. UCLA's defense continued to shut down opponents, but the game was not settled until UCLA scored two touchdowns in the final stanza. Despite a 3–0 record, UCLA dropped from No. 4 to No. 6 in the AP poll. On October 9, the defending Big 10 champion Wisconsin Badgers made a return trip to Los Angeles after losing at home to the Bruins the previous year. The two Dons, Foster and Stalwick, gave the Badgers fits all day, and UCLA won the rematch, 13–0. UCLA was 4–0 on the season. The defense was allowing fewer than two points per game. The Bruins were motivated and hungry for a PCC crown.

The fifth game of the year turned out to be an unexpected battle. When the Bruins arrived in Palo Alto, they expected another successful trip, another win on the résumé. But the Stanford Indians had other plans. UCLA's offense came to play on this day. They scored 20 points, a number usually high enough to come away with a resounding victory. Stanford's offense was the best UCLA had seen so far, however, and they would not only refuse to be shut out—like the Beavers, Webfeet, and Badgers had been—but they would instead push the Bruins around the field. Bob Garrett was a fine runner, passer, and punter. He was assisted by Samuel Morley and John Steinberg Jr., who consistently got open against the Bruins and made sure catches. UCLA led in the second half, but when Garrett, who scored all three touchdowns for the Indians, crossed the goal line for the third time, the Bruins were finished. The offense couldn't respond. UCLA would not leave Palo Alto with a victory, but rather a stunning defeat. Stanford won, 21–20.

After losing to Stanford, UCLA dropped to No. 12 in the polls. It was likely that the Bruins' chances of being voted the National Champion had taken a fatal blow, but coach Sanders would not let his team think that way. He had them focus on winning the PCC, one win at a time, and if the Bruins sneaked back into the national picture, they would think about it then. The Bruins would get back on track by dismantling three straight unranked opponents. On October 12, UCLA beat WSU, 44–7. One week later, they beat Cal Berkeley, 20–7. After a bye week, UCLA returned and beat the University of Washington, 20–6. Paul Cameron was an unstoppable force. Against the Cougars, he averaged more than 15 yards per play, pass or run. Seventy thousand fans packed the stadium for the Cal game, knowing that, despite the loss to Stanford earlier in the year, UCLA was one of the best teams in the nation. When UCLA took on the Huskies, it was less football and more comedic entertainment as the two teams slopped around in the mud during a major rainstorm. The game may have been amusing to some observers, but not to the failing Huskies. Importantly, the Stanford Indians lost on November 7 to USC, thus opening the door for the Bruins to still win the conference.

On November 21, the Bruins, who had climbed all the way up to No. 5 in the nation, had their chance for revenge against the Trojans. Due to a Halloween meltdown against Oregon, the No. 9 Trojans were tied with the Bruins and Indians in the conference standings. In order for UCLA to win the PCC, they would have to defeat the Trojans and hope for Stanford to falter against Cal. Regardless of standings, this is the game the Bruins had waited 12 months to play. Unlike the previous year's close 14–12 USC win over UCLA, there was little drama in the '53 matchup. The better team won, and did so handily. That team was the Bruins of Westwood. After defeating the Trojans, UCLA was left to sit, wait, and wonder what was happening up north. When news spread that Stanford had indeed slipped up, tying Cal, 21–21, Bruins coaches, players, and fans were overjoyed: UCLA was headed to the Rose Bowl. Bring on the Michigan State Spartans!

What came with the Rose Bowl was pageantry. This was a game of utmost importance, with teams clinging to the chance of being named National Champions—it was a college football tradition revered by fans far and wide. On January 1, 1954, America saw the Rose Bowl game televised in color for the first time. When the game began, it was a heavyweight battle. UCLA was 8–1 and ranked No. 5 in the country. MSU was 8–1 and ranked No. 3. The defending National Champion Spartans were angry over their loss to Purdue earlier in the season, which had snapped their 28-game winning streak. With the Rose Bowl game broadcast throughout the entire country, teams were determined to prove they were the best in the nation, regardless of what the final rankings said. With MSU wearing their home uniforms and UCLA in their white road uniforms, the game kicked off. Despite being the notable underdog, the Bruins came out and took what seemed to be an early commanding lead. After recovering a Spartans fumble, Bill Stilts hauled in a pass from Paul Cameron and took it to the end zone. UCLA was up, 7–0. Another fumble in the second quarter led to the second Bruins score. This time, Paul Cameron took it in himself from a few yards out, and the Bruins were suddenly ahead, 14–0. The Spartans were stunned, but not out. With just minutes to go in the half, MSU came up with the big play that ultimately changed the momentum and direction of the game. Ellis Dockett recovered the ball after blocking a UCLA punt and rushed to the end zone. At halftime, UCLA was happy to be ahead, 14–7, but disappointed in the way the first half had ended. In the third quarter, MSU physically imposed its will on the Bruins. The Spartans marched down the field and scored from one yard out. After stopping the Bruins, they marched down and scored again. UCLA's defense, usually dominant against the run, was being pushed around. MSU led, 21–14, but UCLA was not done. Paul Cameron had one last moment of brilliance in him. After recovering another fumble, the UCLA offense struck quickly, with Cameron finding Rommie Loudd for a 28-yard score. All in attendance were wondering the same thing. Would the game end in a tie? What many failed to think about, and what became a crucial play, was the extra point. It was missed, and UCLA was still down by a point, 21–20. The offense had two more chances but could not again reach the end zone. With just under five minutes to play, after a disappointing offensive series, UCLA punted, and it was returned by Billy Wells of MSU for a touchdown. UCLA lost the Rose Bowl game, 28–20. Though UCLA had gone one step further in '53 than in the previous year, the season again ended in a defeat. With the no-repeat rule, UCLA would be ineligible to compete in the '55 Rose Bowl. UCLA would have to wait at least two years to return.

The Downtown Athletic Club named Johnny Lattner from the University of Notre Dame the 1953 Heisman Trophy Winner.

The Associated Press named the University of Maryland the 1953 National Champions.

## Paul Cameron

The life story of Paul Cameron differs from that of most athletic superstars. Cameron was born on August 17, 1932, and from the time he set first foot on an athletic field, he could do it all. Though Cameron reached the National Football League for a brief time, little has been written about his life. The memory of his sports accomplishments has faded with time. Those fortunate to have seen the Bruins of the 1950s play, however, are not likely to forget the accomplishments of a young Paul Cameron. He was a superstar. Thirty-five years after the Southern Branch was founded, they were National Champions. Though unquestionably deserving of all accolades, head coach Red Sanders could not have accomplished what he did in Westwood without talented players, and perhaps no man was more skilled than Paul Cameron.

After a standout athletic career at Burbank High School, Cameron was off to Westwood to play for Coach Sanders. While the Bruins varsity was rapidly improving under Sanders's tutelage, Cameron thrived on the freshman team. When the fall of '51 came around, the war in Korea was not the only conflict on Cameron's mind. It was time for him to play with the big boys. He was a varsity football player, and with expectations reaching new heights for the Bruins, much was expected of the all-around sophomore performer. Cameron was a solid defensive back—ultimately, that was the position he would play in the NFL—but he was also a standout with the ball in his hands on offense. He was a halfback, and in those days the backs would typically throw more passes than the quarterback. He was effective through the air, but his main

Paul Cameron, 1951 (Southern Campus Collection)

weapon was his legs. In 1951, Cameron was not yet a star. The team failed to improve on the 1950 season, instead slipping to 5–3–1. They finished second in the conference behind the Stanford Indians, ranked No. 17 team in the nation. More important, however, to many fans was that the Bruins beat the University of Southern California Trojans, 21–7. After having defeated USC, 39–0, in 1950, the win in '51 marked the first time UCLA had beaten USC two years in a row. Though USC dominated the first half of the twentieth century, Coach Sanders and company were proving that the early part of the second half of the century would belong to the squad from Westwood.

By 1952, UCLA proved to be an emerging college football powerhouse. The Bruins' scoring offense was No. 21 in the nation, averaging 24 points per game. On defense, the Bruins had the No. 4 unit in the land, giving up only 6.1 points per game. Cameron was a key member on both sides of the ball, and though his production on offense would bring him glory, it was his performance on defense that helped the Bruins win games. Cameron finished the 1952 season sixth in the Heisman Trophy voting, but it was the team's season record that many would remember, whether good or bad. Coming off a solid '51 campaign, UCLA was ranked No. 18 to start the season. After reeling off wins against the Oregon Webfeet, top-10 TCU, the University of Washington, and Rice University, the Bruins found themselves in a place they had rarely been before: in the top 10. With the meat of the schedule still ahead, there was no time to look back at what had already been accomplished. The team had to look forward, and they did just that. UCLA won the next four games, including wins over three ranked teams. With one game to play, UCLA was the No. 3 team in the nation. A win over No. 4 USC would put the Bruins in the Rose Bowl and into the National Championship conversation. UCLA, however, was not ready to emerge as a national contender. That would have to wait, but it would come. Coach Sanders would remember the loss to the Trojans for the rest of his life. He was determined to never let it happen again. In '53, Cameron was a major reason why it wouldn't.

The Bruins of 1953 were brilliant. Though they would lose to Stanford by one point to spoil an undefeated regular season, they would nonetheless win the Pacific Coast Conference and head to the Rose Bowl. Paul Cameron's performance on both sides of the ball once again earned him All-America acclaim and Heisman consideration. When the voting was concluded, Cameron had placed third in the 1953 voting. Cameron, together with Bob Davenport, Donn Moomaw, and Coach Sanders, had helped take UCLA to a position never before reached in school history. They were on the verge of a National Championship. Though the team would win the coveted national title in 1954, it would be without Cameron. He was off to the NFL. After being drafted by the Pittsburgh Steelers in the 1954 NFL draft, Cameron agreed to a contract via long-distance telephone call. As simple and quiet as contract negotiations were for Cameron when joining the Steelers, so his life has been since. He played only one season in the NFL before moving on in his postplaying career. Much as he had done for the Bruins of 1954, Paul Cameron excelled. He led the Steelers with seven interceptions. He was fourth in the NFL with 118 interception return yards. He forced one fumble and recovered three. And then, just like that, he was gone. Paul Cameron retired from football at 22 years old, but his contribution to the game lives on. In 1984, he was named to the inaugural UCLA Athletics Hall of Fame class, and his number 34 has been retired by UCLA football. In 2008, he was named to the inaugural Burbank High School Athletics Hall of Fame class. Though much of Paul Cameron's life may be relatively unknown, the influence he had on UCLA football should never be dismissed.

## 1954

In 1954, the United States was at peace. With the Korean War over, Americans at home could finally fully focus on what they aspired to in life. No longer did they have to fear receiving the fateful knock on the door or the letter in the mail. Americans could focus on family, on education, on work. They could focus on their favorite baseball teams, their favorite heavyweight boxers, and their favorite football teams. UCLA was entering its thirty-sixth season. The program had achieved the kind of success under Red Sanders that it had only dreamed of before his arrival. Yet the 1952 season ended in crushing defeat at the hands of the Trojans. The 1953 season ended in defeat at the hands of the Spartans. Coach Sanders loved the success of both teams; he felt the '52 team especially was National Champion caliber. In '54, the goal was not to get to the big stage once again and fail, but to complete the journey this time. Though the nation was at peace, Red would not find peace of mind unless the Bruins got over the hump. Early season wins meant little. They were a stepping stone. Difficult trips to Kansas and Washington were part of the challenge. Nothing mattered except winning. The quote that Coach Sanders is now famous for (though some misattribute it to Vince Lombard) fit perfectly for the Bruins: "Winning isn't everything. It's the *only* thing." In 1954, it was the only thing deemed acceptable. The Bruins were up to the task.

The success of the 1954 season was not only dependent on the efforts of Coach Sanders and the players, but on the assistant coaches, as well. Prowling the sidelines, doing much of the dirty work, and getting little attention compared to Coach Sanders was a fine staff. Tommy Prothro and Bill Barnes certainly had fine futures ahead of them in the coaching business. George Dickerson, Johnny Johnson, Jim Meyers, and "Deke" Brackett also did their best to teach the players the intricacies of the game. When the season kicked off, all the work by the head coach, players, and assistants was put to the test, and UCLA was not only ready to prove they were well prepared, they were ready to dominate. Led by three men who would be named All-Americans—Jim Salsbury, Jack Ellena, and Bob Davenport—the Bruins were simply too talented to be stopped on opening day. The game pitted the Bruins against the San Diego Navy on September 18. UCLA's staunch defense of the previous years was just as strong in '54, and the Bruins offense was not only consistently good, but explosive, a team that could score quickly. Navy's subpar defense had no chance against the Bruins. John Peterson, Sam Brown, Garry Okuneff, Steve Palmer, and Bob Davenport all played particularly well, and the Bruins won by an overwhelming margin, 67–0.

1954 UCLA cocaptains John Peterson (left) and Jack Ellena (right) (Southern Campus Collection)

Scoring points was rarely a problem for the Bruins in '54. Only once did they score fewer than three touchdowns. UCLA finished the season with the number one offense in the nation, scoring almost 41 points per game. The defense, always a strong suit under Coach Sanders, also finished number one in the nation, giving up only 4.4 points per game. The Bruins team of '54 was truly dominant, but season statistics alone do not tell the entire story. Games like the blowout over the San Diego Navy can skew statistics, and just because a team averages a high number of points does not guarantee they will win every game. After beating the Kansas Jayhawks in Week 2 by a score of 32–7, the Bruins had their two toughest challenges of the season ahead of them.

On October 4, the long-awaited nonconference matchup between the No. 4 UCLA Bruins and the No. 6 Maryland Terrapins had arrived. The "Terps" had traveled over 2,600 miles from College Park, Maryland, to take on the Bruins at the Coliseum, and they didn't plan on traveling all that way to lose. In 1953, Maryland, led by head coach Jim Tatum, won the AP National Championship. UCLA was seeking the same glory the Terps had already achieved. In a rare night game, more than seventy-three thousand fans showed up at the Coliseum, most of them to cheer on the Bruins. In such an important game, nerves can often play a factor, and though UCLA was the team hoping to knock off the defending champions, Maryland was the team that made the first major miscue. After the Bruins defense held Maryland and forced a 4th-and-long situation, the Maryland punter mishandled the snap, and UCLA fell on the ball on the Terps' 11-yard line. UCLA quickly capitalized, as Bob Davenport crossed the goal line. The extra point was missed, and UCLA led, 6–0. The game would be a battle decided mostly by strong defense and excellent punting, until the fourth quarter. Early in the fourth, the Terps punched the ball into the end zone, capping a 63-yard drive with a touchdown. The extra point was good, and Maryland led, 7–6. The defending champions had their first lead of the game, something they were accustomed to having. Riding a regular-season winning streak dating back three years, the Terps were confident their strong defense would hold and send the large Bruins crowd home disappointed. UCLA's offense had been stagnant all night, looking nothing like the team that had destroyed the San Diego Navy two weeks earlier. UCLA would catch a break, however. After another strong series by its defense, UCLA forced Maryland to punt deep in its own territory. The ball was snapped, and UCLA got a strong rush from its defensive line. The Maryland punter was rushed and shanked the ball out of bounds. UCLA took over at the 15-yard line. Down one point, it was now or never for the Bruins. The 5'10", 172-pound Primo Villanueva ran a power sweep to the right, found a seam, and took the ball all the way to the 1-yard line before being tackled. On the next play, Davenport plowed into the end zone, and the Bruins took the lead! UCLA's defense would hold, and the Bruins went on to win, 12–7. UCLA gained only 231 yards on the day, with a mere six of those coming through the air. Maryland fared no better, however, as the Bruins held them to just 206 total yards. The Bruins had proved they could score points early in the year, and the defense proved to be just as strong in '54 as in the previous two years. UCLA's offense would get even better the rest of the way. The defense never faltered.

After beating the Maryland Terrapins in a hard-fought clash between two college football heavyweights, UCLA had the difficult task of traveling to Seattle to take on the Washington Huskies. UW was a poor team in '54 but had a penchant for playing tough football against the Bruins. The October 9 meeting was no exception. UCLA, sensing that Washington was no pushover, came out of the tunnel and instantly went to work. Davenport and Villanueva led a balanced attack for the Bruins offense, and after three quarters, UCLA, led 21–0. The Huskies, though inferior in talent and coaching, were strong of will and mounted an amazing comeback. With three fourth-quarter touchdowns of their own, they were back in the game. If not for a missed extra point, the Huskies may have spoiled the Bruins' perfect season. UCLA held on to defeat UW and move to 4–0.

After barely escaping the game against Washington, UCLA dropped from No. 2 in the AP Poll to No. 3. Coach Sanders, staff, and players used this as motivation. They could simply make no mistakes in their pursuit of the PCC crown and national title. The only doubt that the Bruins left in the game against the Stanford Indians was whether or not spectators actually saw the Bruins win, 72–0, or if they had been dreaming. The crowd of 70,555 fans saw a beatdown of epic proportions. At halftime, UCLA led Stanford by a score of 27–0. In the second half, they didn't slow down, but sped up. Fifty seconds into the second half, UCLA scored again and led, 34–0. After the fifth UCLA touchdown of the day, Coach Sanders pulled his starters and began playing backups. Though lesser in talent, experience, and readiness, the Bruin backups were eager to show the large crowd what they were capable of. Touchdown

Bob Long leads the way for Jim Decker, 1954 (Southern Campus Collection)

after touchdown after touchdown, the Bruins were unstoppable. The UCLA defense intercepted eight Stanford passes and recovered two fumbles. It was a shocking display of superiority. Stanford was a 3–1 team at the time, with a win over a ranked Oregon team, but UCLA proved that, on this day, they were the greatest team in America.

After the win over the Stanford Indians, UCLA kept the momentum going, and no team could stop them. Only 8,500 fans showed up in Corvallis to see the hometown Beavers lose, 61–0, to the Bruins. UCLA then easily defeated Cal, 27–6, in front of a large crowd in Berkeley. UCLA allowed the Bears to gain only 28 yards on the ground. The Bruins had become a team on a track with destiny. The only question was, where would the pollsters rank them? On November 1, the Associated Press named UCLA the No. 1 team in America. The Ohio State Buckeyes were number two.

Newly minted the top team in the country proved to be no distraction for the Bruins. In the eighth game of the year, UCLA took on the Oregon Webfeet. Oregon coach Len Casanova would say after the game, "We played our worst game offensively and defensively." Surely, the strong and fast 4–4 Bruins defense and the unstoppable UCLA single wing offense had something to do with that. Coach Casanova would make the trip back to Oregon knowing that the Bruins were a team on a mission. UCLA had one game to play. It was the big one. Coach Sanders didn't need to motivate his team during the week but instead had to try to keep them calm. Though USC posed a challenge and was the last hurdle before the finish line, the Bruins would have to play a complete game to come out victorious. They could not think of pollsters, but rather only of their mission: to destroy Troy.

Though the participant of the Rose Bowl game had already been decided, the battle for Los Angeles still had great significance. Due to the "no-repeat" rule for the Rose Bowl game, the Bruins were ineligible to participate. The USC Trojans would be going to the Rose Bowl, regardless of outcome. The winner of the Pacific Coast Conference, however, was up for grabs. When the two teams met at the Coliseum on November 20, UCLA was angry and determined. Despite destroying Oregon two weeks earlier, UCLA had dropped to No. 2 in the AP poll. Ohio State, coming off of a 28–6 win over unranked Purdue, jumped ahead of UCLA in the poll. November 20 would be the biggest day in college football in 1954, and many believed it would be the week to decide the National Champion. The No. 2-ranked Bruins took on the No. 7 USC Trojans, and the top-ranked Ohio State Buckeyes took on the No. 12 Michigan Wolverines.

A crowd of 102,548 fans packed the Coliseum on an unusually warm November day. It was 110 degrees at kickoff. Though 57 fans were treated for heat exhaustion, nothing could stop the Bruins. Exhaustion came only from the USC Trojans, as UCLA once again showed brilliance on both sides of the ball. Herman Hickman of *Sports Illustrated* called the game the "Slaughter in the Coliseum." UCLA went on to win by a score of 34–0. Primo Villanueva, known by teammates as the "Calexico Kid," Bob Hadenfield, and the rest of the Bruins offense proved to be too strong and too fast for the Trojans. The UCLA defense was once again marvelous. USC gained a total of only 108 yards for the day, with only five of those yards coming on the ground.

Ohio State went on to beat the University of Michigan, 21–7. The only thing left for the Bruins to do was wait to see how the polls would judge them. Two days after the final regular season game, the AP announced Ohio State as the No. 1 team in the nation and the AP National Champion. But the title in '54 would be split. UCLA was named National Champion by the Coaches Poll. With UCLA's season over and Ohio State going to the Rose Bowl, UCLA was in an uncomfortable position. Though they were already National Champions, they felt slighted by the AP and wanted everyone to know they were the true champions. Ohio State was playing USC in the Rose Bowl, and though the Bruins did not need USC to beat the Buckeyes, they wouldn't mind if somehow both teams lost. Of course, this was not possible, and Ohio State would go on to beat USC, 20–7. Though there were many polls that named college football champions, it was the two previously named polls that carried the most weight. Looking beyond the AP and Coaches Polls, however, we see that other voters were just as undecided as those.

UCLA was named the 1954 National Champion by the Coaches Poll, as well as the College Football Researchers Association (cochampions), Dunkel System, Football Writers Association of America, Helms Athletic Foundation (cochampions), Litkenhous, National Championship Foundation (co-champions), and United Press International.

Ohio State was named the 1954 National Champion by the Associated Press, as well as by Berryman,

Billingsley Report, Boand System, College Football Researchers Association (cochampions), DeVold System, Helms Athletic Foundation (cochampions), International News Service, National Championship Foundation (cochampions), Polling System, Sagarin Ratings, and Williamson System.

Both Woody Hayes and Red Sanders led their teams to miraculous seasons. Due to the "no-repeat" rule, players, coaches, and fans were robbed of what many believed would be the "Game of the Decade." Without the experience of seeing the two teams play, one can only anticipate what would have happened. One must analyze the teams and the results to determine who the best team in America was that year. On October 2, OSU defeated Cal, 21–13. Four weeks later, UCLA defeated Cal, 27–6. In the Rose Bowl game on January 1, 1955, OSU defeated USC, 20–7. Weeks earlier, UCLA defeated USC, 34–0. It would be 44 more years until college football had a National Championship system that pitted the No. 1 team against the No. 2 team in one final game.

Top: Jim Salsbury (64), Jack Ellena (77), and Bob Davenport (27) were all named All-Americans in 1954 (Southern Campus Collection)

Middle: Primo Villanueva follows the blocking of Bob Davenport and Terry Debay against Oregon State University in 1954 (Southern Campus Collection)

Bottom: The Bruins kicked off their 1954 National Championship season by beating the San Diego Navy, 67–0 (Southern Campus Collection)

The 1954 coaching staff, left to right, Tommy Prothro, Bill Barnes, George Dickerson, Red Sanders, Johnny Johnson, Jim Meyers, and Deke Brackett (Southern Campus Collection)

The Downtown Athletic Club named Alan Ameche from the University of Wisconsin the 1954 Heisman Trophy Winner.

## 1955

Coming off a shared National Championship in 1954, the Bruins of 1955 had several major goals. In addition to winning another national title, the Bruins were still eyeing the Rose Bowl. The "no-repeat" rule, which was five years away from being discontinued, cost the Bruins a berth in the '55 Rose Bowl and a chance to play the Ohio State Buckeyes in a dream matchup. UCLA had lost the '54 Rose Bowl to Michigan State. The next Rose Bowl was scheduled for January 2, 1956, and UCLA would settle for nothing less than a Pasadena date with a Big 10 foe.

On September 16, the top-ranked UCLA Bruins took on Paul "Bear" Bryant and the Texas A&M Aggies at the Coliseum. Though UCLA had lost a fair amount of talent from its 1954 championship team, one of the biggest losses came from the coaching staff. Tommy Prothro, the excellent backfield coach for the Bruins, accepted the head coaching job at Oregon State University. Though Prothro was gone (for now), the Bruins returned many experienced players, most notably Sam Brown, Jim Brown, Hardiman Cureton, Bob Davenport, Jim Decker, Gil Moreno, and Ronnie Loudd. Hardiman and Moreno were named team cocaptains, and both were named All-Americans at the end of the season. Bear Bryant was entering his second season at TAMU. The man who would, in time, become a legend had already built an impressive résumé, including an eight-year run at Kentucky that rivaled Red Sanders's success at UCLA. His teams won the Sugar Bowl and the Cotton Bowl in back-to-back years. His overall record at Kentucky was 60–23–6. Bear Bryant was without a doubt a great coach, but his first year at TAMU was not so pleasant. Though it wouldn't take Bryant long to turn it around (with an undefeated record in his third season), his 1954 team, The Junction Boys, struggled mightily, finishing with a 1–9 record. A total of 63,334 fans attended the season opener at the Coliseum to see the defending champions in a night game, and they were not disappointed. The first touchdown of the season came in the second quarter on a 25-yard pass from Cal Berkeley transfer Ronnie Knox to John Herman. Knox would add two more touchdown passes, one to Jim Decker and one to Chuck Holloway. UCLA's 4–4 defense held strong, allowing TAMU to cross the 15-yard line only once but never score. UCLA won the season opening test, 21–0, and was on to a big challenge in Week 2.

After the Bruins defeated No. 6 Maryland, 12–7, in '54, Terrapins fans had to wait a year to see their team face the opponent who had knocked them out of championship contention. Now, in '55, UCLA was ranked No. 1 and the Terps were No. 5, but this time the game was in College Park. If UCLA was to have a realistic shot at the National Championship, they would have to pass a monumental road challenge. When the game began, the teams were not only battling their opponents, but also a driving rainstorm. The game was played on a 100-yard mud puddle, with a constant pelting rain adding to the mess. The style of play necessary to win in such elements seemed to improve the odds of the home team. Though UCLA was a physical squad, with a tough defense and strong running game, their passing attack would be hampered greatly. Maryland, led by bruising middle linebacker Bob Pelligrini and halfback Ed Vereb, could play in any weather. The first legitimate scoring opportunity for either team came in the second quarter. UCLA pounded the ball to the Terps 1-yard line. On 2nd-and-goal, Doug Peters received the handoff but before crossing the goal line was pounded by Pelligrini. The ball came loose, and Maryland recovered at the 1-yard line. At halftime, the game remained scoreless. Maryland received the opening kickoff of the second half and proceeded to march down the field. After eight plays, they were at the Bruins 17-yard line. On the ninth play, Vereb took the ball on a sweep to the right and found running room. Seventeen yards later, Vereb was in the end zone, and the Terps were on the scoreboard. The extra point was good, and Maryland led, 7–0. UCLA was never able to mount another serious drive. The loss to Maryland was the first regular-season loss in over two years for coach Sanders and the Bruins. With the dreams of a National Championship now no more than a hope and a prayer, UCLA set its sights on winning the Pacific Coast Conference title.

Johnny Hermann against Oregon State, 1955 (Southern Campus Collection)

UCLA fell to No. 7 in the rankings following the loss to Maryland. When conference play began in Week 3, the Bruins had some frustration to let out, and the Cougars and Beavers were the teams to feel their wrath. UCLA beat Washington State by a score of 55–0 before facing former assistant coach Tommy Prothro's Oregon State Beavers. Coach Prothro had no luck in his first trip back to the Coliseum. UCLA won, 38–0. Despite the decisive wins, UCLA fell to No. 9 in the Associated Press rankings before taking on Stanford in Palo Alto. A crowd of about 52,000 fans saw the Bruins take on the Indians in a surprisingly tight game. UCLA, which had roughed up Stanford the year before, appeared well on its way to another decisive victory. At the end of the first quarter, UCLA led, 21–0. In the second quarter, the UCLA offense stalled, but the defense remained strong. With the score still 21–0, the Stanford Indians mounted a solid comeback attempt. John Brodie would throw for two touchdowns and drive the ball one last time deep into Bruins territory. With under a minute to go, Stanford had reached the UCLA 3-yard line. It was first-and-goal, but the clock was ticking. After back-to-back negative plays by the Stanford offense, the clock ran out, and UCLA survived. The 5,500 Bruins fans who made the trip to Palo Alto could breathe again and enjoyed the trip home.

After defeating Stanford in a close game, UCLA played a stretch of games in which they gave the AP voters something to think about. It would take chaos in the college football world for the Bruins to have a chance at another title, but in case that chaos occurred, Coach Sanders was ready for his team to be the benefactors. UCLA defeated Iowa, 33–13, as 75,692 fans saw Sam Brown score three touchdowns against the Hawkeyes. The next week, UCLA handed the California Golden Bears their worst loss in 15 years. After losing, 47–0, Cal coach Lynn Waldorf proclaimed, "One of these days, we got to go back into this conference. UCLA and USC are so much stronger than everybody else in the league, it's pretty much a two-man show." UCLA would then defeat out-of-conference opponent College of the Pacific, 34–0.

Despite Coach Waldorf of Cal claiming that the conference was a two-man show, the Washington Huskies would come to play on November 12 and threaten UCLA to a degree that very few expected. UCLA was now the No. 4 team in the nation, and the Huskies were 4–3, coming off a 14-point loss to the Cal Bears. With the game 7–7 in the second quarter, UCLA was driving the ball against the fierce, but tired, Huskies defense. UCLA appeared to be heading for a score when Gerry McDougald was intercepted by Jim Jones, who returned the pass 61 yards for a score. At halftime, UCLA trailed, 14–7. In the second half, UW kicked a field goal and UCLA scored another touchdown before the dramatic end unfolded. With just under five minutes to go and the UCLA defense pushing the Huskies offense back deep into their own territory, UW Coach John Cherberg decided to intentionally take a safety rather than risk punting out of their own end zone. After the safety, the score was 17–16 Huskies. On the ensuing kickoff, Sam Brown took the ball at the Bruins' 31-yard line and returned it 25 yards to the Huskies' 44. Six plays and 28 yards later, the Bruins lined up for a field goal attempt. With eighteen seconds to play, Jim Decker knocked the field goal through the uprights, and the Bruins survived, 19–17. The team was 8–1 on the season and 5–0 in conference play.

When the Bruins took on the USC Trojans on November 19, the nation was watching: 95,000 fans packed the Coliseum, and millions more watched on TV in the rare nationally televised PCC game. Right from the start, it appeared UCLA had a fight on its hands. On the opening kickoff, USC's John Arnett fielded the ball at the 3-yard line and promptly raced 97 yards for a touchdown. As would be the case in the rest of the game, the joy the Trojans felt was short-lived; the return was called back due to a penalty. UCLA would then score 10 first half points and hold the Trojans scoreless in the firstt half. In the fourth quarter, the men of Troy once again snagged momentum, only for it to be short-lived. USC scored a touchdown early in the fourth, but UCLA responded with a long, steady drive. Thirteen plays and 59 yards later, Bob Davenport crossed the goal line. UCLA beat USC, 17–7, the third consecutive victory for the Bruins in the rivalry. UCLA was the Pacific Coast Conference Champion and was off to the Rose Bowl.

On January 2, 1956, UCLA played in the Rose Bowl game for the fourth time in school history—this time against Michigan State University. In 1943, UCLA had lost the Rose Bowl to Georgia. In 1947, they lost to Illinois. In 1954, they lost to Michigan State. Now, in 1956, they looked to reverse their luck and finally win the big game. Due to the no-repeat rule, UCLA and Ohio State were once again barred from playing each other. Though the '55 Buckeyes were also a notch below their '54 team, they finished undefeated in Big 10 play, having avoided MSU on the schedule. The Spartans, however, were the higher-ranked team, with their lone loss coming at the hands of the Michigan Wolverines three months earlier. When the game kicked off, MSU was ranked No. 2 in the country and the Bruins No. 4. After Decker intercepted a pass for the Bruins early in the game, Davenport pounded the ball into the end zone from two yards out. The Spartans would respond, however. Michigan State made steady charges in the second and third quarters, playing sound defense and winning the field position battle. Twice they were able to turn their successful drives into touchdowns. With the score 14–7 MSU, the season entered its final quarter. In the fourth, UCLA went hard for the win. Ronnie Knox led a drive to the Spartans 1-yard line, and Doug Peters finished for the final yard's touchdown. The extra point was good, and the score was tied. MSU marched the ball down the field on the next drive but then appeared to give UCLA the break it needed by missing a field goal. That gave the ball to UCLA with a chance to take the lead in the fourth quarter, but UCLA faltered and had its worst drive of the game. After several penalties pushed the Bruins back, Knox poorly kicked a punt and the Spartans took over at the Bruin 25-yard line with under two minutes to play. Though the Bruins had outplayed the Spartans on the day, the game would come down to one final field goal attempt. Head coach Duffy Daugherty called on Dave Kaiser to kick a 41-yard field goal for the win, his first career collegiate attempt. The kick was up and good. Michigan State won the Rose Bowl, 17–14. UCLA finished the season with a 9–2 record, but still without a Rose Bowl victory. Sam Brown finished the season as the new single-season rushing champion at UCLA, breaking Kenny Washington's record, and finishing with 892 yards. Bob Davenport played his last game in a Bruins uniform and finished his career with 25 touchdowns. The 1955 season concluded a stretch in which the Bruins had 34 wins and only five losses in four years. UCLA would have to replace a lot of talent in '56, but Red Sanders was seen as the man to do it.

The Downtown Athletic Club named Howard Cassady from Ohio State University the 1955 Heisman Trophy Winner.

Chuck Hollway intercepts a pass against Washington State, 1955 (Southern Campus Collection)

The Associated Press named the University of Oklahoma the 1955 National Champions.

## 1956

In 1956, Dwight Eisenhower was reelected president after winning all but seven states over Adlai Stevenson, the same man Eisenhower had defeated four years earlier. Red Sanders and the UCLA Bruins had winning records, as well. They had won three consecutive Pacific Coast Conference championships, and though the talent lost from the '55 team would make winning a fourth extremely difficult, the Bruins set their eyes on nothing less.

But in the spring of 1956, what eventually led to the downfall and collapse of the Pacific Coast Conference became public. Several institutions, UCLA included, were investigated for a "pay-for-play" scandal. UCLA and USC were hit hardest by the sanctions, though they had proven to do no more than any other team. UCLA was fined $93,000, sentenced to a four-year Rose Bowl ban, was also banned from participating in any postseason play in any sport for one year, banned from participating in any nationally televised games, and all players who participated in any 1955 varsity or freshman games would be ruled permanently ineligible unless they could prove they were not paid. The PCC cited that Bruins players received $40 above the maximum NCAA limit at the time. Stanford alumnus Goodwin Knight, who was then Governor of California, publicly called for the Board of Regents to look into the PCC to investigate the harsh punishment. He said, "It is hard for me to believe UCLA is much different than the other members of the conference." UCLA's Public Information Manager, Andrew Hamilton, would respond to the punishment in July by saying, "What it all boils down to is this: people in the Los Angeles area consider that both UCLA and USC have been unjustly dealt with by the rest of the conference. Here are some of the opinions frequently expressed: The PCC Code is unrealistic—it's been broken by all institutions and their booster clubs, so why pick on UCLA and USC? Why penalize student athletes when educators have for years winked at subsidization? Why were the entire Trojans and Bruins squads declared ineligible when 29 football players at California were given the right to 'buy back' their eligibility? Why were Washington, UCLA, and USC banned from the Rose Bowl and their receipts confiscated—and not California? Furthermore, who gets the shares of the banned schools, those who voted for the heavy financial penalties? What has the Commissioner's office been doing all this time? Seems like only those who were honest with the PCC are the ones that were penalized." Though a vote would come up to expel both UCLA and USC, neither would happen, but the PCC had made a major mistake in specifically targeting the two conference cash cows. It was believed for many years that Stanford and California Berkeley were behind the hit job. UCLA and USC would not forget the actions of both the PCC and some of the member institutions. One must remember, prior to 1960 (and beyond, though more subtle), paying players was not only the norm, it was visible. It was not hidden, and it was regular. In 1959, the PCC would disband. The pay-for-play scandal could have been a minor bump in the road, in which UCLA, USC, and the other offending schools paid a punishment, but the attack on UCLA and USC specifically signaled the end. The member institutions did not need the PCC, but the PCC needed member institutions.

[Insert photo: Don Long runs the ball against Washington with a caravan of blockers leading the way, 1956 (Southern Campus Collection)]

With a depleted and completely inexperienced roster, Red Sanders and the Bruins took the field angry in 1956. The season would be a challenge even with a full roster in place, but without it many believed the season would be a disaster. The fact is, Coach Sanders could win with anyone. Could the Bruins win the PCC, even though the Rose Bowl was not an option? They would try. The season finally kicked off on September 21 against the University of Utah. A small crowd of approximately 38,000 saw the Bruins defeat Utah, 13–7. Doug Bradley and Edison Griffin each scored a touchdown for the Bruins in the season opener. In Week 2, UCLA would not be as fortunate. The Bruins traveled to Ann Arbor to take on the University of Michigan and suffered their worst loss in six years. The Wolverines outrushed the Bruins, gaining 231 yards to 97 yards on the ground en route to a 42–13 win.

A week later, the Bruins returned to the win column. The game against the University of Oregon was a battle. For three quarters, neither team scored. In the opening minutes of the fourth quarter, with Oregon backed up near their own goal line, UCLA forced a fumble that was recovered by Dick Wallen at the 1-yard line. Don Long then crossed the goal line for the only score of the day. UCLA defeated Washington State the next week, 28–0. UCLA was a surprising 3–1 on the season, but the next three games were the ones that the Bruins wanted the most.

On October 20, UCLA traveled to Berkeley. One year earlier, Cal coach Pappy Waldorf had famously exclaimed, "One of these days, we got to go back into this conference. UCLA and USC are so much stronger than everybody else in the league, it's pretty much a two-man show." There was little if any subtlety in the disdain the players from UCLA and USC felt for Cal and Stanford following the pay-for-play scandal. Though California was also involved, it was clear that the PCC rulings were an attack on the Bruins and Trojans, an attempt not to even the playing field, but to dismantle the more successful football programs. Though the Bruins came out motivated, the game was sloppy. The teams together accounted for more than 200 penalty yards, and those penalties shackled the Bruins offense. UCLA could have scored 50+ points but instead settled for 34. UCLA scored in every quarter and twice in the first period, beating the Bears by 14. UCLA would lose the following week to Tommy Prothro and the eventual PCC champion Oregon State Beavers before taking on No. 10 Stanford on November 3. Five minutes into the game, UCLA caught its first break. After a Stanford fumble, Barry Billington crossed the goal line, and Don Duncan's point after touchdown attempt was good. UCLA scored again in the first quarter when Pete O'Garro caught a blocked punt in the air, courtesy of Hal Smith, and returned it 46 yards for a touchdown. UCLA took a 14–0 lead and would hold on to win, 14–13, behind the ferocious UCLA pass rush that harassed Stanford passers all game.

With wins over California and Stanford, UCLA had only one game left to look forward to. Though UCLA was in the hunt for the PCC crown, with no Rose Bowl in their sights, the remaining two games were seen by many as just playing out the strings. On November 10, UCLA defeated the University of Washington, 13–9, and one week later defeated the University of Kansas, 13–0. Despite the postseason ban for both teams, the UCLA and USC intracity game was always meaningful on both campuses. UCLA was 7–2 on the season with only one conference loss, and the Trojans were 6–2 with two conference losses. In the first half, the Bruins defense could not get off the field. USC played a ball control offense that was effective in keeping the ball away from UCLA's single wing, which had given them fits for years. USC ran a total of 47 plays, compared to the Bruins' 18. Despite the discrepancy in time of possession, the game was scoreless at halftime. In the third quarter, USC quickly changed that with an early passing touchdown. The Trojans added a fourth-quarter field goal before UCLA finally got on the board with a Stu Farber touchdown. UCLA was unable to mount another drive challenging the Trojans' defense and fell by the score of 10–7.

Though UCLA finished the season with a 7–3 record and tied for 2nd in the PCC, an achievement few thought possible at the outset of the scandal-ridden season, coach Sanders was furious. He was furious at the PCC and member institutions. He was furious at Stanford and Cal. He was furious he lost to USC. It was the first time USC had beaten UCLA since '52. Coach Sanders vowed to take UCLA back to the top. Little did he know, he had only twenty months to live.

The Downtown Athletic Club named Paul Hornung from the University of Notre Dame the 1956 Heisman Trophy Winner.

The Associated Press named the University of Oklahoma the 1956 National Champions.

## 1957

In 1957, Coach Sanders had one more chance to preach his 10 football commandments:

1. The team that makes the fewest mistakes wins.
2. Press the kicking game, for it's here the breaks are made.
3. Play for and make the breaks; when one comes your way, score.
4. If at first the game or a break goes against you, don't slow down. Put on more steam.
5. Cover and pursue relentlessly—here is the winning edge.
6. Linemen, protect your kicker and passer. Rush their kicker and passer. Backs, protect your kicker and passer.
7. Carry the fight to your opponent and keep it there all afternoon. Hit hard and hit first.
8. Be mentally alert at all times and leave nothing to chance.
9. Be determined to carry out your assignment.
10. Win the surest way.

The season kicked off on September 20, 1957, against the United States Air Force Academy. The Bruins season was not supposed to begin against the Academy. Due to a flu epidemic in Gainesville, Florida, a large portion of the Gators squad was infected, and the Bruins were forced to find a last-minute fill-in. With the Air Force season not scheduled to begin until the following week, they were the final choice. It was the first time the AFA had ever played a team in a major college conference. In only its third year in existence, AFA brought little resistance to the Bruins. UCLA won, 47–0.

Though Illinois would provide a stiffer challenge in Week 2, the Bruins again prevailed. The game was evenly played, but UCLA capitalized on scoring opportunities, something the Illini were not able to do. Final score: UCLA 16, Illinois 6. The shocker of the season came in Week 3. Though the Bruins prepared for a strong Oregon team, no one expected the game to end the way it did. As is often the case, when the Bruins went north to face Oregon at Multnoman Stadium in Portland, the game was played in less than ideal weather. The field was wet, the air was cold, and the Bruins were soundly defeated. It mattered little under what weather the game was played. UCLA could not stop the ground game of Jack Crabtree, Jack Morris, and Jim Shanley and could not break the strong Oregon defense. For the first time since 1948, Oregon beat UCLA. When the game ended, the scoreboard read Oregon 21, UCLA 0. The Webfeet would go on to win the Pacific Coast Conference and play Ohio State in the Rose Bowl.

After suffering defeat at the hands of Oregon, UCLA had the tough task of then taking on the Washington Huskies. In the first half, the game was in great doubt. It was a defensive struggle, with neither team threatening the end zone. Punting was essential, and field position was thought would be a key factor in the second half. When the Bruins came out after halftime, it was no longer a battle but a beatdown. UCLA marched downfield, and Don Long plunged across the goal line from a yard out to get the Bruins on board first. UCLA added two more touchdowns, one by Barry Billington and another by John Pierovich, and went on to win, 21–0.

With the Bruins at 3–1 on the season, they entered a three-game stretch similar to the one so important to the team in '56. On October 19, UCLA took on the No. 7 Oregon State Beavers and head coach Tommy Prothro. With their own unblemished record, aspirations for a PCC crown, and dreams of the Rose Bowl, the Beavers were the clear favorites on this day. Prothro vs. Sanders was a matchup of two of the best coaches in the country, and many believed that Prothro was a man on the rise. On this day, Sanders had no intention of being outcoached. UCLA would start the scoring early. After taking the opening kickoff, UCLA drove down the field with ease. There was nothing the Beavers could do to stop the Bruins' single wing offense. The drive was capped by a 1-yard score from Billington up the middle. UCLA also scored on a pass from Long to Bill Mason, then a 1-yard run by Long, and finally a rush by Chuck Kendall. With the Bruins up, 26–0, Coach Sanders brought in reserves, and OSU would get on the board late to make the final score 26–7 Bruins. The following week, the Bruins were victims of an untimely letdown. The Stanford Indians had three drives deep into Bruins territory and scored touchdowns on all three. The Bruins, who recovered a fumble at the Indians' 1 early in the game and didn't score, squandered opportunities all game. The final: Stanford 20, UCLA 6. The Bruins defeated Cal for the seventh straight time in their rivalry the following week. After Long and Ray Smith each scored a touchdown in the first half, the Bears made a charge of their own. With UCLA up 13–0, Cal would score for the first time. UCLA's Kirk Wilson kicked a field goal to extend the Bruins lead, and though Cal scored once more late, the game was decided and the Bruins were victorious, 16–14.

Though the Bruins would not go to the Rose Bowl, they still had pride, and the last three games were key if the Bruins were to call the season a success. The stretch would include three opponents that UCLA could beat, and all three were on the road. A crowd of 27,000 fans saw the Bruins beat Washington State in a thrilling game in Spokane. After Long scored an early touchdown for the Bruins, the Cougars came right back with two TDs of their own to take a 13–6 lead. In the third quarter, Long crossed the goal line once again, and the Bruins tied it up. Though Washington State would have more scoring chances, the Bruins defense held, and with just 40 seconds left, Ray Smith leaped into the end zone for UCLA's game-winning touchdown, 19–13. College of the Pacific presented less of a challenge the following week. Despite the Bruins experiencing a rash of injuries, especially in the offensive backfield, UCLA defeated the physically imposing Tigers, 21–0.

In what turned out to be coach Sanders's last game against USC, the Bruins did what he loved: they beat the Trojans. At halftime, the Bruins led only 7–0 after Steve Gertoman scored on a 19-yard pass from Long. The offense struggled for much of the half, but the 4–4 Bruins defense stifled the Trojans. In the second half, UCLA kicked into high gear and ran away with the victory. Long, Billington, and Mason repeatedly ripped off long runs and left the Trojans chasing. The second Bruins touchdown came on a 1-yard Long run, and UCLA stretched the lead minutes later on an 18-yard touchdown reception by Dick Wallen from Long. The final score was UCLA 20, USC 9. The Bruins finished the season with an 8–2 record. Tackle Bill Leeka and Dick Wallen were named to the All-PCC team, and Wallen was named a consensus All-American.

When Coach Sanders died of a heart attack the following August, the college football world was shocked. UCLA had lost a man who had taken the team to new heights. The Bruins were forced to find a new coach. For UCLA, Coach Sanders's death was the end of an era.

The Downtown Athletic Club named John David Crow from Texas A&M University the 1957 Heisman Trophy Winner.

The Associated Press named Auburn University the 1957 National Champions.

Red Sanders's 10 Football Commandements (Southern Campus Collection)

# CHAPTER 8
# William Barnes (1958–1964)

William Barnes was not supposed to be the UCLA head football coach. At least not in 1958. When Red Sanders died on August 14, 1958, just five weeks before the start of the 1958 UCLA football season, Bruins assistant coaches, players, and fans were sent into a state of shock. Even when UCLA named a new head coach to replace Sanders, it wasn't Barnes. He wasn't supposed to be the man to lead the Bruins. Red Sanders was only 53 years old when he died. William "Bill" Barnes was just 10 days away from his forty-first birthday when he coached his first game for the Bruins. The path that led Barnes to college football and the head coaching job at UCLA, and the way he carried himself the rest of his life, was defined by his upbringing.

Bill Barnes was born on October 20, 1917, in Cape Girardeau, Missouri. He was a child of the Great Depression. Growing up, Barnes loved football. With the collapse of the stock market in 1929 when Bill was a young boy, he was required to work with his father and mother. Though he was expected to continue his education for several more years, upon finishing 8th grade, like many others, attending high school was not a given. But Bill loved football, and his parents loved their son. In 1931, Bill enrolled at Central High School. His family had moved from Missouri to Tennessee, and though Bill didn't know it at the time, it was the break he needed. With an understanding that education and football were a privilege, Bill took both very seriously while at Central. In 1936, Bill not only graduated high school, but found a university to call home for the next four years. Bill would enroll at the University of Tennessee and play for legendary coach General Robert Neyland. Though he stood at only 5'9" and weighed 160 pounds, Bill would be an integral part of

Head Coach Bill Barnes reaches out to shake Washington Coach Jim Owens's hand as his players carry him off the field, 1963 (Southern Campus Collection)

three very successful teams. As a sophomore, Barnes and the Volunteers finished with a 6–3–1 record. As a junior, the team was brilliant. Bill Barnes and the Volunteers went 11–0 in 1938 and split the National Championship with Notre Dame and TCU. In '39, Tennessee was once again great. As a senior, though Barnes was an All-American, he knew he didn't have a future beyond his final collegiate season playing ball, but coaching was already on his mind. When the 1939 team made a miraculous run to the Rose Bowl without being scored on all season, Barnes knew that coach Neyland was a football genius. He learned from his coach and absorbed his teachings. Despite finally being scored upon and losing to USC in the Rose Bowl, Bill Barnes learned the lessons that would eventually make him "Coach Barnes." After one year as an assistant to Coach Neyland at Tennessee, Bill was all-in. He loved football and would dedicate his life to teaching the game he loved. He had a direction and an idea of what he wanted to do with his life, but the Japanese had other plans, and Bill Barnes would sooner be fighting in the Pacific than urging anyone to fight for first downs again on the gridiron.

Following the attack on Pearl Harbor, Barnes joined the United States Army and was quickly sent off to the south Pacific. He earned the rank of major and was part of the original Alamo Scouts, considered by many to be the first United States Special Forces. While with the Alamo Scouts, Barnes was responsible for missions with small teams operating deep behind enemy lines. These small, tactical units would free American POWs. The Alamo Scouts performed 106 known missions behind enemy lines without losing a single man. For his efforts in the war, Bill Barnes was awarded two Bronze Stars, a Silver Star, the Legion of Merit, a Philippine Ribbon, and an Alamo Scout Recommendation.

When the war was over, Barnes, like war heroes everywhere, went back to his life. Though his dream was put on pause for four years, Barnes was a football man, and he would return to coaching. For four years, Barnes faithfully served as an assistant coach for John Barnhill at the University of Arkansas. Barnhill succeeded Neyland at the University of Tennessee when General Neyland joined the U.S. fighting force in World War II. When Neyland returned, Barnhill took the job at Arkansas and brought Barnes with him. The Razorbacks finished with a 22–17–3 record from 1946–1949. Barnhill retired from coaching in 1949 after being diagnosed with multiple sclerosis. Otis Douglas was hired to replace Barnhill, and Barnes was out of a job. When another Tennessee man came knocking, Barnes was ready, and in 1950, the Southern boy, who was a Tennessean through and through, packed up and headed west to join what was a uniquely Southern staff operating in Los Angeles.

For eight seasons, Bill Barnes was an assistant coach for one of the greatest coaches in America. After playing under General Robert Neyland at Tennessee, his football education continued to grow under Red Sanders. He learned the nuances of the single wing (an offense many believed his devotion to as a head coach ultimately hurt him) and the 4–4 defense. Coach Sanders demanded all assistants know both sides of the ball, so as to better understand their opposition. Barnes was a member of the 1953 coaching team that won the Pacific Coast Conference. He was a member of 1954 team that won the PCC, shared a national title, and just missed out on the "Game of the Decade" due to the Rose Bowl no-repeat rule. He was a member of the 1955 team that again won the PCC. As an assistant, he learned the importance of beating USC. He also was around during the scandal that ultimately brought down the PCC altogether. In his eight years in Westwood as an assistant, Bill was being mentored by one of the greatest teachers in America. Sanders was close with all his assistants, and being a man from Tennessee himself, he had a special friendship with Barnes. John Wooden, the UCLA head basketball coach, also developed a friendship with Barnes that would last for decades. Bill was a kind man, and it often seemed to be to the detriment of the team.

The two men were different in some respects. Bill Barnes was principled. Red Sanders was able to balance toughness with compassion; he was a "players' coach" who could send a message. Bill Barnes often struggled finding the balance between caring individual and dictatorial leader. In 1958, Barnes was thrust into a position he was perhaps not ready for. With the sudden death of Bill's mentor, UCLA needed a new coach, and they needed one quickly. George W. Dickerson, a UCLA alumnus, captain of the 1936 Bruin team, and long-time assistant coach, was the man originally called on to replace Sanders. With just weeks until the season kicked off, Dickerson, a workaholic, was feeling overwhelming stress and exhaustion. On August 30, Dickerson was admitted to the UCLA Medical Center. Thirteen days later, he returned to coaching the Bruins. Though Dickerson was able to coach the first three games of the '58 season, he was not physically well, and on October 10, 1958, Bill Barnes was named the new UCLA football head coach. Dickerson would recover and go on to work for a construction company in Alhambra, ultimately rising to senior vice president before retiring at the age of 71. Barnes coached at UCLA for the rest of the 1958 season, and for an additional six years. In 1964, Barnes resigned after learning that Athletic Director J.D. Morgan was not going to renew his contract.

Bill Barnes, 1958 (Southern Campus Collection)

Bill Barnes would have a roller-coaster career at UCLA. He was not Red Sanders, and perhaps he was chosen before he was ready. From 1958 to 1964, UCLA would sink back into mediocrity. Though he would twice win the Athletic Association of Western Universities (AAWU, predecessor to the Pac 8) title and once go to the Rose Bowl, Barnes was not able to meet the expectations that had been raised by Red Sanders.

After resigning from UCLA, Barnes spent time as an NFL scout for multiple organizations before becoming a real estate developer late in his career. His biggest accomplishment in the real estate business was the development of the Coto de Caza complex in south Orange County. John Wooden remained friends with Barnes until Barnes's death on April 23, 2009, at the age of 91. Sam Boghosian, who played at UCLA and coached with Barnes before moving on to the NFL, would say of his friend, "He was a man of great character. Sometimes he was maybe too nice."

## 1958

When Red Sanders died and Bill Barnes took over as the head football coach at UCLA, it was just one of several major changes in the Los Angeles sports scene. First, and historically most memorable, the Bruins and the USC Trojans would welcome a new tenant into the crowded Los Angeles Coliseum. On April 18, 1958, a crowd of 78,672 watched professional baseball in the Coliseum for the first time. Walter O'Malley, Vin Scully, and the Dodgers came west, and with them came the excitement of the most popular sport in the nation. On this day, the Dodgers beat the San Francisco Giants—who later followed the Dodgers but landed a little farther north—by a score of 6–5. The iconic Dodger Stadium would open in 1962.

While the sports scene was very lively in Southern California, one change in Westwood went largely unnoticed. In 1958, the University of California at Los Angeles changed its name. The word "at" was removed and the University of California Los Angeles was the new name. Many people had simply ignored the "at" for decades, so in '58 when it became official, many didn't even notice. With the excitement of the Dodgers distracting many people for most of the spring and summer, the college football offseason seemed to fly by. While many were mentally preparing themselves for the start of the season and looking forward to another year of Bruins dominance on the field, Red Sanders died. Fans everywhere were stunned, but the calendar slows for no one, and despite a rush to ready the team for kickoff, George Dickerson's and Bill Barnes's task in '58—fielding a team that would suffer no significant drop-off—was something very few men would be able to accomplish. But Coach Barnes and staff would give it their best shot. On September 20, 1958, it was time to move past the death of Red Sanders. Football was to be played.

On college football's opening Saturday, the No. 19 Pittsburgh Panthers came to the Coliseum. The Bruins captains, Jim Dawson, Jim Steffen, and Don Long, would have much responsibility. Not only was there a leadership void that needed to be filled, but the team was young and several seniors would be allowed to play in only a handful of games due to the earlier PCC penalties. The Bruins would have the big play that day, but not the big team that day.

With under a minute to go in the first half, sophomore Bill Kilmer was surrounded in the Bruins backfield by Panthers and seemed destined to go down for a loss, but he somehow escaped and launched a 58-yard pass to Marv Luster, who took the ball to the Panthers 3-yard line. Kilmer would then take the ball left and into the end zone for the first Bruins touchdown of the season. The Pitt Panthers, the superior team, dominated most of the game, but at the start of the fourth quarter, the score was only 15–6. After two Bruins fumbles, both recovered by Pitt, and two ensuing touchdowns, the season opener, the first game of the George Dickerson era, ended with UCLA losing, 27–6.

George Dickerson, 1958 (Southern Campus Collection)

The '58 season had several highs, but many lows. After UCLA defeated a strong University of Illinois team on the road in Week 2, they returned home and were soundly defeated by Tommy Prothro and the Oregon State Beavers. Paul Lowe, a Southern California native and future Los Angeles and San Diego Charger, and at the time a star halfback for the Beavers, ran through the Bruins defense all game. Lowe accounted for both OSU touchdowns, and UCLA went down, 14–0. Following the OSU game, George Dickerson could handle no more. After being hospitalized for nervous exhaustion in August, doctors and Dickerson agreed that he could return to work. But after three games the nervous exhaustion was too much, and Dickerson never coached again. It was Bill Barnes's team now. On October 10, the University of Florida came to the Coliseum, and despite the success of the Bruins passing attack, something that stunned observers who had heard of Barnes' reliance on the single wing and running the ball, the Bruins went down in defeat once again. Don Long and Dick Wallen had put on a show for the Bruins, but it wasn't enough. Fans enjoyed theatrics and superstar play, but more than anything they appreciated winning. The Bruins were just 1–3 with six games to go.

Though the Bruins would defeat the University of Washington on October 18, the joy of winning a conference game was something not often seen in 1958. Following the win over the Huskies, UCLA would lose the next three games, including two heartbreaking losses to their archrivals, Stanford and California. Stanford and UCLA matched each other in the touchdown column, but UCLA missed an extra point early in the game and failed on a late two-point conversion. Final score: Stanford 21, UCLA 19. The California Golden Bears, the Pacific Coast Conference representative in the Rose Bowl, would be given an unexpected scare when the Bruins went north. UCLA trailed, 14–3, early in the contest but finally crossed the goal line in the fourth quarter when Skip Smith rushed off tackle and into the end zone. The extra point failed, and when Cal responded with a touchdown of their own, the game seemed all but over. UCLA continued to fight, however. Chuck Kendall threw a touchdown to Phil Parslow. Kendall found Jim Steffen for the two-point conversion, and the score was 20–17. UCLA failed to overtake the Bears, but the crowd was stunned that the Bruins had hung in as close as they did. After defeating Oregon, 7–3, the following week in dramatic fashion, the Bruins had one game left.

When the Bruins faced the Trojans on November 22, neither team had anything to play for other than pride and the Victory Bell. UCLA's record was 3–6, and USC was 4–4. Oddsmakers had the Trojans as 15-point favorites, but though their record didn't show much success for the Bruins all season, the team continued to play hard for coach Barnes, and often in what some consider "meaningless" games, the team that continues to stay focused and motivated is the one to beat. A crowd of just over 59,000 saw the two battle, and the vast majority expected to see the Trojans come out on top. Despite a scoreless first half, fans who stayed saw a thrilling second half. The first touchdown of the game was set up by a 66-yard run by Trojans halfback Don Buford. After falling behind, UCLA got two breaks that they desperately needed. Twice, USC quarterback Tom Maudlin was errant on pitches to his back, and twice the Bruins came away with the ball. Both times, UCLA would capitalize and reach the end zone. With UCLA up 15–7 in the fourth quarter, they kicked off, and Trojan Luther Hayes returned the kick 74 yards for a touchdown. USC succeeded with the two-point conversion, and the score was 15–15. Each team had more chances, but neither could break away. The final score was a 15–15 tie, not what coach Barnes and the Bruins wanted, but it was more devastating for the Trojans. After losing to Notre Dame in the final week of the season, USC finished with a losing record. UCLA's first season post-Red Sanders was also a disappointing one. When the final seconds ticked off in the final game, the Bruins saw themselves with a 3-6-1 record. It was the first season UCLA had finished with a losing record in 10 years.

The Downtown Athletic Club named Pete Dawkins from the United States Military Academy (Army) the 1958 Heisman Trophy Winner.

The Associated Press named Louisiana State University the 1958 National Champions.

## 1959

By 1959, the pay-for-play controversy in the Pacific Coast Conference had entered its fourth year. UCLA and USC were at the center of the issue, and after a long, harassing process, they had simply endured enough. Though Cal was also implicated in the scandal, they were not hit as hard by sanctions as the two Los Angeles schools. Nevertheless, they wanted out. Cal and UCLA would be the leaders that helped bring together several of the former PCC members into a new conference. In 1959, UCLA, USC, California, Stanford, and Washington played in the newly formed Athletic Association of Western Universities (AAWU). For two years, the AAWU had no written agreement with the Rose Bowl, though the Rose Bowl took the AAWU winner anyway. Three years later, Washington State joined the AAWU, and two years after that Oregon and Oregon State joined. In 1968, the conference changed its name to the Pacific 8 Conference.

Coming off a 3–6–1 record, the Bruins of '59 were tasked with a new challenge. After the implosion of the Pacific Coast Conference and the establishing of the Athletic Association of Western Universities, the Bruins had only four conference opponents to play and would have to schedule a significant number of out-of-conference opponents. In '59, the plan was for UCLA to sever ties to West Coast rivalries and become more of a national brand. They would play more teams from across the country and bring necessary exposure to the University. The schedule that coach Barnes was tasked with playing was a difficult one, but the team was much improved. The season kicked off against the No. 11 Purdue Boilermakers. Seniors Ray Smith and Rod Cochran were team cocaptains. When the game finally began, the Bruins cared little about being 15-point underdogs. They came to win, and the defense certainly did its job. Three times Purdue drove inside the Bruins' 20, and three times they were denied. UCLA would hold the Boilermakers scoreless on the day. With UCLA not yet on the scoreboard, Bobby Smith attempted a short field goal late in the final period, but it sailed wide left, and though not what the Bruins were hoping for, their achieving a scoreless tie against powerful Purdue was a shock to college football fans everywhere.

Two weeks after that season opener, the Bruins traveled to Pittsburgh, Pennsylvania, to take on the University of Pittsburgh Panthers. UCLA led at halftime after two touchdown receptions by Marv Luster, one thrown by Bill Kilmer and the other by Gene Gaines. The aerial artwork was not limited to just the Bruins, however. Despite falling behind, 21–6, Pitt and their star quarterback Ivan Toncic gave everything they had. Trailing by 15 with 10 minutes to play, Toncic took over the game and threw for three touchdowns. He did what star players are expected to do: steal victory from opponents when few believe it is possible. UCLA lost to Pitt, 25–21. When the California Golden Bears came to Los Angeles for the third game of the season, they brought with them a fighting spirit that kept the game close throughout. UCLA had not lost to Cal at home since 1949 and were favored once again to beat them. Though Cal went ahead early, Ray Smith put the Bruins ahead in the second quarter, and the team never relinquished the lead. Up 13–12 in the third quarter, Marv Luster pounded the ball in from the 1-yard line and the Bruins led, 19–12. The defense held, and UCLA won their first game of the season.

The following two weeks were ones to be forgotten, though, surprisingly, the Bruins were able to bounce back. On October 23, the Bruins lost to the Air Force Academy. It was a dismal showing. After playing the Falcons to an even score at halftime, the Bruins were dominated in the second half and went down by a score of 20–7. The following week brought no better results for Coach Barnes. Though the Bruins would lead the Washington Huskies, 7–0, early in the game, the story of the day was Bob Schloredt, the quarterback for the Huskies, who despite being legally blind in his left eye after a fireworks accident, accounted for three touchdowns. UCLA lost, 23–7.

UCLA was 1-3-1 with five games to play. Fans and enemies of the Bruins alike all thought the same thing. The common belief was that the season was over. Coach Barnes was not Red Sanders, and rallying the team to finish strong was not going to happen. That belief, however, was wrong. The Bruins finished the season with a roar that would make coach Sanders proud. He did rally the troops and the fight to the finish began with a beat down. On November 7, the Bruins took on the Stanford Indians in Palo Alto and left their longtime rival wondering what had happened. Thirty-five thousand fans saw the Bruins flip the script on the Indians. Stanford, known for their passing game, was beaten through the air and on the ground for a 55–13 UCLA victory. Six days later, the Bruins were back at home, and though the score was much closer, the team was again impressive. UCLA jumped ahead of North Carolina State, 21–0, behind strong performances by Bill Kilmer, Marv Luster, and Skip Smith. Though the Wolfpack made a late charge behind the prolific passing of Roman Gabriel, UCLA won, 21–13.

With seven games down and three to go, nothing mattered more to the Bruins than the next opponent on their schedule. What happened early in the season meant little compared to what lay ahead. On November 21, UCLA took on the University of Southern California. The Trojans were the No. 4 team in the country, and though the AAWU didn't have any tie-in to the Rose Bowl, many expected the Rose Bowl committee to take a western power, and that would likely be the winner of the new conference. With a win, the Trojans were all but a lock. With a loss, the door was open for UCLA or the University of Washington. A large crowd of 85,917 was in the Coliseum to see the two local teams battle. Though Bill Kilmer was thought to be out with a severe ankle injury, the thrill of the sport and the intense passion that one has for beating a rival can often help an individual block out pain. With the Bruins trailing 3–0 in the third quarter, Kilmer had seen enough from the sidelines. When he entered the game, he did so not for show, but for the purpose of leading his team to victory. The Bruins offense instantly took on new life. After getting possession on their own 13-yard line, the Bruins drove downfield 72 yards, and Ivory Jones tied the score with a field goal. On the next Bruins drive, the march continued. With the Bruins at the Trojans 17, Kilmer launched a high pass into double coverage, risky from a coach's perspective, but the pass was in a position from which only the intended Bruins receiver, Marv Luster, could make a play. Though the ball landed on the ground, UCLA accomplished its goal. Pass interference! The ball was placed at the Trojans 7-yard line. First and goal. It took Ray Smith three tries, but on the third he crossed the goal line, and the vaunted USC defense had been broken. For the rest of the day, the Bruins defense played with tenacity and will, perhaps inspired by the bravery of Kilmer. UCLA won the crosstown matchup and brought home the Victory Bell with a final score of 10–3. Though the University of Washington would go to the Rose Bowl, UCLA, along with the Trojans, tied the Huskies in the conference standings. The three-way tie for first place is something that had been only a dream for the Bruins just four short weeks earlier.

The final two games of the season could have been viewed as potential letdown games, but Coach Barnes and the Bruins continued to play hard. One week after beating the Trojans, the now No. 20-ranked Bruins beat the University of Utah, 21–6. Finally, the Bruins finished the season with the No. 1-ranked Syracuse University Orangemen. Led by Ernie Davis, the Orangemen were undefeated. After dismantling the Bruins, 38–6, Syracuse was headed for the Cotton Bowl for a New Year's Day matchup with the University of Texas, and UCLA was headed for the offseason.

The Downtown Athletic Club named William Cannon from Louisiana State University the 1959 Heisman Trophy Winner.

The Associated Press named Syracuse University the 1959 National Champions.

## 1960

A new decade. The '50s were over and the '60s were rolling in. John Fitzgerald Kennedy was elected president. John Wooden started his thirteenth season as the UCLA basketball coach, and Bill Barnes started his third as the football coach. After the strong finish to the '59 season, fans, coaches, and players alike all hoped that the Bruins could carry that momentum into the new season. UCLA would have a successful season, and, as in many years past, the game with the USC Trojans would be the game fans would remember most.

The UCLA football season began with a bang. On September 17, the Bruins took on the No. 7 University of Pittsburgh Panthers at the Coliseum. With memories of the heartbreaking loss in '59 fresh on the minds of all returning players and coaches, the Bruins were sure to compete for the entirety of four quarters. After falling behind, 7–0, early in the game, the Bruins continually drove the ball into Panther territory, only to be turned away. Entering the fourth quarter, the Bruins still trailed, 7–0. In the fourth quarter, Ezell Singleton made his mark as a Bruin. For the first time in his young career, Singleton was called on to lead the Bruins offense. With only 30 seconds left, after marching 80 yards, the Bruins scored. Rather than kick the extra point and settle for an opening game tie for the second season in a row, coach Barnes went for the win. The two-point conversion was good! UCLA knocked off the highly ranked Panthers and began the season 1–0. When the new Associated Press rankings were released, the Bruins had soared all the way to No. 8.

Head Coach Bill Barnes, 1960 (Southern Campus Collection)

In Week 2, the Bruins traveled to West Lafayette, Indiana, to take on the Purdue University Boilermakers. Despite UCLA being so highly ranked by the AP, oddsmakers preferred the Boilermakers. UCLA was a five-point underdog and early in the game looked as if they had been insulted by the betting line. Bill Kilmer scored two touchdowns early for the Bruins before the Boilermakers could strike back. In the fourth quarter, UCLA led, 27–20, with minutes to play. Kilmer had scored all four times for the Bruins, but now it was time to rely on the defense. Unfortunately, the defense couldn't hold, and Purdue went on to tie the score. The offense couldn't muster up a final, winning drive, and the second game of the season ended in a disappointing tie. After a three-week break, the Bruins finally hit the field once again, this time in Seattle. When the now No. 15 Bruins took on the No. 13 Huskies, there were obvious AAWU implications on the line. The Huskies, Bruins, and USC Trojans had tied for the conference title the previous year, and the Huskies went to the Rose Bowl. UCLA started this game slowly and fell behind the Huskies, 10–0, at the end of three quarters. It would be tough for the Bruins to come back, but they would give it their best shot. UCLA marched downfield for the longest sustained drive of the afternoon in the fourth quarter, and Kilmer capped the drive with a short pass to Jim Johnson for the score. UCLA went for two, and the attempt was successful. Down 10–8, there was hope for a Bruin miracle, but the reality is that the team was inferior to the Huskies. Washington was able to run out the clock, and the Bruins fell to 1-1-1 for the second year in a row.

Also for the second year in a row, the Bruins would go on a run. But this time, in 1960, the winning streak started earlier. On October 22, UCLA dismantled Stanford. Kilmer was his usual brilliant self, and Almose Thompson scored three touchdowns. The following week, UCLA took on North Carolina State. The defense was dominant. Kilmer and Roman Gabriel would make the pregame headlines, but the solid front and speedy defensive backs stole the show. The final: UCLA 7, North Carolina State 0. When the Bruins took on big brother California the following week, the Bears simply did not show up. They could not compete with the Bruins, who put on an offensive and defensive performance that made fans proud. Thompson and Skip Smith would each score, and Kilmer added two touchdowns himself. It was 28–0 Bruins. Riding a three-game winning streak, the Bruins took on Air Force Academy on November 12. For the third game in a row, the Bruins defense dominated and shut out their opponent. Kilmer once again proved he was one of the best players in America. He scored three touchdowns on the day, including one from 88 yards out, the longest touchdown of his career.

The Bruins were 5–1–1 and ranked No. 11 in the country by the AP when they took on the USC Trojans. John McKay and USC had struggled thus far and were 3–5 when they met the Bruins. The University of Washington had already clinched the AAWU crown and would go on to their second consecutive Rose Bowl. Despite the reality that neither team was in contention for the conference title, the game between the two rivals was always a major event. If the Bruins could beat USC and finish the final two games of the season with victories, they would likely finish ranked in the top 10. USC, despite the poor season, could find a silver lining just by defeating the Bruins. If USC could finish the season with wins over the Bruins and the Notre Dame Fighting Irish, they could avoid a losing record and finish 5–5. But past records have a way of losing their meaning when it comes to rivalry games. Though the Bruins came in riding a four-game winning streak, and the Trojans came in dragging a two-game losing streak, the Trojans thoroughly dismantled the Bruins. UCLA's offense struggled all game, and the defense did not play up to the standard it had set in previous weeks. The Trojans defeated the Bruins in a stunner, 17–6.

UCLA finished the season by defeating the University of Utah, 16–9, and whipped Duke University, 27–6. A large audience saw the Bruins' season finale against the No. 11 ranked Duke Blue Devils in a nationally televised game. Kilmer, Thompson, Smith, and Don Vena all played well, and though the USC loss would sting for the entirety of the offseason for fans, and lifetimes of many players, the Bruins of 1960 were a solid team. UCLA finished with a 7-2-1 record and were the No. 22 team in the nation in the final Associated Press poll.

The Downtown Athletic Club named Joe Bellino from the United States Naval Academy (Navy) the 1960 Heisman Trophy Winner.

The Associated Press named the University of Minnesota the 1960 National Champions.

UCLA Cheerleader, 1960 (Southern Campus Collection)

## 1961

UCLA had improved each year under coach Barnes. After a dismal 1958 season, UCLA had two consecutive winning seasons, and though they were not back to the level that coach Red Sanders had Bruins fans accustomed to cheering for, the 1961 team could once again focus their eyes on the Rose Bowl. With a plethora of talented players occupying the roster, coach Barnes had his deepest and most talented team. The '61 season would be one to remember.

Along with Coach Barnes, assistant coaches Johnny Hermann, Bob Bergdahl, Jim Dawson, Sam Boghosian, Deke Brackett, Johnny Johnson, and Dan Peterson were responsible for preparing the team for battle each Saturday. The culmination of the work put in by the players, the assistants, and Coach Barnes was finally put on display on September 23 in Denver, Colorado. The season kicked off against Air Force Academy, and despite a cold, rainy atmosphere, Bobby Smith and the Bruins played well enough to win. Smith, a backup to Bill Kilmer for two years, was now a key part of the offense. His season started with an excellent performance. Smith finished with

178 yards on the ground, and he was responsible for all three Bruins scores in a 19–6 win.

Though the Bruins were off to a good start, the next two games would prove to be challenges that could crush the dreams of any team. In Week 2, the Bruins were once again on the road, this time in Ann Arbor, Michigan. When the Bruins met the Wolverines in Michigan Stadium, more commonly known as "The Big House," they were simply outclassed in every way. The Associated Press ranked the Bruins as the No. 8 team in the country, and the Wolverines were unranked, but it was the first game of the season for Michigan coach Bump Elliott and his squad, and the pollsters were quite simply wrong. After two early Bruins fumbles, Michigan led, 13–0, at the end of the first quarter. The Wolverines tacked on a field goal in the second quarter, then added two more touchdowns in the second half, one coming on a 92-yard interception return, and the Bruins found themselves down, 29–0. Though UCLA would add a late touchdown on a short run by Mitch Dimkich, it was too little and too late. UCLA lost, 29–6, and the following week provided another tough opponent. After losing to Michigan at The Big House, they took on Ohio State University at Ohio Stadium, more commonly known as "The Horseshoe." UCLA played well against the No. 8 Buckeyes. The 82,992 fans saw an unexpectedly close game. UCLA's defense played very well, led by Andy Von Sonn and Mel Profit. OSU's offense was predicated on a ground game, and All-American fullback Bob Ferguson was not accustomed to being slowed down the way he was on this day. UCLA held Ferguson to just 29 yards on the day. Entering the fourth quarter, UCLA led by a score of 3–0 on a Bobby Smith field goal. UCLA made a valiant effort, but in the fourth quarter, the better team came alive. OSU scored twice in the final frame and won by a score of 13–3.

UCLA had started the season with three consecutive road games, two of which were against traditional powerhouse programs of the Big 10 Conference. When the Bruins made their way back to Los Angeles and played in front of their home crowd at the Los Angeles Coliseum, it was a relief, but even that schedule was not easy. UCLA still had two nonconference opponents to play before the conference season began, and both were formidable opponents. On October 14, the Vanderbilt University

Rob Smith converts a fake punt against Michigan, 1961 (Southern Campus Collection)

Commodores made their way to Los Angeles, and with them came a fighting spirit that would challenge the Bruins for four quarters. Despite it being UCLA's first home game of the season, a very small crowd of just over 23,000 fans showed up to see the two opponents battle. The reason for this was the extreme heat. Temperatures reached a reported 119 degrees. One could not blame the UCLA secondary for a sluggish performance in such extreme temperatures. Vanderbilt was three times able to beat the Bruins through the air for touchdowns, but the UCLA ground game more than made up for it. Sophomore tailback Mike Haffner performed admirably, finishing with 157 yards and one touchdown on the day. Bobby Smith added two touchdowns, and Kermit Alexander added another. UCLA won, 28–21. In the final week before conference play began, UCLA took on a now-familiar foe, the Pittsburgh Panthers. As the temperature dropped back into the normal October range, the Bruins played a more complete game. Haffner and Smith once again led the Bruins offense. The UCLA defense hounded the Panthers all day, and following a Carmen di Paulo interception and long return, the Bruins sealed the game on a short Almose Thompson touchdown: 20–6 Bruins.

When conference play began, the Bruins were 3–2. They had lost to two tough opponents but also had three quality wins. The first game of the AAWU season was against the Stanford Indians. Through the first quarter and a half, UCLA could get nothing going on offense. The defense held firm and the game was scoreless. With the second quarter winding down and halftime nearing, Mike Haffner led an 82-yard drive, capped by a Haffner score from the 1-yard line. Stanford, with just enough time before half for one last possession, got into field goal range, or so they believed. On the last play of the half, the Stanford kick was caught out of the air by Kermit Alexander and returned 94 yards into the end zone! UCLA's defense continued to dominate in the second half, and the offense added another score. UCLA passed its first conference test. Bobby Smith and the Bruins would go on to trounce the California Golden Bears, 35–15, the following week, when Smith rushed for 177 yards and scored three touchdowns. Following the win over California, UCLA took on Texas Christian University in a late season nonconference game. The Horned Frogs were no match. UCLA 28, TCU 7.

The annual Homecoming matchup pitted the UCLA Bruins and the two-time defending AAWU champion Washington Huskies. A crowd of approximately 33,000 fans showed up at the Coliseum and saw a thriller. Perhaps too caught up in the Homecoming festivities, the Bruins started a step slow and were quickly down on the scoreboard. Charley Mitchell of the Huskies fielded the opening kickoff at the 6-yard line and 94 yards later crossed the goal line. On the Bruins' first drive they fumbled, and Washington converted the miscue into a field goal. Before the crowd could settle in, UCLA was down, 10–0. While the Huskies' scores came in the blink of an eye, the Bruins' comeback was slow and deliberate. UCLA moved the ball, playing a field position game, and twice took advantage of steady progress. Both Bruins scores came on short runs by Haffner after long, sustained drives. Entering the fourth quarter, UCLA led, 13–10. If the Bruins could hold on, they would clinch a berth in the Rose Bowl. If not, the season would once again come down to a final matchup with the Trojans. UCLA's defense was tough but ultimately made two major mistakes that put the Huskies in position to score. After the Bruins were twice called for defensive penalties, UW had the ball deep in Bruins territory. There were just minutes to go when Bill Siler broke free and found the end zone. UW took the lead, 17–13. With little time on the clock, UCLA was forced to abandon the run game and let the ball fly through the air. The desperate attempt at a comeback failed, and UCLA fell. Dreams of the Rose Bowl would not become a reality on this day. McKay and the Trojans had soundly defeated the heavily favored Bruins in 1960 and had plans to do the same in '61. UCLA was once again the better team but would have to finish the job this time in order to win the conference title and head to the Rose Bowl. Fifty-seven thousand fans braved the elements and sat in the rain to see the two crosstown teams battle. After an early Trojans fumble, Bobby Smith put the Bruins on the scoreboard first with a short field goal. Neither offense could muster up much in the first half, and the only other scoring would come from the special teams. After the UCLA offense was pushed back near their own goal line, Pete Beathard of the Trojans hauled in a punt near midfield and raced to the end zone for the first touchdown of the day. At halftime, USC led, 7–3. If coach Barnes and staff were to avoid being upset by the men of Troy for the second year in a row, they would have to play an inspired second half. In the third quarter, the Bruins defense supplied the play of the day. USC dropped back to pass. UCLA end Mel Profit reached up, deflected the pass, and Joe Bauwens ran underneath it, made the interception, and returned it to the Trojans 33-yard line. UCLA's offense took over from there and, inspired by the big play of Profit and Bauwens, marched into the end zone. Touchdown Bruins! UCLA held on to beat the Trojans, 10–7, and were headed to the Rose Bowl!

On January 1, 1962, UCLA played in their fifth Rose Bowl game. In their previous four appearances, UCLA had not yet scored a victory. They lost to Georgia in 1943, Illinois in 1947, Michigan State in 1954, and Michigan State in 1956. Though the Bruins team was not as strong as the team that lost to MSU less than a decade earlier, this team was hitting its stride just in time for the big game. Kermit Alexander, Mike Haffner, Almose Thompson, Ron Hull, Mitch Dimkich, Foster Anderson, Steve Bauwens, Tony Fiorentino, Joe Rosencrans, Chuck Hicks, Bobby Smith, Ezell Singleton, and the rest of the Bruins didn't plan on just competing in the Rose Bowl; they were determined to be winners. In order to win the first Rose Bowl game in school history, the No. 16-ranked Bruins would have to defeat the defending National Champion and No. 6-ranked Minnesota

Kermit Alexander runs against the University of Minnesota in the 1962 Rose Bowl (Southern Campus Collection)

Golden Gophers. UCLA got off to a fine start. After receiving the opening kickoff, marching down the field with relative ease, and kicking a field goal, it appeared the Bruins would be serious contenders for the win. The Gophers, however, responded in a way the Bruins could not handle. Following a successful stop by the Bruins defense, the UCLA offense took over deep in their own territory and then made a momentum-changing mistake. The Bruins fumbled, and Minnesota recovered the ball and punched in for a quick touchdown. The Gophers led, 7–3, and never looked back. In the second quarter, Minnesota added another touchdown to make the score 14–3, and in the fourth they added an insurance score and went on to win, 21–3. The first Rose Bowl victory for the Bruins would, again, have to wait. UCLA finished the season with a 7–4 record.

The Downtown Athletic Club named Ernie Davis from Syracuse University the 1961 Heisman Trophy Winner.

The Associated Press named the University of Alabama the 1961 National Champions.

## 1962

After the successful season of 1961, the 1962 season was a disaster. UCLA had gone from two wins in Bill Barnes's first year to five in his second season to back-to-back seven win seasons. In 1962, all momentum the Bruins may have appeared to have was lost, and the debacle of the new season proved to be the beginning of the end for coach Barnes in Westwood.

The UCLA season started off with a matchup that eight years earlier was the one everyone wanted. For the second year in a row, UCLA took on the Ohio State Buckeyes, and this time Woody Hayes had his team ranked No. 1 in the country. Despite its Rose Bowl berth the previous season, UCLA was unranked. The biggest change UCLA made was a switch to a different primary offense. Coach Barnes, though often criticized for holding onto his belief in the single wing offense, did have success in running it. But in '62, he'd had enough of the criticism and decided to upgrade the offense by switching to the now-popular T formation. With the team's new offense and a largely inexperienced roster, many fans knew that it could be a long season for the Bruins. The thought of taking on the top-ranked team in the country weighed heavily on the minds of even the most dedicated fans. UCLA played well, however. After all, Kermit Alexander was back, and he would prove to be one of the best players in America. Forty-eight thousand fans saw the Bruins take on the Buckeyes at the Coliseum. UCLA was a 14-point underdog, and few expected them to actually compete with the powerful squad from Columbus, Ohio. On the opening kickoff, UCLA made a statement. They would not only compete; they were there to win. After kicking off to the Buckeyes and making a hard tackle, the ball came free, and UCLA recovered. On the first offensive play of the game, Alexander found a seam off left tackle and raced 45 yards to the end zone. Just like that, the Bruins were on top, 6–0, and the Buckeyes were stunned. The UCLA offense struggled for the rest of the day, but the defense held strong. Ohio State would drive to the Bruins' 1-yard line four times, but, miraculously, UCLA held the Buckeyes scoreless on three of those trips. Still, the difference on the scoreboard came on an extra point. Ohio State led, 7–6, late in the game. With minutes to go, UCLA had the ball and was driving. With now under a minute, the fate of the game would be in the hands, or foot, of sophomore Larry Zeno. As the clock ticked down, Zeno and the Bruins lined up for a field goal. The snap was perfect. The hold was flawless. The kick was up and straight through the uprights from 24 yards out. There was never any doubt. UCLA stunned Woody Hayes and the

Buckeyes. They stunned the college football world. UCLA 9, Ohio State 7.

Despite beating the top-ranked Buckeyes, the Bruins were still unranked when they took on Colorado State in Week 2. UCLA would have no problem dismantling a porous CSU team that, in the midst of a 19-game losing streak, was quite a significant drop-off in competition from OSU. After leading by only 13–7 at halftime, the Bruins finally woke up and dominated the second half to win by a score of 35–7. Despite the 2–0 start, the collapse of the Bruins turned out to be inevitable. In Week 3, UCLA lost a close game to the University of Pittsburgh. After a scoreless first half, the Panthers scored the first touchdown of the game in the third quarter, and after a bad snap on the point after touchdown attempt, the holder, Jim Traficant, picked up the snap, scrambled around, directed traffic, and hit Rick Leeson in the end zone for the fluke two-point conversion. UCLA came right back and scored on the Bruins' next possession but failed on a two-point try. The Bruins then turned the ball over twice in the fourth quarter and suffered their first defeat of the season. In Week 4, the Bruins struggled again. The game was poorly played on both sides. The Stanford Indians, coming in as nine-point underdogs, proved not to be better than expected, but UCLA proved to be worse. The two teams combined for 11 turnovers, and when the game was finally over, the Indians led on the scoreboard, 17–7. It was an embarrassing loss for coach Barnes and the Bruins, and when they entered the month of November with a 2–2 record, all excitement generated by the opening week win over Ohio State was gone. The team was lost and needed something, or someone, to get them back on track.

When the Bruins went to Berkeley to take on the California Golden Bears on November 3, they desperately needed a win. After suffering an embarrassing defeat at the hands of the Stanford Indians, the season was on the brink of collapse. UCLA scored first on a 24-yard rushing touchdown by Kermit Alexander. A senior in '62, Alexander was the clear leader of the team. He would go on to play in the National Football League for 11 seasons with the 49ers, Rams, and Eagles. Before he was a professional, however, he was a Bruin, and against Cal his team needed him most. After his first-quarter touchdown, Cal came back with a touchdown and a field goal to take a 9–6 lead. Before halftime, Alexander found the end zone once again, and the Bruins took a 13–9 lead into the break. The game was a back-and-forth seesaw match. Cal scored first in the second half to take the lead, but Alexander score for a third time, and the Bruins took the lead once again. After the Bruins stopped the Bears, Alexander scored his fourth touchdown of the day, and UCLA went on to win, 26–16. It took a brilliant performance from a brilliant player, but UCLA was back in the win column.

The rest of the season brought very little success for the Bruins. After defeating the Golden Bears, UCLA lost to 10-point underdog Air Force Academy. Things went from bad to worse the following week, when the Bruins traveled to the University of Washington and lost, 30–0. Huskies fullback Junior Coffey dominated the Bruins' weakened defense, and the offense was shut out for the first time in 36 games. The 30-point loss was the worst for the Bruins since 1950. The team was now 3–4 on the season when they were tasked with playing the top-ranked USC Trojans. John McKay's undefeated squad was led by Pete Beathard, Bill Nelson, Ben Wilson, Willie Brown, and a strong defense. Though the Bruins were battered, they had beaten the top-ranked Ohio State Buckeyes in Week 1 and they planned on beating the top-ranked Trojans in their annual rivalry matchup. The largest crowd the Coliseum had held for a college football game since 1955—86,740—crammed in to watch the big game. They saw the Bruins dominate the Trojans physically for much of the game. Despite looking like the better team for three quarters, UCLA only led, 3–0, entering the final frame. The Bruins' defense had stopped USC in its tracks all game, but the offense continually wasted opportunities. After a brilliant goal-line stand by the Bruins defense in the fourth quarter, UCLA's offense was pinned deep, and after three unsuccessful plays, they were forced to punt. USC got great field position, and with the game on the line, they were forced to go for it on fourth down and long. Beathard launched a pass to Willie Brown, who jumped and made a spectacular catch before going down at the Bruins' 2-yard line. The UCLA defense was unable to replicate the goal-line stand of minutes earlier, and USC scored the go-ahead touchdown. UCLA turned the ball over on downs deep in its own territory, and USC took over. The Trojans scored a meaningless touchdown at the end of the game and went on to win, 14–3. The Trojans were off to the Rose Bowl.

Larry Zeno attempts a pass against Cal, 1962 (Southern Campus Collection)

UCLA would play the final two games of the disappointing season against Utah and Syracuse. The Bruins beat the Utah Redskins, 14–11, in dramatic fashion to claim their fourth win of the season but would fall to the Orangemen, 12–7, in the final game of the year. The 1962 season had been a step back. Coach Barnes and company were looking to build off a Rose Bowl berth in '61 but fell to only four wins in '62.

The Downtown Athletic Club named Terry Baker from Oregon State University the 1962 Heisman Trophy Winner.

The Associated Press named the University of Southern California the 1962 National Champions.

## 1963

What turned out to be a memorable, albeit sad, year for the United States was a forgettable one for the UCLA Bruins football program. The season started on September 20 against the University of Pittsburgh Panthers. When the season kicked off, coach Barnes, staff, and players were solely focused on football. Two short months later, the world would stand still. While many fans were focused on the gridiron, a deranged man named Lee Harvey Oswald had his sights set on a plan to change the world and would carry out his deed on November 22.

The UCLA season started off not with a bang, but with a beatdown. Pittsburgh dominated the Bruins. The Panthers gained 409 yards and held the Bruins to just 103. UCLA's defense struggled to get off blocks from the Pittsburgh offensive front and failed to tackle when they finally reached the ball carrier. The Bruins offense were unable to protect their three quarterbacks and couldn't open up any holes for the backfield. The quarterbacks completed just four of 19 passes. The Bruins offense failed to light up the scoreboard even once, and the defense gave up three scores. The first game of the season resulted in not only a disappointing loss, but a depressing one. The 20–0 score could have been much worse, and the Bruins looked inadequate to start the season. The second game of the season for UCLA was against another opponent from the state of Pennsylvania, this one taking place on the road. The Penn State Nittany Lions, led by Coach Rip Engle and superstar Assistant Coach Joe Paterno, were another formidable opponent. They had opened the season with an impressive victory over the University of Oregon and entered this second game with supreme confidence. The Bruins and the Nittany Lions traded touchdowns for the first three-and-a-half quarters. The two Bruins scores came on passes from Larry Zeno to Mel Profit and Bobby Richardson. The score was 14–14 with five minutes to play when Penn State Kicker Ron Coates hit the go-ahead field goal. On the Bruins' last drive, Zeno drove the offense down the field and into Nittany Lions territory. With the ball at the 28-yard line, Zeno dropped back and fired a pass, which was tipped in the air and landed in the hands of a waiting Penn State defensive back. The game was over. UCLA's record dropped to 0–2.

The third game of the season was the Bruins' first realistic chance at victory. UCLA went north to Palo Alto, and after receiving the opening kickoff, they marched down the field with ease. Despite the successful drive, UCLA was forced to settle for a field goal after being stopped at the Indians' 3-yard line. Though UCLA's offense continued to struggle, it appeared they would enter the halftime break with a lead. The score was still 3–0 when Larry Zeno took a chance he should not have. His pass was intercepted, and the Indians capitalized on the mistake with a 22-yard touchdown. UCLA trailed at halftime, 7–3. UCLA's offense struggled in the second half, as well. The only scoring came on a Stanford safety, and the score was 9–3 in the fourth quarter. If UCLA were to win, they would need a big play. Down by only six points, Bob Richardson had victory in his sights and was determined to be the hero. Late in the fourth quarter, he intercepted an Indians pass and returned it all the way to the Stanford 5-yard line. Johnny White then raced to the outside and into the end zone for the game tying touchdown! Zeno kicked the extra point, and the Bruins won, 10–9! It was their first victory of the season.

The following week, the Bruins began a losing streak that ultimately lost Coach Barnes the support of the majority of Bruins fans who still clung to hope that he was the coach to take them to the next level. For two consecutive weeks, UCLA was not competitive in losses to nonconference opponents. Syracuse University beat the Bruins, 29–7, on October 11, and the University of Notre Dame beat the Bruins, 27–12, the following week. With No. 4 University of Illinois on the schedule, things were not looking good for the Bruins.

Bill Barnes was the head coach of the UCLA Bruins, and he would do what he saw fit even if it wasn't working. When the Bruins took on the Illinois Fighting Illini, the things that Coach Barnes had preached for years started to work a little better. UCLA was the inferior team and entered the game as 10-point underdogs. The Bruins, however, came out of the tunnel ready to play football. They led for most of the game, but holding the opposing talent back for four quarters is often a task impossible for the weaker opponent. Illinois took a fourth-quarter lead, 18–12, and the Bruins were still in a position to do what they had done against the Stanford Indians. Down a score, they needed to mount one drive to knock off one of the best teams in the land. But, unlike the Stanford game, there would be no theatrics and no hero returning to Westwood. The Illini held, and UCLA lost, 18–12, for the its third consecutive defeat.

The losing streak would eventually reach five games. After a hard-fought battle with Illinois, the Bruins were steamrolled by a California Berkeley team that was only 2–3–1 at the time. The Bears beat the Bruins, 25–0. A week later, UCLA was once again handily beaten. The Air Force Academy Falcons had a strong offense, and when the Bruins traveled to Colorado Springs, they knew they had to stop one man in order to have a chance. Terry Isaacson was one of the best players in AFA history, and on this day, he single-handedly beat the Bruins. Isaacson himself accounted for 258 yards, more than the entire Bruins team. The final score, 48–21, represented a new low point for Coach Barnes and the Bruins. It was the most points UCLA had given up in a single game since 1930.

On Saturday, November 16, Coach Barnes and the Bruins were at the Coliseum taking on the Washington Huskies. UW would go on to win the AAWU and represent the conference in the Rose Bowl for the third time in four years. The Bruins were just a lowly 1–7 entering the game. To the surprise of all in attendance, the Bruins were simply the better team on this day. The University of Washington was shocked when UCLA played its best game of the season. Quarterbacks Zeno and Steve Sindell were sensational. Sophomore fullback Byron Nelson caught two touchdown passes, and the Bruins defense shut out the high-powered Huskies offense. All-American fullback Junior Coffey struggled to crack the Bruins code and finished with only 28 yards. The final score was 14–0 Bruins. UCLA's players carried Bill Barnes off the field on their shoulders. It was the team's best win of the season. But the joy and pleasure of the Bruins and their fans—indeed, of the entire nation—would be short-lived. In one week, all would mourn.

The Bruins were supposed to take on the rival USC Trojans on November 23, 1963. But plans would change. On Thursday, November 21, Air Force One landed in San Antonio, Texas. President Kennedy traveled to Houston and Fort Worth, and then it was on to Dallas the following day. it was there that the president was killed, assassinated in Dallas.

The nation mourned, and sports was no longer on the minds of most Americans. Most college football games were pushed back one day. UCLA's final game would not be played until the following Saturday. USC Coach John McKay was adamant that no game should be played on Sunday and insisted that the matchup be pushed back a week. Though the annual UCLA-USC football game was always one of the most grandiose sporting events in the nation, hardly anyone seemed to care in 1963. The final score was USC 26, UCLA 6. Mike Garrett, Pete Beathard, and the Trojans were simply too much for a beaten-down Bruins squad. UCLA finished the season with a disappointing 2–8 record.

The Downtown Athletic Club named Roger Staubach from the United States Naval Academy (Navy) the 1963 Heisman Trophy Winner.

The Associated Press named the University of Texas the 1963 National Champions.

## 1964

1964 was the beginning of a dynasty at UCLA—but in a different sport. John Wooden and the UCLA men's basketball team won the National Championship. UCLA was a well-balanced team. Gail Goodrich was the leading scorer, averaging over 21 points per game, and Walt Hazzard, Keith Erickson, and Jack Hirsch each averaged double figures, as well. UCLA capped the season by defeating the Duke University Blue Devils in the National Championship game on March 21. Coach John Wooden was named the National Coach of the Year. Bill Barnes and the football program had a different task. They were not competing at the national title level, but rather were looking to at least have a winning season. Nineteen sixty-three had been one of the worst seasons in UCLA football history, and if '64 wasn't to be any better, Coach Barnes would not be long for Westwood.

When UCLA took on the University of Pittsburgh on September 12, it was the seventh consecutive season the two teams faced each other (they would end up playing 14 out of 15 years). To that point, UCLA had a 2–4 record, with every game having been played between the two teams during coach Barnes's tenure. The 1964 matchup took place in Pittsburgh, and after being embarrassed the year before by losing 20–0, the Bruins would achieve a turnaround, upsetting the Pitt Panthers in Week 1 by a score of 17–12. In Week 2, the Bruins again avenged a loss from the previous year. When the Penn State Nittany Lions traveled to Los Angeles, they were in for a rude awakening. The Bruins would come out on top, and it was a long trip home for the Nittany Lions, who must have expected to make the journey to Los Angeles a victorious one. When conference play began, the Bruins had no plans to slow down. In Week 3, UCLA defeated Stanford University by a score of 27–20. To the shock of observers, most of whom had good cause for low expectations, the Bruins were 3–0. They had surpassed the previous season's win total through only three games. Maybe coach Barnes would save his job after all.

Though the early season success was something to be cherished and enjoyed by all, astute observers were aware that the season was only going to get much tougher. The opponents that lay ahead were no slouches. On October 10, reality set in for the Bruins when they traveled to Syracuse to take on the Syracuse University Orangemen. The team from upstate New York had a man that no one could contain. Floyd Little would carry on the running back tradition at Syracuse and would wear number 44, just like previous greats Jim Brown and Ernie Davis. Little was a freshman in '64, however, and though he would go on to be a three-time All-American, he was ineligible as a freshman. In 1983, he was elected to the College Football Hall of Fame. But Little's teammates didn't need him on this day, and the Orangemen dismantled the Bruins, 39–0. The following week, UCLA was on the road

UCLA football, 1964 (Southern Campus Collection)

once again. This time, they took on No. 4 Notre Dame. The Fighting Irish, behind Coach Ara Parseghian, would go 9–1 on the season and finish No. 3 in the Associated Press poll. Their lone loss? Not at the hands of the Bruins. The Irish would lose only to USC in their final game of the season. They beat UCLA by a score of 24–0. Then, in their third consecutive away game, the Bruins lost again. The University of Illinois beat UCLA, 26–7, on October 24. After a surprising 3–0 start, the Bruins were now 3–3 following three blowout defeats in a row. With four games to go in the season, there was still hope the Bruins could finish with a winning record, but they would have to do what they couldn't in previous years—finish strong.

When UCLA played its fourth consecutive away game on Halloween, the team was desperate for a win. Record-setting quarterback Larry Zeno, Kurt Altenberg, Dick Peterson, Jim Sykes, and the rest of the Bruins offense had only scored a total of seven points over the last three weeks. Bob Richardson, Mike Hafner, Gerald Jones, and the rest of the defense had given up almost 30 points per game in the losing streak. When the Bruins went to Berkeley, the offense woke up, the defense did enough, and their luck changed. UCLA escaped with a win in a wild game by a score of 25–21.

With the Bruins now at 4–3, they were back above .500, and though it may have seemed like a small task to the National Champion team of a decade earlier, a winning season was a worthwhile goal to the '64 bunch. To come out with a winning record, they would need to win two of the remaining three games. To avoid a losing record, they would need to win one. Their opponents, however, cared little about UCLA's goals and were intent on taking them down. UCLA still had to face the Air Force Academy, University of Washington, and the University of Southern California. It was a tough schedule, but the games were set and there was no backing out

When the Bruins took on the Air Force Falcons, it was their first home game in over a month. After trips to Syracuse, South Bend, Champaign, and Berkeley, the familiarity of the Coliseum was a welcome sight. Air Force, which had scored 48 points on the Bruins the year before, had no issues heading west to face the improved opposition. The Falcons beat the Bruins once again, this time by the score of 24–15. When UCLA hit the road once again, they had another tough task. They had upset the Washington Huskies in '63, but doing so again proved to be too difficult to repeat. Washington beat the Bruins, 22–20. When the Bruins took on the USC Trojans in the final game of the 1964 season, it was no contest. John McKay was building a legacy at USC, while building a constant winner. Bill Barnes was finished at UCLA. Though he took one team to a Rose Bowl, his overall tenure as the UCLA head coach was disappointing. He was perhaps not yet ready for the job, but with the sudden death of Red Sanders in '58, he was forced into duty. UCLA finished the 1964 season with a 4–6 record, and in '65, they would start a new era.

The Downtown Athletic Club named John Huarte from the University of Notre Dame the 1964 Heisman Trophy Winner.

The Associated Press named the University of Alabama the 1964 National Champions.

# CHAPTER 9
# Tommy Prothro (1965–1970)

James Thompson "Tommy" Prothro was a born football coach. He was a natural. Prothro learned from two men: his father and Red Sanders. "Doc" Prothro taught Tommy about life, responsibility, and competition. Red Sanders taught him leadership. Behind the greatest football teams in UCLA history, there was Tommy Prothro. When Red Sanders was building a dynasty, Prothro was building a résumé. The education of Prothro, which led him from Memphis, Tennessee, to the College Football Hall of Fame, was a lifelong venture. Prothro would never stop learning and never stop spreading his influence. He was a tactical master. It began in 1920.

Tommy Prothro was born on July 20, 1920. Tommy's father, Doc, was a dentist. The story of Doc's life itself can fill a book. He was a fascinating man who raised a fascinating family. Doc was a baseball man. While pitching for a local semipro team in Dyersburg, Tennessee, he was spotted by Major League Baseball scout Joe Engel of the Washington Senators. Engel liked what he saw and decided to come back to see Doc play several more times. After speaking with Engel, who had enormous power for a scout, Doc signed a Major League Baseball contract with the Senators and was paid a generous salary of $500 per month. Though Doc only played football, basketball, and ran track, in high school, he had made it big in baseball. His life in dentistry would be put on hold. Doc skipped the minor leagues altogether and went directly to the Majors, where he debuted on September 26, 1920, at the Polo Grounds in New York. Tommy was just two months old when his father made the career switch from dentist to Major League Baseball player. He grew up in sports. The path his father would take would be one of many twists and turns, but Tommy was there for the ride, learning from the man he would come to admire throughout his life.

After a brief stint with the Washington Senators, Doc was back to dentistry and semipro ball the following year. When the Senators chose to send him down to the minor leagues, Doc refused and instead decided to return to his old life. In 1923, Doc gave baseball another shot. Though Tommy was just three years old, he would later come to see this as a teaching moment. One should never give up on his dreams. In '23, Doc was reinstated to the Washington Senators roster, but immediately his contract was sold to the Memphis Chickasaws, a Class A minor league team. For 12 years, Doc would play professional baseball. The dentist who was seen at a local semipro game played the most popular sport in

Tommy Prothro looking on, 1968 (Southern Campus Collection)

America on the biggest stage. He would spend time with the Senators, Chickasaws, and the Boston Red Sox. He spent eight years as a player-manager. After retiring from the game as a player, he continued to manage. After four years as minor league manager in the Red Sox system, Doc became the manager of the Philadelphia Phillies. For three years, he managed the low-budget Phillies before returning home to Memphis in '42, taking ownership of the Chickasaws, and managing for six more seasons. Doc was a baseball man. His son, Tommy, who was along for the ride, would blaze his own trail. He preferred the game on the 100-yard field. He preferred football.

Just after Tommy's father had finished his final season managing the Little Rock Travelers, Tommy enrolled at Duke University. A tall, imposing man, Tommy was a natural on the offensive line. He had a passion for learning the game of football and had coaching on his mind from the day he set foot on the Durham campus. Tommy played for legendary Duke coach Wallace Wade and was a key member of the 1941 Southern Conference Championship team and 1942 Rose Bowl participant. As a senior, Tommy was named the Jacob Award Winner as the best blocker in the conference. After a successful playing career, Tommy's career in coaching began, but it wouldn't be long until he hit a speed bump.

Though drafted by the New York football Giants in 1942, Tommy knew that coaching was the career path best suited for him. His first stint on the sideline would be at Western Kentucky University, where he coached for just one year. When the United States entered World War II, everything changed. Tommy joined the United States Navy and served for 39 months. Upon completion of his duty, Tommy returned to his passion. While serving for over three years, he had constantly thought about the game of football and became a master tactician. He thought about strategy and how to counter different defenses. In 1946, Tommy joined the staff at Vanderbilt University. After one year as the freshman coach, he was promoted to the varsity staff. In 1949, he went west with Red Sanders and became the architect of one of the greatest offensive units of the 1950s.

For six seasons, Tommy Prothro was the backfield coach for the greatest offense in the Pacific Coast Conference and one of the best in the nation. Coach Sanders lived by the single wing offense, and Prothro lived to outthink the opposition. He was a strategist and a philosopher. Coach Prothro was the brains and coach Sanders was the leader. In his six seasons as an assistant in Westwood, coach Prothro learned to blend the two. When Prothro took the head coaching position at Oregon State University in 1955, he brought something to the Pacific Northwest that was missing: toughness. Wearing his fedora, always carrying his briefcase full of game notes and scouting reports, and donning a cigarette, Prothro went to Corvallis and changed a culture. His Oregon State teams were typically neither big nor fast, but they were always good. They were disciplined and worked hard. After coming off a National Championship with the Bruins, Prothro had a monumental task ahead of him in 1955. He took over a team that had won one one game the previous year. Tommy Prothro was a complex man, but his position on leadership was basic. He was a master motivator. If he could get his teams to play hard and give maximum effort, he could live with the results. He knew that strategically there were few, if any, coaches in the nation who grasped the game as well as he did. Prothro prided himself on identifying the weaknesses of his opponents and exploiting them. He moved players from position to positon until he found the fit that would maximize their talents. Though seen as aloof by some, he was loved by many more. One player said he felt like a pawn on Coach Prothro's chess board. Prothro responded, "I don't think of players that way, particularly off the field. I develop a real affection for football players that play for me. They put out tremendous effort, but winning is the most important thing to most football players. To achieve that, a player has to blot out any sentiment that would affect his judgement of his efforts toward helping the team win." Prothro had a fine line to walk. He truly cared for his players and was deeply insulted by the thought of him using them as pawns. For those he developed a closer relationship with, he would cherish not only the discussions about football, but about life. He fiercely defended his players from public scrutiny. Wesley Grant, a black player and defensive lineman, learned valuable lessons from his mentor during their weekly chess matches. Prothro would get to know Grant as an individual. He would encourage and challenge him to stand up for himself when faced with racial inequality. Prothro would say,

"A black man who didn't do anything about certain situations wasn't worth his salt." Gary Beban would speak with Prothro about history and world events. Prothro fought the label of disinterested and aloof his entire career. He was far from either.

At Oregon State, he was an immediate success. After he took over a bottom feeder of a program, OSU won six games in his first year, then seven, then eight. OSU won the PCC two years in a row and went to the 1957 Rose Bowl. Before Prothro's fifth year, the PCC disbanded, and OSU became an independent team. Because of the difficulty in scheduling games, Prothro changed his style and went to something completely foreign to him and mastered it. In 1958, Oregon State University was still running the single wing offense, but because more teams were now using the T-formation offense, scheduling became difficult. Opponents did not want to schedule a single wing team and spend significant time preparing for an offense they would only see once per season. In 1959, Prothro changed his offense, and though he initially struggled, his great football mind would prevail. OSU won only three games in '59, but Prothro continued to study his new formation. OSU would once again dominate. John Ralston would say of Prothro, "He always felt he teaches blocking techniques better than anyone. It's been his main forte. I'm not so sure he isn't right." In 1962, he was right. Oregon State went 9–2 and won the Liberty Bowl. In 1964, OSU, now in the Athletic Association of Western Universities, won the conference and went to the Rose Bowl. A year later, he was at UCLA.

Tommy Prothro brought the Bruins back. After a dominant run under Red Sanders, UCLA struggled for much of Bill Barnes's tenure in Westwood. When Prothro went south, the Bruins' winning percentage went north. Tommy Prothro would lead the Bruins to their first Rose Bowl win in school history. His teams would finish first or second in the conference in all but one year. He would coach UCLA's first Heisman Trophy winner. He would win two-thirds of his games. He would be the first UCLA coach to move on to become a head coach in the National Football League.

Following the 1970 season, Tommy Prothro's reign at UCLA was over. Dan Reeves convinced Prothro he was the man to take the Los Angeles Rams to the next level. Prothro enjoyed the challenge and felt that the NFL game was more complex, more of a thinking man's game. It was a challenge he felt he could not pass up. The Rams were an old team, but Prothro was nearly able to guide them to the playoffs in his first season. After finishing with an 8-5-1 record, the Rams were on the brink of the playoffs. Prothro and the Rams needed the 49ers to lose to the Detroit Lions, and they nearly got the break they needed. The 49ers trailed all game but mounted a fourth-quarter comeback to end the Rams' season. After finishing 6-7-1 the following year, new owner Carroll Rosenbloom fired Prothro. He would not be unemployed for long. The San Diego Chargers, a struggling franchise, quickly hired Prothro. For four seasons and four more games, Prothro was the head coach in San Diego. In '78, he resigned. Following his stint in San Diego, Prothro was on the move again. For three years, he was the Director of Player Personnel for the Cleveland Browns. In 1982, he retired and moved back home to Memphis, Tennessee.

In 1985, Tommy Prothro was diagnosed with prostate cancer. He fought the illness for nearly a decade, but in January, 1993, he was a fragile, nearly broken man. What he said in 1985 was something that helped him battle the disease so long. "I have cancer and nobody knows how it's going to go from there. It's certainly nothing to give up on, but it's certainly something to worry about. I certainly don't intend to give in." The school that he gave so much to was returning the favor. Due to experimental treatments at the UCLA Medical Center, Prothro was able to extend his life. In 1993, after a rest period from treatments, he went home to Memphis. Two years later, Tommy Prothro died. Though a Hall of Fame coach, Prothro preferred to be called a teacher. In his eulogy, it was said, "He was a teacher who took boys and turned them into men . . . Prothro type men of character and integrity."

## 1965

As American soldiers entered Southeast Asia in the early stages of the Vietnam War, Tommy Prothro entered Westwood, and the Bruins' football present and future suddenly changed.

Though the Bruins were picked to finish at the bottom of the now-eight team Athletic Association of Western Universities Conference, there was more talent on the Bruins roster than preseason prognosticators had given them credit for. With the tactical magician and master motivator Tommy Prothro now at the helm, such talent would come to be recognized when games began on September 18. Though coach Bill Barnes had struggled in his time as UCLA's coach, he left a gift for his successor. In 1965, Gary Beban would be eligible for varsity football. After a year on the freshman team, Beban took over as the starting quarterback, and in his first year under center he was named First Team All-Conference and Honorable Mention All-America. Beban was not alone, however. The Bruins were filled with star power. Halfback Mel Farr, split end Kurt Altenberg, offensive tackle Russ Banducci, defensive back Bob Stiles, linebacker Dallas Grider, and the defensive end trio of John Richardson, Edwin Dutcher, and Jim Colletto each joined Beban on the All-Conference team. The 1965 season would be one for the ages. *Sports Illustrated* would name UCLA "The Miracle Bruins," but the name that would stick, to the enjoyment of some and the annoyance of others, was "The Gutty Little Bruins." UCLA was not big, but they were good. With the memory of the Red Sanders era fading into history, Tommy Prothro was the man to bring the Bruins back into national contention.

But the 1965 season did not start out the way Coach Prothro had hoped. With a new coach, a new quarterback, and a new culture of accountability, Prothro would have preferred to start the season with an opponent the Bruins could easily handle. Instead, they opened against the Michigan State Spartans. Little was expected of either team when the season began, but the story of triumph for the '65 Bruins is one that essentially ran a parallel course with the season of the Spartans. Coach Prothro knew better than to believe the preseason hype, or lack thereof. He knew his team was better than predicted, and he knew that any opponent with the quality of athletes on the MSU squad could be as good as any team in the land. The game was played in East Lansing and was nothing if not a snoozer. UCLA struggled offensively, and though the score would not indicate the extent of the mismatch, it was clear that, on this day, UCLA was the inferior team. Despite stopping MSU four times inside the Bruins 30-yard line, UCLA lost, 13–3. The career of a brilliant quarterback began with a loss. Gary Beban finished with 122 yards. But Beban and the Bruins would see the Spartans again.

The first win of the Tommy Prothro era in Westwood came in Week 2, a thriller at Beaver Stadium in University Park, Pennsylvania, against Penn State University. PSU was a fledgling program under head coach Rip Engle. In 1964 they had finished 6–4. In '65, they would finish 5–5. (One year into the future, in '66, they would make a change that would reverse their fortunes as a football program. One year later, the Nittany Lions' Assistant Coach, Joe Paterno, would be the head coach and start a run as one of the greatest college football coaches of all time.) But now, when the Bruins headed east, Joe Paterno was in his final year as an assistant coach. UCLA played well throughout the game until the final minutes. After jumping out to what seemed an insurmountable three-score lead, the Bruins allowed two late touchdowns to let the Nittany Lions creep back in. The Bruins were able to hold on and defeat PSU, 24–22. Beban ran for two touchdowns, and Mel Farr added a TD on a 58-yard dash to the end zone. UCLA took on the Syracuse Orangemen a week later and prevailed once again. The explosiveness of the Bruins offense was on full display, and the strength of the Bruins defense was something to behold. UCLA had proved to be a team to keep an eye on out West. After the defense stopped the Orangemen on the first drive of the game, Beban took advantage of the short field and ran for 27 yards and a touchdown on the first play from scrimmage. The Bruins' second play from scrimmage would have similar results. Beban found Kurt Altenberg for 79 yards and a touchdown. UCLA's defense held All-American Syracuse halfback Floyd Little to 27 yards on 16 carries. UCLA was 2–1, with one game to go before conference play began. UCLA's fourth game of the season was a battle with Big 8 opponent the University of Missouri. Though most people believed the Bruins stood little chance against the team from Columbia, the Bruins dominated in two of the three categories. Offensively, the Bruins were far superior to the Tigers: Beban threw two touchdowns, each from 34 yards out; Byron Nelson was on the receiving end of the first, and Altenberg on the receiving end of the second. The UCLA defense was better than Mizzou's: the Bruins held the Tigers to a total of 146 yards. Where the Tigers outplayed the Bruins was in the special teams category: Missouri had two kick returns that ultimately haunted the Bruins. The better team did not win, but they did not lose. The game ended in a tie, 14–14.

Though the result of the Missouri game did not satisfy the Bruins, plenty of evidence was now available to prove that UCLA was a real contender for the conference crown and national attention. Conference play began on October 23 against the California Berkeley Golden Bears. The game was no match. Prothro, Beban, and the Bruins outsmarted the Bears and outplayed them. Three men reached the end zone multiple times: Beban, Farr, and Norman Dow. Placekicker Kurt Zimmerman also had a fine day, breaking a school record with eight successful extra points. The defense was a wall, stopping the Bears in their tracks. UCLA 56, Cal 3. It was the largest victory for the Bruins in the history of the rivalry. Though the Bruins would have a bit of a letdown the following week against the Air Force Academy, they came away with another victory. UCLA came out flat offensively, and Beban was slowed for the first time since the season opener. The Bruins finally got on the board late in the third quarter on a 31-yard run by Farr and added three more points on a 31-yard field goal by Zimmerman. UCLA 10, AFA 0.

With four games left in the regular season, the Bruins were entering a critical stretch that would define their season. 1965 would either be considered a solid start to a new coaching regime or it could be a truly special season, remembered for decades. UCLA already had as many wins in '65 as they did in all of '64, but they aimed for more. On November 6, the No. 8-ranked Bruins took on the University of Washington. UCLA got off to a slow start, and dreams of the Rose Bowl suddenly became nightmares that the upset-minded Huskies could actually prevail. After seven minutes, UCLA trailed, 14–0. UW quarterback Ted Hullin threw a pair of touchdown passes, both to Dave Williams. The UCLA defense struggled for the entirety of the first half, but the offense gained a bit of momentum. At halftime, UCLA trailed, 24–14. In the third quarter, UCLA's big-play offense would strike quickly. Beban ran 60 yards for a touchdown on the first play of the half and then hit Dick Witcher for a 60-yard score later in the quarter. The Bruins led, 28–24. The defense, atrocious in the first half, was brilliant in the second. Washington was able to mount four drives into Bruins territory in the second half, but all four times they were turned back. UCLA won, 28–24. The Bruins train rolled on the following week. Beban and Farr would each score twice for the Bruins as they handily defeated the Stanford Indians, 30–13.

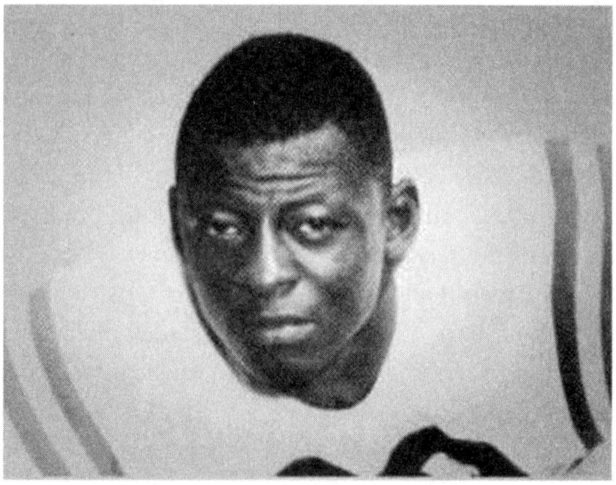

Mel Farr, 1965 (Southern Campus Collection)

Tommy Prothro and John McKay took the UCLA-USC rivalry to a new level. Coach Sanders had instilled in the Bruins a decade earlier a hatred of their crosstown opponent. When Prothro came to Westwood, he came as a peer with John McKay. The Trojans coach would go down in history as a legend, but Tommy Prothro never backed down. He planned on beating the Trojans. He planned on breaking their hearts. On November 20, 1965, the No. 7 Bruins took on the No. 6 USC Trojans before 94,085 fans who packed the Coliseum to see the game that would decide the AAWU conference crown. Both teams sported identical 6–1–1 records, and both had stars on offense who would eventually win the Heisman trophy. The game was a slugfest throughout, and for all fans of either team the pressure was enough to make a man turn away, too nervous to watch. USC received the opening kickoff, and the Bruin defense immediately showed their strength. Three plays and nine yards later, the Trojans punted. The start was exactly what the Bruins hoped for. Their offense came out on fire. After starting at their own 17-yard line, the Bruins drove 24 yards on eight plays before the ball rested in Trojans territory. On the ninth play of the drive, Mel Farr sprinted through a massive hole on the left side and raced 49 yards into the end zone. Just like that, the Bruins were ahead. Zimmerman's PAT attempt was blocked, his first miss in 25 tries, and the Bruins were ahead, 6–0. Though the Bruins got off to a great start, the game was far from over. For much of the battle, the Trojans physically dominated the smaller Bruins. USC back Mike Garrett ran over, around, and through the UCLA defense. He totaled 210 yards on 40 carries for the day. USC reached the end zone just twice, however, on Mickey Upton and Rod Sherman touchdowns. With five minutes to go, UCLA trailed, 16–6. Since the opening drive, Beban, Farr, and the Bruins were continually pushed back by the strong USC defense. The game appeared all but over when Garrett raced around right end to the Bruins 47-yard line, but a clipping penalty brought the ball all the way back to the USC 23. On the next play, momentum changed, and it changed dramatically. USC quarterback Troy Winslow ran to the left, and UCLA linebacker Dallas Grider seemingly came out of nowhere to decleat the USC ball carrier and force a fumble. The ball was loose, and Edwin Dutcher was the Bruin nearest the ball. Dutcher recovered at the USC 34-yard line. Less than a minute later, Beban found Dick Witcher for a score. UCLA went for a two-point conversion, which was good on a short pass from Beban to Byron Nelson. UCLA's situation had gone from hopeless to hopeful. Following the score, it was time for an onside kick by Kurt Zimmerman, who executed perfectly. The ball was kicked diagonally and Grider caught it on the first bounce at the Trojans' 49-yard line. The Bruins quickly got a first down but then were pushed back once again. It was third-and-24 at the USC 48. The play was sent in: X Post 11. The Bruins had called the same play earlier in the game; that time, Beban's pass had been intercepted. This time, the game was on the line. Beban dropped back and delivered a high pass. Altenberg ran under the ball, caught it at the 5-yard line, and raced past the goal line. Touchdown Bruins! USC took over with one final chance to steal the Rose Bowl bid from the Bruins. Garrett ran twice and Winslow threw twice, but it was not enough. USC turned the ball over on downs, and UCLA had completed the comeback. The Bruins would go to the Rose Bowl!

But before the trip to Pasadena, the Bruins played a game that was a rarity on their schedule. After defeating the Trojans in the biggest game thus far in years, UCLA played a nonconference opponent, a good one. On December 4, the No. 5 Bruins took on the No. 7 Tennessee Volunteers in Memphis. The letdown was inevitable. Coach Prothro tried to motivate his players and keep them focused, but it wasn't to be. They had just defeated their arch rivals to win the AAWU and would be taking on the top-ranked team in the nation in the Rose Bowl. UCLA fell to Tennessee, 37–34. Their minds were clearly back in Pasadena.

A crowd of 100,087 packed the Rose Bowl on January 1, 1966. The vast majority expected the Michigan State Spartans, a team that had defeated the Bruins handily in the first game of the season, to clinch the National Championship on this day. For the first time, the AP and Coaches Poll voters would decide the National Champion after the bowl games. UCLA hoped to play spoiler. MSU was 10–0. They had a massive offensive line and a defensive front that most believed was impenetrable. UCLA had played in the Rose Bowl five times in their history and five times came away dejected after being defeated. The Spartans themselves had beaten the Bruins twice in the Rose Bowl, in close affairs in 1954 and 1956. Coach Prothro, a man aware of his place in history and of that which had come before him, cared little about keeping with tradition. He planned on beginning a new tradition, one in which the Bruins go to Pasadena and come back victorious. The game began with a shock. The defense that no one could run on was penetrated. UCLA took possession at its 27-yard line after the opening kickoff. On the first play, Beban ran 27 yards off right tackle, weaving in and out of traffic before being planted at the MSU 46-yard line. The UCLA drive stalled, but the Beban run had flipped field position. After punting, the UCLA defense proved that, although physically much smaller than their opponent, the Bruins were every bit as talented and could stand up to the Jolly Green Giants. Fifty million people watching on television saw the Bruins defense and the Spartans defense battle in the first quarter. It turned into a punting contest as neither offense could threaten the opposition's end zone. With the first quarter coming to a close, UCLA punted again, and Spartans captain Don Japinga fielded the ball at the 6-yard line. Byron Nelson, a Blue-and-Gold special teams ace, raced down the field and made a hard tackle, forcing the ball to come free. UCLA's John Erquiaga recovered, and the Bruins were in business. Beban took advantage of the Spartans miscue and raced left for the end zone. Touchdown Bruins! The extra point was good, and UCLA led, 7–0. After the first touchdown of the game, Coach Prothro made a call that would astound writers one way or another, depending on the result. It was an onside kick! For the second game in a row, Zimmerman executed the kick perfectly, and the Bruins recovered again! Dallas Grader was once again the man who landed on the loose ball. Suddenly, the Bruins were no longer a team that might make the game interesting but eventually falter; they were in position to take a two-score lead. Farr ran for 21 yards. Altenberg pulled in a 27-yard reception. Beban rushed for a 1-yard touchdown! UCLA led, 14–0. The Spartans and the large crowd in Pasadena were stunned. MSU, a proud team, would not quit. They would mount drive after drive in a comeback attempt. UCLA continually stopped them. UCLA's Jim Colletto recovered a fumble. MSU missed a short field goal. With the third quarter winding down, UCLA still led, 14–0, and was looking for more of a cushion. After Bob Stiles intercepted his second pass of the day, Coach Prothro called a trick play. Offensive tackle Larry Stagle gained 35 yards on a tackle eligible play. The drive continued, and UCLA marched to the MSU 12-yard line. On the next play, rolling left, the ball slipped out of Beban's hand. It was free on the ground and Beban dove to recover, but missed. MSU's Don Bierowicz fell on it, and the scoring opportunity was wasted. The Spartans, who all game appeared to be in a funk, suddenly came alive. They gashed the Bruins for long runs. They passed the ball with relative ease. The Spartans reached the UCLA 31-yard line. Fourth and 1 to keep the drive alive. Dwight Lee was the ball carrier. Stuffed! No gain! UCLA took over on downs. MSU had several more chances, and they came in desperation time, but they had the heart of champions and would not quit. Once again it was fourth down and 1. Another handoff to Lee. Another fourth down stop by the Bruins! Down two touchdowns with less than half a quarter to go, the Spartans did what they hadn't done all day—score. After UCLA punted once again, MSU had control, and two plays and 80 yards later, the Spartans were on the board. MSU lined up for the extra point but had no plans to kick the ball. It was a fake! The attempt was futile, and the score was 14–6. UCLA, still ahead, 14–6, with just under half a quarter to play, simply needed to move the ball on offense and keep the clock running. The offense had gone cold, however, and after MSU partially blocked a Larry Cox punt, the unthinkable just minutes earlier was now a possibility. The Spartans took over at their own 49-yard line, down by eight. Now with under five minutes to play, the Spartans had plenty of time to score. Thirteen plays later, it was fourth and 1 again. The ball was at the 2-yard line. Quarterback Jimmy Raye took the ball up the middle on a quarterback sneak and gained the first down by inches. On the following play, Steve Juday crossed the goal line. It was 14–12, and, with just 31 seconds on the clock, the two-point conversion would likely be the deciding play. UCLA would tie in the Rose Bowl or they would win the first in school history. MSU would be the National Champions or they would nervously wait for the results of the voting. The ball was placed on the left hash. The ball was snapped, reverse pivot, pitch to the right to Bob Apisa. This was the same play that had scored a Spartans touchdown earlier. The Bruins' Colletto cut through the backfield and raced for Apisa. He grabbed hold but did not have a strong grip. Apisa fought to break free. Colletto held on with everything he had, and Grider latched on as well, but Apisa would not go down. Finally, with Apisa breaking free and lunging toward the goal line, Stiles knocked Apisa down with a thunderous hit that not only sent Apisa flying to the natural grass of the Rose Bowl field, but sent shockwaves throughout the college football world. UCLA defeated the top ranked Michigan State Spartans, 14–12, in the Rose Bowl! Tommy Prothro had inherited a team that won six games over the previous two years combined and had won eight in his first year. He beat the top-ranked team in the land and won the first Rose Bowl in school history. Tommy Prothro went from being a West Coast name to a national icon. He was named the 1965 National Coach of the Year.

The Downtown Athletic Club named Mike Garrett from the University of Southern California the 1965 Heisman Trophy Winner.

The Associated Press named the University of Alabama the 1965 National Champions.

1966 Rose Bowl (Southern Campus Collection)

Tommy Prothro is carried off the field after the Bruins won the 1966 Rose Bowl (Southern Campus Collection)

## 1966

1965 had been that "special season" the Bruins longed for. "The Gutty Little Bruins" beat the top-ranked Michigan State Spartans in the Rose Bowl. 1966 would prove to be a special season, as well. The success of Tommy Prothro, Gary Beban, and Mel Farr had not been a fluke. UCLA was again a national power. The team was nationally competitive. After a half decade of mediocrity, the Bruins once again had dreams of glory. The Rose Bowl. A National Championship. Coach Prothro brought hope. The players brought grit. The fans brought enthusiasm. The basketball program was thriving under John Wooden. Coach Prothro would try to escape the ever-growing shadow being created by the legendary Wooden. The season began on September 17. The Bruins were the No. 4 team in the land.

The momentum that many believed UCLA had going into the offseason would carry into the new season. UCLA started the fall of 1966 on fire. Led by Coach Prothro and Assistant Coaches Tony Kopay, John Jardine, Ron Siegrist, Bob McKittrick, John Cooper, Jerry Long, Lew Stueck, and Pepper Rodgers, the Bruins handily defeated long-time foe the Pittsburgh Panthers. The "dream backfield" of Beban and Farr opened in 1966 where they had left off the previous year. The Bruins received the opening kickoff and promptly marched downfield for a touchdown on the first drive of the season. At halftime, UCLA led, 29–0. In the second half, Coach Prothro played many of the reserves. After Beban left the game, quality backup Norman Dow led the Bruins to three more touchdowns. UCLA went on to win the season opener, 57–14.

UCLA would play four more nonconference games before the conference season started. In Week 2, the Bruins hit the road for their first away game. For the second year in a row, the Bruins defense stifled Syracuse's All-American, Floyd Little, holding him to just 18 yards on the ground. UCLA started the scoring on a Gary Beban short run, following a Mike Roof fumble recovery. Final score: UCLA 31, Syracuse 12. On October 1, the Bruins were ranked the No. 2 team in the nation as they took on the University of Missouri. Just one year earlier, many viewers had been convinced that UCLA would lose to the Tigers, but times and feelings had changed since then, and now the Bruins were heavily favored. UCLA struggled a bit for the first time in the young season. The Bruins entered the game as the highest-scoring team in the nation but seemed stuck in the mud early. At halftime, their lead was only 3–0. The defense, which was brilliant, kept UCLA ahead in a game in which they could otherwise have found themselves in a deep hole. In the second half, the offense regained the form it had shown in the previous two games. Mel Farr scored twice and Steve Stanley reached the end zone before the Tigers could respond. Respond, they did, however. Mizzou scored two touchdowns before Farr once again reached the end zone, his third TD of the day, and that sealed the game for the Bruins. Though the Bruins now enjoyed a record of 3–0, they had just played their worst game of the season so far, and the challenge would only get tougher. When UCLA next played the Rice Owls, that game would come down to a dramatic finish. The Bruins once again struggled in the first half. At the break, UCLA trailed, 10–8. They would once again need a second-half surge to seal victory, just as they had the week before. Unfortunately, the third quarter came and went, and the UCLA deficit only increased. With fewer than four minutes left to play in the game UCLA trailed, 24–16, when they got the break they needed. Wade Pearson recovered a fumble at the Rice 40-yard line, and three plays later Gary Beban threaded the needle between two Owl defenders to Harold Busby, who held on for the 33-yard score. UCLA was down, 24–22. They would be forced to go for two. The Bruins would go to their bread and butter, a handoff to Mel Farr. The attempt was good! The game was tied, but there was still enough time for the Owls to mount a scoring drive to break the hearts of the unsuspecting Bruins. When great teams play their worst, they still seem to finish strong and make their own breaks. That was the case for UCLA on this day. On the kickoff, the Owls fumbled once again and Larry Agajanian dived on the loose ball. UCLA would run the ball to the 1-yard line before trusty kicker Kurt Zimmerman knocked in a short field goal to win the game. The Bruins escaped, 27–24. Following the close call, UCLA dropped to No. 4 in the rankings. Perhaps it woke the team up. When the Bruins took on the Penn State Nittany Lions and first-year Head Coach Joe Paterno, they were once again at their best. The Bruins offense dominated the program that would years later become known as "Linebacker U." The offense racked up 533 yards, reaching the end zone seven times. Beban and Farr each scored twice for the Bruins. UCLA won, 49–11, and was 5–0 for the season.

The conference opener took place on October 22 in Berkeley against the rival Golden Bears. Though the Bears would put up quite a fight and control the ball for the majority of the game, UCLA was once again too strong. The 1–2 punch of Beban and Farr was spectacular once again, and the UCLA defense was tough enough when the chips were on the line. Sophomore Mark Gustafson intercepted two Berkeley passes, junior Don Manning intercepted one, and senior John Richardson made 10 tackles. UCLA 28, California 15. After the successful conference opener, UCLA was pitted against a nonconference opponent for the final time in 1966 when they took on the Air Force Academy. In the first half, Beban was breathtaking. He finished the day with one touchdown through the air and another two on the ground. The UCLA defense intercepted four passes, one each by Sandy Green, Don Manning, Andy Herrera, and Tod Friend. The Bruins were 7–0 for the first time in 11 seasons.

The Bruins were the No. 3 team in the nation when they took on the University of Washington. All seemed to be going well, and UCLA appeared to be headed for an undefeated season and a possible National Championship. The Bruins were better than the Huskies. UW was a formidable opponent but entered the game with just a 4–3 record. Their team appeared to be better than their record, however. Four weeks prior to the clash with the Bruins, the Huskies had lost a close game to the No. 6 USC Trojans and followed that with a close loss to the Golden Bears. Since the loss to Cal, the Huskies had won two games in a row. They appeared to be playing better football when they took on UCLA. On November 5 against the Bruins, they played their best game of the season. Would it be enough to upset Coach Prothro and the men from Westwood? In the first quarter, UCLA got on the board early with a Kurt Zimmerman field goal. Though UCLA's offense was slowed from its typical pace, they still moved the ball throughout the game. UCLA outgained the Huskies, 267–191, but struggled to finish drives in their customary fashion, which usually wound up in the end zone. The Huskies caught two major breaks that helped them in their hopes for an upset. After an 84-yard kickoff return put the ball deep in Bruins territory, Washington scored on a short drive. They also returned an interception for a score. UW kicker Don Martin added a field goal. When the game was over, UW had scored 16 points. It was the second highest point total UCLA gave up all season, but in each of the first seven games of the season, UCLA had scored at least 27 points and had scored over 30 in five of the seven games. Against the Huskies, Gary Beban was a one-man show, but unfortunately for the Bruins on this day football is a team game. UCLA drives continually stalled. Gary Beban would set a school record for total offense in this game, but UCLA went down by a score of 16–3. It was the first time in two years that the Bruins had failed to reach the end zone. This would no longer be an undefeated season. UCLA had two games left, and they were big ones. The Bruins would defeat the Stanford Indians on November 12, but the win would come with a cost. The game was ugly. Stanford fumbled nine times. UCLA recovered six of those fumbles, which set a conference record. But UCLA also fumbled, four times. Beban got the Bruins on the board in the first quarter with a 24-yard run around left end into the end zone. This would be the final big play of the season for Beban. Though UCLA tacked on a field goal in the fourth quarter, there was no celebration after the game: Gary Beban broke his ankle and would be unavailable for the final game of the season against the hated USC Trojans.

When the Bruins took on the Trojans in the regular season finale on November 19, they were without the services of "The Great One," Gary Beban. Instead, they were forced to rely on super sub Norman Dow, a man who—if not for being behind one of the greatest players in school history—would have been the starting quarterback. Teammates and coaches trusted Dow, but replacing Beban was an impossible task. UCLA was the No. 8 team in the nation. USC was ranked No. 7. It was Homecoming Week in Westwood, and 81,890 fans came out to the Los Angeles Coliseum for the big game. Those who could not attend could watch on national television. The first half was like the early rounds of a boxing match. The opponents took shots but were cautious. The defense prevailed, and, while neither team entered the break punished, neither had put their best foot forward. It was scoreless when coach Prothro of UCLA and coach McKay of USC gathered their men at intermission and urged them to fight for victory. In the third period, UCLA landed the first major shot of the day. Norman Dow and the Bruins offense capped a seven-play drive with a Dow 5-yard run around right end. The PAT was good, and UCLA led, 7–0. Though UCLA had taken the lead, they had sustained another devastating injury. Star linebacker Don Manning had separated his shoulder earlier in the quarter. When USC took possession of the ball, it became clear they would not go quietly. After fullback Mike Hull broke past the first line of defense and ran 57 yards to the 1-yard line before being dragged down from behind, USC evened the score seconds later. With the score tied, 7–7, it was time for Dow and the Bruins to remember the joy they felt when they defeated the Trojans in shocking fashion the year before. The situation was less dire, but they would need to play with the same intensity. They did just that. In the final quarter, UCLA marched 53 yards on seven plays. On one play, Dow sneaked through the line and weaved his way for 26 yards. The final play of the drive came on a 21-yard run by Cornell Champion for a touchdown. Up 14–7, it was up to the Bruins' defense to hold. Defensive lineman Mike Roof made sure his unit would not be defeated on this day. After what turned out to be his eight-tackle performance, he was named Lineman of the Game. UCLA held on to win, 14–7, giving the Bruins a record of 9–1. USC had a 7–2 record, but because the Trojans played one more conference game than the Bruins, a vote would be needed to decide who would go to the Rose Bowl. UCLA finished 3–1 in AAWU play, and the Trojans finished 4–1. Prior to the game, it was widely believed that the winner of the crosstown matchup would receive the Rose Bowl invitation. When Gary Beban broke his ankle, the matter became more complex. The AAWU wanted to send the best team in the conference to the biggest bowl game of all. Despite the excellent performance by Dow and the Bruins win, the question of conference best was still debated. When it was time to vote for the Rose Bowl representative two days after the final game, the Trojans were the team selected. There are many reasons people speculate as to why the Trojans were picked ahead of the Bruins. One of these is that in 1964, when Prothro was at Oregon State, the Beavers were selected over the Trojans, and this was a way to even it out. Despite the Bruins clearly being the better team, an imperfect system ultimately hurt them. While many can point to the poor voting of the coaches as an insulting message to UCLA, the one Coach Prothro chose to express to his players was different. Though they had a great season, the decision was left in the hands of those who didn't deserve it. If the Bruins had defeated the Washington Huskies, they would have been in the Rose Bowl. USC would go on to lose to top-ranked Notre Dame, 51–0, in their final regular season game and lose to No. 7 Purdue, 14–13, in the Rose Bowl. UCLA finished the season ranked as No. 5 by the Associated Press. USC finished unranked.

The Downtown Athletic Club named Steve Spurrier from the University of Florida the 1966 Heisman Trophy Winner.

The Associated Press named the University of Notre Dame the 1966 National Champions.

## 1967

Gary Beban and the UCLA offense, 1967 (Southern Campus Collection)

Coach Tommy Prothro was entering his third season as the UCLA football head coach. Gary Beban was a senior. The Bruins would reach as high as No. 1 in the nation in the Associated Press poll. The era of athletic prosperity in Westwood appeared to have arrived. UCLA had already won three championships in men's basketball under Coach John Wooden, and, in 1967, the team went undefeated. A sophomore by the name of Ferdinand Lewis Alcindor Jr., later to be known as Kareem Abdul-Jabbar, had burst onto the college basketball scene and already established himself as an all-time great. When the football season kicked off on September 16, the Bruins had a simple goal: win every game. It started with the University of Tennessee.

The season opener pitted the No. 8 Bruins and the No. 9 Volunteers in an early-season thriller. In the previous meeting between the two teams, the Volunteers had upset the Bruins in 1965, and UCLA looked forward to avenging that loss. Coach Prothro held back very little when asked about the importance of this game. He wanted to win. Badly. UCLA struggled early. On the first two offensive plays, the Bruins' ball carrier fumbled, and on both occasions a Volunteer was there to recover. Tennessee was quickly up by two touchdowns. The Bruins' running game struggled in the first half. They were still trying to replace a player the caliber of Mel Farr, who was on his way to a Rookie of the Year season in the National Football League. In the second half, sophomore Greg Jones and junior Rick Purdy found their rhythm, and the Bruins offense hit its stride. With four minutes to go, UCLA still trailed. The score was 16–13 in favor of Tennessee, but one man, for whom this would be a miracle season, soon made it known to all in attendance that he was the best player on the field. Gary Beban would not accept defeat. On fourth-and-1, with the ball in Tennessee territory and the game essentially on the line, Beban ran a sweep to the right. He was past the first down marker when he cut left and outraced the desperate Tennessee defenders into the end zone. UCLA won, 20–16. Senior Gary Beban had left his first mark on the new season. It would be far from his last.

Beginning in Week 2, the Bruins had three consecutive games on the road. They would travel over 12,000 miles in total and play three quality opponents. UCLA dismantled the Pitt Panthers, 40–8, then defeated former Pacific Coast Conference and now-Athletic Association of Western Universities opponent Washington State by a score of 51–23. In the final game of the three consecutive road games, the Bruins took on Penn State. After finishing with a 5–5 record in coach Joe Paterno's first season, the Nittany Lions of '67 were a much improved team that would finish the season as the No. 10 team in the nation. UCLA struggled that day. The crowd was hostile in Happy Valley, and the Bruins were sluggish. The first touchdown of the game came on a blocked punt by Vic Lepisto that teammate Hal Griffin recovered and took to the end zone. UCLA would need all the breaks they could get. It took another sensational finish by Beban and the Bruins, but UCLA escaped with a 17–15 victory.

The lineup of opponents didn't get easier, though the travel schedule did. On October 14, the now-No. 4 Bruins were relieved to be back home to take on the California Golden Bears. Rick Purdy averaged six yards per carry, and Beban found Dave Nuttall for two touchdowns. UCLA defeated Cal by a score of 37–14. Stanford kept the game much closer the following week, but once again the Bruins' record remained unscathed. Beban scored two more touchdowns himself and Mike Garratt added one, but still the game's outcome was uncertain until the final minute. The Indians had the ball and a chance to steal a victory, but the UCLA defense held. The Bruins' record climbed to 6–0, and they were now ranked the second best team in the nation when they took on the Oregon State Beavers. What many in the West had known for years was becoming a national story: Gary Beban was a superstar. The rumors that Beban could be a contender, or even the frontrunner, for the most prestigious award in football were growing louder. Beban simply tried to block out the noise.

On November 4, the Bruins' run of outstanding play came to an end. When UCLA took on the Oregon State Beavers, the general public underestimated unranked OSU. They had lost consecutive games earlier in the year to Washington and BYU, but two weeks prior to the game against the Bruins, they had beaten then-No. 2 Purdue, 22–14. The game against Purdue was the first of a stretch of four games for the Beavers that ranks with any of the best four-game stretches for any team in college football history. After beating WSU handily, the Beavers took on the now-No. 2 Bruins. The Bruins were able to penetrate the end zone only once, while OSU scored 16 points. But UCLA kicker Zenon Andrusyshyn kept the Bruins in the game. His three field goals, including a then-school record 52-yarder, meant the score was tied late in the fourth quarter. UCLA received the ball with just over a minute on the clock after the Beavers had tied the game on a field goal. Beban, a late-game magician, went to work. After he quickly moved the ball downfield, Andrusyshyn had one final job to do: kick one through the uprights for a three-point win. The ball was snapped. The hold was good. The kick was blocked! Coach Prothro would say after the game, "The field goal attempt didn't get much height, and if it doesn't get up too high, it's going to get blocked." The final score was 16–16. A disappointing result for the Bruins. For their part, the Beavers would go on to finish their four-game stretch by defeating the top-ranked USC Trojans the following week.

Despite the disappointing tie, the Bruins were still in the picture for the AAWU conference crown and a national title. After avenging the only loss of the '66 season by rolling over the Washington Huskies, 48–0, the Bruins jumped all the way from No. 4 to No. 1 in the Associated Press rankings. UCLA would take on the No. 4 Trojans in their annual rivalry. Gary Beban entered the game beat up. He would have to struggle through a rib injury but was not going to miss the biggest game of the year. USC was led by a junior college running back transfer named Orenthal James Simpson, nicknamed "The Juice." Despite the rib injury and a USC defense that pounded him all game, Beban was brilliant. He connected with George Farmer for a 53-yard touchdown, found Dave Nuttall for a 20-yard strike, and Greg Jones added a 12-yard touchdown run. There could have been more UCLA points on the scoreboard, but Beban threw one interception, the Bruins had two field goals blocked, and the usually reliable Andrusyshyn even missed an extra point. Despite leaving points on the field that should have been on the scoreboard, the Bruins still led, 20–14, with the clock ticking down in the fourth quarter. Facing a crucial third down and 7 in their own territory, O.J. Simpson broke off one of the first memorable runs in the history of color television coverage of college football. Millions of people saw the nationally televised game in which Simpson found a hole off left guard, jumped over a defender, bounced to the outside, raced down the sideline, cut inside at the 30-yard line, and outraced the entire defense to the end zone. Simpson's run was magical. What would have been a short gain for most backs turned into a heartbreaking play for the Bruins. USC would convert the PAT and defeat the Bruins by a score of 21–20. It was a stunner. Simpson finished with 177 yards. Many Bruins players, coaches, and fans would never forget this loss. ESPN would rank the 1967 UCLA-USC game as the greatest game in the history of the rivalry. For the Bruins, the 1967 season would not end with a final triumphant battle, but with another difficult loss. Following the heartbreaking loss at the hands of the Trojans, UCLA faced unranked Syracuse in the final game of the season and was handily defeated. Larry Csonka was unstoppable, and the Bruins never got anything going. It was the final game of Gary Beban's career.

Though the season ended in painful disappointment, one must not overlook the brilliant career of Gary Beban. He had taken over the starting quarterback role in 1965 and helped turn the Bruins program around. In his freshman season, when he was ineligible and Tommy Prothro was still at Oregon State, the Bruins won just four games. In his first season on the varsity squad, the Bruins won the Rose Bowl. The Bruins would defeat the Trojans twice in his three years (though he missed the 1966 game with injury) and helped bring a program back to national prominence. When Beban graduated, he held UCLA records for pass completions in a game (17), total offense in a game (333), touchdowns scored in a game

(3), total offense in a season (2,073 yards), yards passing in a season (1,483), touchdowns scored in a season (14), total offense in a career (5,458 yards), most yards passing in a career (4,087), most passes attempted in a career (465), most passes completed in a career (243), most touchdowns in a career (35), most points scored in a career (214), and touchdowns responsible for in a career (58). In 1967, Beban would win a plethora of individual awards, among them the Maxwell Award. He was named to the All-Conference team three times and was a consensus All-American in 1967. He is a member of the College Football Hall of Fame. Beban was also a Heisman candidate in 1967. When the results of the Heisman voting were announced, it turned out the talking heads were correct. A man from Los Angeles won the Heisman Trophy. It was not O.J. Simpson. He would have to wait.

The Downtown Athletic Club named Gary Beban from the University of California Los Angeles the 1967 Heisman Trophy Winner.

The Associated Press named the University of Southern California the 1967 National Champions.

In 1967, Gary Beban won the Heisman Trophy (Southern Campus Collection)

## Gary Beban

On August 5, 1946, a UCLA legend was born. The boy who would one day be known as "The Great One" grew up in Redwood City, California. His childhood was not typical of many of the boys who grow up to be college football players, but his story is altogether distinctly American. Gary Beban was the son of Frank Beban, a Croatian immigrant. His mother was Italian. Before Gary learned English, he spoke Italian. From the time he was strong enough, Gary was tasked with helping his father, a San Francisco longshoreman. The worst job was moving the banana boats. He would much rather move the coffee bags. Neither was easy for a boy who would rather be out playing with friends. Watching his father work motivated Gary to lead a different kind of life. While Gary was a natural on the football field, and as a man would be one who attracted the public's rapt attention, his father was not often there to see his boy. It was the 1960s, and though Frank loved and supported his son, he had to work. Gary would shine on the field, but football was not the only motivation driven by his father's hard life. Gary was an excellent student and knew that if he applied himself, he could be as successful in the classroom as he was on the football field. He knew that one day it would lead him to a different life. In describing work with his father, he would say, "I would come home and I could barely move. How hard they worked. . . . It was enough to make me realize that I should hit the books a little harder." As it turned out, Gary would excel in both the classroom and on the football field. One would ultimately provide him with the skills to be successful in life. The other made him a legend.

After leading Sequoia High School in both rushing and passing in 1962 and 1963, earning All-League honors both years, Gary Beban took his athletic and academic talents to the University of California Los Angeles in 1964. He played on the freshman team in 1964, then won the starting quarterback job in the spring of 1965. Prior to the start of the season, the media claimed that the Bruins were both small and slow, certainly not a winning combination. What they didn't know, however, was that Coach Prothro had watered down the field in practice so that sportswriters would underestimate the speed of the team. Nor did they know how great Beban would be. Terry Donahue, a defensive lineman and future coach of the Bruins, would claim that the team had two great players, Mel Farr and Gary Beban, several

Gary Beban finished his UCLA career with 13 school records (Southern Campus Collection)

good players, and a bunch of "ragamuffins." Though expectations entering the '65 season were low among outsiders, the team itself believed in coach Tommy Prothro and in their quarterback. UCLA stormed out to a surprising 4–1–1 start before the Associated Press finally ranked the Bruins in their top 25. By the time UCLA met USC in the final regular game of the season, they were No. 7 in the country. USC was led by eventual Heisman Trophy winner Mike Garrett and were ranked No. 6. The winner of the game would go to the Rose Bowl. USC led for much of the game and Beban struggled, turning the ball over twice. With four minutes to play, USC led, 16–6 when Garrett fumbled, and suddenly the Bruins were back in the game. Beban found Dick Witcher for a touchdown and then hit Byron Nelson for the two-point conversion. Minutes later, Beban threw another touchdown, and the Bruins went on to win 20–16. With a National Championship on the line for the Michigan State Spartans in the Rose Bowl, the Bruins played the role of spoiler and played it well. Beban would say of the Spartans, "They were so big, they didn't have to tackle you. They could just throw you down. The field tilted when they came out. Bubba Smith was so big and so strong. George Webster hit me so hard I wasn't sure my bones stayed in the same place." The size of the Spartans only added to the fairytale story that unfolded. The Bruins may not have had the size advantage, but they had a genius in coach Prothro, and the man under center was perfectly able to execute the game plan of his tactically brilliant coach. Assistant coach Pepper Rodgers, teamed with Prothro, came up with new wrinkles to the offense, and UCLA pulled off one of the biggest upsets in Rose Bowl history. The Bruins won, 14–12, and finished No. 5 in the final Associated Press poll.

If Beban's sophomore campaign was his hello to the college football world, the next two years would prove he was there to stay, forever mentioned with the greatest to play the game. As a sophomore, Beban had thrown for 1,483 yards and nine touchdowns and added 590 on the ground with 14 more scores while earning All-Conference honors. As a junior, he threw for 1,245 yards and six scores and rushed for another 10 touchdowns on 454 yards. Even so, his stats did not tell the entire story. Beban executed Coach Prothro's single wing offense to perfection, and in 1966 the Bruins finished 9–1 and were again the No. 5 team in the final AP poll. As a senior, Beban was predictably brilliant and would leave his mark on college football history. With two weeks left in the season, coach Prothro and his star quarterback had the Bruins in a position to pull off a feat achieved only once before in school history. They were ranked No. 1 in the nation. The game that would stick with Beban for the rest of his life was the matchup against O.J. Simpson and the USC Trojans. A crowd of 90,772 fans packed the Los Angeles Memorial Coliseum to see the top-ranked Bruins take on the No. 4 Trojans. The game would go down as a classic. UCLA lost to the Trojans and missed a shot at championship glory. O.J. Simpson's 64-yard touchdown run in the fourth quarter to win the game is considered one of the greatest plays in college football history. Gary Beban passed for 301 yards on the day and appeared to be the best player in America for most of the afternoon. Two weeks later he was named the Heisman Trophy winner, the only winner in UCLA history, in a controversial vote over Simpson. Beban added the Maxwell Award, as well as *Sporting News* Player Of the Year, and numerous First-Team All-America honors to his résumé.

Following a brilliant college career, "The Great One" moved on to the professional ranks, but his greatness came not on the football field, but rather in another venture. In 1968, Beban was drafted by the Los Angeles Rams, but after he failed to come to terms on a contract agreement, his draft rights were traded to the Washington Redskins. That year, Beban played behind veteran quarterback great Sonny Jurgensen. The team finished with a 5–9 record. The next year, coach Vince Lombardi came out of retirement to coach the Redskins. Though the team finished 9–5, Beban still sat on the bench. In September of 1970, the Redskins released Beban. He would be without a team for all of the 1970 season. His final chance would come with the Denver Broncos, who signed him after the 1970 season ended but released him prior to the start of the 1971 season. In the final game of his career, Beban distinctly remembers sitting on the bench for the final play, wondering if he would ever get his shot. Professional football did not work out for Beban the way college did, but his legacy as an athlete will never be forgotten. Beban's impact as a football player can best be described by those closest to him and those who competed against him. Coach Prothro would say of Beban, "It is inconceivable that anyone could be more of a value to a football team than Gary Beban is to ours. He truly is a great one." Penn State football coach Joe Paterno, who lost to Beban and the Bruins in each of his first two seasons, would compare Beban to Roger Staubach. For fans of the UCLA Bruins, he will always simply be "The Great One.'"

Following his retirement from professional football, Beban joined CBRE, Inc., one of the largest real estate groups in the nation. Beban climbed from industrial salesman in 1971 to senior executive managing director in 1998. Gary Beban had found a new passion in life, and the duties that he enjoyed about working for CBRE are the same challenges that made him a brilliant quarterback. In describing his love for the real estate business, he said he most enjoyed: "developing strategies, executing on those strategies, hard work and camaraderie." He sounds like a football player. He sounds like coach Prothro. Gary Beban retired from full-time work in 2008 after 37 years with CBRE. He is still active as a company advisor.

For UCLA and college football fans alike, no player in Bruins history has matched the prestige of Gary Beban. He is the only player in Bruins history to win the Heisman Trophy, and though he rooted for Troy Aikman and Cade McNown to join him, he still stands alone. The memories of "The Great One" will live in Bruins lore forever. In 1984, Gary Beban was honored as a charter member of the UCLA Athletics Hall of Fame. In 1988, he was elected to the National Football Foundation Hall of Fame and the College Football Hall of Fame. He was inducted into the San Mateo County Sports Hall of Fame in 1989 and the Rose Bowl Hall of Fame in 1991. His number 16 jersey is retired by UCLA football, and in 2009, the Bruins wore 1967 throwback jerseys to honor the legacy of Gary Beban. In the half century since Beban won the Heisman Trophy, many great UCLA players have come and gone. Many have had successful NFL careers, and many have earned college football acclaim. Many are more widely known across America and many have made more money than Gary Beban, but no other has won the ultimate individual prize. As Gary Beban eyes his Heisman Trophy, he still thinks back to the days when he took the field in the magnificent blue-and-gold uniforms of the Bruins. He thinks of the game in 1967 against the Trojans, and though the defeat has stuck with Beban for over 50 years, fans think not of defeat, but of the memories. They think of the 1965 team, the ones called "The Gutty Little Bruins," the ones said to be inferior to Michigan State in every way. The ones who toppled the giants. Fans think of the day the "The Great One" was ours.

## 1968

1968 was a year of shock and change for both UCLA and the United States of America. Though U.S. troops had already been fighting for three years in Vietnam, most engagements were relatively small skirmishes with guerrilla fighters. In '68, the war would change with a surprise attack from the North Vietnamese—the Tet Offensive—on January 30 that changed the course of the war.

Back in the United States, the 1960s represented the height of the Civil Rights Movement. No man better represented the Civil Rights Movement than Dr. Martin Luther King Jr. On April 4, 1968, the nation would be shocked once again when Dr. King was shot and killed by James Earl Ray. The Civil

Rights Movement would go on, but it had lost its greatest leader.

In '68, the Bruins would return their highly successful head coach, Tommy Prothro, for his fourth season, but Heisman-winning quarterback Gary Beban was now gone. Replacing him would prove to be very difficult. The leader of the free world would soon also be replaced. President Lyndon B. Johnson decided not to run for reelection in '68, and former Vice President Richard Nixon's "law and order" campaign beat out Democrat Hubert Humphrey and Independent George C. Wallace. The year of '68 would be memorable in the West Coast college sports world for one more off-field change. The Athletic Association of Western Universities was no more. The conference would officially rename itself the Pacific 8 Conference, shortened by many to the Pac 8. The member schools were UCLA, USC, California, Stanford, Washington, Washington State, Oregon, and Oregon State.

The Bruins season was difficult to predict. Coming off three brilliant seasons, the expectations were sky-high for the '68 team. Many believed UCLA was underrated when they started the season ranked No. 16 in the nation. Those who had a say in the rankings had questions about the team's quarterback slot and took a "wait and see" approach. The season began on September 21 against the Pittsburgh Panthers. Bruins fans remembered the season of 1965, when they broke in a sophomore quarterback and eventually won the Rose Bowl. This new season would start with similar promise. As it turned out, the Panthers had no chance. On the first drive, UCLA marched downfield and into the end zone. Though Pitt would move the ball early, UCLA blocked a field goal, and momentum was back with the Bruins. Bill Bolden was impressive at quarterback before injuring his shoulder. Backup quarterback Jim Nader replaced him and kept the train on the tracks. Mike Garratt, Ron Copeland, Gwen Cooper, and Bob Manning would each score as UCLA routed the Panthers, 63–7. The voters who held out ranking the Bruins in the top 10 in the initial polls had seen enough, and the Bruins shot all the way up to No. 8 the following week. Though the Bruins would come away victorious in Week 2, the high praise seemed to be premature. UCLA beat Washington State by a score of 31–21, a disappointing result considering many had believed WSU to be a pushover.

When the Bruins traveled to Syracuse, New York, in Week 3, the season began to unravel. With the belief that Week 2's subpar performance had been due to a lack of motivation and focus rather than deep-seated issues, expectations remained high for the rest of the season. Assistant Coach Lew Stueck expected the Bruins to be ready for their matchup against the strong Syracuse opponent. Stueck said before the game, "If we can't get up for Syracuse, we're in trouble." Getting up for the game was not the issue; the fact was, the Bruins were simply inferior to the men across the field. Though UCLA did a fine job stopping the powerful Syracuse running game in the first half, they were still down at halftime, 13–0. The Orangemen were able to reach the end zone once and kicked two field goals, while the Bruins struggled to move the ball. UCLA teams under Prothro were always known for strong second-half showings and dramatic comebacks. They would need precisely that if they were to come away victorious on this day. Still down 13–0 in the fourth quarter, Greg Jones finally crossed the goal line for the Bruins with eight minutes to play. Coach Prothro called for an onside kick. Unlike the successful attempt in 1965 that had sparked the Bruins to victory over the Trojans, this one did not work. Syracuse marched down the field and scored a touchdown to seal the victory. UCLA was 2–1. The slide had just begun.

Following the tough loss in upstate New York, the Bruins came home to face the No. 3 Penn State Nittany Lions. Linebacker Mike Ballou was UCLA's player of the game and Larry Agajanian and Floyd Reese each played well, but PSU was too strong. Quarterback Jim Nader was harassed all game by the ferocious PSU defense. The Bruins fell again, 21–6. The Nittany Lions would finish the season 11–0, ranked No. 2 in the Associated Press poll. When it was time for the Bruins' Pacific 8 opener on October 19, they were battered, but ready to take on the California Golden Bears. Unfortunately for UCLA, Ray Willsey and the Bears had their strongest team in years. The Bruins suffered a rash of injuries against Cal, losing Bill Bolden, George Farmer, and Vince Bischof. On top of the physical pain was the emotional scar of losing their third game in a row. Cal 39, UCLA 15.

UCLA's season record was 2–3 when they took on the Stanford Indians. They continued to struggle in a way very few had thought possible a month earlier. The Bruins were down, 14–0, at halftime and appeared destined for a fourth consecutive loss. A minute into the second half, Bolden, injured a week earlier, found Gwen Cooper for a long touchdown that got the Bruins on the board. The two-point attempt failed. Two minutes later, fullback Rick Purdy found the end zone again for the Bruins. Once again, the two-point attempt failed. UCLA was down, 14–12, and when the Indians added a field goal at the start of the fourth quarter, UCLA would be forced to score a touchdown to win. Backup quarterback Jim Nader entered the game and led the Bruins on a drive that put them in a position to steal the victory. After a 50-yard completion to Ron Copeland put the ball at the Stanford 3-yard line, Greg Jones took the ball into the end zone on his first try. Jones carried again on the two-point attempt and this time was successful. UCLA led, 20–17, and though Stanford sophomore Jim Plunkett was able to move the ball, the Indians were unable to get on the board again. UCLA's losing streak was over, and the team was back to .500 for the season.

Though the streak was over, the task ahead was daunting. Three of the final four games were against ranked teams, and three of the four were on the road. The win over the Indians seemed to have sapped all the energy out of the Bruins, and in the following two weeks, they were crushed by superior teams. On November 2, the No. 5 Tennessee Volunteers beat the Bruins, 42–18. UCLA was down, 35–0, at halftime, and the string of injuries continued. Six players were injured in that game, the most serious of which was sustained by John Chrestman, who suffered a life-changing neck injury and was immediately taken to the hospital. After severing his spinal cord, Chrestman was diagnosed a quadriplegic. He would prove doctors wrong and would walk just months later but never played football again. UCLA followed up the Tennessee loss with a 45–21 loss at Oregon State the following week. After that loss, Agajanian said, "It'll be a matter of pride now. If we have it, we'll win the next two games." The team had pride and they played hard the final two games, but pride doesn't always equate to victories. UCLA was shut out for the first time in the Tommy Prothro era. The Bruins defense played well against the Washington Huskies on a cold day in Seattle but would nevertheless go down by the score of 6–0.

When the Bruins took on the USC Trojans in the final game of the season, the two teams were going in different directions. UCLA's season had fallen apart. After a spectacular three-year run, the '68 team not only took a step back, but had regressed more than many thought possible. The USC Trojans were No. 1 in the country. The Bruins played one of their best games of the year against the men from Troy. Sophomore Mickey Cureton scored two touchdowns and had a spectacular punt return into USC territory. A national television audience saw the Bruins compete "tough" against the Trojans, but O.J. Simpson was simply too strong. USC went on to win, 28–16. Though UCLA lost and the long and disappointing season was finally over, they could take a bit of joy in knowing they had knocked the Trojans back in the AP poll following their better-than-expected performance. USC would tie Notre Dame the following week and face the No. 1 Ohio State Buckeyes for the National Championship in the Rose Bowl. What the nation was robbed of 14 years earlier, when UCLA was denied the Rose Bowl berth due to the no-repeat rule, they were allowed to see now. As for the Bruins, they would be forced to regroup. The '68 season was one to forget for fans. It was left to coach Prothro and his players to remember the pain of a 3–7 season.

The Downtown Athletic Club named O.J. Simpson from the University of Southern California the 1968 Heisman Trophy Winner.

The Associated Press named Ohio State University the 1968 National Champions.

## 1969

"That's one small step for man, one giant leap for mankind." When President John F. Kennedy had announced before a Joint Session of Congress on May 25, 1961, that the United States would set a goal of sending a man to the moon by the end of the decade, many thought it an impossible task. Apollo 11 touched down on the moon on July 20, 1969, at 4:18 pm EST, and the dream was realized. Upon landing, Astronaut Neil Armstrong called Mission Control saying, "The Eagle has landed."

On that day in '69, the nation celebrated an astounding accomplishment for all the world to remember. In Westwood, the thought of the previous

'68 season was one that coaches, fans, and players wanted to forget. The success that coach Tommy Prothro had enjoyed in his earlier three seasons gave Bruins fans confidence in his ability to take the team once again to the pinnacle of the college football world. The Bruins of '69 set out to prove that the past year had been nothing other than a fluke.

On September 13, UCLA kicked off the season against a familiar Pac 8 foe. When the Bruins took on Coach Prothro's former team, the Oregon State Beavers, they kicked off a season that would restore faith in their leader. UCLA's first touchdown of the season came early, and it was a sign of things to come. With just over a minute gone in the season opener, Long Beach City College transfer quarterback Dennis Dummit hit Gwen Cooper in the left flat on a third-and-6 situation at the Bruins' 40-yard line. Cooper made an Oregon State defender miss and raced down the sideline for a 60-yard touchdown. It was the first pass of the season for Dummit, and it was memorable. His last pass of the season would be memorable, as well. The Bruins defeated the Beavers, 37–0.

UCLA would go on a winning streak to start the season that immediately put the rest of the conference on notice. Following the dominant victory over the Oregon State Beavers, the Bruins beat the University of Pittsburgh, 42–8. Over the following three weeks, UCLA was scheduled to play three road games. On September 27, the Bruins beat the University of Wisconsin Badgers, 34–23. They followed that up with a masterful performance against the Northwestern University Wildcats. UCLA 36, Northwestern 0. When the Bruins returned to conference play, the Washington State University Cougars, who had hung around and competed well with the Bruins in the previous year, were no match this time around. UCLA sported a 5–0 record after defeating the Cougars in Spokane by a final score of 46–14. The Bruins were firing on all cylinders. Through the first half of the season, the offense averaged 39 points per game, and the defense allowed just nine points per game. In Week 6, the California Golden Bears proved to be no match, either. Finally, back at the Coliseum, the Bruins continued to dominate with a shutout over Cal, 32–0.

When the Bruins took on the Stanford Indians on October 18, the varsity squad had risen to No. 8 in the Associated Press poll. Stanford, led by Jim Plunkett, was ranked No. 19 by the AP. Plunkett would go on to establish Pac 8 single-season records in passing yards (2,673), TDs (20), and total yards (2,786) in 1969. UCLA had a challenge beyond just Plunkett, however. The Stanford offense was dynamic and multifaceted. Leading rusher Bubba Brown gave the Bruins fits all game. Randy Vataha scored a touchdown on a spectacular leaping catch, and on defense All-Conference safety Rick Keller intercepted a Dummit pass to put the ball deep into Bruins territory. Despite the Indians being a formidable opponent, the score was tied, 20–20, with just minutes to go in the game. UCLA's trusty kicker Zenon Andrusyshyn had a chance to give the Bruins the lead but missed a short field goal. With little time on the clock, even the most ardent Bruins fans were now rooting for a tie. Plunkett drove the ball deep into Bruins territory, but the attempted game-winning field goal by Stanford was blocked by Steve Horowitz. The game ended in a 20–20 tie.

UCLA's perfect season was over, but the loss column still read "0." The Bruins were 6–0–1, and the next two games would serve to set the stage for another dramatic rivalry game against the Trojans. After the tie against the Indians, UCLA took on the University of Washington at the Coliseum and dismantled them by the score of 57–14. Though the following game was close, the Bruins escaped from a squeaker in Eugene, Oregon, by a score of 13–10. UCLA's season record was 8–0–1 when they faced the University of Southern California Trojans on November 22. The Bruins were ranked No. 6 in the country, and the Trojans, with an identical 8–0–1 record, were No. 5. The winner of the crosstown rivalry game would win the Pac 8 Conference and go to the Rose Bowl. In the biggest of games, everyone involved wants the final result to be decided by the men wearing the pads. To the present day, it is debatable as to whether that game was decided not by the players, but by the men in black-and-white stripes. The buildup for the game and hype surrounding the showdown were noticeable to all right away. Quarterback Dennis Dummit was reported as saying, "We would usually get there four hours before the game and maybe 50 people would be there. That day, we walked in, and there were 75,000 people already in their seats." More than 90,000 would pack the Coliseum by the time the ball was kicked, and perhaps just as many would have opinions as to what actually happened in the fourth quarter. Celebrities watched from the sidelines. Defenses dominated early in the game. Dummit would get sacked nine times and be intercepted five. UCLA's defense held the leading rusher in the nation, Clarence Davis, to just 37 yards. Because of UCLA's tie being in a conference game, and USC's tie coming in nonconference, there was added pressure on the Bruins. They needed a win to go to the Rose Bowl. The Trojans simply needed a tie. It would change the Bruins' strategy and play a key role in the outcome. UCLA trailed USC, 7–6, when Dummit found Gwen Cooper for the go-ahead score with 3:07 left to play in the fourth quarter. As the Bruins had done earlier in the game, they were forced to go for two, and for the second time, they were unsuccessful. The Bruins led, 12–7, and would need a defensive stop to secure a Rose Bowl berth. Though USC pushed the ball to near midfield, the Bruins appeared on the brink of victory. It was fourth down-and-10 with the game on the line. The next play would be debated for years. USC receiver Sam Dickerson ran a curl route, just past the first down marker. The pass was thrown, Dickerson jumped in the air, stretched his arms, and felt contact on his back. UCLA defensive back Danny Graham slipped and crashed into Dickerson. Pass interference was called. Bruins coaches, fans, and players were irate, not because of any dispute about contact, but because of the pass that was thrown. The ball was so high over Dickerson's head that the thought of him catching it was nothing other than imaginary in the minds of USC fans. Graham would say, "Yeah, he could have caught it . . . if he were on stilts." USC was given another chance. The game would go on, and a classic controversy was only a play away. On the next play, USC quarterback Jimmy Jones rolled deep to his right, planted his back foot, and threw to the corner of the end zone. The ball was high in the air, and Dickerson had it in his sights. As he slid to the ground, catching the ball in the back right corner of the end zone, the referees signaled touchdown! To this day, Bruins fans swear he both came from out of bounds and reentered—making him ineligible for the reception—and also that his knee hit down out-of-bounds before his foot hit inbounds. The opinion of fans didn't matter, though, and when the referees signaled touchdown, the Bruins suddenly trailed. The UCLA offense marched to the USC 38-yard line, now down by two points, but Dummit's final pass of the season was intercepted, and the Bruins lost, 14–12. UCLA's season was over. Coach Prothro was said to never get over that loss, and the pain of losing in '69 ultimately played a factor in his leaving UCLA after the 1970 season to take over as head coach of the Los Angeles Rams.

The Downtown Athletic Club named Steve Owens from the University of Oklahoma the 1969 Heisman Trophy Winner.

The Associated Press named the University of Texas the 1969 National Champions.

## 1970

The Rose Bowl game that the Bruins so narrowly missed out on ushered in a new decade. The Bruins watched from home as the USC Trojans beat the Michigan Wolverines in the game the Bruins believed they should have played in. The 1970s had arrived. The Tommy Prothro era was winding down. Quarterback Dennis Dummit was back for his senior season to lead the Bruins offense. Nineteen seventy would be a season of both heartbreak and triumph. Football was a game of inches. UCLA would learn that the hard way.

Coach Prothro was joined by assistants Larry Weaver, Jerry Long, Tony Kopay, Rich Brooks, John Becker, Earnel Durden, Bobb McKittrick, and Dick Vermeil on the coaching staff. A key assistant coach for the Bruins in Prothro's first three seasons, Pepper Rodgers, was now the head coach at the University of Kansas. On Rodgers's staff was a young Terry Donahue, a man who had played on the defensive line under Prothro. The future of UCLA football for the next 25 years would be in the hands of three men: Rodgers, Vermeil, and Donahue, who were all directly influenced by Prothro. The man who would help shape the future of the next quarter century of UCLA football had been thinking about the NFL for quite some time. The loss to USC in '69 weighed heavily on Coach Prothro's mind when it was time to decide his future. For now, he was focused on winning in Westwood. The NFL was a matter for another time.

UCLA came out not on fire, but winning nonetheless. The Bruins squeaked by Oregon State in Week 1 by a score of 14–9 and edged out the Pittsburgh Panthers, 24–15, in Week 2. The Bruins extended their winning streak when they defeated the Northwestern Wildcats, 12–7, in the third game of the year. Though the Bruins averaged only a tad under 17 points per game, they were winning, and that was ultimately what mattered most. The defense was off to an excellent start, giving up just over 10 points per game.

On October 3, a monumental challenge was at hand for the Bruins. They would travel to Austin, Texas, to take on the defending National Champion Texas Longhorns, led by a powerful wishbone offense. Despite the Bruins coming in at No. 13 in the Associated Press rankings, the No. 2 Longhorns were 22-point betting favorites. Texas was riding a 22-game winning streak, and the matchup between Tommy Prothro and Longhorns Head Coach Darrell Royal was billed as one of the best coaching matchups in football. UCLA started the game by proving they were no pushover, and that installing them as such underdogs was a slap in the face. They didn't simply plan on covering the spread; they planned on winning the game. Though the Bruins forced a turnover on the second play of the game and capitalized on the mistake with a 19-yard field goal by Bruce Barnes, they trailed at halftime by a score of 13–3. Coach Prothro had implemented a "mirror" defense to combat the wishbone attack of the Longhorns, but the UCLA offense was struggling to keep the ball, and the Bruin defense was on the field too long. In the third quarter, the UCLA offense came alive. On the day, Dennis Dummit would complete 19 of 30 passes for 340 yards and two touchdowns, both of which came in the third quarter. At the end of that quarter, UCLA led the Longhorns, 17–13. The Bruins were one quarter from ending Texas's long winning streak and vaulting themselves into the National Championship picture. With just over two minutes to go, UCLA's defense was in a position to make the play of the game. It was fourth down-and-4, with the Longhorns driving into Bruins territory. As Jim Bertlesen raced trying to get to the outside, he slipped and fell short of the first down. UCLA took over on downs! But after three offensive plays, UCLA was forced to punt. Texas was out of timeouts when they received the punt with 52 seconds left to play. After giving up a first down, the UCLA defense stiffened and on second down forced Texas quarterback Eddie Phillips to retreat. When they brought him down, he fumbled! The ball was loose, but it rolled out of bounds. On third down and 19, coach Royal of the Longhorns called "86 Pass, Ted Crossing, Sam Post." The ball was at the UCLA 45-yard line when Phillips dropped back and fired. He connected with Cotton Speyrer. The ball was launched just over three Bruins defenders, who leaped in the air but could not reach the ball. Speyrer caught it at the Bruins' 15-yard line, and with the remaining defender out of positon to make a tackle, he jogged into the end zone for the go-ahead touchdown with just 12 seconds remaining on the clock. It was a heartbreaking defeat. Texas's 23rd consecutive win set a new Southwestern Conference record.

The loss to the Longhorns was just one game in a season full of thrilling finishes. A week after losing to UT, UCLA went down at the hands of the University of Oregon. Leading 40–20 entering the fourth quarter, the Bruins simply fell apart. Oregon quarterback Dan Fouts led a spirited comeback, and the Bruins fell, 41–40. The Bruins alternated wins and losses for the rest of the season. Week after week, thriller after thriller, the season went on. UCLA defeated California in a close game, 24–21, before losing to Jim Plunkett and the Stanford Indians, 9–7. UCLA had nearly defeated the No. 8 men from Palo Alto, but a late Bruins fumble in Indians territory cost them the game. Despite just a 4–3 record, UCLA was ranked No. 19 when they took on the Washington State Cougars on October 30. UCLA handily defeated WSU by a score of 54–9. While the Bruins felt the thrill of a blowout victory that one week, they would feel the agony of a blowout loss the following week, being trounced by the University of Washington, 61–20. UCLA was 5–4 on the season. The 1970 season was surely a disappointing one, but when the Bruins took on the Trojans, the game that every member of each team had thought about for a year, the struggles against prior opponents were set aside amid the fervor of renewed motivation of a team out to avenge the previous loss because of an official's "bad call." UCLA's players, as well as coach Prothro, remembered the result of the 1969 game and were determined that, this year, the referees would *not* decide the end result. Sure enough, on this day the Trojans were no match for the motivated Bruins. UCLA beat USC by a score of 45–20, the third largest margin of victory for UCLA in the history of the rivalry. This was Tommy Prothro's final game as the UCLA head football coach. He took the head coaching job with the Los Angeles Rams. Prothro's record at UCLA was 41–18–3. UCLA beat USC three out of Prothro's six seasons, and his teams finished in first or second in the conference five times.

The Downtown Athletic Club named Jim Plunkett from Stanford University the 1970 Heisman Trophy Winner.

The Associated Press named the University of Nebraska the 1970 National Champions.

Dennis Dummit, 1970 (Southern Campus Collection)

# CHAPTER 10

# Franklin "Pepper" Rodgers (1971–1973)

Franklin "Pepper" Rodgers can best be described by one word: interesting. Pepper Rodgers was born on October 8, 1931, in Atlanta, Georgia. Rodgers would have an up-and-down coaching career. He won as many as nine games in a college football season (twice), and he also lost nine games in a season. His life, however, was always interesting. I.J. Rosenberg of the *Atlanta Journal-Constitution* would write of Rodgers long after he retired, "If football came down to personality, Franklin 'Pepper' Rodgers never would have lost a game."

Pepper Rodgers, 1972 (Southern Campus Collection)

Coach Rodgers's first love was not football, but dancing. In *Pepper! The Autobiography of an Unconventional Coach*, Rodgers claimed, "If I weren't coaching football, I might be dancing on a television reality show. I could have been a tap dancer. Or a vocalist. But not a clarinetist." Luckily for the sports world, and even luckier for the entertainment world, Rodgers's first love was not his only love. Though Pepper started taking dance lessons at three, and would perform in the *Kiddie Review* in Atlanta for two years, by the time he was six years old, it was clear he had another gift. He was smarter than most kids his age. Pepper was so advanced that his mother convinced his principal that Pepper would be better skipping the third grade. He did just that and continued to thrive. Pepper grew up in a middle-class family. He didn't consider himself privileged, but he knew his family was always able to feed him. His father was an insurance salesman, and his mother always held a steady job. One of the largest influences in his young life, however, came from his grandfather. Pepper's love for sports grew because of the stories his grandfather, J.B. Upshaw, told him and his brother, Allen, while working his farm. Pepper's imagination would grow wild at a young age. He imagined he was Ty Cobb, "The Georgia Peach." He imagined he was Civil War General Jeb Stuart. He was young and he was ambitious.

One of Pepper's earliest times being exposed to sports up close and personal came when he was a young boy and his Boy Scout Group 22 was allowed to usher peanuts at Grant Field for the Georgia Tech vs. University of Georgia football game. The winner would go to the Rose Bowl, and Pepper rooted hard for the home team Yellow Jackets. When UGA defeated GT, Pepper was crushed. He was not shy, however, and he knew that, as poorly as he felt after the loss, the players must have felt worse. Pepper decided after the game to do the best he could to offer condolences to the GT players. He picked up a phone and called star Clint Castleberry in an attempt to cheer him up. Pepper was hooked. He loved football. He loved Georgia Tech.

In 1945, Pepper was off to high school. At Boys High, Pepper passed on playing football. As a small child, he saw the size of the players and the tough exterior that they displayed and felt he was better off playing the clarinet. Though Pepper was not on the team, his love for football continued to grow. He continued to watch Georgia Tech games and further learn the game he loved. In 1946, the city's four high schools were abolished, and the neighborhood system that was used for junior high was instituted for high school. There were now seven high schools, and Pepper was reacquainted with the children he grew up with, the ones he was comfortable with. Pepper attended Brown High School and was no longer afraid to play football. He played football, as well as basketball and baseball. Though he believed basketball was his best sport, football was his love and his future. After a year on the B team, Pepper took over as the starting quarterback. Before the season, Pepper was able to use his charm and forward thinking to help himself and the team. Knowing that Charlie Brannon was the best quarterback on the team, Pepper convinced Brannon and the coaches that Brannon was so good he could be used elsewhere. Pepper sold the coaches on the idea that he himself was too slow and too small to play any other position but was an excellent quarterback who could be even better with a great athlete like Brannon on the field with him. It worked. As a junior and senior, Pepper was the quarterback for the city champions. Pepper considered himself a thinking man's quarterback. Though a better athlete than he would admit publicly, he knew that he didn't have all the best physical tools. He would have to understand defenses and how to lead his team. He thrived. On the basketball court, Pepper was the best player in the city. He led the city in scoring. And in baseball, he was a solid infielder. His team went to the city championship when he was a senior but lost, 10–9. Throughout Pepper's entire life, there is an interesting story in every twist and turn. After a stellar high school career, Pepper was in the situation that thousands of excellent high school athletes are in every year. They know they can play at the collegiate level, but no schools are interested. Rather than feeling helpless, Pepper made his own break. When he saw Georgia Tech assistant coach Ray Graves in his neighborhood, he made his move. Graves was there to see four of Pepper's teammates. He would end up meeting another. When Graves made his first stop, Pepper jumped into his car and started rattling off his high school statistics. He was selling himself. After hounding Graves for some time, the GT assistant finally had enough. He would say to the young, enthusiastic man sitting in his car, "Pepper, if you'll leave me alone, I'll get you a city scholarship for one year." Pepper lived at home for that year, but by the fall of 1951, when he was eligible for the varsity squad, he was on full scholarship.

On Georgia Tech's freshman team in 1950, Pepper would excel, but it was on the varsity that he became a household name, even if not as a player. Pepper was not a great player, far from it, but he was a great entertainer and clutch performer. As a sophomore, playing for coach Bobby Dodd, Pepper's goal was to be the backup quarterback, but he was beat out by Bill Bringman and relegated to third string. Pepper, however, was multitalented. He was also a fine kicker. Coach Dodd rarely used his kicker for field goals, and Pepper was not always the man to get the nod, but on January 1, 1952, Pepper's opportunity came. Georgia Tech was undefeated and ranked No. 5 in the country by the Associated Press when they took on No. 9 Baylor in the Orange Bowl. The night before the game, the ever-optimistic Pepper said to his roommate, Larry Morris, "Larry, I'm going to bed because I have a feeling I'm going to kick a field goal to beat Baylor." With seconds to play, the score was 14–14. It was fourth-and-3 at the Baylor 8-yard line when Coach Dodd turned to the sideline and asked, "Who can kick field goals?" Pepper raised his hand, and Coach Dodd pointed in his direction. It was the biggest moment of his athletic life. It was a difficult angle, so Pepper suggested taking a 5-yard penalty. His teammates refused to allow it. The ball was snapped. Pepper was afraid it would be blocked. It was not. He kicked the ball, and before it went through, he raised his hands in celebration. Georgia Tech won the Orange Bowl!

As a junior, Pepper expected to be the starting quarterback. When he was not named the starter, he was momentarily crushed but motivated to find a way to help his team. In 1952, Georgia Tech went undefeated again in the regular season and this time faced Ole Miss in the Sugar Bowl. The Yellow Jackets beat the Rebels, 24–7, and were named National Champions by several outlets (the AP named Michigan State the National Champions). As a senior, Pepper was injured before the season began, and, after missing three games, he struggled when he came back. Following his best game of the year, coming in with the game well in hand against Vanderbilt University, Pepper was promoted back to the starting position with four games to play. After finishing 9–2, Georgia Tech was off to the Sugar Bowl. Pepper threw three touchdowns and kicked a field goal in his last collegiate game. The Yellow Jackets won, 42–19. Pepper's playing days were over, and though he would only direct the action from the sidelines in his future, he continued to entertain for years to come.

Like so many young men in his era, Pepper Rodgers had a duty to fulfill. After serving as a student assistant coach under Bobby Dodd in 1954, Pepper's country came calling. He was a member of ROTC at Georgia Tech, so in 1955 he joined the United States Air Force. He had been offered a full-time position at the University of Virginia and wished to take it, but instead he was sent to Spence Air Force Base in Southern Georgia. After two years in the Air Force, Pepper took a coaching job at the Air Force Academy. He believed he was obligated to remain at the Academy, but years later he would learn he had been free to coach anywhere. His contract stipulated only minimal service, but he remained an officer while coaching at the Academy. He would have preferred to coach at the University of Florida. In 1960 he got his wish. Ray Graves, the man who recruited him to Georgia Tech, offered him a job as the backfield coach for the Gators. Pepper coached at Florida for five years. His most famous player was a young Steve Spurrier, who would win the 1966 Heisman after Pepper left. The two remain friends to this day. By 1964, Pepper had become a burden. His personality clashed with other members of the staff, and he was said to be blamed for things over which he had no control. Graves was in the tough position of firing a man whom he adored personally. He told Pepper to look for another job and he would delay the announcement of the firing. Pepper met, and interviewed with, Tommy Prothro at Oregon State University. Prothro offered him a job. What no one yet knew was that the job was not at OSU, but at UCLA. Tommy Prothro was coaching the Rose Bowl game for OSU, and the news of him taking the UCLA job was not going to be released until after the game. Pepper kept it a secret. He was off to Westwood.

For two years, Pepper was an assistant coach at UCLA. The Bruins beat USC both years and won the first Rose Bowl in school history. Pepper called the offense from the press box. He was an excellent coach, and his so-called "divisive personality" that caused problems at Florida was never an issue at UCLA. In 1967, he became the head coach at the University of Kansas. When Pepper became a head coach, he would do things his way. He was well prepared for every game and every practice. He took his job very seriously. What one might consider "goofy," he considered important. He didn't consider the game of football to be a life-or-death situation, but he felt that every man should make the best of his ability. When playing under Bobby Dodd at Georgia Tech, he learned that football should be fun. Players will perform best when they are happy to be on the field. In his four years as the head coach at Kansas, he fine-tuned his coaching technique. His style was shaped by both wins and losses. In his second year, the Jayhawks had a record of 9–2 and went to the Orange Bowl. In his third season, they finished 1–9. In 1971, he took the head coaching job at UCLA when Tommy Prothro left for the NFL. At UCLA, his team won only two games in his first year, then he was named Pac 8 Coach of the Year in his second and third seasons. Ultimately, his love for Georgia Tech and his dreams of coaching at his alma mater led him back to Atlanta. He coached at Georgia Tech for six seasons with moderate success. Outwardly, he was a showman. Inwardly, he was a strategist. He did cartwheels on the field. He drove a Harley Davidson motorcycle. He invited television crews into his locker room to televise his halftime speeches live. He had his own talk show. He sometimes wore a wig. He played the guitar for his team. He sang Christmas carols on television.

Pepper Rodgers loved life, and when he was fired from Georgia Tech University following the 1979 season, he was expected to love life performing another occupation. What you expect from Pepper Rodgers you seldom get. In 1984, Pepper Rodgers was named the head coach of the Memphis Showboats of the United States Football League. In his first season, the Showboats finished with a 7–11 record. In typical Pepper Rodgers fashion, he turned it around in year two. The Showboats finished the 1985 season with an 11–7 record and a playoff appearance. While with the Showboats, Rodgers had the privilege of being Reggie White's first professional coach. The team folded in 1986. Rodgers would finish his coaching career with one final stanza. In 1995, he coached the Memphis Mad Dogs, a team that played in the Canadian Football League and hoped to eventually build a state-of-the-art stadium and transition to the National Football League. They folded after one year. In 2001, Pepper took a job with the Cleveland Browns. He was named director of football operations and served in that capacity for four seasons. Pepper has four children and two stepchildren. He has eight grandchildren and one great-granddaughter. He now lives in Renton, Virginia, and has been married to his wife, Janet, for over 40 years. We stated at the outset that Pepper Rodgers is a smart man. Indeed, and an accomplished one.

## 1971

When William Spaulding left UCLA prior to the 1939 season, the school's football program hired Edwin Horrell, and the success of the Spaulding era turned into the struggles of the Horrell era. When Red Sanders died in 1958 and William Barnes became the coach one month into the season, the glory faded away. UCLA slid into mediocrity. The Bruins would have a third chance to replace an elite coach in 1971 when Tommy Prothro left Westwood to take the head coaching position with the Los Angeles Rams. Prothro had helped bring back the Bruins to the status of national contender. With Pepper Rodgers named the head coach, there were high expectations, but after one year, the man with the goofy personality was still a question mark. Could Rodgers lead the Bruins into the future as an elite program? Time would tell. Rodgers made a habit in his career of turning programs around. In '71, he was tasked not with turning one around, but keeping it afloat.

UCLA started the 1971 season with high hopes. The Associated Press ranked the Bruins No. 15 in the country. The schedule was tough, and the Bruins would have to prove week in and week out that they deserved to be considered one of the best teams in the land. On September 11, the Bruins took on the University of Pittsburgh Panthers in the first game of the Pepper Rodgers era. Coach Rodgers struggled to find an offense that best fit his personnel. Ultimately, he would settle on the wishbone offense. Along with Rodgers, assistants Dick Tomey, Ken Blair, Terry Donahue, Jerry Long, Tony Kopay, Lynn Stiles, Floyd Reese, and Billie Matthews filled out the coaching staff. UCLA would rely all season on wide receiver Reggie Echols, wide receiver Terry Vernoy, kicker Efren Herrera, punter Bruce Barnes, quarterback Mike Flores, tight end Bob Christiansen, defensive lineman Mike Pavich, halfback Marv Kendricks, and team MVP center Dave Dalby to lead the team. The season opener did not start the way Bruins fans had hoped. Neither did the entire first month. UCLA lost to the Panthers, 29–25, at the Coliseum. The following week, the No. 3 Texas Longhorns came west and took on the Bruins in L.A. UCLA got on the board first. The upset-minded Bruins had come to play. Their 10-play, 83-yard drive that took over six minutes was capped by a 42-yard touchdown pass from Flores to Echols. At the end of the first quarter, you could sense a feeling of serenity in the crowd. It was 73 degrees. The Bruins were winning. All was good. Then the second quarter rolled around. Soon the serenity turned into anxiety. Bruins fans still clung to the hopes of an upset, even as the Longhorns smashed through their team. But the dream was fading. Texas scored 14 unanswered points in the second quarter and went into the halftime break leading, 14–7. UCLA got on the board first in the second half. Coach Rodgers, known for running the ball, simply did what he knew best. Ronald Reagan would years later ask Rodgers why he didn't throw the ball more. He needed nothing other than to point to the first scoring drive of the second half. After 20 plays, UCLA got on the board again. Unfortunately, they were unable to get seven, settling instead for three on a Herrera 41-yard field goal. It was 14–10. UCLA would never get closer. Texas scored two fourth-quarter touchdowns and won, 28–10. The Bruins were 0–2. The following week, they would lose again. UCLA's first road game came against the Michigan Wolverines. They had no chance. Michigan 38, UCLA 0. When the Bruins lost their Pac 8 opener the following week to Oregon State, 34–17, fans became suspicious of the Pepper Rodgers decision. Had UCLA once again hired a coach not capable of continuing the winning ways of his predecessor?

The Bruins were 0–4 when they took on Washington State University on October 9. Looking ahead, it was clear the next two weeks would be critical. If UCLA lost to WSU and then the University of Arizona in the following week, it was possible and probable that they would finish the season winless. The Bruins soon put those worries to rest. UCLA beat the Cougars, 34–21, in Spokane. The following week, they won again, beating the University of Arizona Wildcats, 28–12. Coach Rodgers's Bruins were 2–4. With four games to play, there was still hope of finishing with a winning record. The positive feelings generated from a budding winning streak proved to be short-lived. More troubles lay ahead.

UCLA lost to the University of California Berkeley on October 23 and followed that up with another loss the following week at the hands of the University of Washington. With two weeks left to play, the season appeared all but over. UCLA took on the Stanford Indians in the ninth game of the season. Though Heisman winner Jim Plunkett was now off to the NFL, the defending Rose Bowl champions were still very strong. Stanford's offense that season would score 82 fewer points than the 1970 squad, but the defense was significantly improved. Though the Bruins played the Indians tough, Stanford ultimately won, 20–9. They would go on to repeat as Rose Bowl champions. There was one week left on the Bruins' schedule. USC was the No. 15 team in the nation. The Bruins were playing strictly for pride. On this day, pride would win, but the Bruins wouldn't. USC was the much better team. They were 6–4. They had beaten a ranked Washington team the week before. They had defeated No. 6 Notre Dame in October, and three out of their four losses came against ranked teams. But pride has a way of putting its thumb on the scale, and in this game, UCLA played USC to a tie. The final score was 7–7. The nightmare season was over for Pepper Rodgers and the Bruins. They would be back in nine months. Coach Rodgers was determined to fix the problems of '71 and produce a winner in '72. He just needed a quarterback. He would find one.

The Downtown Athletic Club named Pat Sullivan from Auburn University the 1971 Heisman Trophy Winner.

The Associated Press named the University of Nebraska the 1971 National Champions.

## 1972

Nineteen seventy-two was the season that Pepper Rodgers would have to prove himself as a coach. The Bruins faithful were patient, but unwilling to see the team across town continue its dominance unobstructed. The Bruins had two new men in '72 who would have to perform at the highest level to make sure the season of '71 would not be repeated: Homer Smith, the former halfback at Princeton and a man rising up the coaching ranks, was tasked with offensive coordinator duties, and the man tasked with executing the offense on the field was quarterback Mark Harmon. With the 1–2 punch of Smith and Harmon, Coach Rodgers's luck turned around. Smith was a brilliant wishbone play caller. Harmon was tough as nails. He mastered the wishbone offense and knew which players to hand the ball to at the appropriate time. On the defensive side, the Bruins were young and talented. The only senior starter was the excellent defensive back Allan Ellis. UCLA excelled on special teams. Bruce Barnes led the conference in punting for the third year in a row, and junior kicker Efren Herrera was one of the best in the nation.

Though the Bruins would be much improved in '72, the season-opening opponent was one of the greatest teams in history, or so everyone thought. When UCLA took on the University of Nebraska on September 9, 1972, the Huskers were riding high. They had a 32-game winning streak and were the two-time defending National Champions. They were ranked No. 1 in the nation by the Associated Press and expected to continue their stranglehold on college football's greatest prize for the third season in a row. Coach Rodgers had a bit of a dustup with a coach from Nebraska prior to the game. The last time Nebraska had been beaten was by the Pepper Rodgers-led Kansas Jayhawks in '68, and after initially agreeing with Huskers Coach Bob Devaney to exchange game film, the two had a falling-out, and the exchange never happened. Nebraska was a talented team, to say the least. Pepper felt he could outstrategize anyone if he had ample time to prepare beforehand. Without the tape, it would be more difficult, but then again Nebraska was the known entity. Homer Smith and Mark Harmon were the unknown.

It played into UCLA's hands. Nebraska entered the Coliseum as 21-point favorites. Little did they know they were in for a battle that would be remembered for decades. On the first play of the game, Bruins running back James McAlister broke off a 40-yard run. The Bruins would get on the scoreboard first on a 27-yard field goal by Efren Herrera. It was time for the powerful Nebraska offense to go to work. The Huskers were breaking in a new quarterback in Dave Humm but returned the man who would go on to win the Heisman Trophy, wide receiver Johnny Rodgers. UCLA's defense was strong, however. After a Nebraska field goal, defensive end Cal Peterson of the Bruins recovered a Nebraska fumble on their next possession, and on the very next play Harmon completed his first pass as a Bruin: a 46-yard touchdown to wide receiver Brad Lyman. It was 10–3 Bruins, and the Huskers were shocked. Great teams stay composed, and Johnny Rodgers and the Huskers stayed calm. Rodgers scored the first touchdown for Nebraska on an 11-yard run just before halftime, and when the teams went into the break, the score was tied, 10–10. UCLA had outplayed the defending champions yet were only tied on the scoreboard. Observers may have thought it was an opportunity wasted, but the Bruins knew they could play even better in the second half. After UCLA's Jimmy Allan intercepted Humm and returned the ball deep in Huskers territory, Harmon scored from two yards out, and the Bruins were back ahead. The Cornhuskers would continue to fight. One minute into the final quarter, they scored again. Humm found tight end Jerry List from 44 yards out, and the score was tied. The teams exchanged punts, but the Bruins still had a bit of magic left in them. After they drove deep into Nebraska territory, the game was on the line, and Pepper Rodgers, the man who had kicked the game-winning field goal in the Orange Bowl as a sophomore at Georgia Tech 20 years earlier, would now call on his kicker to win this game over the nation's top-ranked team. Only 22 seconds remained on the clock. Efren Herrera lined up for a 30-yard field goal. Perfect snap. Perfect hold. Perfect kick! UCLA led, 20–17, with 17 seconds remaining. The Bruins defeated the Huskers, and Pepper Rodgers was forgiven for the entire previous 1971 season. It was clear '72 would be a much better year for the men from Westwood. After the final seconds ticked off the clock, the crowd stormed the field. McAlister, Harmon, and the rest of the team would remember the thrill and talk about the game for many years. UCLA offensive lineman Bruce Walton, brother of legendary UCLA basketball player Bill Walton, would always remember the disrespect he felt the Huskers showed the Bruins. "They expected us to mail it in. That didn't happen." Though the thrill of victory is sweet, the season would continue in just seven days. Coach Pepper Rodgers displays in his home just one game ball from his UCLA tenure. It comes from the day the Bruins beat the Cornhuskers. In Week 2, the journey continued. UCLA had another game to play; there was no time to rest on their laurels.

The Bruins had a powerful offense. Though the win over Nebraska was impressive and brought attention to the Bruins as legitimate contenders, the offense got even better as the season went on. UCLA would score 38 against Pittsburgh (win), 65 on Oregon (win), 42 against Arizona (win), 37 on Oregon State (win), 49 on Cal (win), 35 on Washington State (win), 28 on Stanford (win). The offense was loaded. Four backs each rushed for more than 500 yards. Kermit Johnson led the team with 989, McAlister had 825, Harmon 521, and Rob Scribner 511. The Bruins rushed for more than 4,000 yards on the season. Over the first nine games of the season, UCLA's only loss came at the hands of the University of Michigan. The Wolverines slowed down the Bruins' wishbone offense and held them to only nine points.

When UCLA traveled to the University of Washington on November 11, they were 8–1 and ranked No. 8 in the country. But marching into Husky Stadium, they were hit by a train they could not stop. Washington had a lethal passing attack and a defense that did enough to slow down the potent Bruin offense. Final score: Washington 30, UCLA 21. The last game of the season would put a bookend on the 1972 season, with UCLA facing once again the top-ranked team in the country. The University of Southern California Trojans were 9–0 and had dreams of a national title. Coach John McKay's squad was led by Mike Rea, Pat Haden, Anthony Davis, Sam Cunningham, and a stingy defense. The Rose Bowl was on the line. The winner would head to Pasadena for the most prestigious bowl game in America. UCLA, if defeated, would go home and not be heard of until the following September. USC would play Notre Dame a week later regardless, but a defeat would dampen the mood from their otherwise incredible season. The game was nationally televised, but unlike UCLA's opener against Nebraska, this time would be no upset. USC defeated the Bruins, 24–7. It is hard for many to judge the 1972 season. The Bruins won eight games compared to just two the year before. The offense was brilliant, setting a Pac 8 rushing record. The team found a sophomore quarterback who was a wizard with the football. But they had lost to USC, and the Trojans went on to win the National Championship. Just months later, John Wooden and the UCLA basketball team would win the National Championship again, their seventh straight. Bruins fans rejoiced when Bill Walton raised the trophy after a brilliant championship performance. They also dreamed of the day when Bill's brother and the rest of the football team could raise a championship trophy themselves.

The Downtown Athletic Club named Johnny Rodgers from the University of Nebraska the 1972 Heisman Trophy Winner.

The Associated Press named the University of Southern California the 1972 National Champions.

## 1973

The 1973 UCLA Bruins were loaded with talent. Five players would be named to the All-America team, and 10 would be named to the All-Pac 8 Conference team. Pepper Rodgers had worked out the kinks that slowed the 1971 team and had now built a contender. The Bruins would use two quarterbacks, Mark Harmon and Josh Sciarra. The two combined would throw for only 774 yards on the season and six touchdowns. No problem. The Bruins led the nation in rushing. Kermit Johnson was an All-American. He rushed for 1,129 yards and 16 touchdowns. James McAlister added 714. Harmon and Sciarra rushed for 532 and 496, respectively. Charlie Schumann and Wendell Tyler each rushed for five touchdowns, and Russel Charles and Eddie Ayers were each solid contributors to the running game. The UCLA wishbone offense was a juggernaut.

The UCLA season began again with the Nebraska Cornhuskers. On September 8, the No. 10-ranked Bruins took on the No. 4 Huskers in front of a crowd of 74,996 fans at Memorial Stadium in Lincoln. Following the '72 season, Huskers coach Bob Devaney had retired, and Tom Osborne was named his successor. Nebraska was set on revenge, and the Bruins would have to play even better in '73 to defeat the motivated men opposite them. On the opening drive, Nebraska drove 56 yards into the end zone. Backup quarterback Steve Runty, filling in for the injured Dave Humm, scored the first touchdown of the Tom Osborne era, and UCLA found themselves trailing early. Before the Bruins knew what hit them, Nebraska delivered a massive blow. On UCLA's first offensive drive, they went three-and-out and were forced to punt. Randy Borg hauled in the punt at the Husker 23-yard line and raced 77 yards into the end zone. Less than nine minutes into the game, UCLA trailed, 14–0. UCLA scored for the first time of the '73 campaign on a 12-yard run by Kermit Johnson on their next drive, and at the end of the first quarter, UCLA trailed, 14–7. In the second quarter, the two teams exchanged scores, with UCLA's touchdown coming on a 3-yard run by Harmon. Nebraska's point after touchdown attempt was blocked, and the halftime score was 20–13 Huskers. UCLA had an opportunity to win, trailing by only seven at halftime, but on this day, the Huskers were not to be denied. Nebraska dominated the Bruins in the second half, scoring three touchdowns and holding the Bruins scoreless. The season would start with a 40–13 loss at the hands of Nebraska. The Tom Osborne era had begun in Lincoln.

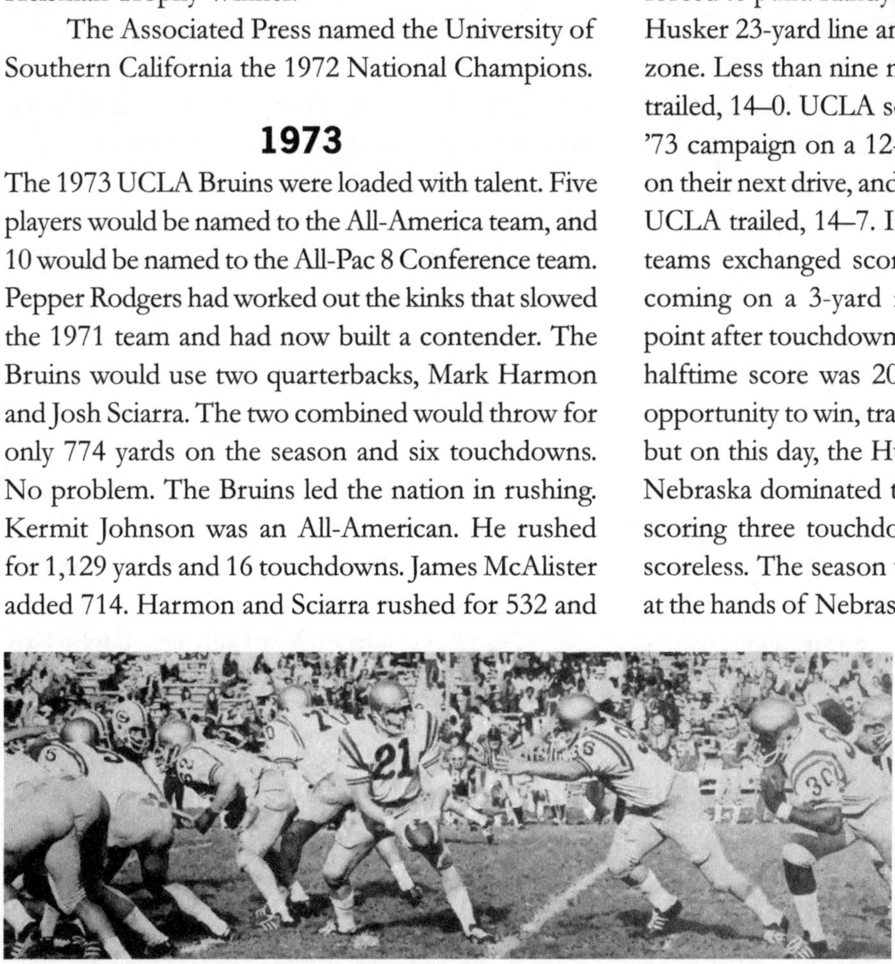

UCLA's offense, 1972 (Southern Campus Collection)

After the game against Nebraska, the coaches held a meeting. Pepper Rodgers asked every assistant, "If your jobs depended on the next game, who would you start at quarterback?" The answer was unanimous. John Sciarra was the new starter. Just two years earlier, Pepper didn't have any-quarterback he trusted. Now he had two. Though the coaches were working hard to correct the issues that had doomed the team in Week 1, the players were not happy. Many of the seniors marched into Coach Rodgers's office and voiced their complaints. They didn't like the play calling. They didn't like their preparation before the game. They didn't like the food they ate on game day. Coach Rodgers responded, "Look, you're not going to blame the coaches and the coaches are not going to blame you. Individually, we'll accept the blame; collectively, I'll take the responsibility." After the Nebraska game and ensuing meeting of the minds, UCLA dominated. In the second game of the season, UCLA beat Iowa, 55–18. On September 29, they beat Michigan State, 34–21, and one week later, they steamrolled the University of Utah, 66–16.

When the conference season began, the Bruins were 3–1 and averaging 42 points per game. Then, something amazing happened. When the Bruins took on the Stanford Cardinals (changed from the "Indians" one year earlier and would be changed again to "Cardinal" in 1982), they set a record that still stands today. On October 13, the Bruins rushed for 621 yards, breaking the record of 532 they had set just the previous year. Then, the second-highest rushing performance in school history came just three weeks later when the Bruins rushed for 566 yards against Washington. Their 10th greatest rushing performance also came in 1973, when the Bruins rushed for 455 yards against California. In coach Rodgers's three seasons as the head coach of the UCLA Bruins, his teams were responsible for five of the top 10 rushing performances in school history. Against Stanford in '73, Kermit Johnson rushed for 168 yards on just 11 carries, and James McAlister rushed for 117 yards and three touchdowns on just 14 carries, before being removed because of a knee injury. The 1973 season produced rushing stats that are looked upon as astounding to this day. Those Bruins rushed into the school record book, accumulating 4,403 yards, 400.4 yards rushing per game, 6.4 yards per carry, and an impressive 56 rushing touchdowns.

After defeating the Cardinals, the Bruins beat Washington State despite one of their worst performances of the year, squeaking by 24–13, before hammering Berkeley, 61–21; Washington, 62–13; Oregon, 27–7; and Oregon State, 56–14. For the second year in a row, the fate of the Pacific 8 Conference came down to the game between the Bruins and the Trojans. UCLA was 9–1 and ranked No. 8 in the country, having gone unbeaten since the season opening loss to Nebraska. USC was 8–1–1 and ranked No. 9. UCLA halfback James McAlister was ready to play again after having missed significant time following his knee injury against Stanford, and Coach Rodgers was convinced it was the proper move to play his 6'1", 205-pound back who had Olympic speed and long jumping ability. Assistant Coach Homer Smith was not so sure. He preferred to lean heavily on Charlie Schumann, who had filled in more than admirably since McAlister went down. Ultimately, head coaches win these arguments, and McAlister was relied on to keep the Bruins offense on a winning path. In hindsight, coach Rodgers admitted that Smith was right and McAlister was used more than he should have. Regardless, UCLA had a strong team and should have defeated USC with or without McAlister at his best. UCLA certainly had the ability to beat the Trojans. They were the top offense in the nation. They had steamrolled strong opponents all season, but the Trojans were a team that reportedly mystified Pepper Rodgers. This time, when the Trojans beat the Bruins again, it was the most disappointing loss of the Rodgers era. USC slowed down the Bruins wishbone like few thought was possible. UCLA scored only 13 points, and USC cruised to a 10-point victory despite being the underdogs. UCLA's season was over. They would finish 9–2 and ranked No. 12 in the final AP poll. USC was off to another Rose Bowl. Pepper Rodgers got a call after the season he could not ignore. His childhood love, the Georgia Tech Yellow Jackets, had a coaching vacancy, and they had a man in Westwood in mind.

The Downtown Athletic Club named John Cappelletti from Penn State University the 1973 Heisman Trophy Winner.

The Associated Press named the University of Notre Dame the 1973 National Champions.

# CHAPTER 11
# Richard "Dick" Vermeil (1974–1975)

Dick Vermeil is a blue-collar man, a hard-working mechanic. He just so happened to be one of the best football coaches in America. Richard "Dick" Vermeil was born on October 30, 1936, in Northern California. Vermeil grew up in the small town of Calistoga in northern Napa Valley. To Louie and Alice Vermeil, Calistoga was more than just a wine attraction; it was the place they could raise their family. After marrying and having four children, the Vermeil parents instilled discipline and toughness. They instilled something in Dick that would make him work harder than anyone in his profession. It all started in Calistoga. The story of Dick Vermeil included stops in Los Angeles, Philadelphia, St. Louis, and Kansas City. He would reach the pinnacle of success in professional football, thanks to a life shaped by long hours in a garage in Calistoga.

Louie Vermeil worked at the Owl Garage, a converted barn, and expected his sons to work as hard as he did. Louie learned from his father, also a mechanic, and he would teach his sons the lessons taught to him. Nothing great comes without sacrifice, and what Louie sacrificed most to build a great life for his family was time. When speaking about the influence he had on his children, Louie would say, "I always worked long hours. I guess it rubbed off on them. I used to go out at 7:30 or 8:00 a.m., come in at 5:00 or 6:00 p.m. and eat, then go back to work until midnight. Then I'd get up in the morning and do it all over again." This was an everyday routine for Louie, and what he passed down to his son Dick was something he would take with him to the NFL. Unfortunately, along the way he encountered challenges that would make the rigor of coaching more difficult than it already is. So he just worked even harder. The sign that Louie hung in the garage summed up what others would feel working for Dick on a coaching staff: "Anyone Who Enjoys Work Can Have a Helluva Time in This Place."

Though Dick was an accomplished mechanic already by the time he reached high school, he had other interests besides working on cars. His home was a place where all the athletes would gather. Dick was a social child, a boy who had aspirations of reaching the highest level. At Calistoga High School, Dick played four sports: football, baseball, basketball, and track. His mother, Alice, would say of Dick, "He was a leader. He was always being chosen captain." Though only 5'5", 125 pounds, Dick was the quarterback at Calistoga and ran the option for coach Bill Wood. Dick would learn the value of a strong running game from coach Wood and also the belief in long practices, perfecting every detail planned. Wood would say of his quarterback, "Dick was a great competitor. You could see right off he didn't want anybody to get the best of him." Very few got the best of Dick. He was an excellent quarterback and an excellent all-around athlete. When he got home from school or competition, he would head to the garage to work with his father for the rest of the night. The long hours in the shop and spending more time with his new girlfriend, Carol, did pose one major problem for the star athlete. He was falling behind in school. After a successful career at Calistoga High School, he was not off to a large university to continue his education and playing career; he would instead attend Napa Junior College.

By now, Dick was up to 140 pounds, still small but an excellent option quarterback. The team finished his sophomore season with a 6–4 record. In 1956, Dick was on to the next stage of his life. He married Carol and enrolled at San Jose State University, where he would continue playing football. He knew he would likely get very little time at quarterback since he weighed only 155 pounds, but he would use this opportunity to learn more about the game. He was ready to be a coach and just wanted to learn. When not in the classroom, practice field, or back home in the garage, Dick would spend his time all across the state attending coaches' clinics. He fully immersed himself in something he planned on doing for the rest of his working life. After graduating with a Master's degree in 1959, Dick began coaching. He was an assistant at Del Mar High School before earning his first head coaching job the following year at Hillsdale High School. In his three seasons there, he went 17–9–1 before moving on to coach the backfield at the College of San Mateo. One year later, he was named the head coach at Napa Junior College, where he compiled a 7–2 record in his only season. By 1965, he had worked his way through the high school and junior college ranks and was ready to take on a major college football program.

The head coach at Stanford University was John Ralston, a man Vermeil had grown to admire. He studied Ralston, and the two became friendly when they met at a coaches' convention. Ralston would remember that Vermeil always sat in the front row with his tape recorder and yellow legal pad, feverishly taking notes. When he got home, Carol would organize the notes, Dick would study them, and the following morning he would have them rewritten, perfectly legible and organized. In '65, Ralston offered a job that Dick was thrilled to accept. "How'd you like to be the freshman coach at Stanford?" Dick's response was swift and simple: "How soon do you want me to report?" In their time together, Dick continually amazed Ralston with his day in, day out work ethic. Ralston would say of his propensity to outwork everyone, "No question, it was phenomenal. No one worked harder than Dick Vermeil . . . He's just the best coach that I can think of. Everything he did was perfect. I've never seen a guy like him."

In 1969, he got his first taste of Los Angeles and his first taste of the National Football League. The head coach of the L.A. Rams was George Allen. He was ahead of his time with his emphasis on special teams. It was an honor for Dick to be named the special teams coach of the Rams in '69, but it was a short-lived duty. In 1970, he was still in Los Angeles, but with another team. The UCLA Bruins, coached by Tommy Prothro, wanted Vermeil, and Prothro got what he wanted. Dick was named the UCLA offensive coordinator. It was the first time in his career that he called plays at a major school, and he did extremely well. Though the team had lost significant talent from the 1969 season and took a step back, Vermeil was considered one of the best coaches on staff. Tommy Prothro would later recognize the great job Vermeil had done for the 1970 team when it came time to fill a staff position in the NFL. UCLA scored 40 points against Oregon, 45 against USC, and 54 against Washington State. When Prothro left UCLA after the 1970 season to take the job with the Los Angeles Rams, he brought his top assistant with him. Dick Vermeil was back with the Rams. He coached the quarterbacks for the Rams for three seasons. One of the players he coached was a cocky, long-haired young man from Youngstown State by the name of Ron Jaworski. The two would reunite years later and stand side by side as they led a team to the Super Bowl. After three years on Prothro's staff, Vermeil moved again. This time he was the head coach. He would make the decisions. Never again would he be an assistant. Now it was time to do things Dick Vermeil's way—at the University of California Los Angeles.

Just four years before, he had come to Westwood to work for Tommy Prothro. Now he was in charge, and he planned to take the team that Pepper Rodgers had succeeded with and take it to the next level. Vermeil set no barriers. He believed he could turn UCLA into the best team in the land. Of course, there was an adjustment period. Most coaches are not accustomed to what Vermeil considered normal hours. Longtime UCLA assistant coach Dick Tomey was one who objected to the 5 a.m.–12 a.m. days that were often standard. Tomey would later say, "I'm for Dick Vermeil. I have the greatest respect for Dickie. He's a very, very close friend, but to contrast myself with him, well, football is not the most important thing in my life. If you've got to work all day and all night every day to be a football coach, I don't want to be one." Despite the frustrating demands of the head man—or perhaps because of them—UCLA thrived under coach Vermeil. After a good opening season, Vermeil's second season was brilliant. UCLA would pull off one of the greatest upsets in college football history on the grandest stage. His time in Westwood, however, like much of his early career, was short-lived. He was on to the next stage. The National Football League came calling, and Dick couldn't say no.

For seven years, Dick Vermeil was known as "The Little Dictator," as head coach of the Philadelphia Eagles. When his team struggled, he simply worked harder and worked longer. The team motto under Vermeil: "No one ever drowned in sweat." One problem for the ultracompetitive Vermeil was that the Eagles were a below average franchise. He inherited a bad team, and when the Eagles won only four and five games in Dick's first two seasons, the man drove himself harder than many considered healthy. He worked more. He was determined to build a winner. In 1977, Ron Jaworski was traded from the Rams to the Eagles, and in his second season in Philadelphia, "Jaws," as he would come to be known, led the Eagles to the playoffs. After four wins in Vermeil's first year, they won five, then nine, then 11, then 12. In 1980, the Eagles were on the verge of doing something no one thought possible before the arrival of Vermeil. They made it to the Super Bowl. The players who could not handle the work that Vermeil demanded of them were traded or released. The coaches who refused to commit to the long hours were let go. By 1980, Vermeil had his team. Though not as talented as many teams in the league due to poor draft trades arranged before Vermeil arrived, the Eagles made up for their talent deficiencies with toughness and discipline. Jaws, Wilbert Montgomery, and Harold Carmichael led the offense. Veteran Herm Edwards was the leader of the defense. After winning the NFC Championship game, Vermeil would say, "I can't even visualize going to the Super Bowl." By the time the game started, he was ready. He worked just as hard to prepare for this game, though he told the press otherwise. The Eagles lost to the Tom Flores-led Oakland Raiders, 27–10. Dick Vermeil would be back to the Super Bowl, but it would take nearly 20 years.

Following the loss in Super Bowl XV, Dick Vermeil was crushed, but motivated. It seemed impossible to the outside observer for Vermeil to work any harder, but he believed that, in order to reach the next step as a team, he would have to lead by example, and that meant more hours. The 1981 Eagles finished with a 10–6 record and a disappointing first-round playoff exit. Due to the 1982 players' strike, the season was shortened from 16 games to nine. Dick Vermeil's final game as the coach of the Philadelphia Eagles came on January 2, 1983. The Eagles lost on a last-second field goal, and Dick Vermeil would leave the game he loved. His hectic work schedule had caught up to him. During the '82 campaign, he was said to be on the verge of a mental breakdown. He worked until 4:00 in the morning on many days and would then be up and ready to address the team by 7:00. He was mentally and physically worn out. Dick Vermeil retired from NFL coaching at the age of 46.

Following his sudden retirement, Vermeil was courted by network television companies almost immediately. He went to work as an NFL analyst. From 1983 to 1987, he worked for CBS. From 1988 to 1996, he worked for ABC. He could rattle off statistics quicker and with more accuracy than any other announcer in the business. Vermeil was, of course, known for overpreparing. He failed to come off as a "natural." He was interesting because he was a human statistical data base, but he failed to connect to the audience on a human level, talking football amongst acquaintances. By staying close to the game, Dick was able to stay happy. He enjoyed his time in the booth, but he always considered himself a football coach. He was not alone.

On December 18, 1994, Dick Vermeil was added to the Philadelphia Eagles Honor Roll. The rumors followed. The Eagles were struggling. With Dick in attendance and rumors swirling of a possible return to the sideline, the crowd chanted, "We want Dick! We want Dick!" Vermeil eventually passed on the opportunity to return to the Eagles, but his interest in a return to the NFL was strong. When Vermeil's old friend, Rams owner Georgia Frontiere, called Dick in January of 1997, he finally made the decision to return. Vermeil had turned down the Rams in 1991, 1994, and just a month prior to getting hired. When he took the job, he was torn. Vermeil was pleased to return to the sidelines and the game he loved but disappointed that his old friend Jim Mora, whom he would replace, was now out of a job. He signed a five-year contract worth eight million dollars. Dick Vermeil was back.

Many fans were skeptical. Analysts agreed. Dick Vermeil was a great coach in the '70s and '80s, but the game had changed. John Madden would say of Vermeil's return, "Dick Vermeil is not coming back to the game he left. I'm not saying he can't do it. I'm saying I don't think *I* could, and it's going to be difficult for him. It's a different game." Though Madden and others doubted Vermeil, he believed in himself. He had stayed close to the sport and believed his work in television helped him understand the game even better. The Rams won the first game of the Dick Vermeil era, 38–24, over the Mike Ditka-led New Orleans Saints. It would be one of the rare bright spots in Vermeil's first two seasons in St. Louis. The team won only five games in 1997 and four in 1998. In the offseason prior to the 1999 season, the Rams hired Mike Martz as their new offensive coordinator. They also drafted Torry Holt in the first round, traded for Marshall Faulk, and had a new quarterback. Coach Vermeil was excited and had high expectations for 1999, but when the man he trusted to execute the offense was injured in preseason, Vermeil was devastated. Trent Green was out. Kurt Warner, a man working in a grocery store five years earlier, was the new quarterback. Warner had played in the Arena League before coming to the Rams, and little was known about him entering the season. What happened next was miraculous. The Rams went 13–3. Faulk was brilliant. Kurt Warner was the MVP of the league. He passed for 4,353 yards and 41 touchdowns. The offense was known as "The Greatest Show on Turf." After beginning the postseason with a bye week, the Rams beat the Vikings, 49–37, behind Warner's five touchdown passes. The following week, they beat the Buccaneers, 11–6. Dick Vermeil reached the Super Bowl 19 years after his first appearance. This time he was relaxed. He knew his team was well prepared, and the best team in the NFL. The game was close. Tied with Tennessee, 16–16, with two minutes to play, Martz called 999-H Balloon. Isaac Bruce caught the underthrown ball and raced to the end zone for the 73-yard score. But Steve McNair and the Titans would not quit. First-and-goal at the 10-yard line. Five seconds left. McNair dropped back and found Kevin Dyson streaking inside and toward the goal line. He caught the ball near the end zone, but linebacker Mike Jones grabbed him and brought him down one yard short as his arm stretched out for the goal line. Close, but not close enough . . . and the Rams won the Super Bowl!

Dick Vermeil retired following the 1999 season. After a year off, he returned to the game. His final coaching stint came with the Kansas City Chiefs from 2001 to 2005. The Chiefs would win as many as 13 games, and Vermeil would finish with a 44–36 record. Over his career, Vermeil had a 120–109 record. He was a head coach in the NFL for 15 years. For UCLA fans, Vermeil was not only the man who led the Rams to a Super Bowl victory in 1999, or led the Eagles to the Super Bowl in 1980. He wasn't just the man who coached the Chiefs or had a long broadcasting career. He's the man who coached the Bruins for two seasons. He's the man who led one of the greatest upsets in college football history. Dick Vermeil and Carol have been married over 50 years. They have three children and 12 grandchildren. From Calistoga to the heights of the football world, Dick Vermeil has done it all.

## 1974

This was a year of intrigue. The nation watched as the events of the Watergate scandal unfolded. After two years of rumors, hearings, conspiracies, and cover-ups, the drama reached a climax. On August 8, 1974, President Richard Nixon resigned, the first and only president ever to do so. Gerald Ford would be sworn in as the 38th President of the United States. A month after Nixon's resignation, the college football season began. For UCLA, it was a year of question marks. Pepper Rodgers had moved on to Georgia Tech. UCLA's high-powered, record-setting offense under Rodgers was an exciting brand of football, but he had never defeated USC. The man who would take his place had no previous head coaching experience. Dick Vermeil's first game as the UCLA head coach came against a tough opponent, the Tennessee Volunteers.

When the No. 12-ranked Bruins took on the No. 16 Volunteers on September 7, the nation was watching. The game was nationally televised on ABC, and the network would be debuting much-hyped football sideline reporters for the first time. The two working this game were both college students. Don

Tollefson, a senior at Stanford University, would report from the UCLA sideline. Jim Lampley, a graduate student at the University of North Carolina, reported from the Tennessee sideline. The two men would not be satisfied with their performances during the game. They were awkward, rushed, and appeared nervous. Very little of the information they reported on was considered significant by viewers, who nonetheless enjoyed the experiment and felt that with time the football sideline reporter could be a valuable broadcasting asset. The game itself was a thriller. Coach Vermeil, like Bruins fans everywhere, was uncertain going into the year how the team would perform. Mark Harmon was gone and on his way to becoming a Hollywood actor. John Sciarra was back, however, at quarterback. In the backfield, James McAllister and Kermit Alexander were both off to the World Football League. There were holes to fill, and coach Vermeil had a difficult task trying to replace established stars. The Bruins of '74 would lean on Sciarra, as well as Russel Charles, Wendell Tyler, and Norm Alexander on offense, to replace those who were now gone. The starting quarterback and leader of the offense for the Volunteers was Conredge Holloway, the first black quarterback at the University of Tennessee and first to start in the Southeastern Conference. On Tennessee's first drive of the game, Holloway made his mark. After running a fullback dive for a short gain out of the veer formation, the Vols went without a huddle. Holloway faked a dive, dropped back, and threw a long pass to Stanley Morgan, who had gotten behind the defense. Seventy-four yards! Touchdown! Both teams added field goals before the halftime break. The score was 10–3 Tennessee. But before the break, the Vols appeared to have suffered a major setback. Holloway was hurt. He fractured his shoulder and was taken to the hospital. Sciarra and the Bruins moved the ball well. They finished the game with over 400 total yards, but UCLA's offense had yet to break through and reach the end zone. In the third quarter, with Tennessee pinned against its own goal line, backup quarterback Pat Ryan fumbled! UCLA recovered and scored. The game was tied, 10–10, when the crowd erupted. Holloway had left the hospital and returned. He had convinced doctors that he could play through the pain. Would he have enough time? That was the question. UCLA added another touchdown in the third quarter and led, 17–10. Holloway was not interested in simply returning, he would do everything in his power to win the game. After driving the ball down the field, Holloway would show his grit. The drive was capped by a diving, hurdling leap into the end zone. Touchdown Volunteers! The extra point was good, and the score was once again tied, 17–17. Though Sciarra didn't have Holloway's flash, he was every bit the great quarterback. After driving down the field in the final minutes, UCLA was in field goal range, but the kick missed. The final score was 17–17. Coach Vermeil's first win would have to wait.

Unfortunately for Coach Vermeil, his assistant coaches, players, and fans, that first win would have to wait more than just one more week. In Week 2, the Bruins traveled to Iowa City, Iowa, and lost to the Hawkeyes, 21–10. The following week, the Bruins took on old nemesis Michigan State in the Los Angeles Coliseum. Final score: UCLA 56, MSU 14. The Bruins were in the win column. It would be the first of many wins for Dick Vermeil as a head coach. The Bruins were 1–1–1 with one nonconference game remaining. On October 5, the Bruins took on the struggling University of Utah. The Bruins won by a score of 27–14. Now it was time for conference play. After four games, many of the same questions asked at the beginning of the season were still unanswered. Coach Vermeil, as well as Sciarra and the other leaders, would have to prove themselves in conference play.

The Bruins began conference play with a disappointing tie. When Stanford came south to take on the Bruins, UCLA hoped to begin the Pac 8 slate with a win. It wasn't to be. Final score: UCLA 13, Stanford 13. Following the tie, UCLA would win consecutive games for the second time that season. On October 19, the Bruins beat Washington State, 17–13, and the following week they roughed up the No. 20 California Golden Bears, 28–3. UCLA had dropped out of the top 25 rankings after their early-season loss to Iowa, but after beating the Bears they reentered the list, and when the Blue and Gold took on the University of Washington, they were ranked No. 18 in the country. Jim Owens and the Huskies started the game with a 3–4 record. They had won their first two games of the year before losing four straight. One week before their meeting with the Bruins, Washington had broken a losing streak by crushing the University of Oregon, 66–0. While the Bruins were difficult to judge in '74, the Huskies were impossible to figure out. Washington beat the Bruins, 31–9. It was a disappointing loss for the workaholic Vermeil, who believed his team was ready to take the next step and compete consistently each week. UCLA won the next two games—over Oregon, 21–0, and Oregon State, 33–14—before taking on their hated rival, the USC Trojans.

The Bruins had won two consecutive games early in the year before failing to win a third, against Stanford. They later won two in a row again, then lost to Washington. Now, they were riding another two-game winning streak when they took the field against the Trojans. USC was ranked No. 8 and entered the game with a 7–1–1 record. Though only in his first year, there was pressure on Dick Vermeil. UCLA fans, who had grown accustomed to beating USC in the 1950s and '60s, were tired of losing to John McKay and the Trojans in the '70s. Coach Vermeil would get a victory over the Trojans that would ultimately become a fond memory for Bruins diehards, but he would have to wait a year to get the job done. In 1974, the Trojans were too strong. The Bruins turned the ball over five times, and Anthony Davis rushed for 195 yards against the Bruins defense. As the final seconds ticked off the clock, the scoreboard read USC 34, UCLA 9. The 25-point loss was the Bruins' largest margin of defeat by the Trojans since 1944. The Bruins finished the season with an overall record of 6–3–2, for a third-place finish in the Pacific 8 Conference.

The Downtown Athletic Club named Archie Griffin from Ohio State University the 1974 Heisman Trophy Winner.

The Associated Press named the University of Oklahoma the 1974 National Champions.

## 1975

In 1975, the Vietnam War came to a close, as did the career of legendary UCLA basketball coach John Wooden. Coach Wooden would go out on top. His '75 Bruins were led by Dave Meyers, Richard Washington, and Marques Johnson. They finished with a 28–3 record and a 92–85 victory in the National Championship over the Kentucky Wildcats. It was a fitting way to end the career of the greatest coach in college sports history. John Wooden teams won 10 National Championships, including a stretch of seven in a row from 1967 to 1973. Though UCLA had considerable talent, the team hoops program always stood above the individual. While players like Walt Hazzard, Gail Goodrich, Lew Alcindor, Sidney Wicks, Bill Walton, Keith Wilkes, and Marques Johnson came and went, Wooden remained, and success was always near. The Wizard of Westwood was a Hall of Fame player and coach. His was, and is, the standard that still stands today. It would be another 20 years before UCLA would win a National Championship in basketball without Wooden. By 1975, it had been 21 years since the UCLA football team won the National Championship in a split decision by the numerous polls. The gridiron Bruins of '54 had shared the title with the Ohio State Buckeyes, and the nation was robbed of what was seen by many as the potential "Game of the Decade." When Dick Vermeil's second season in Westwood came to a close, the situation was similar. But this time—on January 1, 1976—the nation got the matchup it had wanted 21 years earlier.

The Bruins of '75 had a loaded roster. All-American John Sciarra was a senior; junior halfback Wendell Tyler was back and poised for a breakout season. Cliff Frazier led the defense from the nose guard position, and Terry Tautolo, Raymond Bell, Pat Schmidt, Dale Curry, and Raymond Burks helped form one of the best Bruins defenses in years. The season kicked off on September 13, when the Bruins took on the formidable Iowa State Cyclones at the Los Angeles Memorial Coliseum. The Associated Press tabbed the Bruins as the No. 16 team in America, and in order to keep their ranking, they would have to prove they could live up to the hype. UCLA would have to avoid the injury bug that plagued them during the '74 season and ultimately perform at a high level on the field. They would have to show the consistency that the team lacked in coach Vermeil's first season. The first two games of the season proved to be strong showings for the Bruins. After defeating the Cyclones, 37–21, in Week 1, it was time for the rematch with the Tennessee Volunteers that fans from both sides had looked forward to for an entire year. When the No. 10 Vols traveled to Los Angeles, they got a rude awakening. The Bruins, now No. 12 in the nation, beat Tennessee, 34–28. UCLA was 2–0 with a matchup against highly ranked Ohio

State just two weeks away. But first, before they got to the Buckeyes, UCLA would have to take care of the Air Force Academy Falcons. Perhaps with their focus diverted on Archie Griffin and the Buckeyes, UCLA struggled against AFA and stumbled to a 20–20 tie in a game plagued by turnovers. It was most assuredly a disappointing outcome for the Bruins, but they had no time to sulk. They had a challenge just seven days away that would keep Coach Vermeil awake and working long hours. Teams were unable to slow down Heisman winner Archie Griffin in '74, and the Bruins had a monumental task ahead to crack the code. On October 4, it was time to face the Ohio State Buckeyes.

After the disappointing tie, the Bruins were ranked down a notch to No. 13 when they took the field against the No. 2 Buckeyes at the L.A, Coliseum. Though the Bruins had beaten a highly ranked Tennessee team just weeks earlier, few thought they could compete with OSU. The Bruins got off to a quick start. The day's scoring began when Sciarra hit James Sarpy for a 13-yard score. OSU bounced back, however, to tie the score with a touchdown of its own. At the end of one quarter, the score was still tied, but the Buckeyes would show their strength in the second quarter. Three times Ohio State ran for touchdowns in the second quarter, and the Bruins were unable to answer after any of them. At halftime, the score was 28–7, OSU. The monumental task of beating the Buckeyes seemed impossible. Woody Hayes's squad was too strong. In the second half, Eddie Ayers ran for two Bruins touchdowns, but the UCLA defense could not slow down the potent OSU offense. Final score: OSU 41, UCLA 20. Despite the result, coach Hayes predicted that the Bruins and Buckeyes would meet again.

The Bruins were 2–1–1 when they began conference play. Despite a disappointing two-week stretch, the main goal remained the same. UCLA had eyes on the Rose Bowl. The Pacific 8 Conference opener pitted the Bruins against the Stanford Cardinals. UCLA won, 31–21, and after having briefly fallen out of the AP rankings reentered the following week at No. 18. UCLA went on to beat Washington State, 37–23, and California, 28–14, before facing their old nemesis, the Washington Huskies. UW was 3–4 when they traveled south to take on Coach Vermeil and the Bruins. Huskies Coach Don James was in his first year at Washington and was playing a difficult schedule. They had been crushed by highly ranked Texas and Alabama earlier in the season, were battle-tested, and improving as the season went on. To the surprise of those in attendance, and many of those playing and coaching, Washington stunned the Bruins. UCLA's normally powerful offense struggled for much of the night and scored only 13 points, the fewest they would score all season. Washington reached the end zone twice and added a field goal to win, 17–13. It was a disappointing loss for the Bruins, but it was not debilitating. UCLA had only one loss thus far in conference play, and because of their victory over the California Golden Bears one week earlier, their destiny was still in their hands. If they could win their final three conference games, they would be Pac 8 Champions and head to the Rose Bowl.

On November 8, the Bruins offense reawakened after that one-week slumber. The Oregon Webfeet had no chance. The final score was UCLA 50, Oregon 17. A week later, UCLA dominated once again: UCLA 31, Oregon State 9. The regular season came down to one final game. When the Bruins took the field against USC on November 28, the familiar roles were reversed. USC was a strong team, but the UCLA Bruins were favored. If UCLA beat USC, they would head to the Rose Bowl. If they lost, Cal would get the January 1 date. Just a month earlier, USC had a record of 7–0 and was ranked No. 3 in the country, but a three-game losing streak had dropped the Trojans out of the AP rankings and out of the chase for the conference title. UCLA was the superior team but almost fumbled away an opportunity to beat its rival. UCLA fumbled the ball an astounding 11 times and lost eight of them. Multiple backs coughed the ball up, and coach Vermeil tried everything to resolve the issue. He would say after the game, "Wendell Tyler was a fumbler and he fumbled it. Then I went to my next running back, Carl Zaby, and he fumbled. Then I went to my next running back, Kenny Lee, and he fumbled it." Coach Vermeil explained that fumbling had no prejudice. He would say, "I remember turning to my coaches and saying, 'We had a black guy fumble it, a white guy fumble it, and an Oriental guy fumble it. Let's go back to the best running back and we'll see what he does.'' The best running back the Bruins had, and one of the best in UCLA history, was Wendell Tyler. He rushed for 130 yards on the day. Eddie Ayers added 98 yards. The game was close, but the Bruins escaped by a score of 25–22. UCLA beat USC for the first time in five years. The Victory Bell was carried back to Westwood, and the Bruins would be off to Pasadena to take on the team that had clobbered them earlier in the season, the Ohio State Buckeyes.

Ohio State was 11–0 and ranked No. 1 in the nation. Archie Griffin was a brilliant running back who would go down in history as one of the greatest to ever play college football. The pregame festivities on the day of the Rose Bowl are always part of the show, and on this day it was no different. Kate Smith was the Rose Bowl parade grand marshal. By tradition, the UCLA band performed along the parade route. They donned roses on their instruments in salute to the greatest bowl game of them all. More than 105,000 fans packed the Rose Bowl in what most presumed would be the final game to cap another National Championship season for Coach Hayes and the Buckeyes. UCLA was a 15-point underdog, but coach Hayes felt UCLA was the best team they had played all season and should not be taken lightly. Coach Vermeil considered the time between their game against USC and the Rose Bowl game as an opportunity to perfect their craft. UCLA spent countless hours fine-tuning his game plan and perfecting its execution. The first half was unexpectedly uneventful. OSU dominated the line of scrimmage and moved the ball seemingly at ease, but the Bruins held time and again to keep the score close. UCLA's offense was anemic and appeared unable to do anything against their strong opposition. At halftime, UCLA had accumulated only 48 yards yet trailed just 3–0 after a 42-yard field goal by Tom Kleban. At the break, one thing was clear: the Bruins would not roll over and simply hand the crown to the Buckeyes. Coach Vermeil and the Bruins planned on beating Coach Hayes and sending them back to Columbus wondering what had happened. Only 30 minutes remained for the Bruins to pull off one of the greatest upsets in college football history. Still, they trailed. UCLA's offense came alive in the second half. Opening the third quarter, the UCLA offensive line and backfield dominated as they marched down the field for their strongest drive of the game to that point, and Brett White knocked in a 33-yard field goal to tie the game. The crowd was stunned: the underdog Bruins were hanging in with the best team in America. UCLA forced a punt on OSU's next drive, and Sciarra again led the Bruins down the field. Six plays and 61 yards later, Sciarra hit Wally "Hollywood" Henry for a 16-yard touchdown. After another defensive stop, the two connected again. This time Henry beat OSU safety Craig Cassady, and Sciarra threw a perfect pass as Henry outraced the defense 67 yards for another score. UCLA led the top-ranked team in the nation, 16–3! The Buckeyes would not go quietly. Despite a deficit few on the OSU squad had expected, they still had their sights on victory. After a 12-play, 65-yard drive, Pete Johnson scored from three yards out, and the lead was cut to six. Twice more, OSU drove into Bruins territory, both times seemingly ready to retake the lead and break the hearts of the Bruins, but both times UCLA stood tall. All Big 10 quarterback, Cornelius Greene, was intercepted first by Barney Person and then by Pat Schmidt to end both threats. With just under four minutes to play, UCLA had the ball, still holding a six-point lead. The ball was handed to Wendell Tyler, and with the OSU defense selling out in an effort to stop the run and get the ball back as quickly as possible, Tyler broke through the first line of defense and raced toward the end zone. No one would catch him! Fifty-four yards, touchdown! The Bruins beat the Buckeyes, 23–10! The college football world was shocked. Heisman trophy winner Archie Griffin, who broke a bone in his hand in the first quarter, finished with 93 yards. Wendell Tyler finished with 172 yards. Sciarra threw for 212 yards. UCLA was the only team to score at least 20 points on the OSU defense all year, doing so in both meetings. The 10 points scored by the OSU offense was their lowest point total all season. The Bruins were the Rose Bowl champions! Coach

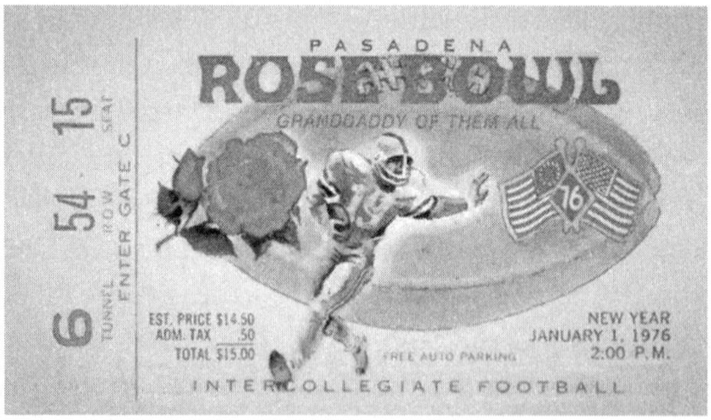

1976 Rose Bowl ticket (Southern Campus Collection)

Vermeil's stint in Westwood was short-lived. He was off to the NFL, but he left UCLA with a memory to cherish forever. For the fans of the 1954 Bruins, the win over OSU in January of '76 may not be the redemption they sought, but victory on the biggest stage is always sweet.

The Downtown Athletic Club named Archie Griffin from Ohio State University the 1975 Heisman Trophy Winner.

The Associated Press named the University of Oklahoma the 1975 National Champions.

Dick Vermeil and family following the 1976 Rose Bowl (Southern Campus Collection)

John Sciarra and the Bruins shocked the world in the 1976 Rose Bowl (Southern Campus Collection)

# CHAPTER 12
# Terry Donahue (1976–1995)

The man who would one day become the Pacific 12 Conference's all-time leader in wins was born on June 24, 1944, in Los Angeles, California. Terry Donahue was not a natural athlete. He was a worker. Growing up, he wasn't big. He wasn't particularly fast. He wasn't recruited by schools around the country. Yet, he still made it. Terry Donahue's path from a high school athlete largely ignored, to a Division 1 football player, to a successful coach, and ultimately to the College Football Hall of Fame was filled with speed bumps. After attending St. Charles Borromeo Elementary School, Donahue attended Notre Dame High School in Sherman Oaks. After high school, Donahue needed a home. He wanted to continue playing football and believed he could play at the college level, but his options were limited. Terry Donahue enrolled at one of the few schools that would let him play, San Jose State University.

Terry Donahue, 1978 (Southern Campus Collection)

Despite finding a place he believed he could settle in for four years, Donahue found San Jose State to be not all that welcoming. As a walk-on, he would have to continually prove his worth and work extra hard, something that was not a problem for him. What was a problem, however, was a coach who simply didn't believe Terry could ever make anything of himself as a player. After one year, Donahue left SJSU because he was told that, at 170 pounds, he wasn't big enough to play linebacker, and the Spartans no longer wanted him. Once again, he was forced to look for a new place to continue his football career.

After his brief stint with San Jose State University, Terry Donahue enrolled at tiny Valley College, just north of Los Angeles. In the meantime, he got serious about another sport: boxing. He bulked up to 190 pounds and trained relentlessly. He wanted to be the best athlete he could be. Boxing would ultimately help make him a better football player, he believed. After one year at Valley College and one amateur boxing bout—a win—Donahue gained the title he had been working at for years: he became a UCLA football player. In 1965, Donahue enrolled at UCLA, and, though he was still small for a linebacker, Coach Tommy Prothro believed he was suited to be a defensive tackle. Yes, he was small, but he was strong and he was quick. Though he was still a walk-on, Donahue contributed almost immediately. In 1965, he earned a starting spot and was part of a magical season. After losing the opening game of the season to Michigan State University, UCLA would go 7–1–1 the rest of the regular season, including an upset over highly favored USC. In the Rose Bowl game rematch against Michigan State, the Bruins would get their revenge, beating MSU, 14–12 and denying the Spartans the National Championship. The 1965 team would be nicknamed "The Gutty Little Bruins," and Terry Donahue epitomized the nickname. Winning the Rose Bowl is something that Terry Donahue would later become accustomed to.

After the 1966 season, in which Terry was a senior and the Bruins finished 9–1, beat USC, and only missed out on the Rose Bowl once again due to bureaucratic shenanigans, it was time to start a new phase. Despite being a good college player, Donahue knew that his future was not in playing, but rather in coaching. After graduation, Terry Donahue followed UCLA Assistant Coach Pepper Rodgers to the University of Kansas. Rodgers had taken over as the Jayhawks head coach, and Donahue asked his former coach if he could join his staff. "Yes," said Rodgers, but there was no room for him in the budget. He would have to be a volunteer, unpaid coach. Donahue did just that, eventually becoming part of the full-time, paid staff and coaching the defensive line at Kansas through the 1970 season. In 1971, Pepper Rodgers returned to UCLA, this time as the Bruins head coach, and Donahue came with him to coach the UCLA offensive line. For five years, Donahue was an assistant, teaching his unit the intricacies of blocking, taking proper angles, and the importance of knowing and executing assignments. All the while, he was learning on the job, as well. Donahue would later credit three men for teaching him the ways of coaching. Donahue would say of Tommy Prothro, for whom he played, "Prothro would teach me the value of fundamentals." Of Pepper Rodgers he would say, "Rodgers was brilliant in his way of teaching technical features." Lastly, he would say of Dick Vermeil, who would take over for Rodgers in 1974 when the latter left for Georgia Tech, "Vermeil taught me the value of organized drills and hard work." By 1976, when Dick Vermeil was off to the NFL, Donahue, though only 31 years old when hired, was the man selected for the job. UCLA Athletic Director J.D. Morgan initially thought Donahue would take an assistant job with Vermeil or Prothro in the NFL, but Donahue wanted to stay at UCLA. The final decision came down a choice between Donahue and UCLA Defensive Coordinator Lynn Stiles. Once again, the underdog came out on top. Donahue took over the UCLA football program and would leave a lasting legacy.

In Terry Donahue's 20 seasons as the UCLA football head coach, he racked up a list of accomplishments that made UCLA Bruins fans, alumni, and boosters quite proud. The Bruins won the Pac 10 Conference titles in 1982, 1983, 1985, 1987, and 1993. He was twice named Pac 10 Coach of the Year. He is the Pac 12 all-time leader in wins. He had a winning record against the rival USC Trojans. He repeatedly turned down NFL head coaching opportunities with the Cowboys and Falcons, and he is the longest-tenured UCLA football coach in history. Donahue's teams won three Rose Bowls. His teams won eight consecutive bowl games from 1982 to 1989, including a stretch of four consecutive New Year's bowl games from 1983 to 1986. During his tenure, the Bruins had a winning percentage of .665, finished ranked in the top 20 by the Associated Press 12 times, and were ranked in the top 10 five times. Terry Donahue coached 34 first-team All-Americans, and more than 100 players who played under Coach Donahue were drafted into the National Football League. The luxury suites at the Rose Bowl are now named the Terry Donahue Pavilion. He was named to the Rose Bowl Hall of Fame and the Sun Bowl Hall of Fame. He has been named to both the UCLA Athletics Hall of Fame and the College Football Hall of Fame.

Looking back on Terry Donahue's career, it may come as a bit of a shock to many that he retired from coaching at the age of 51, and in good standing with UCLA administrators, but rumors had been circulating for years before he announced his retirement in December of 1995. When Donahue accepted the job in 1976, he was told by athletic director Morgan that if he made it to the age of 40, he would be a good coach in his mind. Terry had an itch for television, and an itch to try something new. Looking back on his young retirement from coaching, Donahue became convinced that he left too early, but he is also proud of the things he has done since leaving UCLA. In 1996, he became the lead college football analyst for CBS Sports. It was a role he filled for three seasons before moving on to the next stage of his career.

In 1999, Bill Walsh hired Donahue as director of player personnel for the San Francisco 49ers. Walsh handpicked Donahue knowing that Walsh himself would be retiring soon and wanted the 49ers in capable hands. In 2001, Donahue was named general manager of the 49ers. But Donahue would not have the success in the NFL he had in college. After four seasons, he was fired. As the UCLA football program began to flounder, Donahue could only think, "What if?" In 2005, he was back on television, working as a lead game analyst for FOX. As of this writing, Donahue works for the NFL Network as an analyst.

Since retiring from coaching following the 1995 season, Donahue has continued to stay connected to UCLA and dreams of one day seeing his alma mater win another National Championship. He is part of the UCLA Campaign Cabinet, devoting time speaking to various groups. Terry was very close to former UCLA Basketball Coach John Wooden and has represented UCLA well throughout his life. Donahue still attends UCLA football games on occasion; he is eager for the day the Bruins reach the college football mountaintop. "Somebody—probably Jim [Mora], but if not him, somebody else—will win a National Championship." When they do, Terry Donahue, a Bruin always, will celebrate.

## 1976

By 1976, the Vietnam War was over, and the presidency of Gerald Ford was coming to a close. On November 2, former Governor of Georgia Jimmy Carter defeated incumbent President Ford by a 297–240 electoral margin. The nation would soon have a new leader, just like UCLA football. After a successful 1975 season had culminated in a Rose Bowl victory, Dick Vermeil was off to the NFL, and Terry Donahue was eager to start the next era of UCLA football. As the United States celebrated its bicentennial, the Bruins celebrated a good season. Donahue would pick up right where Dick Vermeil left off. The Bruins of '76 were good, damn good, but the season is long. They would have to show up and perform each and every week if they were to make another Rose Bowl. The Terry Donahue era began on September 9, 1976.

UCLA began the season as the No. 17 team in the nation, according to the Associated Press. Though defending Rose Bowl Champions, there were question marks entering the 1976 season beyond coaching. Star quarterback John Sciarra was gone, off to the Canadian Football League. Future Hall of Fame offensive lineman Randy Cross was off to the NFL, as well as Cliff Frazier, Norm Anderson, Dale Curry, and others. The Bruins had holes to fill and a tough opponent to open the season. When the Bruins traveled to Tempe, Arizona, to take on the Arizona State Sun Devils, they were underdogs. ASU, members of the Western Athletic Conference, were the No. 3 team in the nation and were riding a 17-game winning streak. ASU head coach Frank Kush had built a team that could compete with Pac 8 opponents and win. They would soon join the conference themselves. In this season opener, ASU would get on the board first. After Sun Devils defensive end Willie Scroggins recovered a Theotis Brown fumble at the UCLA 39-yard line, ASU kicker Dan Kush knocked in a field goal, and the Bruins trailed, 3–0. Following the ASU field goal, the Bruins began to hit their stride. Late in the first quarter, UCLA began their first scoring drive of the season. Following a nine-play, 80-yard drive, the Bruins reached the end zone for the first time just 40 seconds into the second quarter on a 32-yard touchdown run by quarterback Jeff Dankworth. The UCLA defense dominated the first half, shutting down the ASU offense and keeping them out of the end zone. UCLA's offense mounted another long drive in the second quarter. On the 12th play of the drive, Dankworth reached the end zone again, and the Bruins led, 14–3, at halftime. When the teams reentered the field in the third quarter, many expected the highly ranked Sun Devils to adjust and come out in the second half with a better performance. That wasn't the case. UCLA dominated the third quarter. Theotis Brown scored twice on the ground, from two yards out and then from 26, taking over after All-Pac 8 cornerback Levi Armstrong recovered a fumble, and then when Harold Hardin intercepted a pass. Though ASU would finally reach the end zone in the fourth quarter, it was too little too late. Coach Donahue and the Bruins had passed their first test of the season by defeating the No. 3 Sun Devils on the road, 28–10.

After the impressive showing, it was clear that voters responsible for the rankings had taken notice. When the Bruins took on the Arizona Wildcats in Week 2, they had risen all the way to No. 5 in the nation. The Wildcats had no chance. UCLA 37, Arizona

9. On the following week, the Bruins won again, this time defeating Air Force Academy, 40–7. On October 2, the Bruins took on the team they had beaten 10 months earlier in Pasadena, the Ohio State Buckeyes. UCLA was ranked No. 4 and the Buckeyes No. 8 when the two teams clashed in Columbus. The game was billed as "the rubber match" because the two teams had split their two games in '75. A crowd of 87,969 packed The Horseshoe to see the two powers face off. The game was dominated by both defenses. Jeff Dankworth, Theotis Brown, and Wendell Tyler struggled to move the ball, and it was apparent that the post-Archie Griffin era Buckeyes were still looking to fill the enormous void left by the graduation of their two-time Heisman Trophy-winning running back. The first score of the game came in the second quarter. After a 17-yard punt return by Ray Griffin put the ball into UCLA territory, the OSU offense came to life, and fullback Pete Johnson capped the Buckeyes drive with a touchdown from four yards out. Fewer than six minutes into the third quarter, the Bruins finally got on the board with a 47-yard field goal. Later in the half, UCLA scored again. After recovering a Buckeyes fumble deep in their own territory, UCLA drove 83 yards to take a 10–7 lead. The drive had appeared to be stalled, but on fourth-and-1 at the OSU 49-yard line, Coach Donahue called for a fake punt, and Theotis Brown carried the ball 25 yards to keep the drive alive. OSU bounced back on their next drive and tied the game on a 25-yard field goal. With time ticking away in the fourth quarter, legendary OSU coach Woody Hayes appeared to be playing for the tie. It was fourth-and-1 with the ball on UCLA's 48-yard line. UCLA's defense was strong, and coach Hayes felt it better not to risk turning the ball over on downs, which would give UCLA a shot to win in the final minute. He chose to punt. The game ended in a 10–10 tie. The two teams had both pushed hard in their rubber match. The debate would continue, and the teams would have to wait.

After their 3–0–1 start and the slight disappointment against the Buckeyes, UCLA caught fire. On October 9, they beat Stanford, 38–20. They followed up with wins over Washington State (62–3), California (35–19), Washington (30–21), Oregon (46–0), and Oregon State (45–14), before taking on the Trojans. UCLA was 9–0–1 and ranked No. 2 in the nation. USC was 8–1 and ranked No. 3. Once again, the winner of the game would go to the Rose Bowl. Although this was a contest in which everything was on the line for both teams, it ended up being a stinker. USC dominated. The final score was 24–14, but it could have been much worse. USC led at one point, 24–0. The Bruins struggled to contain Ricky Bell and Vince Evans and never really managed to get their own offense going when it counted. Wendell Tyler was playing injured, and Dankworth was mostly ineffective. The Bruins' season had been a success through the first 10 games, but the 11th would leave a bad taste in their mouths for the entire offseason.

UCLA went to the postseason Liberty Bowl in Memphis, Tennessee, and took on the No. 16 Alabama Crimson Tide, coached by Bear Bryant. After the disappointing regular season finale, there was nothing to play for except pride, and Coach Donahue and staff were unable to rally their men for one final performance. UCLA was thoroughly beaten. The final score was 36–6 Alabama. Coach Donahue's first season had fans dreaming of the Red Sanders era, but the greatest of teams are able to finish the season with wins against the toughest opponents. UCLA had lost to USC once again. They ended their season in a bowl game, but not the one they had hoped for. The team finished 9–2–1, a record that, ironically, in most years would have been considered a fine achievement in Westwood, and were ranked No. 15 in the final AP poll of the season.

The Downtown Athletic Club named Tony Dorsett from the University of Pittsburgh the 1976 Heisman Trophy Winner.

The Associated Press named the University of Pittsburgh the 1976 National Champions.

## 1977

By 1977, one thing was clear. It was Terry Donahue's team. The young, energetic coach had led the Bruins to a 9–2–1 record in '76, and in '77 they set their sights on an even better season. Star linebacker Jerry Robinson, already one of the best players in school history, was a junior, and a new man arrived on campus who immediately made his mark. Kenny Easley was a freshman who would soon join Robinson in the hearts and minds of Bruins fans everywhere. Like Robinson, Easley would go down as one of the best players to ever put on a blue-and-gold uniform. On the defensive line, Manu Tuiasosopo anchored the unit and would earn All-America acclaim. On the offensive side of the ball, Rick Bashore was the new quarterback. Wendell Tyler was off to the Los Angeles Rams of the National Football League, but Theotis Brown returned, and James Owens emerged as a premier offensive weapon. Freshman Freeman McNeil would provide a spark in limited action, and Homer Butler would lead the Bruins in receiving. Offensive lineman Gus Coppens was an All-American. The Bruins also signed what many considered the best recruiting class in the nation in 1977. The season would begin with a challenge. Expectations were high. The Associated Press named UCLA the No. 14 team in the nation.

The 1977 football season kicked off on Monday, September 12, in Houston, Texas, against the No. 9 Houston Cougars of the Southwest Conference. The Bruins got off to a quick start. At halftime, they led by a score of 13–3. Placekicker Frank Corral had knocked in field goals from 30 and 36 yards out, and quarterback Rick Bashore found Homer Butler for the first touchdown of the season on a 20-yard pass. The defense was stingy and allowed only three first-half points. In the second half, the UCLA offense continued to move the ball seemingly at will but repeatedly made crucial errors that prevented them from scoring. On three consecutive possessions, UCLA fumbled deep in Houston territory. The Bruins fumbled at the Houston 6-yard line, then the Houston seven, then the Houston nine. Each time, their opponent recovered and the Bruins were kept off the scoreboard. The Houston offense in the second half took advantage of the Bruins miscues. Though the UCLA defense performed fairly well, it was not enough, and the two second-half Houston scores were the difference in the game. UCLA lost, 17–13, and started the season 0–1.

For the next four weeks, inconsistency plagued the Bruins. After beating Kansas, 17–7, in Week 2, UCLA was whipped by the Minnesota Golden Gophers, 27–13, in Week 3. In UCLA's final non-conference game, they got back in the win column by beating Bob Commings and the Iowa Hawkeyes, 34–16. When conference play began, the Bruins brought with them a record of 2–2. They had won, then lost, then won, then lost. They hoped to break the trend against the Bill Walsh-coached Stanford Cardinals (they didn't change the name to "Cardinal" until 1981). Offensively, Stanford presented a challenge to Robinson, Easley, Tuiasosopo, and the rest of the Bruins. Quarterback Guy Benjamin was one of the best passers in the nation, and wide receiver James Lofton and tackle Gordon King would go on to be drafted in the first round of the NFL draft. A crowd of 64,500 fans showed up at Stanford Stadium to see the two California rivals on October 8. They would get a show, but those who made the trek north from Westwood would leave disappointed. Stanford won, 32–28. UCLA's record dropped to 2–3, certainly a disappointment thus far—with already more losses than in the entire previous year—but Coach Donahue and his talented roster would plug along until they finally hit their stride.

After beating Washington State, 27–16, in Spokane on October 15, UCLA took on their old foe, the California Berkeley Golden Bears. Cal was having a strong season, 5–1 to that point, and were ranked No. 15 in the nation. Coach Mike White had a strong offense, but a mediocre defense. UCLA believed they could score on the Bears and slow down their strong offense enough to come away with an upset over the favored opponent. The Bruins had defeated the team from up north five times in a row, and though Berkeley had a strong team in '77, the Bruins had no intention of letting their oldest rival taste victory anytime soon. Coach Donahue's confidence in his team was justified. UCLA's defense held the Bears to just 19 points, and the offense scored just enough to escape with a win. UCLA 21, California 19.

After defeating WSU and Cal, the Bruins had their first winning streak of the season. On October

UCLA vs. Cal, 1978 (Southern Campus Collection)

29, they extended their winning streak to three with a 20–12 win over the University of Washington. One week later, the win streak was four when the Bruins beat the Oregon Webfeet, 21–3, in Eugene. The Bruins saved their best offensive performance of the year for their tenth game, a matchup with the Oregon State Beavers. The Bruins dismantled the Beavers defense and went on to win by the score of 48–18. The winning streak had reached five, but the biggest game of all was still ahead.

On November 25, 1977, the red-hot UCLA Bruins, now ranked No. 17 in the nation, took on the unranked 6–4 USC Trojans. Head coach John Robinson and the Trojans had just come off a loss to the Washington Huskies and were playing for nothing more than bragging rights. UCLA, on the other hand, was one win away from clinching a Rose Bowl berth. The Bruins got off to a good start. At the end of the first quarter, they led, 10–0, but the second and third quarters could be described as nothing other than disastrous. The Trojans scored 26 unanswered points and took a lead into the fourth that seemed insurmountable. USC coaches, however, sensing victory at hand, got very conservative with their play calling, and UCLA stormed back into the game. Rick Bashore would not go down without a fight. Bashore's coaches, teammates, and fans had not even expected him to play. He had bruised ribs and suffered a collapsed lung, but days before the game doctors cleared him, and his toughness was never clearer than during his valiant fourth quarter. Bashore led drives of 63 and 48 yards that ended in a touchdown and a field goal. The Bruins trailed 26–20. In the middle of the fourth quarter, UCLA once again had the ball, and this time they could take the lead and complete an improbable comeback. The Bruins took over at the USC 20-yard line and proceeded to march down the field like General George Patton and the United States Third Army marched across Europe during World War II. They were unstoppable. The drive culminated with their third late score, a 1-yard pass from Bashore to tight end Don Pederson. The extra point was good, and the Bruins took the lead, 27–26, with 2:51 to go. The comeback was complete, but the game was not. Rob Hertel and the USC offense began their march. Short pass after short pass, they suddenly found themselves in a position to steal victory, but it took a break to get them there. On third-and-10 from the 50-yard line with under a minute to play, Hertel dropped back and looked for Kevin Williams. He delivered a pass, and UCLA defensive back Johnny Lynn was all over it, meeting Williams and the ball and breaking up the pass. The fans cheered. They were one play away from sealing victory, but a flag had been thrown! Just as in the 1969 game, there was controversy. Pass interference! The drive continued. The game would come down to the leg of USC kicker Frank Jordan. The ball was snapped. The hold was good, and the ball sailed right through the uprights from 38 yards out. The Bruins were crushed. With just two seconds left, Jordan had ended their season and their bid for the Rose Bowl. Coach Donahue would long remember the pass interference call and years later say, "A very bad call. We were down and came storming back and fought like crazy, and to have that thing decided in the final seconds on that kind of call . . ." He couldn't finish. He was too upset. UCLA finished the season with a 7–4 record.

The Downtown Athletic Club named Earl Campbell from the University of Texas the 1977 Heisman Trophy Winner.

The Associated Press named the University of Notre Dame the 1977 National Champions.

UCLA Cheerleaders, 1977 (Southern Campus Collection)

UCLA fans, 1978 (Southern Campus Collection)

## 1978

On September 9, 1978, the UCLA Bruins were matched against the University of Washington Huskies in a much-anticipated season opener. UCLA was ranked No. 12 in the country, and the Don James-coached Huskies were ranked No. 11. Both teams figured to compete for the conference title. Along with the usual conference powers, two new teams were joining the competition. Unlike the conference expansion that would take place three decades later, the one in '78 was not driven by money alone, but rather by two men looking to improve the exposure of the conference and of their schools. UCLA chancellor Charles Young and University of Arizona president John Schaefer were the driving forces behind the change. In May of '76, chancellor Young had sent UCLA Vice President John Sandbrook to Arizona to explore the option. Ten months later, Young, Sandbrook, and Schaefer concluded that adding UofA to the conference would not only work, it would be beneficial to all members. Though the deal to add UofA and Arizona State University met some opposition, most notably from ASU football head coach Frank Kush and University of Washington president John Hogness, the deal was approved on December 12, 1976. The two schools would play one final season in the Western Athletic Conference before joining the Pacific 10 in 1978. UCLA's first game against one of the new conference foes would not come until the eighth game of the season. Their first task was taking on the talented Huskies. A crowd of 55,780 fans showed up at Husky Stadium eager to see their beloved team in the season opener, but when the clock hit :00 in the fourth quarter, they found themselves on the losing side. UCLA had pulled off an impressive 10–7 win. The UCLA defense dominated. The core of the '77 team was back. Senior Manu Tuiasosopo was a second-team All-American in '78, and fellow senior Jerry Robinson was a consensus first-team All-American for the third season in a row. Sophomore Kenny Easley was also named a consensus first-team All-American. Though the Bruins offense would have strong performances in the middle of the year after a slow start, the Bruins defense carried the team.

UCLA won again in Week 2, again on the road. After beating Tennessee, 13–0, at Neyland Stadium, the No. 8 Bruins took on Bud Moore and the University of Kansas Jayhawks. UCLA entered the game as 17-point favorites but were in for a rude awakening. The 0–2 Jayhawks came to play, and they came to win. UCLA played fine football for much of the day, but a stretch of just under three minutes ultimately doomed them. With the game tied, 7–7, Kansas freshman Sam Smith plunged in from one yard out to give the Jayhawks a 14–7 lead. On the ensuing kickoff, UCLA running back Theotis Brown fumbled after a jarring hit from Buford Johnson, and Kansas recovered. The Jayhawks took advantage of the miscue, and after a pass interference call put the ball at the UCLA 1-yard line, they converted and went ahead, 21–7. The avalanche continued as UCLA was quickly stopped and forced to punt. Jimmy Little returned the punt to the UCLA 3-yard line; one play later, Kansas was in the end zone again. In the blink of an eye, Kansas was up, 28–7. The Bruins were stunned. In the second half, however, the team regrouped. Kansas's offense gained only 26 yards in the entire half, but it was up to the Bruins' offense to make up the difference. They scored 17 unanswered points to get back in the game with minutes to go. Finally, UCLA had one last chance. Down four, the Bruins needed a touchdown to win. Fourth down-and-3 with 2:09 to play. Rick Bashore dropped back, but he was rushed and sacked. The game was over. UCLA lost, 28–24. The Jayhawks would not win another game the entire season. They finished '78 with just one victory, but it came against the Bruins. Thirty-seven years after the game was played, *SB Nation* named the defeat over the Bruins on September 23, 1978, the greatest upset in Kansas football history.

The Bruins were 2–1 and ranked No. 18 when

they finally played their first home game of the season. The loss to the Jayhawks one week earlier was demoralizing, and it was also humbling. UCLA defeated the Minnesota Golden Gophers, 17–3, before Pac 10 play the following week. More than 54,000 fans saw the Bruins defeat Bill Walsh, Steve Dils, and the No. 17 ranked Stanford Cardinals. Much as in the previous year, UCLA would go on a midseason winning streak following the Stanford win. On October 14, UCLA beat Washington State University, 45–31. It was the best performance of the season for the Bruins offense, but, ironically, the worst for the Bruins defense. The following week, they were finally able to play a complete game. With a record of 5–1, and a three-game winning streak, they took on the California Golden Bears. Over 15,000 UCLA students, alumni, and fans traveled to Berkeley and saw a spectacular, balanced effort. The Bruins offense was able to repeat their performance of a week earlier and again score 45 points. What amazed the crowd, however, was the performance of the UCLA defense. They intercepted an astonishing 10 passes and shut out the Bears. The Bruins were rolling. Then, in their first meeting as conference opponents, UCLA beat the University of Arizona, 24–14, on October 27. All that was left for the Bruins before their annual big game against the Trojans were the lowly teams fielded by the University of Oregon and Oregon State University. Though the Bruins struggled, they beat the Ducks, 23–21, on November 4. One week later, Coach Donahue and the Bruins were shocked once again. The Oregon State Beavers were coming in with a 2–5–1 record. UCLA was 8–1 and ranked No. 9. It mattered little. The Beavers won, 15–13. UCLA's two losses on the season had been to two college football bottom-dwellers. Their next challenge would be a college football powerhouse.

On November 18, 1978, UCLA took on USC in what was once again a battle for city bragging rights and a Rose Bowl appearance. USC was 8–1, its only loss coming at the hands of Pac 10 newcomer Arizona State. The Trojans were ranked No. 5 in the country. Charles White was the latest USC star running back. They had dreams of a National Championship. But coach Donahue and his Bruins knew they could play with anyone. If not for the two upsets that defined the season thus far, the Bruins could have been in a position for a national title themselves. Still, they dreamed of roses. In what seemed to be a theme for the season, the Bruins inexplicably came out flat. USC marched out to a 17—0 lead before the Bruins finally awakened from hibernation. UCLA would score the next 10 points to get back into the game but had to stop Charles White one final time to get the ball back. With just over a minute to play, it was third-and-six for the USC offense. Predictably, they handed the ball to White. He broke through the first line and gashed the defense for 12 yards and the game-clinching first down. White rushed for 145 yards on the day, and on his final carry he became the Pac 10's all-time leading rusher. Terry Donahue had a strong record through three years, but one thing stood out to UCLA fans: he was 0–3 against the Trojans. The season would not end, however, for the Bruins that day. They still had one game to play: a bowl game.

Though the Bruins were grateful to play in the Fiesta Bowl on Christmas Day, 1978, against the No. 8 Arkansas Razorbacks, they also knew that their hated rival was playing in the bowl they had coveted. Nevertheless, Arkansas was a strong team and presented an opportunity for the Bruins to prove they were a quality team. A total of 55,227 fans showed up to see the two teams battle at Sun Devil Stadium in a nationally televised game. Coach Terry Donahue and Coach Lou Holtz proved to be equals on this day. Donahue made the decision to start second-string quarterback Steve Bukich, who provided the lone touchdown for the Bruins. UCLA senior linebacker Jerry Robinson went out with one final, brilliant performance. He had 15 tackles and held the Razorbacks' offense to just 10 points. The final game of the season ended in a tie. The Bruins finished with an 8–3–1 record.

The Downtown Athletic Club named Billy Sims from the University of Oklahoma the 1978 Heisman Trophy Winner.

The Associated Press named the University of Alabama the 1978 National Champions.

## Jerry Robinson

Long before Albert Pujols, nicknamed "The Machine," came to Southern California to play for the Los Angeles Angels, and long before people would dub Kobe Bryant's fadeaway baseline jumpshot "automatic," there was a man dominating the sports scene in Los Angeles with as much consistency and greatness as either of those two legendary athletes. His name was Jerry Robinson, and he was marvelous.

Jerry Robinson was born on December 18, 1956, in San Francisco, California. By the time Jerry reached high school, he was a sight to behold. At Cardinal Newman High School in Santa Rosa, he captained the football team, as well as the basketball and track teams. On the gridiron, Jerry was an All-American playing on both sides of the ball. In one game, he rushed for 350 yards and five touchdowns. In basketball, he averaged 25 points per game as a senior. He had blazing speed. He ran the 100-yard dash in 9.5 seconds. He high-jumped 6' 5". He long-jumped 23' 2". There was nothing Jerry Robinson could not do. In 1975, Jerry came south to UCLA, turning down the hometown teams and giving the stiff-arm to college recruiters across the country, just as he had done to opposing tacklers in high school. UCLA Head Coach Dick Vermeil coveted Jerry, and Assistant Coach Lynn Stiles helped finish the job of recruiting him to Westwood. The multitalented athlete arrived at UCLA in 1975. The only question was, what position would he play?

The 1975 Bruins were a team of destiny. The team began the season ranked No. 16 in the country, but Coach Vermeil had higher goals than that. The Bruins got off to a 2–0–1 start before meeting the No. 2 Ohio State Buckeyes on October 4. Though the Bruins lost, 41–20, OSU Head Coach Woody Hayes recognized how good the team was and predicted that the two squads would meet again. UCLA finished the regular season 8–2–1 and did indeed prove Coach Hayes to be right. They met the Buckeyes on January 1, 1976, in the Rose Bowl. The Bruins were ranked No. 11, the Buckeyes No. 1. OSU was almost assuredly going to beat the Bruins and win the National Championship. Where was Jerry Robinson this whole time? He was playing tight end, a position that many coaches and recruiters believed was his best position. Coach Vermeil initially thought so, as well, but in the back of his mind, he knew he had an uncommon athlete, a man who could dominate every week, and with the Bruins' offense focused on the run, he was not going to let Robinson's talent go to waste. On New Year's Day, the Bruins stunned the Buckeyes, pulling off one of the greatest upsets in the history of college football. While the press watched with amazement and wondered how coach Vermeil had led his team to such an accomplishment, one thing was overlooked. Jerry Robinson was not a key player on that 1976 Rose Bowl winning team, but he would be a star from then on. During preparation for the big game, Coach Vermeil moved Robinson to linebacker. With this move, Coach Vermeil did not create a legend, he released one. Any coach could see the athletic ability of the 6'2", 218-pound Robinson; it was Coach Vermeil who didn't try to overcoach it, he simply freed it.

In 1976, Coach Vermeil was off to the National Football League to coach the Philadelphia Eagles, and Jerry Robinson was about to make his name known throughout the college football world. In '76, Robinson was a full-time linebacker and a full-time beast. As a sophomore, he finished with 159 tackles, a new school record. On September 25, 1976, in just his third game, Robinson finished with 28 tackles, a school record that still stands today. The Bruins finished with a 9–2–1 record, and Robinson was a consensus All-American. One year later, Robinson was a known commodity. He was just as great, finishing his junior season with 147 tackles, the second-best mark in school history. His 23-tackle performance against USC is still the second-best performance in the history of the rivalry. He was again a consensus All-American. Robinson made it three-for-three his senior season, when he was again named a consensus All-American. He was the first Bruin to earn consensus All-American honors three times and the first player in college football to do so since Doak Walker of SMU had been so honored from 1947 to 1949. As a senior, Jerry broke his own single-season tackles record, finishing with 161. He finished his career with five games racking up at least 20 tackles and three interception returns for touchdowns. Robinson was named Linebacker of the Year in 1977 and 1978 by the Downtown Athletic Club. He was given the Pop Warner Award in '78, awarded to the best player on the West Coast. In his senior season, Robinson finished 10th in the Heisman Trophy voting. Coach Vermeil had made the right call in 1975, and when coach Donahue set Robinson free, Bruins fans were simply left in awe. His incredible speed, instincts, and tackling ability were a sight to behold. Despite playing for only three years on defense and playing a shorter season, Jerry Robinson held the all-time tackles record at UCLA for 36 years.

When Jerry Robinson graduated and left for the NFL, the Bruins had a void to fill, but for his former coach Dick Vermeil, Robinson had the reverse effect. Vermeil drafted Robinson for the Philadelphia Eagles in the 1979 NFL draft, and Robinson immediately made an impact. In his second year, Robinson was named a second-team All-Pro by the Associated Press. In his third year, he was again named second-team All-Pro by the AP, and first team by the Pro Football Writers Association. Robinson was a mainstay with the Eagles for six seasons and spent another seven with the Los Angeles Raiders. The former Bruins star would have a long professional career and was a fan favorite in both cities in which he played. He was gracious to the media. He was dependable. He was Mr. Right. But he would prove to not be Mr. Perfect. In 1987, Jerry Robinson was arrested for being under the influence of drugs, as well as possession of four rocks of cocaine, codeine pills, and a pipe. On top of the multiple felony charges, Robinson was charged with five misdemeanors. He had a drug problem. So did many in the NFL and the NBA. As a first-time offender, Robinson got off without serving any prison time. Instead, he paid a fine and was placed on probation. For the Bruins great, and at the time NFL star, it served as a wake-up call. Robinson turned his life around. In 1991, he retired from the National Football League. For fans of the Eagles, the Raiders, and especially the Bruins, a "thank-you" is owed to Dick Vermeil: because Vermeil was able to see Robinson's talent on defense, the American public saw greatness. Jerry Robinson is arguably the best defensive player in UCLA history, and one of the best ever to play college football. In 1991, Robinson was inducted into the UCLA Athletics Hall of Fame, and in 1996 he was inducted into the National Football Foundation Hall of Fame and the College Football Hall of Fame. In 2011, he was named to the all-time Pac 10 Conference team, one of three Bruins. Jerry Robinson's number 84 is retired by the UCLA football program, never to be worn again. Nor is it likely that we will again see a linebacker like Jerry Robinson. He was everything a coach dreams of. He was fast. He had incredible instincts. He was a machine. He was automatic. Jerry Robinson was a Bruin, and for that UCLA fans are forever thankful. For those who saw Robinson, the images of him flying across the field, making tackle after tackle, will never die. Jerry Robinson was otherworldly. He is a legend. And legends are forever.

## 1979

Over Coach Terry Donahue's first three seasons, the Bruins failed to finish seasons in strong fashion. In his fourth season, '79, they failed to finish games. The season began on September 8 against the Houston Cougars. The Bruins were young, but they returned a superstar. Kenny Easley was a junior. He was an All-American. On offense, Freeman McNeil, also a junior, was poised for a breakout season. Though UCLA would play the highly rated Cougars close, they would ultimately go down to the Bill Yoeman-led squad. While quarterback Delrick Brown and his teammates would eventually go on to win 11 games and finish in the top five in the country, the loss was seen as nothing other than just that: a season-opening defeat. The Bruins were 0–1.

One week after losing to the Cougars, the Bruins were looking at a possible 0–2 start to the season. They were tasked with taking on the No. 5 Purdue Boilermakers of the Big 10 Conference. Though oddsmakers would declare the Bruins heavy underdogs, they had no plans of losing this one. On the first play of the game, Freeman McNeil, who would go on to be named a third-team All-American, broke free for 51 yards. It was a sign of things to come. UCLA beat Purdue by a score of 31–21. It was their finest moment of the season. After beating Purdue, the Bruins entered the Associated Press rankings in Week 3. On September 22, the No. 20 Bruins took on the Wisconsin Badgers in Madison. Motivated in part by a local sportswriter calling them a bunch of "beach boys," and insinuating that the Bruins were soft, they simply took apart their opponent. With McNeil out with a groin injury and the flu, the offense relied on sophomore Anthony Edgar. He filled in more than admirably, finishing with 168 yards on the day. While the Bruins proved they could stand up to a bullish press and a team that finished eighth in the Big 10, the following three weeks presented a challenge much more demanding. They would have to play their best football to come out alive.

A quarter century after the nation was robbed of "The Game of the Decade" between UCLA and Ohio State due to the Rose Bowl's no-repeat rule, UCLA and OSU took the field to square off.

A small crowd of only 47,228 showed up to see the Big 10 powerhouse take on the hometown team at the Coliseum, possibly because the game was seen on ABC-TV in millions of homes nationwide. UCLA got on the board first against the Buckeyes. After Billy Don Jackson blocked a Tom Orosz punt, quarterback Rick Bashore found Willie Curan for a 10-yard touchdown. Kicker Pete Boermeester knocked in the extra point, and UCLA led, 7–0. After a defensive stop, the UCLA offense was on the move again. Bashore hit Jojo Townsell for 15 yards. He hit Tim Wrightman for 11 yards. The Bruins were in OSU territory, at the 12-yard line, and looking to jump ahead by two scores. On third-and-10, they were called for a delay of game. Deciding to play it safe, Donahue called for a run by McNeil and then a field goal from Boermeester. The kick was good, and UCLA took a 10–0 lead over the No. 14 Buckeyes. The Bruins were strong in every aspect of the game. Ohio State tried a fake punt, but the Bruins shut it down for a loss of 14 yards. They tried passing. They tried running. Early on, there was nothing they could do against Kenny Easley and the UCLA defense. In the second quarter, the Buckeyes offense was finally able to break through as Calvin Murray took a draw, bounced to the outside, and raced 34 yards to the end zone. At halftime, the score was 10–7 Bruins. On the first possession of the second half, the Buckeyes proved that the Bruins would have to play an entire game to come away with a win. After marching down the field, Ohio State knocked in a short kick and tied the game at 10. After UCLA converted a field goal with 11 minutes to play to take the lead, the two teams exchanged punts. UCLA then went on a long, punishing drive. They repeatedly handed the ball to McNeil, Edgar, and Toa Saipale and asked them to carry the team. But after marching deep into OSU territory, the Bruins failed to finish—a theme for the season not once, but twice. After being stopped at the OSU 20-yard line, Boermeester went in for a 37-yard field goal attempt. The kick was missed, but there was a penalty! Roughing the kicker. The Bruins had new life. First and goal at the OSU 10-yard line. The Bruins ran the ball three times. On third down, Edgar was stopped for no gain. It was the twenty-fourth consecutive Bruins running play. They would have to settle for a field goal. Boermeester lined up for the 23-yard attempt but missed! With two minutes and 21 seconds to go, OSU had the ball at their own 20-yard line, down three points, with two timeouts. It didn't take long before the Buckeyes were marching down the field. A series of short passes and one long strike put the ball at the Bruins 3-yard line with exactly one minute to play. On first and goal, the ball was handed to OSU's Cal Murray, but he was immediately hit by Billy Don Jackson and Arthur Akers. Denied. OSU took their last timeout. On second down, OSU called "Pass Play 21," a play that would give the OSU quarterback a run-pass option. He took the snap, rolled to the right, but straight into the onrushing defense. Unfortunately for the Bruins, they did not take away the second option. Paul Campbell was wide open in the end zone and scored the game-winning touchdown.Though UCLA would reach the OSU 46-yard line, the final play, a Hail Mary pass, failed. The Bruins played a strong game but could not close.

Following the heartbreaking loss to Ohio State, it was time for conference play, but it was not time for the heartbreak to end. The Bruins would lose to Stanford, 27–24, on a 54-yard field goal that bounced off the left upright and ricocheted through the uprights. The following week, the downcast Bruins lost, 17–14, in Pullman to the Washington State Cougars. It was the first time UCLA had lost to WSU in 20 years. UCLA was 2–4 when they took on the California Golden Bears. The season had unquestionably been a disappointing one thus far, but when UCLA took on the Bears, all past failures were forgotten. They had a rival to beat, and they did just that. UCLA got back in the win column by flipping the season script. They trailed big at halftime but came back and won in dramatic fashion, 28–27. Homecoming week was a success.

Coach Terry Donahue and Tom Ramsey, 1979 (Southern Campus Collection)

UCLA vs. USC, 1979 (Southern Campus Collection)

With four games to play in the season, the Bruins were not playing for the Pac 10 title but still had reason to finish the season strong. They had hopes of a winning record and always played USC with a passion for victory. The Bruins finished the final four games the way they had played all season—inconsistently. UCLA lost to a strong Washington team, 34–14, before defeating Arizona State, 31–28, in their first meeting as conference foes. On November 17, the Bruins traveled to Eugene, Oregon, and beat the Ducks, 35–0. They were 5–5 with one game to play. Just as was the case so many times before, the Rose Bowl was on the line when UCLA and USC met. The Bruins had been eliminated from contention, but an upset over their crosstown rival could knock the Trojans out of the big game. Instead, UCLA was overpowered. Though many believed they had found their answer at quarterback two weeks earlier, when Tom Ramsey replaced Bashore, nothing worked on this day. Ramsey was ineffective, and though Bashore would come in late to throw two touchdown passes, it was meaningless in the end. USC won, 49–14. Though Freeman McNeil broke Wendell Tyler's single-season rushing record from 1975, and finished his junior campaign with 1,396 yards, it came in a losing season. In 1980, there was significant pressure on Coach Donahue. He was 0–4 against USC. He had 19 returning starters. It was time to win.

The Downtown Athletic Club named Charles White from the University of Southern California the 1979 Heisman Trophy Winner.

The Associated Press named the University of Alabama the 1979 National Champions.

## 1980

It was 1980. A new decade. A new president-elect. A new reality for UCLA football. After the two best decades in Bruins football history, the 1970s were a setback. UCLA fielded good teams in '72, '73, '75, '76, and '78, but they finished the decade with just a 2–7–1 record against USC. Coach Terry Donahue was 0–4 against USC, and Bruins fans were becoming exceedingly impatient. The victory in the 1976 Rose Bowl now seemed like a distant memory. It was time to start winning again. Memories of Red Sanders and Tommy Prothro were all that fans seemed to have. Recruits had only seen disappointment. While the changing of the year represented a wake-up call for the Bruins, the year 1980 also was a time of decision for the United States. After four years of Jimmy Carter in the oval office, Ronald Reagan was elected president in a landslide. The final electoral count—Reagan 480, Carter 49. The beating that Carter took at the ballot box is what it must have felt like to be a Bruins fan in the late '70s, but with the turning of the decade came change. While the election of 1980 marked the beginning of the "Reagan Revolution," the UCLA football team would come alive, as well. The UCLA football season began with a bang.

When assistant coach Homer Smith returned to UCLA to assist the offense, he immediately proved

Tom Ramsey, 1980 (Southern Campus Collection)

his worth. The season began on September 13, 1980, and the Bruins put on a stellar first-half show. Led by quarterback Tom Ramsey, receiver Cormac Carney, and All-American running back Freeman McNeil, the predictable, conservative offense of '79 had turned into the flashy, exciting offense of 1980. Though the Bruins would lose the second half to Colorado, 14–0, the story was what happened in the first half: UCLA had jumped out to an astonishing 56–0 lead at halftime. The Buffaloes had no chance, and the nation was put on notice. A week later, pollsters were still skeptical. One game does not make a season, but one game can grab the headlines. UCLA certainly did so in Week 1 but would have to follow up its dominant performance week in and week out. The second game of the season pitted the Bruins against the Purdue Boilermakers in West Lafayette, Indiana. Though the performance wasn't as flashy as that of Week 1, the end result was, nonetheless, a victory. After beating the Boilermakers, 23–14, Coach Donahue's squad entered the Associated Press rankings for the first time of the season and would remain ranked for the rest of the schedule.

A crowd of just 40,018 fans showed up at the Los Angeles Memorial Coliseum on September 27 to see the Bruins take on the 0–2 Wisconsin Badgers. The Bruins, with a big game coming up, could have looked past the struggling Wisconsin team and fallen into the inevitable trap that so many teams fall into. However, the 1980 team was different, at least it looked to be so far. Freeman McNeil and the offense ran up 35 points on the weak Wisconsin defense, and Kenny Easley and the Bruin defense had no problem shutting out the Badger offense. The 35–0 win was not only the third convincing win of the season thus far, but a signal to the next opponent on the Bruins' schedule. This team was good. Damn good. The final nonconference game of the season came against the No. 2 team in the nation, the Ohio State Buckeyes. As they had done the week before, the UCLA defense dominated. The offense did their part, and the Bruins came away with a stunning 17–0 victory. UCLA was 4–0 with conference play looming.

By the time UCLA took on Stanford in the conference opener on October 11, the Bruins had risen to the No. 5 position in the AP poll. The Cardinals were also a strong team. After a 4–1 start, including a win at No. 4 Oklahoma, Stanford was ranked No. 15 in the AP poll. The Bruins, perhaps suffering an emotional letdown after the victory over OSU, struggled early. After scoring first on a 7-yard touchdown pass from Ramsey to Ronnie Debose, UCLA fell apart. Stanford scored 21 unanswered points to take a two-score lead heading into the halftime break. Down 21–7, coach Donahue rallied the troops. In the third quarter, Freeman McNeil scored twice, once from 12 yards out and the second time from 72. In the fourth quarter, McNeil continued to dominate. He scored twice more, once from six yards and once from 42 yards. His four second-half touchdowns set a school record for most in a half. The UCLA defense blanked the Stanford offense in the second half for the come-from-behind win.

After dominating Cal in Berkeley the following week, the Bruins were 6–0 and ranked No. 2 in the country when they took on the Arizona Wildcats. With Alabama losing earlier in the day to Mississippi State, the Bruins appeared primed to take over the No. 1 ranking in the country. But first, they had to get by the Wildcats. At halftime, though the game was close, it appeared UCLA was well on its way to doing that. However, many of the players, who hadn't yet known about the result of the Alabama game, learned about it during the break, and how they handled the pressure would determine how the game ended. UCLA led, 17–14, when the teams returned from the locker rooms for the final 30 minutes of play. Instead of running away with the game in the second half, the Bruins knew they were in for a battle when Arizona freshman quarterback Tom Tunnicliffe, only 18 years old and making his second career college start, found tight end Bill Nettling for a 39-yard score on the opening drive of the half. That gave the Wildcats the lead, 21–17. The Bruins' offense struggled all half but had one final chance for a victory. Backed up near its own goal line, UCLA needed a long drive and a touchdown to win, but with fewer than two minutes to play, Ramsey was sacked in the end zone for a safety. UCLA would go down by the score of 23–17. Their dream of being No. 1 was killed in the desert.

While the loss to the Wildcats may have been a stunner, the loss to the Oregon Ducks the following week was every bit as painful. UCLA lost its second game in a row on November 8 and fell out of the top 10 rankings, down to No. 17. Though momentum was gone and hopes of a National Championship gone with it, there were still two games left in the season. The Bruins got back in the win column after beating Arizona State, 23–14, before taking on rival USC. No matter how much the team had improved in 1980, the season would be seen as a failure if they lost to USC again. The Trojans of 1980 were once again a good team. Their offense was led by star tailback Marcus Allen, and Ronnie Lott led the defense. The media jokingly called the 1980 matchup between the two teams "The Probation Bowl," as both teams were banned from appearing in the Rose Bowl. It mattered little. The University of Washington was the best team, with the best record in the Pac 10, and would go to the Rose Bowl regardless of the outcome of this contest. This game was about pride. And hate. UCLA hated to lose to USC, and the emotion continued to grow each year that passed. By 1980, it was time for coach Donahue to beat the Trojans. Using an eight-man front on defense for the first time all season, UCLA shut down Marcus Allen, holding him to only 72 yards on 37 carries. All-American Kenny Easley was playing hurt, but he would never surrender. After a serious shoulder injury in the first half, Easley was told he must go to the hospital. He refused. He would not finish his career without beating the Trojans. He played through the injury and deflected three passes in the second half. The offense did just enough to give the Bruins a shot. Down, 17–14, with two minutes to play, UCLA's season was on the line. With the ball at the UCLA 42-yard line, Jay Schroeder, who had replaced Ramsey at quarterback in the first quarter, heaved the ball deep to Freeman McNeil. The pass was badly underthrown, and USC Cornerback Jeff Fisher camped under the pass, waiting for the easy interception. What happened next was miraculous . . . for the Bruins. USC Coach John Robinson would say, "It happened 15 feet from me. It was one of the first times in a game that, while the ball was in the air, I was saying, 'It's over. Jeff will intercept and we'll win.' I can still close my eyes and see it." Except Jeff Fisher didn't intercept the pass. He tipped it in the air and McNeil caught it and ran into the end zone for the game-winning 58-yard score. UCLA beat the Trojans, 20–17. Coach Donahue saved his job, and the Trojans' dominance of the 1970s had turned into the Bruins joy of the 1980s. UCLA would go on to play their final game of the season in Tokyo, Japan, in front of a crowd of 80,000 in the Mirage Bowl. They beat the Oregon State Beavers, 34–3, and finished the season with a 9–2 record.

The Downtown Athletic Club named George Rogers from the University of South Carolina the 1980 Heisman Trophy Winner.

The Associated Press named the University of Georgia the 1980 National Champions.

UCLA vs. Wisconsin, 1980 (Southern Campus Collection)

## Kenny Easley

While Jerry Robinson may have been coach Terry Donahue's first superstar, he was not the only man dominating on the defensive side of the ball in the late 1970s. Kenny Easley was a man forged through fire. He was symbolic. He was fierce. He was great. Kenny Easley was born on January 15, 1959, in Chesapeake, Virginia. He was a military boy. His father, Kenneth Easley Sr., a former sergeant in the Marines, was his coach. He was his mentor. He was a disciplinarian. He shaped the man who would become a college football icon.

When Kenny Easley was six years old, he was like many other young boys. He had no future plans. Why would he? He was young and carefree. His life changed when he watched his first football game. On October 17, 1965, six-year-old Kenny watched the Baltimore Colts, led by Johnny Unitas and John Mackey on the field, and coached by Don Shula, take on Sonny Jurgensen, Charley Taylor, and the Washington Redskins. The game mesmerized him. Recalling the game years later, Easley would say, "Looking at all those people in the stands, and listening to the announcers, and all that excitement, I was hooked right there on the spot." He was young, but he was motivated. He would do anything to one day be on the same stage as the players who caught his eye at six years of age. "I said that day, 'This is what I want to do. I want to be a pro football player.'"

Kenny Easley, 1979 (Southern Campus Collection)

As a kid, Kenny was impatient. He had a drive to be a great athlete. He would run on his own. He would lift weights. He was blessed with athletic ability and a motivation to make it in his desired profession. Still, like any young athlete, he had a lot to learn. Kenny Sr. would push him to work harder and to play better. He played multiple sports, and along the way his father was always there. His dad was a coach and a mentor. Recalling the way his father made him work at all sports, Kenny would later say, "He always drove me harder than he did the other kids on the team." Not only did Kenny want to make his father proud, his father wanted to make his son tough. Nothing would come easy, and the pair worked relentlessly. In Little League baseball practice, Kenny Sr. would hit fly balls directly to all the players. To young Kenny, he would hit them high to left and make Kenny chase them from center field. If he didn't catch them, he would have to do it again. In basketball, if Kenny made five shots in a row, it wasn't good enough. He had to make more. In football, he would be scrutinized in tackling drills, in pursuit drills, in quarterback drills. Kenny Easley was a unique talent, and his father helped shape him. Ultimately, no man can force his son to be talented. That was a gift, for which football fans are forever thankful.

By the time Kenny Easley reached Oscar F. Smith High School in Chesapeake, he was ready for a larger stage. As a sophomore, he was the starting quarterback on the varsity squad, and an immediate star. As a junior, he played both sides of the ball for the first time. Knowing his team needed more athleticism on defense, his coach let him play free safety. Kenny was a natural, but he never stopped working. On offense, Easley continued to shine. As a senior, he rushed for over 1,000 yards and passed for over 1,000. He was the first player in Virginia state history to accomplish that feat. Despite his success on offense, Easley preferred defense. He was a ferocious hitter, but that was not why he loved playing. He was thinking long-term. "I knew, even at that age, that black quarterbacks were a rarity in the NFL. I thought if I played safety, I had a much better chance of playing in the NFL than if I played quarterback." As a senior in high school, he was recruited by 350 colleges. He was one of the most coveted athletes in the history of prep athletics in the United States.

When Kenny Easley ultimately decided to travel 2,700 miles across the country to attend UCLA, it was not because coach Donahue and staff saw him as a safety; they also thought his best fit was at quarterback. Easley chose UCLA because he considered it the best fit for him. He could make it anywhere, but to the delight of alumni, fans, and coaches, he chose to "wow" the city of Los Angeles for four years. In 1977, Easley did not line up at quarterback, but rather at the position that he wanted to play. He was a safety, and when he first stepped foot on the grass at the Los Angeles Memorial Coliseum, it was a show. Jerry Robinson was already an All-American linebacker, and teamed with Kenny Easley, the two would form one of the greatest defensive combinations in history. While Robinson was a tackling machine, Kenny

Easley was different. He was symbolic, and he was ruthless. His greatest demand of himself was to play hard at all times. He believed he had an obligation to become an All-American. Kenny Easley wore number 5, and he was a force. He had a mindset that he would be the greatest of all forces, a Force 5 Hurricane. Easley wore a sticker on the back of his helmet that simply said "F5." Before every game, he would turn his helmet around, stare at the sticker on the back, and say to himself, "If you're not going to be the biggest force on the field today, do not put this helmet on." Kenny Easley would say of himself, "I was a force to be reckoned with, the biggest force known to mankind." As a freshman, Easley made 93 tackles, intercepted nine passes, and was named first-team All-Pac 8, the only freshman ever to be named to the first team. He was named the National Freshman of the Year. His 1977 season was great. And he was just getting started. As a sophomore, Easley was named a consensus All-American, just like his teammate Robinson. As a junior, he was again a consensus All-American. One year later, one more time. For the third year in a row, he was a consensus All-American. Easley finished his UCLA career with 324 tackles and a school-record 19 interceptions. He was named to the Pac 8/10 first team all four seasons, still the only player in conference history to achieve that feat.

Kenny Easley was drafted fourth overall in the 1981 NFL draft by the Seattle Seahawks, the highest a defensive back had ever been drafted. Though Easley wanted to play for the 49ers, who drafted eighth, he would give everything to Seattle and create a legacy with the Seahawks that is only topped by his legacy with the Bruins. In his rookie pro campaign, Easley was an immediate starter and immediate sensation. Though playing strong safety instead of free safety, the position he much preferred, Easley intercepted three passes and returned one for a touchdown. When the season was over, he returned home with something else: the AFC Rookie of the Year Award. Over the next six seasons, Easley was named All-Pro four times and went to five Pro Bowls. In 1983, he was voted AFC Defensive Player of the Year and one year later was named NFL Defensive Player of the Year. He was voted the Seattle Seahawks team MVP twice. He was at the height of his powers. And then it was over.

Kenny Easley was the ultimate NFL tough guy. He played through pain, blocking out what was uncomfortable, for fear of losing a battle with time. He would be able to play football for only so long. Worrying about the aches and pains and injuries that accumulate when playing a violent game was not a consideration for Kenny. He had four knee surgeries, but ultimately what ended his career was not a break or a sprain, but something much more serious. To cope with the pain of being an NFL player, Easley had been given painkillers repeatedly by team trainers and doctors. Following the 1987 season, it finally caught up to him. On April 22, 1988, the Seahawks traded their star safety to the Arizona Cardinals. They needed a quarterback, and Easley had stopped throwing passes twelve years earlier. In what is normally a routine occurrence, Cardinals team doctors found something that was life-threatening. Following his team physical, Kenny Easley was diagnosed with a life-threatening kidney disease called *idiopathic nephrotic syndrome*. The trade was voided, and Kenny Easley was forced into early retirement. He was shocked. He sued the Seattle Seahawks, who had reportedly told him to take 15–20 Advil per day while recovering from his 1986 ankle injury. The case was settled out of court years later.

For Kenny Easley, a great player forced to leave the game too soon, the loss of his first love, his passion, his job, was heartbreaking. Though Easley received a kidney transplant in 1990, his medical issue is ongoing. "I have battles to fight, and I continue to fight them with the same will and fortitude that I fought with on the football field. My battles are long-term. There's nothing that's going to change the course of my situation in the medical industry." For Easley, one change occurred in 2002. After fifteen years of severed ties with the Seahawks, he returned. Following his retirement, Easley was deeply hurt by the franchise that had played a role in the demise of his brilliant career. With new club ownership, however, Easley was able to forgive, and able to move on with his life. On October 13, 2002, Kenny Easley was added to the Seattle Seahawks Ring of Honor. He would say of the estranged relationship of the past, "Time heals everything. This is a new organization. These people that run the team now had nothing to do with what transpired back in the '80s. It would be foolish not to take advantage of the generosity these folks are extending to my family and to myself. All the stars lined up correctly. It was time to do it."

For Seahawks fans, reconciliation between their beloved franchise and the man who once roamed the defensive backfield with a ferocity uncommon in professional football, was everything. Kenny Easley was back where he belonged. For UCLA fans, the memory of Kenny Easley will live on forever. He was a Force 5 Hurricane. He was the most ferocious player to ever wear a Bruins uniform. Kenny Easley's number 5 jersey was retired, not years down the line, but immediately. Coach Donahue knew the impression that Easley had made on the Bruins, and it was announced during the team banquet following Easley's senior season that the number 5 uniform at UCLA will never be worn again. In 1991, Kenny was inducted into the UCLA Athletics Hall of Fame and the College Football Hall of Fame. He was a member of the 1980s NFL All-Decade team and was named a member of the Seattle Seahawks' 25th and 35th anniversary teams. For a man who was once one of the greatest athletes in the world, being limited to watching football has been difficult. He knows the pain of the players and what they go through. He knows the struggle of a career cut short. In 2015, he was named an honorary Seattle Seahawks captain in Super Bowl XLIX. It was the first Super Bowl Easley had watched in full in over thirty years. It was too much to handle. In 2017, Kenny Easley finally received the call he had been waiting for. He was inducted into the Pro Football Hall of Fame, taking his deserved place alongside the greatest football players of all time. For fans of the Bruins, the Seahawks, and football fans in general, Kenny Easley was a player of a different era, the likes of which will never be seen again.

## 1981

It certainly was no surprise in 1981 to see both the UCLA Bruins and the USC Trojans field good teams. What was surprising in '81 was not what happened on any competitive field or court. The moment that shocked the nation came on March 30. Eighteen years after President John F. Kennedy was assassinated in Dallas, Texas, and just 69 days into the presidency of Ronald Reagan, John Hinckley Jr. tried his best to duplicate the feat that Lee Harvey Oswald had completed. He attempted to kill the president but failed.

For fans of Los Angeles sports, there was much going on to take their minds off the turmoil in Washington D.C. The Los Angeles Lakers were bidding for a repeat in the NBA playoffs. Though they fell short, another team would pick up the slack. Perhaps just as shocking to some as the Reagan assassination attempt was the rise of a man named Fernando Valenzuela. The rookie left-handed pitcher from Mexico had turned the normal grind of a long baseball season into the magic of fairy tales. "Fernandomania" swept over Los Angeles, and on October 28, 1981, the fun of the season was capped by the jubilation of victory. Across the country, 56,513 fans packed Yankee Stadium to see the Dodgers defeat their beloved Bronx Bombers and capture the 5th World Series title in Dodger history. For Terry Donahue at UCLA and John Robinson at USC, the expectations would also be high. The bar had been set. Los Angeles wanted winners.

The UCLA football season kicked off against the University of Arizona on September 12. The Bruins of '81 were a balanced team. They had a solid mix of experience and an influx of young talent. Quarterback Tom Ramsey, All-American tight end Tim Wrightman, tackle Luis Sharpe, and receiver Cormac Carney led the offense. On defense, safeties Tom Sullivan and Don Rogers were the leaders of an excellent unit. The No. 12-ranked Bruins put their talent on display early and often in Week 1 against the Wildcats, and then played well in Week 2 against the Wisconsin Badgers. Just one week earlier, the Badgers had knocked off top-ranked Michigan, but when the Bruins came to Madison, it was a different story. UCLA 31, Wisconsin 13. By Week 3, the Bruins were No. 6 in the country in the AP rankings, but as they had done so many times in the past, they were unable to build off their early season success. UCLA lost the third game of the season, all of which were on the road, this time to Iowa, 20–7. The Bruins were 2–1, with one nonconference game to play. In the fourth game of the season, the No. 16 Bruins got back in the win column after beating Big 8 foe Colorado, 27–7. It was time to return to conference play, and to make a push for the Rose Bowl.

The return to conference play began not in joy, but in fear. When games come down to the wire, players and coaches, although they rarely admit it, and fans suffer from extreme anxiety. Such was the case when the Bruins and the Stanford Cardinals met on October 10. UCLA lost, 26–23. It was a heartbreaking defeat.

The following week, the Bruins improved, but only slightly. Playing in their fifth away game out of six, the Bruins tied the No. 18-ranked Washington State Cougars. It was a disappointing start to conference play for the Bruins, but they would make a run. Refusing to write off the season as a lost cause, the Bruins would rally.

UCLA vs. USC, 1981 (Southern Campus Collection)

On October 24, they began the stretch that would put them back in the Pac 10 title picture. Coach Donahue and the Bruins beat the California Golden Bears, 34–6, at the Los Angeles Memorial Coliseum. Four days later, the Dodgers won the World Series. Three days after that, the Bruins beat the Oregon Ducks, 28–11, and one week after that, UCLA played its best game of the season. Before the Bruins took on the Washington Huskies on November 7, many had believed the Pac 10 race was a two-team battle between the Huskies and the Arizona State Sun Devils. Not only did the Bruins demand that others make room for them, they did so by destroying one of the frontrunners. Final score: UCLA 31, Washington 0. One week later, the Bruins took out the other Pac 10 frontrunner. UCLA 34, ASU 24. There was one week left, and the Bruins were playing for the Rose Bowl.

When UCLA took on USC in 1981, the game was like so many before it: Rose Bowl implications were on the line. But this time, only for the Bruins. USC had a strong season. They were 8–2. Their record was better than UCLA's (7–2–1), but the Trojans had lost two conference games. Their job in this game was to play spoiler. If the Bruins won, they would go to the Rose Bowl. If USC won, the University of Washington would go. Though the Trojans entered the game as the No. 10 team in the country and a betting favorite against the No. 15 Bruins, the '81 Trojans were not a balanced team. They depended heavily on tailback Marcus Allen. The USC passing attack was almost nonexistent. Allen led the nation in both attempts and yards. The UCLA game plan was clear. Shut down Marcus Allen. The Bruins did not stop Allen from gaining yards. He racked up 219 in total on 40 carries, but he fumbled three times. USC's turnovers kept the Bruins in the game. For the second year in a row, the game would be decided by one final, memorable play. Trailing 22–21 with seconds to go and the game on the line, UCLA kicker Norm Johnson came onto the field. The 89,432 fans rose to their feet in anticipation of the one play that would either give or deny bragging rights to the fans of each team. The ball was snapped. The hold was perfect. Johnson kicked the ball. Blocked! A 6'5", 260-pound USC defensive lineman, George Achica, had squeezed his massive frame between center and right guard and smothered the kick. Johnson had no chance. USC defensive line coach Marv Goux was said to have noticed the gap in film study. For coach Donahue and the Bruins, it was heartbreaking. They had rallied late in the season in hopes of getting to Pasadena on January 1. With one blocked kick, the hope was gone, and the Bruins would have to wait once again. Donahue would say of the loss, "It's a tough game to lose. I couldn't be prouder of our players. It's a big disappointment for our players and coaches. I thought our team played with great character. We're obviously disappointed, but we've accepted a Blue Bonnet Bowl invitation to play against Michigan." The Bruins had a bowl game to play, though once again not the one they had hoped for. In the bowl game, Bo Schembechler and the Wolverines overwhelmed the Bruins. At one point in the second quarter, UM had gained 212 yards to the Bruins' 0. Ramsey threw two late touchdowns to Wrightman, but UCLA went down, 33–14. The Bruins finished the '81 season not like the Dodgers, but rather like the Lakers. They were a good team but didn't do enough. The rivalry with USC would change going forward. USC's coach was on his last legs, and the Bruins had a new home.

The Downtown Athletic Club named Marcus Allen from the University of Southern California the 1981 Heisman Trophy Winner.

The Associated Press named Clemson University the 1981 National Champions.

## 1982

In 1982, UCLA finally had a stadium of its own to call home. Though they would share the Rose Bowl with Caltech for 11 years, the Bruins were no longer roommates with their most hated rival, the USC Trojans. It was time for UCLA to differentiate itself from USC. The Trojans dominated the 1970s, but the Bruins and Coach Terry Donahue would not let the status quo remain. The 1980s would belong to UCLA. The Rose Bowl was the team's new home. While USC continued to play in the historic, yet rundown Los Angeles Memorial Coliseum, the Blue and Gold took the field in the most pristine, glamorous, beautiful football setting in the nation. Though UCLA changed the game day route and headed to a new stadium, the goal remained the same: games in September at the Rose Bowl are great, but those in January at the Rose Bowl are where legends are born.

The 1982 Bruins entering the field (Southern Campus Collection)

In 1982, Terry Donahue was in his seventh season as the UCLA football head coach. He enjoyed a 43–21–3 record, had fully implemented his system, and was seeing results not only on the field, but in recruiting. However, over Coach Donahue's first six seasons, there were two glaring flaws. He had a 1–5 record against USC, and he had yet to win the Pac 8/10 Conference title. His Bruins finished in second place four times, but fans were anxious for a return to the Rose Bowl. It had been seven years since UCLA played Ohio State in the Rose Bowl. The quest to return started once again on September 11, 1982. When UCLA took on Long Beach State at the Rose Bowl in the '82 season opener, it was the beginning of a new era. Quarterback Tom Ramsey, receivers Jojo Townsell and Cormac Carney, running backs Kevin Nelson and Frank Cephous, as well as All-American defensive tackle Irv Eatman and defensive back Lupe Sanchez, may have all been returning from the year before, but none would experience anything like the thrill of the upcoming '82 season. The Bruins began ranked No. 18 in the Associated Press poll, and with the christening of the new home stadium, the Bruins kicked off the season in style. UCLA 41, LBSU 10.

The Bruins were 1–0 and hungry for more. In Week 2, they dismantled the Wisconsin Badgers in Madison, 51–26. The team was hot. The conservative label that had been given to Coach Donahue was being shed slowly, game by game. His offense no longer lay back and let opponents dictate the action, but rather they were explosive and took the fight to opponents. At least that's what many had hoped. The first half of the Michigan game proved otherwise. A crowd of 105,413 fans packed The Big House as the No. 12 Bruins took on the No. 20 Wolverines, the team that had whipped the Bruins 10 months earlier in the Bluebonnet Bowl. UCLA fans believed things would be different in '82. Not so fast. Michigan stormed out of the gate with a pounding offense and a tactically brilliant passing attack. Anthony Carter had 8 catches for over 100 yards and a touchdown, as they jumped out to a 21–0 lead. UCLA's offense struggled, but finally got on the board when Tom Ramsey hit Dokie Williams for a 47-yard score. Ramsey then scored on a 1-yard quarterback keeper. UCLA had cut the lead to seven and looked to be going into the half down by only one score, but then came the moment that proved to many doubters that Terry Donahue was not soft and would not back down to anyone. With the clock running out in the first half, Michigan took its final timeout. Coach Donahue was furious. The clock appeared to have expired before the timeout was called, but the referees granted the timeout request and Michigan kicker Ali-Haji Sheikh knocked in a 47yard field goal as the half ended. UCLA trailed, 24–14. UCLA players ran into the locker room, but Coach Donahue continued to argue with the referees, and Michigan head coach Bo Schembechler—in an attempt to intimidate Donahue—screamed as he raced past him, "That's three more points, Terry!" The taunting did nothing to scare the Bruins' young coach. He had played for Tommy Prothro. He had coached with Dick Vermeil. He had coached against Frank Kush and Woody Hayes. He wasn't scared of Bo Schembechler. Instead, his halftime rant inspired the team. Ramsey would say of his coach, "He was screaming and yelling and throwing things in the locker room. He gave one of the most inspiring halftime speeches ever. It rattled our cages." Coach Schembechler would regret taunting Coach Donahue on this day. The 21–0 lead that once seemed insurmountable was gone. UCLA came out on fire. Ramsey hit Townsell for a touchdown. Kevin Nelson rushed for a short score, and kicker John Lee knocked in a field goal. The defense held the Wolverines to three second-half points, and UCLA won, 31–27. The Big House was stunned. Coach Donahue was jubilant. The Bruins were 3–0 and would close nonconference play with one final game against the Colorado Buffaloes. UCLA won, 34–6. Now it was time to battle for conference supremacy.

UCLA was a well-tested team when conference play began, but that did little to stop them from a poor performance. In the conference opener against Arizona, UCLA led, 21–14, in the fourth quarter, but they let their foot off the gas, and Arizona scored 10 points to take the lead with just minutes to go. Ramsey, the once-highly criticized quarterback, had won over doubters in the first four games and was now being called upon to save the Bruins in the final drive. Ramsey did just that, but it was not enough to come away with a win. Instead, John Lee would be tasked with attempting a 36-yard field goal with just two seconds left for the tie. The kick was good, and UCLA's perfect record was gone. They were still undefeated, but the tie was nothing less than a disappointing result. The first half against Washington State the following week looked eerily similar to much of the Arizona game, but the second half more closely resembled the Michigan game. UCLA trailed in the third quarter but went on a tear and wound up dismantling the Cougars 42–17. UCLA and California were tied, 31–31, in the seventh game of the, season, but Ramsey once again stepped up late and carried the team. UCLA scored 16 unanswered points and won the game, 47–31. Ramsey set a school record by throwing for 397 yards. The Bruins' winning streak reached three games when they beat the Oregon Ducks, 40–12, on October 30. UCLA's record was 7–0–1, but if they were to achieve their goals and reach the Rose Bowl game, the next three games would define their season.

While the Bruins were beating the Oregon Ducks, Stanford was beating the Washington Huskies. The upset win for the Cardinal (they had changed their name from the Cardinals) made the following UCLA matchup with the Huskies all the more important. The winner of the game would be in the driver's seat in the Pac 10 Conference race. UCLA was ranked No. 9 in the country when the team went north to take on the No. 10 Huskies. It was a cold, wet day, and for UCLA the weather was symbolic of the game itself. The Bruins struggled, never warming up the engine of their fine offense. Ramsey and the running game never got going. The defense performed admirably, but ultimately, Washington came away victorious by a score of 10–7. The dream of the Rose Bowl was not dead, but it would take a run of luck to get there. UCLA, UW, and ASU all had a shot at the title. It would take a six-game parlay for the Bruins to make it. The next game was against the Stanford Cardinal and the brilliant John Elway. Ramsey and Elway went mano a mano, and when the dust settled, UCLA came away with a squeaker win. The final score of the shootout: UCLA 38, Stanford 35.

With one game remaining in the regular season, the Bruins still had a shot at Pasadena. UCLA had to beat archrival USC, and the lowly Washington State Cougars had to upset the University of Washington Huskies, in order for the Bruins to get the Rose Bowl nod. USC, though out of the picture for the Rose Bowl, was a very good team. The Trojans were ineligible for postseason play, as well as placed on probation, banned from television, and handed recruiting limitations because of their role in academic fraud, improper employment, player eligibility issues, and an elaborate ticket-selling scheme used to funnel cash to players. Head Coach John Robinson was in his last season as the USC coach, and the game was played for nothing other than pride and bragging rights for the Trojans. Attendance at the Rose Bowl was 95,673 to see the two teams battle. For two years, once at the Rose Bowl and once at the Coliseum, the teams would split ticket distribution 50/50. Both teams were considered home teams, and both would wear home uniforms. The game would again be a classic. UCLA scored 14 points early, but USC clawed back in the game. In the third quarter, UCLA defensive tackle Mark Walen recovered a USC fumble, and John Lee kicked a short field goal to give UCLA a 20–10 lead. That is all UCLA would score for the day. It was up to the defense to hold the lead. USC tacked on a field goal before the real drama began. On the last play of regulation, USC quarterback Scott Tinsley threw a spectacular touchdown pass to tight end Mark Boyer. The score was 20–19, Bruins. There would be one untimed down. USC head coach John Robinson was leaving USC for the NFL. He was not interested in a tie game. He decided to go for two. There were three options on the play. Tinsley could hit Jeff Simmons in the flat, Timmy White in the back corner of the end zone, or Boyer in the middle of the field. UCLA lined up in a 5–3 defense. Linebacker Neal Dellocono blitzed up the middle. Tinsley looked up and cocked his arm to throw, but he had no chance. He was sacked! Karl Morgan had sliced through the USC offensive line and sealed the win for UCLA. The game was over! UCLA beat USC, 20–19, and coach Donahue, who would always remember the heartbreaking result of the 1969 battle between the rivals, was jubilant. The year 1982 was a season of destiny and a season of redemption. No longer were the Bruins to be second-rate citizens in Los Angeles. Washington State beat the University of Washington, and UCLA was off to Pasadena. The Rose Bowl was not just a home stadium, it was a winter destination, and UCLA had a date once again with Coach Bo Schembechler and the Michigan Wolverines.

When UCLA took the field against Michigan on January 1, 1983, it was the third time in two seasons the two teams had met, and the deciding matchup would be in the "Granddaddy of Them All," the Rose Bowl game. The setting was perfect. The skies were clear. The mountains were beautiful, and the football was masterful. When the No. 5 Bruins played the No. 19 Wolverines, each team had a chip on its shoulder. UCLA was doubted by the media. Yes, they had beaten Michigan in the regular season, but UM was said to have taken its foot off the gas. The Wolverines were motivated to finish what they

Fans cheering on the Bruins in the 1983 Rose Bowl (Southern Campus Collection)

started three-and-a-half months earlier. The streets outside the Rose Bowl proved to be a place families and friends would ring in the New Year. Campers, sleeping bags, and tents lined the streets. Tailgaters rose early. It was more than a game. It was a spectacle. The crowd was vivacious. UCLA scored, the crowd roared. Michigan scored, the crowd roared. In the end, the Bruins won the rubber match, 24–14. Tom Ramsey was once again brilliant. He was named Rose Bowl co-MVP, along with teammate Don Rogers. As the players carried Coach Donahue off the field on their shoulders, the crowd applauded. They didn't want to leave. Bruin fans dreamed of the days of Red Sanders, of Tommy Prothro, of Dick Vermeil. Coach Donahue hoped one day to join the elite status of the men who came before him. The 1982 season was a start. UCLA had won the Rose Bowl! The Bruins would finish the season with a 10-1-1 record, No. 5 in the final AP poll, and with sky high expectations for the 1983 season.

The Downtown Athletic Club named Herschel Walker from the University of Georgia the 1982 Heisman Trophy Winner.

The Associated Press named Penn State University the 1982 National Champions.

## 1983

Coming off a 10-win season and a Rose Bowl victory, fans of the UCLA program expected and hoped that the momentum of '82 would continue into the future. They expected Rose Bowls and dreamed of National

Championships. When faced with reality, however, they could see that the team taking the field in September of '83 was not the same as the one a year earlier. Tom Ramsey was gone. So were Cormac Carney and Jojo Townsell. Irv Eatman was gone and so was Blanchard Montgomery. The team taking the field in '83 was an unknown entity. There were holes to fill, but there was also a wellspring of talent. Rick Neuheisel was the new starting quarterback, though backup Steve Bono would provide one of the more memorable moments of the season. Running back Kevin Nelson and receiver Mike Sherrard were the two most effective playmakers on offense, and defensive back Don Rogers led the defense. Though relatively inexperienced in key positions, Terry Donahue was optimistic going into the season. Fans were excited to see the new product, and Donahue was excited to show off his new team. When the season began, the Bruins still had some kinks to work out. It also didn't help that they would be facing the toughest schedule in the nation.

The UCLA football season kicked off on the road in Athens, Georgia, against the No. 15-ranked Georgia Bulldogs of the Southeastern Conference. UGA, which had been one game away from winning the '82 title themselves, faced a daunting task, as well. Coach Vince Dooley had to replace the reigning Heisman Trophy winner and one of the greatest college football players of all time, Herschel Walker. A capacity crowd filled Sanford Stadium, and millions more watched at home on ABC-TV. Rick Neuheisel, in his first collegiate start, would finish 19-for-25, picking up 208 yards. Walk-on receiver Mike Sherrard led all receivers with six catches for 72 yards, but the Bruins fell, 19–8.

Things would only get worse for the Bruins. As the team returned to L.A. in Week 2 and opened up Pac 10 play against the Arizona State Sun Devils, they learned that home field advantage was not enough to overcome poor play. The Bruins found themselves down, 26–10, in the fourth quarter and staring an 0–2 start right in the face. In what would become a theme for the season, UCLA mounted a comeback. After a touchdown and a successful Kevin Nelson two-point conversion run, the Bruins were down just eight when Joe Gasser intercepted a Sun Devils pass at the Bruins 47-yard line. On the eighth play of the ensuing drive, Neuheisel found Mike Young for the score. Nelson was again successful on the two-point conversion run, and the score was tied, 26–26. With 1:36 remaining in the game, ASU's offense took the field, but UCLA held, and the game ended in a tie. The momentum of the fourth quarter was not enough to carry the Bruins to victory the following week, when they took on the top-ranked Nebraska Cornhuskers in Lincoln. The 76,510 fans who packed Memorial Stadium saw what they came for. UCLA jumped out to a 10–0 lead in the second quarter, but the hometeam Huskers stormed back and scored 42 unanswered points. Nebraska quarterback Mike Rozier would go on to win the Heisman Trophy, and the Huskers would finish the season ranked No. 2 in the nation. The last of the Bruins' three brutal nonconference games came on October 1 against Brigham Young University. It was a shootout. Steve Bono, who had replaced Neuheisel at quarterback, and BYU's All-American Steve Young went toe-to-toe for four quarters. Bono threw for a school-record 399 yards, including touchdown passes of 33, 58, and 36 yards. Young was great, as well. Besides his usual running ability, he also had a stellar day through the air, throwing for 270 yards on 25 for 36 passing. When the game was finally over, the BYU Cougars had escaped with a 37–35 victory. It was a crushing defeat for the Bruins, but both BYU and UCLA would surge and finish the season strong. The Cougars finished with an 11–1 record to finish No. 7 in the final AP poll, and UCLA would once again make a charge for the Rose Bowl.

Following their difficult nonconference slate, the Bruins were relieved to once again play familiar opponents from the Pac 10 Conference, though those teams were no slouches, either. On October 8, Bono once again started at quarterback. Coach Donahue, obviously impressed by his performance the previous week, named him the starter for the remainder of the season. But the plans of man are rarely executed without bumps in the road. In just the first quarter, Bono went down after a hard shot from a Stanford defender and separated his shoulder. Rick Neuheisel was back in the game. The job was again his, and on this day he did enough to lead the Bruins to victory, 39–21 over the Stanford Cardinal. UCLA had its first winning streak of the season when the Blue and Gold knocked off Washington State a week later by the score of 24–14. Statistically, the Bruins were beaten soundly by the Cougars, but the numbers on the scoreboard are the only ones that matter. Despite once again not looking dominant on the field, the Bruins came away with another win on October 22 when the California Golden Bears came to Pasadena on an unusually hot fall day. Final score: UCLA 20, Cal 16.

Despite a 3–0–1 record in conference play, the Bruins had still yet to earn the respect of the media. The 0–3 nonconference start had turned many away from the team, considering them to be only a shell of what they had been a year earlier. So they were still unranked and heavy underdogs when they took on a team that was becoming a Pac 10 powerhouse, the Washington Huskies. UW was ranked No. 11 in the country and still highly motivated by the end of season collapse of '82 that had cost them the Rose Bowl. In this matchup, the Bruins would play their finest game of the year on offense. Kevin Nelson ran for 145 yards, and Rick Neuheisel completed an NCAA-record 25 of 27 passes, 287 yards, and one touchdown. Neuheisel had a stretch of 17 consecutive passes completed. He picked apart the Huskies defense with the accuracy and anticipation of an NFL veteran. It was the finest moment of his season to that point. It would not be his last. The Bruins winning streak reached five games on November 5, when they dismantled the Oregon Ducks in the rain in Eugene. Neuheisel was once again effective, and Nelson rushed for over 100 yards for the third consecutive game. Though outsiders still failed to recognize the Bruins as an elite team, the members of coach Donahue's team undoubtedly had their eyes once again on the Rose Bowl. With two games to go, the Bruins had their destiny in their own hands, but the Arizona Wildcats had no plans to simply roll over and hand over the conference title. In the 10th game of the season for UCLA, Arizona toppled the Bruins on a late drive. The winning streak was over. Arizona 27, UCLA 24.

Entering their intracity rivalry game with UCLA, the USC Trojans had been struggling mightily. Their 4–5–1 record put them on the verge of doing something they hadn't done in 12 years: finish with a losing record. John Robinson was gone, off to the NFL. The new head coach of the Trojans was Ted Tollner, tasked with not only dealing with continued NCAA sanctions, but also a depleted roster. The Bruins, though not as talented as the team of a year prior, found themselves in the same exact position. They once again needed the Washington State Cougars to defeat the Washington Huskies, and to beat the Trojans themselves, in order to win a spot in the Rose Bowl. In the first half, UCLA seemingly could not get on track. USC led, 10–6. Up north, WSU was doing its part, beating UW. If the Bruins were to miss out on the Rose Bowl, losing to their archrival was the worst way to do it. The Bruins were aware of what was happening in the other critical game. Coach Donahue informed the team. They got the message and dominated the second half. UCLA would score three touchdowns in the first 11 minutes of the third quarter, and the game was essentially over. USC added a late touchdown, but it was meaningless to the end result. UCLA 27, USC 17. Washington State finished the job by beating Washington, and for the second year in a row, UCLA was headed to the Rose Bowl.

UCLA players celebrate, 1983 (Southern Campus Collection)

In 1984, New Year's Day fell on a Sunday, and because the Rose Bowl was never played on Sundays, the game took place on Monday, January 2. Entering the game, the Bruins were still feeling disrespected. Despite winning the Rose Bowl a year earlier, and winning the Pac 10 Conference, UCLA was still unranked. They entered the game with a modest

6–4–1 record, but three of their losses had been to the nation's top teams. Their opponent in Pasadena would be another top team, the University of Illinois Fighting Illini. It was the 70th Rose Bowl in history, the ninth for the Bruins, and they were looking for their fourth win in the classic. The field condition was perfect, and the weather was spectacular. The game was televised nationally on NBC, and Dick Enberg was at the mic, as the Bruins played their best game of the year. Illinois was ranked No. 4 in the country. They had a 10–1 record and were considered Goliath to the Bruins' David. The Big 10 Conference was seen as superior, but on this day the Pac 10 representative was better in every way. It was clear from the beginning: this day was meant for UCLA. After placekicker John Lee's field goal was blocked on the opening drive, Illinois fumbled the return and UCLA recovered, gaining 12 yards and a new set of downs. UCLA went on to score on a Neuheisel-to-Paul Bergmann pass and took the lead, 7–0. The huge Rose Bowl crowd of 103,000 fans were stunned, overjoyed, and—for those who had come confidently from the Midwest—depressed. UCLA took a 28–3 lead at halftime. Neuheisel was on fire. He found Young, Bergmann, Sherrard, and Karl Dorrell over and over again. It had become a pattern. Neuheisel threw for four touchdowns, including two to Dorrell. Both men would eventually coach their Westwood alma mater. For now, they celebrated. The final score was 45–9. The team that was disrespected all year had won the Rose Bowl for the second season in a row. They were unranked entering the game and watched the final minutes with backups on the field. They had dominated their opponent. The Bruins not only made a statement about themselves, but about their conference. The Pac 10 had been seen by some as inferior to the Big 10. With the Bruins' win, the Pac 10 had now won 13 of the last 15 Rose Bowl games. The team that started the season 0–3–1 was a team of magic, a team of destiny, a team of grit. The '83 Bruins were not the best team in UCLA history, but they were champions.

The Downtown Athletic Club named Mike Rozier from the University of Nebraska the 1983 Heisman Trophy Winner.

The Associated Press named the University of Miami the 1983 National Champions.

## 1984

In 1984, the country was strong, and so was the UCLA football program. President Ronald Reagan won the '84 presidential election in a landslide. Democratic candidate Walter Mondale would win one state, his home state of Minnesota. President Reagan's 525–13 win in the Electoral College was reminiscent of some of UCLA football's earliest scores when, in the 1920s, the Bruins had often been on the losing end of lopsided margins. By the 1980s, however, UCLA was thriving on the gridiron. In '84, as Head Coach Terry Donahue entered his ninth season in Westwood, the Bruins had won the Pacific 10 Conference two years in a row and followed up both seasons with victories in the Rose Bowl. Coach Donahue was returning UCLA to the days of glory seen decades earlier under Red Sanders and Tommy Prothro. Once again, 1984 would present the Bruins with a new challenge. Talent was lost to graduation. Expectations had been raised. But the Bruins of '84 were capable of rising to a challenge. Though winning a third consecutive Pac 10 title seemed a daunting prospect, the Bruins were ready to give it a try. Other teams were anxious and ready to dethrone Coach Donahue's team. The Pac 10 was strong, and the fight for conference superiority would be a heavyweight battle.

Entering the season, not only were UCLA fans expecting a strong season, but preseason national prognosticators were, as well. *Football News* would rank the Bruins No. 7 in the country. *Athlon Publications* believed the Bruins were No. 6. The most widely used national ranking was the Associated Press, and they named the Bruins the No. 4 team in the nation, as did *The Sporting News*. One publication, however, with as much clout as anyone named the Bruins No. 1 in the country! When the *Sports Illustrated* college football preview issue was released, the Bruins stood at the top. Not only were the eyes of the West Coast on Coach Donahue's squad, but so were the eyes of the entire college football world. Despite the high expectations, the Bruins had areas to work on after Week 1. Though they escaped by a score of 18–15 over San Diego State, the Bruins failed to reach the end zone. Only the steady leg of kicker John Lee helped the Bruins avoid embarrassment. Lee would finish the day with six field goals, tying the NCAA record for most in one game.

The disappointing performance in Week 1 was

only a sign of things to come early in the season. In Week 2, UCLA once again barely came away victorious over an inferior opponent. UCLA's offense would reach the end zone just twice against Long Beach State, and Lee added three more field goals. Quarterback Steve Bono completed 11 of 18 passes for 141 yards but left early with an ankle injury. The UCLA defense dominated LBSU's offensive line, allowing only 10 net rushing yards on the day, but the 49ers consistently beat the Bruins through the air, finishing with 312 passing yards. UCLA's defense was saved by the ability to force turnovers. The Bruins intercepted three passes and recovered three 49ers fumbles. UCLA 23, LBSU 17. Following two games that the Bruins were barely able to squeak by, they fell to No. 8 in the AP poll, and though they were at the Rose Bowl on September 22, they were the clear underdogs. When UCLA took on the top-ranked Nebraska Cornhuskers, the Bruins were taught a lesson in what a top team looks like. Lee would once again have a successful day, but he was alone. The Bruins finished with a dismal 206 total yards, their only points of the day coming on Lee's 10th field goal of the season. Nebraska 42, UCLA 3. Following the blowout loss, the Bruins would hit the road for their final nonconference game of the season. Now ranked No. 17, the team had been humbled. After being crushed a week earlier, Coach Donahue's squad played their best game of the season thus far. Due to injuries, the Bruins would field some of their younger talent in extended roles. At quarterback, sophomore Matt Stevens got the start and completed 13 of 23 passes for 193 yards and a touchdown. Freshman running backs James Primus and Gaston Green each proved effective, rushing for 88 and 81 yards, respectively. John Lee knocked in four more field goals and surpassed Gary Beban as UCLA's all-time leading scorer. Final score: UCLA 33, Colorado 16.

When conference play started, one team on the field at the Rose Bowl was ready and one was not. Stanford jumped out to a 20–0 lead on the Bruins in the Pac 10 opener and forced them into an almost unwinnable situation. The team was outplayed and outcoached, but they were not outworked. The Bruins continued to fight, and despite four turnovers, they still had a chance late in the game. After Stevens led a brilliant fourth-quarter comeback, the game came down to a final play. Trailing 23–21, the Bruins had just scored and were forced to go for two. James Primus get the carry, but Stanford held and the Bruins lost. It was a disappointing start to the conference season. UCLA would have to improve and rally, in order to have a shot at the Pac 10 title for the third year in a row.

Rally, they did. Following the loss to the Cardinal, UCLA made its move, but it was not easy. On October 13, the Bruins beat the Washington State Cougars, 27–24. Despite leading, 24–7, early in the fourth quarter, the Bruins found themselves looking at a possible loss in the final minutes. Luck, however, was on the their side. After tying the game, 24–24, WSU lined up for the go-ahead field goal when the snap sailed high over the holder's hands. The Bruins would take over in Cougars territory, and six plays later, Lee knocked in the game-winning field goal. He was 16 for 16 on the season. To the surprise of few, the game the following week against Cal again came down to Lee's talented and dependable leg. Though Cal was a porous team and the Bruins had not lost to the Bears in 13 years, the game was tied, 14–14, in the fourth quarter. After recovering a Cal fumble, Lee came through in the clutch and hit the game-winning 18-yard field goal. Though UCLA played its best game in conference play the next week against Arizona State, that game was still tight. The defense would shine on this day, and the Bruins came away with a 21–13 victory over the Sun Devils. Despite having underwhelmed fans all season long, the Bruins still enjoyed a respectable 6–2 record when November rolled around and were still battling for the conference crown with a 3–1 record. But when UCLA met the Oregon Ducks on Homecoming Day, they would experience one of their darkest times in years. After losing, 20–18, UCLA was eliminated from Rose Bowl contention. They could now simply play spoiler. They beat Oregon State, 26–17, and then had only one thing on their minds: beat the Trojans!

Though the USC Trojans were heavy favorites and had just beaten the top-ranked Washington Huskies in the previous week to clinch a trip to the Rose Bowl, the Bruins proved to be the superior team when the rivals met on November 17. That became clear to the 90,096 fans who saw Gaston Green and the Bruins offense dominate the Trojans. Green finished with 134 yards. The defense stifled the USC attack, holding them to just 10 points. Dennis Price had the highlight play of the game for the Bruins defense, intercepting a pass and returning it 63 yards for a touchdown. As fans could by then come to expect, kicker John Lee was once again fabulous, finishing with five more field goals and breaking the NCAA single-season field goal record in the process. The Bruins had beaten the Trojans for the third time in a row, and though UCLA would not be returning to Pasadena on January 1, they would have a game to play on New Year's Day.

UCLA vs. USC, 1984 (Southern Campus Collection)

On January 1, 1985, UCLA took on the defending National Champion Miami Hurricanes in the Fiesta Bowl in Tempe, Arizona. "The U" was now coached by first-year man Jimmy Johnson, and though the team was not as strong as in the year prior, they still presented a challenge to the Bruins. Miami was the No. 13 ranked team in the country. The Bruins were No. 14. Just as the two were closely matched in the polls, so they were on the field. The game finished exactly as one would expect having watched the Bruins all season. Gaston Green finished with 144 yards, but the game was won by John Lee. He nailed the game-winning field goal to give the Bruins a 39–37 win. UCLA finished the season with a 9–3 record and a No. 9 ranking in the final Associated Press poll.

The Downtown Athletic Club named Doug Flutie from Boston College the 1984 Heisman Trophy Winner.

The Associated Press named Brigham Young University the 1984 National Champions.

## 1985

The 1985 offseason was a year of reflection for many UCLA fans. It had been 10 years since the miracle team of Coach Dick Vermeil that shocked the nation in the Rose Bowl. The '85 season would be Coach Terry Donahue's tenth in Westwood. He had provided stability that the Bruins lacked in the 1970s. After a decade in which UCLA saw Tommy Prothro bolt for the NFL, Pepper Rodgers leave after just three seasons to return to his alma mater, Dick Vermeil spend just two seasons, and Coach Terry Donahue get off to a slow start, the struggles of the 1970s were now a distant memory. The 1980s saw a turn in not only the success of the Bruins as a team, but in the success they were having against their greatest rival. The Bruins had won four of the most recent five games against the USC Trojans after losing the previous four. Despite being a frequent occupier of a top 10 position in the national polls for the previous half decade, UCLA was now starting the 1985 season as a bit of an outsider. Yes, pollsters knew they were good. What they didn't know was how good. The Associated Press named UCLA the No. 20 team in America in their first poll of the season. It was an insult.

The 1985 season, as in so many seasons of late, kicked off against a fantastic opponent. Coach Donahue and the Bruins would play anyone, anywhere, at any time. In season openers, this can be especially challenging, considering an information shortage about opponents that teams must deal with. On September 7, UCLA took on the defending National Champion Brigham Young University Cougars. The game would go down as a classic. Ever-reliable kicker John Lee scored the first points of the season for UCLA in the first quarter with a short 25-yard field goal. From then on, the game swung back and forth. BYU's Gary Webster tied the game with a field goal, then Craig Rutledge intercepted a pass and raced 65 yards to put the Bruins back on top at the end of the first quarter. In the second quarter, BYU scored two touchdowns, and UCLA could only counter with another field goal. At halftime, the score was 17–13 Cougars. The second half was much of the same for the Bruins. Their offense drove down the field only to stall, perhaps burdened by conservative play calling. Lee made two more field goals to temporarily regain the lead, before the Cougars' Robbio Bosco reached the end zone on a short run. UCLA, despite seemingly outplaying BYU all game, was down, 24–19.

Lee had kicked four field goals, but another would not help the Bruins. They needed a touchdown, and that's what they got. After driving down the field, Gaston Green finally reached the end zone for only the second touchdown of the day for the Bruins. It was enough, however, and after a successful two-point conversion, the score was 27–24. The score held, and the Bruins left Provo with a big opening game victory. The Bruins were 1–0. The second game of the season once again pitted the Bruins against a tough opponent. A Tennessee crowd of 94,370 fans, most of them for the home team, cheered for their Volunteers when UCLA came to town. Both fan bases, though one more than the other, would come away disappointed. UCLA got off to a quick start. On the third play of the game, Gaston Green raced 72 yards for a score, and minutes later Lee booted a 39-yard field goal to give UCLA a 10–0 lead. Tennessee stormed back. After a Matt Stevens interception, Tennessee kicker Carlos Reveiz hit a 49-yard field goal. Later in the half, Tennessee reached the end zone for the first time of the day, tying the game at 10. Later in the second quarter, after a second Stevens interception, Tennessee got on the scoreboard again on a field goal, taking a 13–10 lead. Coming out of the halftime break, the Vols showed no signs of slowing down. In fact, they looked to crush their opponent. On the third play of the half, quarterback Tony Robinson hit wide receiver Joey Clinkscales for a 68-yard score, extending the lead to 20–10. The game appeared over when Tennessee knocked in a field goal on the first play of the fourth quarter and three minutes later made another field goal. Despite the belief that the two scores may have doomed the Bruins, holding the Vols to just field goals served to keep the Bruins alive. Down by 16, they would rally. David Norrie came in to replace Matt Stevens at quarterback, and though Norrie himself threw an interception, he proved to be the spark the Bruins needed. After taking over at their own 3-yard line, the Bruins offense went to work. An eight play, 97-yard drive was capped by an 8-yard touchdown pass from Norrie to wide receiver Al Wilson. The two-point conversion was successful on a pass to tight end Jeff Nowinski. The Bruins were down just one score when they took over at their own 27-yard line with just over a minute and a half to play. Eight plays later, the Bruins found themselves within reach of the end zone. The ball was snapped at the 25; Norrie looked and found Flipper Anderson. Touchdown Bruins! The score was 28–26. A win was nearly impossible at this point, but a tie is better than a loss. Gaston Green took the two-point conversion carry around right end and into the end zone. The final score was 26–26. Though Norrie would be the story for many, the real star of the game was Gaston Green. On 24 carries, Green rushed for 194 yards and a score. At the time of the game, Tennessee was unranked, but they would go on to win the SEC and finish No. 4 in the final Associated Press rankings.

When the Bruins returned home, it may have been difficult for some to appreciate the moment: two classic games to open the season and an inferior opponent on the schedule. The game was not always pretty, but when the clock hit :00, the Bruins were 2–0–1 after beating San Diego State in the home opener. The Bruins did not fare as well, however, in the conference opener the following week. Even without the services of Gaston Green, UCLA led the Washington Huskies, 14–11, at halftime. But in the second half, the lead quickly evaporated, and UCLA fell by the score of 21–14.

Though the Bruins were a disappointing 2–1–1 and had fallen to the depths of the unranked by the time October rolled around, Coach Donahue would lead his team to his usual midseason winning streak. UCLA returned to its home field, the Rose Bowl, for the fifth game of the season and soundly defeated Arizona State, 40–17. The following week, the Bruins dismantled Stanford, 34–9. In the next game, a third win in a row, they barely escaped Pullman, Washington, with a 31–30 victory. Three more wins ran the Bruins winning streak to six: 34–7 over Cal, 24–19 over Arizona, and 41–0 over Oregon State. The Bruins were once again in the Rose Bowl hunt, something that had become a regular occurrence under Coach Donahue.

In order for the Bruins to reach the Rose Bowl once again, they would have to beat their rival Trojans, or have Arizona beat Arizona State. Coach Donahue and his squad had no plans to depend on the Wildcats. They counted on winning it themselves. Of course, the plans one has are often misaligned with the reality to come. The No. 8 Bruins were upset, 17–13. Ultimately, the inability of the offense to score touchdowns instead of field goals haunted them.

USC quarterback Rodney Peete scored the game-winning touchdown from one yard out to give USC the victory. Once again, however, UCLA was lucky. Arizona beat Arizona State, 16–13. As a result, the Bruins were the Pac 10 champions and would head to the Rose Bowl for the third time in four years.

The January 1 clash between the No. 13 Bruins and the heavily favored No. 4 Iowa Hawkeyes would turn out to be one of the most talked about UCLA games in history, though not for the reasons many might expect. The Bruins beat Iowa by a score of 45–28. With Norrie out due to a thigh injury, Stevens was back under cnter. He played efficiently and led the Bruins to 488 total yards. The story, however, was the running backs. UCLA freshman Eric Ball ran for 227 yards and four touchdowns. Iowa star running back Ronnie Harmon would not have as good a day; in fact, he had the worst day of his collegiate career. Following his four-fumble performance, many in the media and many Iowa fans believed he threw the game. He was simply too good to fumble away what they was anticipated would be a sure victory. Whether Harmon threw the game or not, it mattered little to the Bruins. They were simply the better team, with or without the fumbles. The Bruins finished the season with a 9–2–1 record and were voted the No. 7 best team in the nation in the final AP poll.

The Downtown Athletic Club named Bo Jackson from Auburn University the 1985 Heisman Trophy Winner.

The Associated Press named the University of Oklahoma the 1985 National Champions.

## 1986

In 1986, the goals remained the same: win the Pacific 10 Conference, win the Rose Bowl, compete for a National Championship. Another thing remained the same: the schedule was brutal. Five of the 11 regular season games would come against ranked teams, including three against top 10 teams. UCLA was unquestionably strong, and going into the season pollsters took notice. Having won three of the previous four Rose Bowls, UCLA was not a team simply in the midst of a successful stretch, sure to fade back to the pack. Rather, they were a burgeoning college football powerhouse. For three and a half decades, UCLA had been one of the best football programs in America. It was time to take the next step. The memory of Red Sanders and the '54 Bruins faded further and further into the distance. Bruins fans yearned for another National Championship. Looking at the past, some might say that UCLA fans were spoiled. It is more accurate to say, they dreamed of more.

For the second year in a row, UCLA opened the season against the defending National Champions. After beating BYU in '85, fans, coaches, and players were anxious to see what the Bruins could do against the University of Oklahoma in '86. UCLA was ranked No. 4 in the nation by the Associated Press, and the Sooners were dubbed the top team in the land. It was a marquee matchup, televised nationally, and the premier game in the entire country. The Sooners were led on offense by quarterback Jamelle Holieway, who, after taking over for an injured Troy Aikman the previous year, had revitalized the Sooners wishbone offense. On defense, they were led by All-American linebacker Brian Bosworth. UCLA, which led the nation in rush defense in '85, was bringing back eight starters on defense, and the Oklahoma wishbone vs. the UCLA rushing defense figured to be the matchup to watch. Linebackers Ken Norton and Carnell Lake, and safeties Craig Rutledge and James Washington,

UCLA Cheerleaders, 1985 (Southern Campus Collection)

led the Bruins defense. On offense, quarterback Matt Stevens was back for his fifth year, but the UCLA offense was led by the slew of talented running backs on the roster. Gaston Green, Eric Ball, and Mel Farr Jr. were all individually capable players, but as a group they formed one of the best units in the nation. The game started slow on both sides, but one team picked up play after the first quarter and one was left in the dust. Not only were the Bruins badly beaten, they were wounded. Receiver Karl Dorrell left with a knee injury, but the worst pain was that inflicted to the Bruins' psyche. It was the first-ever meeting between the two schools, and UCLA was not likely to forget it. Final score: Oklahoma 38, UCLA 3.

Two weeks after the beatdown in Norman, Oklahoma, UCLA took on San Diego State University. Gaston Green starred for the Bruins, finishing with 131 yards and three touchdowns. UCLA defeated the Aztecs, 45–14. For the second week in a row, when they took on Long Beach State, UCLA looked more like the dominant team predicted by the pollsters than the team that had been dominated in Week 1. After leading by just 10 points at halftime, the Bruins scored 24 straight points to put the game away. James Primus rushed for a career-high 160 yards on the day.

As September turned to October, the focus of the team turned from nonconference to conference opponents. The conference opener would not be easy. The two Arizona schools, both fielding strong teams in '86, were the first two on the conference slate. Despite playing a strong first half, UCLA lost its conference opener, 16–9, to Arizona State. The Bruins defense didn't allow even a single first down until two minutes before halftime, but the offense was unable to carry its weight. Quarterback Matt Stevens struggled, and ASU came away on top. The quest for a fourth Rose Bowl in five years was not off to a strong start. By October 11, the team once ranked No. 4 in the nation was now unranked. Their opponent, the Arizona Wildcats, which had lost out on a Rose Bowl trip the year before on the final Saturday, was ranked No. 11. UCLA, it seemed, was now inferior to the Wildcats, who were hell-bent on returning to Pasadena in January. UA jumped out to an 18–0 lead, but the Bruins stormed back. With six minutes to play in the game, the deficit was erased. The comeback was complete. The UCLA lead did not last, however. UA quickly scored to retake the lead, 25–24. Finally, with 41 seconds left, UCLA got the last laugh, scoring the game-winning touchdown and securing a much-needed win. The Bruins were 3–2 on the season and 1–1 in conference play.

The middle of the Pac 10 schedule had long been a Bruin strongpoint under coach Donahue, and 1986 was no exception. After their big win over the University of Arizona, the Bruins carried the momentum into Berkeley the following week. Offensively, it was a true team effort. Stevens completed nine of 15 passes for two scores, both coming to split end Flipper Anderson. Gaston Green added 134 yards in the Bruins' dominant performance. UCLA defeated Cal for the 15th consecutive time. Final score: UCLA 36, Cal 10. On October 25, the Bruins returned to the Rose Bowl and continued their winning ways. The offense racked up yards and points, while the defense stifled opponents. Though UCLA started slow against Washington State and fell behind,16–7, when they finally awoke, the Cougars had no chance. UCLA scored 47 consecutive points. Gaston Green rushed for 162 yards and two touchdowns. James Primus added 78 yards and three scores. The following week, the offensive output was similar. Green ran for 123 yards against the Oregon State Beavers, and Primus scored two touchdowns. The defense, however, was even better. They shut out the Beavers and intercepted eight passes, returning two for touchdowns. The Bruins were again looking like the team that America had seen in the Rose Bowl on January 1.

After winning four straight games, the Bruins were back in a position to win the Pac 10 Conference. The next three games would decide if they were to return to the big game on New Year's Day or watch at home. On November 8, the No. 12-ranked Bruins took on unranked Stanford. The Cardinal jumped out to a 14–0 lead in the first quarter, and the Bruins were once again tasked with coming back. Unlike the game against Washington State weeks earlier, the comeback attempt would be much more difficult. Down, 28–16, in the third quarter, Green scored his third touchdown of the day to cut the lead to 28–23, but neither team was able to score the rest of the way. Winning the Pac 10 would now require help. All the Bruins could do was focus on what lay ahead. The tenth game of the season pitted the No. 19 Bruins against the No. 10 Washington Huskies.

With the score tied, 14–14, UCLA kicker David Franey knocked in a go-ahead field goal with 1:42 to play. The disappointed faces in the Washington crowd soon realized, however, that the game was not over despite the kick. Their offense was marching downfield. Though they threatened the Bruins defense and reached as far as the UCLA 10, time was not on Washington's side. They were forced to kick a field goal on the final play of the game, which was successful from 27 yards out. The game ended in a tie. Since each team desperately needed a win, the tie solidified Arizona State's spot in the Rose Bowl game.

Members of UCLA's rally committee guard the Victory Bell during rivalry week, 1986 (Southern Campus Collection)

With one week to go, the game against USC was not about winning the conference, though the Bruins were still technically alive; it was about avenging the loss of the previous year. The Bruins entered the game ranked No. 18 in the country, and the Trojans No. 10. Beyond the normal rivalry motivation, UCLA's players were amped up for the game for another reason. Teammate and friend Al Wilson had died one week earlier, and the Bruins were dedicating the USC game to Wilson. They honored him the best way they knew how. They destroyed USC. Gaston Green rushed for 224 yards and four touchdowns. Matt Stevens was 14 for 19, picking up 190 yards in the air. Karl Dorrell was unstoppable. At halftime, UCLA led, 31–0. The final score was 45–25. The Bruins would not go to the Rose Bowl, but they would play in a bowl game. On December 30, UCLA took on BYU in the Freedom Bowl. Green shined once again, rushing for 266 yards and three touchdowns. The careers of Matt Stevens and Karl Dorrell came to a close in proper fashion. UCLA won its fifth consecutive bowl game and once again had Bruins fans excited for football. It would be a long offseason, having to wait for the next kickoff.

The Downtown Athletic Club named Vinny Testaverde from the University of Miami the 1986 Heisman Trophy Winner.

The Associated Press named Penn State University the 1986 National Champions.

## 1987

In 1987, the Bruins were loaded. Not only did Gaston Green return, but he had a new star quarterback to relieve pressure. The man handing him the ball was not just good, he was great. When Troy Aikman left Oklahoma following the 1985 Sooners' National Championship season, his future was up in the air. He was coming west, back to Southern California, back to where he had grown up. Aikman simply didn't fit in at Oklahoma. At UCLA, he would stand out. He was a superstar. Though UCLA had been a good team for some time, consistently finishing in the top half of the AP rankings for most of the 1980s, the belief in Westwood in 1987 was that if Aikman could prove to be the quarterback everyone believed him to be, the Bruins would be special. It was perhaps the best UCLA team since the brilliant one of 1982.

UCLA started the season ranked No. 3 in the country. When they took on San Diego State on September 5, it was expected to be a cakewalk for UCLA, an easy victory to help prepare for the big Week 2 matchup. That was exactly the case. Aikman, Green, and Flipper Anderson all shined and the Bruins cruised to a 47–14 season-opening win. One week later, UCLA played in a game that already had National Championship implications. The No. 3 Bruins traveled to Lincoln, Nebraska, and took on the No. 2 Huskers. UCLA got off to a strong start, scoring first on a 4-yard Green touchdown run toward the end of the first quarter. Though still early in the season, the crowd was nervous. It was the 150th consecutive sellout at Memorial Stadium, and fans did now show up to see their beloved team lose. In the second quarter, Nebraska scored twice before the Bruins could answer. Huskers quarterback Steve Taylor, who was brilliant on the day, threw to Tom Banderas and Ken Clark for the two touchdowns. UCLA answered with a field goal before the half ended but would head into the locker room trailing, 14–10. Though the first half brought action, it was nothing compared to the rapid pace of both offensives in the second half. Nebraska scored the first two touchdowns of the second half to seemingly put the game away, but UCLA came storming back. Eric Ball scored from six yards out, and Green added two touchdowns. The offense was never an issue that day, racking up 361 total yards, compared to the Huskers' 334. Though UCLA's running game was slowed, the passing game thrived. Tight end Charles Arbuckle and receiver Flipper Anderson each had a big day. Nebraska's offense was simply better when it came to converting scoring opportunities. Steve Taylor threw for five touchdowns, and Nebraska went on to beat UCLA by the score of 42–33. After dropping 10 spots in the AP poll, UCLA had something to prove. They had played well against powerhouse Nebraska and probably should have won the game, but that was unimportant. They had lost. But they wouldn't feel that pain again for quite some time. In Week 3, the offense didn't have its best day, but the defense carried the team. Ken Norton Jr., Carnell Lake, Darryl Henley, and Terry Tumey led the unit that completely shut down Fresno State, blanking them all game. The offense did enough, and UCLA won, 17–0. They were 2–1 when conference play began. It was time to make a run for the roses.

UCLA kicked off conference play on September 26 against the University of Arizona with a sound 34–24 victory. One week later, they were even better. When UCLA traveled to the farm to take on the Stanford Cardinal, they came with a purpose. Stanford was a poor team. UCLA got a big lead and never gave the heavy underdog a chance to win. They were not only successful in doing so, they embarrassed their opponent. The *New York Times* would say of the game, "UCLA trounces Stanford." Gaston Green ran all over the Stanford defense and into the UCLA record book. He would finish with 139 yards on the day and pass Freeman McNeil to become UCLA's all-time leading rusher. The performance by the Bruins was not just by one man, but by the entire team. Aikman threw two touchdowns to Paco Craig. Alfredo Velasco made four field goals. The UCLA defense intercepted six passes, including two that were returned for touchdowns, one each by Ben Hummel and Eric Turner. UCLA won by the score of 49–0.

When the Bruins hit their stride, as they so often did midseason under Coach Donahue, it seemed that nothing or no one could stop them. In game number six, UCLA had a stiff challenge, but it proved to be nothing they couldn't handle. On October 17, the Bruins took on the No. 17-ranked Oregon Ducks, and as they had done one week earlier, they rolled over their opponent. UCLA won, 41–10. It was becoming more and more evident each week that the team of 1987 was a damn good one. As the Bruins continued to win, they rose in the rankings. After beating Cal on October 24, they climbed to No. 7. After beating Arizona State and dismantling Oregon State, they were No. 5. Only one opponent stood between them and USC: the Washington Huskies. The Bruins once again showed they were too strong. UW went down by the score of 47–14. UCLA had won eight games in a row, and their final regular season matchup would be the biggest game of the season.

When UCLA took on USC on November 21, it was the most significant game between the two rivals since 1978. The winner would once again win the Pacific 10 Conference and go to the Rose Bowl. USC, under first-year head coach Larry Smith, was a strong team, with a 7–3 record, but the Trojans were clear underdogs. UCLA was one of the best teams in the nation, and USC was unranked. The man they did have, however—who gave them a chance in every single game—was Rodney Peete. The rivalry game would be a battle of quarterbacks. Through 10 games, Aikman had thrown for over 2,000 yards and 16 touchdowns and was number one in the nation in passing efficiency. UCLA appeared to be on its way to a convincing win in the final seconds of the first half. With the Bruins leading, 10–0, USC faced a first and goal at the UCLA 5-yard line with just 14 seconds to play, when momentum shifted drastically. Rodney Peete looked and fired toward the left corner of the end zone, but the pass was tipped by UCLA linebacker Marvcus Patton and landed in the arms of defensive back Eric Turner. Turner saw green grass and raced down the sideline. He would say after the game, "I saw the end zone. I saw daylight. I thought I was gone." He was wrong. He wasn't gone. Rodney Peete was the only man who could catch the speedy Turner, and he did just that, finally dragging him down at the USC 11-yard line with no time on the clock. UCLA took a 10-point lead into the half, but the tackle by Peete kept the Trojans alive. Early in the third quarter, UCLA extended the lead to 13 on a field goal by Alfredo Velasco, but the game was far from over. USC would score the next 10 points and were within striking distance in the fourth quarter. Down three, USC found themselves with the ball and a chance to take the lead. On first down with the ball on the Bruins' 33, the UCLA defense was set to stop a run, but Coach Smith called for a bomb. Marcus Turner bit on a double move, and USC receiver Erik Affholter got behind the defense. Though it appeared to half the fans watching that Affholter bobbled the ball and never gained control until he was out of bounds, the referee signaled touchdown, and the USC comeback was complete. The score was 17–13. Aikman would not be the hero on this day. After he threw an interception with a minute to go, the game was over. USC had spoiled UCLA's otherwise brilliant season. Though the Bruins would go to the Aloha Bowl and beat the University of Florida on Christmas Day for their sixth consecutive bowl victory, the season was ultimately a disappointment. The team coming back in '88 would have holes to fill. The greatness of college athletics is the endless cycle of players coming and going. The careers of the great Gaston Green, as well as Ken Norton Jr., Flipper Anderson, James Washington, and others, were over.

The Downtown Athletic Club named Tim Brown from the University of Notre Dame the 1987 Heisman Trophy Winner.

The Associated Press named the University of Miami the 1987 National Champions.

## 1988

The 1988 presidential election mirrored what many saw happening with the UCLA football program. After a steady eight years under Ronald Reagan, the Republican Party nominated his vice president, George Herbert Walker Bush. This was seen as a continuation of the Reagan doctrine. At UCLA, the 1980s had been a decade to be proud of. They consistently challenged for Rose Bowls and every year entered the season with grand hopes of taking home the title of National Champions. After a mass exodus of talent to the National Football League following the 1987 season, however, there were questions to be asked and answers that could only be given on the gridiron. Coach Donahue was back for his thirteenth season as the UCLA head coach. Troy Aikman was back to lead a largely inexperienced, yet talented, roster, and with Gaston Green gone, it was Aikman's time to soak in the individual glory—although more important to him and to the fans was the team. The Bruins of '88 would once again start with high expectations. Rose Bowl or bust.

The first two games of the 1988 season were against the same teams the Bruins faced to start the 1987 season, but only one had similar results. In the season opener, UCLA easily defeated San Diego State University, just as they had done a year earlier. Though a small crowd of just over 46,000 fans saw the UCLA season-opening victory at the Rose Bowl, fans would show up in much greater numbers the following week. The Nebraska Cornhuskers were in town, once again ranked No. 2 in the nation. UCLA was the No. 5-ranked team, and for the second year in a row, the two squared off on national television in the biggest game of the day. Most of the 84,086 fans who showed up at the Rose Bowl to see the two heavyweight teams play were not disappointed. Despite Nebraska's legendary home crowd attendance figures at their stadium in Lincoln, the size of the crowd at the Rose Bowl was the fourth-largest the Huskers had ever seen. UCLA fans looking for revenge from the defeat a year prior got exactly what they wanted. The fans in attendance and those watching on ABC-TV saw the Bruins thrash the Cornhuskers. By the end of the first quarter, UCLA led, 28–0. Aikman had found Charles Arbuckle for the first score of the game from 57 yards out. Six minutes later, Shawn Wills ran 50 yards for a touchdown. Arbuckle caught his second touchdown of the day a few minutes later, and finally, with a minute to go in the first quarter, Darryl Henley returned a punt 75 yards for a score. The crowd at the Rose Bowl was wild with excitement. It was the worst first quarter in Nebraska history. UCLA went on to win by the score of 41–28. Aikman's three-touchdown performance put him right at the top of many pundits' Heisman

Trophy list. The Bruins played their third home game in a row to start the season one week later, and, predictably, they destroyed Long Beach State by a score of 56–3.

When conference play began, the Bruins were eyeing much more than a Pacific 10 Conference title. They had dreams of winning the national title. Following their 3–0 start, UCLA climbed to No. 2 in the latest polls when they took on the University of Washington on the 1st of October. The Huskies were a strong team, ranked No.16 in the country, and the Bruins had the added test of playing in their first away game of the season. It would be a battle throughout, but the better team came away with the win. UCLA 24, Washington 17. While UCLA had become known for going on long, midseason winning streaks during the Coach Donahue era, the streak of '88 would start at the beginning of the season. After starting 4–0 with impressive victories over two ranked opponents, UCLA began the easier part of their schedule. On October 8, they beat Oregon State, 38–21, and one week later defeated California Berkeley by the exact same score. It was the seventeenth consecutive win for the Bruins over the Bears. More notable than just the victory over California, the win put UCLA in a position they had rarely held. The top-ranked Miami Hurricanes were on a bye week, and the Bruins' impressive showing was enough to catapult them over the "U" in the next rankings. UCLA entered the game against Arizona as the number one team in the nation! UCLA's defense, led by a terrific secondary, dominated. Final score: UCLA 24, Arizona 3.

The Bruins' record was 7–0, with four games to play in the regular season. An epic finish to the season was on the horizon. Across town, USC was also undefeated and anticipation was growing for the big matchup, but that was still a month away. Coming in to the game against Washington State University on October 29, Troy Aikman had thrown 19 touchdowns and was considered by many the Heisman front-runner. At halftime, it appeared that UCLA was on track to win again and maintain its position as the top-ranked team in the nation. They led, 20–6, at the break, but in the second half, the Cougars fought back. UCLA's offense scored 10 more points, but ultimately the defense failed them. After a strong first half, UCLA gave up four touchdowns to fall behind, 34–30. Washington State struggled all season on special teams, and it almost came back to bite them in the end. After a big return, UCLA had the ball at the WSU 6-yard line, but four plays later, the Bruins found themselves not in the end zone, but rather in the loss column for the first time in almost a year. WSU Head Coach Dennis Erickson won his biggest game as the Cougars coach, and the loss for coach Donahue and the Bruins was heartbreaking. Their chance at a National Championship had slipped through their hands. UCLA fell to No. 6 in the rankings, and after two consecutive 10-point wins, they were in the same position as they had been one year earlier: 9–1, and facing USC for a shot at the Rose Bowl.

When UCLA and USC met in 1988, it was more than just a normal late fall game. It was a showcase. Troy Aikman was sure to be the number-one pick in the NFL draft. The only question for him individually was, would he have a Heisman Trophy on his mantel at home come December? USC in '87 had upset the Bruins to go to the Rose Bowl. In '88, there would be no upset. UCLA was the No. 6 team in the country. The Trojans were the No. 2 team. Oddsmakers considered the game a toss-up. Anything could happen. While Aikman was a top Heisman Trophy candidate, he was not the only one playing in Southern California. Rodney Peete from USC was a serious candidate, as well. Many in the local and national media dubbed Aikman-Peete II not only a battle for the city, but a contest for the most famous trophy in sports. Five days before the much-anticipated showdown, however, news came out that could derail the storylines of USC's hopes. Rodney Peete had the flu. He was stuck in a hospital bed, and it was unknown whether or not he would play. He had to change hospital rooms three times to avoid reporters hounding him. By Friday, to the dismay of the Bruins, whether they would admit it or not, Peete was feeling much better. He would play on Saturday. All of 100,741 fans showed up at the Rose Bowl, the largest crowd to see the two teams play since 1954. For UCLA fans, it was a day to forget. Though Aikman won the battle of the statistics, throwing for more than 300 yards to Peete's 189, USC won on the scoreboard. Neither man would win the Heisman. One week later, USC would fall to Notre Dame. The loss for the Bruins was much like the one the previous year. The Bruins finished with a 10–2 record after beating No. 8 Arkansas in the Cotton Bowl, but the loss to USC would sting. Aikman went on to win three Super Bowls with the Dallas Cowboys, and is a member of the Pro Football Hall of Fame. His two years at UCLA were brilliant, but the losses to USC would hurt forever.

The Downtown Athletic Club named Barry Sanders from Oklahoma State University the 1988 Heisman Trophy Winner.

The Associated Press named the University of Notre Dame the 1988 National Champions.

## Troy Aikman

The first and only UCLA Bruins football player ever taken number one overall in the National Football League draft is Troy Aikman. Troy was born on November 21, 1966, in West Covina, California. From a young age, Troy had one goal: to become a professional athlete. Which sport? It didn't much matter for the youngster. Troy's two older sisters, Terrie and Tammy, were cheerleaders. His parents were his biggest fans. He grew up around sports and dreamed of playing on the biggest stage. Though he had a mild form of club foot, nothing could keep Troy from competing. An already experienced playground ballplayer, Troy's first experience in organized sports came when he was eight years old. He played football, baseball, and basketball. He played year-round, and though he had an inkling that his future was in football, he respected the process. Troy would have to climb the ladder. He continued playing multiple sports as he grew up. At the age of twelve, Troy's life changed drastically. In the California suburbs, Troy had always been able to find friends to go out and play with him at any time. When his family packed up and moved to Henryetta, Oklahoma, with a population of just over 6,000 people, he was forced to adjust. Living in rural Oklahoma was a major change. The hyperactive kid who rode his bike everywhere suddenly had to slow down. There were fewer people, initially fewer friends, and fewer paved roads, which meant he had to walk instead of ride. Though Troy missed his friends back in California, he eventually got used to living in a small town and grew to really enjoy it. The people of Henryetta were close-knit, and supportive of the local high school. As he grew older, Troy appreciated the hard-working, yet laid-back lifestyle that Oklahoma presented. Like most who would later become star athletes, Troy played multiple positions

Troy Aikman, 1987 (Southern Campus Collection)

in multiple sports growing up. In football, he was the quarterback and middle linebacker. In basketball, he was the center. In baseball, he was a shortstop and pitcher. At Henryetta High School, Troy not only competed in multiple sports, he thrived. As a senior, he was seen as a top baseball prospect and potentially a player who could forgo college to play professionally. Prior to the MLB draft, Troy was contacted by the New York Mets and asked what it would take for him to skip college and pursue a baseball career. Troy, who hadn't much considered the thought of ending his football career quite yet, didn't know what to say. When pressed for an answer, he said, "I don't know, $200,000." The response, "$200,000? Darryl Strawberry is not even making that much money." Aikman, firm on his stance and knowing football was still his best option, replied, "Well if you want me, that's what it's going to take." They replied: "You have a nice football career at Oklahoma." That was the end of the baseball discussion.

Following high school, Troy did indeed head off to the University of Oklahoma on a football scholarship. Though he was courted by teams across the country, he believed his home state Oklahoma Sooners, under legendary coach Barry Switzer, was the best fit. Troy enjoyed college and the challenge it presented. He truly believed he had a future in football, but he had other interests, as well. He studied business, finance, and marketing. On the football field, however, things were not going as he had hoped and planned. In 1984, he became the starting quarterback as a freshman, admittedly before he was ready. Injuries forced him into a tough situation, but Oklahoma nonetheless entered the 1985 season ranked No. 1 in the nation. Expectations were high, and Sooners fans dreamed of another National Championship. The season started off as expected. Oklahoma dominated the first three games of the season before facing the Jimmy Johnson-coached Miami Hurricanes. Troy started the game on fire but would finish on the sideline . . . and in pain. After being tackled by two Hurricanes defenders, Troy fell on his left leg, and his ankle bent underneath his body. His ankle was broken, and his season was over. The Sooners lost the game to Miami, and Troy would lose his starting spot for good. After the injury, Jamelle Holieway stepped in at quarterback and led the Sooners to the national title. Oklahoma went 11–1 on the season. Holieway was an All-Conference performer and a perfect fit for Coach Switzer's famous wishbone offense. The writing was on the wall for Troy at Oklahoma. Though he loved the University of Oklahoma, he knew his future there would consist of sitting on the bench. He needed a new home.

In 1986, with the help and support of Switzer, Troy Aikman transferred to UCLA. The only major available for him that would transfer all his units from Oklahoma was sociology, so he majored in that. After sitting out one season, Aikman became the starting quarterback for Terry Donahue and the Bruins in 1987. As a first-year starter for the Bruins, he excelled. Troy threw for over 2,500 yards and 17 touchdowns, as the Bruins finished with a 10–2 record. He was named Pac 10 Offensive Player of the Year and led UCLA to a Christmas day bowl matchup against the Florida Gators. UCLA would go on to defeat Florida, 20–16, in the Aloha Bowl, finish the season ranked No. 9 in the country, and have sky-high expectations for the 1988 season.

When the 1988 season rolled around, Troy was even better. He finished his senior year with over 2,700 yards and 24 touchdowns, again with a 10–2 record, this time as the No. 6 team in America. Troy would win the Davey O'Brien Award, handed out to the best quarterback in America. He was a consensus All-American and won a handful of other individual awards. He finished third in the Heisman Trophy voting and capped his career with a game for the fans . . . Dallas Cowboy fans. On January 2, 1989, UCLA took on the No. 8 Arkansas Razorbacks in the Cotton Bowl in Dallas, Texas. Though for many involved, the thought of Troy being drafted number one overall in the upcoming NFL draft was simply a rumor, it was to most a certainty. Troy was the best quarterback in America, and the Cowboys desperately needed a gunslinger to resurrect the glory days under "Captain America," Roger Staubach, who had retired 10 years earlier. Cowboys fans, looking to catch a glimpse of the future in the Cotton Bowl, were not disappointed. The Bruins beat the Razorbacks, 17–3, and Troy was named Cotton Bowl MVP. Troy Aikman was off to the NFL and, yes, to Dallas.

Though Troy would win the starting job with the Cowboys during his rookie season, not all was ideal. The Cowboys were terrible. Troy finished his rookie season with an 0–11 record as the starter, picking up 1,749 yards, with nine touchdowns and 18 interceptions. The Cowboys finished the 1989 season with a 1–15 record in Head Coach Jimmy Johnson's first season in the NFL. Though the general public, and die-hard Cowboys fans, saw the season as a complete disaster, there was a glimmer of hope. Michael Irvin was in his second season. Troy Aikman was in his first. The Cowboys also pulled off one of the most famous trades in sports history. Running back Herschel Walker was sent to the Minnesota Vikings in exchange for a slew of high draft picks. In 1990, the Cowboys drafted Emmitt Smith, and the famous trio was set. Along with Daryl Johnston, the Cowboys premiere players were personally close off the field and dynamic on it. Troy was able to see through the tough exterior of Michael Irvin and get to understand and adore the man. He was able to see the importance of balance, and understand the value of Emmitt Smith. Troy understood Jimmy Johnson on a deeply emotional level. Though they did not always have a lot in common, they shared a burning desire to win, and to prove themselves at the highest level. By 1990, the team was starting to improve. In Troy's second season, the Cowboys went 7–9. In his third season, they went 11–5 and reached the playoffs for the first time in nine years. Though they beat the Bears, 17–13, in the Wild Card round, they were routed by Barry Sanders and the Lions, 38–6, the following week. For the first time in Troy's pro career, there were high expectations heading into the 1992 season.

In 1992, the Cowboys would achieve an outstanding 13–3 record in the regular season. Troy threw for 3,445 yards and 23 touchdowns. They trounced the Philadelphia Eagles in the Division round, 34–10, and defeated the San Francisco 49ers, 30–20, in the Championship round. They were off to the Super Bowl! Super Bowl XXVII was a special game for Troy, one he will remember for the rest of his life. The game was played at his old college home stadium, the Rose Bowl. When his name was called and he ran onto the field to the roar of his hometown crowd, he felt a rush like nothing he had ever experienced before. Though he was admittedly nervous and started out shaky, Troy was his usual brilliant self, and his teammates were, as well. Final score: Cowboys 52, Bills 17. In Troy's first season in the NFL, the Cowboys had gone 1–15. In his fourth, they won the Super Bowl. In his fifth, they would be back in the big game. After finishing 12–4 in the regular season, the Cowboys beat the Packers and the 49ers in postseason play and advanced to the Super Bowl once again. Standing in their way, as in the previous year, were the Buffalo Bills. Hungry to avenge that earlier loss to the Cowboys, the Bills planned to knock the champs off their throne. It wasn't to be. The Cowboys again won the Super Bowl, defeating Buffalo, 30–13. Aikman would later say that the second Super Bowl season was not as much fun as the first. It was more of a grind, but the victory was just as sweet.

In 1995, the Cowboys won again. A year earlier, Jimmy Johnson left the Cowboys, and Troy was reunited with his former college coach at Oklahoma, Barry Switzer. In Switzer's second season, the Cowboys finished 12–4. The trio of Aikman, Irvin, and Smith dominated on offense, and cornerback Deion Sanders put on a show on defense and special teams. The Super Bowl was played at Sun Devil Stadium, and the Cowboys beat the Pittsburgh Steelers, 27–17. It was the fifth Super Bowl in Cowboys history, the third in the last four years. Statistically, Troy was good. But he believed he could have been great. He knew he was as good as Elway, Marino, or Favre, but it didn't matter. Winning percentage was the stat that he cared most about, and in his time in Dallas, the Cowboys did plenty of winning. Troy would play five more seasons, but the core of Dallas's championship rosters was getting old. Following the 2000 season, Troy Aikman announced his retirement from the National Football League. In his career, Aikman threw for 32,942 yards and 165 touchdowns. He won three Super Bowls. In 2005 Aikman, Irvin, and Smith were honored in the Cowboys Ring of Honor. In 2006, Troy was elected to the Pro Football Hall of Fame. In 2008, he was elected to the College Football Hall of Fame. In 2014, his number 8 was retired by UCLA. Troy Aikman was a great football player. He was a leader, and he was a winner. After football, Troy would not simply fade into the background. He is still a star.

In 1999, Troy had written a brief autobiography titled *Mind, Body, and Soul.* In his book, he writes about the things that drive him. He talks about the ways he approaches life and what he might do after retirement. He talks about his childhood, his upbringing, and how he came to be the man he is today. He talks about how he prepares for games and dedicates himself to his craft. He talks about how he takes care of his body, both for personal reasons and because of the responsibility he feels toward his team. He talks about how he overcame skin cancer. He talks about life and his reasoning behind doing the things he does. He talks about love of family and love of work. Troy hinted that he would like to stay involved in football but wasn't sure exactly how. He didn't have plans for coaching, but the thought of being involved in a front office intrigued him. He has thought about sports ownership. He loves golf, but it's not something he could do every day in retirement. Fortunately for football fans, Troy found a postplaying career. In 2001, he joined Fox's NFL coverage as a color commentator. In 2002, he was part of the lead crew. He has broadcast five Super Bowls and has been one of the best color commentators in football for over a decade. Aikman has also done radio shows, television advertisements, and made cameo appearances. He has worked with the National Football Foundation, as well as with many schools throughout Texas, Oklahoma, and California. He has invested in auto racing and is a part owner of the San Diego Padres. In 2009, Aikman participated in the UCLA Sociology commencement ceremony after finishing his degree. Troy Aikman is one of the best players in college football history and one of the best players in NFL history. He is an excellent NFL announcer and a good businessman. Troy Aikman is a quintessential Bruin.

## 1989

The 1980s were a decade of dominance for the UCLA Bruins. After Coach Dick Vermeil left UCLA following the 1975 season, UCLA struggled in the second half of the 1970s. Coach Terry Donahue was young. He was smart. He was innovative. He won games, but he struggled in the big moments. By 1980, UCLA had transitioned to an offense Coach Donahue had envisioned. He turned UCLA into a West Coast powerhouse, both on the football field and on the recruiting trail. By 1989, the Bruins were strong, but there was a crack in their armor. UCLA would struggle in 1989. After winning 79 games in the first nine years of the decade, including back-to-back 10-win seasons in '87 and '88, the Bruins of '89 were an entirely different team. Long gone were the defensive stars of Donahue's earliest years. Gone were the quarterbacks who carried UCLA to Rose Bowl victory after Rose Bowl victory. Coach Donahue would call the 1989 season a rebuilding one. The question remained, would they rebuild or would they collapse?

Despite a revamped roster depleted by departures to the National Football League, pollsters had faith in the Bruins. After they had finished in the top 10 in the Associated Press rankings throughout much of the 1980s, the public, and UCLA fans, began to look past the initial struggles of the Bruins under Coach Donahue and finally appreciate the program he built. UCLA was ranked the No. 6 team in the country to start the season. When the Bruins took on the unranked Tennessee Volunteers in the season opener, there were questions that needed to be answered. How would UCLA replace Troy Aikman? Was freshman Bret Johnson going to be the man to carry on the tradition of fine quarterback play in Westwood? Would UCLA be physical enough to make up for the lack of speed on the roster? Was the defense too young and inexperienced to compete for a conference title? When the opening game was over, Coach Donahue not only felt some questions were left unanswered, but some had been answered in a way he didn't like. Bret Johnson? Good. He had completed 26 of 42 passes for 253 yards. Would they be physical enough? It didn't appear so. Coach Donahue would say, "Up until Saturday night, I didn't feel our defense was unphysical, but I'd certainly say that Saturday night we were unphysical." Tennessee ran the ball on UCLA at will. The Bruins starting defense included five newcomers, and their first taste of college football was not a pleasant one. Tennessee ran for 247 yards. When the game was over, the scoreboard read Tennessee 24, UCLA 6. In a moment of honesty, Coach Donahue said, "I'm not sure I can remember an opening game where we played any poorer." While the Bruins entered the game with questions, they left with fear. Would the season be this poor, or was it only one game? Coach Donahue noted, "They were clearly such a dominant team over us, it's frightening. Either they have been grossly misevaluated or this might be as poor a football team as I've ever had." He continued, "At this time, it's still very difficult to make a clear diagnosis, but I don't like the preliminary reports. It doesn't look very nice and it doesn't look very encouraging."

Coach Donahue's initial instincts were correct. The opening game loss was not only a setback, it was a shocker. UCLA's schedule would only get more difficult. In Week 2, UCLA took on San Diego State University, a team they had beaten handily in the past, and a team they desperately needed to beat before hitting the meat of their schedule. A total of 31,639 fans were in attendance at Jack Murphy Stadium in San Diego to see the No. 20 Bruins and the home-town Aztecs battle for four quarters. UCLA had beaten SDSU 11 of the 12 previous meetings, with the lone tie coming in 1924, and in order to preserve their unbeaten streak, they would need a fourth-quarter rally. When SDSU scored on a 73-yard run on a fake punt in the first quarter, it was the first time SDSU had ever even led in a game against the Bruins. Though UCLA led, 14–10, at halftime, the Bruins defense struggled mightily and were lucky to have given up only 10 points. They gave up 234 yards in the first half, the same amount they gave up the entire game one year earlier, when UCLA had won by a score of 59–6. This was clearly not the same SDSU team, nor was it the same Bruins team. UCLA entered this fourth quarter with a 21–10 lead, but it wouldn't last. SDSU scored two touchdowns to take a three-point lead with just over four minutes to play. UCLA was staring an embarrassing defeat and an 0–2 record in the face. The Bruins would have to drive, and they did just that. On the ninth play of the drive, quarterback Bret Johnson crossed the goal line from one yard out on a QB Sneak, and the Bruins escaped with a victory.

UCLA was 1–1 when the Michigan Wolverines traveled to the Rose Bowl in Week 3. UM was undefeated, ranked No. 5 in the nation. UCLA was No. 24 but hardly looked worthy of being ranked at all. If they played once again the way they had in the first two weeks, they were in danger of getting blown out in front of an anxious home crowd. Instead, UCLA played its best game of the season. Leading by eight to start the fourth quarter, the Bruins were back on track and playing the quality football fans had become accustomed to. Collapse, a major theme of 1989, was what the Bruins wanted to avoid. After Michigan scored, and failed on the two-point conversion, UCLA's eight-point lead was cut to two. And after Michigan made a field goal with no time remaining to win, 24–23, the collapse was complete. It was still September, but it was clear that the 1980s, a decade in which the Bruins had thrived, would not end with one of Coach Donahue's better teams. They would have to finish the season strong in order to salvage a winning record.

When conference play began, even the most skeptical of fans would have to admit that Coach Donahue's Bruins had gone on a long midseason winning streak almost every year. Though the Bruins were 1–2, had fallen to the depths of the unranked, and hardly looked like a team that could compete for a Pac 10 title, none of the previous games mattered in the conference race. It was a new season. When conference play began, UCLA began to look like the team that had so often thrilled fans throughout the decade. On September 30, the Bruins beat California Berkeley for the eighteenth consecutive year. One week later, they crushed Arizona State, 33–14. Maybe the Bruins weren't so bad after all. Did UCLA have another long winning streak in them? Could they make a run for the Pac 10 crown?

When the Bruins took on the Arizona Wildcats in Tucson on October 14, the team was supremely confident, though still flawed. After winning two consecutive games to open conference play, there was an underlying belief that the Bruins had been here before, and that they would once again find themselves in a position to win the conference when November rolled around. That hope for a turnaround, however, was short-lived: the Bruins' winning streak turned into a losing one. Arizona dismantled UCLA, 42–7. One week later, UCLA lost a heartbreaker, 18–17, to Oregon State. The trail of tears continued when Washington beat UCLA, 28–27, the following week. It was the second consecutive loss by one point and the third of the season. Though UCLA would not lose any more games by a single point, they would continue to get their hearts broken. On November 4, they lost, 17–14, to Stanford and a week later lost, 38–20, to Oregon. It was the worst season for the Bruins since 1971, Head Coach Pepper Rodgers's first year in Westwood.

With one game to go, UCLA had nothing to play for. Their season would end following their annual rivalry showdown with the USC Trojans. Their five-game losing streak was the longest for the Bruins since 1943, and they wished for no other way to end the streak than by beating the Trojans. USC entered the game ranked as the No. 8 team in America, led by quarterback Todd Marinovich, a man raised by his father with the single goal of becoming a professional quarterback. While Marinovich looked like a future Heisman candidate, his old high school rival Bret Johnson looked like he might not even be the answer for UCLA at the same position. Though UCLA struggled for most of the 1989 season, they did play well against USC. With the game tied, 10–10, in the fourth quarter, UCLA recovered a fumble on its own 12-yard line and had a chance to score and steal a victory. After Johnson hit Scott Miller for a 52-yard completion, the 17-point underdog Bruins found themselves in a position to pull off a shocking upset. Shawn Wills carried the ball to the Trojans' 35-yard line on first down. On second down, Johnson kept the ball up the middle for a 1-yard gain. On third down, Wills carried outside and was stopped for a 3-yard loss. Conservative play calling had certainly hurt the Bruins. Rather than risk putting the ball in the air, Coach Donahue and staff believed it best to run three times and go for the game-winning field goal. Kicker Alfredo Velasco lined up for a 54-yard attempt, about five yards farther than Coach Donahue was comfortable with. He had no other option at this point. The snap was good. The hold was good. The ball was up in the air. It was straight, and if it could make it far enough, it would shock the Trojans and give the Bruins a much-needed boost heading into the offseason. The ball came down and hit the crossbar, bounced high into the air, and finally came down just short. The clock was at :00. The game was over. Though UCLA's losing streak came to an end with a 10–10 tie, the result of the game and of the season was nothing less than disappointing. Overall, despite the way they ended, the 1980s were a decade of great accomplishment for UCLA football. Now they were over. It was on to the '90s.

The Downtown Athletic Club named Andre Ware from the University of Houston the 1989 Heisman Trophy Winner.

The Associated Press named the University of Miami the 1989 National Champions.

## 1990

A new decade brought new challenges for UCLA football. Coach Donahue had successfully brought UCLA out of the funk of the late '70s and into an era of prosperity throughout the 1980s. In the first nine years of the '80s, UCLA won four conference titles. They won three Rose Bowls. They won seven consecutive bowl games. They had a winning record against USC. In 1989, however, it had all come crashing down. The Bruins finished with a 3–7–1 record. They finished in ninth place in the Pac 10 Conference. They suffered through the longest losing streak in 46 years. As '89 turned to '90, the once-confident Bruins faithful were now uncertain if the failure of '89 was just a blip on the radar, sure to be forgotten, or if the disappointing season was a sign of things to come. Expectations were no longer sky-high. Excitement had been dampened. UCLA would once again play a difficult schedule. It was time to prove the naysayers wrong. Or at least attempt to.

Despite the rough season in 1989 and question marks at the quarterback position, Associated Press pollsters voted UCLA the No. 19 team in the nation to start the 1990 season. On September 8, UCLA's schedule kicked off at the Rose Bowl against another ranked opponent, the No. 23 Oklahoma Sooners of the Big 8 Conference. UCLA got on the board first on a Brad Daluiso 30-yard field goal and extended the lead to six on a Daluiso 39-yard field goal minutes later. The good start for the Bruins proved to be insufficient. They would pay for not reaching the end zone, and instead of settling for field goals, reaching the end zone proved to not be an issue for the Sooners. OU pounded the ball at the Bruins, scoring four touchdowns on the ground. UCLA's only touchdown of the day came on a 2-yard Shawn Wills run in the second quarter. After Jim Bonds found Randy Austin for the two-point conversion, UCLA had 14 points, but it wasn't near enough. Final score: Oklahoma 34, UCLA 14.

Tommy Maddox vs. Oklahoma, 1990 (Southern Campus Collection)

Conference play started early in 1990. UCLA's second game of the season came against the Stanford Cardinal in an increasingly important early-season game. UCLA could not wait to find its rhythm in nonconference games. The Bruins had issues they had to figure out. It was time to make a run. No issue was more important to the success of the team than that of the quarterback position. On defense, the Bruins struggled all season. They would go on to give up more than 30 points per game. Without a capable quarterback, the Bruins simply had no chance to have a competitive season. In Week 2, the problem was solved: the Bruins went on to beat

Stanford, and Tommy Maddox was the man under center. One week after getting their first win of the season, the Bruins faced the Michigan Wolverines at The Big House. A crowd of 104,992 fans packed into Michigan Stadium to see the No. 7 Wolverines take on Coach Donahue and the Bruins. UM was 0–1, having lost their season opener to top-ranked Notre Dame by the score of 28–24. In a season in which the Wolverines were expected to compete for a national title, falling to 0–2 was seen as entirely unacceptable in Ann Arbor. If the Bruins were unaware of how much of a monumental task it would be to pull off an upset on this day, it didn't take long before it was made clear. After Michigan received the opening kickoff in the end zone for a touchback, the potent UM offense went to work. On the first play of the game, Jon Vaughn raced through the front line of the UCLA defense and broke off a 43-yard run. Six plays later, Allen Jefferson was in the end zone for the first score of the day. It took all but two minutes and three seconds for UM to march 80 yards for a touchdown. After UCLA punted on its first possession, Michigan showed there were two sides to its offense. The quick-score, explosive offense was evident on the first drive, and a pounding, physical offense was evident on the second. Fifteen plays, 76 yards. The Bruins defense was helpless in trying to stop Vaughn, Jarrod Bunch, and Ken Sollom: 14–0 Michigan. There would be no looking back for the Wolverines. Though the game was still close at halftime, only 23–15, UCLA went on to lose, 38–15. The defensive secondary did a fine job of slowing UM All-American Desmond Howard, limiting him to just 48 yards on four catches, but Michigan's running game was the difference. Vaughn rushed for 290 yards and three touchdowns. The Bruins were 1–2 on the season.

The theme that had developed to start the season—the Bruins had lost, then won, then lost—was one that lasted throughout the entire year. When they took on Washington State University on September 29, they were due for a win, and they got just that. The Bruins beat the Cougars in Pullman by a score of 30–20, before falling to the No. 25 Arizona Wildcats, 28–21, the following week. Looking ahead at the schedule, it now appeared time for the Bruins to make the midseason charge that they had so often achieved during the Terry Donahue era. The next three games would come against opponents that UCLA had regularly beaten in recent years. Entering the game against San Diego State University, this should be the time to "get right," especially on offense. SDSU ranked last in the nation (106th) in total defense, giving up 509.3 yards per game. Coach Donahue, understanding that his offense had become predictable and largely ineffective for long stretches, presented a new wrinkle to the game plan against the Aztecs. UCLA ran the option at times. It had worked. The Bruins ran for 376 yards and passed for only 139. The 376 on the ground was the most for the Bruins since the 1986 Freedom Bowl, and the 45 points they scored were the most since defeating Long Beach State, 56–3, two years earlier. Though the UCLA defense was less than impressive, they did just enough, and the Bruins beat the Aztecs, 45–31. The following week, they took on old foe and traditional punching bag, California Berkeley. The Bruins had beaten the Bears eighteen consecutive times! They were sure to make it 19. The Bruins needed to win, and they saw Cal as nothing but an inferior opponent. But the opinions of fans, players, and coaches mattered little. California was the better team on this day. The streak was over. Cal beat UCLA by a score of 38–31. The Bruins closed out the month of October with a win over Oregon State the following week, and the win one, lose one pattern continued. The Bruins had yet to build a winning streak, nor suffer a losing streak, all season. When they took on the University of Oregon, they hoped to reverse that trend.

The final three games of the UCLA football season would come against three very strong opponents. On November 3, the 4–4 Bruins took on the No. 22 Oregon Ducks in Eugene in front of a raucous crowd. Once again, UCLA was unable to string together two consecutive winning performances, this time falling to the Ducks, 28–24. Now, with the hopes of continuing the trend for at least one week, the Bruins' task seemed all but impossible. They were floundering. Their season was going nowhere, and they were playing one of the best teams in America. When the Bruins traveled to Huskies Stadium to take on the No. 2-ranked University of Washington on November 10, few in attendance believed they could come away victorious. Don James and the Huskies were peaking. They were strong, they were physical, and they were eyeing the National Championship. Terry Donahue and the Bruins were in a rebuilding phase. The Bruins were inconsistent. They were able to play well one week, and play seemingly uninspired the following week. UCLA entered the game as 21-point underdogs. If they were to have a chance, they would need to start fast and prove to not only themselves, but to their opponent, that they were capable of playing with a top team for four quarters. Just minutes into the game, UCLA running back Brian Brown provided the spark the team needed. On third-and-1 from the Bruins' own 12-yard line, the Huskies blitzed, the UCLA line held, and Brown broke free 88 yards untouched for the first score of the game. UCLA took the lead into the second quarter, and though the Huskies would tie the game on a 1-yard run by quarterback Mark Brunell following an 18-play, 95-yard drive, the Bruins had an answer. On the last play of the second quarter, Coach Donahue shed his conservative reputation, and, instead of kicking a field goal with the ball at the 1-yard line, the Bruins went for the touchdown, and Maddox found tight end Corwin Anthony for the score just before halftime. On the point after touchdown attempt, the snap was poor and UCLA failed to convert. At the half, the score was 13–7 Bruins. Like any good team, the Huskies responded in the second half. Late in the third quarter, the Huskies took the lead for the first time of the day after a 47-yard pass from Brunell to wide receiver Orlando McKay put the offense in position to score. Running back Beno Bryant capped the drive with a 4-yard plunge across the goal line. UCLA had played well for 45 minutes but still trailed. Entering the fourth quarter, UCLA was down, 14–13. It would take the best 15 minutes of football the team could muster up to shock the Huskies. Though down, the Bruins were not deflated. They believed they could win. After a field goal and a touchdown, the Bruins led, 22–14. Another missed extra point now played a critical role. UW was down only eight points, one possession. UCLA's defense, which had struggled for most of the year, was now charged with holding the lead and completing the monumental upset. After forcing a Huskies punt, it appeared the Bruins were up to the challenge. On the punt, however, UCLA return man Scott Miller muffed the reception, and UW recovered. Four plays later, Brunell and the Huskies took advantage of the Bruins miscue. After finding wide receiver Mario Bailey for a touchdown, Brunell then ran in the two-point conversion himself to tie the score at 22 with 2:36 to play. Tommy Maddox and the UCLA offense would have a chance to win the game, but they were stopped. After UCLA punted, it suddenly appeared as though the Huskies might survive. The ball was in the hands of Brunell, the brilliant tactician who had led the Huskies all season. Brunell was not the only masterful player on the field, though. Eric Turner, the All-American safety for the Bruins, would not go down without making an impact on the game. Turner intercepted Brunell and gave the Bruins the ball at midfield. Four plays later, the ball rested at the 26-yard line. Kicker Brad Daluiso was in for the game-winning attempt. There was never any doubt. The kick was good, and the Bruins pulled off the upset! Washington's National Championship dreams were over. The Huskies would go on to win the Rose Bowl. The Bruins, at least for one week, could pride themselves on a job well done.

Like so many times before, the UCLA-USC rivalry game would define the feelings of fans and players alike during the upcoming long offseason. The Bruins had struggled all year to consistently perform at the level to which their fans had become accustomed. If they could knock off the Trojans, they would enter the offseason with two consecutive quality wins. USC was the No. 19 team in the country, and though the two rivals had engaged in battles with far more on the line many times in the previous 60 years, few games would provide the drama that the 1990 matchup provided. The game would forever after be known as "The Shootout." It would be called "The Game That Never Died." It would haunt players for decades. It would bring joy to the men who came away victorious. Tommy Maddox, the new kid on the block, was playing against the man who one year earlier had been in the same position. Maddox and Todd Marinovich would have a memorable back-and-forth battle that started not with glory, but with regret. Fifty-two seconds into the game, Maddox was intercepted by Stephen Pace, who raced 27 yards down the sideline for a score. It was the quickest touchdown in the history of the rivalry. Maddox bounced back, however, and got a touchdown by the end of the first quarter. In the second quarter, Maddox ran for a 9-yard score and added a 47-yard touchdown pass. While the Bruins offense was performing well, so was the USC offense. Entering the fourth quarter, USC led, 24–21. The fireworks were just beginning. Early in the fourth quarter, it appeared the game had finally taken a turn in favor of the Trojans. Maddox was once again intercepted, and this time Jason Oliver returned the pass 34 yards for a touchdown. USC led, 31–21, but just as he had following his first-quarter blunder, Maddox responded. He hit Scott Miller for touchdowns on two consecutive drives. The first score came from 29 yards out and the second from 38. The Bruins took the lead, but it was now Marinovich's turn. With 3:19 to play, he hit Johnnie Morton for a touchdown, and USC regained the lead, 38–35. Maddox's turn. He responded. In exactly two minutes, Maddox led the Bruins on a 75-yard drive, capped by a 1-yard score from Kevin Smith. UCLA led, 42–38. The much-maligned defense would simply need to hold USC out of the end zone to pull off an upset for the second week in a row. The 98,088 fans of both teams at the Rose Bowl cheered every play, prayed for victory, and winced every time their beloved team missed a tackle or dropped a pass. This was UCLA and USC. This was the epitome of a rivalry. This was why the game is so great. Marinovich found his top target, Gary Wellman, for two consecutive big pass plays, and USC was once again in scoring position. The ball rested at the UCLA 23-yard line with 26 seconds to play. Marinovich dropped back and eyed Johnnie Morton. The quarterback trained since before his first birthday for this very moment lofted the ball high into the back corner of the end zone. Free safety Michael Williams was in perfect position. The throw would have to be even better. One on one. Pride on the line. As the ball reached its peak and then dropped down toward the two players, the crowd could barely watch. Bruins fans were biting their nails. Trojans fans were hoping for a miracle. The ball spiraled down and Morton leaped, hands outstretched, and snagged the ball. Touchdown USC. It was a heartbreaker. Maddox finished the day with a school-record 409 yards passing and three touchdowns, but it wasn't enough. UCLA finished the season with a 5–6 record.

The Downtown Athletic Club named Ty Detmer from Brigham Young University the 1990 Heisman Trophy Winner.

The Associated Press named the University of Colorado the 1990 National Champions.

## 1991

By 1991, the United States was at war once again. The conflict actually began in August of 1990, when Iraqi leader Sadaam Hussein ordered the invasion of neighboring Kuwait. Hussein's move to invade Kuwait set off a chain response. The world condemned the Iraqi leader, but Hussein would not back down. Saudi Arabia and Egypt called for the United States to intervene. The United Nations Security Council demanded that Iraq withdraw. Still, Hussein didn't care. In January 1991, the Persian Gulf War, code named Operation Desert Storm, began. For 42 days, the United States-led coalition launched a massive air strike against Iraqi forces. Soon the war was over. The United States military was able to flex its muscles and prove that they were the undeniable greatest power on Earth. Back in Los Angeles, the UCLA Bruins were unable to flex theirs. Their defense was poor. The offense was inconsistent. The Bruins had finished the 1989 season with just three wins. The following year, they mustered up only five. By 1991, fans were starting to believe that coach Terry Donahue had run his course. True, he led the Bruins in a decade of prosperity. But Bruins fans had no plans on seeing a decade of downturn. They wanted to win. The 1991 Bruins were nothing like the teams of the previous two years. They had hit rock bottom in 1989. There was no going back.

When UCLA started the season in 1991, they were tasked with not only taking on a good team, but a great individual player. At quarterback for the Bruins was Tommy Maddox. UCLA had struggled in 1990, but they had found their on-field leader. In 1991, there were high expectations for Maddox. When searching for a player whom Maddox could hope to emulate, all he had to do was look to the other sideline on September 7. UCLA football kicked off the 1991 season against No. 25-ranked Brigham Young University, led by defending Heisman Trophy-winner Ty Detmer. All of 61,542 fans showed up to the Rose Bowl to see the man they hoped would be a star take on the man who was already a star. It was 68 degrees at kickoff, and just as the weather offered a great day for football, the UCLA football team provided great excitement for Bruins fans. The

Blue and Gold scored first on a 20-yard pass from Maddox to Sean LaChapelle in the first quarter. Ricky Davis added a 7-yard touchdown run, and UCLA led, 14–3, at the end of the quarter. In the second quarter, BYU scored its first touchdown of the season, but Maddox again hit LaChapelle to extend the Bruins' lead. The extra point attempt failed, and UCLA took a 20–10 lead into the half. In the third quarter, the Heisman Trophy winner came alive. Detmer hit Bryce Doman from 19 yards out for a score and then hit Eric Drage from two yards out for his second touchdown of the quarter. Entering the fourth, BYU led, 23–20. In previous seasons, UCLA would likely have lost a close game in the end. In 1991, it would be different. Kevin Williams scored the only points of the fourth quarter, and UCLA won, 27–23. The Bruins were 1–0.

Kevin Williams, 1991 (Southern Campus Collection)

One week after playing in the utopian conditions of Southern California that draw so many people out West, UCLA played in one of the most physically demanding games of all time. Yes, their opponent was good. The Tennessee Volunteers, ranked No. 11 in the country, presented the Bruins with a difficult challenge. Of even greater impact on the game, however—for both teams—was the weather. Coach Terry Donahue would say of the 112-degree temperatures on the AstroTurf field of Shields-Watkins Field at Neyland Stadium, "I can't remember more uncomfortable weather for a game. The heat was a bigger factor than the crowd. Of course, Tennessee had to play under the same conditions. Guys were cramping up, and we both had to do a lot more substituting than usual." Coach Donahue was right. Both teams had to play in the same conditions, and as difficult as they may have been, the Volunteers played better. A determined crowd of 97,117 fans fought the conditions to see the Vols play, and they came away pleased. Tennessee 30, UCLA 16. UCLA's nonconference slate ended with familiar opponent San Diego State University. The Bruins remained undefeated against the Aztecs in their fifteenth meeting, by winning, 37–12.

The Bruins seemed to be a better team in '91 than they had been the previous two losing seasons when conference play began, but time would surely tell. The Bruins had climbed into the top 25 rankings at No. 24 when they took on the No. 18 California Golden Bears on October 5. With six minutes to play, UCLA held a 10-point lead over the Bears, who were looking for their first win in Pasadena in 20 years. A win over a ranked California team would be a sign that the Bruins were back. It wouldn't come easy, however. Following a Cal field goal, Russell White, who was suffering from illness all day, tied the game on a rushing touchdown with four minutes to play. After Cal stopped the Bruins, White and the Bears offense went back to work. White carried the ball on six consecutive plays, and the Bruins were powerless to stop him. Cal won the game on a field goal and went on to their best season in decades. Though the Bruins were an improving team, they still were unable to win consecutive games. The win one, lose one trend had now dated back almost a full season and a half, uninterrupted.

While inconsistency had been the theme of the 1990s thus far, the theme of the '80s for UCLA was midseason-long winning streaks. Though the decade was new, the coach remained, and following the loss to Cal, the Bruins were able to do what they had done so many times in years past. They got on a roll. On October 24, the Bruins trounced the Arizona Wildcats, 54–14. One week later, they beat Oregon State, 44–7. The third win in a row came against Arizona State, and on November 2, the Bruins beat the Washington State Cougars, 44–3. Suddenly, the Bruins were 6–2 and looked like a contender.

On November 9, the No. 22-ranked Bruins lost to Stanford, 27–10. It was their worst performance of the season. Though a second conference loss didn't mathematically eliminate the Bruins from Rose Bowl contention, their dreams of returning to

Pasadena on January 1 took a major hit. One week after the loss to the Cardinal, the Bruins got back to their winning ways by defeating the University of Oregon, 16–7. With one game to play in the regular season, the Bruins were 7–3 and ranked No. 25 in the nation. They would win that final game, the one that always meant the most to the coaches, players, and especially the fans. When UCLA beat USC, 24–21, in 1991, fans expected to celebrate the victory for one year. Instead, they celebrated for eight.

The Bruins did not reach the Rose Bowl, but they did reach a bowl game. On New Year's Eve 1991, UCLA took on the University of Illinois in the John Hancock Bowl, later renamed the Sun Bowl. Tommy Maddox and quarterback Jason Verduzco, both highly touted by the press, were used as marketers for the game, but it was defense that ruled on this day. With both offenses struggling to move the ball all game long, the winner would in the end be decided by the placekickers. UCLA's Louie Perez made two of his three attempts, and the Bruins defense held Illinois to just one field goal. The Bruins held on to win, 6–3. UCLA linebacker Arnold Ale was named the game MVP. The Bruins finished the 1991 season with a 9–3 record, and Coach Donahue came away with another victory in a bowl game.

The Downtown Athletic Club named Desmond Howard from the University of Michigan the 1991 Heisman Trophy Winner.

The Associated Press named the University of Miami the 1991 National Champions.

## 1992

Football was not the only thing on the minds of sports fans in Westwood in the summer of 1992. After a strong season in 1991, the Bruins faithful were excited to once again see Coach Donahue's squad take the field in September. But first, there was the Olympics. And the Dream Team. In 1992, the United States Olympic Committee allowed professional basketball players to play on the Olympic team for the first time ever. Basketball was America's sport. We had always dominated, but in 1988 things began to change. The United States team, coached by John Thompson, didn't win. We took home the bronze medal. It was a national disgrace. Four years later, a team was assembled that not only would win the gold medal, they would send a message. In the United States of America, you do not beat us in basketball. The glory of USA Basketball was restored, and the nation was mesmerized. When the Olympics ended, summer rolled into fall, and it was time, once again, for football.

UCLA entered the season ranked No. 16 by the Associated Press, and their opener kicked off on September 12 against Cal State Fullerton. Despite the hype coming into the season, only 37,965 fans showed up at the Rose Bowl to see the Bruins take on the Titans. A majority of fans preferred to wait for the tougher opponents that lay ahead. After defeating CSUF, 37–14, the Bruins were back home to take on the BYU Cougars in Week 2. No longer was the BYU-UCLA contest hyped for the quarterback matchup. Gone were Ty Detmer and Tommy Maddox. The Cougars would start John Walsh under center and bring in Steve Clements off the bench. Both men struggled. For the Bruins, the QB situation wasn't as dire, at least for one game. Rob Walker started and completed 18 of 26 passes for 198 yards. The UCLA offense was not the story, however; rather, it was the defense. The Bruins held the Cougars scoreless until midway through the third quarter, and after jumping out to a 17–0 lead behind two Daron Washington rushing touchdowns and a Louis Perez field goal, the Bruins held on to win, 17–10. One week later, the Bruins took on an opponent that they had dominated for decades, the San Diego State Aztecs. SDSU, once seen as a team simply to fill the nonconference schedule, was now much improved. They were coached by Al Luginbill and entered the game against the Bruins 2–0 and ranked No. 21 in the country. The Bruins may have been the better team, but the Aztecs had the best player. Running back Marshall Faulk was a Heisman Trophy contender. After finishing the 1991 season with six consecutive 100+ yard rushing games, he didn't disappoint in the first two games of the '92 season. Stopping Faulk would be the primary objective of the UCLA defense. Controlling the ball and wearing down the inferior SDSU defense was the goal of the UCLA offense. They accomplished both. The game was effectively over in the first period, when UCLA scored two touchdowns in a 57-second span. Though Faulk was the man with the hype entering the game, UCLA's backs were the men with the superior production on this day. Faulk rushed for

118 yards on 23 carries, with his best run of the day a 46-yard touchdown in the fourth quarter, coming when the game was out of reach. While Faulk was a one-man wrecking crew, the Bruins running game was by committee. The team rushed for 330 yards, with 114 coming from Daron Washington, 96 from Kevin Williams, and 68 from Sherman Shaw. When the game ended, the Bruins were on top, 35–7, and when the month of September came to a close, the Bruins were 3–0. But October wouldn't be so kind.

When UCLA took on the University of Arizona on October 3, the Blue and Gold was on the verge of cracking the top 10 for the first time in the 1990s. The Bruins were ranked No. 11 and appeared to be on their way back to the glory days of the 1980s. In 1991, Coach Donahue had led the Bruins to a 9–3 record, but what made his success in the middle part of his career so impressive was the ability to field great teams year after year. The Bruins ascent into the top 10 would have to wait, however. The University of Arizona crushed UCLA, 23–3. One week later, UCLA faced a tougher opponent, the Stanford Cardinal. Coach Bill Walsh and the men from Palo Alto entered the game with a four-game winning streak and were on their way to a top 10 finish in the season-ending rankings. The Cardinal offense was led by multitalented back Glyn Milburn and quarterback Steve Strenstrom. Stanford's defense was one of the top units in the nation. Coming off a loss, UCLA was at a crossroads. The Bruins were entering the toughest stretch of their schedule. For the second consecutive week, the Bruins offense struggled mightily. After falling to the Cardinal, 19–7, they dropped out of the AP rankings. The losing streak reached three when they were defeated by Washington State on October 17, and the offense was once again dismal a week later when Arizona State University shut out the Bruins, 20–0. UCLA, which was once 3–0, lost its fifth consecutive game on Halloween in Berkeley. The midseason winning streaks that Coach Donahue-led teams were so often able to ride were a thing of the past. The 1992 Bruins were in a tailspin.

Bruins fans were finally put out of their misery on November 7, when UCLA beat Oregon State by a score of 26–14. Though the Bruins would not make a bowl game, there was still hope for a winning season. With two games to play, they would need to win both. The matchup with USC in the final week of the season had always provided drama, and the Bruins always focused on beating the men from across town. Before the Trojans, however, another task was in their way. In the tenth game of the year, the Bruins were simply trying to get back to .500 when they took on the Oregon Ducks in Eugene. Though the game was not aesthetically pleasing, the result worked in UCLA's favor. All-American cornerback Carlton Gray and the UCLA defense dominated. The offense did just enough, and the Bruins came away with a 9–6 victory.

In a year that began with promise, but would otherwise be disappointing, an astonishing thing happened. A story unfolded in front of 80,568 fans at the Rose Bowl and millions more viewing on ESPN. John Barnes was a walk-on, a fifth-string quarterback, but on November 21, 1992, he would become a legend—at least in Bruins circles. USC was coached by Larry Smith and entered the game against the Bruins with a 6–2–1 record and a No. 15 national ranking. Months before the two rivals took the field in front of a national audience, John Barnes made an impression, not to the public, but to one man. Before the season began, Barnes entered Coach Terry Donahue's office, dressed in a suit, and asked if he could walk on to the team. While Donahue was impressed at the time with Barnes's confidence and his wardrobe, he would be more impressed months later with the young man's final performance of the season. After other players' injuries and ineffectiveness pushed Barnes onto the field against the Trojans, the fairy tale unfolded. Trailing, 31–17, entering the fourth quarter, the Bruins needed magic from the man under center, and that's what they got. With 12:49 remaining in the game, Barnes hit J.J. Stokes for a 29-yard score to bring the Bruins within a touchdown. Five minutes later, Barnes hit Stokes for another big play, this one going 59 yards to set up the game-tying score with seven minutes to play. The UCLA defense, which had struggled most of the day, forced another USC punt, and UCLA would take over at their own 4-yard line. After two running plays brought the ball to the 10-yard line, it was third-and-4. Quarterbacks coach Rick Neuheisel had noticed earlier that USC had seemingly picked up on the Bruins hand signals and told Barnes to change the signs. Neuheisel told Barnes to change from a tap of the helmet to a nod in the direction of his receiver, to signal a streak route against the USC press coverage if the situation called for it. Deep in their own territory, if the Bruins were forced to punt, they could very well give USC the opportunity they needed to win and break the hearts of the Bruins. For their part, UCLA simply needed a first down to continue the drive. Barnes was not interested, however, in simply getting a first down. Instead, he wanted to score. When he walked up to the line, he saw the Trojans in press coverage and nodded to J.J. Stokes. After beating his man off the line, Stokes was behind the defense. Barnes floated the ball up, and it came down in Stokes's hands at the Bruins 40-yard line. Stokes zigzagged his way across the field and finally reached the end zone for the go-ahead score! While sports writers were gleefully preparing their story about the brilliance of Barnes and Stokes, the game was far from over. USC was not interested in a feel-good story. They wanted to win, and with just 41 seconds to play, USC scored to bring the score to 38–37. There would be no tie on this day. The Trojans were going for two! On the two-point attempt, linebacker Nkosi Littleton knocked away the pass, and the Bruins held on to win! Barnes finished the day with 385 yards passing and three touchdowns. He had 204 yards and two scores in the fourth quarter alone. J.J. Stokes finished the game with a school record 263 receiving yards. Barnes, the "walk-on" substitute, would cherish the memory his entire life. Years later, he would say of his miraculous performance, "There's times where I've had a crappy day or week and I'll put in the tape and watch it and it brings back all the good feelings." Perhaps one day, Barnes will have something else to watch. In 2005, Disney acquired the rights to the UCLA–USC miracle of '92. A script was written, but a movie never was made. The story was simply too unbelievable. Even for Disney.

The Downtown Athletic Club named Gino Torretta from the University of Miami the 1992 Heisman Trophy Winner.

The Associated Press named the University of Alabama the 1992 National Champions.

## 1993

The Bruins of 1993 were loaded. Star power was not an issue. Six men would be named All-Americans, three of whom were consensus selections. Marvin Goodwin and Jamir Miller led the defense. Craig Novitsky and Vaughn Parker anchored the offensive line, and J.J. Stokes was a star receiver. Bjorn Merten was one of the best placekickers in America. After a resurgent season in 1991, the Bruins had taken a step back in 1992. Entering the '93 campaign, many fans didn't know what to think. It was Terry Donahue's eighteenth season as the UCLA football head coach. Was he still motivated? Was he still the man to lead the Bruins in the future? Had he lost it? UCLA would answer those questions on the field. It had been eight years since the Bruins played in the Rose Bowl. There would be no plans to make it nine.

When the season began on September 4, 1993, the hopes and dreams of Bruins fans were crushed. After losing, 27–25, at home to the California Golden Bears, a team they had once dominated, it appeared a run at the Rose Bowl was unlikely. UCLA had once won eighteen consecutive games over the Bears, but following the season-opening loss, the Bears had now won four straight against the Bruins. Things would go from bad to worse two weeks later. While many believed the first game of the season was not only a winnable game, a must-win game, the Bruins' next opponent would be a much better team—the Nebraska Cornhuskers, one of the best teams in America. Following a bye week, the Bruins took on not only a great team, but a motivated one. The Cornhuskers had their eyes on the National Championship. In Week 1, they had slammed North Texas, 76–14. One week later, they beat Texas Tech, 50–27. Slowing down the powerful Huskers offense would be the toughest challenge for the Bruins, but in the first quarter, they were up to the task. Fifteen minutes in, the Bruins led, 3–0, on a 39-yard Bjorn Merten field goal. Skip Hicks extended the Bruins' lead in the second quarter on a 6-yard run to make the score 10–0. Lawrence Phillips got the Huskers on the board in the second quarter with a 5-yard touchdown. In the third quarter, Nebraska took the lead for the first time on an 11-yard touchdown pass from Tommie Frazier to Gerald Armstrong. With the Bruins trailing by four points in the fourth quarter, it was up to running back Skip Hicks and quarterback Wayne Cook to rally the Bruins to victory. The 12,000 Huskers fans who had made the trip from Lincoln to Pasadena to watch were admittedly nervous. However, the UCLA offense was only able to muster up a field goal in the fourth, and Nebraska held on to win, 14–13. Nebraska would go on to an undefeated regular season and a two-point loss in the Orange Bowl to Florida State in the de facto National Championship game.

The Bruins were 0–2, and though they had played a great team to within a point, nothing changed the fact that a loss by one is still a loss. If the Bruins were to be competitive in 1993, they would have to improve and would have to start winning. The first win of the season for the Bruins came on September 25 against the No. 17-ranked Stanford Cardinal. One week later, they beat up San Diego State, a team they had regularly handled with ease, 52–13. The final nonconference game of the year pitted the Bruins against No. 19 Brigham Young University. Though the nonconference matchup would mean nothing in terms of Pac 10 implications, it meant everything to fans, coaches, and players alike in terms of pride. The Bruins were 2–2, and with two consecutive impressive showings, believers wanted confirmation that what they were witnessing was real: that the Bruins were once again a good team. What they got was not just confirmation, they witnessed a spectacle. The Bruins got on the board twice early with field goals by Merten, but it is hard to win games three points at a time. No longer would UCLA settle for field goals. The barrage began. Cook hit Stokes for a 15-yard touchdown. Cook hit Stokes for a 19-yard touchdown. James Milliner ran for a 35-yard score. Cook hit Stokes for a 3-yard touchdown. Cook found Kevin Jordan for a 59-yard touchdown. Suddenly, it was 40–0. BYU got on the board just before half, and the score was 40–7. If there was any doubt that the Bruins were for real, it was likely gone by the time the two teams ran into the tunnel for the midgame break. In the third quarter, the scoring barrage continued. Donovan Gallatin intercepted a pass and ran it back 42 yards for a score. Ricky Davis rushed for a 1-yard touchdown. Derek Akers rushed for a 9-yard touchdown. Jeff Ruckman rushed for another 9-yard touchdown. UCLA led, 68–7, and would go on to win, 68–14. The Bruins dismantled a ranked opponent and made a statement in doing so. They had started the season with consecutive losses. They had no plans to continue that trend.

After the big nonconference win over BYU, the Bruins were determined to avoid a letdown performance against the University of Washington. UW was the No. 12 team in the country, and though the Bruins were the home team and were now ranked No. 22 themselves, they certainly had to play well to come away with a victory. Though the Bruins started slow and fell behind, 15–0, in the first quarter, they mounted a comeback one J.J. Stokes touchdown at a time. Stokes caught four touchdowns on the day and finished with 190 yards to lead the Bruins to a 39–25 win. The UCLA winning streak reached five when the Bruins traveled to Corvallis and escaped with a three-point win. On October 30, the Bruins took on their fifth ranked opponent in eight games, downing the No. 7 University of Arizona Wildcats by a score of 37–17. The Bruins were not only back on track, they had eyes on the Rose Bowl once again. The month of November began the way the month of October ended. UCLA extended its winning streak to seven by beating the Washington State Cougars, 40–27. Though the Bruins were playing great football, they would have a setback in the game against WSU. Quarterback Wayne Cook left the game with a bruised kidney, and one week later, he was on the sidelines, unable to play, when the Bruins took on Bruce Snyder and the Arizona State Sun Devils. Backup quarterback Rob Snyder struggled, throwing three interceptions and passing for just 120 yards. Skip Hicks rushed for 132 yards, but turnovers ultimately cost UCLA the game.

The attendance at the Los Angeles Memorial Coliseum totalled 93,458 fans when UCLA and USC met in the last regular season game of the year. UCLA entered the game ranked No. 16, and with Wayne Cook back, they believed they were even better. USC was ranked No. 22, and once again the winner of the game between the two rivals would head to the Rose Bowl on January 1. At halftime, the Bruins led, 17–0. They were 30 minutes away from their third consecutive victory over the Trojans, and the first trip to the Rose Bowl in eight years. Fans of this rivalry know better, however, than to think that anything is a given. Drama is an annual occurrence, and USC provided the drama when they marched back into the game in the second half. USC scored 14 unanswered points before the Bruins could respond. Cook found Stokes for a touchdown, but USC once again responded with a touchdown of its own, and the Bruins added a field goal. It was 27–21 Bruins with three minutes to play. USC quarterback Rob

Johnson completed two long passes, and suddenly the ball was at the UCLA 2-yard line. While almost all in attendance believed the Trojans would score, one man cared not about the expectations of thousands. Instead, he made his own reality. Marvin Goodwin intercepted Rob Johnson in the end zone, and the Bruins held on to win, 27–21! UCLA won the Pac 10 Conference and were headed to the Rose Bowl!

When January 1 came around, Bruins fans were in a somewhat familiar place. They were not only in their home field, they were in a stadium where many longtime fans had been over and over on New Year's Day throughout the years. For the Wisconsin Badgers, it was not so. The Badgers had never won a Rose Bowl before, and after they won the Big 10 Conference, fans traveled in droves from Madison to Pasadena to see their beloved team play. To fans in attendance, it appeared that 70 percent of the stadium was filled with red. UW entered the game as the No. 9 team in the country, and the Bruins came in as No. 14. Coach Barry Alvarez said before the game, "We have one goal left—to win." The game simply meant everything to Wisconsin fans. They were determined to turn the Rose Bowl into "Camp Randall West." Coach Alvarez used everything he heard from radio and television, everything he read from newspapers and magazines, to motivate his team. In the end, it worked. Wisconsin came away with a 21–16 victory. Brent Moss rushed for 158 yards, and the Badgers defense forced five turnovers. It had been a great season for the Bruins, but it ended in disappointment. The Bruins were the reigning Pac 10 Champions entering the 1994 season, and all questions about the ability of coach Donahue to rally his men had dissipated. The Bruins were back.

The Downtown Athletic Club named Charlie Ward from Florida State University the 1993 Heisman Trophy Winner.

The Associated Press named Florida State University the 1993 National Champions.

## 1994

Coming into the 1994 season, expectations were again sky-high. The Bruins were the defending Pac 10 champions and started the season as the No. 14 team in the country. Quarterback Wayne Cook returned, and so did All-American J.J. Stokes. Offensive tackle Jonathan Ogden was now a sophomore and would become one of the most dominant offensive tackles in college football. Kevin Jordan was an All-American in '94, and the defense, though young, was extremely talented. While football always filled the minds of many year-round, there was another story in Los Angeles that grabbed even more headlines. On June 17, 1994, former USC star running back O.J. Simpson was charged with murder. The case would play out over the following 16 months with the United States citizenry hanging onto every detail. O.J. would be found not guilty in what many consider one of the worst jury decisions in history. The case was closed.

The 1994 UCLA football season began on September 3 against the University of Tennessee. The Bruins entered the season as the No. 14 team in the first Associated Press rankings, and the Volunteers came in at No. 13. The game was broadcast nationally on ABC-TV, and while the two teams played a close game, ultimately finishing with the Bruins on top, 25–23, the game is most known for the appearance of a UT freshman quarterback by the name of Peyton Manning. Senior quarterback Jerry Colquitt had gone down early with an injury, and in the second quarter Manning saw his first glimpse of college football. Coach Phillip Fulmer played four quarterbacks that day, and Manning only saw action on one series, handing the ball off three times before a Volunteer punt. Manning's first college football game may not have contained the heroism that many of his later games would, but it was the first time the nation was exposed to the man who would later become a football icon. Manning said of his first game, "I'm glad the coaches had confidence in me. I know I will get my chance." Manning did get his chance, and he never looked back. After a long NFL career, breaking nearly every passing record in the books, Manning retired in 2016 after winning his second Super Bowl. It may have only been three handoffs, but the path to greatness passed through Pasadena.

The Bruins would win their second game of the season, as well, over Southern Methodist University. The Bruins were 2–0, but the next team on the schedule provided an entirely different challenge. The previous year, UCLA had played the Nebraska Cornhuskers close, but the 1994 Nebraska team was special. After losing in the National Championship game nine months earlier, Tom Osborne and his talented squad would not only come back better, they would cement their legacy as one of the all-time greatest teams. The Bruins were simply standing in the way. Nebraska went on to beat UCLA, 49–21, and would go on to win the National Championship.

When conference play began, the Bruins were 2–1 and for the second consecutive year had a front-loaded schedule. The first two conference games came against the ranked schools from the state of Washington. Though the Bruins were able to beat SMU in Week 2, and hadn't figured to beat Nebraska in Week 3, they finally felt the impact of having lost one of their best players to injury: J.J. Stokes, the consensus All-American, was hurt in Week 1. He would play against Washington State for the first time since bruising his quad in the season opener but would leave early after catching just one pass and reaggravating the injury. Without one of the best players in UCLA history, the offense struggled. The Bruins were shut out and lost, 21–0. One week later, the University of Washington, ranked No. 12 in the nation, avenged the loss to the Bruins from one year earlier. The losing streak reached four when California beat UCLA, 26–7, for the Bears' fifth win in a row over the Bruins. UCLA reached a new, unexpected low when the losing streak went from four to five, and then five to six. Oregon State beat UCLA, 23–14, and the University of Arizona defeated the Bruins, 34–24.

With three games to play, UCLA was already assured a losing season for the first time since 1990, and only the fifth time in the last quarter century. The remaining games were in a sense meaningless, but, successful or not, the Bruins played for pride.

1994 Bruins Marching Band (Southern Campus Collection)

On October 29, the losing streak ended. UCLA beat Stanford by a single point, 31–30. One week later, the Bruins had a winning streak. They played their best game of the year and beat Arizona State, 59–23. The only game left was against the hated USC Trojans. While the match itself generated the usual drama and hatred, the rivalry took a new turn prior to the game. Both student bodies participated in a series of pranks, ranging from the low-creativity stunts of splashing paint on school statues, to the spreading of player phone numbers, to the attempted poisoning of food. Entering the game, the Trojans still had hopes for a Rose Bowl berth. With a win over the Bruins and an Oregon loss to Oregon State, USC could make the big game once again. UCLA cared little about the Trojans' hopes. Sharmon Shah and Wayne Cook would lead the Bruins offense and Donnie Edwards would lead the Bruins defense to victory in front of 91,815 fans at the Rose Bowl. It was the Bruins' third consecutive win to end the season, and their fourth consecutive victory over the USC Trojans.

The Downtown Athletic Club named Rashaan Salaam from the University of Colorado the 1994 Heisman Trophy Winner.

The Associated Press named the University of Nebraska the 1994 National Champions.

## 1995

1995 was Terry Donahue's twentieth season as the UCLA football head coach. He was only fifty-one years of age but still had thoughts of a postcoaching career. This would be his last season with the Bruins. Over two decades, Donahue had won more games than any other coach in Pac 10 history. While there were plenty of doubters in the late '70s, there were far more believers throughout the 1980s. As coach Donahue led the Bruins into the 1990s, questions had surfaced once again. Fans wondered aloud if he was the man for the job. When coach Donahue took over from Dick Vermeil following the stunning upset of Ohio State in the 1976 Rose Bowl, no one yet knew if Donahue was ready to be a head coach. In the 1990s, it appeared to some that Donahue had lost his touch. Though he had led the Bruins to the 1993 Pac 10 championship and a berth in the 1994 Rose Bowl, Angelinos clamored for more. Coach Donahue would lead the Bruins for one final season, and with his departure came the end of an era. UCLA had been a top 15 football program for the better part of half a century. As the 20th century neared an end, and new leadership was sure to take the Bruins into the 21st, no one could predict what would happen. But in hindsight, one thing is sure: Coach Donahue has been missed.

The 1995 season kicked off for the Bruins against a college football powerhouse. UCLA entered the season ranked No. 15 in the Associated Press poll. Their first game came against the No. 12 Miami Hurricanes. Though the Bruins had lost significant talent to graduation from the year before, the 1995 Bruins had two players who would make names for themselves. Karim Abdul-Jabbar, formerly known as Sharmon Shah, was the starting running back who would rush for a school single-season record 1,571 yards. At quarterback, a freshman by the name of Cade McNown took over, and when his time in a Bruins uniform came to a close, he would be remembered as one of the greatest players in school history. Before McNown became a household name, he was a backup quarterback. In the season opener against the Hurricanes, Ryan Fien got the nod. Though Fien would exit in the second quarter with an injury, the story was not the man under center, but rather the offensive line and the man carrying the rock. The UCLA offensive line was brilliant. From left to right saw the names Jonathan Ogden, James Christensen, Mike Flanagan, Matt Soensen, and Chad Overhauser. Ray Lewis and the Miami defense were simply dominated. Abdul-Jabbar rushed 29 times for 180 yards and two touchdowns. The quarterbacks did just enough, and UCLA started the season with an impressive 31–8 victory. One week later, the Bruins were victorious again. McNown and Fien both played, but again the story was the defense and the running game. The Bruins defense held BYU quarterback Steve Sarkisian and the Cougars offense to just six points, while Abdul-Jabbar rushed for 147 yards. UCLA was 2–0 and ready for conference play.

On September 16, the impressive Bruins were tasked with proving that they could play as well against conference opponents as they had against nonconference foes. The first conference matchup pitted the No. 12-ranked Bruins against the No. 20 Oregon Ducks. Bruins fans, still basking in the glory of the National Championship won by their men's basketball program six months earlier, dreamed of seeing the football program make a similar dash to greatness. Instead, it came down to a dash for the end zone. Down, 38–31, with under a minute to play, the Bruins broke the huddle. Seeing that the Ducks had substituted out their middle linebacker for an extra defensive back, McNown ran a quarterback sneak on first down from the 3-yard line. He gained only a yard. On second down, he fired for Eric Scott in the end zone. Incomplete. On third down, McNown looked for Abdul-Jabbar in the flat. Denied. It was fourth-and-goal from the 2-yard line with the game on the line. When the Bruins broke the huddle, Ducks players already knew what the Bruins were trying to do. Oregon defensive end Troy Bailey would say after the game that the defense knew the Bruins were going to run. But knowing what was coming and stopping it are two entirely different things. Abdul-Jabbar was a great back, and he was running behind a great offensive line. There were four seconds on the clock when McNown took the snap and handed off to Abdul-Jabbar. He avoided a tackler almost immediately, bounced to the outside, and sprinted for the pylon at the front left corner of the end zone. Cornerback Lamont Woods hit him first, but Abdul-Jabbar stayed up, fighting to reach the paint. Safety Jaiya Figueras hit him next, and the two together brought him down just inches short of the goal line. The Bruins fell, 38–31. Troy Bailey would say after the game about the AP pollsters, "The voters are idiots." On this day, at least, Bailey and the Ducks proved they were the better team.

One week after the heartbreaking loss to the Ducks, Coach Donahue and the Bruins lost again, this time to the Washington State Cougars. Though the Bruins beat Fresno State by a score of 45–21 to close out the month of September, the team was 0–2 in conference and would have to likely win out in order to make the Rose Bowl once again. The Bruins went on a winning streak, but would it be enough? Time would tell. Two weeks after beating the FSU Bulldogs, the Bruins defeated the University of Arizona, 17–10. One week later, they traveled to Palo Alto and beat a ranked Stanford team by a score of 42–28. The Bruins improved to 6–2 the next week by downing California, 33–16. The Bruins had won four games in a row, including three in conference play, and with the victory over the Bears, Coach Donahue tied the record for most conference wins in Pac 10 history. Maybe the Bruins had a run in them after all. With three games to play, the Bruins simply needed to keep winning.

With the chance to take sole possession of the all-time wins leaderboard and be in a position to reach another Rose Bowl, Coach Donahue and the Bruins fell to Arizona State on November 4. UCLA led, 27–10 at halftime, but in the second half, Jake Plummer and the ASU offense dominated. The Bruins offense fell apart. On the first four possessions of the half, UCLA fumbled three times and punted. Plummer would finish with 312 yards passing and complete the comeback. The third loss of conference play eliminated the Bruins from Pac 10 title contention. One week later, the Bruins lost their fourth conference game to the University of Washington. Entering the final game of the season, UCLA was 6–5, and with an expanded bowl game schedule, the Bruins would need to win one final contest to reach a bowl game. USC came in as the No. 11 team in the country and had already clinched a berth in the Rose Bowl. Despite the rankings and the opinions of the pundits, UCLA stormed out of the gate to take a 21–0 lead. You could call the Trojans the better team, but the Bruins were there to prove you wrong. USC made the game close, but with under a minute to play, Cade McNown clinched a UCLA victory by scrambling for 21 yards on third-and-13. The Bruins held on to win, 24–20. The game had a great deal of significance for Coach Donahue. With the victory, he took over sole possession of the Pac 10 record for career wins and moved his record against the Trojans to 10–9–1. The Bruins' fifth consecutive win over the Trojans marked a record in the rivalry. Donahue would say of the streak, "That was a significant accomplishment. I was around that rivalry for a long time and I can tell you it really was rewarding to win five straight over USC." Donahue would later say that his first victory over USC, and now his last, were the two that he enjoyed most. "There were some games in between that might have been more important in terms of Rose Bowls or something like that, but those were certainly the two that stand out as most rewarding." The Bruins were unable to send Coach Donahue into his postcoaching life with a win. In the Aloha Bowl, the Bruins lost to the Kansas Jayhawks, 51–30. In Coach Donahue's 20 years as the head coach of the UCLA Bruins, his teams finished with a 151–74–8 record. UCLA had a monumental task in moving on to the next phase of their football story. The Terry Donahue era was officially over. Bob Toledo was handed the torch.

The Downtown Athletic Club named Eddie George from Ohio State University the 1995 Heisman Trophy Winner.

The Associated Press named the University of Nebraska the 1995 National Champions.

Terry Donahue after his final game in 1995 (Southern Campus Collection)

## Jonathan Ogden

What Jerry Robinson and Kenny Easley were to defense, what Troy Aikman and Cade McNown were to the quarterback position, Jonathan Ogden was to the offensive line. He was mammoth. He was quick. He was extremely athletic. He is also the greatest of all time. Though Ray Lewis, Ed Reed, and the Baltimore Ravens defense have received most of the acclaim for the success of the Ravens at the turn of the century, no single player was better than Jonathan Ogden. Offensive linemen rarely get the same attention as quarterbacks, or running backs, or star linebackers. But Ogden was simply too great to ignore. When he retired following the 2007 NFL season, football fans lost a legend. He was young. He could still play. He was still the best.

Jonathan Ogden grew up in Washington D.C. By the time he reached high school, he was a star not only on the football field, but in another sport: track and field. He was kind. He was quiet. He was humble. He avoided trouble and strived to be the best. On the football field, his massive frame and unbelievable athletic ability made him one of the most coveted recruits in the nation. Ogden was raised by his father, a single parent raising two boys. Shirrel Ogden would call his role as a father "his greatest accomplishment in life." One reason Shirrel could be so proud was the way his boys turned out. Jonathan was not just a star athlete, but a fine man. Shirrel would say he didn't want his son to turn out like Michael Irvin or Dennis Rodman. He admired Grant Hill. "Not from an endorsement point of view, but because of what he can do for kids. Contrary to what Charles Barkley has said, kids do emulate athletes, and you, the athlete, are a role model. And sports need better role models." Jonathan would turn out to be an excellent role model, and the standard bearer for what it means to be a left tackle. While football would ultimately lead Ogden to fame and fortune, he was even better in track and field. His senior season, he threw a nation's-best 63.09 feet in the shotput and 186.12 feet in the discus. Following high school, Ogden made the trip west to UCLA, where he soon became a household name. With the support of his father, he set out on an adventure 3,000 miles away from home that would lead him to the top of his profession.

When Jonathan Ogden came west in 1992, he came with a stipulation. He chose UCLA over the University of Florida and other suitors because the Bruins let him participate in track and field. It was a great tradition at UCLA to play multiple sports, and Ogden carried on the mantle like no one else could. He was a four-year starter for the Bruins in football. In his sophomore season, the Bruins went 8–3, won the Pac 10 Conference, and went to the Rose Bowl. The following two years, the behemoth lineman turned from good to great. He would allow only two sacks in his final two years. As a senior, he was a consensus All-American. He won the Outland Trophy, Morris Trophy, Jim Parker Award, and was named the UPI Offensive Lineman of the Year. In track and field, he was just as dominant. In 1996, he won the National Championship in the shotput. Many in his situation would gloat and proclaim their greatness. Not Ogden; success would not change the man behind the face mask. In 1996, two of the marquee names heading into the NFL draft were Ogden and USC receiver Keyshawn Johnson. For Johnson, who would be drafted number one overall, his style was much different. He was loud, brash, and arrogant. Ogden never changed. He was a once-in-a-generation talent, but his coaches at UCLA remember him more for the kind of man he was. Coach Donahue would say, "Never set foot in my office in four years because he was in trouble or needed something special." His track coach, Art Venegas, would one day ask Ogden what he wished for in life. Ogden would say, "I just don't have that many things I want. I'm not a things person. I'm not dreaming of having fourteen different cars and four mansions here, there, and everywhere." He simply focused on the task at hand. His job was to get an education and be the best athlete he could be. He would graduate from UCLA with a history degree, and at the NFL combine he would finish with one of the highest Wonderlic scores. There was nothing more Jonathan Ogden could do for the Bruins. He was on to the next phase of his life. It was time to add to his legend.

Ogden didn't want cars or houses in every vacation spot in the world. He didn't want publicity or any extra attention. He simply wanted to play football, and the Baltimore Ravens wanted him to play for them. Ogden was drafted as the fourth overall pick in the 1996 draft, the first pick in the franchise's history. Ogden was known for his size, but it was his unbelievable athleticism that made him the best offensive lineman in NFL history. He had tremendous footwork. He was a master tactician. He was a student of the game, and he was competitive. He was the entire package. For one season, Ogden did not even play his natural position, and yet he dominated. As a rookie, he started the entire season at left guard. He was named to the All-Rookie team and to the All-Pro team. When he moved to left tackle in his second season, he got even better.

In 1997, Ogden was selected to his first Pro Bowl and second All-Pro team. In '98 and '99, he was All-Pro Second Team. For the entirety of Ogden's career, without a single major injury or off year, he was brilliant. He never failed to make the NFL All-Pro team. In 2002, he was named NFL Offensive Lineman of the Year. In 2003, he helped teammate Jamal Lewis rush for over 2,000 yards. In 2007, his final year, he was named to his eleventh consecutive Pro Bowl. His greatest feat, however, came in 2000. In just the fifth season in the franchise's history, the Ravens won the Super Bowl. When Jonathan Ogden retired following the 2007 season, many quietly wondered why. He was still the best offensive lineman in the NFL. For Ogden, the reason was simple. He had nothing left to accomplish. He had lived his dream. He played at the highest level, and he dominated.

Jonathan Ogden was inducted into the National Football League Hall of Fame in 2013. He was the youngest member of the Hall of Fame. For Ogden, his enshrinement was just one of many honors bestowed upon him. On February 3, 2013, he was named an honorary captain for the Ravens in Super Bowl XLVII. After the Ravens beat the San Francisco 49ers, Ogden was given a championship ring, just like the rest of the team. He was said to be the foundation upon which that the franchise was built, and though he had retired five years earlier, winning another Super Bowl was not possible without him. In addition to the Pro Football Hall of Fame, the accolades bestowed upon Ogden are too numerous to count. He was named to the NFL All-Decade team of the 2000s. He is part of the Ravens Ring of Honor. He is a member of the UCLA Athletics Hall of Fame and a member of the College Football Hall of Fame. His number 79 is retired by the Bruins, never to be worn again. The legacy of Jonathan Ogden is not just that of a man who was able to stop the best pass rushers dead in their tracks. It is that of a man who, despite unbelievable success, has remained true to himself. A man raised by a single father, taught to be humble and gracious, who never steered away from the lessons of his father. Prior to the NFL draft in 1996, Ogden would say, "Now I can't think of a better way of making a living. I want to do something to help people, and I know that sounds bad—very corny—but I always felt I was here and as good as I am because I'm going to be in the public's eye with a chance to do something positive for people or the community. I'm not sure what, but something." After a legendary career, one can only say it was a job well done.

# CHAPTER 13
# Bob Toledo (1996–2002)

When Bob Toledo was announced as the UCLA football head coach beginning with the 1996 season, there was immense pressure. It had been 20 years since UCLA had hired a new head coach. The man who preceded Toledo became the Pacific 10 Conference's all-time leader in wins. Terry Donahue had won a Rose Bowl as a player. He had taken the Bruins to four Rose Bowls as a coach, winning three of them. He had a winning record against USC and retired with a five-game winning streak against the Trojans. He would go down as one of the greatest coaches in Pac 10 and UCLA history. He is a member of the UCLA Athletics Hall of Fame and the Rose Bowl Hall of Fame. Bob Toledo was being tasked with the job of taking the team back to Donahue's prime years: the 1980s. Sure, beating USC every year will always thrill fans, but when Coach Toledo took over the Bruins program, it had been more than 40 years since UCLA's lone National Championship. If Toledo was to be the man to take the Bruins to the top, he would have to work hard for it, something he had done all his life.

Bob Toledo is a college football lifer. That is how people may describe him now, but before there was college football, there was childhood. There was his upbringing. There was a career as a player that would help him transition into the profession of coaching. Bob Toledo was born on March 4, 1946, in San Jose, California. Like so many of the men who become successful coaches later in life, as a child Bob was "different." He never rooted for a team. He loved sports, but it wasn't the individual players or the roar of a home crowd that attracted him, but rather the strategy, the on-the-spot decision making that would change the course of a game that hooked him. Toledo grew up poor. His mother was a cannery worker. His father was a truck driver who would later become a school custodian. Though money can enhance one's life, lack of money could not deter young Toledo from chasing his dreams. He played board games and talked strategy with youth football coaches. He analyzed plays and players and tried to understand tendencies. Bob was a boy who liked to always be in control, to always be informed, to make decisions with a firm understanding of the potential effects of any decision. He was a natural coach.

After starting at quarterback for three years at Lincoln High School in San Jose from 1961 to 1963 and winning 27 out of 30 games, Toledo was off to college. Though he stood only 5'9" with a chubby build, Toledo was a brilliant passer. His understanding of offensive schemes and his ability to break down a defense were unnatural at his age. In 1964, Toledo enrolled at local San Jose State University. Much like his coaching career, his playing days were filled with many stops. Bob spent only one year at SJSU before transferring to San Jose City College and leading his team to a successful season while earning Junior College All-America honors. A year later, Bob was on the move once again. He would finish his career at San Francisco State University. In two seasons as the starting quarterback, he led the Gators to a 16–5 record. His senior season, he finished with a bang, named the 1967 Northern California Player of the Year for Division II. He was named a second-team All-American after throwing for more than 3,500 yards and 45 touchdowns. He set eight Division II NCAA records in 1967 and led his team to a Far Western Conference title. Though Bob would not have much of an NFL career—he was cut by the San Francisco 49ers as a rookie—his legacy was much more than that of a coach. His playing career should not be forgotten. In 1982, he was inducted into the San Francisco State University Athletics Hall of Fame, and in 1996 he was inducted into the San Francisco State Gridiron Hall of Fame.

Following the end of his playing career, Bob Toledo immediately went into coaching. In 1969, at the age of 23, Toledo took his first coaching position as the head coach of Archbishop Riordan High School's freshman team in San Francisco. One year later, he was the head coach of the varsity team. In three years coaching the varsity squad, Coach Toledo's teams accumulated a 26–5–1 record and would win two Catholic Athletic League titles. It was clear Toledo had a future in coaching, and in 1970 he sought a bigger stage. Following his four years at Archbishop Riordan High School, Toledo took his first college job. In 1973, he became the offensive coordinator at the University of California Riverside. One year later, he was named the UCR head coach. Coach Toledo had shot through the coaching ranks. After just seven years of coaching, he was now a head coach, and at just 28 years old. In two years as the head coach of UCR, Toledo's teams finished with a 15–6 overall record and two conference championships. Despite the success, the UCR athletic program was not doing well financially, and in 1975, the football team folded.

Though he was temporarily out of work following UCR dropping its football program, Coach Toledo was a hot commodity and would not be free for long. In 1976, John Robinson reached out to Toledo and offered him the defensive backs coach position at USC. For three seasons, Coach Toledo served well on Robinson's staff, and though he was an offensive coach, he credits his time coaching defense with helping him further understand offense. He coached Ronnie Lott and Dennis Thurman, among others. Though the obvious next progression in the career of a football coach would not be to step back to lower competition, Toledo did so in 1979 by taking the head coaching position at University of the Pacific. For the first time in Coach Toledo's career, he failed. In four seasons at Pacific, he compiled a 14–30 record.

Though Toledo was unable to turn the University of the Pacific program into a consistent winner, he received another shot at big-time college football in 1983 and would never look back. From 1983 to 1988, Coach Toledo was the offensive coordinator at the University of Oregon and coached two of the most prolific quarterbacks in the Pac 10 Conference, Chris Miller and Bill Musgrave. In 1989, Toledo was on the move again. From 1989 to 1993, he was the offensive coordinator at Texas A&M University. In Coach Toledo's five years in College Station, the Aggies won three Southwest Conference titles and five straight bowl games, including three consecutive Cotton Bowls, and fielded some of the best offenses in school history. In 1990, the Aggies averaged a school record 471.1 yards per game, and against the University of Louisiana at Lafayette set a school record with 774 yards.

When Bob Toledo came to Westwood in 1994, few could have guessed that this would be the place he would stay the longest. Toledo coached at 10 schools in his career but is mostly known today for his time with the Blue and Gold. In 1994, Toledo became the offensive coordinator at UCLA under Head Coach Terry Donahue. In his two years as the OC, the Bruins finished with just a 12–11 record but beat USC both years. When Coach Donahue retired following the 1995 season, few thought the job would go to Toledo. One of the names mentioned at the top of the Bruins' search was a young coach by the name of Rick Neuheisel. His time would come more than a decade later. In Toledo's time as head coach of the UCLA Bruins, fans would see some of the best football in school history. They would also feel a level of frustration many had never felt before. Coach Toledo would finish with only four winning seasons in seven years. He was the man in charge of the Bruins program when USC made a resurgence. He would lead UCLA into a new millennium, a new century, a new decade. Coach Toledo would coach two of the finest football teams in UCLA history and would bring the Bruins closer to a National Championship than at any other time since 1954. Under Coach Toledo, the Bruins won two Pac 10 titles and a school record 20 consecutive games. In 1998, the Bruins set school marks for total offense, passing yards, and passing touchdowns, and Coach Toledo was named Pac 10 Coach of the Year. Ultimately, the success of the Bruins under Coach Toledo was short-lived. Though the team would have moments of mastery, and frustrated fans would be revitalized, his tenure was nothing other than a flash of brilliance surrounded by mediocrity. On December 9, 2002, Bob Toledo was fired.

Following his seven-year run with the UCLA Bruins, Bob Toledo, a man who had bounced around for 33 years, was on to his next stop. That stop, however, was not at a football school, but back home. Bob Toledo retired, at least temporarily. After three years away from coaching, Toledo retuned to the sideline, this time at the University of New Mexico. For one year, Toledo served as the offensive coordinator for the Lobos. Under his direction, running back Rodney Ferguson rushed for over 1,300 yards and was named First-Team All-Mountain West. Coach Toledo's stay in New Mexico would be brief, however. In 2007, he was once again given the opportunity be a head coach, this time at Tulane University. Though the Green Wave finished with a 4–8 record in Coach Toledo's first season, the offense gained national attention when senior running back Matt Forte finished with 2,127 yards, a number that was the seventh best in NCAA history at the time. Toledo was never able to relive the brilliance of his two best seasons at UCLA. He finished his career at Tulane with a 15–40 record and resigned midway through the 2011 season. The final coaching stop for a man who had dedicated his life to the business was at San Diego State, where in 2013–2014, he served as the offensive coordinator. Following the 2014 season, Bob Toledo announced his retirement from coaching. His final career record was 93–108. Though Toledo and his wife, Elaine, had three daughters, he claimed to have 105 boys every year. He was a coach. He was a father. He was a Bruin, and for a brief time it seemed he would bring the Bruins back to levels unseen by many fans. For those not old enough to see or remember the teams of the 1950s under Coach Sanders, or those of the late '60s under Tommy Prothro, or the 1975 team under Dick Vermeil, or the early 1980s teams led by Terry Donahue, they cling to the memories of the 1997 and 1998 teams under Coach Toledo. There is one word alone that can describe the feelings many fans have for Coach Toledo: *Almost*.

## 1996

For the UCLA Bruins, the 1996 football season was one of new beginnings. The program was under new leadership. After 20 years, Terry Donahue retired. Bob Toledo was the new coach. Though the UCLA offense returned Cade McNown and Skip Hicks, the product on the field was different under a new coach. McNown and Hicks had breakout seasons, as Coach Toledo brought trickery to the table. The element of surprise was used as a weapon. Reverses, double passes, fake kicks—they were all on the menu. For the United States, 1996 was not a time of change, but rather a continuation of the present. President Bill Clinton easily defeated Bob Dole of Kansas in

Bob Toledo, 1996

both the popular and electoral votes and would serve for four more years. In professional sports, the New York Yankees won the World Series, the first for the storied franchise in 18 years and the first with new shortstop Derek Jeter. In the NBA, Michael Jordan was back from his brief stint playing professional baseball, and the Chicago Bulls won the 1996 NBA Finals. As for Coach Toledo at UCLA, he was tasked not with duplicating the success of baseball's Joe Torre or basketball's Phil Jackson, but rather with proving the skeptics wrong and showing fans that he was the man for this pigskin job. His shot at a championship would come later.

If coach Toledo was to get off to a good start in his UCLA head coaching career, it would not be easy. Per tradition, the Bruins played an extremely difficult nonconference schedule. The season opener pitted the Bruins against the No. 2-ranked Tennessee Volunteers in Knoxville. Neyland Stadium was packed with 106,297 fans who left with the win they so coveted. Quarterback Peyton Manning was a junior, a Heisman Trophy candidate. The Vols were eyeing a National Championship. For coach Toledo in his first game, this was simply too much. UT 35, UCLA 20. The first win of the Bob Toledo era would come in Week 2, when the Bruins took on the University of Louisiana Monroe at the Rose Bowl. The Bruins crushed the Warhawks, 44–0. With a bye week before their next big matchup, the Bruins believed they were primed to play more like they had in Week 2 than in Week 1. When UCLA walked into the Big House in Ann Arbor, not only were the Michigan Wolverines waiting, but 111,238 fans, the largest crowd UCLA had ever played in front of, greeted them, as well. UM entered the game ranked No. 7 in the country, and on this day they destroyed the Bruins. For the UCLA defense, nothing worked. Defensive coordinator Rocky Long commented later, "Maybe we have piled up too much defense too fast, so much defense that we can't play it all. I've been saying all along that there are still things we don't know." From the very beginning, UCLA had no answers for Michigan running back Chris Howard, who found the end zone four times. Michigan scored 38 points on the day. Though the defense would prove to be a problem for UCLA all year, the offense was one of the best in the nation—but not against the mighty Wolverines. UCLA's offense was stifled, to the point of surprising UM head coach Lloyd Carr. He would later say, "I never dreamed that we would do the things we did to UCLA. I thought with their speed and movement that they would score some points, and I was very pleased with the way we played, with our effort." UCLA, in fact, didn't score any points besides an early field goal and a touchdown on an interception return by linebacker Phillip Ward off third-string quarterback Tom Brady in the fourth quarter. The final score read Michigan 38, UCLA 9. It was a setback for the Bruins. The losses to the Volunteers and Wolverines in nonconference play proved that the team was not yet ready to play with the big boys of college football. Nevertheless, the season moved on. It was time for conference play.

The Bruins would open league competition with a win in '96 by beating Mike Bellotti and the Oregon Ducks, 41–22. One week later, the Bruins faced their third opponent in the top seven in the Associated Press Poll, the Arizona State Sun Devils. ASU, coached by Bruce Synder, was ranked No. 4 in the country and led by superstar quarterback Jake Plummer when they went west to take on the Bruins. The Bruins played the Sun Devils close, but once again, the defense let them down. The final score was 42–34. ASU would go on to finish the regular season undefeated and head to the Rose Bowl for a chance at a National Championship. They would lose to Ohio State and fall just short of claiming the biggest prize. After the loss to Arizona State, UCLA was 2–3. The team had yet to gain traction. All three of their losses had come to elite teams in the nation, a place the Bruins wished to be but were simply not yet there. One week after losing to the Sun Devils, the Bruins took on another ranked team, the No. 25 Washington Huskies, and once again the Bruins failed to come away with a win. Final score: UW 41, UCLA 21.

UCLA snapped out of its two-game losing streak against California Berkeley on October 26 with a 38–29 victory. It was their second win in a row over the Bears. Before UCLA won in '95, California had won the previous five meetings, and Coach Toledo hoped to turn back the clock in the battle of UC schools. Prior to that Bears' five-game streak, the Bruins had won 18 in a row against their older brother from the north. The frustrating season of '96 continued as the calendar turned from October to November. After defeating California, the Bruins lost a heartbreaker to Stanford. They then crushed Washington State but lost handily to the University of Arizona. The Bruins were 4–6 when they entered the final game of the regular season against the USC Trojans. Coach Toledo's first season had not gone the way he and fans alike had hoped. The Bruins would not make a bowl game, but at least the offseason would be a lot sweeter with a victory over the Trojans.

USC entered the final game of the season in a similar way as the Bruins. Both teams had disappointing seasons, and both fan bases were frustrated. The Trojans (5–5) struggled to pass the ball and leaned on the running trio of LaVale Woods, Delon Washington, and Rodney Sermons, who accounted for over 1,500 yards combined over the season. On the Bruins' side of the ball, the offense was not the issue. McNown was having an excellent year, Skip Hicks rushed for over 1,000 yards, and the receiving corps was deep. The Bruins' problem was the defense, which had given up almost 29 points per game. Many times over the years, the Bruins and Trojans have met with more on the line, but few, if any, games have had such dramatic endings. The 1996 battle was a classic. UCLA trailed, 17–0, after the first quarter. It appeared the frustrating season would come to an end in a nightmare scenario. Nothing was worse than losing to USC, and on top of that nothing was worse than losing in embarrassing fashion. The Bruins made no progress in the second quarter in trying to put a dent in the Trojans lead. When the teams ran for the Rose Bowl tunnels at halftime, the score was 24–7. The Bruins tried to peck away at the lead in the second half, but the Trojans kept responding, and late in the game, UCLA still trailed by two touchdowns. The score was 38–24 with 2:49 to play when Keith Brown scored from a yard out to cut the lead to seven, and one minute and 19 seconds later, the Bruins got the break they needed when USC fumbled and the Bruins took over at their own 38. Cade McNown was the man who spearheaded the comeback, but Skip Hicks was the man trusted to finish the job. After McNown and the offense worked the ball down to the USC 11-yard line, Hicks raced through a massive hole up the middle to tie the game at 38! It was an amazing comeback. The Bruins were down by 17 and had somehow found a way to tie the game, but it was not over! USC quickly worked the ball downfield, and with seconds to go it looked as though UCLA's comeback would be for naught. Trojan kicker Adam Abrams lined up for a 39-yard kick, but the field goal attempt was blocked! Travis Kirschke's block sent the game to overtime, the only overtime game in the history of the rivalry. In the first overtime period, both teams made field goals. The score was 41–41 at the start of the second overtime period. On the first play of double overtime, Skip Hicks took a handoff up the middle. Like a ball shot out of a cannon, he blasted through the front line of the USC defense and three yards downfield found himself in a mass of bodies, surrounded by teammates and would-be tacklers. But he somehow escaped, cut to the right, made a defender miss, and raced to the front right corner of the end zone for a touchdown! UCLA led, 48–41! The Rose Bowl crowd went wild! It was Skip Hicks's second touchdown of the day and 20th touchdown on the season, a new UCLA record. As he left the field, coach Toledo gave him a massive bear hug. He was the man of the moment, but the game was not over.

Shaun Williams makes a tackle against Washington State, 1996 (Southern Campus Collection)

On first down, USC running back Delon Washington ran for seven yards. On second and 3, quarterback scramble, no gain. On third down, USC receiver R. Jay Soward, who had killed the Bruins all day, found himself wide open in the right flat for a first down but dropped a perfect pass. It was fourth-and-3 with the game on the line. The ball was snapped. The Bruins' Phillip Ward broke through the line immediately and wrapped up USC quarterback Matt Koffler, who threw the ball up in the air in desperation, and on the other end was UCLA defensive back Anthony Cobbs for the interception. The game was over! UCLA won, 48–41! It was the sixth consecutive victory for the Bruins over the Trojans. The 1996 season was a disappointment for Coach Toledo, his players, and their fans everywhere, but the thrill of beating USC never gets old. UCLA enjoyed the offseason, but in 1997, Bruins faithful wanted more, and their wishes would come true.

The Downtown Athletic Club named Danny Wuerffel from the University of Florida the 1996 Heisman Trophy Winner.

The Associated Press named the University of Florida the 1996 National Champions.

## 1997

On paper, the Bruins of 1997 were loaded with talent, but games are played not on paper, but on the field. In Coach Bob Toledo's first season, the Bruins finished with an uninspiring 5–6 record. Several weeks into the 1997 season, it was not uncommon to hear the rumblings of disappointed fans wondering out loud if hiring Coach Toledo a year earlier had been a cataclysmic error. Much to the delight of the fans, however, Toledo would rally his men and lead the Bruins to one of the best seasons in their history. The Blue and Gold offense was led by third-year quarterback Cade McNown, as well as All-America running back Skip Hicks, All-America offensive guard Chad Overhauser, and big-play tight end Jim McElroy. The offense would average 41.7 points per game, which was good for third in the nation. On defense, Shaun Williams was a leader and would be selected in the first round of the 1998 NFL draft. Special teams were led by the brilliant kicker Chris Sailer. The 1997 season would have a period of disappointment, but it would also have a long stretch of brilliance. By the time the regular season ended, Coach Toledo turned many of his biggest doubters into believers.

When UCLA kicked off its season on August 30, it was the first time in school history that the team had played in the month of August. It would be one of their biggest games of the season. The Bruins traveled to Pullman, Washington, to take on Ryan Leaf, Michael Black, and the tough Washington State Cougars. Though both teams came in unranked, the season would prove that the Associated Press pollsters severely underrated both squads. Each team would earn their respect, but when they took the field to play each other, it was not yet about garnering national attention, but rather to launch the season on a positive note. For both offenses, starting on a positive note was easy. For the defenses, it was not so easy. The first half was a shootout. At the end of the first quarter, UCLA led, 21–14. At halftime, the Cougars led, 35–28. On personal performances alone, McNown and Leaf

Skip Hicks, 1997 (Southern Campus Collection)

could hardly imagine a better way to begin the season. The second half would tell a different story. The Cougars' only points would come on a safety, and though the Bruins were able to muster up two field goals, they still trailed, 37–34, late in the fourth quarter. After driving down to the 1½-yard line with just under three minutes to go, Toledo decided to roll the dice. Rather than tapping in a short field goal to tie the game, the UCLA offense remained on the field on fourth down. They would go for the lead. The Bruins went to a heavy formation. Three tight ends. Two men in the backfield, lined up in the I formation. McNown took the snap, opened left, and handed to Jermaine Lewis, who pounded forward off left guard but was hit at the line of scrimmage by Cougars defensive lineman Leon Bender. The Bruins went on to lose, 37–34. The small crowd of 26,000 in Pullman went wild. For Coach Toledo, it was another disappointing loss. It was a decision, and a game, that would come back to haunt the Bruins.

Chris Sailer, 1997 (Southern Campus Collection)

For UCLA, the upcoming schedule looked daunting. Preseason prognosticators may have predicted the Bruins to beat the Cougars to open the season, but few thought they would beat either Tennessee or Texas the next two weeks. When the Vols came west to the Rose Bowl, they brought with them two problems: 1. Coach Toledo worried about how his offense would block Leonard Little, the middle linebacker turned defensive end; 2. The Vols returned Heisman Trophy favorite Peyton Manning. It didn't take long for Toledo's fears to be brought to life. Early in the first quarter, Little sacked McNown for a safety. Minutes later, Little hit McNown while he was throwing, forcing an errant pass that was intercepted by Cory Gaines and returned for a 57-yard touchdown. Manning would also have a big first half, throwing for two touchdowns. McNown, Hicks, and the Bruins offense had no such luck. At halftime, the score was 24–3 Volunteers. Much like in the season opener, the Bruins would make a comeback, only to fall at the end. The Bruins defense was much better in the second half and in the fourth quarter trailed by only 30–24. With a Bruins chance to drive down and take the lead, Little once again wreaked havoc on the Blue and Gold offense. He chased down Hicks and forced a fumble that essentially put the game away. Final score: Tennessee 30, UCLA 24. Manning said after the game, "I was frustrated during the second half that we weren't performing better offensively." Frustration from the opponent would be a major theme going forward, but for the Bruins, all they could see was an 0–2 record and another top opponent standing in front of them.

On September 13, 1997, the Bruins played one of the most memorable games in school history. It was not, however, memorable for its drama as a close contest, or because of the significance of the situation, but rather for the shock value. The University of Texas Longhorns entered the contest with a record of 2–0, and coming off a stunning upset over Nebraska the previous year to win the Big 12 Championship, fans in Austin thought the 1997 team could make a run at the National Championship. Quarterback James Brown was being hyped as a possible Heisman Trophy contender, but entering the game against the Bruins, he was hurt, and backup Richard Walton and third-string QB Marty Cherry, who had spent much of his offseason as an underwear model, were now called into duty. With Brown out, the Longhorns would rely heavily on running back Ricky Williams, but with the attention of the UCLA defense focused squarely on him, carrying the offense would be a tough task. As it turned out, the task proved impossible for Williams, and for the Longhorns, the first half was a nightmare. At halftime, the score was 38–0 UCLA. McNown threw for a school-record five first-half touchdowns. The Bruins defense pounded the Texas offense, hammering Walton and third-string quarterback Marty Cherry over and over. Williams rushed for just 36 yards on the day. With the score 45–0, the Longhorns finally got on the board with a field goal. When the game finally came to a close, the score was 66–3. It was the second-worst loss in UT history, the worst since losing, 68–0, to the University of Chicago in 1904. Cherry would soon discover that his heart was not in football. The thought of taking a beating like the one he had suffered against the Bruins was horrifying. He quit football and became a model. UT wide receiver Wane McGarity said of his former teammate, "I remember sitting back watching Marty take a beating. They beat us so bad they sent the guy into modeling." For the two programs, the game that would forever be remembered as "Rout 66" would send the teams in different directions. UCLA entered one of the most memorable periods in school history. Texas lost all hopes of being a national contender under Head Coach John Mackovic. They finished that season with a 4–7 record and fired Mackovic. They hired Mack Brown, who would in time lead the Longhorns to the Promised Land.

Though the Bruins were only 1–2, after beating UT they entered the AP top 25 for the first time. Following a bye week, they were back on the field and back to their winning ways. The Bruins beat the University of Arizona Wildcats, 40–27, and then took on the Houston Cougars with a script that was familiar to those who saw the team dismantle the Longhorns just three weeks earlier. The Bruins once again scored 66 points and gave up only 10. This game may not be remembered as "Rout 66," but it was the third consecutive win for the Bruins and gave them a 3–2 record. The winning streak continued to grow week after week, as the Bruins continued to play near-flawless football. They played a close game against the University of Oregon on October 11, escaping with a 39–31 win. The rest of their opponents didn't get as close. OSU went down, 34–10. UCLA beat Cal for the third consecutive season, 35–17. The Bruins ran the winning streak to seven when they beat Stanford, 27–7. Finally, the Bruins reached the top 10 in the AP rankings with just two regular season games to play. A crowd of 85,697 fans showed up at the Rose Bowl to see the Blue and Gold take on the Washington Huskies, who entered the game ranked No. 13 in the nation and proved they were a quality team from the minute they ran out of the tunnel. At the end of the first quarter, the Bruins trailed, 17–3. Their hopes for a January 1 Rose Bowl appearance were in serious doubt. For the next 45 minutes of game play, however, the Bruins proved they were one of the best teams in America. They dominated a strong opponent, outscoring them by 11 in the second quarter, 13 in the third quarter, and 14 in the fourth quarter. When the game ended, the scoreboard read UCLA 52, Washington 28. The dream was still alive.

Entering the final regular season game of the year, the Bruins had won eight games in a row. They were ranked No. 7 in the country and had a 7–1 conference record. Still, they found themselves in need of help. The Washington State Cougars, who had beaten the Bruins, 37–34, on August 30, had an identical conference record, but because of the head-to head win over the Bruins, they would go to the Rose Bowl with one more victory. UCLA needed to beat the USC Trojans and have Washington State fall at the hands of the Washington Huskies, the team UCLA had just crushed one week earlier. The Trojans entered the game with a 6–4 record. They had struggled for much of the season but entered the crosstown rivalry game with a modest two-game winning streak. Los Angeles Memorial Coliseum was packed with 91,350 fans, and though the Bruins didn't play particularly well, they were methodical and eventually wore down the inferior Trojans. UCLA trailed, 21–17, at halftime and the score was tied at 24 entering the fourth quarter. The only points in the fourth would come on a UCLA touchdown, and the Bruins won, 31–24. UCLA's 1997 winning streak reached nine games, and the winning streak over rival USC now stood at seven games. Unfortunately for the Bruins, Washington State beat Washington, 41–35, in the Apple Cup and would go to the Rose Bowl.

Though the Bruins did not play in the game they had hoped for on January 1, they did play in a marquee game. The Bruins took on the No. 20 Texas A&M Aggies in the Cotton Bowl in Dallas, Texas, and as they had done for much of the year, they started slow. Though facing a long layoff can be challenging, even more challenging is facing a strong defensive line. The Aggies possessed the men to challenge the Bruins' offensive front, and in the first half they did just that. After falling behind, 16–0, the Bruins finally got on the board on a 22-yard touchdown pass from

McNown to Jim McElroy with just two seconds to play in the first half that brought the score to 16–7 at halftime. In the second half, McNown was brilliant. He engineered three touchdown drives and mesmerized the crowd with his arm, his legs, and even his foot. He punted 76 yards on a quick kick. The comeback was complete. The Bruins won by a score of 29–23. It was the second-greatest comeback in Cotton Bowl history and the Bruins' 10th consecutive victory, the first time they had achieved such a feat since 1946. McNown was named Most Outstanding Player of the Cotton Bowl; he had completed a full season passing for over 200 yards in every game. His 24 touchdown passes tied a school record, and his 168.6 passer rating was the highest in the nation. He finished eighth in the Heisman Trophy voting and was named a third-team All-American. For the Bruins, however, McNown was only one piece of the masterful offensive puzzle. Senior running back Skip Hicks was brilliant, as well. He finished the 1997 season with a school record 26 touchdowns and finished his career with a school record 55 career touchdowns. The Bruins finished the season ranked No. 5 in the country, and even though Hicks would be gone in 1998, the team would have even higher expectations. The year 1997 was a fun season for Bruins fans. The 1998 season would be even more memorable. It would bring great times. It would also bring great heartbreak.

The Downtown Athletic Club named Charles Woodson from the University of Michigan the 1997 Heisman Trophy Winner.

The Associated Press named the University of Michigan the 1997 National Champions.

## 1998

UCLA entered the 1998 football season hoping to continue what they had started in 1997. The Bruins were riding a 10-game winning streak, and with All-American Cade McNown entering his senior season as one of the top Heisman Trophy candidates, expectations were understandably high. At the same time, there was a change in college football that would have an enormous impact. After six decades of relying on the Associated Press poll and Coaches Poll, and over 50 years more of relying on numerous other polls, there was a new way to compare the teams: in 1998, the Bowl Championship Series was founded. In the BCS format, there were four bowl games decided by BCS rankings and by conference affiliation. Those games, called BCS bowls, were the Rose Bowl, Sugar Bowl, Fiesta Bowl, and Orange Bowl. The big change, however, came with the addition of a National Championship game determined by the BCS rankings. Often throughout college football history, there had been a de facto national championship game, but many times there were also shared championships. This would no longer be the case because the top two teams would now square off every year in a title game. For 16 seasons, the BCS determined college football's National Champion, and though it would stir a lot of debate, it was the natural next step in the college football progression. Fans may not have liked the way the BCS rankings were determined. A complex set of polls and computer calculations created the rankings. They did, however, like the concept of a National Championship game. The BCS had served to help the game of college football grow at the turn of the century, and it now finally provided fans, coaches, and players what they craved: a true National Champion.

Though the BCS rankings would determine the National Championship game finalists, the first BCS rankings would not come out until midseason. For comparison's sake, observers would still mostly use the AP poll in the beginning of the year. To start the season, the AP believed the Bruins were one of the best teams in America. UCLA began the season ranked No. 6 in the country and would play Mack Brown and the University of Texas in the season opener. Despite its porous season one year earlier, UT was talented and with new leadership had high expectations. Heisman Trophy candidate Ricky Williams led the Longhorn offense, and the team entered the game ranked No. 23 by the AP. When the teams finally hit the field, the Bruins did so in style. This was a good team. They were riding the longest winning streak at UCLA in more than 50 years, and they had swagger. Coach Bob Toledo, known for trick plays, used his deep bag of tricks early. The Bruins' first touchdown of the season came through the air, but it was not McNown who threw the pass.It was wide receiver Freddie Mitchell, who found Brian Poli-Dixon for a 34-yard score. The game would not be the memorable blowout of a year earlier, but the Bruins were nonetheless impressive in their opening game. Running back Jermaine Lewis scored twice in the first quarter, and McNown threw two touchdowns—one to Danny Farmer and one to Poli-Dixon—in the second quarter. The defense held Ricky Williams and the Longhorns offense to just three first-half points. The halftime score was 35–3, and though the Longhorns would score four second-half touchdowns, the Bruins did enough to come away with a win. They were 1–0, and their winning streak reached 11.

The Bruins ran their winning streak to 12 in Week 2, when they beat the Houston Cougars, 42–24. Next on the schedule: the Miami Hurricanes. Due to a real hurricane, Georges, however, UCLA would not travel east to face Miami on September 26 but instead would have to wait. The game was rescheduled for December 5, two weeks after the regular season was scheduled to end for the Bruins. With the postponement of the Miami game, the Bruins had a week off, and when they returned to the field on October 3, they had revenge on their minds. The Bruins were now ranked No. 4 by the AP and were taking on the team that kept them from the Rose Bowl one year earlier. Washington State no longer had star quarterback Ryan Leaf, who had gone to the NFL, and were no longer one of the top teams in the nation. They came into the game unranked and left feeling the full wrath of an angry Bruins team. Final score: UCLA 49, WSU 17.

After starting the season 3–0, the Bruins faced the meat of their schedule. On October 10, the No. 3 Bruins took on the No. 10 Arizona Wildcats in Tucson. UofA was led by Keith Smith at quarterback and Trung Canidate at running back. The Wildcats would go on to finish their season with a 12–1 record and the best season in school history. Their lone loss, however, came against the Bruins, as 58,738 fans packed into Arizona Stadium, the fourth largest crowd in the venue's history. For 50 minutes, the two teams were evenly matched, with the Bruins holding a 31–28 lead. But the final 10 minutes belonged to the Bruins. Cade McNown and the entire offense were unstoppable. McNown hit Danny Farmer for a touchdown. After forcing a three-and-out, the Bruins regained possession, and on the first play Keith Brown raced 64 yards for another score. With desperation setting in, the Wildcats took to the air, but to no avail. Tony White intercepted a pass, and on the next play, Brown ran for another TD, this one from 20 yards out. UCLA rolled up 229 yards in the fourth quarter alone and won, 52–28. The Bruins were 4–0 and riding high, but in the chase for a National Championship, every game matters, and the dreams of the Bruins almost came crashing down when they played the No. 11 Oregon Ducks. The Bruins got off to a quick start and led, 24–7, but the leaky Bruins defense and flat offense allowed the Ducks back in the game. Suddenly, after allowing 24 unanswered points, the Bruins found themselves trailing in the fourth quarter. Finally receiving a wake-up call, UCLA's offense quickly scored two touchdowns to retake the lead. The Bruins needed a stop to secure victory, but the Oregon offense came back and scored with 22 seconds remaining to tie the game at 38. After UCLA returned the Oregon squib kick to the Ducks 42-yard line with 17 seconds to go, McNown entered the game.. He took the snap and dropped back. Buying time as his receivers ran down the field, he shuffled to the right and let go a long pass down the left sideline to backup quarterback-turned-receiver Drew Bennett. The pass was caught at the 5-yard line with eight seconds to play! All-American kicker Chris Sailer, nursing an injured right groin, lined up for the 21-yard field and missed! The kick was wide left. The Bruins would have to win in overtime if they were to keep their winning streak alive. On the first play of OT, UCLA linebacker Brendon Ayambadejo shot through the line of scrimmage and chased down Oregon quarterback Akili Smith for a 9-yard loss. One play later, Ayambadejo got to Smith again, bringing him down for a loss of three more! It was third-and-22. Incomplete pass. Fourth down. Smith bobbled the snap, picked the ball up, and was instantly feeling the heat from the ferocious Bruins pass rush. He scrambled left, in desperation threw the ball up, and was intercepted by Ryan Roques, his fourth consecutive game with an interception. UCLA began its offensive series at the 25-yard line. On first down, Keith Brown banged ahead for six yards. One play later, he ran for seven more. After three short carries, the ball sat at the Oregon 6-yard line. For Chris Sailer, it was a chance to redeem himself. He lined up for a 23-yard field goal to win the game and knocked it right through! The Bruins remained unbeaten. The winning streak reached 15 games, and the remaining scheduled appeared much easier. For

Coach Toledo, the doubters of two years ago were now firmly in his corner. For the team, the season was not quite half over.

After beating the Ducks, the Bruins traveled to Berkeley to take on the California Golden Bears and came away with a 28–16 win. The Bruins were 6–0. Two days later, when the first BCS rankings came out, there was much nervousness and suspense. People were unsure of how the computers would compare to the human polls. For UCLA, the formula turned out to be perfect: On October 26, 1998, the first BCS poll was released, and UCLA was the No. 1 team in the country! The pressure increased. The Bruins were ranked at the top, and if they could win their final five games, they would play for the National Championship for the first time in 44 years. The pressure may have been felt by the Bruins, but it didn't lead to any losses soon after. They beat the Stanford Cardinal (28–24), Oregon State (41–34), and Washington (36–24). Though the Bruins fell to No. 2 in the BCS rankings, they were still in a prime position to play in the title game as they reached late November. In what was originally scheduled to be the final game of the season for the Bruins, they took on the USC Trojans. At halftime, the Bruins led, 27–10. When the game ended, the score was 34–17 Bruins. A crowd of 88,080 fans showed up to see the game that many thought had clinched a position for the Bruins in the title match. They had one regular season game remaining, the one that had been rescheduled because of Hurricane Georges. On December 5, the Bruins had a date with the University of Miami Hurricanes.

When the Bruins went east to take on Miami in the final game of the 1998 season, they had already won the Pac 10 Conference and clinched a berth in the Rose Bowl. They had won 20 consecutive games, the longest streak in school history. They were 10–0 and ranked No. 2 in the country, one win away from a berth in the BCS National Championship. The eyes of the nation were on the two teams. The Bruins were the heavy favorite, but "The U" would not back down. Seven minutes into the game, the Hurricanes got on the scoreboard first on a 45-yard touchdown run by Edgerrin James. The two teams went back and forth for much of the first half. Cade McNown had a hot hand, but the UCLA defense was powerless to stop the rushing attack of James. With seven minutes to play in the first half, James scored again, giving the Canes a 21–14 lead. Chris Sailer knocked in a field goal before halftime, and the score was 21–17 at the break. When the second half began, it appeared the Bruins were on their way to another win. They scored first on a Danny Farmer 14-yard reception from McNown. Two minutes later, the Bruins regained possession and McNown hit Poli-Dixon for a 61-yard touchdown to extend the lead to 31–21. The Bruins scored again in the third quarter, this time on a 59-yard pass from McNown to Brad Melsby. The lead was 38–21. It would take a Bruins collapse to miss out on a National Championship game appearance. The Hurricanes scored their only points of the third quarter with under a minute remaining, when running back Najeh Davenport raced 23 yards for a touchdown. Though the Bruins held a 10-point lead entering the fourth quarter, their defense was tired, and they were beaten down. James was on his way to a 300-yard rushing performance. Win or lose, it would be an area of concern for the UCLA coaches going into the postseason. On the first play of the fourth quarter, one that is remembered by the most die-hard fans but forgotten by many others, the direction of the game changed. While minutes earlier it had appeared that UCLA was firmly in control, the latest Miami touchdown meant the game was still in question. On that opening play, McNown found Poli-Dixon at the Miami 46-yard line. Poli-Dixon had his sights on the end zone. After breaking a tackle, he cut back to the middle of the field and, avoiding Miami defensive back Ed Reed, was hit from behind and fumbled. Miami defensive back Al Blades recovered at his own 13-yard line. In the fourth quarter, the Miami running game continued to pound the ball. After repeatedly handing the ball to James and Davenport, the Canes finally took a shot over the top of the defense. Quarterback Scott Covington faked a handoff to Davenport to the right, set, and fired a deep strike to wide receiver Santana Moss near the left sideline. Moss got behind the defense and raced to the end zone untouched. The score was now 38–35 with over 12 minutes still remaining. After a long drive resulted in a 1-yard Cade McNown rushing touchdown, the Bruins were back in a solid position to win the game. But Miami again responded. It took the Canes just 46 seconds to march down the field and answer the Bruins' score with a 29-yard touchdown of their own. The score was 45–42 with six minutes to play.

Then, with 3:30 remaining on the clock, the play that has been debated ad nauseam occurred and changed the course of Bruins football history. It was third-and-8 on the Miami 44-yard line. McNown took the shotgun snap, looked left, stepped up in the pocket, and fired a bullet down the middle of the field to Brad Melsby, who caught the ball at the 35-yard line, made a man miss, and was crushed by Ed Reed at the 27-yard line. The ball came loose. Four officials came together to converse, and when a decision was made, the line judge pointed first down Hurricanes. Coach Toledo was livid. It appeared to him that Melsby's knee was down, ending the play before the ball came loose. Replays to the TV audience confirmed his knee was down, but this was in the era before instant replay and coaches' challenges. It was a bad call, but Miami's ball, and UCLA would need a stop to secure their spot in the championship game. On the final drive, James and Davenport continued to shine, and Miami quarterback Scott Covington had come alive. With 54 seconds to play, Miami had the ball at the UCLA 1-yard line. First and goal. Covington took the snap, reverse pivoted, and pitched the ball to James to the left, who again had a massive hole in front of him. He raced into the end zone to give the Hurricanes the go-ahead score with just under a minute to play. The Bruins were stunned. The Miami Hurricanes had a long history of ending winning streaks for opponents. They had ended winning streaks of 23, 22, 20, 16, and 14 in the previous 15 years, but the Bruins had no intentions of forfeiting their 20-game streak. As long as there was time on the clock and the ball was in the hands of Cade McNown, there was a chance. With the ball at the Miami 30-yard line with three seconds left, the Bruins had time for one final play. McNown took the snap, dropped back, and effortlessly heaved a long pass into the end zone to Drew Bennett, the receiver with the highest vertical leap on the team. He went up, but the defense was too tight and the ball was just too high. UCLA was shocked. They had lost, 49–45. Cade McNown had thrown for a school record 513 yards on the day, but the two late fumbles by Poli-Dixon and Melsby were critical errors, and the magnificent performance of Edgerrin James beat the Bruins. Danny Farmer and Poli-Dixon each went over 100 yards receiving on the day, and freshman running back Deshaun Foster finished with 90 yards rushing. For all their gaudy offensive statistics, no one could take away the sting of the loss. The 1998 Bruins were a great team, but they could not finish the job. For the first time in school history, they "settled for" the Rose Bowl.

Cade McNown in the 1999 Rose Bowl against the University of Wisconsin

When UCLA took on the University of Wisconsin on January 1, the Badgers were not the only opponent facing the Bruins. Stopping Ron Dayne would prove to be a challenge, but just as difficult for some was getting over the loss to the Hurricanes. The team was heartbroken. They had dreamed of a national title. If Hurricane Georges had not moved the game back to December, if Melsby was ruled down before fumbling, if the defense could slow Edgerrin James, perhaps the Bruins would not be in Pasadena, but instead in the Fiesta Bowl battling for the National Championship against the Tennessee Volunteers. Wisconsin coach Barry Alvarez, a master motivator, used the words of CBS analyst Craig James, who called the Badgers "the worst team I can remember playing in the Rose Bowl," as motivation to whip his team up for the game. Stopping Ron Dayne was like stopping Edgerrin James; it was impossible for the porous UCLA rushing defense. Dayne finished the day with 246 yards and four touchdowns. McNown threw for 340 yards, but it was not enough. Just as five years earlier, the Badgers beat the Bruins in the Rose Bowl. UCLA finished the season with a 10–2 record. They had been one minute away from a trip to the National Championship game. The offseason would be a long one. Star quarterback Cade McNown was off to the NFL, and fans, players, and coaches have been stuck

Jermaine Lewis in the 1999 Rose Bowl

for decades with nightmares of the game played on December 5 in Miami.

The Downtown Athletic Club named Ricky Williams from the University of Texas the 1998 Heisman Trophy Winner.

The Tennessee Volunteers beat Florida State University, 23–16, in the BCS National Championship game.

## Cade McNown

UCLA football has a strong quarterback history. Bob Waterfield was UCLA's first star quarterback. As a rookie in the NFL, he was named MVP. Billy Kilmer led the nation in total offense in 1960. Gary Beban won the 1967 Heisman Trophy. Troy Aikman is in the Pro Football Hall of Fame. Steve Bono, Wayne Cook, Tom Ramsey, John Sciarra, Brett Hundley, and Josh Rosen have all had success. When discussing the best quarterbacks in UCLA history, the man who stands eye-to-eye with any who came before him, or have walked the hills of Bruin Walk since, is Cade McNown. He was a four-year starter. He took the Bruins to sights unseen in decades. He had a strong arm, good feel in the pocket, and the ability to read a defense in the blink of an eye. He was a winner, and he was a Bruin.

Cade McNown was born on January 12, 1977, in Portland, Oregon. In high school, Cade had success at two different stops. After moving to California as a boy, Cade attended San Benito High School in Hollister, California. Much as would be the case in his college career, Cade was a good player from his first moment on the scene but would quickly make the leap from good to great. He was an all-around athlete and played multiple sports. As a sophomore at San Benito in 1992, Cade was named Honorable Mention All-Monterey Bay League. His best sport was not even football. In track and field, Cade set a school record with a 15 foot 0 inch clearance in the pole vault. He also threw the discus 142 feet, threw the shotput 48 feet 3 inches, and high-jumped 6 feet 2 inches. As a junior, he improved in football, but his time on the gridiron was cut short. After four games, he underwent an emergency appendectomy that ended his season. In track and field, he was once again an all-league performer. As a junior, Cade's varsity athletic exploits were not limited to football and track and field; he was also a starter on the varsity basketball team. Though his junior football season had been cut short, Cade was recognized as one of the top quarterback recruits on the West Coast, and as a senior he transferred to West Linn High School in West Linn, Oregon. Though he was a star quarterback, Cade played defensive back, as well. He accumulated a total of 81 tackles, four interceptions, four pass breakups, and he forced one fumble. His future, however, was not in the defensive backfield, but at the quarterback position. As a senior, he passed for 1,711 yards and 17 touchdowns. He also ran for 631 yards and nine touchdowns. He garnered national attention from recruiters and was named a Blue Chips Illustrated All-American, USA Today All-American, First Team All-State as both a quarterback and defensive back, and was rated the third-best quarterback recruit on the West Coast. Cade's ultimate college decision was not fully his own but was instead decided by another prep star. Brock Huard was one of the top recruits in the nation, the QB at the top of every West Coast team's recruiting short list. In the spring of 1994, both Cade and Huard were still uncommitted. They both were now only considering UCLA and the University of Washington. Cade would say of his decision, "It was simple. We had both gotten our choices down to Washington and UCLA. He was everyone's number one guy. I just decided wherever he went, I would go to the other place." Ultimately, Huard chose the Huskies, and Cade went to UCLA. For both parties, the decisions worked out just fine. Despite committing to play football for the Bruins, Cade had one season more of basketball and one more of track to compete in. After once again starting on the basketball team, Cade went on to track and set a school record in the pole vault (15 feet 2 inches) and recorded personal bests in the discus (150 feet 11 inches) and shotput (53 feet ¼ inch). He was named Outstanding Male Athlete at West Linn High School and was named to the All-League team in track. Over four years in high school, Cade showed his athletic prowess. He was a natural. He could do everything. For Coaches Terry Donahue and Bob Toledo, they could only hope he would be as successful in college. They got what they hoped for.

When McNown took the field for the first time in 1995, he did so not as a starter, but as a backup. Junior Ryan Fien had been named the starting quarterback by Head Coach Terry Donahue, but it didn't take long for McNown to get his shot. Due to the ineffectiveness of Fien, who was dealing with nagging injuries, McNown got his chance just four games into the 1995 season and never looked back. Though he struggled for much of his true freshman season, McNown was recognized not only as the team's future, but as the best option in the present. It was Donahue's final season as the head coach of the Bruins, but a new era was beginning. The late 1990s would not be defined so much by the success of Donahue's successor, Bob Toledo, but rather by the brilliance of the program as McNown continued to improve. As a freshman, he completed just 49.8% of his passes and threw for only seven touchdowns. He rushed for 311 yards, the most by a Bruins quarterback since Rick Bashore in 1977. He finished second on the team with five rushing touchdowns. Overall, it is inaccurate to say that McNown was a sensation from the beginning, but he was the only answer. Against USC, McNown was his typical freshman self. He did not put up gaudy stats. He completed only 8 of 17 passes for 131 yards, but when the game was on the line, he came through. With the Bruins leading, 24–20, late in the fourth, McNown scrambled for 21 yards and a first down. The Bruins were able to run out the clock and secure the victory. McNown's freshman season was not as memorable as that of other Bruins greats, but it resulted in a seven-win season and a victory over USC, something McNown would make an annual tradition.

As a sophomore, McNown took a step back, and following the 1996 season, it was hard to believe that he would one day become a Bruins legend. He upped his completion percentage to 52.4 and his touchdown passes to 12, but his rushing dropped to just 58 yards, he threw 16 interceptions, and finished ninth in the Pac 10 Conference in pass efficiency. The Bruins finished Head Coach Bob Toledo's first season with a losing record. For McNown, his best game of the season came against the rival USC Trojans. With seven minutes to play in the game, the Bruins trailed USC by 17 points. Trojans fans believed their losing streak to the Bruins, which had reached five games, was finally coming to an end. McNown had other plans. He led the Bruins to 17 unanswered points, sending the game into overtime, and in the extra period, the Bruins came away with another win. His sophomore season had been a disappointment. Coach Toledo's first year was underwhelming. It appeared to be a lost season, but with one fourth-quarter comeback, the quarterback who had struggled all season turned the page. He was 2–0 against the Trojans. It was time now to build a legacy.

In 1997, the Bruins started the year 0–2. The same constant chatter about Coach Toledo, questioning whether he was the right man for the job, continued. As for McNown, he was relatively ignored by the naysayers. His freshman mistakes were written off as rookie errors. In McNown's sophomore season, Coach Toledo had shouldered most of the blame. Now, as a junior, there was pressure on the quarterback as well as on his coach. It was time to perform. McNown had spent the entire offseason working on every facet of his game. He regularly threw with his receivers and came back in '97 with a transformed body. He had spent the entire offseason in the weight room, and it showed. He was bigger, tougher, smarter, and much better. In '97, Cade claimed that the goal of the offense the coming season was to average 30 points per game. Writers laughed. The team instead averaged 40. Cade spearheaded one of the most miraculous team performances in UCLA history, leading the Bruins to a 66–3 victory over the University of Texas. The game has since been dubbed "Rout 66." Cade McNown would go on to lead the nation in passing efficiency, and his team on an impressive winning streak. The Bruins closed out the '97 regular season with nine consecutive victories. Their lone conference loss, in the first game of the year to Washington State, prevented the Bruins from going to the Rose Bowl. Instead, they played in the Cotton Bowl, beating Texas A&M, 29–23. For Cade, it was a stunning turnaround. His dedication to perfecting his craft was seen on the field, and the public took notice. He was named an All-American by the Associated Press and *Sporting News*. He finished eighth in the Heisman Trophy voting, and the Bruins finished the season ranked No. 5 in the final AP poll. For fans of the Bruins, the 1997 season was fun. The 1998 season would be a roller-coaster ride of emotions.

As Cade entered his senior season, the expectations for him and UCLA were sky-high. He started the year as one of the top Heisman Trophy candidates in America, and the Bruins as one of the top teams. They would once again average 40 points per game, and Cade was once again the man who spearheaded the attack. After starting the season 10–0, the Bruins' winning streak reached 20 games—including the previous season—and when they took on the Miami Hurricanes in a game rescheduled from months earlier, the Bruins were one win away from appearing in the first-ever BCS National Championship game. But the Bruins lost to the Canes, and then to the Wisconsin Badgers in the Rose Bowl. Cade's college career came to a disappointing close, but for Bruins everywhere he had been a joy to watch. He finished his senior season with 3,470 yards and 25 touchdowns. He broke school records in passing yards, touchdowns, and total offense for a season and once again led the Bruins to a victory over USC, the eighth in a row for the Bruins. When McNown's career came to a close, he was the first Bruins quarterback to go 4–0 against the Trojans. In the 1999 NFL Draft, Cade was selected by the Chicago Bears with the twelfth overall pick. His time in a Bruins uniform had come to an end, but his legacy would live on forever.

After being drafted by the Bears, Cade would say, "To have things work out the way they did, I couldn't have pictured it, written it any better. Going from a young Bruin to a Bear is really an exciting thing." The city of Chicago initially embraced McNown, and the relationship seemed to be working. In 1999, he became only the fifth rookie to start at quarterback for the Bears. He established Bears rookie records with 127 completions in 235 attempts and was second in passing yards and touchdowns in Bears rookie history. For McNown, the story of his NFL career would not mirror his college career. In 2000, he was named the starting quarterback, but playing through an injured shoulder, he struggled, and after eight games, he was benched. Prior to the 2001 season, he was traded to the Miami Dolphins. He was relegated to third string and saw no playing time during the season. In the 2002 offseason, he was traded to the San Francisco 49ers. His former coach, Terry Donahue, was now the general manager of the 49ers and believed McNown still had some magic in his strong left arm. He was wrong. McNown again injured his shoulder and missed the entire season. In 2003, he was released, and he retired.

Cade McNown, 1998

While McNown was not able to recover in the NFL any of the magic from his college playing days, he was able to find something else at which he excelled: business. Following his playing career, Cade went to work in the investment advisory business, working for UBS Investment Bank and JP Morgan Chase. In 2008, McNown was named senior vice president of investor development for Thompson National Properties, LLC. In 2013, he took a job as the vice president of Lourd Capital Management in Beverly Hills. McNown would say of his "revised dream," his new career: "When it comes to work or investing or anything else, discipline and focus and commitment are all things that you need to be successful in a business career, and those are all certainly things that you develop when you're on a football team." In 2013, the *University Herald* named McNown one of the five best former or current professional football players on Wall Street. For McNown, success came in a way perhaps not imagined by him in 1999. He found success in the business world. For UCLA football fans, McNown is, and will forever be, a legend. He led the Bruins to two of the greatest seasons in school history. He was a man who elevated the UCLA football program to levels unmatched in the two decades following his departure. He took the

Bruins on a ride closer to the pinnacle of the college football world than had been seen in over 40 years. Cade McNown may not have had the NFL career of Troy Aikman or Bob Waterfield, but when he put on the Bruins blue and gold, he was a wonder to watch. His 4–0 record against the USC Trojans has yet to be duplicated by another player since his departure. McNown was inducted into the UCLA Athletics Hall of Fame in 2009, and in 2015, he was a nominee for the College Football Hall of Fame. For Bruins fans, Cade was more than just a football player, he was an icon. His smooth style, confident approach, crafty running ability, and cool under pressure have not been seen since. The Bruins will field a new team every year with a different man under center. They will win big games and lose in heartbreaking fashion. Quarterbacks will have great games, and eventually all of McNown's records will be broken. For a time much longer than that which will see his name in the record book, the memory of number 18 in the blue and gold will live on. Cade McNown was not big, he was not particularly fast, but he was a winner, and when summer turned into fall in the late 1990s, there was no better attraction than watching Cade McNown and the UCLA Bruins.

## 1999

1999 was a year of unknowns. As Y2K conspiracy theorists believed the end of the millennium would come the end of the world, and were thus preparing for the end times, Coach Bob Toledo was preparing for life without quarterback Cade McNown. The Bruins had finished the 1998 season in disappointment. After losing the final regular season game of the year that cost them a National Championship game appearance, and then losing the Rose Bowl to underdog Wisconsin, the Bruins limped into the offseason. Players, coaches, and fans alike were all heartbroken. And replacing McNown was a challenge that would ultimately prove to be too difficult for Coach Toledo and his next two successors. With the loss of McNown came the deterioration of a program. The Bruins would sink into a sustained period of mediocrity not seen since the earliest days of Bruins football. While certain years were better than others, giving fans hope that playing in the Rose Bowl was again possible, a feeling of inferiority soon set in. For Coach Toledo and the Bruins, the 1999 season was a turning point. Unfortunately, that turn was in the wrong direction.

Even before the season began, the Bruins took a beating. A story that had unfolded for several years was now becoming clear. There was a scandal on campus, and it involved the football team. Many players had received fraudulent handicap parking decals, and up to two dozen were arrested and/or suspended, including former greats now off to the NFL. Before the team even set foot on the field to prepare for their opening opponent, the Bruins had lost the battle of public opinion. When the season started in September, losing would become a normal activity. Replacing Cade McNown proved to require a group effort, and in the 1999 season, two was not greater than one. In the season opener, however, the quarterbacks played well enough, and so did the entire football team. The Bruins opened the season as the No. 17-ranked team by the Associated Press and on September 4 proceeded to trounce the Boise State Broncos. Cory Paus and Drew Bennett shared time under center, while Deshaun Foster and Jermaine Lewis split reps at running back. Kicker Chris Griffith scored the first points of the season on a first-quarter 37-yard field goal. In the second quarter, the Bruins kicked into high gear. Foster scored from four yards out. Julius Williams intercepted a pass and returned it 53 yards for a score. Gabe Crecion scored the first passing touchdown on a 5-yard toss from Paus five minutes before halftime. At the break, the Bruins led, 24–0. In the third quarter, Bennett found Randy Hakes for a 65-yard score, and Lewis ran in a touchdown from five yards out. The Bruins led, 38–0, entering the fourth quarter and went on to win, 38–7. Joey Strycula led the defense with nine tackles and an interception. Ricky Manning Jr. added seven tackles and a sack, and Joe Hunter had an interception and two pass breakups. The UCLA quarterbacks combined to complete 20 of 34 passes for 248 yards and two touchdowns. But the first game was not a complete success—they did throw three interceptions. The Bruins quarterbacks would have to play much better going forward for the team to have a successful season. For any coach there are always things to worry about, but after Week 1, Coach Toledo and staff could at least come away happy with a victory. There wouldn't be too many more.

When the Bruins entered The Horseshoe on

September 11, 1999, to play before 93,238 fans in person and millions more on ABC-TV, they came with a loud confidence, and a quiet unease. The Bruins were ranked No. 14, and the Ohio State Buckeyes were No. 13. As Brad Nessler and Gary Danielson were on the call, the nation saw the end of the brief Bruin era. UCLA took a 7–0 lead, but on this day, they were clearly the inferior team. The Buckeyes, who went on to a meager 6–6 record themselves, stormed past the Bruins and won by the score of 42–20. Despite the loss, the Bruins remained ranked. In Week 3, they were now No. 21 in the country, according to the AP, and were back home to take on the Fresno State Bulldogs. The Bruins won, 35–21. The team was 2–1, right where the pundits expected them to be, heading into conference play. But things would not go as predicted in the Pac 10.

The conference opener did not go the way UCLA had hoped. The Stanford Cardinal beat the Bruins, 42–32, in Palo Alto. The Blue and Gold entered the game as the No. 18 team in the nation. They would leave with a second loss in their record and a dent in their confidence. If the loss to the Cardinal was a shock to the system, it didn't work to jump-start the Bruins. One week later, they played the Arizona State Sun Devils, and the game would come down to the wire. The Bruins kicked off the scoring in the first quarter with a 50-yard dash to the end zone by running back Keith Brown. In the second quarter, the Bruins struck again on a big play, this time an 85-yard touchdown pass from Paus to Danny Farmer to bring the score to 14–0. Arizona State's comeback was not sudden, but rather a slow, methodical march back into the game. Each team scored again in the second quarter, and at halftime, the Sun Devils still trailed by 14 points. ASU got a quick strike of their own in the third quarter on an 80-yard touchdown run by J.R. Redmond. In the fourth quarter, Redmond scored again, his third of the day, but two field goals by Griffith helped the Bruins maintain a six-point lead. For two years, the Bruins seemed to always come through in the clutch, but 1999 was neither '97 nor '98. Things were different now. The Sun Devils scored on a 49-yard pass and won, 28–27. The box score showed it to be a close game. The Sun Devils gained just four more yards than the Bruins. The difference came in the turnovers. UCLA lost the turnover battle and lost the game. One week later, the Bruins played another close game but this time came out on top. After beating the Oregon Ducks,34–29, the Bruins' record was 3–3. In the not-so-distant past, one could expect the Bruins to make a midseason run and start a long winning streak, just as they had done so many times under Coach Donahue. Under Coach Toledo, at least in 1999, just the opposite happened.

Entering the game with the University of California Berkeley, the Bruins had a four-game winning streak in the series matchups. Though the Bruins were certainly not a strong team, neither were the Bears. Entering the game, Cal had a 2–3 record, but all wins would eventually be vacated due to the changing of players' grades for eligibility purposes. To the Bruins, this mattered little. They lost, 17–0, and the fact that Cal would later vacate their win didn't make losing feel any better. One week later, the Bruins lost again, this time in even more embarrassing fashion. The Oregon State Beavers were coached by Dennis Erickson and boasted a solid, yet unspectacular, offense and defense. Both units ranked in the top 35 nationally, and both dominated the Bruins. When the clock hit :00, the final score read Oregon State 55, UCLA 7. Oh, how the mighty had fallen. One week later, the Bruins' losing streak hit three with a 33–7 loss to Trung Canidate and the Arizona Wildcats. There were two games left in the regular season. The Bruins could now not avoid a losing record. They were 3–6 on the season, and the possibility of going into the offseason with a five-game losing streak was looking ever more likely. On November 13, the Bruins took on the highly favored Washington Huskies, coached by former UCLA quarterback Rick Neuheisel and led by current quarterback Marques Tuiasosopo. For the Bruins, who would finish the season in ninth place in the conference, this was the game they could hang their hat on. The Bruins beat the Huskies, 23–20. There was one game left, the one that could make a poor season a bit more bearable. It was also the one that could make a poor season feel like the end of the world.

When the Bruins took on the USC Trojans on November 20, there was nothing on the line but pride. UCLA had a forgettable season and would not reach a bowl game. The Trojans, under Coach Paul Hackett, started the season in the top 25 but entered the game against the Bruins with an equally poor 4–6 record. What mattered most to both teams was not being able to say that they had won five games instead of four, but rather the history of the rivalry and its current implications. The Bruins had defeated the Trojans eight times in a row, something never before accomplished by either team, and were looking to make it nine. The two teams had more than just the same record; they had the same quarterback issue to overcome. Cory Paus had emerged as the Bruins' best option at QB, but he would be missing the game against the Trojans with a broken collarbone. USC quarterback Carson Palmer quite literally knew the pain Paus was going through: he, too, would miss the game with a broken collarbone! As many expected, when two below-average teams meet, the game gets ugly. On this day, the two teams combined for 25 penalties for 194 yards. The Bruins turned the ball over five times, and neither offense mounted many serious threats. USC scored two touchdowns, one of which came on a controversial call in which receiver Kareem Kelly caught a ball in the end zone, but his foot landed out of bounds. The referee nearest the play ruled it a touchdown, and USC led, 17–7 late in the game. For the Bruins, there would be no magic. Final score: USC 17, UCLA 7. The miserable season was finally over. It was time to turn the page on the decade of the '90s, one that started poor and ended poor, but which fielded three of the finest teams in school history. It was time to forget about Cade McNown and Skip Hicks. It was time to forget all about the 1999 season. The Bruins entered the new millennium on a downturn. Fans only hoped they could turn it around quickly.

The Downtown Athletic Club named Ron Dayne from the University of Wisconsin the 1999 Heisman Trophy Winner.

Florida State University beat Virginia Tech University, 46–29, in the BCS National Championship game.

## 2000

To the surprise of those lacking common sense, the world did not end on January 1, 2000. The Y2K scare blew over, and people celebrated the New Year as they had done every other year. For the Bruins, the era of dominance was over. The 1999 season had been a disaster. Replacing the star power gone to the NFL was a task that proved to be daunting. But in 2000, the team improved. Cory Paus got the lion's share of the calls at quarterback. Deshaun Foster had a strong season at running back, and Freddie Mitchell emerged as a star wide receiver. The team was certainly entertaining to watch. Coach Bob Toledo continued to dig deep into his bag of tricks. The offense was unpredictable, and they were good. The Bruins would average nearly 30 points per game, but the defense was leaky. They would finish 86th in the country in scoring defense, giving up just over 30 points per game. While the Bruins certainly had strong defensive performers, such as Ricky Manning Jr., Rodney Leisle, and Marques Anderson, inconsistency on defense ultimately hurt the team and led to a mediocre season. The 2000 season saw an improvement over '99, but the Bruins were still far away from the level of the '98 squad. The schedule would open against a college football powerhouse.

On September 2, 2000, the UCLA football season began in front of 76,640 fans at the Rose Bowl against the No. 3 Alabama Crimson Tide. For a brief moment, it appeared the season was destined for disaster. On the first play of the game, UCLA quarterback Cory Paus separated his shoulder. Two plays later, UCLA punted, and Alabama's Freddie Milons returned the punt 71 yards for a touchdown. Coach Toledo was obviously worried. After the game, he would say, "When they scored right off, I thought they'd score 200 points." Luckily for Coach Toledo and the Bruins, that was not the case. Ryan McCann came off the sideline to replace Paus and led the Bruins on three consecutive scoring drives to give them a 21–7 lead late in the second quarter. The Tide made a charge, however, and eventually retook the lead after a Reggie Myles interception that he returned 91 yards for a score. Alabama led, 24–21. McCann pleaded with Toledo to not lose confidence in him. The coach stood by his quarterback. The Bruins would close out the game by scoring two touchdowns, the first coming on a 46-yard connection from McCann to Mitchell, and the second coming on an 8-yard score by Foster. McCann threw for 194 yards and helped the Bruins offense enough to pull off the stunning upset, but the star of the game was Deshaun Foster. After missing much of the previous season with a nagging ankle injury, he entered the 2000 season healthy, and he dominated. He finished the game with a school record-tying 42 carries, 187 yards, and three touchdowns. The Bruins were 1–0, and it didn't take long for the chatter to start. Were the Bruins back? Time would tell.

One week after beating the Crimson Tide, the Bruins got another win. In Week 2, they beat the Fresno State Bulldogs, 24–21. Unlike the first game of the season, McCann was not the best quarterback on the field this day. He finished with just 106 yards passing, and his counterpart for the Bulldogs clearly outplayed him. FSU quarterback David Carr finished with 249 yards passing, three touchdowns, and no interceptions. The Bruins run defense was solid, however, and held the Bulldogs to just 30 yards on the ground. For the second week in a row, Deshaun Foster was the best player on the field. He finished with 140 yards rushing and two touchdowns. The Bruins were 2–0, and when the Michigan Wolverines came to the Rose Bowl on September 16, the eyes of the nation were on Pasadena. UCLA was ranked No. 14 by the Associated Press; the Wolverines were No. 3. The game was televised nationally on ABC, and a crowd of over 88,000 showed up to see the two teams battle. For the second time in three games, the Bruins beat the No. 3 team in the country. It was a true shocker. For the second week in a row, Ryan McCann struggled in the first half, but his teammates once again supported him. Despite the slow start, coach Toledo believed in his quarterback, telling him: "This is your game to win. Don't look behind you." McCann didn't, and the Bruins came through. The final score was 23–20 UCLA. Foster finished the game with 95 yards, and Mitchell added 137. The temperature during the second half soared over 110 degrees, and Toledo admitted that both teams were wearing down as the game unfolded. For the Bruins, the temperature outside could only be matched by the success of the team. The Bruins were on fire. They started the season 3–0, and the memory of 1999's disappointment began to fade. McCann would say after the game, "I think we proved we were the number one team in the nation. I don't know who else we can beat or what else we can do."

The Bruins started conference play on September 23 and entered the game against the Oregon Ducks with "a chip on their shoulder." UCLA had climbed up to No. 6 in the AP rankings, and though there was still a month until the first BCS rankings would be released, the Bruins had built quite a résumé and were looking to build on their success. But after three consecutive wins, the Bruins felt defeat. Against the Ducks, not only were the Bruins beaten; they were outplayed in every facet of the game. Joey Harrington outplayed McCann, though both struggled. The Ducks rushed for 208 yards, the Bruins only five. Freddie Mitchell had 158 yards receiving, but only four Bruins caught passes, and only 41 percent of those passes found their intended targets. The Ducks knocked in three field goals, and the Bruins only one. When the game mercifully came to a close, the final score was Oregon 29, UCLA 10. The illusions of grandeur were gone, and though UCLA remained ranked for several more weeks, the most honest of observers could see this team still had a ways to go.

The Bruins defense had performed admirably over the first three games of the year, but in conference play, they simply fell apart. Though the Bruins would beat the Arizona State Sun Devils, the defense gave up 31 points. One week later, the seemingly dead California Golden Bear offense came to life. Cal was averaging just 13 points per game in their first five contests but exploded for 46 against the Bruins. Kyle Boller would have a career day, and ultimately the Bruins offense was unable to do enough to come away with a victory. Cal beat UCLA in thrilling fashion, 46–38, in three overtimes. One week later, the Bruins defense struggled mightily again. The Bruins led by 10 points in the fourth quarter against the Oregon State Beavers, but the game eventually was decided by the Bruins defense. OSU overcame the deficit to win, 44–38. Jonathan Smith threw for four touchdowns. Patrick McCall rushed for 146 yards. Ken Simonton rushed for 100. Chad Johnson had 104 yards receiving. The strong individual performance at quarterback by Cory Paus, back from injury and in the starting lineup, was not enough. The Bruins lost their third game in the last four. They were on a downward spiral, and dreams of BCS relevance were gone. The new goal was simply to finish with a winning record.

With five games left in the season, Coach Toledo had the challenge of motivating his team. Just one month earlier, there were hopes and dreams of being a national contender. Now, they simply needed a win. On October 28, the Bruins entered the game against the Arizona Wildcats riding a two-game losing streak and staring at a possible third. UofA was the heavy favorite, but if one thing was to be learned from the Coach Toledo era at UCLA, it was to expect to be surprised. The Bruins beat the Wildcats, 27–24, and one week later beat the Stanford Cardinal, 37–35. The team was back on track, or so it seemed. On November 11, the Bruins took on the Washington Huskies, the No. 6 team in the BCS rankings, led by second-year Head Coach Rick Neuheisel. The Bruins played well. They stayed close, but quarterback Marques Tuiasosopo and an inspired Huskies team—which had dedicated their season to teammate Curtis Williams, who suffered a serious neck injury that left him paralyzed—were too much for the Bruins to handle. The Huskies would go on to win the Rose Bowl. The Bruins were simply hoping to win their final regular-season game.

The game against the Trojans was, once again, about nothing more than pride. The Bruins were 6–5. The Trojans were 4–6. In the end, the result of the game would come down to one final play. With the score tied at 35, USC kicker David Bell, who had missed three previous attempts on the day, lined up for a 36-yard field goal. The Bruins' regular season ended in a way entirely unpredictable when compared to the way it started. Bell knocked the field goal through with nine seconds to play, and the Bruins fell to a lowly USC squad. The Trojans celebrated the win, but for Head Coach Paul Hackett, his time of joy would be brief. It was his final season coaching the Trojans. UCLA played one more game, the Sun Bowl, against old foe Wisconsin. Though the season had been a disappointment, and the meeting was not on the same stage as when the two teams had met in January of 1994 or 1999, it was an opportunity for the Bruins to finish with a winning record. UCLA's Freddie Mitchell would set a Sun Bowl record with 180 receiving yards, but it wasn't enough, as UW running back Michael Bennett scored a touchdown midway through the fourth quarter to give the Badgers a 21–20 lead. The Bruins were unable to overtake Barry Alvarez's team, and the season came to a close in disappointing fashion once again. The Bruins finished with a 6–6 record and a three-game losing streak.

The Downtown Athletic Club named Chris Weinke from Florida State University the 2000 Heisman Trophy Winner.

The University of Oklahoma beat Florida State University, 13–2, in the BCS National Championship game.

## 2001

When the 2001 college football season began, it was a time of joy. For fans, the offseason is a time of anxiety. With football season comes passion, enjoyment, and love. But in 2001, the tone and feelings of the nation would soon change. The season kicked off for the Bruins on September 1. Beating a top team at home is very different from winning one on the road. A year earlier, the Bruins began their season by beating the No. 3 Alabama Crimson Tide at the Rose Bowl. Despite finishing only 6–6, the Bruins entered the 2001 season ranked No. 17 in the country. This time Alabama, led by new Head Coach Dennis Franchione, was ranked No. 25. Unlike the previous year, the Bruins would not have home field advantage. The game would be played at Bryant-Denny Stadium, and the crowd would be loud. The Crimson Tide would get off to a fast start. Just six minutes into the game, Tyler Watts hit Antonio Carter for a 78-yard touchdown pass. In the second quarter, the Alabama lead would stretch to 10–0 after a short field goal. UCLA's first touchdown of the season came on a 10-yard run midway through the second quarter by Ed Ieremia-Stansbury to cut the lead to three. When the two teams went to the locker room at halftime, one thing was clear. Both teams were in for a tough battle for all four quarters. For Alabama coach Franchione, it would be his first test. Would he be able to make the necessary adjustments to keep the Tide ahead and ultimately win the game? In the third quarter, it was all Bruins. Cory Paus threw his first touchdown of the season, a 53-yard strike to Tab Perry. Chris Griffith added a 30-yard field goal, and a minute and a half into the fourth quarter, he added a 45-yard field goal to stretch the lead to 10 points. Though Alabama would quickly strike back after the Griffith field goal with a long touchdown of their own, the 20–17 score held. The Bruins were 1–0. One week later, the Bruins were on the road again and came away with another victory. Paus, Perry, Craig Bragg, and senior star running back Deshaun Foster led the offense. Ryan Nece, who intercepted a pass and returned it for a touchdown, led the defense. Final score: UCLA 41, Kansas 17. The Bruins were off to a great start. Everyone in Westwood was pleased. That would all change, however, three days later. An event that shocked the nation and changed the world happened in front of our very eyes. The United States was under attack.

At 7:59 a.m. EST on the morning of Tuesday, September 11, American Airlines Flight 11 took off from Boston, Massachusetts. Sixteen minutes later, United Airlines Flight 175 took off from Boston. Neither flight would reach its intended destination. At 8:46 a.m., American Airlines Flight 11 crashed into the North Tower of the World Trade Center. The 76 passengers and 11 crew members on board, as well as hundreds in the tower, were killed instantly. Seventeen minutes later, the South Tower was hit. All 51 passengers and nine crew members, as well as hundreds more in the tower, were killed instantly. By now, television media were all over the story. When the second building was hit, the public saw it. It was now clear the United States was under attack. At 9:37 a.m., tragedy once again struck. Flight 77 hit the Pentagon in Washington D.C. At 9:59 a.m., the South Tower collapsed. Nearly 1,000 people died instantly. Four minutes later, Flight 93 met its fate, but thanks to the heroism of those on board who perished, American lives were saved. Just 20 minutes away from Washington D.C., Flight 93 crashed into a field in Shanksville, Pennsylvania, after crew members rushed the cockpit to try and retake control of the plane. Finally, at 10:28 a.m., the North Tower, which had burned for 102 minutes, collapsed. More than 1,600 people were killed instantly. The attacks were over, but reality was just setting in. Islamic terrorists, who were affiliated with al-Qaeda, had carried out the largest attack on the United States homeland in history. Nearly 3,000 Americans died. We were at war.

Suddenly, football didn't seem so important, or perhaps it was more important than ever. The attacks on September 11 were a wake-up call, a notice that we were vulnerable. Returning to sports was a return to normalcy, at least for a brief time. The nation rallied around President George W. Bush. They cheered the Yankees and the Mets. Fans watched with tears in their eyes when Mike Piazza hit the game-winning home run in the first baseball game in New York following the attack. For the Bruins, there would be no game on Saturday, September 15. They would wait another week. Before the game against the No. 21 Ohio State Buckeyes, a moment of silence was observed to honor those who had fallen 11 days earlier and those still waiting for answers. As the silence was coming to an end, one fan in attendance yelled, "God Bless America, yeah!" The crowd cheered. Sixty thousand patriotic placards with an American flag that read "United, we stand" were handed out, and though the Buckeyes and the Bruins opposed each other on the field, the overwhelming feeling in the stands was somber. It was not the best-played game in recent history, but it was one of the most memorable. The Bruins fumbled seven times, losing four, including two by Foster. Ohio State's first-year Head Coach Jim Tressel would lament not being able to capitalize on the Bruins' mistakes. While the offense struggled, the UCLA defense shined. They held OSU to just eight first downs and 166 total yards. The final score read UCLA 13, OSU 6. The Bruins were 3–0.

UCLA opened conference play against a tough opponent, the Oregon State Beavers. OSU was ranked No. 19 in the country and were led by Ken Simonton and Steven Jackson on offense. Dennis Erickson had turned the Beavers into a consistent winner, but Coach Toledo had his best team since 1998, and the Bruins easily defeated OSU, 38–7 in Corvallis. Following a bye week, the Bruins played their fourth ranked opponent in five games, the Washington Huskies. By October 13, the Bruins had climbed all the way to the No. 4 team in the nation, so when Washington came to town, it was a top 10 matchup. Coach Rick Neuheisel had done a great job at UW, but there was nothing he, nor any of his assistants or players, could do to stop UCLA running back Deshaun Foster on this day. Foster finished with a school record 301 rushing yards. It was the eleventh 100+ yard performance of his career, and his four touchdowns moved him into sole possession of third on the all-time UCLA rushing touchdown list. The Bruins won, 35–13. They followed up the impressive victory against the Huskies with another convincing win over the California Golden Bears, routing them, 56–17. The record was now 6–0. Deshaun Foster looked to be one of the Heisman Trophy frontrunners. In the blink of an eye, however, everything would change.

The seventh game of the season, a matchup between the No. 20 Stanford Cardinal and the No. 4 Bruins, looked like many of the other games early in the 2001 season. The Bruins got off to a great start. Ryan Nece recovered a fumble and raced 39 yards for the first touchdown of the game. Nothing about this game was normal, however. Stanford would score the next 31 points, and the game was essentially over. The Bruins added 14 points, but it was too late. The perfect season had ended, and it would only get worse. One week later, the Bruins lost again, this time, 20–14, to the Washington State Cougars. Their season was falling apart. What they needed was a win. What they got was bad news. UCLA's best player, Deshaun Foster, would not play in the next game, nor would he ever play for the Bruins again. Before the team was set to take on another top opponent, they were hit with the news. It was discovered that Foster was seen driving an SUV owned by actor/director Eric Laneuville. This was dubbed an extra benefit and against NCAA rules. His season, his Heisman chances, his career—it was over.

The Bruins took on the Oregon Ducks in their ninth game of the year, and though the Ducks were ranked No. 6 in the country by the BCS, the Bruins hung around. The game came down to a field goal . . . and the Bruins missed. Final score: Oregon 21, UCLA 20. When UCLA took on USC, it was not the last game of the season. They had one more game to play, one that had been rescheduled due to the 9/11 attack months earlier. For the Trojans under new Head Coach Pete Carroll, it didn't matter when the game was played. They were there to prove things would be different under new leadership. The Trojans beat the Bruins, 17–0. It was an embarrassing defeat, and beating Arizona State one week later did little to make the Bruins feel better about their season. UCLA had a 7–4 record and declined to go to a bowl game for financial reasons. The season that once seemed so promising came to a close, not with glory, but rather inaction. As bowl games were being played, as stars were showing their talent, UCLA was sitting it out. Deshaun Foster was sitting it out. The UCLA-USC rivalry had turned a page. Pete Carroll was in, and soon Coach Bob Toledo would be out.

The Downtown Athletic Club named Eric Crouch from the University of Nebraska the 2001 Heisman Trophy Winner.

The University of Miami beat the University of Nebraska, 37–14, in the BCS National Championship game.

## 2002

In the summer of 2002, the Southern California sports scene was buzzing. The Lakers had just won the NBA championship, their third in a row. The Dodgers, led by outfielder Shawn Green and closer Eric Gagne, were in the thick of a division race. In Orange County, the Angels were in the midst of their best season in history, which ultimately culminated in a World Series title. At USC, there was hope once again. In Pete Carroll's first year, fans had seen promise; in his second year, they expected more. Under Coach Bob Toledo, the UCLA Bruins had steadily improved since 1999, but the brilliant seasons of '97 and '98 were drifting further and further into the rearview mirror. Though UCLA's best player, Deshaun Foster, was off to the NFL, the 2002 Bruins looked to be loaded with talent. The question that many fans wondered aloud when Coach Toledo was hired six years earlier remained: was he the man to lead the Bruins to the pinnacle of the college football world? He would have one more season to prove himself. Coach Toledo was on the hot seat.

The 2002 Bruins sported a list of new names unfamiliar to many casual fans. While Cory Paus and Ricky Manning Jr. would provide veteran leadership and playmaking, newcomers such as Drew Olson, Tyler Ebell, and Spencer Havner burst onto the scene. The 2002 season was a make-or-break one for Coach Toledo, and in the season opener he got exactly what he needed, a big win. The young Bruins entered the season unranked. Their first opponent, the Colorado State Rams, led by Sonny Lubick, were ranked No. 19 and had already played two games, winning both. For much of the game, the Bruins trailed. CSU jumped out to a 10–0 lead before UCLA got on the board for the first time on a second-quarter touchdown. For three quarters, UCLA's offense could do nothing else. Coach Toledo swore to play Drew Olson at least one series under center, and he played him two, but entering the fourth quarter, the Rams still led, 13–7. Five minutes into the fourth quarter, the Bruins offense finally broke through. Akil Harris scored from a yard out, and Manual White scored a 16-yard touchdown 64 seconds later. The Bruins took a 21–13 lead, and though the Rams scored a touchdown with under two minutes to play, their two-point attempt was unsuccessful. White added a late touchdown, and the Bruins won, 28–19. One week later, the Bruins won again, this time beating Oklahoma State, 38–24. Bruins fans had seen this act before.

On September 21, the No. 20 UCLA Bruins returned to the Rose Bowl to take on Big 12 opponent Colorado. With the Bruins already down, 13–7, Colorado Coach Gary Barnett called for the kind of trick play that would make even Bob Toledo proud. Quarterback Robert Hodge took the snap under Center and fired the ball backwards to Receiver Barry Kunkel, who looked left and then turned and threw the ball back to Hodge. The quarterback had a wall of blockers in front of him and took the ball all the way down to the UCLA 12-yard line. The Buffaloes went on to score and won the game, 31–17. In their final nonconference game of the regular season, the Bruins got back to their winning ways. UCLA improved its all-time record against San Diego State to 17–0–1 by beating them, 43–7.

When conference play kicked off, the schedule appeared decidedly easier than it had been one year earlier. Two of the toughest games for UCLA would come in the first two weeks. On October 5, the Bruins dodged Oregon State, winning 43–35. One week later, they were back at home, but their opponent was the Oregon Ducks, led by Jason Fife at quarterback and Onterrio Smith in the backfield. For the Ducks, replacing Joey Harrington was the big question mark entering the season, but Fife proved to be a valuable commodity. He would account for almost 3,000 yards and finished with 27 touchdowns for the season. UCLA outplayed the No. 7 Ducks for much of the game, but as had been common in the recent history of the series, the game would come down to the wire. Fife had another great game, completing 14 of 18 passes for 202 yards, but it was his scrambling that made the difference. The UCLA offense, which had gained 605 yards one week earlier, racked up 477, almost 100 more than their opponent. In a game that could have been a blowout, the Bruins were held back by turnovers. Paus threw for 316 yards and three touchdowns, all three of which went to Receiver Craig Bragg, but he also threw three interceptions. With just under two minutes to play, the Bruins found themselves in a familiar situation. A year earlier, they had lost to the Ducks on a late missed field goal by the usually reliable Chris Griffith. Now the game was again in the hands, or on the foot, of the kicker. Earlier, the Bruins had an extra-point attempt blocked and now trailed, 31–30. The previous miscue could be forgiven if they were able to execute now. Griffith lined up for a 46-yard field goal. This one would not be blocked, but it sailed wide left. History repeated itself. The Ducks held on. Final score: 31–30 Oregon.

For UCLA, the 2002 season was another frustrating one. They should have beaten Oregon. They should have been better than they actually were. The team was talented, but something was off. After the heartbreaking loss to the Ducks, the Bruins fell again one week later to the University of California. Quarterback Cory Paus separated his shoulder and was replaced by Drew Olson. The offense was never able to get on track, and the Bruins ultimately lost, 17–12. The Bruins' record fell to 4–3, and they were once again mired in mediocrity. For fans, the only thing left to look forward to was the future, and that future was now under center. Drew Olson got his first start at quarterback on October 26 against the Stanford Cardinal. Only 54,116 fans showed up at the Rose Bowl. UCLA won by a score of 28–18. One week later, they beat the University of Washington, 34–24, and on November 9 they traveled to Tucson, Arizona, and stomped the Wildcats, 37–7. In a season that seemed typical of the past four years, there was a bit of hope. The future was on display, and his toughest test was the next team on the schedule.

The Bruins entered the game against USC with a three-game winning streak and an extra week to prepare following a bye. Second year USC Head Coach Pete Carroll had turned the Trojans from a doormat to a contender. Entering the rivalry game, the Trojans were No. 8 in the BCS rankings and boasted a strong 8–2 record. The game was a tale of polar opposites. The Trojans were sharp, and the Bruins struggled mightily. On the opening kickoff, Tab Perry fumbled, and USC recovered. One play later, USC quarterback Carson Palmer hit Kareem Kelly for a 34-yard score. The game would never be in doubt. USC led, 21–0, at the end of the first quarter, 28–7, at halftime, 42–7, after three, and wound up winning by a score of 52–21. After the Bruins had won eight in a row over USC in the 1990s, USC had now won the previous four. UCLA had one remaining game on the schedule, and again they fell short to a good team. Washington State, the No. 6 team in the BCS rankings, beat the Bruins, 48–27.

The Bruins were invited to participate in, and accepted an invitation to, the 2002 Las Vegas Bowl on Christmas Day against the New Mexico Lobos, but head coach Bob Toledo would not be on the sidelines. On December 10, 2002, UCLA fired Toledo and named Assistant Coach Ed Kezirian the interim coach for the bowl game. Newly hired Athletic Director Dan Guerrero would say of his decision, "This was an extremely hard decision to make but one I felt was necessary for the future of the program. During the last five months, I developed a very good relationship with Bob and learned to have respect for all that he has accomplished at UCLA. This made the decision even more difficult. That being said, I believe that in order to revitalize our program and move it forward, a change of leadership is required. The circumstances over the past four years, both on and off the field, created an environment that, in my opinion, hindered long-term success." The Bruins would go on to win the Las Vegas Bowl, 27–13, over New Mexico and finish the season with an 8–5 record.

The Yale Club of New York City named Carson Palmer from the University of Southern California the 2002 Heisman Trophy Winner.

Ohio State University beat the University of Miami, 31–24, in the BCS National Championship game.

# CHAPTER 14
# Karl Dorrell (2003–2007)

When Bob Toledo was fired as the head coach of the UCLA football team in December of 2002, Dan Guerrero and the athletic administration were sending a clear message. The team needed new leadership. The mediocrity that defined Coach Toledo's final four years ultimately led to his termination, and in typical UCLA fashion, replacing him would not be without historic precedent. When Toledo was shown the door, the man who walked in was Karl Dorrell, the first minority head coach in Bruins football history. He was a UCLA alum, and, just as comes with the hiring of any new coach, excitement filled the program. He was not a household name to many younger fans at the time, but he was young, he had won multiple Rose Bowls as a player, and he was charged with taking UCLA to the next level.

Karl Dorrell, 2005

Karl Dorrell was born on December 18, 1963, in Alameda, California. He was the son of a military man. His father, John, was a member of the United States Navy, and as a young child, Karl moved to San Diego. It didn't take long for Karl to have the logistical skills and the discipline of his father. By the time he was eight years old, he was the local quarterback during street football games. In his spare time, he would also put together written playbooks. Playing with friends was fun, but so was thinking about the game and putting his ideas on paper. As a coach years later, he would be responsible for motivating others and convincing them to do things they might not otherwise feel necessary. As a boy, he did the same. He had a neighborhood newspaper delivery job, but often he was able to get out of work by convincing others that they should climb the San Diego Hills and deliver the papers for him because it would strengthen their legs and make them better athletes. For Karl, by the time he reached high school, the jump in competition was nothing he couldn't handle. At San Diego Helix High School he competed in multiple sports, but his best, and the one he was most passionate about, was football. While Karl was no longer a quarterback, he did have the ball in his hands often. He played wide receiver and as a junior led Helix High to a sectional championship. One year later, they would lose in the sectional championship, but Karl's career was far from over. Following his All-American senior season, it was time for him to make a decision about where he would attend college. Local school San Diego State recruited him fiercely and he considered the Aztecs, but ultimately the choice was UCLA.

As a freshman in 1982, Dorrell saw the field in limited action, finishing with just three catches for 48 yards. The Bruins went on to beat the University of Michigan in the Rose Bowl and finished as the No. 5 team in the Associated Press rankings. One year later, the Bruins were once again good, but now Dorrell was a key reason why. He finished his sophomore season with 390 yards receiving and six touchdowns. He saved his best performance for last. The Bruins again won the Pac 10 Conference and returned to the Rose Bowl on January 1. A crowd of 103,217 packed into the stands to see UCLA take on the University of Illinois, the No. 4 team in the country. Dorrell would finish the game with five catches for 61 yards and two touchdowns. The Bruins won, 45–9. His teammate and also future UCLA coach, Rick Neuheisel, was the game MVP.

Entering Dorrell's junior season, much was expected of him and the team. They had won two consecutive Rose Bowls, and Dorrell was improving each year. In 1984, the team was again successful, but Dorrell missed most of the season following a shoulder injury. The NCAA granted him an extra year of eligibility, and though the team won the Fiesta Bowl without him in '84, they welcomed him back with open arms in '85. As a fourth-year junior, he finished with a career-best 565 yards, and the Bruins once again won the Rose Bowl. One year later, he capped his career with another solid season and another bowl win, this time in the Freedom Bowl. Over five years, Dorrell finished with 1,517 yards, nine touchdowns, and five bowl wins, including three Rose Bowls. His 108 receptions ranked second in school history at the time of his departure. In 1987, he graduated from UCLA with a degree in psychology. Though he had a brief professional career with the Dallas Cowboys before being placed on the Injured Reserve, and retired shortly thereafter, his life in football would not be limited to wearing shoulder pads. He was a coach, and like the man who came before him at UCLA, his journey has shown that the life of a coach often includes many stops. He would eventually come home to the Bruins. But in 1988, he was just getting started.

Following his brief stint with the Cowboys, coaching was not even on the mind of Karl Dorrell. He was a computer enthusiast and dreamed of working for IBM. If not for the nudging from his former coach at UCLA, Terry Donahue, a man who would become a football lifer may have otherwise been a computer whiz. As a player, Dorrell rubbed off on others quite easily. Coach Donahue saw how meticulous he was with the details of the game. He recognized in Dorrell a man who enjoyed the Xs and Os, as well as the motivational aspect of bringing a team together. Donahue would say to Karl, in a push to convince him to join the coaching profession, "Karl, as a young minority coach you'll climb the ladder so fast you won't know what hit you." He was right. In 1988, Dorrell joined the UCLA staff as a graduate assistant. The team, led by Troy Aikman, finished with a 10–2 record and won the Cotton Bowl. In 1989, he got his first full-time position, spending one year as the receivers coach at Central Florida. Just as coach Donahue had predicted, Dorrell climbed the ladder in the coaching ranks at rapid speed. In 1990, he was named the offensive coordinator at Northern Arizona, directing them to a school record for first downs, and second-best total offense in school history. As Dorrell continued to build a résumé, he did so at many stops. He spent two seasons at Colorado State as the receivers coach, and then one at Arizona State. He spent four seasons as the offensive coordinator at the University of Colorado, and then one as the OC at the University of Washington. In 2000, Dorrell left the college coaching scene and was off to the NFL. For three seasons, he was the receivers coach for the Denver Broncos. In Dorrell's first season, veteran wide receiver Ed McCaffrey had the most productive season of his career, finishing with 101 catches and 1,307 yards. His teammate, Rod Smith, was even better, finishing with 100 receptions and 1,602 yards, a new franchise record. One year later, McCaffrey was injured early in the season, but Smith continued to shine, catching a franchise-record 113 passes. There was nothing more Coach Dorrell needed to prove. He was as ready as he'd ever be for a head coaching job. When the phone rang, he answered.

In 2003, after stops in seven other cities in his coaching career, Karl Dorrell was hired on his 39th birthday as the head coach of the UCLA football program. One of the reasons AD Dan Guerrero chose Dorrell was his experience facing the USC Trojans. Coach Bob Toledo had lost four consecutive games to USC, and Guerrero would say of Dorrell, "He knows something about rivalries . . . and the importance of those things in a city like Los Angeles." Not only was Dorrell's understanding of the UCLA-USC rivalry one of the reasons he was hired, but he was also expected to clean up the off-the-field issues that had plagued the Bruins under Coach Toledo. The results, in that aspect, were clear. Dorrell demanded accountability off the field and a commitment first and foremost to one's own integrity. On the field, the results didn't come so fast. In Coach Dorrell's first two seasons, it appeared the team was heading in the wrong direction. They finished both years with mediocre to subpar records, and entering 2005, pressure was once again starting to build. Fans were anxious. They wanted a winner. The 2005, season would ultimately be Coach Dorrell's best. He led the team back into the national spotlight. Though the Bruins would have memorable moments in Dorrell's final two seasons, such as the shocking upset of the Trojans in '06, they were never able to either replicate the season of '05 or improve on it. Following the 2007 season, Karl Dorrell was fired. His time at UCLA was not as satisfying as a coach as it had been two decades earlier as a player. But for a coaching lifer, this was not the end of the road. He would continue his coaching career, making pit stops throughout the country.

Though Dorrell would seek other head coaching opportunities following his firing by UCLA, he would find none. He may have struggled as a head coach, but he had a proven record as an assistant coach for 15 years. In 2008, the Miami Dolphins hired Dorrell as their wide receivers coach. For three years, he would coach WRs, and then in 2011, he was moved to the position of quarterbacks coach. In 2012, he coached quarterbacks for the Houston Texans, leading Matt Schaub to a Pro Bowl season. Dorrell had never failed as an assistant coach in his career, but in 2014, he was hired by the Vanderbilt Commodores as their offensive coordinator, and after just one year, in which the offense averaged only 17 points per game, he was relieved of his duties. Since 2015, he has coached receivers for the New York Jets. Coach Karl Dorrell has proven to be an effective position coach for almost 30 years. He was a winner in college as a player and can individually coach with the best of them. As for his time as the UCLA head coach, he had many believers when he was hired. Troy Aikman would say, "I am excited that Karl Dorrell is our head coach. When he was a graduate assistant coach in my senior year, you could tell he had the makings of an outstanding head coach." Terry Donahue would add, "Karl is an outstanding choice to head up the UCLA football program." NFL Head Coach Mike Shanahan showed his support for Dorrell by saying, "I think Karl Dorrell will do a great job at UCLA. Number 1, he's a great person. He's a very intelligent guy. He possesses a great work ethic and great morals. I think UCLA made a great decision." Coach Shanahan was correct. Karl Dorrell's intelligence was never questioned. His work ethic was never berated. By all accounts, he is a tremendous person. When Dorrell was fired following the 2007 season, the UCLA community did not have an angry word for him. They only wished to win more games. It's a goal that will never go away.

## 2003

When Karl Dorrell ran through the tunnel onto Folsom Field in Boulder, Colorado, on September 6, 2003, he did so for the first time as the UCLA football head coach, and he did so with a talented team running behind him. The UCLA defense was led by Spencer Havner, a human tackling machine at linebacker. Justin London and Brandon Chillar, along with Havner, created one of the most formidable linebacker units in the country. On the defensive line, Rodney Leisle was back for his senior season, and Jarrad Page was a leader in the defensive backfield. On offense, Drew Olson and Matt Moore would both play under center, and each had a plethora of talent surrounding him. Maurice Drew, Tyler Ebell, and Manual White created a strong 1-2-3 attack in the running game, and Craig Bragg, Junior Taylor, and Marcedes Lewis were the primary targets in the passing game. For Coach Dorrell, the question was not whether the team had talent, it was whether he could rally the team effectively enough to have a strong first season. Many of the best players were young, and all were new to Coach Dorrell. In 2003, the defense would perform well throughout the year. The offense was another story.

The first game of the Karl Dorrell era was a road matchup against the No. 24 Colorado Buffaloes. A Boulder crowd of 48,534 fans showed up to see the two teams kick off the new season, and they saw a close game. At halftime, the Bruins trailed, 10–7, but they were down not just on the scoreboard; they were without starting quarterback Matt Moore, who had injured his knee on a low hit in the first half. Drew Olson came in, and in the second half the Bruins offense suddenly came alive. After driving down the field, the Bruins were in a position to tie the game just minutes into the third, but kicker Justin Medlock missed a 35-yard field goal wide left. After the defense forced a fumble and recovered at the Buffalo 37-yard line, the offense was back on the field. The great break the Bruins received appeared to be wasted when, after two consecutive penalties, the Bruins faced third and 30. But Olson was able to find tight end Marcedes Lewis for a 38-yard gain that brought the ball all the way inside the Colorado 10-yard line. After another penalty brought the ball back to the 13-yard line, Olson found Lewis again, this time for the go-ahead score. Entering the fourth quarter, UCLA led, 14–10. With five minutes to play, the score had not changed, and the Buffaloes took over the ball at their own 37-yard line. Eleven plays later, quarterback Joel Klatt hit Joe Klopfenstein for a 6-yard touchdown. Brandon Chillar blocked Mason Crosby's extra-point attempt, and the score was 16–14, with just over two minutes to play. On the ensuing kickoff, the Bruins nearly lost any hope of victory after Maurice Drew fumbled, but he recovered it himself at the 10-yard line. The Bruins needed a field goal to win. It was not to be, however, and the drive ended after four straight incomplete passes by Olson. The Karl Dorrell era started with a loss to Colorado, 16–14.

One week later, the UCLA offense struggled again. Justin Medlock kicked two field goals in the first half. The offense was unable to score the rest of the game, but the Bruins' defense made up for the poor offensive play, holding the Illinois Fighting Illini to just one field goal and winning, 6–3, for Karl Dorrell's first victory as a head coach. The next game would be a tougher test. On September 20, the Bruins traveled to Norman, Oklahoma, to take on Bob Stoops and top-ranked Oklahoma. The Sooners' 83,317 fans who cheered on the home team saw something that had never before been done in college football history. Oklahoma's special teams ace Antonio Perkins returned three punts for touchdowns on the day, an NCAA record. His 277 total punt return yards also set an NCAA record. Star Oklahoma quarterback Jason White passed for two touchdowns on the day but also threw a key interception to Spencer Havner, who returned the pick 72 yards to the Oklahoma 6-yard line, where Manual White took it in for the score. UCLA was ahead, 10–7, but the lead would not last. When the Sooners needed a big play, they got it from Perkins. Final score: Oklahoma 59, UCLA 24. In the final nonconference game for the Bruins, it was a relief for their fans to see the San Diego State Aztecs instead of the Oklahoma Sooners. UCLA had historically dominated SDSU, and they continued to keep the series one-sided by winning, 20–10. UCLA was 2–2. In Coach Dorrell's first nonconference slate as a head coach, there were certainly positives. The defense had played well in three of the four games. There were also negatives, however. The offense and the special teams had struggled mightily. It was now time for conference play. Time for the Bruins to ride the roller coaster that would be their 2003 season.

In the conference opener, the Bruins were without the services of defensive lineman Rodney Leisle for the first half, suspended for punching an SDSU player in the stomach one week earlier. Without Leisle, the Bruins defense was without its leader, and without a great player. The Bruins offense continued to struggle, scoring just seven points. This time, however, at least in the first half, UCLA was unable to make up for the poor offensive play with a strong defense. The No. 18 Washington Huskies scored on three consecutive drives and took a 16–7 lead into the break. With the return of Leisle, however, came an immediate flip of the switch. The Bruins defense held the Huskies scoreless in the second half. Leisle himself scored a touchdown on a fumble recovery and intercepted a pass. Defensive end Dave Ball was a terror for the Huskies offensive line, and the Bruins offense suddenly looked formidable. Tyler Ebell, Maurice Drew, and Manual White all had touchdowns, and Jarrad Page had an interception return for a score. When the game mercifully came to a close for the Huskies, the favorites saw themselves on the wrong end of a beatdown: UCLA 46, UW 16. One week later, Leisle was again the difference. For the second week in a row, the 294-pounder performed more like a defensive back than a defensive lineman. With UCLA trailing the University of Arizona,

21–17, in the fourth quarter, Leisle intercepted a Kris Heavner shovel pass and returned it 55 yards for the decisive score. Halfway through Coach Dorrell's first season, the Bruins were 4–2, and undefeated in conference play.

The Bruins continued to win in thrilling fashion to begin the second half of the season. They found the end zone against the California Golden Bears three times on October 18. Quarterback Drew Olson threw for two touchdowns, but the Blue and Gold would also once again find a way to score a non-offensive unit touchdown. Spencer Havner blocked two field goals on the day, the second of which was returned 65 yards by Brandon Chillar for a score. The Bruins led, 20–12, with just seconds remaining on the clock, but the Golden Bears had a dangerous quarterback by the name of Aaron Rodgers, and he was marching his offense down the field. With 11 seconds to play, the Bears faced fourth-and-10 at the Bruins 35-yard line. Rodgers took the snap and fired for receiver Burl Toler, who hauled in the pass for a 35-yard touchdown. The score was 20–18. Cal was able to convert the two-point conversion, and the game went to overtime. In OT, it was a battle of the kickers, and UCLA had the better one. Justin Medlock knocked in a 41-yard field goal, and Cal kicker Tyler Frederickson missed from 50. The game was over. The Bruins escaped with another victory. One week later, a star was born. When the Bruins took on the Arizona State Sun Devils, fans were thrilled with the Bruins' perfect conference record but worried about the struggling offense. Freshman running back Maurice Drew rushed for 176 yards on the day, all of them in the second half. Matt Moore returned as the starting quarterback and struggled for much of the day, but Drew's dominant performance helped the Bruins come away with another win, this time by the score of 20–13.

The Bruins were undefeated in conference play and were riding a five-game winning streak entering the month of November, but that was deceiving. They were a flawed team. They had escaped with victory thanks to timely touchdowns from their defensive unit, and the defense, though strong, could not win games alone for the entirety of a conference season. On November 1, it all came crashing down. UCLA lost to Stanford, 21–14, and one week later they lost, 31–13, to No. 15 Washington State. What slight hopes UCLA may have had for a Rose Bowl appearance were now fading, and when they lost to the University of Oregon one week later, they were gone for good. The Bruins had won five games in a row earlier in the season, but now they were mired in a three-game losing streak. The offense was averaging just over 13 points per game in the losing streak, and the defense had slipped to giving up an average of 27 points per game. The Bruins were falling apart, and the next opponent was a National Championship contender.

When UCLA faced the USC Trojans on November 22, the two teams were going in opposite directions. Pete Carroll and the Trojans had won six games in a row, took the field with a 9–1 record, and enjoyed a No. 3 ranking in the BCS. Coach Dorell and the Bruins were simply trying to get through the season after falling apart in November. From the opening drive, it was clear that this was a mismatch. Just three minutes into the game, USC quarterback Matt Leinart found receiver Mike Williams for a touchdown. Seven minutes later, running back Lendale White scored, and in the blink of an eye, the Trojans led, 14–0. On the first play of the second quarter, Leinart hit Mike Williams for another score, and the floodgates were now open. USC would go on to win, 47–22, and finish as the No. 3 team in the final BCS rankings. Despite just a 6–6 record, the Bruins accepted an invitation to the Silicon Valley Bowl on December 30 against the Fresno State Bulldogs. UCLA's offense once again struggled, and the Bruins lost, 17–9. Coach Dorrell's first season was a disappointment. The Bruins finished with a 6–7 record. At one point, they had won five consecutive games, but they finished the season with a five-game losing streak. In 2004, coach Dorrell and staff would have to get better results from the talent that its offense possessed. Year one was over. There would be no more grace period.

The Yale Club of New York City named Jason White from the University of Oklahoma the 2003 Heisman Trophy Winner.

Louisiana State University beat the University of Oklahoma, 21–14, in the BCS National Championship game.

## 2004

2004 was a year of celebration and reflection for the

UCLA football program. It had been 50 years since Red Sanders led the Bruins to their lone National Championship—20 years since Terry Donahue led the Bruins to the Fiesta Bowl and beat the University of Miami. 2004 was also a time of turmoil. George W. Bush won his presidential reelection bid, and one of the largest topics throughout the campaign season was a new world conflict, the Iraq War. As the political arguments raged on, so did the fighting. For Coach Karl Dorrell, the UCLA Bruins, and the rest of the college football world, so did the games. In 2004, UCLA fans were clamoring for, and expecting, a jump in the UCLA win total. They expected a better team in year two of the Dorrell era than they had been granted in year one. They didn't get it.

When the Bruins took on the Oklahoma State Cowboys on September 4, there was a contrast of styles apparent to all watching. The Bruins were a balanced team. They passed the ball 36 times and ran the ball on 33 plays. The Cowboys were unable to pass the ball at all. They put the ball in the air just eight times and ran the ball 67 times. For Head Coach Les Miles and the Cowboys, there was simply no need to pass the ball. UCLA's Drew Olson passed for 252 yards and OSU quarterback Donovan Woods threw for just 23, but that was not the story. Manual White rushed for 145 yards and Maurice Drew added 44, but the Bruins combo was outperformed by the Cowboys' stellar running back group. Greg Jones rushed for 65 yards and Seymore Shaw added 64. But the star of the game was running back Vernand Morency, who finished the game with 261 rushing yards. The Bruins fell in their opener, 31–20. In Week 2, the Bruins took on the Illinois Fighting Illini. One year earlier, the Bruins had won, 6–3. For the UCLA offense, this was a game in which they aimed to demonstrate that they were no longer the porous offense they had been the previous season. In beating the Illini, 35–17, they were able to prove just that. In fact, the 2004 offense would turn out to be one of the most improved units in the entire nation, finishing in the top 30 in total offense in the entire country.

On September 18, the Bruins traveled to Seattle, Washington, to take on Head Coach Keith Gilbertson, Casey Paus, and the Washington Huskies. For fans of the Bruins, the Huskies, and all watching on television, this would be no ordinary game. It would be one for the ages. The first quarter surprised those just settling into their seats expecting the action to come at a normal pace. The opening quarter was a shootout. It was Hearns vs. Hagler circa 1985. It was instant and unending action. UCLA's Maurice Drew had runs of 47, 62, and 58 yards, racking up three touchdowns in his first four carries of the game. It was a spectacle. The 5'8" back with massive legs, excellent power, and blazing speed was the best player on the field; no one else was even close. Despite that, the UCLA defense, the strength of the team one year earlier, didn't help in any way during that first quarter. At the end of one, somehow the Bruins trailed the Huskies, 24–21. The rest of the game was played at a slower pace, but Drew was still brilliant. At halftime, UCLA led, 27–24. On just 13 carries, Drew had 235 yards rushing at the break, just 52 yards short of the NCAA record for a half. On the first drive of the second half, Drew proved he was more than just a 30-minute player; he scored on a 37-yard burst for his fifth touchdown of the day. UCLA led, 34–24, but the game was far from over. The Huskies added a touchdown of their own in the third quarter. After a UCLA field goal in the fourth, the score was 37–31 Bruins. The Huskies would have one final chance late in the game. With 39 seconds to play, UW took over on the UCLA 41-yard line and promptly drove to the Bruins 1-yard line. There was time for one final play. Paus took the snap and handed to Charles Frederick, who was immediately smothered by the Bruins at the ½-yard line as time expired! The Bruins hung on to win, 37–31, their fourth consecutive win over the Washington Huskies. Maurice Drew rushed for a school record 322 yards on the day and five touchdowns! The Bruins offense proved again that they were much improved one week later, with another strong performance. Final score: UCLA 33, San Diego State 10.

On October 9, the Bruins won their fourth game in a row, scoring at least 33 points in each game, by beating the Arizona Wildcats, 37–17. The Bruins looked to be an improved team, but the season would not be considered a success based on a nice winning streak alone. In the previous year, UCLA had won five consecutive, only to finish the season losing five in a row. The season would be judged by how the Bruins bounced back from an eventual loss. After beating the Wildcats, they didn't have to wait long. On October 16, the Bruins traveled north to

Berkeley to take on Heisman Trophy candidate Aaron Rodgers and the California Golden Bears. The team that UCLA once owned was now fielding one of its strongest teams in their history. The Bears were No. 8 in the country and had their eyes on the Pac 10 crown. Rodgers threw for a career-high four touchdowns against the Bruins, but he was not the only Bear to find success. J.J. Arrington ran for a career-high 205 yards and scored two touchdowns. Drew Olson also threw four touchdown passes, but it wasn't enough. Cal 45, UCLA 28. One week later, the Bruins were tasked with reversing the trend of a year earlier. They could finish the season competitively, or they could fold up their tents and go home. The Bruins took on the No. 18 Arizona State Sun Devils in Tempe and got off to a blazing start. The UCLA offense once again clicked. Drew and White each ran for a score, and Olson threw for a career-high 325 yards, including touchdowns to Marcedes Lewis and Tab Perry. The Bruins led, 42–31, in the fourth quarter, but if not for four Olson interceptions, the game would have been well out of reach. With 6:36 to play, Arizona State quarterback Andrew Walter took the game into his own hands. After hitting Derek Hagan for a 46-yard touchdown, the Devils trailed, 42–38. The Bruins offense then went three and out, and the ball was back in the hands of Walter, who knew exactly what to do with it. He found Terry Richardson deep for a 65-yard score, and suddenly the comfortable Bruins lead was now a deficit. After the successful two-point conversion, the score was 45–42 ASU, with just under five minutes to play. The Bruins were unable to do anything on offense the rest of the way. The Sun Devils added a field goal and won, 48–42. UCLA had outplayed ASU for much of the day, but turnovers and a leaky defense killed them. Walter threw for a career-high six touchdowns. The Bruins were 4–3.

Coach Dorrell and staff were able to right the ship, unlike the previous year. Following the defeat at the hands of ASU, the losing streak would extend no further. UCLA rebounded against Stanford, 21–0, but were unable to play consistently enough the rest of the way to finish with a hot streak. Washington State squeaked by UCLA, 31–29, and then UCLA beat Oregon, 34–26. With one game left, everyone knew whom the Bruins would be facing. On December 4, 2004, Coach Dorrell and the UCLA Bruins took on the No. 1 team in the nation, the USC Trojans. This time the challenge was monumental, and everyone knew it. USC was the best team in the land. They had Heisman candidates at quarterback, running back, and receiver. They had a strong defense and superior talent at nearly every position, but anything could happen in a rivalry game. Drew Olson vs. Matt Leinart appeared to be a mismatch on paper, but when the clock hit :00, Olson could be proud to say he had held his own against a star player. Olson threw for 278 yards to Leinart's 242. Olson threw for one touchdown and two interceptions. Leinart had no touchdowns and one interception. The statistical difference between the two teams came in the running category. USC running back Reggie Bush rushed for 204 yards on the day, and Lendale White added 75. Maurice Drew, Manual White, and the rest of the Bruins ground attack struggled throughout, finishing with just 17 yards rushing as a team. Still, the game remained close. At the end of the first quarter, the Bruins trailed, 10–0, but by halftime the Bruins found their stride and were comfortable being on the same field as the Trojans. In the second quarter, Craig Bragg returned a punt 96 yards for a touchdown, the longest punt return in school history. When the teams went to the tunnels, the score was 20–10. With the score 29–17 in the fourth, Olson found Marcedes Lewis for a short score with 2:20 to play, to cut the deficit to five. UCLA was unable to stop the USC running attack, and it appeared the game was over. But the Bruins got one last chance. With 53 seconds to play, Bush fumbled, and UCLA linebacker Spencer Havner recovered at the UCLA 14-yard line. On the next play, however, Olson was intercepted by Jason Leach, and the Trojans went on to win, 29–24. It was USC's sixth consecutive win over the Bruins, their longest streak in school history. UCLA would again go to a bowl game with just six wins, and on December 23, they lost to the Wyoming Cowboys, 24–21, in the Las Vegas Bowl. For Coach Dorrell, his second season was only minimally better than his first. The Bruins finished with a 6–6 record. In 2005, he would have to turn it around. His seat was getting hotter.

The Heisman Trust named Matt Leinart from the University of Southern California the 2004 Heisman Trophy Winner.

The 2004 BCS National Championship title is vacant.

## 2005

In 2005, Karl Dorrell had a breakthrough. In two years under his leadership, the Bruins were just 12–13. They lost to USC twice and lost in lower-tier bowl games both years, as well. Entering the 2005 season, the Bruins were an unknown. They had a talented roster, but compared to their rivals across town, they were beaten at nearly every position. Patience was wearing thin with the Bruins, who had done little more than tread water for the past six seasons. The once-solid Bruins defense of 2003 struggled in 2004 and lost key players in 2005. The offense, which was abysmal in 2003, was better in 2004 but lacked the depth that USC and California had. In 2005, Drew Olson would finally have a breakout year, and though the running back across town received more national attention, the man in the backfield for the Bruins, number 21, was a marvel to watch. In 2005, the Bruins were back, but could they finish the job?

On September 3, 2005, the Bruins took on the San Diego State Aztecs in the season opener. It was the 21st all-time meeting between the two teams, and UCLA had yet to lose, only once tying the Aztecs in 1924. UCLA's key players began the season in dominant fashion. Quarterback Drew Olson finished 10 for 15 for 152 yards, a solid performance, but he was bested by the other two big names on offense. Maurice Jones-Drew finished with 114 yards and two touchdowns on the ground, as well as a 72-yard punt return for a touchdown. Tight end Marcedes Lewis had seven catches for 131 yards on the day. On defense, Spencer Havner was once again great, intercepting his first pass of the year, and cornerback Michael Norris added an interception. The Bruins won easily, 44–21. In the second game of the year, the Bruins were even better. After the game, Rice Head Coach Ken Hatfield would say, "It was a physical mismatch. They're just plain better than us." He was simply speaking the truth. The Bruins scored on their first six possessions. Olson threw for 296 yards, three touchdowns, and no interceptions before UCLA's offensive starters were pulled just one possession into the second half. Jones-Drew scored twice, including another punt return touchdown. Receivers Junior Taylor and Brandon Breazell accounted for three touchdowns through the air. When the UCLA starters left the game, the Bruins led, 49–15, and went on to win, 63–21. In the Bruins' third and final nonconference game, they took on the team that had whipped them in Norman one year prior. When the Oklahoma Sooners came to the Rose Bowl on September 17, they brought with them the label of the No. 21 ranked team in America. They would not be ranked one week later, after the Bruins beat the Sooners, 41–24. Oklahoma's super sophomore running back and Heisman Trophy candidate Adrian Peterson was held to just 58 yards on 23 carries. Olson was again spectacular, finishing with 314 yards passing, three more touchdowns, and again no interceptions. The Bruins were 3–0. It was time to take on the Pac 10 Conference.

The Bruins began conference play in the same fashion they had ended nonconference play, with a win. After falling behind, 10–0, at halftime and trailing, 17–7, entering the fourth quarter, the Bruins finally awoke from hibernation, scored 14 unanswered points, and squeaked by the Washington Huskies, 21–17. UCLA was 4–0, but their next test would be their toughest one yet. On October 8, the No. 20 Bruins took on the No. 10 California Golden Bears. UCLA entered with a modest four-game winning streak, and the Bears came to the Rose Bowl sporting an impressive 12-game winning streak. Coach Jeff Tedford worried that his Bears would be unable to stop UCLA's elusive back, Maurice Jones-Drew. His worries were confirmed when the two teams hit the field. The Bears were the more complete team. They had a running attack that the Bruins were powerless to stop. They sported two backs, Justin Forsett and Marshawn Lynch, who could take any carry the distance. Their star receiver, Deshaun Jackson, was the fastest man on the field. He ran precise routes and was unguardable one-on-one. Forsett would finish the day with 153 yards and a touchdown. Lynch finished with 135 and a score. Jackson caught 10 passes for 128 yards and a touchdown. Cal's offense was dynamic, and after a 36-yard field goal by Tom Schneider early in the fourth quarter, the Bears led, 40–28. UCLA would obviously have to score two touchdowns to take the lead, but just as important, and perhaps more difficult, they would have to stop the Bears. Following the Cal field goal, Olson marched the Bruins quickly downfield and capped the drive by plunging in on a quarterback sneak from a yard out to bring the score to 40–35. After the Bruins stopped the Cal offense, they had the ball and a chance to take the lead. For UCLA, there was utmost confidence in Olson's ability to lead the team to the winning score, but it was Jones-Drew who would be the man with all eyes on him. He had two rushing touchdowns already on the day and another punt return score. After moving the ball to the California 29-yard line, the Bruins faced a third-and-1. All in the stadium and those watching on television knew that UCLA would try to get the ball to Jones-Drew. Cal stacked 10 in the box to stop the run. The Bruins lined up with their tight end to the left and three in the backfield. Jones-Drew lined offset to the right in a three-point stance. At the snap, Olson rolled to the right, and Jones-Drew sprinted to the right flat. Jones-Drew caught the ball at the 28-yard line, turned up the sideline, and, like a man running on an airport moving walkway, sprinted past the defense as if they were standing still. At the 3-yard line, there was only one man who had a chance to stop him. Jones-Drew hurdled into the end zone, bounced off the defender, and scored! It was Jones-Drew's fourth touchdown of the day, and the crowd went wild! The Bruins went for two, but the attempt failed. With 1:35 remaining on the clock, the Bears simply needed a field goal, but 16 seconds later, Trey Brown intercepted a pass to seal the deal. Jones-Drew scored a final touchdown as time expired, and the Bruins won, 47–40. Jones-Drew finished the day with 299 total yards: 162 on punt returns, 65 rushing, 52 receiving, 20 on kick returns—and five total touchdowns. The Bruins were 5–0.

One week after beating the California Golden Bears, the Bruins were committed to avoiding a letdown, and though the Washington State Huskies played them close, the game ended 44–41 with the Bruins on top. When the first BCS rankings of the season came out on October 17, the Bruins saw themselves in the No. 9 spot, certainly a shock to those preseason prognosticators who had seen UCLA as nothing more than an average team. The Bruins kept their winning streak alive the following week when they took on the Oregon State Beavers. Jones-Drew was once again brilliant, finishing with 120 yards on the ground, 67 through the air, and another near punt return for a touchdown. The star of the game, however, was Drew Olson. He threw for six touchdowns, a school record. UCLA powered past Oregon State, 51–28. The team was cruising. They had won seven games in a row, and after beating the Stanford Cardinal one week later, the winning streak reached eight.

On November 5, the No. 5-ranked Bruins took on the Arizona Wildcats in Tucson. UofA, led by Mike Stoops, was just 2–6 on the season. They had one of the worst offensive attacks in the conference and a middle-of-the-road defense. While the game was on paper a mismatch in favor of the Bruins, it turned out to be a mismatch on the field in favor of the Wildcats. Coach Stoops's primary goal on defense was to slow down Jones-Drew and make Olson, who was more than capable, beat him through the air. Jones-Drew was held to just 41 yards rushing and 25 receiving. Olson finished with 232 yards passing and two touchdowns, both of which went to Marcedes Lewis. Olson's two touchdown passes gave him 25 on the season, tying a school record. But UCLA's offense was able to muster up nothing more, and the UCLA defense was abysmal all game. UofA freshman quarterback Willie Tuitama, starting just his second career game, threw for 204 yards and two scores. Gilbert Harris rushed for 113, and the Wildcats ran up 52 points. The Bruins were no longer undefeated, and they were embarrassed. Coach Dorrell said after the game, "Obviously we did not play to our capabilities as an offense, defense, special teams, and we got outcoached, as well. It was one of those humble butt-kickings that you're going to have to take and get yourselves ready to play again next week." As UCLA players and coaches watched Arizona fans storm the field when the clock hit :00, they could see their dreams of a BCS crown all but disappear. With two games to play, however, dreams of a Pac 10 title were still alive.

One week after the stunning loss to the University of Arizona Wildcats, the Bruins got back on track against Arizona State. Olson and ASU quarterback Rudy Carpenter dueled for four quarters, but ultimately the Bruins' gunslinger came out on top. Carpenter finished with 334 yards and three touchdowns. Olson's final line read 22 of 27 for 510 yards, 5 touchdowns, and 0 interceptions. It was a fitting way for the Bruins to head into a break. UCLA would not play for three more weeks. Their next opponent was the No. 1-ranked USC Trojans. Entering the final game of the season, the Bruins were ranked No. 12, and though USC was a heavy favorite and one win away from a berth in the BCS National Championship game, there was something on the line for the Bruins, as well. It was the 75th game between the two rivals. UCLA would not be going to the Rose Bowl with a win because the Rose Bowl was to be the National Championship game, but they could knock the Trojans out and win the Conference title at the same time. For UCLA, the issue was not the offense. Olson, Jones-Drew, and Lewis had led the Bruins to one of the best offensive seasons in their history, and a top five offensive ranking in the country. The problem was their defense. The rushing defense was No. 115 in the country, and the two backs in Trojans uniforms were two of the best in the nation. As it turned out, the game would not be competitive from the very beginning. Reggie Bush was unstoppable. He rushed for 260 yards. Lendale White added 154. At halftime, USC led, 31–6. At the end of the game, the scoreboard read USC 66, UCLA 19. The Bruins were 9–2. Coach Dorrell had led the Bruins to their best season since 1998, but the regular season ended in disappointment. USC won its seventh consecutive game against the Bruins, only one short of the eight consecutive the Bruins had won in the 1990s. USC was off to the National Championship game. The Bruins were off to the Sun Bowl. The Bruins' bowl game would be the final appearance in blue and gold for Olson, Jones-Drew, Lewis, and star linebacker Spencer Havner. All had memorable careers. Olson finished his career second all-time in passing yards and touchdowns for the Bruins. Havner was a four-year starter and All-American. Jones-Drew and Marcedes Lewis would each have long NFL careers, mostly as teammates with the Jacksonville Jaguars. Jones-Drew was an All-American in 2005 and the first Bruin to lead the country in punt returning since Jackie Robinson. Lewis was also an All-American in 2005 and won the John Mackey Award, presented to the best tight end in America. The star players had received attention for much of the year, but in the bowl game, it was Brandon Breazell who made the highlight reel. With 2:29 remaining in the game, Northwestern cut the Bruins lead to 36–31 and lined up for an onside kick. The kick went to Breazell, and, rather than fall on the ball, he returned it 43 yards for a touchdown. With 23 seconds remaining, the teams were in the same position. The Wildcats had scored again and once more needed an onside kick recovery. For the second time, Breazell recovered the kick and raced for a touchdown. The Bruins won, 50–38, closing out a strong season with a wild bowl win. The Bruins finished with a 10–2 record. In 2006, Coach Dorrell was tasked with improving his team despite massive losses to the NFL.

The 2005 Heisman Trophy is vacant.

The University of Texas beat the University of Southern California, 41–38, in the BCS National Championship game.

## Maurice Jones-Drew

Maurice Jones-Drew, 2004

Maurice Jones-Drew, the most exciting player at UCLA in a generation, was born on March 23, 1985, in Oakland, California. As a boy, he loved the Oakland Raiders and idolized such Raiders stars as Tim Brown, Rich Gannon, and Napoleon Kaufman. As a young athlete, however, it was not a Raider he patterned his game after, it was a Detroit Lion. It was the best player in Lions history, Barry Sanders. Before the pros, however, and before dominating the Pac 10 Conference, there was high school. There was

De La Salle, the place where a legend was born, the place where a 5 foot 7 inch running back first made his name. MJD, as he would become known, was not just a football player, he was a multisport athlete. Known then as Maurice Drew, he competed in football, track and field, and in his free time enjoyed snowboarding and swimming. On the track, he was a sprinter and a member of the De La Salle 4x100 State Championship relay team. While he was fun to watch on the track, he was breathtaking on the football field.

As a sophomore, Drew was part of a championship team, something he would become accustomed to; but he was not the star. The De La Salle Spartans would finish the season undefeated and win the mythical high school national title. In 2001, as a junior, Maurice Drew made a name for himself. He rushed for nearly 2,000 yards on the season and finished with 26 touchdowns, but it was one game and one performance that opened the eyes of the high school and college football world. On October 6, 2001, De La Salle, the No. 1 team in America, took on Long Beach Poly, the No. 2 team in the nation, in a rare nationally televised high school game. The Spartans were talented. They were disciplined. But compared to the Long Beach Poly Jackrabbits, they were small. De La Salle entered the game with a winning streak dating back almost a decade. The Jackrabbits came in with a slew of division one recruits, including Drew's eventual college and NFL teammate, Marcedes Lewis. It was the first-ever meeting between the top two ranked teams in high school football, and Drew did not disappoint. Before the game, Drew asked announcer Jim Watson to hype him up if he ever got the chance. It wouldn't take long for him to get his wish. On the opening kickoff, Drew fielded the ball at the 7-yard line, shot through a seam, and picked up 33 yards on the return. On the first offensive snap, he rushed for 13 more yards. Three minutes later, Drew took a screen pass on the Long Beach Poly 25-yard line, made one cut inside, weaved back toward the sideline, and sprinted toward the end zone. At the Jackrabbits' 13-yard line he dipped down to take on a would-be tackler and ran right through the defender. Nearing the end zone, Drew jumped from the 2-yard line, did a front flip, and landed into the end zone for the first touchdown of the game! Watson had no need to hype up Drew; the young man had earned it on his own. Drew would prove he was worthy of all the attention he received. Nearly 15,000 fans had showed up to see the two best teams in the nation, and instead of coming away talking about how the bigger Long Beach Poly players had worn down the smaller Spartans, all the buzz was about the short running back no one could stop! Drew finished with four touchdowns on the day, and the Spartans won, 29–15. The Spartans went on to finish the season undefeated and won another National Championship. For Drew, this game was his coming-out moment. In a game filled with stars, none were better than the back often overlooked. The Spartans would again finish undefeated in Drew's senior season, but no more was he ignored. He became one of the top recruits in the nation, and luckily for Coach Karl Dorrell and UCLA fans, he chose the Bruins.

Coach Dorrell and the UCLA football coaching staff knew they had an obvious talent on their hands when Drew arrived on campus. The question for them was, how do they use him? He played linebacker in high school, but he was much too short to play there in college, or so they thought. He was a star with the ball in his hands, but his potential durability was questioned, again due to his size. Playing cornerback was an option, and he actually saw action there four times during his college career, but he was too dynamic with the ball in his hands to take him away from offense permanently. Drew was short, but he was not small. He had been doubted his entire life. He was said to be too short to play running back. A 5 foot 7 inch back couldn't possibly take the beating that came with college and professional football. He just continued to prove them wrong. Ultimately, offense was his destiny. He had a powerful build. His legs were built like redwood tree trunks. His upper body was carved out of stone. He had impeccable balance and the ability to play with such a low pad level that he rarely took on major contact despite being a power runner. He had sprinter speed, perfect vision, and the instincts that all great running backs have. He was the perfect package. As a freshman, he was a sensation, but not just on running plays. He was a great pass catcher and an even better return man. Drew would be named a Third Team Freshman All-American in 2003. His 582 yards rushing led the team. His 26.65-yard kickoff return average was the 14th best in the country. His 83-yard rushing touchdown against Arizona State was the longest in the Pac 10 for the season, and his 99-yard kickoff return for a touchdown against USC was the longest by a Bruin in 23 years.

Despite a season shortened due to injury, Maurice was again brilliant as a sophomore. In just eleven games, in two of which he left early because of injury, he accumulated 1,606 all-purpose yards, good for fourth best in UCLA history at the time. He averaged 6.3 yards per carry on the season and was just as dynamic in other facets. He became the first UCLA Bruin to finish a season with at least 100 total yards in each of the four all-purpose categories. He was named to the Second Team All-Pac 10 team and was named the Offensive Team MVP. His best individual moment as a Bruin came on September 18, 2004, when he rushed for a school record 322 yards against the University of Washington, breaking Deshaun Foster's previous school record of 301. For Drew, his sophomore season was dynamic. His junior season would be even better.

As a junior, much went right for Maurice Drew, but it started with tragedy. In the second game of the season for UCLA, Maurice's grandfather was watching the Bruins take on the Rice Owls when suddenly he had a massive heart attack and died at the Rose Bowl. Coach Dorrell had a duty to his team to try to win the game, but as a man he had a duty to do what was right in the moment. On the sideline, Coach Dorrell walked up to Drew and broke the news to him. Maurice had been raised by his grandparents, and the loss hurt him deeply. His grandfather was his idol, and now he was gone. Maurice dedicated the rest of his season, and the rest of his career, to his grandfather. He would from that moment on have his entire legal surname, Jones-Drew, be a part of his uniforms to honor that legacy. His grandfather, was unable to see his grandson shine from the Rose Bowl seats during his junior year, but he had a view from the heavens as MJD dominated college football. MJD would finish his junior season, his final as a UCLA Bruin, with a spectacular campaign. He was named a consensus All-American as a returner, a role in which he thrived, in historic fashion. In 2005, he became the first UCLA Bruin to lead the country in punt returning since Jackie Robinson sixty-five years earlier, and his 29.5 yards per punt return is still an NCAA record today. The Bruins finished the season with a 10–2 record, the best for UCLA since 1998. For the man who was doubted in high school, and then again in college, he was off to the NFL. He had to prove more doubters wrong.

In preparation for the NFL draft, MJD went through the same process as thousands of potential football players have done throughout the years. He trained. He went to the NFL combine. He participated in the UCLA pro day. For him, unlike many others, it was not a time to check the boxes and prove to NFL coaches that he was everything his film said he was; it was a time to prove he was even better. He was a first-round talent, but again the same issues surfaced. He was said to be too small. He was said to be inferior to the running back across town, Reggie Bush. He was said to be a receiver out of the backfield and a return man, but not someone who could carry the workload as a lead back. At the combine, he weighed an impressive 207 pounds. He ran the 40-yard dash in a blazing 4.39 seconds. He was everything a first-round back should be, but he was overlooked once again. Maurice Jones-Drew was selected by the Jacksonville Jaguars, 60th overall, in the 2006 NFL draft. The Jaguars had also selected his UCLA teammate, Marcedes Lewis, but in the first round. Jones-Drew wore number 21 in college, but in the NFL he would change to number 32. The symbolism was not a secret. He told a national audience on Sirius XM NFL Radio that he chose 32 because all 32 teams had passed on him in the draft. He would make them pay.

As a rookie, MJD was used primarily as a third-down back behind veteran Fred Taylor, but as the season went on, it became more evident that the Jaguars could no longer keep their dynamic talent contained. Against the Indianapolis Colts, he rushed for 166 yards and added a 93-yard kickoff return for a touchdown. He averaged nearly six yards per carry for the season and finished with 16 touchdowns, finishing second in the Rookie of the Year voting. As MJD's career went on, he defied the odds and he continued to star, but no longer in a secondary role. As Fred Taylor's usage went down, MJD's went up, and by the time he reached his fourth season with the Jags, Maurice Jones-Drew was a household name. He finished the season with almost 1,400 yards, 15 rushing touchdowns, and a berth in the Pro Bowl. MJD had reached the top of his profession. In 2011, he won the NFL rushing title. He was a three-time Pro Bowler, a 2011 All-Pro back, and one of the most dynamic players in the NFL. By 2014, however, he was wearing down. The shelf life of an NFL back is short, and MJD had maximized his talents. After joining the Raiders in 2014 and rushing for just 96 yards, it was clear his career was over. On March 5, 2015, Jones-Drew announced his retirement from the NFL. Fifty-four days later, he signed a one-day contract with the Jaguars and officially retired with the team that had given him a shot. Upon his retirement, fans were able to reflect on the career of one of the league's best running backs. He retired as the Jaguars' all-time leader in rushing touchdowns and total touchdowns. He finished with over 8,000 career rushing yards and nearly 3,000 receiving yards.

Jones-Drew returned to UCLA to finish his studies and in 2013 said he envisioned one day getting a law degree, becoming an NFL general manager, and gaining a partnership in an NFL ownership group. For MJD, his postretirement plans first dealt with two of his greatest personal qualities: teaching and entertaining. In 2015, he returned to De La Salle as a part-time football coach. No longer was the legendary football coach Bob Ladouceur roaming the sideline for the Spartans, but Jones-Drew's alma mater was still the best high school team in the state. With one De La Salle coaching legend now enjoying retirement, it was a welcome sight to see another legend join the coaching staff. When not helping young running backs hit the correct holes, he was helping viewers on NFL Network understand their favorite teams. In August 2015, MJD joined the on-air staff for the NFL Network and appears as a regular analyst on *NFL Now*, as well as serving as an analyst on *NFL Fantasy Live, Madden NFL Live,* and *The Top 100 Players*. In 2017, MJD started his own fitness training business.

Maurice Jones-Drew and his wife, Ashley, have three children, and his legacy lives on not only in his offspring, but in the minds of every fan who ever saw him play. He was unlike anyone ever seen before. He was so short, yet so powerful, so fast, and so electrifying. Bruins fans will long remember his performance against the Washington Huskies, his game-winning touchdown against the California Golden Bears, and all the kickoff and punt returns he took to the end zone. As a public figure, Jones-Drew never hides his love for the Bruins, and fans never hide their love for the player who took their breath away. Maurice Jones-Drew may have left for the NFL in 2006. He may be a coach and a TV star. He may go on to be an executive in the NFL. He may do anything he wishes, but for the fans who saw him in the blue and gold, he is a Bruin, and he always will be.

## 2006

2006 was a big year for coach Karl Dorrell and the UCLA Bruins. For two years under Dorrell's leadership, UCLA had been a middling program, but in his third year, suddenly the Bruins were one of the best teams in the country. They reached as high as No. 5 in the BCS rankings and played for the Pacific 10 Conference title in the final regular-season game of the year. Still, they had lost to USC in 2005, the third year in a row under Dorrell, and though Dorrell's seat was no longer blazing hot, he would need to have another strong season in 2006 to keep the pressure from mounting. On offense, the Bruins of 2006 would have a new look. Gone was Drew Olson as the starting quarterback, and in were Patrick Cowan and five-star quarterback transfer Ben Olson. Maurice Jones-Drew was gone to the NFL, and Chris Markey and Kahlil Bell would be taking the bulk of the carries. Marcedes Lewis was gone, and the Bruins had no man to replace his production in the passing game. Instead, the UCLA offense would rely on Brandon Breazell, Marcus Everett, Junior Taylor, Logan Paulsen, and the rest of their weapons to make up the difference. On defense, Spencer Havner was gone, and so was Marcus Cassel. Losing Cassel's production was something his teammates could make up for, but, tragically, they lost much more than that: in November, 2006, Cassel passed away after suffering injuries in a car accident. The Bruins' defense was still talented in 2006. Bruce Davis and Justin Hickman would emerge as stars. Rodney Van and Reggie Carter were key contributors. None, however, were more important than Dewayne Walker, the new defensive coordinator for the Bruins who would turn the unit into one of the most formidable in the country, and when all eyes were on the team in their biggest game of the year, the defense turned in one of the best performances in school history.

Entering the first game of the season, all the questions that had been asked during the offseason were finally answered, at least for one game. How would the much-hyped new UCLA quarterback fare? Ben Olson threw for 318 yards, three touchdowns, and no interceptions against the Utah Utes. Would Markey and Bell be able to replace Maurice Jones-Drew? They didn't fare as well. The two combined for just 66 yards. What about Marcedes Lewis? Tight end Logan Paulsen did a fine job. He finished with 90 yards receiving. While the offense was certainly strong, it was the defense that opened eyes. Trey Brown intercepted his first pass of the year, and a true freshman by the name of Alterraun Verner intercepted another one, taking it back for a 34-yard touchdown. Verner, just a three-star recruit coming into UCLA, was expected to redshirt, but not only would he have an excellent freshman year, he finished as a freshman All-American and would go on to have an excellent four-year career. Verner was a solid tackler and had a propensity for intercepting passes and returning them for touchdowns. He would eventually earn the nickname "Pick Six." The Bruins passed their first test of the season. Final score: UCLA 31, Utah 10.

For the Bruins, only so much could be learned from the first game. With a slew of new players, they were sure to have their share of both ups and downs. The Bruins won their second game of the year over the Rice Owls but fell in the conference opener against Tyrone Willingham and the Washington Huskies. With a 2–1 record, but 0–1 in conference play, the fourth game of the year had significant impact. If the Bruins were to prove themselves a good team, they would need to avoid an 0–2 conference start that usually signifies doom. On September 30, the Bruins took on the Stanford Cardinal at the Rose Bowl. The Cardinal were struggling, so they were just the team the Bruins needed to face. Though the Blue and Gold were sluggish for much of the first three quarters, with their only points coming on a blocked punt and a fumble recovery, UCLA came alive in the fourth quarter, outscoring Stanford 17–0 in the final frame. Freshman Chane Moline scored two touchdowns on the ground, and the Bruins beat the Cardinal, 31–0. It was UCLA's first shutout in two years, and Stanford's 0–5 start was its worst in 23 years. For the Bruins, the month of October started in the same way that the month of September ended. On October 7, the Bruins dismantled the University of Arizona, 27–7. The rest of the month wouldn't go so well.

The Bruins were 4–1, but the schedule ahead looked daunting. On October 14, they traveled to Eugene, Oregon, to take on the Oregon Ducks, led by star quarterback Dennis Dixon. Going into the game, UCLA's run defense was tops in the Pac 10 and second in the country. Oregon's offense was premised on running the ball first to open up the passing game. It was a battle of two strengths, and the Ducks prevailed. Oregon ran for 256 yards, 121 of which came from running back Jonathan Stewart and 69 from Dixon. Patrick Cowan was now the man under center for the Bruins, filling in for Olson, who had been injured one week earlier. Cowan finished with only 112 yards passing, no touchdowns, and one interception. Markey ran for 97 yards, but it was not enough. Oregon 30, UCLA 20. One week later, the Bruins found themselves in an even tougher game, with an even better opponent. The Bruins traveled to South Bend, Indiana, to take on the Notre Dame Fighting Irish, ranked No. 8 in the BCS rankings. Notre Dame presented a stark contrast at the quarterback position to the Bruins, who were without Olson, the man they were counting on to be their next big star. Cowan proved to be a reliable backup, but he was no Brady Quinn, the Golden Domer quarterback who was one of the best in the nation. Still, UCLA put up a battle. Notre Dame may have had the advantage at quarterback, but up front it was a different ball game. The Bruins defensive attack was relentless, pressuring Quinn all game. With 2:25 remaining and the Bruins leading, 17–13, the Irish faced a fourth-and-1 at the Bruins 35-yard line. Quinn took the snap, dropped his center of gravity, and pushed for the first-down marker. He hit a wall! He was stopped. The Bruins took over at the 35. Despite the prediction of the announcers, the game was far from over. Notre Dame had all three timeouts remaining, and the Bruins had a struggling offense. For three consecutive plays, Cowan turned and handed the ball to Markey, who was able to gain only one total yard. On fourth down from the 36-yard line, Aaron Perez punted. It was a poor punt, and after the return, the Irish had the ball at their own 37-yard line. There was a holding penalty on the Irish, however, and Coach Dorrell chose to rekick. Perez boomed the next punt into the end zone. Notre Dame took over at their own 20-yard line with 1:02 to play, trailing by four. Within just 16 seconds, Quinn and the Irish had the Bruins on their heels. They had advanced the ball to the Bruins 45-yard line with 46 seconds still remaining. On first-and-10 with the clock running, Quinn took the snap. He had a great pocket—the Bruins pass rush got nowhere. Quinn stepped up, looked middle, pump-faked to the middle of the field, and scrambled right. Just as he reached the hash mark, he fired a laser throw to Receiver Jeff Samardzija at the 30-yard line. Samardzija broke one tackle, and at the 10-yard line he cut inside, broke another tackle, and raced for the end zone! Notre Dame took the lead, 20–17, and held on to win. It was a heartbreaking loss for the Bruins. For just the third time in Notre Dame history, they scored the game-winning touchdown with under 30 seconds to play. Brady Quinn would go on to be a first-round NFL pick and have a brief pro career. Jeff Samardzija chose to play Major League Baseball rather than pursue the NFL and has had a long, successful career. For the Bruins, the loss was crushing. They were a young team who dared take on a college football power. They would not come out victorious this day but would again face a top team—with a different script—later in the year.

Recovering from the heartbreaking loss in South Bend was not easy, and neither was the schedule that lay ahead. One week after losing to Notre Dame, the Bruins took on Washington State University and lost, 37–15. The losing streak reached four one week later in Berkeley. The Bears were ranked No. 10 in the country and beat the Bruins, 38–24. UCLA was now 4–5. A once-promising season had turned to one of disappointment, but the season wasn't over, and the Bruins would rally. For two consecutive games, the Bruins again looked like the team of September, not October. The offense was never explosive, but facing Oregon State and then Arizona State, it did just enough. Against the Beavers, the offense scored 25, and the Bruins defense was dominant, holding former Bruin Matt Moore and the Beavers offense to just seven points. Against the Sun Devils, the Bruins used the same formula to come out on top. Final score: UCLA 24, ASU 12. There was one game left on the schedule, and it was the big one.

When the Bruins took on the USC Trojans on December 2, few gave them a chance of winning. USC was the No. 2 team in the BCS rankings and with a victory would head to their third consecutive BCS Championship game. Like the Bruins, the 2006 USC Trojans were not the same team as the previous year. Matt Leinart, Reggie Bush, and Lendale White were all off to the NFL. The new Trojans were led by John David Booty at quarterback, Dwayne Jarrett at receiver, Chauncey Washington at running back, and a menacing defense. Unlike the Bruins, the Trojans were able to handle the loss of personnel without a major drop-off. Conversely, unlike the Trojans, the Bruins were disrespected. They were tired of playing well and coming up just short. They were tired of USC beating them. The Trojans had won seven consecutive times against the Bruins. The record winning streak in the UCLA-USC series was eight—by UCLA in the 1990s—and the Bruins had no intentions of letting the Trojans match that number. Early in the game, it was clear to the Bruins, and to quarterback Patrick Cowan, that the Trojans defense was unlike anything they had seen all season. They were big. They were fast. They hit harder than any team in America. Still, they were not tougher. They did not have more heart. Cowan repeatedly dropped back, and, when his receivers weren't open, he quickly tucked the ball and ran, and at the end of every run there was a USC defensive player ready to unload on him. The first score of the game would fittingly come on a Patrick Cowan run. With one minute remaining in the first quarter, Cowan rolled right, looking for Markey in the front corner of the end zone, but he wasn't open. Cowan cut in, dived for the goal line, took a hit, and crossed the chalk for a touchdown. After a safety, the Trojans were within five points when Booty, CJ Gable, and the Trojans offense mounted their best drive of the game, capping it with a short touchdown run one minute before the half to bring the score to 9–7 USC at the break. The game was predictable, or so many thought. Underdogs can often hang around with the heavy favorites for a half, but seldom can they do it for four quarters. The Bruins had no plans of stopping after 30 minutes. In the third quarter, Cowan, Marcus Everett, and the Bruins continued to march. Medlock knocked in a field goal, and again the Bruins led. Their defense was relentless. The pass rush was a force. The run defense was a wall. After another field goal, the Bruins extended the lead to 13–9, and with six minutes to play, UCLA had the ball and was looking to put the game away. On third-and-10, Cowan rolled right, decided to keep the ball, cut upfield toward the sideline, and after seven yards met USC linebacker Ray Maualuga, who hit Cowan with what SportsCenter anchor Scott Van Pelt described as a hit that "would have killed either one of us." The Bruins were short of the first down, but not short on emotion. Cowan bounced to his feet, up before Maualuga, as if to prove that the hit would not stop the Bruins. UCLA punted. During the break, Coach Dorrell brought his entire team together and in his finest moment as a coach inspired in his team a fighting spirit that cannot be described with simple words. The Bruins as an entire team, one unit, bounced up and down, staring at their rivals, challenging them to come take this game from them. USC had the ball at their own 39-yard line. Fourth and 1. The game was on the line. Booty took the snap and executed a quarterback sneak for a first down. The Trojans were in business. With two minutes to play, Booty hit Steve Smith at the 25-yard line. Forty-five seconds later, it was third-and-four at the UCLA 18-yard line. Booty took the snap and dropped back five steps. To his left, Steve Smith was running a short out to the sideline. Rodney Van was all over Smith. Booty threw it anyway. Coming off the right edge for the Bruins was fifth-year senior Eric McNeil. As Booty released the ball, McNeil jumped, tipped the ball, landed on the ground, quickly did a full 180-degree counterclockwise turn, and dived for the ball. McNeil intercepted the pass, and the Bruins won! It is arguably the single greatest defensive play in UCLA football history. The Trojans would not go to the BCS Championship. The era of USC dominance was over. As of this writing, they have not been to the Championship since. The 13–9 victory by the Bruins was more than just another game. It is a memory that will live on forever in Westwood. Pete Carroll stood on the sideline with a blank look on his face as the clock hit :00, and Coach Dorrell was showered with Gatorade. The Rose Bowl crowd went wild. The Bruins had scored the upset. UCLA defensive end Bruce Davis famously said after the game, "They overlooked us. They thought they were on their way to the National Championship. Lee Corso, Kirk Herbstreit, we had another thing coming! Thank you, and that's all I gotta say!"

The Bruins season would not finish with the thrilling victory over their hated rival, but rather in a bowl game. The Bruins took on Florida State University in the Emerald Bowl on December 27 and fell, 44–27. It was a fitting way for the season to end. The joy of victory over the Trojans would certainly not be squashed with a disappointing bowl performance, but when the entire season is judged, it can be seen as nothing other than disappointing. The Bruins finished with a 7–6 record and unranked. Looking ahead to 2007, Coach Dorrell was in an uncomfortable position. USC was still good, but they had fallen from their absolute peak. The Pac 10 Conference was welcoming to any team that could knock the Trojans off their pedestal. For one game, the Bruins did it in '06. Fans were hoping to do it for an entire season in '07. It was a daunting task, and fans were hoping that, with an experienced roster, their team would be up to the challenge. It would be nine more months until it all started again.

The Heisman Trust named Troy Smith from Ohio State University the 2006 Heisman Trophy Winner.

The University of Florida beat Ohio State University, 41–14, in the BCS National Championship game.

## 2007

2007 was coach Karl Dorrell's last season with the UCLA Bruins. In five seasons, he cleaned up the Bruins' off-the-field image. The team was accountable, but they weren't winning enough. Coach Dorrell and staff did not recruit at the level of Coaches Bob Toledo or Terry Donahue before him. Nor did they recruit to the level that was expected of UCLA coaches. The team was thin on talent and, save for the occasional big game, short on toughness. Coach Dewayne Walker had instilled in the Bruins defense what coach Dorrell had hoped to instill in the entire team, but it was simply not enough. The Bruins were mediocre, and they had been for some time. The 2007 season again lacked star power on offense. They lacked flash, and, ultimately, they lacked enough victories.

The season began with high expectations. The Bruins were ranked No. 14 by the Associated Press to start the season. On September 1, Coach Dorrell and staff traveled to Palo Alto to take on the Stanford Cardinal. For the second year in a row, Ben Olson began the year under center, and he put on a show.

Stanford was a poor team. They had finished the 2006 season with just one win, and following the season, they hired University of San Diego coach Jim Harbaugh to take over. Harbaugh would ultimately have success, but not in his first game. UCLA's Olson threw for 286 yards and five touchdowns. Kahlil Bell ran for nearly 200 yards. The power offense that Harbaugh hoped to utilize was futile. The Cardinal rushed for only 52 yards. Receiver Richard Sherman was the only bright spot for Stanford, finishing with 100 yards receiving and a touchdown. The Bruins won, 45–17. It was a good start to the season, though entirely expected.

The Bruins' first two games of the nonconference slate were against two old rivals from the state of Utah, and the results would be vastly different. Against the BYU Cougars, Olson struggled, but Trey Brown intercepted a pass, returning it for a touchdown, and Kai Forbath knocked in two field goals to help the Bruins to a 27–17 win. One week later, they took on the University of Utah Utes, and the game didn't go as well. The Bruins came into the game No. 11 in the country and left wondering what had happened. Olson passed for 290 yards, but for no touchdowns, and threw three interceptions. The offense finished with just 83 yards rushing, and a meager six points. On the other side, Utah was flawless. They didn't physically pound the Bruins, and they didn't have a quarterback throwing pinpoint passes, but they executed and were mistake-free. Final score: Utah 44, UCLA 6.

The Bruins were 2–1. They were crushed by a Mountain West Conference opponent, and now two conference games were next on their schedule. UCLA would go on to beat the University of Washington and Oregon State in back-to-back weeks. The Bruins' victories were impressive. At the end of September, they were 4–1. In their four wins, they averaged 39 points per game and were giving up just under 20. On October 6, the Bruins had revenge on their minds, but they ran into a problem they couldn't overcome. For two years, Olson and Patrick Cowan shared the quarterback responsibility, alternating as the starter depending on who was healthy enough to play. Olson had been named the starter to open the 2007 season, but he was hurt and missed the game against the Washington Huskies three weeks later. While Olson was healthy enough to take on the Notre Dame Fighting Irish, Cowan was not. The Bruins needed Olson to play, and needed him to get through uninjured. When Notre Dame came to the Rose Bowl, they did so for just the second time in school history. In their only other appearance in Pasadena, legendary ND coach Knute Rockne and the "Four Horsemen" had defeated Pop Warner and the Stanford Indians, 27–10, in the 1925 Rose Bowl. Now, in 2007, the Irish were not the caliber of the Four Horsemen, nor were they even as good as their 2006 team. Brady Quinn was gone, and the Irish relied on heavily touted freshman quarterback Jimmy Clausen. Through five games, he had yet to show the promise that every recruiter in the nation saw in him when he played at Oaks Christian High School. The Irish were 0–5. Early in the game, the Bruins' worst nightmares came true. Ben Olson went down with another injury, this time to his knee on an awkward tackle by Notre Dame safety Tom Zbikowski. McLeod Bethel-Thompson, a walk-on, was pressed into emergency duty for the Bruins. This would not be a fairy tale. Bethel-Thompson threw for only 139 yards. He finished with four interceptions and a fumble that was returned for a touchdown. The Bruins defense was spectacular, holding the Irish to just 159 yards on the day. The Bruins racked up 322 yards, but ultimately it was turnovers that cost the Bruins the game. Final score: Notre Dame 20, UCLA 6. McLeod Bethel-Thompson is remembered most by Bruins fans for his performance against the Irish, but it is not the only story of his life. Following the season, he transferred to Sacramento State, and though he put up scant numbers there as well, he never gave up on his dream. Bethel-Thompson played on five NFL teams, including three stints with the 49ers and two each with the Vikings and Dolphins.

The Bruins were now 4–2, and after a bye week, they welcomed a strong team to the Rose Bowl. On October 20, the No. 12 California Golden Bears took on the Blue and Gold. It would be a thriller. Patrick Cowan was back under center for the Bruins, and the crowd of 83,494 who showed up at the Rose Bowl was happy to see him, as well as Cal's best player and one of the best receivers in America, Desean Jackson. Cal would strike first on the day, but it was not to Jackson. Quarterback Nate Longshore found Craig Stevens for a 21-yard score in the first quarter, and in the second quarter the offenses loosened up, and action was at a furious pace. The Bruins scored 10 straight points, including a touchdown from Cowan to tight end Logan Paulsen, but the Bears answered back. Longshore hit Jackson for a 39-yard score to give the Bears a 14–10 lead. Kai Forbath tacked on a short field goal, and at halftime, the Bruins trailed, 14–13. In the third quarter, the two teams exchanged touchdowns. The Bruins' score came on a trick play. Receiver Brandon Breazell found Dominique Johnson for a 29-yard score. The Bears answered in a more conventional manner: they found their best player. Jackson scored his second touchdown of the day on a 2-yard pass, and the score was 21–20 at the end of three. The game would come down to the wire, but it was not any offensive play that defined the game, but rather a defensive play. After Kai Forbath kicked a field goal from 27 yards out with just over three minutes to play, it was up to the defense to hold onto the lead. Unfortunately, it appeared the defense would fail them, as Cal had an attempt at a field goal for the win. With 1:46 on the clock, the Bears were already in field-goal range. The ball rested at the UCLA 30-yard line. Cal coach Jeff Tedford wanted to gain a few more yards, possibly pick up a first down, to give his kicker a better shot. It was third-and-5. Quarterback Nate Longshore took the snap and looked left. He haphazardly turned his body and lobbed a throw into the left flat for Jackson. But UCLA star cornerback Alterraun Verner would not be beaten on this play. He undercut the route, picked off the pass at the UCLA 25-yard line, and raced down the sideline. From the moment he caught the ball, all in attendance and watching on ABC-TV knew he would not be touched. Verner raced for the end zone, and as he crossed the goal line, he crushed the dreams of the Bears faithful. Touchdown Bruins! Victory Bruins! The man they called "Pick Six" delivered in the most crucial moment. The crowd at the Rose Bowl was in a frenzy. At one point in history, the California Golden Bears were nothing but a toy for the powerful Bruins. Now the Bears were the favorites, and they had been toppled.

Following the dramatic win over the Bears came the disappointing collapse that ultimately led to the end of the Karl Dorrell era. The Bruins were 5–2 but would suddenly see their promising season turn into another forgettable fall. The Bruins went on to lose to Washington State, Arizona, and Arizona State in successive weeks. On November 24, the script that had played out a month and a half earlier was reversed. The Oregon Ducks were ranked No. 9 in the country and had their sights firmly on a Rose Bowl berth. Their star quarterback, however, Dennis Dixon, had torn his ACL nine days earlier and would miss the rest of the season. Oregon's backup quarterback Brady Leaf wouldn't last long. In the first quarter, Leaf exited with an injury, and the Ducks were stuck with two inexperienced signal callers, Cody Kempt and Justin Roper. Neither was able to restart the once-electrifying Oregon offense. Kai Forbath kicked three field goals, including a career-long 54-yarder. The Bruins were able to add only one touchdown, but the defense held Oregon scoreless, the first time they had been shut out in 22 years.

The Bruins were 6–5. They would go to a bowl game regardless of how they fared against the USC Trojans, but that was not good enough. Coach Dorrell heard the rumblings and knew that he would likely have to pull off an upset over the Trojans once again to keep his job. On December 1, the Bruins took on the No. 8 USC Trojans. The motivation was there, but the magic of the previous year was not. USC jumped out to a 17–0 lead and went on to win, 24–7. One day later, Karl Dorrell was fired as the head coach of his alma mater, the UCLA Bruins. Coach Dorrell was given an option to coach in the bowl game but declined. Defensive coordinator Dewayne Walker was named the interim coach, and the Bruins accepted an invitation to the Las Vegas Bowl against the No. 17 BYU Cougars, a team they had beaten three and a half months earlier. UCLA was the better team on the day but as so often before was unable to clinch the deal. Kai Forbath made field goals of 22, 52, and 50 yards. UCLA's lone touchdown came on a Bethel-Thompson 4-yard hookup with Breazell. With seconds to play, Forbath lined up for another field goal. This time, he wasn't successful. Defensive lineman Eathyn Manumaleuna jumped up and blocked Forbath's low kick. The Bruins finished the season with a 6–7 record. It was time to turn the page. A new era was beginning. Read on if you dare.

The Heisman Trust named Tim Tebow from the University of Florida the 2007 Heisman Trophy Winner.

Louisiana State University beat Ohio State University, 38–24, in the BCS National Championship game.

# CHAPTER 15
# Rick Neuheisel (2008–2011)

In 2008, the Bruins once again started a new era. After the Bob Toledo tenure came to an uninspired close, Coach Karl Dorrell had been given his shot, and again the Bruins failed to recapture past glory. When Rick Neuheisel became the UCLA football coach, there were again high hopes. He was an accomplished coach with an impressive résumé. He had been a UCLA quarterback who led the team to a Rose Bowl victory. He was a master public speaker, a natural with a microphone in his hand. He had a past that led to constant message board chatter. He had a life that some would envy, while some have chastised. Despite everything Coach Neuheisel brought with him to Westwood in 2008, none of it mattered. The fans wanted wins. They wanted to see Coach Neuheisel again at the Rose Bowl on a January afternoon, but this time with a headset on. Coach Neuheisel was a Bruin through and through, but passion alone does not make a great coach.

Rick Neuheisel was born on February 7, 1961, in Madison, Wisconsin. As a boy, Rick was not a product of the Badger State, but of the Grand Canyon State. Rick and his three sisters grew up in Tempe, Arizona. Though Rick was a three-sports star at McClintock High School, no coaches and no recruiters ever came knocking on his door. He was a whiz kid. He was smart and could go to almost any school in the country, but he wanted to play football. He was the best athlete at his school, but that honor would have meant little if his sports career had ended at 18 years of age. As a senior, Rick was considering two schools, Princeton and Dartmouth. He valued his education but wanted to not only attend a fine academic institution, but also play on the biggest college football stage. In the Ivy League, he could achieve only one of those goals. He was set to head east, likely to play football for four years, get a great education, go to law school, and live the life of an attorney. That is, until coach Terry Donahue came calling. There would be no scholarship. There would be no guarantee of playing time. There would be no luxurious recruiting pitch. For Rick, the decision was simple. At UCLA, he could receive the same Ivy League-level education *and* could play in a top football conference. He was sold. He chose UCLA.

For Rick, UCLA was everything he was told it would be. He majored in political science, and he was a scout team quarterback. Getting a UCLA degree is challenging, but for Rick beating out other quarterbacks proved just as difficult. Neuheisel was at first relegated to scout team duty and holder for kicker John Lee. He was seen as less essential than most contributors and underwent full contact practice sessions against the first-team defense. He volunteered to also be on the kickoff team in practice, and though he was slow and small, he ran downfield and attempted to help the team in any way possible. Rick would use his time as a practice punching bag not to weep, but to challenge himself. As a boy, his father, Dick, would regularly challenge him. He would say, "If you can beat me, Ricky, maybe you can get a new bicycle." Rick would come close, but his father always won. The inner challenges that Rick faced in his first years at UCLA were not the only time his competitive juices got flowing, however. In the beginning of practices, Neuheisel would challenge the other quarterbacks during warmups. Soon they had a routine. They would compete for the title of most accurate by throwing passes at the field goal crossbar. It was an ongoing challenge, and Rick usually won.

In 1980, the Bruins went 9–2. They beat USC in thrilling fashion and went on to win the Mirage Bowl in Tokyo, Japan. Rick, however, was not the man under center. That was Tom Ramsey. One year later, Ramsey was still the man, and Steve Bono was waiting in the wings. For Rick, not playing was frustrating, but he understood he was a walk-on quarterback. He never expected to play significant snaps. He simply had to stay ready, just in case. When he was a junior, the Bruins won the Rose Bowl, and Neuheisel saw his first action. He finished the year with just 22 attempts, 13 of which he completed for 235 yards, two touchdowns, and two interceptions. One year later, the unthinkable happened. As a senior in 1983, Rick Neuheisel finally got his shot at quarterback. After coming to UCLA as a walk-on, with no major scholarship offers, he was the starter for the defending Rose Bowl champions. Things didn't go according to his plan, however, at least not in the beginning. The Bruins started the season 0–2–1. They had played a difficult schedule, including the No. 1-ranked Nebraska Cornhuskers, but it mattered little. Rick wasn't getting the job done. After three games, he was benched. Steve Bono took over. For Rick, it was a familiar sight. He had watched from the sideline for three seasons. His time on the sideline, however, would not last long. Bono was injured in his first game as the starter. The Bruins lost to BYU and fell to 0–3–1. When Rick was inserted back into the starting lineup, it already seemed like a lost season. He would prove the doubters wrong.

Rick finished his senior season with 2,245 yards and 13 touchdowns. His 69.3 percent completion percentage is still the highest in UCLA history. His career was not defined by season statistics, but by two of his greatest moments. On October 29, 1983, the 3–3–1 Bruins took on the No. 11 Washington Huskies. Rick finished the day completing 25 of 27 passes, and the Bruins pulled off an upset. His 92.6% completion percentage set a then-NCAA record. The mark is still highest in UCLA history. With Rick's success came team success. After he was reinserted into the starting role, the Bruins won five in a row, six out of seven, and they beat the USC Trojans on November 19 to win the Pac 10 title and a berth in the Rose Bowl. Rick was named Honorable Mention All-Pac 10, but his dream story didn't end with a conference crown. Despite winning the Pac 10, the Bruins entered the Rose Bowl game unranked. Their opponent, the No. 4 Illinois Fighting Illini, still had an outside shot at a National Championship. The Bruins were heavy underdogs, but the day before the game Rick had another problem: his stomach. The Bruins had their team dinner at a local steakhouse, and a handful of players came down with food poisoning. None, however, were more high profile than the quarterback, and he was in bad shape. Backup QB and roommate David Norrie would later explain how bad Neuheisel was feeling when describing the sound of his vomiting at 3:30 in the morning. By the time warmups were over the next day, and viewers were settling in across the country to watch the biggest spectacle in college sports, Rick was still struggling. His face was pale. His body was shaking. He told his father that morning, "Dad, I'm sick. I don't know if I can play." Rick heard the message he needed. His father, who regularly challenged him growing up, was there to do so once again. Dick would say to his son, "This is the most important game of your life. You've got to pinch yourself." Rick pushed through his illness and was brilliant. He threw for 298 yards on the day and four touchdowns. The Bruins not only upset the highly favored Illini, they crushed them. The final score was 45–9 Bruins. Rick Neuheisel was named the Rose Bowl MVP, and 15 years later he was inducted into the Rose Bowl Hall of Fame. Much had changed in the life of Rick Neuheisel since leaving McClintock High School. He had gone from walk-on to MVP. He had gone from scout team punching bag to star quarterback. While the aura around Rick Neuheisel may have changed, one thing stayed the same. He was always up to a challenge. It was time for the next phase of his life.

Rick played two years in the United States Football League and had a brief, five-week career in the NFL in 1987 as a replacement player during the NFL players strike. As a rookie in the USFL, he threw for over 2,500 yards, but his future would not be as a player, but rather as a coach. Rick's objectives were lofty. He set the bar high. His first goal was to climb the ladder as fast as possible. He wanted to be an offensive coordinator, and he didn't want to wait long. He wanted to be a head coach eventually, and he wanted to be like the man who had coached him in college. He wanted to be young when he got to that point, and he wanted to run the show. In 1986, Neuheisel returned to UCLA as a graduate assistant. While attending law school across town at USC, his major job in '86 was to tutor a young transfer quarterback from Oklahoma, Troy Aikman. In 1988, he received his first full-time coaching position. For two years, he coached the quarterbacks, and in 1990 he became the receivers coach at UCLA. In his time with the wideouts, he helped tutor some of the finest receivers in school history: J.J. Stokes, Kevin Jordan, and Sean LaChapelle. Not everything went as planned, however, for Neuheisel at UCLA. In 1993, he was eyeing the offensive coordinator position. He believed he was the frontrunner, having been at UCLA for eight years, but was passed over. Coach Terry Donahue instead hired Bob Toledo to run the offense. Rick's sister, Nancy, later described his disappointment as "a kick in the stomach." Coach Neuheisel was passionate. He believed he had earned the job. He was hurt, and then he was gone.

In 1994, Coach Neuheisel got the title he coveted, but not at the school he had hoped for. He was named offensive coordinator for the University of Colorado Buffaloes, and once he set foot on campus in Boulder, he made a splash. Television cameras frequently caught the youthful Neuheisel running up and down the sidelines, cheering on his team. His quarterback, Kordell Stewart, was a national name, and the offensive coordinator was the man who encouraged him. Kordell's greatest moment as a college player, and Neuheisel's greatest as an OC, came against the Michigan Wolverines. The Buffaloes trailed almost the entirety of the game, but on the final play, the star quarterback unleashed a Hail Mary that found the hands of Michael Westbrook in the end zone. The game was dubbed the Miracle at Michigan. It would not be the only big break Neuheisel had that year. When coach Bill McCartney resigned near the end of the season, the Colorado administration began a national search, but their answer was already on the staff. Neuheisel was considered an outside contender for the Colorado head coaching position, but his lifelong charisma paid off when he interviewed for the job. Neuheisel nailed it. At age 34, Rick Neuheisel was named the head coach of the University of Colorado. He was the youngest big-time college coach in the nation.

For four seasons, Rick Neuheisel was head coach of the Colorado Buffaloes. He was nicknamed by many around the program "Kid Genius," and he proved why in his first season. Colorado finished with a 10–2 record and a New Year's Day victory in the Cotton Bowl. Both the AP and the Coaches Poll named the Buffaloes a top-five team in the final rankings of the season. One year later, they won 10 games again, and again finished as one of the best teams in America. But 1997 would not be a third consecutive great season under Neuheisel. After falling to the Michigan Wolverines early in the season, the Buffaloes collapsed and finished with just a 5–6 record. In 1998, however, the team rebounded and finished 8–4. In four seasons, Coach Neuheisel compiled a 33–14 record, but his team in Boulder was not perfect, nor was his NCAA slate 100 percent clean. Neuheisel was a ferocious recruiter, and he demanded the same from his staff. He was a legal scholar, having finished law school in 1990 and passed the bar in 1991. He looked for loopholes. He found some. He created more. The NCAA was watching. Neuheisel would park across the street from players and call them. Colorado staffers would hand out sweatshirts, tee shirts, and shorts on visits. He committed violations, but many were considered minor. Fans looked past the minor infractions. They liked having a coach who could relate with young players. They liked hearing him play his guitar on his weekly radio show. They liked his youthful energy. Though Coach Neuheisel would have run-ins with the NCAA at Colorado, it was only the beginning.

In 1999, Rick Neuheisel left Boulder for Seattle. He became the head coach of the Washington Huskies, and as he had done at Colorado, he won games and also blurred the lines of what was right and wrong. In 1998, the Huskies had finished 6–6 under head coach Jim Lambright. In 1999, under Coach Neuheisel—no longer a young coach flying under the radar—the Huskies improved, ever so slightly. Coach Neuheisel was making one million dollars per year, making him one of the five highest-paid coaches in the nation. Fans expected more than seven wins, and in year two they got it. The Huskies were led by star quarterback Marques Tuiasosopo, and though expectations were high going into the season, the

Huskies even exceeded them. UW finished with an 11–1 record and the No. 3 ranking in both major national polls. The next two years were difficult. Replacing a star like Tuiasosopo can set a team back, and though the Huskies had to replace one of the best players in school history, they still reached consecutive bowl games, finishing with a two-year overall 14–10 record. Coach Neuheisel was the answer for UW, but again he found himself in trouble. In March 2003, Neuheisel participated in an NCAA Basketball Tournament Pool. Simply filling out a bracket was not a problem. Gambling was. Initially, Neuheisel denied gambling but later admitted to it. He was fired by the University of Washington, though his infraction was neither beneficial nor harmful to the image of the program. Neuheisel sued both the NCAA and the University of Washington for his termination and in March of 2005 was awarded $4.5 million in a settlement. Neuheisel felt vindicated, but he had lost two seasons of high-level coaching. It was time to get back to work.

In 2005, Neuheisel was named quarterbacks coach for the Baltimore Ravens of the National Football League. One year later, with new quarterback Steve McNair, the Ravens finished with a 13–3 record, and after the season Rick was promoted to offensive coordinator. Though Rick was again a success, he wanted back into the college football world and hoped to be back with his alma mater. He got his wish. On December 29, 2007, Rick Neuheisel was hired as the 15th head coach in UCLA football history. He arrived in Westwood with a 66–30 coaching record. Neuheisel would say of his hiring, "I am thrilled to be returning to my alma mater as its head coach. UCLA is a special place and I want to thank Dan Guerrero and chancellor [Gene] Block for the opportunity to come home. We are going to build a program our supporters will be proud of, both on and off the field. I can't wait to get started." For the most part, fans rallied behind Coach Neuheisel. His passion and commitment was unquestioned. In Los Angeles, Neuheisel's personality shined. He regularly appeared on local radio and never could say no to an open microphone. He was a media darling, but he had to win. Coach Neuheisel's first major move as head coach of the Bruins was to hire what was called a "Dream Team" coaching staff. Defensive coordinator Dewayne Walker was retained, and Norm Chow was named the offensive coordinator. Hopes were high entering the 2008 season. Coach Neuheisel gleefully claimed that the monopoly in Los Angeles was over. The Bruins were going to end the reign of USC dominance. It was time to prove it on the field. But over four years, coach Neuheisel never was able to find the success at UCLA that he had in Boulder and Seattle. Following the 2011 regular season, Neuheisel was fired, and though the Bruins would participate in the postseason, his coaching career at UCLA was over. Following his final practice, Coach Neuheisel was carried off the field by his players. The team loved him, but he worked in a results-oriented business, and his 21–29 record at UCLA was simply not good enough.

Following his termination by UCLA, it didn't take long for Coach Neuheisel to find a new passion. In December of 2011, he was hired by CBS Sports as a college football analyst. Four months later, he joined the Pac 12 Network. Neuheisel was a natural on television. He's smart. He's witty. He's personable. In 2014, he was nominated for an Emmy Award for Outstanding Studio Analyst. In his brief career on television to date, Neuheisel has been a star, but his greatest personal moment came not while he sat behind a desk, but rather when he sat in front of a television set. On September 13, 2014, Coach Neuheisel was working for the Pac 12 Network while his son, a back-up quarterback for the UCLA Bruins, was in Texas. UCLA was taking on the University of Texas in Dallas at AT&T Stadium, home of the Dallas Cowboys. The stadium had been nicknamed "Jerry's World," but on this day, it was not Jerry Jones to whom the nickname belonged, but Jerry Neuheisel. After quarterback Brett Hundley exited with an early injury, in came Jerry. Meanwhile, his father watched from the San Francisco studio. With three minutes to play, Jerry pump-faked to the left and found receiver Jordan Payton streaking down the sideline. He let the ball go, and it landed perfectly in Payton's hands for the game-winning touchdown. Rick, unaware that the cameras were rolling, stood up, pumped his fast, and yelled, "Yeah! That's my son." Jerry was carried off the field just as his father had been three years earlier, this time not in sadness, but in joy. Rick Neuheisel couldn't help but cry as he watched his son deliver on national television. In March 2015, Neuheisel became an analyst for *College*

*Football Today* on CBS. In the three and a half decades since Coach Neuheisel first stepped on campus, his life has taken many twists and turns. He was the Rose Bowl MVP. He was a successful college football coach. He coached in the NFL, and he came back to coach his alma mater. Though his time on the Bruins sideline was not the success that many had hoped for, his greatest achievement may be yet to come. He is the father of a man who has his own aspirations of coaching. Coach Neuheisel is a Bruin, and he loves his school. He once declared his dreams of seeing UCLA hoist a National Championship trophy. Maybe one day that dream will come true, and maybe the coach will be a different Neuheisel. Rick Neuheisel is no longer a paid football coach; he is a member of the sports media, and he has found a new career. If he ever decides to rejoin the coaching profession, he will have suitors, and he will have fire. For Coach Neuheisel, the "Passion Bucket" never ran dry. He served the Bruins with pride, and he gave everything he had. That much can never be questioned.

## 2008

When the 2008 UCLA football season began, few knew what to expect. Karl Dorrell was gone, and Rick Neuheisel was the new man in charge. Neuheisel had been successful in both of his previous stops as a head coach, but turning around his alma mater was all that Bruin fans cared about. It had been 10 years since the Bruins won the Pac 10 Conference and nearly made the BCS Championship game. Coach Neuheisel assembled a staff that was dubbed "The Dream Team," and fans hoped to no longer see lackluster offensive performances. With a first-year coach, there is always a grace period. Fans, media, and other observers knew that Coach Neuheisel was unlikely to be able to turn the Bruins around in year one. They were confident and hopeful that he would end USC's monopoly in Los Angeles college football, but it would take time. In 2008, the Bruins simply needed to show promise. They needed to be competitive. For Coach Neuheisel and staff on one spring day, the plan would change, and so would the expectations.

On April 24, 2008, the injury bug hit the Bruins, and it hit them hard. After Patrick Cowan beat out Ben Olson for the starting quarterback job, they both went down, and the storyline changed. Cowan injured his knee, and Olson broke his foot. Neither would play again for UCLA. The Bruins had several other QBs on the roster, but none with any experience. Osaar Rasshan became a quarterback-turned-wide receiver-turned quarterback once again. He was ineffective in brief playing time. McLeod Bethel-Thompson was ineffective as well, and he would ultimately transfer out of UCLA. Chris Forcier was a redshirt freshman, and though he was athletic, there were questions about his passing ability and maturity. Kevin Prince was an option, but he was a true freshman, and Coach Neuheisel wanted to redshirt him. There was only one man for the job, and it was Kevin Craft. A junior college transfer, Craft came to Westwood with high expectations. After two years at San Diego State, starting five games as a redshirt freshman, Craft transferred to Mt. San Antonio College, where he played under his dad, the offensive coordinator, and led the Mounties to the State Championship game. At UCLA, he would have a different challenge. Mt. SAC was a junior college powerhouse. They ran a spread offense and got rid of the ball quickly. At UCLA, he had a porous offensive line, one of the worst in school history, and a running game that lacked star power. Despite the tough situation, the clock stops for no one, and on September 1, it was time to play football.

Rick Neuheisel's first game as the UCLA head coach was played on a big stage. It was a Monday, Labor Day. The nation wanted to watch football. After a long offseason, the nation wanted to enjoy the game it loved. The Bruins took on Phillip Fulmer and the No. 18 ranked Tennessee Volunteers. The game was exciting. Kevin Craft struggled mightily and at halftime had a miserable stat line—just 66 yards passing and four interceptions. For Coach Neuheisel, that performance was nothing new. Twenty-five years earlier, he himself had thrown four interceptions in the opening half of his first start, but Coach Donahue had stayed with him. In the second half of this game, Neuheisel saw a new Craft. The Bruins had trailed, 14–7, at the break, and though Craft was taking a physical beating and struggling, he was not down. He bounced back for a brilliant second half. At the end of three, the Bruins still trailed, 14–10, but the action was just getting started. The Bruins were without three offensive starters due to first-half injuries: running back Kahlil Bell with an injured ankle, receiver Marcus Everett with a toe injury, and tight end Logan Paulsen with a fractured foot. Still, the game was close, and midway through the fourth quarter, the Bruins took the lead on a 3-yard Raymond Carter run. The Vols, however, came back, and with just under two minutes to play, running back Montario Hardesty raced 20 yards to the end zone to reclaim the lead. With the score now 21–17, the Bruins needed a touchdown, and they needed their third-string quarterback to lead the way. Craft, though one might imagine he lacked confidence, kept his composure. He quickly marched the Bruins downfield. On the ninth play of the drive, with the Bruins on the Volunteer 3-yard line, and under a minute to play, Craft found tight end Ryan Moya for the go-ahead score! It was a dramatic turnaround for Craft, but the game was not over. Tennessee's offense had 27 seconds remaining, and after four quick plays, they reached the Bruins' 30-yard line. There was time for one final play. Kicker Daniel Lincoln lined up for a 47-yard field goal attempt, and he knocked the ball through the uprights as time expired! The score was 24–24. If Coach Neuheisel was to get his first win as the Bruins head coach, he would have to do it in overtime. UCLA received the ball first but was unable to move the ball very far. Kicker Kai Forbath knocked in a 42-yard field goal, and the Bruins led by three when the Vols took over. On first down, the Vols put the ball in the hands of Hardesty again, and this time he was stopped for a 1-yard loss. On second down, Tennessee quarterback Jonathan Crompton found running back Arian Foster for a 4-yard gain. It was third-and-7. Crompton took the snap, had time to throw, but no one was open. He scrambled left and turned upfield, searching for the first down. At the 17-yard line, UCLA cornerback Alterraun Verner brought him down, and the Vols faced a fourth and short. Daniel Lincoln lined up for a 34-yard field goal, and a chance to send the game into double OT. He was only one-for-three on the day thus far, but his last attempt had forced overtime, and now he was called upon to force another OT period. He lined up just inside the left hash mark and never straightened out the kick. The ball missed left, and the Bruins stormed the field! The game was over. The Bruins upset the Volunteers and were 1–0. Coach Neuheisel was overjoyed. After the celebration, Neuheisel grabbed a microphone and addressed the crowd. Much to the delight of many in the beginning of his tenure, and ultimately the chagrin of most in the end, this would become a Coach Neuheisel tradition. On this day, however, there was nothing but joy. The Bruins were victors.

One week later, the Bruins again took on a strong opponent, but this time the result was much different. While the thrill of victory is sweet and ultimately keeps the die-hard fans coming back each year, the pain of defeat is often even worse. Not only were the Bruins defeated by the BYU Cougars in Week 2, they were destroyed. BYU quarterback Max Hall threw for seven touchdowns, two of which went to star receiver Austin Collie. When the clock ran out, the score was 59–0 Cougars. It was a shocking shutout. The 59-point loss was the worst for the Bruins since 1929. One week later, the Bruins lost again. The University of Arizona, led by Rob Gronkowski's two receiving touchdowns, beat the Bruins, 31–10. Finally, the Bruins closed September against the Fresno State Bulldogs, losing 36–31, their third consecutive defeat. Suddenly, the win against the Tennessee Volunteers seemed a long time ago.

The Bruins started the month of October in the same way they had the month of September—on the winning side. UCLA beat Washington State, 28–3, and those looking ahead saw a schedule that seemed navigable. The toughest opponent before their season-ending tilt with the USC Trojans was the Oregon Ducks. With their own season record of 2–3, the Bruins had a chance to get back to .500 and on the path to a bowl game. The Bruins defense was able to shut down the Oregon passing attack, holding quarterback Jeremiah Masoli to just 60 yards through the air, but stopping the running game proved to be impossible. Masoli rushed for 170, and LeGarrette Blount added 111. Craft threw for 288 yards, but the ineffectiveness of the Bruins running game led to frustrating drives. The Bruins fell, 31–24. It had been a winnable game, but the Bruins again fell short. This would be a theme that year, but not against the Stanford Cardinal. The Bruins trailed the lowly Cardinal squad, 20–16, with just 16 seconds to play in the game. After driving down the field, the Bruins offense had one final chance. It was first-and-goal at the 7-yard line. Craft took the snap and instantly felt a strong defensive rush up the middle. He was flushed to the right and found the edge of the defense. He looked to run, but just as the Stanford defense committed to Craft, he lobbed a pass over the top of the defense and into the waiting hands of true freshman tight end Cory Harkey. The Bruins won, 23–20. In a season filled with disappointment, the game against coach Jim Harbaugh and the Stanford Cardinal would be one of joy, even if the feeling was ever so brief.

The Bruins would lose three of their next four games heading into the annual rivalry game with the USC Trojans. The team was 4–7 and would not make a bowl game in Coach Neuheisel's first season. The most frustrating game of all for the Bruins was their battle against the Arizona State Sun Devils. Kevin Craft threw three interceptions on the day, all of which were returned for touchdowns. He also fumbled once, which was also returned for a touchdown. The Sun Devils scored four defensive touchdowns, yet finished with a total of only 146 yards. The Bruins racked up 322 yards, but the miscues killed them. The final score was ASU 34, UCLA 9. The problems the Bruins had against ASU were the same ones that haunted them the entire season. The offense struggled to pass the ball. They struggled to run, and they struggled to protect. Coach Neuheisel had proclaimed the monopoly in Los Angeles to be over, and though his promise could still come true, it was not going to happen in year one. The USC Trojans were No. 5 in the BCS rankings and would again go to the Rose Bowl. In their upcoming rivalry game, UCLA was simply trying to play spoiler. Four minutes into the contest, there was a brief moment of hope for the Blue and Gold. Receiver Dominique Johnson found Kahlil Bell for a 21-yard score on a trick play to give the Bruins a 7–0 lead. The moment of euphoria was brief, however. Mark Sanchez and the Trojans controlled the rest of the game, and when it came to a close, the Trojans were ahead, 28–7. The 2008 season was unquestionably another disappointment. The four wins matched the 1999 season as the lowest mark for the Bruins in nearly three decades. In 2009, Coach Neuheisel would be faced with the same challenge he had in 2008. He needed to give the Bruins hope. Their fans were getting impatient.

The Heisman Trust named Sam Bradford from the University of Oklahoma the 2008 Heisman Trophy Winner.

The University of Florida beat the University of Oklahoma, 24–14, in the BCS National Championship game.

## 2009

In 2009, Barack Obama was inaugurated as the 44th president of the United States. The Los Angeles Lakers won their 15th NBA championship. The Pittsburgh Steelers won their sixth Super Bowl, and the New York Yankees won their 27th World Series. Michael Jackson died, and so did Steve McNair. Coach Rick Neuheisel entered his second season as the UCLA head football coach. After going 4–8, his seat was not yet hot, but it wasn't exactly cold; the team needed to improve drastically in year two. The Bruins offense would struggle again, and the defense would have to carry the team. The Bruins had a new quarterback and a new running back. Kevin Prince and Johnathan Franklin would each become a staple of the Rick Neuheisel tenure, but as redshirt freshmen, neither was ready yet to take the mantle of stardom. The defense, though, was loaded with star power. Brian Price and Rahim Moore would be named All-Americans. Alterraun Verner, Reggie Carter, Akeem Ayers, and Kyle Bosworth would each earn All-Pac 10 honors. Jeff Locke was one of the best punters in America, and Kai Forbath was the best kicker in America.

The season began on September 5, and as they had done so many times before, the Bruins beat the San Diego State Aztecs. Coming into the game, the Bruins were 20–0–1 all-time against the Aztecs, and after beating them, 33–14, the streak continued. In Kevin Prince's first game at quarterback, he finished with only 176 yards passing, one touchdown, and two interceptions, but the defensive performance, led by Rahim Moore's three interceptions, helped the Bruins win comfortably. One week later, the test would be tougher, and Prince would prove up to the challenge. A year earlier, the UCLA Bruins and the Tennessee Volunteers had played a thriller at the Rose Bowl. In 2009, the Bruins made the trip to Knoxville to take on first-year head coach Lane Kiffin and the Volunteers. A huge crowd of 102,239 in Neyland Stadium saw another thriller. The Bruins offense struggled for much of the game. After marching down the field on the opening drive, the Bruins settled for a 26-yard Kai Forbath field goal. The Vols scored the next 10 points, but midway through the second quarter,

Prince found running back Chane Moline for a 12-yard score. At halftime, the score was tied at 10. In the third quarter, the Bruins had an opportunity to seal the game. They dominated Tennessee, scoring three times, but each resulted not in six points, but in three. Forbath made field goals of 39, 31, and 47. Still, the Bruins had a two-possession lead heading into the fourth quarter. The score was 19–10, and five minutes into the quarter, the Vols would creep closer, tacking on a 28-yard Daniel Lincoln field goal to draw within six points. Though the Bruins were in the lead, their backs were figuratively against the wall, and literally against the goal line. It was third and 9, and the Bruins had the ball at their own 1-½-yard line. Prince took the snap, opened left, faked a handoff to Franklin, and rolled right. He had a run-pass option, but his intended target was covered. He tried to run but was instead hammered in the end zone by Dennis Rogan for a safety. As the fans at Neyland Stadium celebrated, Prince ran off with blood gushing from his chin. His jaw was broken. The score was now 19–15, and the Volunteers took over. The game would have to be decided by UCLA's defense, and they were up to the task. They stopped the Vols on four consecutive plays and held on for the victory. Kevin Prince had once again struggled. His toughness could not be questioned, but his ability on the field was yet to be displayed. Prince threw for only 101 yards, and the Bruins running game had added only 85. UCLA's defensive secondary was again up to the task. Rahim Moore intercepted two more passes, giving him five for the season, and Alterraun Verner intercepted his first pass of the season. Kai Forbath's four field goals, and Jeff Locke's 47-yard punting average, were key factors in the win. The Bruins were 2–0, and though neither victory was pretty, their Week 2 performance in '09 brought a much sweeter feeling than their Week 2 performance had in '08.

After serving as the starter the previous year, Kevin Craft was now the backup quarterback in 2009, but when Prince went down with a broken jaw, it was time for Craft to take his place on the field once again. His 2008 season had been a disaster. He set the UCLA single season interception record with 20, but instead of sulking about losing his position, he stayed ready, and he improved. Craft threw for 186 yards and one touchdown against the Kansas State Wildcats in the first meeting ever between the two teams. Franklin ran for a career-best 119 yards. The Bruins won, 23–9, and were 3–0 for the first time since 2005. When the Bruins took on the Stanford Cardinal in the Pac 10 opener, they expected to face one of the best offensive players in the nation. They ended up facing two. Senior running back Toby Gerhart was off to a great start in his final season. Two months later, he would go on to finish second in the Heisman Trophy voting in the closest vote in history. Meanwhile, all eyes were on the tough Bruins defense facing the best running back on the West Coast. Gerhart would finish the day with 134 yards rushing and three touchdowns. The Bruins defense zeroed in on Gerhart, and though he was still able to finish with strong statistics, the Bruins made him work for it. Gerhart carried the ball 29 times. Coach Walker and the defense wanted to force the Cardinal to pass the ball. They had a freshman quarterback, and the Bruins had a ball-hawking secondary. Stanford's freshman was up to the task. Andrew Luck finished the day completing 70 percent of his passes and finishing with 198 yards. Luck was a relatively unknown name, but while defenses focused on Gerhart, Luck was building a résumé. UCLA's three-game winning streak came to a close. Soon they would find themselves in a downward spiral, unable to stop their losing streak from growing.

Against the Oregon Ducks, the Bruins were considerable underdogs. After losing their season-opening game to the Boise State Broncos, the Ducks won four straight and entered the game on a roll. At halftime, the score was just 3–0 Bruins, but in the second half, Oregon's offense came alive, while the Bruins continued to struggle. The Ducks scored 21 unanswered points in the third quarter, and though UCLA linebacker Akeem Ayers scored a touchdown on an incredible interception in which he tipped the ball high into the air and then caught it in the back of the end zone, just barely keeping his feet in bounds, the Bruins lost, 24–10. One week later, the losing streak reached three when Jahvid Best and the California Golden Bears rolled over the Bruins, 45–26. Against the University of Arizona, the Bruins fared no better. Kevin Prince struggled, and Kevin Craft came in to replace him. It made no difference. Rahim Moore intercepted two more passes, but the Bruins again fell, this time by the score of 27–13. The losing streak reached five games after Oregon State beat the

Bruins. UCLA trailed, 19–3, but after two consecutive touchdowns and two successful two-point conversions, the game was tied with two minutes left. But UCLA's defense, usually dependable, was unable to stop the Beavers. Receiver James Rodgers scored the game-winning touchdown with 41 seconds to play, and the Bruins lost, 26–19.

After starting 3–0, the Bruins were 3–5, and reaching a bowl game seemed an unreachable goal. They needed to win three more games, and the schedule would not get easier. On November 7, the Bruins donned 1967 throwback uniforms in honor of Gary Beban. Though the uniforms did not help the UCLA offense play like the Tommy Prothro Bruins, they provided enough inspiration to help them win the game. UCLA turned the ball over five times but came away with a 24–23 victory over the Washington Huskies. One week later, the Bruins played their best game of the season and overpowered Washington State, 43–7. There were two games left; the Bruins needed one victory to be bowl eligible. On November 21, in front of a crowd of only 46,151 fans at the Rose Bowl, the Bruins got their sixth win of the season. Final score: UCLA 23, Arizona State 13.

When the Bruins took on the USC Trojans on November 28, the game was not expected to be one of the more memorable in the series history. UCLA's record was 6–5. The Trojans were 7–3 and ranked No. 20 in the BCS rankings. The Bruins again wore their throwback 1967 jerseys, while the Trojans wore their standard home uniforms. USC was the better team. Freshman Matt Barkley had come in as one of the most heralded recruits in the country; he won the starting job as a true freshman. USC led, 21–7, with under a minute to play. The game was essentially over. USC took a knee, and much to the chagrin of the fans of both teams in attendance, and to USC coach Pete Carroll, Coach Neuheisel took a timeout. With 52 seconds to play, Carroll chose not to take a knee, but to line up in an I formation. This was predictable. UCLA was still trying to get the ball back. What was not predictable was the play that was called. Barkley dropped back, faked a handoff, and threw deep for a 48-yard touchdown to Damian Williams. The Bruins were not happy. They didn't like being unnecessarily "piled on." Players walked to the middle of the field toward the USC players, but both coaching staffs separated the teams. The Bruins were in no position to claim they were wronged. The Trojans did what they always do. Pete Carroll did what he always does. The UCLA regular season came to a close in embarrassing fashion.

UCLA would accept an invitation to the Eagle Bank Bowl, played in Washington D.C. on December 29 against the Temple Owls. The temperature was in the teens, and the wind never stopped blowing. It was miserable conditions for a football game, but the Bruins played well enough to win. UCLA trailed, 21–17, entering the fourth quarter, but Kai Forbath knocked in a field goal, Akeem Ayers intercepted a pass and ran it in for a short score, and the Bruins added two points on a bad Temple snap for a safety. The final score was 30–21. The final season record for the Bruins was 7–6. UCLA had improved in Coach Neuheisel's second season, and though the five-game losing streak in the middle of the season and the loss to USC were sure to anger fans, the Bruins were at least progressing. They had won four games in '08, seven in '09, and the Bruins looked to field a stronger team again in 2010. Coach Neuheisel's third season would ultimately define his tenure as the UCLA head coach. They could either get better, or they could flop.

The Heisman Trust named Mark Ingram from the University of Alabama the 2009 Heisman Trophy Winner.

The University of Alabama beat the University of Texas, 37–21, in the BCS National Championship game.

UCLA Spirit Squad, 2009
(Southern Campus Collection)

## 2010

In 2010, the Los Angeles Lakers repeated as NBA champions, and the UCLA Bruins football team repeated as a subpar team. After jumping from four wins in 2008 to seven in 2009, fans expected another jump and clamored for a team that could compete at the highest level. Third-year Head Coach Rick Neuheisel found a weapon on offense. After a quiet redshirt freshman season, Johnathan Franklin rushed for more than 1,000 yards as a sophomore. Derrick Coleman provided the Bruins' rushing attack with a solid second option. However, while the running game improved, the passing game floundered. Kevin Prince was back but again spent much of the season injured or ineffective. Richard Brehaut, once a highly touted recruit in high school, was expected to be a solid backup, but with the injuries to Prince he was forced into duty and struggled. The UCLA defense, once a strength, was now one of the team's weak points. Chuck Bullough was in his second season as the defensive coordinator, and UCLA's defense would fall to number 86 in the nation. Coach Neuheisel had yet to feel much pressure from a frustrated fan base, but in 2010, anger would reach new levels, and he was was feeling the heat.

The UCLA football season kicked off not with a bang, but with a whimper as 51,059 fans showed up at Bill Snyder Family Football Stadium in Manhattan, Kansas, to see the Bruins take on the Kansas State Wildcats. It was the largest crowd for a KSU home opener in history, and the fans got what they wanted—a Wildcat victory. Running back Daniel Thomas rushed for 235 yards and two touchdowns. The Bruins entered the game as favorites and left in shock. One week later, the Bruins lost again. When the Stanford Cardinal came to the Rose Bowl on September 11, they came in as the No. 25 team in the nation. Andrew Luck was now a sophomore and considered one of the best quarterbacks in the nation. The Bruins were on a six-game home winning streak against the Cardinal, but they never stood a chance. At halftime, UCLA trailed, 13–0. The score remained the same until late in the third quarter, when Stanford's two-way player, Owen Marecic, pounded into the end zone from one yard out. The Cardinal went for two and were successful. Nine seconds later, Stanford scored again after the Bruins' quarterback Kevin Prince fumbled on the first play of their drive and Michael Thomas recovered for a 21-yard score. Andrew Luck added a touchdown pass midway through the fourth, and the Bruins were never able to get on the board. Final score: Stanford 35, UCLA 0.

The Bruins were 0–2, and when they returned to the Rose Bowl one week later, only 54,407 fans joined them. The Bruins took on the No. 23 Houston Cougars and put on a better-than-expected performance. Houston's star quarterback, Case Keenum, and backup Cotton Turner were both injured and lost for the year during the game, while UCLA linebacker Patrick Larimore played the best game of his career, finishing with 11 tackles and forcing a Cougars fumble. Larimore was named the Bronco Nagurski National Defensive Player of the Week. The win over the Cougars was surprising, but the game against another Texas opponent one week later would shock the nation. On September 25, the Bruins traveled to Austin to take on the No. 7 University of Texas. The Longhorns had finished the previous season in the National Championship game, and though Colt McCoy was no longer donning burnt orange, Texas was a talented team and was expected to again compete for the Big 12 and national titles. With the Bruins trailing, 3–0, in the second quarter, Texas cornerback and punt returner Curtis Brown fielded a punt at his own 5-yard line, and Sean Westgate was there to meet him. Westgate made the tackle, forced a fumble, and the Bruins recovered. Two plays later, Prince found wide receiver Ricky Marvray for a 1-yard touchdown. UCLA linebacker Akeem Ayers intercepted a pass late in the second quarter, and the Bruins took a 13–3 lead into halftime. In the second half, UCLA's pistol offense shined. The Longhorns had entered the day with the top-ranked rushing defense in college football, but Johnathan Franklin rushed for 118 yards, and the Bruins finished with a total of 264. When the game ended, the final score was UCLA 34, Texas 12. The stadium record crowd of 101,437 left shocked. It was the first time Texas fans had seen their team lose at home in three years. Texas coach Mack Brown would call the loss "embarrassing." The game was not quite the disaster of 13 years earlier, when the Bruins had won by 63 points, but a 22-point victory over a top 10 team on the road is always sweet. It would be up to Coach Neuheisel and staff to build on that achievement. They could play like they had over the last two weeks, or they could revert to the form of their first two weeks. The season depended on it.

As the Bruins entered October, they had a promising two-game winning streak, and against Washington State they extended it to three. The upcoming three weeks, however, would provide an altogether more challenging test. They had three tough opponents ahead, two of whom were highly ranked. On October 9, the Bruins took on the California Golden Bears in Berkeley and fell flat on their faces. The three-game winning streak was snapped. Prince and Brehaut combined to throw for just 150 yards on 15 of 37 attempts, and the UCLA running game accounted for only 26 yards on 26 carries. Final score: Cal 35, UCLA 7. After a bye week, the Bruins traveled to Eugene, Oregon, to tackle one of the best teams in America on a nationally televised Thursday ESPN game. The first BCS rankings of the season came out just four days before the game, and the Oregon Ducks, top-ranked by the Associated Press, were ranked No. 2 by the BCS. Against the Bruins, they would make a statement. Oregon quarterback Darron Thomas threw for a career-best 308 yards and three touchdowns, and the nation's leading rusher, LaMichael James, ran for 123 yards and two touchdowns. Kevin Prince did not play for the Bruins, nursing a knee injury, and Brehaut finished with 159 yards on 16-of-23 passing. But it made no difference who was under center for the Bruins. The UCLA defense could do nothing to stop the Ducks. Final score: Oregon 60, UCLA 13. All Coach Neuheisel could say of his opponent after the game was, "That was impressive. I'll leave it at that. That was impressive." The final game of the tough stretch for the Bruins came against the No. 15 Arizona Wildcats nine days later, and though the Bruins kept the game close, they eventually fell by a score of 30–21.

After beating the University of Texas in 2010, Head Coach Rick Neuheisel addresses the team

The Bruins were 3–5, the same position they had been in each of the past two years. They needed to win three of the next four contests to get into a bowl game. Against Oregon State, the Bruins accomplished their goal, narrowly squeaking by with a 17–14 victory. The following two weeks would not go as well. The Bruins played a Thursday game in front of a large TV audience for the second time in four weeks, against the University of Washington, and though they were not embarrassed quite like they had been against the Ducks, they once again went down in defeat. Washington 24, UCLA 7. The Bruins offense was inept. The defense was weak. All hopes of a bowl game were finally dashed against the Arizona State Sun Devils on November 26. Brock Osweiler threw for 380 yards and four touchdowns. ASU running back Cameron Marshall rushed for 147 yards and a score. Jamal Lewis returned a kickoff 99 yards for a touchdown. Richard Brehaut threw for a career high 321 yards on 56 attempts, but the Bruins fell again, this time by the score of 55–34.

The Bruins were 4–7 and would not go to a bowl game in 2010. The USC Trojans, under first-year Head Coach Lane Kiffin, were also having a down year, but for the Trojans, that meant they were 7–5. One week earlier, the Trojans had lost to Notre Dame, and though the Bruins suffered a miserable season, it would be a slight consolation to force the Trojans to lose to their two main rivals in back-to-back weeks. USC, the stronger team, easily prevented that. Running back Allen Bradford rushed for 212 yards, and the UCLA season mercifully came to a close. Coach Neuheisel was 0–3 against the Trojans, and the rumors of months ago became loud yells. The fans wanted him gone. He would have one more year to turn it around.

The Heisman Trust named Cam Newton from Auburn University the 2010 Heisman Trophy Winner.

Auburn University beat the University of Oregon, 22–19, in the BCS National Championship game.

## 2011

In 2011, a new craze swept over college athletics—conference realignment. The change in conference structure actually began more than a half decade earlier. In 2005, Boston College was added to the ACC, and the Big East welcomed Louisville, South Florida, and Cincinnati. Four years later, the Big 10 Conference announced plans for "evaluations of options for conference structure and expansion." Months later, in February 2010, Pac 10 Commissioner Larry Scott opened the door for Pac 10 expansion, saying, "If the Pac 10 is going to think about expanding, now is our window." On June 10, 2010, the Colorado Buffaloes became the first major college program to jump ship, moving from the Big 12 Conference to the Pac 10 Conference. It was announced they would join for the 2012–2013 academic year, but later the change was moved forward one year to 2011-2012. Three days after Colorado announced it was leaving the Big 12, the Texas Longhorns announced they were not, thus guaranteeing the Big 12 would survive. On June 16, Larry Scott went to his backup plan, the University of Utah, and they accepted an invitation to join the Buffaloes as new members of the Pac 10. Nebraska would join the Big 10. TCU would temporarily join the Big East. Texas A&M left the Big 12 for the SEC. Pittsburgh and Syracuse left the Big East for the ACC. TCU eventually joined the Big 12, Missouri joined the SEC, West Virginia joined the Big 12, Maryland and Rutgers each joined the Big 10, Louisville joined the ACC, and confused fans nationwide were left with a lot to remember. Since the massive conference mix-up, the Pac 10 became the Pac 12, the Big 10 has 14 members, the Big 12 has 10, the SEC expanded its territory, the ACC expanded its influence, and the Big East was no longer a football conference. The Pac 12 added a conference championship game, and the Big 12 lost their conference championship game. The college football world had changed—drastically—but the UCLA football team stayed the same. Head Coach Rick Neuheisel entered his fourth season with the Bruins, following three with less-than-impressive results. When the season kicked off on September 3, Neuheisel was under pressure. ESPN's Mark Schlabach released his 2011 coaches hot seat rankings, and in the category of "scorching" sat Rick Neuheisel.

When the Bruins took on the Houston Cougars in the season opener, both teams had quarterback question marks. Case Keenum was a star, but it was his first game since tearing his ACL against the Bruins the previous year. Kevin Prince was a senior and he was the starter, but he had yet to stay healthy, and Richard Brehaut was clamoring for the job. Both teams would get answers, but only one came away happy. Keenum threw for 310 yards and two touchdowns in his return to action. Prince was again injured, leaving in the second quarter with a concussion. Brehaut replaced him and threw for 264 yards and two touchdowns. The Bruins finished with 554 yards as a team, but it was not enough. The Cougars won, 38–34. In a year when Coach Neuheisel was fighting for his job, it was not a good way to start. The Bruins got on a winning track one week later in their home opener against the San Jose State Spartans, and one week later they took on the Texas Longhorns. UT Coach Mack Brown, a National Championship game winner just six years earlier, was, like Neuheisel, on the hot seat. The Bruins had embarrassed the highly ranked Longhorns in Austin a year earlier, but this time around, the Longhorns were ready for payback. Final score: Texas 49, UCLA 20.

Conference play began on September 24 against the Oregon State Beavers. Kevin Prince, back from his concussion, had struggled against Texas, so Brehaut was now in the starting lineup. On the other side, OSU started redshirt freshman Sean Mannion, who would throw for 287 yards in his first career start, but the Bruins, led by Brehaut's two touchdowns, one on the ground and one through the air, came out on top. The Bruins had alternated wins and losses through the first four games, and if they were to buck the trend, they would next have to beat the No. 6-ranked Stanford Cardinal, led by the best quarterback in the nation, Andrew Luck. The Bruins had no chance. Luck was spectacular, finishing with 227 yards on 23-of-27 passing and three touchdowns. It was not his arm, however, that caught the Bruins off guard, but his hands—or, simply, his hand. Luck also caught a touchdown on the day. As he sprinted down the right sideline on a trick play, Drew Terrell overshot him just a bit, but Luck reached up with one hand to snag the ball and score. Brehaut finished with 202 yards passing, and running back Johnathan Franklin added 96 on the ground, but the Bruins lost, 45–19.

UCLA would continue the trend one week later against the Washington State Cougars. Starting quarterback Richard Brehaut broke his leg in the second quarter, and when Prince came back in, the offense continued to sputter. Entering the fourth quarter, the Bruins were behind, 16–14. Washington State added a touchdown early in the quarter to extend the lead to eight, but the extra point attempt failed, and the Bruins got the key break they needed. They were still within striking distance, down only one possession. With 10:52 remaining, Prince found receiver Josh Smith for a 9-yard score, and though the Bruins were unsuccessful on the two-point try, they were back within two points. WSU countered with a field goal of their own, a 47-yarder from Andrew Furney, and the Bruins were down five. With 3:26 to play, Prince hit Shaquelle Evans for a 7-yard touchdown, and the Bruins had the lead! Prince hit Nelson Rosario for a two-point conversion and the Bruins took a 28–25 lead. Versatile defensive back Andrew Abbott, once a walk-on, sealed the game with an interception, and the Bruins ran out the clock for the victory. Twelve days later, the Bruins lost again, and this time it was ugly. UCLA got routed. With four seconds left in the first half, the Bruins trailed the Arizona Wildcats, 42–7. Things would go from bad to worse. The game was played in Tucson, and a fan dressed as a referee raced onto the field. As security chased after him, fans watched with enjoyment, but something else was going on. There was a fight. Both benches cleared. Referees on the field and coaches on the sidelines were powerless to stop it. Two players were ejected: UCLA receiver Taylor Embree and Arizona cornerback Shaquille Richardson, who had been a Bruin but was kicked off the team for felony theft one year earlier. The Bruins went on to lose, 48–12, and when the Pac 10 Conference reviewed the film, six Bruins were suspended. It was a new low point for Coach Neuheisel and for the UCLA program.

Over the next two weeks, the Bruins snapped their streak of winning one, then losing one. After beating the California Golden Bears, the Bruins took on the No. 19 Arizona State Sun Devils and pulled an upset. Derrick Coleman scored with 49 seconds to play, and following the extra point by Tyler Gonzalez, the Bruins led, 29–28. The Sun Devils quickly marched downfield, but kicker Alex Garoutte missed a 47-yard field goal as time expired, and the Bruins held on. They had won two games in a row, were 5–4 on the season, and their next two games would be critical. With the expansion of the conference came the addition of divisions. In the South Division, UCLA, USC, Arizona, Arizona State, Utah, and Colorado fought for a spot in the Conference Championship against the winner of the North Division. The Bruins stood at 4–2 in conference and were in the driver's seat to win the division. Their next two games would come against their newest division and conference foes. On November 12, the Utah Utes trounced the Bruins, 31–6, and one week later, the Bruins handled the Colorado Buffaloes, 45–6.

Entering the final regular season game of 2011, UCLA's position was set. The Blue and Gold would go to the Pac 12 Championship and represent the South Division. It was, however, a position not earned, but one gained due to circumstances. USC was one game ahead of the Bruins in conference play, but they were banned from participating in postseason play following sanctions handed down by the NCAA for a wide-ranging pay-for-play scandal. The player who took the majority of the heat from the public and from the media was Reggie Bush, but the former Heisman winner was only one of many found guilty of taking extra benefits while at USC. Still, the annual rivalry game was to be played, and if the Bruins beat USC, they would earn their spot in the Pac 12 Championship. UCLA came out of the tunnel flashing new uniforms. They were white from head to toe. Though the Bruins would play six days later in the Pac 12 Championship, it was the Trojans who wanted to prove they were the best team in the conference. USC stormed out to a 29–0 halftime lead, and by the time the game finally came to a close, the score read USC 50, UCLA 0. It was the worst loss for UCLA in the rivalry since 1930. The uniforms would go down as the "surrender whites." USC quarterback Matt Barkley threw for 423 yards and six touchdowns. Wide receiver Robert Woods finished with 12 catches, giving him 111 receptions for the season. Woods's teammate, Marquis Lee, finished the day with 13 catches for 224 yards and two touchdowns. The low point that the Bruins had reached five weeks earlier against Arizona had just sunk further. This was the new low.

Two days after the game against USC, Head Coach Rick Neuheisel was fired. He was allowed to coach in the Pac 12 Championship game against Oregon, but it would be his final game. In his final practice, the players, who generally loved their coach, carried him off on their shoulders. He was a Bruin. He had practiced himself on the same fields a quarter century earlier, but his time was up. The Bruins would lose to No. 9 University of Oregon in the Championship game. Though the Bruins were 6–7, the NCAA ruled that due to USC's sanctions, UCLA was bowl eligible. They were not supposed to play in the Pac 12 Championship but were forced to, which gave them a losing record. For UCLA fans, it hardly mattered. The season was miserable, and it ended with just more pain. Offensive coordinator Mike Johnson was named the interim coach for the Kraft Fight Hunger Bowl, which the Bruins lost, 20–14. UCLA became the first team to ever participate in a bowl game and finish the same season with eight losses. It was not an honor to be proud of. Athletic Director Dan Guerrero led a search for the next UCLA Bruins head coach. Fans had little confidence in their AD, and when the decision was made on the next coach, most had little faith in the hire. The Bruins were once again entering a new stage, but this time it was different. The next coach would bring UCLA back into relevancy, at least for a short time. That next coach was Jim Mora.

The Heisman Trust named Robert Griffin III from Baylor University the 2011 Heisman Trophy Winner.

The University of Alabama beat Louisiana State University, 21–0, in the BCS National Championship game.

UCLA Spirit Squad 2011 (Erkki Corpuz Collection)

# CHAPTER 16
# Jim Mora (2012–2017)

When Jim Mora came to Westwood in December 2011, he had no college experience but boasted a lifetime of football knowledge accumulated over a quarter century in the coaching profession. He was seen by many as an NFL man, not likely to be long for the tedious duties of a college football coach. However, it was not the level of play that his experience came from that mattered, but the process. Every early morning practice, every day of summer conditioning, every hour watching film, and every game on the sidelines had led Jim Mora to UCLA. Football is a game, and whether one builds fame through the professional ranks or college, the game is still the same. Players may be bigger and faster in the NFL, but they all put their pads on the same way. They have the goal of reaching the end zone or stopping the opposing team. While coach Mora built his résumé primarily in the National Football League, the Bruins were simultaneously building a legacy themselves. For half a century, the Bruins were one of the greatest programs in America, but when Jim Mora arrived in Westwood, UCLA had lost much of its former glory. At the turn of the century, the Bruins had suffered a downturn. Coach Jim Mora was being charged with bringing the Bruins back.

Jim Mora, 2012 (Southern Campus Collection)

On November 19, 1961, James Lawrence Mora was born. Like his father, the young boy would go by the name Jim. And, like his son would eventually become, his father was a football coach. After being born in Los Angeles, Jim would spend much of his childhood in Boulder, Colorado, where his father was a defensive assistant for the University of Colorado Buffaloes. In 1973, at just 12 years of age, Jim was on the move again. For one year, he would find a home in a place that would eventually define his career. His father, Jim E. Mora, took a job with the University of California Los Angeles under first-year head coach Dick Vermeil. The Mora family would not be long for Westwood, however, and in 1975 they left for the University of Washington, where Coach Mora would become the Huskies' defensive coordinator.

As the Mora family settled into the Pacific Northwest, Jim started high school. Though his father would eventually leave UW and join the Seattle Seahawks staff, the Mora family was done moving for a while. Jim attended Interlake High School in Bellevue, Washington, and was a versatile star. "I was a receiver, defensive back, linebacker, running back, long snapper. Anything they wanted me to do," Jim would say later. But like the man who came before him at UCLA, he was not heavily recruited. The team would make the state quarterfinals in back-to-back years, but it was not Jim Mora college coaches came to see. They clamored for quarterback Steve Pelleur, who would eventually sign a scholarship and attend the hometown University of Washington. Mora was a man without scholarship options, or at least any good ones. Sure, he was recruited by Montana, Eastern Montana, and Eastern Washington, but none of these were schools that he wanted to attend. Jim preferred the University of Washington and wanted to play under Head Coach Don James. But no scholarship was available. Despite his other options, Jim followed his heart. He chose to walk on at UW, and aside from the fact that several of his friends were attending there, playing for James was a main reason why. Jim would say, "I wanted to have a chance to play for him." He had a chance to be on the team, but to see significant time on the field would be the challenge. Seldom do walk-on athletes get to play meaningful snaps, but even more seldom do players work as hard as Jim L. Mora.

While at the University of Washington, things came together for Mora. Upon arrival, he was seen as an asset by Coach James, though not necessarily someone who would see the field immediately, if at all. Coach James loved having another coach's son on his team. Mora would eventually work his way from scout team player to scholarship recipient and standout special teams contributor. In his four years as a player at UW, the Huskies went to two Rose Bowls, winning one, and under Coach James's leadership, UW established itself as one of the best college football programs in the nation. Still, it was not what happened on the field that shaped Mora's college experience, but something that happened off it. Mora, who had an eye on coaching from a young age, got his foot in the door. He was liked and respected by one of the best coaches in America. He was smart, he was studious, and he had a plan. Coach Don James would later recall that Mora never asked for coaching references from James because he had little interest in coaching in college. He wanted to coach professionally. He saw the recruiting schedule that college coaches had to follow to get top-notch talent. It was something he had personally observed from his father even before attending UW, and he knew the strain on a family was significant. Mora found a profession that he would pursue in the future. He was part of a successful run at UW. Now it was time to get started.

In 1984, Jim Mora, the linebacker/defensive back, became Jim Mora, the football coach. Despite the hopes of coaching professionally, his first option came not only in college, but right where he was. Coach James kept Mora as a defensive graduate assistant, and in 1985, the Huskies were once again a great team. They landed a berth in the Orange Bowl, beat Oklahoma, and once again finished in the top 10 in the final rankings. Still, Coach Mora wanted a change. In 1985, he started his own campaign to find a new job. He wrote letters. Lots of them. He mailed a letter to every coach in the NFL. Every general manager got one, too. If he was rejected, he wrote another letter thanking the team for consideration, and asking that they still consider him in the future. The process was arduous. Handwriting letters to every coach was unlikely to pay off. He had connections. His father had already coached for more than 25 years in major college football, the NFL, and now the USFL. In 1985, Jim E. Mora was the head coach of the Baltimore Stars of the United States Football League. Surely he could help his son get a job. Yes, that would have been an easier path, but it was not the way Jim L. Mora wanted to do things. He wanted to find his own way. He would say of the possibility of his father helping, "I wasn't going to do that. I felt like I needed to establish myself." His persistence paid off. In 1985, San Diego Chargers head coach Don Coryell offered Mora a job. It was not as the defensive backs coach assignment he hoped for, but it was a job nonetheless. Mora became the first-ever quality control coach in the NFL, a position that is now common. Mora's duties were simple. He was to keep the rest of the staff happy, and this mostly meant doing their errands. He would bring them dinner. He would fill up their cars with gas. He would make sure there were snacks in the facility, and he made sure the refrigerators were always full. When coaches grabbed something to drink, there was Mora ready to replace the drink. He would say, "I was obsessive about it . . . to the point where I put one in as soon as somebody would take one out." For most, the job would seem like a pain, but for Mora it was simply part of who he was—and it was a foot in the pro door. He was always organized. His college roommate claimed that Mora always had the vacuum running. Simply making sure the refrigerators were filled and that the Coca-Cola cans always had the label facing forward was just another challenge. He wanted to prove he was an indispensable member of the team, and he did. After four years as a quality control coach, Mora had paid his dues; he got promoted. In 1989, he became the defensive backs coach for the Chargers. His hard work, mostly behind the scenes, had paid off, and now he had the job he wanted. For three years, he was the DB coach for the Chargers, but when Head Coach Dan Henning was fired following the 1991 season, Mora was in need of a job.

In 1992, Coach Mora was in an uncomfortable position. He was out of work in San Diego, but his reputation had grown, and he was considered a hot commodity. The Cincinnati Bengals had an opening, and Jim L. Mora was on their shortlist. The Bengals made an offer, but Mora had his eye on another position. His dream was to return to Seattle and coach for his beloved Seahawks. The Seahawks had just hired Tom Flores, and Mora knew that Flores would need to fill a staff. He hoped for the opportunity to go back home. But the call never came, and it was now too late for him to join the Bengals. Mora would say of the missed opportunity in Cincinnati, "I was not going to accept a job in Cincinnati until I had completely exhausted every opportunity to get even an interview in Seattle." Coach Mora's dream would have to wait, but his problem still remained. By 1992, however, Mora had developed a reputation and a résumé. He was a fiery coach with a fierce secondary. He was just what his father was looking for.

For five years, Coach Jim L. Mora coached the defensive backs for the New Orleans Saints under his father, Jim E. Mora. In his first two years, the Saints boasted the top passing defense in the NFL. After five years, the younger Mora left for the San Francisco 49ers. He was on a fast track to an NFL head coaching gig. For two years, Mora coached the defensive backs in San Francisco under Head Coach Steve Mariucci, and in 1999, he was promoted to defensive coordinator. For five seasons, Mora was the DC in San Francisco, and in his first year, the 49ers finished with the top defense in the league. They also finished second in passing defense with 25 interceptions and had 41 total takeaways. In coach Mora's five years as the DC in San Francisco, he built a powerhouse defense. The team regularly finished in the top five in the NFL in run defense, pass defense, total defense, sacks, and takeaways. Jim Mora was a budding coaching superstar. It was time for the next phase. It was time to call the shots.

In 2004, Jim Mora was named head coach of the Atlanta Falcons. The Falcons were led by quarterback Michael Vick, who was entering his fourth season in the NFL, and the former number one overall pick was expected to have a big year after an injury-riddled 2003 season. In Mora's first season, the Falcons made the jump that fans had hoped for. They finished with an 11–5 record. The 11 wins in coach Mora's first campaign was certainly an impressive feat. He became only the eighth rookie coach in history to win 11 games in a season, and just the eleventh rookie coach to win a division title. The porous Atlanta defense of 2003 was suddenly formidable. Before Mora's arrival, the defense had ranked last in the NFL, and in his first season, they jumped to No. 14 in total defense. The defense set a franchise record and led the NFL with 48 sacks. On offense, the Falcons were physical. They led the league in rushing yards, something that would become a trend under Mora. After finishing with an 11–5 record in 2004, the Falcons had a disappointing 8–8 season the following year and then fell to 7–9 in 2006. The team led the league in rushing in each of Mora's three years, and Michael Vick became the first quarterback to rush for over 1,000 yards in a season in 2006. Despite the declining win totals, Coach Mora was still viewed favorably in coaching circles. The team had won 26 games in three years. The defense went from worst in the NFL to one of the best. The Falcons had a star quarterback, but all was not well. Coach Mora's maturity was questioned, and ultimately that brought him down.

Jim Mora was fired by the Atlanta Falcons in part due to a radio interview. Coach Mora, when speaking with his former college teammate, Hugh Millen, said that the University of Washington head coaching position was his "dream job," and that he would take the position even if the Falcons were in the playoffs. Although Mora claimed he was joking, fans of the Atlanta Falcons were upset.

More important to Mora's future, however, owner Arthur Blank was upset. Mora was summoned to meet with Blank to discuss the issue and was then sent out for an apology press conference. It was an embarrassing mistake, and, coupled with the disappointing end to the 2006 season, it signaled the end of the Jim Mora era in Atlanta. It didn't take long for the accomplished coach to find a job. In January 2007, the Seattle Seahawks announced that Mora was coming home to be their next defensive backs coach. For Mora, not only was this an opportunity to go back to the Pacific Northwest, but it was a chance to get out of the public eye. He would say of his new position under Coach Mike Holmgren: "It was very healthy for me to avoid the spotlight, which I didn't want and I didn't deserve. This was Mike Holmgren's team. Of course, I had aspirations to be a head coach again, but this was an opportunity to watch one of the great coaches of all time up close." Mora interviewed for the Washington Redskins head coaching vacancy one year later, but after Holmgren announced 2008 would be his last year, Mora withdrew his name from consideration with the Redskins. He wanted to coach the Seahawks, and he would get his shot. Mora was announced as the successor to Holmgren, and in 2009, he became the seventh head coach in Seattle Seahawks history. Coach Mora would say of the opportunity, "It's a place that I always wanted to raise my kids because I had such a great upbringing here. I felt so complete here." He continued, "Under no circumstances do I believe I'm allowed to fail. I'm not a mercenary in this city. There's nothing else for me." For Coach Mora and the Seattle Seahawks, the fairy tale story would not play out in the way either envisioned. After going 5–11 in his first season, Jim Mora was fired on January 8, 2010. When the Seahawks fired Mora, they courted USC Coach Pete Carroll, whom they eventually hired. For coach Mora, his dismissal was a surprise and a stab in the back. When Seahawks CEO Tod Leiweke called Mora into his office, Mora believed the discussion would be about the vacant general manager position. Instead, it signaled the end for Coach Mora in Seattle, and in the NFL.

Following his brief stint in Seattle, Coach Mora did what many former coaches and players do; he went to television. In 2010 and 2011, he served as an analyst on NFL Network, and NFL on FOX. Coach Mora was good on TV, but his life in football would not be relegated to color commentary. He was a coach, and he wasn't done coaching. After UCLA fired Rick Neuheisel following a 50–0 loss to USC in 2011, Athletic Director Dan Guerrero and the UCLA athletics administration began a coaching search. Boise State coach Chris Peterson, Houston coach Kevin Sumlin, TCU coach Gary Patterson, and Miami coach Al Golden were all names that fans clamored for, but on December 8, 2011, UCLA hired Jim Mora. Since leaving the University of Washington in 1985, Coach Mora had a experienced a change in his aspirations. He had wanted to coach professionally and did so for 25 years. He was a head coach at two different destinations, but now it was time to return to college, something he was happy to do. Coach Mora would say, "I've given this a lot of thought. This isn't something that just popped up. This has been a goal of mine since I left the Seattle Seahawks. I've had a passion and a real strong desire to get back into coaching football at the collegiate level. I've had opportunities to go back to the NFL over the past year and turned them down in hopes that one day I'd have the opportunity to coach at a college football program like UCLA's." For Coach Mora, the challenge was clear. He had to recruit, something he had little experience doing, but he vowed to do it with ferocity. "We're going to attack recruiting with relentless passion," Mora said. "I'm going to use the credibility I've gained in coaching in the NFL for 25 years to get myself into some of those homes and convince these kids that not only can we help them be great football players, but present them an opportunity to get a great education at one of the outstanding academic institutions in America." He had to awake the Bruins fan base and return the Bruins to their once glorious past. "I think UCLA is truly a sleeping giant, and I realize that an opportunity like this, of this magnitude, doesn't present itself more than once in a coaching career," Mora said. "When the job was offered, I jumped at the chance to be a Bruin."

In Coach Mora's first three seasons in Westwood, he turned the Bruins back into a consistent contender. In 2012, UCLA won the Pac 12 South. In 2013 and 2014, they finished with 10 wins each season. He brought in talent from across the country. UCLA became a recruiting powerhouse. Coach Mora upgraded his staff, though keeping quality coaches and replacing them with equal or better quality proved difficult. He pushed the UCLA football program into the next phase. UCLA's athletic administration has made an increased commitment to football, and though Coach Mora's next three seasons all failed to live up to the hopes of fans, his first three were the best that many young fans have seen at UCLA. Still, UCLA longs for another national title. When Coach Sanders and the Bruins celebrated the 1954 National Championship, Coach Mora had not yet been born. In Coach Mora's tenure at UCLA, he brought back belief, even if for a short time. He stood eye-to-eye with USC and told them, "We own this town." The days of Red Sanders are gone, and so are the days of Tommy Prothro and Terry Donahue. After losing to USC in 2017, and falling to 5–6 on the season, Coach Jim Mora's days as the Bruins coach were also over. He was fired with one game remaining in the season. While in Westwood, Mora had recognizable success, but by 2017, it was perfectly clear that it was time for him to move on . . . and for a new chapter to be written in UCLA football history.

## 2012

For a decade and a half, the UCLA Bruins had suffered through mediocre coaching, constant staff turnover, and below-average quarterback play. In 2012, a change was made. Rick Neuheisel was gone, and Jim Mora was the new man in charge. Mora had a long career in the NFL, but with his move to Westwood came question marks. He hadn't coached in college since he was a graduate assistant at Washington in 1985. As a man in his early 20s, he decided to coach professionally, in part due to his negative feelings about recruiting. Would he now be able to recruit with zeal? He quickly proved he could. He also assembled a staff with a wide range of experience. He hired NFL coaches. He hired experienced college coaches. He hired young assistants who were recruiting wizards. He also changed the culture. Fans clamored for an authoritarian coach who would instill toughness and accountability. For the players, one of their toughest challenges would come not in games, but in practice. UCLA football held its 2012 fall camp in San Bernardino, California. It would become a tradition. Players were roughly two hours away from the distractions of Westwood. They were away from the perfect Los Angeles weather, and the breeze coming off the Pacific. They were in the desert. Temperatures during camp reached 112 degrees. Players who weren't tough enough failed. If they couldn't handle the demands of a driven coach, they didn't make it. One player who not only made it, but thrived under coach Mora, was Brett Hundley. The Bruins' quarterback play had been one of the main reasons for their downturn in recent decades. The memories of Cade McNown were fading further into the past. The Bruins needed a new star under center, and they got it with Brett Hundley. Nicknamed "The Savior," Hundley came in with high expectations. He was recruited by former Head Coach Rick Neuheisel but redshirted in 2011. In 2012, he beat out Richard Brehaut for the starting job. It was his team. He was their destiny.

The anticipated first game of the Mora/Hundley era came on August 30 at Rice University. When the game started, all eyes were on Hundley, but there were other stars ready to finally come into their own. Running back Johnathan Franklin was now a senior, and though he had enjoyed success in the past, he was not yet a household name nationally. He would be, soon. Tight end Joseph Fauria, standing at 6'8", was always an intriguing player, but the Notre Dame transfer had yet to make a mark in college. He, too, would in 2012. On defense, players who were known but not yet key contributors suddenly became stars. Datone Jones, a fifth-year senior, anchored the defensive line. Damien Holmes would have the best season of his career. Sophomore Eric Kendricks led the Pac 12 in tackles. Perhaps no player, however, had a bigger turnaround than Anthony Barr. Barr had come to UCLA as a running back. He stood at 6'5" and was recruited by nearly every school in America. He was a local product, and one of the reasons he ultimately chose UCLA was that he was promised by Coach Neuheisel that he would be allowed to play offense. He did so for two years but didn't find a natural spot. He played tight end. He played H-back. He caught a few passes and ran the ball a handful of times, but he was not a key player. Then, in 2012, he had a breakthrough. After asking Coach Mora if he could move to defense, he did so, and the results were astonishing. Barr was an All-American linebacker. After UCLA forced Rice to punt on the opening drive of the first game, the offense went to work. On the first play of Brett Hundley's career, he took the snap in shotgun formation at the Rice 28-yard line. Franklin lined up to his right. It was a read-option play, and the Owls defensive end crashed hard toward Franklin. Hundley kept the ball, and after gaining five yards, he was surrounded by three oncoming defenders. Hundley split the three defenders and was in the clear. He raced down the sideline. At the 20-yard line, he cut in and set up a block by receiver Shaquelle Evans, then weaved back toward the sideline and into the end zone! On the first play of his career, Hundley ran for 72 yards and a score! It was the start of a new era. Hundley would go on to become a superstar. The Bruins won, 49–24, and were 1–0 on the season.

Anthony Barr, 2012

In Week 2, the Bruins returned home, and with them came the recruits. It was the first chance for most to see Jim Mora's team in person, and to see Anthony Barr terrorize the opposition's offensive line. It was also their first opportunity to see "The Savior" shred a defense. The Bruins took on the No. 16 Nebraska Cornhuskers, and the 71,530 fans in attendance saw a show. With the score tied at 7 in the first quarter, Nebraska quarterback Taylor Martinez, a Southern California native, took a snap at his own 8-yard line, and after splitting the Bruins defense right down the center, he raced 92 yards for a score. The Bruins came back, however, but after every big play for the team in blue and gold, the team in red and white responded. It was a slugfest. The Bruins took a 17–14 lead, only to see Huskers running back Ameer Abdullah juke his way 17 yards for a score to retake the lead. Minutes later, it was the Bruins' turn. Hundley found running back Steven Manfro for a 49-yard touchdown pass, and the Bruins were on top again. The scoring pace in the second half slowed, but the drama never faded. With the score tied at 27 in the fourth quarter, the Cornhuskers were again backed up near their own goal line, and Martinez would again run, but this time the result would be much different. After taking the shotgun snap with his feet on the goal line, Martinez faked a handoff to Abdullah and was instantly crushed by Datone Jones in the end zone. The safety put UCLA up by two points, and with two minutes to play, Johnathan Franklin extended the lead to nine on a backwards pass that he ran in for a short score. UCLA went on to win, 36–30. Franklin rushed for 217 yards on the day, his second consecutive game with at least 200 yards. Suddenly Franklin, the man whom fans called "The Mayor," was a Heisman candidate. Forgotten were his past fumble problems. He was now a fan favorite. In the final nonconference game of the regular season, the Bruins won again, this time defeating the Houston Cougars by a score of 37–6. It was the first 3–0 start for UCLA since 2009.

The Bruins were perfect in nonconference play, but their perfect record ended in the first conference game. The Bruins hosted their third consecutive home game, but the underdog Oregon State Beavers came away with a victory. OSU quarterback Sean Mannion threw for 379 yards. Running back Storm Woods rushed for 96. Brett Hundley had another strong game, throwing for 372 yards and a touchdown and adding another TD on the ground, but Franklin was slowed for the first time that year and finished with just 45 yards. The next week, the Bruins traveled to Boulder, Colorado, and got back on track. Hundley threw for two touchdowns and ran for two more. Franklin rushed for 111 yards. The Bruins won, 42–14, and though the schedule ahead looked manageable, the Bruins ran into a buzz saw that they could not overcome. Their next opponent, the California Golden Bears, was not a special team. They were not better than the Bruins. What hurt UCLA was the inevitable game in which a freshman quarterback performs like a freshman. Hundley had the worst game of his career against the Bears. He threw four interceptions on the day, and UCLA lost, 43–17.

Halfway through the season, the Bruins were 4–2. It was certainly a respectable start, but UCLA fans had seen good starts before. They needed to see more. Fortunately, what they got was the best stretch of the season. The Bruins beat Utah, 21–14, at home and then beat Arizona State University on a last-second field goal by freshman kicker Ka'imi Fairbairn. On November 3, the Bruins took on the No. 22 team in the BCS rankings, the Arizona Wildcats. The Wildcats were led by running back Ka'Deem Carey, one of the best backs in the nation, but it was another back, UCLA's Johnathan Franklin, who stole the show. In the first quarter, the Bruins' offense stormed out of the gates. Three minutes into the game, Franklin rushed for a 37-yard score. Three minutes after that, Brett Hundley rushed for a touchdown from six yards out. Six minutes later, Hundley found receiver Jordan Payton for another. By the end of the first quarter, the score was 21–0. The Wildcats never recovered. The Bruins offense was perhaps motivated by a mark set by their offensive leader. Franklin needed just 21 yards entering the game to become UCLA's all-time leading rusher. On his 37-yard score, he not only broke the record, but started the tidal wave that led to the team's most impressive win of the season. The final score was 66–10 Bruins. After the game, the ever-humble Franklin would say of his accomplishment, "It's a great feeling. All praises to my teammates. They open up the big holes. I just run through them." Franklin did more than just run through the holes. His vision, acceleration, and balance made him one of the best running backs in America, and one of the best in UCLA history. He finished the day with 162 yards, while the Bruins defense held Carey to just 54. One week later, the Bruins found themselves in the BCS rankings for the first time. They came in at No. 18 in the rankings and left with another win. UCLA 44, Washington State 36.

The game between UCLA and USC on November 17 was straight out of a Hollywood script. The Bruins were in the throes of their worst stretch since the 1920s, and USC was fresh off its best decade in a generation. USC entered the 2012 season ranked the No. 1 team in the country by the Associated Press. Though they lost an early game to Stanford, they were still No. 10 in the initial BCS rankings. When the two teams met on November 17, USC was No. 18, and the Bruins were No. 17. One year earlier, the Bruins had been humiliated by USC, dismantled, 50–0, and the memory of Trojan Matt Barkley mouthing the word "scoreboard" from two years prior to that were still fresh on the minds of everyone. The game had conference implications, as well. For the first time, the winner of the rivalry game would go to the Pac 12 Championship. To add to the story line, it was pouring rain at game time. From the moment the game kicked off, one thing was very clear. There was a new sheriff in town. Coach Mora was not like the coaches who had come before him, and his team had adopted his personality. On the very first play of the game, UCLA cornerback Aaron Hester intercepted Barkley, and one minute later, Brett Hundley plowed ahead for a 1-yard touchdown. UCLA added a field goal, and with three minutes left in the first quarter, after Eric Kendricks forced a fumble and the Bruins recovered, Hundley found Joseph Fauria on a corner route in the end zone for a 17-yard score. This was not 2011. Things were different now. UCLA led, 17–0, at the end of the first quarter. Midway through the second quarter, with the score unchanged, Franklin took a handoff and ran off right tackle. He then made a defender miss and raced for a 16-yard score. The Bruins were up, 24–0. USC would not go away, however, and with a chance to take all the momentum into the half, the Bruins defense suddenly looked vulnerable. Barkley threw two touchdowns in the final six minutes of the half, and the score was 24–14 at the break. After a UCLA fumble, the Trojans narrowed the difference again just one minute into the third quarter on a George Oku fumble recovery in the end zone. The extra point attempt failed, and the score was 24–20. All the momentum was with USC, but the Bruins continued to fight. Eric Kendricks blocked a punt. Brett Hundley found his rhythm again. The defense stiffened. After Hundley extended the lead to 31–20 on a short run, the game went back and forth but with no scoring. Both defenses were solid. For more than fifteen minutes of game play, the score remained static, but with seven minutes to play in the fourth, the Trojans finally broke through. Barkley found receiver Marqise Lee for a 14-yard touchdown and then connected with receiver Robert Woods for the two-point conversion. The score was 31–28, and UCLA fans began to fear the worst. But the Bruins offense had no time for fear. They simply executed. The offensive line protected Hundley, who fired strikes across the field. The line opened holes for Franklin, and he gashed through the defense. With four minutes to play, Franklin took a handoff at the USC 29-yard line and found a seam up the middle. Breaking through the first line of defense, he cut to the outside and raced down the sideline for the score. After crossing the goal line, he turned to the fans cheering wildly in the student section and gave a slashing of the throat signal with his hand. The Bruins had taken a 38–28 lead! The Trojans needed to score, and quickly. After marching down the field, USC was in a position to get back in the game. With the ball at the 21-yard line, USC faced a second-and-7. The rain was pouring down. Still, no fans left. They cheered with everything in them. Barkley took the snap and dropped back three steps. He looked to his right, pump-faked toward Marqise Lee, and as his receiver broke for a double move, Barkley got hammered from behind by Anthony Barr! The crowd erupted. The hit heard round the college football world not only symbolized the end of Barkley's college career, it symbolized the end of an era. USC attempted a 38-yard field goal to bring the score to within one possession, but Sheldon Price blocked the kick! The game was essentially over. Franklin ran the ball three times before the Bruins punted to USC, but there was not enough time for USC and no magic left for the Trojans. UCLA won, 38–28. Coach Mora stood on the sideline in the pouring rain and was dumped with blue Gatorade. In his first year, coach Mora had done what few in the preseason thought possible. USC was Goliath, and the Bruins had felled the giant.

UCLA Cheerleader before game against USC in 2012 (Erkki Corpuz Collection)

UCLA would go on to the Pac 12 Championship, but they had one regular-season game left to play. Their final regular-season game was against the No. 8 Stanford Cardinal. Going into that final game, the Bruins' opponent in the Pac 12 Championship was as yet undetermined. It turned out that UCLA would end the season playing Stanford in back-to-back weeks. In the regular-season finale, the Cardinal defense stifled the Bruins. UCLA was unable to relive the high of its USC victory and fell by the score of 35–17. Six days later, the Bruins and Stanford met again, this time in Palo Alto. With much more on the line, high drama was sure to be in the air. On November 30, the No. 17 Bruins took on the No. 6 Stanford Cardinal for the Pac 12 Championship. It was the second consecutive year the Bruins were in the title game. This time they earned it! In the regular season finale, the UCLA offense had been dismal; the running game never got on track. The championship game would be a fight until the very end, and the offense, led by Franklin, came to play. Three and a half minutes into the game, Franklin ran for 51 yards and a touchdown. Stanford and UCLA then exchanged touchdowns in the first quarter, and the score was 14–7 at the end of one. The Cardinal added 10 points in the second and tightened their defensive screws to take a 17–14 lead into the break. UCLA was the clear underdog, but with the Rose Bowl on the line, motivation was at an all-time high, and the 2012 season had thus far been magical. As at the USC game two weeks earlier, it was raining, and it never let up. In the third quarter, the Bruins were able to match the Cardinal's second quarter. Franklin scored and Fairbairn added a field goal. The score was 24–17 Bruins, and a berth in the Rose Bowl was only 15 minutes away. Four minutes into the quarter, the Bruins watched their lead evaporate. Stanford quarterback Kevin Hogan found Drew Terrell for a 26-yard score, and the game was again tied. UCLA had a chance to retake the lead, but the offense was stifled. Stanford kicker Jordan Williamson knocked in a 36-yard field goal with six minutes to play to pull Stanford ahead once again. After the two teams exchanged punts, the Bruins took over with a chance to tie or take the lead. There was 2:18 to play, and the ball was in the hands of a freshman. The Bruins took over at their own 19-yard line and had no timeouts to work with. Soon the Bruins faced third-and-6 at their own 44-yard line. Hundley dropped back and threw a swing pass to Franklin. The senior was sure to get the first down, but he dropped the pass. The man who had led the offense all season let the first down slip through his fingers. On fourth-and-6 the game was on the line, and someone needed to come through. Hundley took the snap, looked middle, and fired to tight end Joseph Fauria for a 12-yard gain. As Fauria was falling to the ground, he flipped the ball to receiver Jerry Johnson, who gained another three before going down. The Bruins were unable to gain another first down. With the Bruins down three, the ball was on the Cardinal 37-yard line. Fairbairn lined up for a 52-yard field goal. Prior to the Championship game, Fairbairn had made only one field goal all season longer than 35 yards, a 48-yarder one week earlier. The snap was good. The hold was good. The kick sailed left. The game was over. Stanford won the Pac 12 Championship, 27–24. UCLA would not go to the Rose Bowl.

The Pac 12 Championship game loss was a disappointment, and the end of the season ended in even more disappointment. UCLA had won the Pac 12 South and beat USC, but the season ended with back-to-back losses to Stanford and a 49–26 loss to the Baylor Bears in the Holiday Bowl. The Bruins won nine games in Coach Mora's first season, a feat accomplished only once by the Bruins since 1999. Coach Mora had changed the attitude at UCLA. He had turned a mediocre team into a winner. He had increased accountability. He had a freshman quarterback who exceeded the lofty expectations placed upon him. The offseason would be long. Fans were once again excited for UCLA football.

The Heisman Trust named Johnny Manziel from Texas A&M University the 2012 Heisman Trophy Winner.

The University of Alabama beat the University of Notre Dame, 42–14, in the BCS National Championship game.

## 2013

UCLA entered the 2013 season with expectations not matched in decades. Johnathan Franklin was off to the National Football League, and replacing him would prove to be impossible in one year. UCLA's backfield was talented, but it would take a team effort to replace the production of "The Mayor." Sophomore quarterback Brett Hundley would lead the team in rushing. Paul Perkins, Jordan James, Malcolm Jones, and Steven Manfro were all being counted on to contribute. Another player, however, did what no one expected. Myles Jack was a freshman linebacker. He was part of a linebacker unit that was the best in the nation. Jack, Jordan Zumwalt, Eric Kendricks, and Anthony Barr led the defense. Jack, however, was multitalented. He would be asked to play on both sides of the ball, finishing with 267 yards rushing and seven touchdowns. He was named Pac 12 Freshman of the Year on offense and defense, the only player to do that in conference history. UCLA had its newest superstar.

UCLA began the season ranked No. 21 in the nation. On August 31, they took on Cody Fajardo and the Nevada Wolfpack. The Bruins struggled early in the game. At halftime, they led by only 17–13, but in the second half the Bruins outscored the Wolfpack, 41–7. Final score: UCLA 58, Nevada 20. Brett Hundley accounted for four touchdowns, two through the air and two on the ground. Running back Jordan James ran for 155 yards and a score. UCLA was 1–0. They had a bye week approaching and were set to take on the University of Nebraska in Lincoln in two weeks. All attention was on the game, but that would quickly change. Tragedy struck. At 1:27 a.m. on Sunday, September 8, UCLA walk-on receiver Nick Pasquale was struck by a car and killed in his hometown of San Clemente. One week earlier, he had played his first snap as a Bruin. Now he was gone. With the Bruins off for the weekend, many players returned home for a few days. Nick was only 20 years old. The UCLA football program was shaken to the core when they heard the news. The 5'7", 172-pound receiver was one of the most popular players on the team. A full year after the tragedy, Head Coach Jim Mora would say, "We think of Nick every day. He's a big part of what we do. His family is a big part of us. We're never going to let go of it. It still bothers me when I think about it. It was a tough, tough deal and still is." UCLA would dedicate the season to the memory of their fallen teammate. When the Bruins took on the Nebraska Cornhuskers on September 14, they took to the field with heavy hearts. Covering those hearts, on the jerseys, the Bruins donned a 36 patch, Pasquale's number. The Cornhuskers showed their respect, as well. They donned a 36 sticker on the back of their helmets, and in the student section, they held a sign reading, "Two Schools. One Team." Another sign read, "N 36." Following a pregame tribute, Nebraska fans released blue and gold balloons into the air. The air was filled with emotion in Lincoln when the game began. Five minutes into the match, the Bruins were behind. Quarterback Taylor Martinez found Quincy Enunwa for an 11-yard score, and after Ka'imi Fairbairn knocked in a field goal for the Bruins, the Huskers pair hooked up again. At the end of the first quarter, the score was 14–3 Huskers. Nebraska extended the lead to 21–3 in the second quarter before something amazing happened. The Bruins were struggling. The crowd of 91,471, a stadium record, was in a frenzy. The game was sold out, not unusual in football-crazed Lincoln. The Nebraska faithful have showed up in droves, and sold out Memorial Stadium, for every home game since 1962, a college football record. With the Cornhuskers ahead, 21–3, the fans were happy. But the Bruins were not in a mood to just fold up their tents and go home. They had a comeback to make. Paul Perkins scored their first touchdown of the day on a 10-yard run in the final minute of the first half. At halftime, the score was 21–10. When the Bruins came out in the second half, they were a new team. They were challenged to "play like Nick." The defense swarmed to the ball. The offense was crisp. After forcing a punt on Nebraska's first series, the offense took the field. Jordan James broke off a long run. Hundley cut through the defense with precision. The drive was capped by a 3-yard James touchdown. UCLA was within four points. After forcing another punt, the Bruins finally took the lead. The final play of the drive was a 28-yard strike from Hundley to wide receiver Shaquelle Evans, who caught the perfectly thrown ball over his shoulder with a defender just a half step behind him. UCLA was ahead, 24–21, and they had no plans to look back. Hundley threw a touchdown to Phillip Ruhl, and then another to Nate Iese. With the Bruins up by 17 in the fourth quarter, Anthony Barr forced a fumble, and safety Anthony Jefferson recovered. While his teammates tried to celebrate with Jefferson, he sprinted to coach Mora on the sideline, gave him the ball, and hugged him tight. With the game now out of reach, Brett Hundley looked into a camera on the sideline and flashed a towel that read "RIP #36." The Bruins had done it. They won for Nick. It was the most emotional game that many would ever play. As members of both teams gathered together after the game to pray, it was a reminder that it could all be gone in an instant. The Bruins were 2–0, and the memory of their fallen teammate would never fade. Receiver Devin Lucien would say, "I don't think 'forget' and 'Nick' should be in the same sentence." Receiver Jordan Payton echoed the same sentiments: "I always remember him. I always take time to pray and talk with him." The season would go on, and after beating the No. 23-ranked Cornhuskers, the Bruins were No. 13 in the nation, according to the Associated Press. In their third game of the season, they dismantled the New Mexico State Aggies by the score of 59–13. UCLA was 3–0, and it was time for conference play.

On October 3, the Bruins took on the University of Utah Utes. The game came down to the wire. The Bruins defense intercepted six Travis Wilson passes, two by Anthony Jefferson and one each by Myles Jack, Kendricks, Ishmael Adams, and Randall Goforth. Still, the game was close. The final interception came on the final drive. With UCLA leading, 34–27, the Utes had a chance to tie the game. The ball was deep in Bruins territory, and after cornerback Brandon Sermons broke up a pass in the end zone seconds earlier, the Utes faced a fourth-and-10 at the Bruins 23. When Myles Jack intercepted the final pass to seal the game, he displayed an athleticism uncommon in a linebacker. This would not be the last time Myles Jack did something special. The Bruins beat the Utes and then went on to beat the University of California Berkeley the following week. UCLA was 5–0, but the games that everyone had eyed coming into the season were the next two on the schedule. If UCLA was going to contend on a national level, these next two would be the deciding factor.

On October 13, the first BCS rankings of the season came out, and UCLA was No. 9 in the country. Their next opponent, the Stanford Cardinal, was No. 12. The Bruins had not beaten the Cardinal since 2008, and though Stanford was a strong team, so were the men in blue and gold. The Cardinal were the more physical team, however, and in football, physicality usually trumps speed. Stanford won, 24–10. Cardinal running back Tyler Gaffney rushed for 171 yards, and the Cardinal defense held the Bruins scoreless in the first half. UCLA's perfect season was ruined, and the challenge would only get harder. While the Bruins slid to No. 11 in the BCS, their next opponent was enjoying an even better season. Marcus Mariota and the Oregon Ducks were No. 2 in the nation. The Bruins defense came to play. Oregon had a high-powered offense, but the first half ended with the score just 14–14. The Bruins were 30 minutes away from pulling the upset of the year in college football. In the second half, however, the Ducks showed they were the superior team. Brett Hundley struggled, throwing for only 64 yards. Mariota threw for 230. The Bruins' offense racked up 219 yards on the ground, but Oregon ran for 325. In the second half, the Ducks scored 28 unanswered points and went on to win, 42–14.

The Bruins were 5–2, riding a two-game losing streak and facing the possibility of a letdown against the Colorado Buffaloes. But UCLA was able to come away with a win. So they were 6–2 when they took on the University of Arizona, a game they went on to win, 31–26. The real story was not the final score, but the performance of an individual player. Myles Jack was a true freshman linebacker who had established himself as one of the best defensive freshman in the nation. Against the Wildcats, he would prove to be even better than the earlier press reports. He made his debut on offense. Yes, Myles Jack was a two-way player. He would finish with eight tackles and a fumble recovery on defense, but the story was not just that he also played offense, but that he wowed the nation. With 11:44 remaining in the second quarter, the Bruins went into a formation they had not yet shown in the year and a half with Coach Mora and offensive coordinator Noel Mazzone in Westwood. Defensive players were scattered throughout the UCLA offensive backfield. Cassius Marsh and Jordan Zumwalt were blockers. Myles Jack lined up behind Hundley in the pistol formation. It was third-and-1 with the ball at UCLA's own 34-yard line. Hundley took the snap, turned to his right, and handed the ball to Myles Jack. After starting to the right, and seeing no hole available, Jack made a sharp cut to his left, shot through a tiny hole, ran into his own blocker, and bounced to the left. He ran through an arm tackle and rumbled for 29 yards on his first career carry. When Myles Jack took the field in the fourth quarter on offense for the first time, the game was still close. UCLA led, 24–19. Jack had 54 yards on five carries, but he was not done. On the next snap, the ball was on the UCLA 34-yard line. It was third-and-2. Jack took the handoff from Hundley and ran off right tackle. He made a sharp cut off his right foot to beat one defender and cross the first-down marker. At the 37-yard line he cut again, this time to the outside, and simultaneously stiff-armed a defender to the ground. Jack had gotten to the outside, but the defender still had an angle on him. He rumbled down the sideline and eliminated the angle. His speed was breathtaking. At the UofA 30-yard line, the defender lunged for him, but like a gnat, he could do nothing to slow Jack. At the 10-yard line, another defender reached for him, but one last stiff-arm and he was in the end zone! Fans on television heard Joe Tessitore yell, "Jacked up indeed!" and Arizona fans in the stadium were left stunned. He was so big and so fast. He finished with 120 yards on six carries. He was named Pac 12 Offensive Freshman of the Week. The Bruins had a phenom.

After the eye-opening performance by Myles Jack against the University of Arizona, ESPN couldn't stop talking about him. Now everyone knew what he could do on offense: he was a weapon. The University of Washington couldn't stop him, either. Six days after the game against Arizona, the Bruins played a Friday night game against the Huskies, and all eyes were on Jack. He finished with four rushing touchdowns, the first Bruin to accomplish such a

(left) Myles Jack, 2013 (Public Domain); (right) UCLA Spirit Squad decked out in their LA Nights apparel (Danielle Alvari Collection)

feat since Maurice Jones-Drew. Jack was not the only defensive player to get in on the fun on offense. Cassius Marsh caught a touchdown pass, as well. The Bruins won, 41–31, and were in the driver's seat to again win the Pac 12 South.

The Bruins took on the Arizona State Sun Devils in a critical game on November 23 and would be forced to play catch-up the entire way. The Devils came in at No. 22 in the BCS rankings, and UCLA came in at No. 15. ASU got off to a quick start. Quarterback Taylor Kelly ran in a 3-yard score just two and a half minutes into the game, but as fast as ASU scored, UCLA would score even more quickly. After the kick return brought the ball all the way to the Sun Devils' 42-yard line, Hundley connected with Lucien on the first play for a long touchdown. The Bruins would temporarily take the lead on a Fairbairn field goal, but the Sun Devils made a run that ultimately put the Bruins in a difficult position. ASU scored three straight touchdowns, and though the Bruins added a field goal in the second quarter, ASU receiver Jaelen Strong scored a touchdown with five seconds to play in the half to give the Devils a commanding 35–13 lead at the break. In the second half, the Bruins would make a charge. Jack and Perkins each ran for a touchdown, and Hundley hit Evans for another 27-yard score. ASU, however, held on to win by the score of 38–33. It was a crushing loss for the Bruins. Their hopes of winning the Pac 12 South were dashed.

Despite the soul-crushing loss, the Bruins still had a game to play, and it was the biggest of the year. USC, which had fired Lane Kiffin earlier in the year, rallied behind interim coach Ed Orgeron, and though the Trojans were inspired by their new coach, the Bruins proved it didn't matter who was calling the shots for the Trojans. Los Angeles was UCLA's town, and they let everyone know it. Though the coaches were certainly not happy about it, UCLA offensive lineman Caleb Benenoch sent a message early on the field, and he did so with one quick, violent act. It was an uprising, and when Benenoch threw the punch that decked J.R. Tavai, it was a sign that the new bully in Los Angeles wore blue and gold. UCLA beat USC, 35–14. Myles Jack ran for a touchdown, and defensive lineman-turned-temporary fullback Eddie Vanderdoes ran for one, as well. Hundley rushed for two touchdowns, and Perkins added one more on the ground. The Bruins physically dominated the Trojans. Cassius Marsh and Anthony Barr terrorized the USC offensive line and punished quarterback Cody Kessler. After the game, the party was on. The Bruins celebrated loudly in their locker room, and recruits who came to see the Trojans begged their way into the Bruins locker room. Coach Mora would say after the game, "You win two in a row in this town and things start to change. If I'm a high school player, I want to play at UCLA." Hundley would say, "UCLA runs L.A. Everybody understands that." Cassius Marsh added, "Oh, we run this town. It's solidified. We're 2–0. We won this game. It's our city now. They can come try to get it next year." For USC fans, it would be a long offseason. The Bruins would enjoy the win for an entire year.

For the second consecutive year, the Bruins finished with nine regular season wins. In 2012, they had been embarrassed in the Holiday Bowl by the Baylor Bears. In 2013, they took on the Virginia Tech Hokies in the Sun Bowl with a chance to reach 10 wins for the first time since 2005. The Bruins crushed VT and won by the score of 42–12. UCLA finished with a 10–3 record and were No. 18 in the final BCS rankings. Under Coach Mora, the Bruins went from mediocre to contender. In two years, he had jump-started the program. Brett Hundley was a redshirt sophomore in 2013, and though he considered a jump to the NFL, he decided to come back for 2014. Expectations would be sky-high.

Brett Hundley, 2013

The Heisman Trust named Jameis Winston from Florida State University the 2013 Heisman Trophy Winner.

Florida State University beat Auburn University, 34–31, in the BCS National Championship game.

## 2014

The 2014 Bruins had star power, and they had much to look forward to. Anthony Barr was gone, off to the NFL, but the defense still had two of the best linebackers in the country. Eric Kendricks would go on to win the Butkus Award, handed out to the best linebacker in the country. Myles Jack, the star two-way player, was now a sophomore, and after a historic freshman season, fans could not wait to see what he would do for an encore. Brett Hundley was now a junior, and he would again excel. He finished the season with over 3,000 yards passing, 22 touchdowns, only five interceptions, and 10 rushing touchdowns. The running game in 2013 had lacked a clear leader. In 2014, a new star would emerge. Myles Jack would again get time in the backfield, but his role decreased on offense because of the emergence of sophomore Paul Perkins, who finished with 1,572 yards on the ground, finishing first in the Pac 12 Conference. The Bruins didn't lack notoriety, and the media didn't ignore them. UCLA entered the season as the No. 7-ranked team in America according to the Associated Press. When ESPN analyst Kirk Herbstreit picked UCLA as a National Championship contender, the country took notice. UCLA was no longer the hunter. They were the hunted. The 2014 season was one of the most anticipated in recent UCLA history. In addition, the entire college football world was excited for a different reason. In 2014, college football finally had a playoff system. From 1998 to 2013, fans had finally gotten from the BCS a true National Championship game. Now, in 2014, they would be getting even more. Four teams would make the playoffs. These teams would be determined by a playoff committee, and as with the BCS, the committee would release weekly rankings beginning midseason. Six bowl games rotated as semifinal sites, and the championship game would be played at a third venue. In 2014, the semifinal games would be held at the Rose Bowl and Sugar Bowl. The National Championship would be at AT&T Stadium in Dallas, Texas. College football entered a new era, and the Bruins hoped to steal the show.

UCLA struggled in nonconference games in 2014. The season kicked off on August 30 at the University of Virginia. UVA was a poor team. Head coach Mike London was on the hot seat. The Cavaliers' defense, however, came to play. UCLA entered the game as 21-point favorites but escaped with just an eight-point win. UCLA's offensive line was dominated from start to finish, but the Bruins were aided by three second-quarter defensive touchdowns, one each by Kendricks, Ishmael Adams, and Randall Goforth. One week later, the Bruins played another tight game, but the storyline was much different. After a poor offensive performance against the Cavaliers, the Bruins' offense came alive in the home opener against the Memphis Tigers. Hundley threw for 396 yards on the day. Receivers Thomas Duarte and Jordan Payton each had over 100 yards receiving, and the Bruins finished with 42 points. UCLA's defense, on the other hand, couldn't stop Memphis quarterback Paxton Lynch and the Tigers offense. The Bruins barely escaped with a 42–35 victory.

After two close calls, the Bruins were 2–0, but there was legitimate concern. UCLA dropped from

No. 7 to No. 12 in the AP rankings, and their next game would come against the Texas Longhorns in Dallas at AT&T Stadium. If the Bruins had any hope to return to Dallas in January, they likely needed to beat the mediocre Texas team in September. It would not be easy. A new name, with a Bruins lineage, was to emerge. UCLA's leader on offense, Brett Hundley, was hurt. After starting the game going 4-for-4, Hundley hurt his elbow. He would not return. It was up to backup quarterback Jerry Neuheisel to lead the team. Having been recruited by his father, Jerry chose to attend UCLA. Then, after grayshirting in 2011, Jerry decided to stick to his commitment and play for UCLA despite his father being fired as coach, and in 2012 and 2013 he bided his time. Now, he had a shot. With Neuheisel at the reins, UCLA's offense went conservative. Passes were short, and handoffs were frequent. The offense struggled to move the ball. Jerry was efficient, but without Hundley, the Bruins lacked big plays in the first half. At the break, UCLA trailed, 10–3. When Brett Hundley didn't come out at the start of the third quarter, it was clear to all fans in attendance that it was now Jerry's game. Three minutes into the half, Neuheisel finally hit Nate Iese for a short touchdown. The game was tied at 10. The offense had seemingly gotten back on track, but as the teams continued trading possessions, it became clear that the game would come down to the wire. UCLA continued to play conservatively on offense, and though they added a field goal in the fourth quarter to take the lead, it was Texas that scored the next touchdown. With 5:13 to play, UT quarterback Tyrone Swoopes found John Harris for an 8-yard touchdown, capping a four-minute, 80-yard drive. The Bruins trailed, 17–13. After taking over at the UCLA 35-yard line, the Bruins offense went to work. On the first play of the drive, Neuheisel threw a screen to Perkins, who saw daylight and scampered for 30 yards, putting the Bruins in a position to score. On first down, the Bruins gained four. Then the momentum shifted. After gaining enough for the first down, UCLA running back Jordan James fumbled. It was the first and only turnover of the game, and it was costly. The Bruins had three timeouts and could still get the ball back, but time was not in their favor, and they had squandered their best scoring opportunity of the fourth quarter. The UCLA defense would step up, however. Defensive lineman Eddie Vanderdoes was a menace and stopped UT on consecutive plays to force a third-and-9 with 3:30 to play. On third down, Myles Jack flushed Swoopes out of the pocket. With the Bruin across his body, the Texas quarterback's short pass was inaccurate, and the Longhorns were forced to punt.

After a booming kick, Ishmael Adams fielded the ball at the UCLA 22-yard line. As Adams raced for the sideline, a wall of blockers was being set. Adams turned the corner and raced upfield. As he sprinted down the sideline, a series of crushing blocks cleared his way. Finally, he was brought down all the way at the UT 33-yard line. On first down, Neuheisel took the shotgun snap and looked left. He dug his back foot and pump-faked to Jordan Payton on the left side. Payton beat his man on a double move. Neuheisel lofted the ball high into the air, and it came down in the hands of Payton for a touchdown! After the extra point, the Bruins led, 20–17. Meanwhile, at that moment in San Francisco, Jerry's father, Rick, the former Rose Bowl MVP for the Bruins and former UCLA head coach, watched in the Pac 12 Network studio. After seeing his son come through in the most important moment of his career, Rick could hardly hold in the tears. UCLA went on to win, 20–17. As fans chanted "Jerry, Jerry, Jerry," teammates carried their hero off the field. The Bruins were 3–0, and while it was certainly a memorable moment, if the Bruins were to fulfill all of their lofty goals for 2014, they would need Hundley back. Their next game would not be for 12 more days. Questions about Hundley's elbow and Jerry's performance would litter the message boards. For at least one game, the Texas stadium nicknamed "Jerry's World" belonged to a Bruin.

On September 25, 2014, Arizona State donned new all-black uniforms. Fans sported black tee shirts, and the crowd and stadium were blacked out. While some may have found the look to be sharp, nothing the Sun Devils did on the field deserved to be complimented. ASU entered the game No. 15 in the country and the Bruins No. 11. During the day, temperatures rose as high as 115 degrees. Even at 7 p.m., the time of kickoff, the temperature was still well over 100. While it was hot outside, the Devils were ice cold. UCLA dominated. Final score: UCLA 62, ASU 27. After three consecutive subpar performances, the Bruins played their best game of the year. Pollsters took notice, and the Bruins reentered the top 10 the following week. As October rolled around, the Bruins entered at 4–0, just where they expected to be. On October 4, they got an unexpected challenge. After a relatively tame beginning to the college football season, the first Saturday of October brought drama in the form of upsets. Three teams in the top 10 lost, and the Bruins hoped to avoid becoming the fourth. The University of Utah Utes jumped out to a nice lead over the Bruins. At the end of one quarter, UCLA trailed, 7–0. At halftime, it was 17–7 Utes, and at the end of three, 24–14 Utah. UCLA's perfect season was in jeopardy. With the Bruins pinned back inside their own 10-yard line, it was make or break. If UCLA let the Utes get the ball back and extend the lead, it might be too much to overcome. Instead, the game was changed on a big play. Hundley hit wide receiver Devin Fuller, who outraced the Utah defense for a 93-yard score. It was just the play the Bruins needed to turn the tide of the game, and though Utah would kick a field goal six minutes later, the Bruins again had an answer. Another receiver, this time Eldridge Massington, stepped up, and with 4:50 to play, the Bruins took their first lead of the game on a 40-yard touchdown by Massington. The Bruins went for two and failed. Leading 28–27, it was up to the defense to seal the deal. The Utes were calm. They had plenty of time, and they quickly marched downfield. After penetrating deep into Bruins territory, Utah was held to a field goal. After Andy Phillips knocked in a kick from 29 yards out, Utah retook the lead with only 34 seconds to play. The Bruins quickly moved the ball downield, as well. With just seconds remaining, there was time for one final play. The ball was on the Utah 38-yard line. Kicker Ka'imi Fairbairn came in to try for a career-long 55-yard field goal attempt for the win. The snap was good. The hold was good, but the kick sailed far right. The Utes stormed the field, but the game was not over. There was a flag on the field. The Utes were penalized for running into the kicker. Fairbairn would have one final chance, this time from 50. Again the snap was good, and the hold was good. Protection held up, and Fairbairn had time. The kick had plenty of leg and started to the center. As the ball neared the goal post, it continued to drift to the right, and when it came down, it was too far off. Utah won. The Bruins' perfect season was over. Following the loss, the Bruins dropped 10 spots, and one week later, they took on a much tougher foe. The Oregon Ducks came to the Rose Bowl and beat the Bruins, this time by a score of 42–20. The Bruins had lost two in a row, and suddenly they found themselves in the land of the unranked.

Following the back-to-back losses, it appeared the Bruins' schedule would get easier. The next two games, expected to be wins, turned out instead to be nail-biters. Hundley outplayed Cal quarterback and future top overall NFL draft pick Jared Goff, but still the game against the California Golden Bears was close. With UCLA leading, 36–34, the Bruins' cornerback Marcus Rios intercepted Goff at the UCLA 2-yard line, and the Bruins won. One week later, the Bruins went to Boulder, Colorado, to take on the 2–5 Buffaloes, and while it took overtime to get it done, the Bruins again came away with a win. UCLA was struggling, and even though they found themselves back in the top 25, there were legitimate concerns. When the No. 25 Bruins took on the No. 14 Arizona Wildcats, all the pregame talk was about the strong UofA offense, but UCLA's defense played their best game of the season on a Friday night in Pasadena. The Bruins debuted gray uniforms, and unlike the Arizona State Sun Devils early in the year, UCLA came to play while wearing their new look. Final score: UCLA 17, Arizona 7. When the first College Football Playoff Committee rankings came out on November 3, the Bruins found themselves at No. 23. It was surely a disappointment when compared to the preseason hype, but UCLA was still in a position to win the Pac 12 South. When the team traveled to Seattle to take on the Washington Huskies, the Pacific Northwest crowd had no plans to welcome them with open arms. Coach Mora had turned down a coaching opportunity from his alma mater, and Myles Jack, who had spent much of his childhood in the Seattle area, had spurned the Huskies for the Bruins. Fans would voice their frustration, and the Bruins simply rubbed it in their faces. UCLA won, 44–30, and Myles Jack, playing both ways, had a spectacular rushing touchdown. The Bruins were 8–2. It was time to take on the Trojans.

While the win over the Trojans in 2012 had signified a changing of the tide, and the victory in 2013 solidified the Bruins as the new bully in town, the 2014 game sealed the deal. The versatile linebacker/running back Myles Jack showed off yet another skill. He was tasked with shutting down

All-American receiver Nelson Agholor and did just that, holding him to three catches for 24 yards. Brett Hundley threw for 326 yards and three touchdowns. Perkins added a touchdown on the ground, and Eric Kendricks intercepted a pass. The 82,431 fans who showed up saw the Bruins dominate, and at the end of three quarters, UCLA led, 38–14. With three minutes to play, USC added a late touchdown, but it meant nothing in the end. UCLA beat USC for the third consecutive season. They were one win away from the Pac 12 Championship. The Bruins entered their game against the Stanford Cardinal ranked No. 9 in the country, and though it was a long shot, there was still a belief that the Bruins could make the college football playoffs. More important, at least in the short term, they could clinch the Pac 12 South with a victory. Stanford entered the game as two-time defending conference champions, but they were just 6–5 on the season. UCLA had everything on the line, but when the game ended, those who were otherwise unaware of the circumstances would have believed the roles were reversed. The game was tied at seven at the end of the first quarter, but Stanford dominated the rest of the way, holding Hundley to just 146 yards in what turned out to be his final home game. Stanford won, 31–10, and instead of reaching the Pac 12 Championship, the Bruins were headed for a layoff. Arizona, the team that UCLA had beaten handily four weeks earlier, would instead go to the Pac 12 Championship. The Bruins would play in the Alamo Bowl on January 2 against Kansas State University. They jumped out to a big early lead, and though they let the Wildcats back into the game, they finished ahead, 40–35. The Bruins under Coach Mora were a new team. Over three years, they had built a new identity. They beat USC three times and changed the way people thought about the rivalry. They had a new swagger and new goals. In 2015, they would have a new quarterback.

The Heisman Trust named Marcus Mariota from the University of Oregon the 2014 Heisman Trophy Winner.

Ohio State University beat the University of Oregon, 42–20, in the CFP National Championship game.

## 2015

In 2015, the Bruins transitioned into their next phase. For three seasons, quarterback Brett Hundley was the rock that held the UCLA offense together. Now he was a member of the Green Bay Packers. The UCLA offense was loaded with talent. Jordan Payton and Thomas Duarte were the primary targets in the passing game. The UCLA rushing attack, thin just two years earlier, was now a strength. Paul Perkins was a star. Nate Starks was a talented sophomore. Two true freshmen, Soso Jamabo and Bolu Olorunfunmi, were reliable options. Finally, Myles Jack was still an option to carry the ball. The offensive line was experienced. The only question on offense was Hundley's replacement. In spring and throughout summer, junior Jerry Neuheisel and true freshman sensation Josh Rosen were in competition for the job. Neuheisel had the experience, but Rosen had the superior talent. As a prep star at local St. John Bosco High School, Rosen was the top player in the country and one of the best quarterback recruits to come out of high school since Jimmy Clausen in 2007. Ultimately, Rosen would win the job and start every game his freshman year. On defense, the team was even more stacked. On every level, UCLA had NFL talent. Myles Jack was the man everyone noticed, but defensive linemen Kenny Clark, Eddie Vanderdoes, and Takkarist McKinley were also valuable. Deon Hollins was a terror off the edge, and the UCLA defensive backs were experienced. Kicker Ka'imi Fairbairn was now a senior and would have the best season of his career, finishing as a consensus First Team All-American. UCLA was set to have a memorable season. It all depended on Rosen, or so many thought. The Bruins would suffer bad luck, something that few, if any, could predict.

UCLA kicked off the season ranked No. 13 in the country, and with all eyes on Josh Rosen, against the University of Virginia the freshman put on a show. On the first offensive play of the game, Rosen took the shotgun snap, dropped back, and launched a deep pass down the left sideline to receiver Kenny Walker. The pass was perfect, but it was dropped. The crowd was upset by the missed opportunity but couldn't help but smile at the prospects of another superstar quarterback. Rosen would finish the day with 351 yards passing and three touchdowns, going 28 for 35, but it was not the stats alone that told the story. It was his throws. Rosen looked like a seasoned NFL quarterback. He was big, he was poised, and he had a rocket arm. The future looked bright. UCLA won, 34–16. Myles Jack scored a touchdown on the ground, Adarius Pickett intercepted his first career pass, and Jamabo rushed for 79 yards in his first game. But all was not well: star defensive lineman Eddie Vanderdoes had torn his ACL and missed the rest of the season.

One week after the exciting season-opening victory, the Bruins went to Las Vegas to take on UNLV, and though they dominated from start to finish, winning 37–3, the celebration would be short-lived. The Bruins had a tough opponent ahead of them one week later, and the injury bug would strike again. For the first time in his young career, Rosen struggled in Week 3. The Bruins came into the game No. 10 in the country; their opponent, the Brigham Young University Cougars, were No. 19. It would be a battle. Rosen threw three interceptions in the first half, but in the second half, he composed himself and played a smooth 30 minutes. Still, UCLA trailed, 17–10, entering the fourth quarter. The BYU lead would reach 10 after a field goal, but with 12:16 remaining, Rosen found Payton for a 19-yard score to bring the Bruins within three. BYU countered with a field goal, but with just over three minutes to play, the Bruins were on the march again, and their drive was capped by a 3-yard Nate Starks run. The game was finally sealed on a Myles Jack interception. UCLA escaped with a 24–23 victory, but again, as in two weeks earlier against UVA, the Bruins had a problem. Cornerback Fabian Moreau broke his foot and was out for the season. Before the next game, linebacker/running back Myles Jack suffered a knee injury in practice and would also be out for the season. UCLA was 3–0, but three of their best players on defense were out for the year. Myles Jack would jump to the NFL. He was an athletic freak in the most positive sense of the word, but his time in Westwood was cut short, and fans were left to wonder "what if." His final play in a Bruins uniform had been a game-winning interception. It was a fitting way to go out. It just came too early.

Without three key defensive players, UCLA was in for a major test the next week. The Bruins traveled to Tucson, Arizona, to take on the University of Arizona Wildcats in a nationally televised game. The crew from the popular ESPN show, *College Gameday*, was in town, and though UCLA was the higher-ranked team, the *Gameday* cast preferred the Wildcats. UCLA passed its first test without the defensive trio, beating UofA, 56—30. One week later, the Bruins fell behind the Arizona State Sun Devils early and could never recover. UCLA lost, 38–23. Twelve days later, UCLA took on the Stanford Cardinal in Palo Alto, and though the extra break would help the Bruins regroup on defense, the bye week couldn't bring back personnel lost to injuries. Jack, Vanderdoes, and Moreau would not come through the tunnel, and they were sorely missed. Stanford running back Christian McCaffrey, who would finish the season as the Heisman Trophy runner-up, cut through the defense and amazed the nationally televised audience. Rosen threw for 326 yards and Perkins ran for 104, but it was not enough to overcome the brilliance of McCaffrey, who finished with 243 yards rushing and 122 yards on two kickoff returns. Stanford won, 56–35, and UCLA's dreams of making the playoffs were over.

But the Bruins were not yet finished. After losing two straight games, they bounced back by winning the next three. One week after the Stanford game, they took on the other team from up North, the California Golden Bears. It was another Thursday game, but this one was at home, and this time the Bruins came out on top. Rosen outplayed Cal quarterback Jared Goff, and UCLA won, 40–24. Next, in UCLA's eighth game of the season, they played another thriller. After leading the Colorado Buffaloes, 21–6, at halftime, the Bruins let their guard down, and the Buffaloes, an improved team over years past, crawled back in. At the end of three, the Bruins still held a 12-point lead, 28–16, but within three minutes of the start of the fourth quarter Colorado not only erased the deficit, but took the lead. The Buffaloes scored two quick touchdowns to go ahead, 31–28, but with 8:28 to play, Soso Jamabo scored a 2-yard touchdown, and the Bruins went on to win, 35–31. UCLA linebacker Jayon Brown, the man who replaced Myles Jack, finished with 18 tackles, a career high. One week later, the Bruins took on the Oregon State Beavers, a Pac 12 bottom-dweller, and won, 41–0. The Bruins were 7–2 and still in a position to win the Pac 12 South.

On November 14, the No. 19 Bruins took on the Washington State Cougars, the most improved team in the conference and one of the most improved in the nation. Washington State, led by head coach Mike Leach, came into the game with one of the best offenses in America. In the first quarter, the Bruins did a fine job of slowing the Cougars. WSU led, 7–6. Nate Starks scored a second-quarter touchdown for the Bruins, and at halftime, the score was 16–14 UCLA. In the second half, the pace ramped up, and excitement was off the charts. The Cougars scored the next 10 points, and midway through the fourth quarter, the score was still WSU 24, UCLA 16. Fairbairn knocked in a field goal with 7:10 to play to cut the lead to five. With 1:09 to play, the Bruins had the ball, needing a touchdown. The ball was at the WSU 37-yard line. Scoring a touchdown would not be the surprise, but how they did certainly was. Josh Rosen, not usually a running threat, saw a massive hole in front of him and rumbled for 37 yards to take the lead! The freshman quarterback looked less like what fans had come to expect, and more like the man who had donned number 17 in blue and gold the previous three years. The Bruins went for two, and Rosen found Duarte to put UCLA in the lead, 27–24. There were 69 seconds remaining, and WSU quarterback Luke Falk was always a threat. In the blink of an eye, the Cougars were on the move. With 11 seconds to play, WSU was already in field goal position. The ball was at the Bruins 21-yard line. On third and 10, Falk took the snap, felt the pressure, rolled right, and lofted a pass into the end zone. Defensive back Ishmael Adams was all over receiver Gabe Marks, and though the referee called pass interference, it didn't matter. Marks caught the ball for the go-ahead score. There were three seconds remaining, and the Bruins were stunned. WSU 31, UCLA 27. The Bruins were 7–3 and trailing the Utah Utes in the Pac 12 South race. When they traveled to Salt Lake City, they needed a win to remain in contention, and they got just that in a low-scoring affair. UCLA 17, Utah 9.

When the Bruins took on the USC Trojans in their regular season finale, the two teams were in the same situation in which they had been so many times before. They were playing for the ultimate prize. In the past, the game was often the determining factor in deciding who would represent the conference in the Rose Bowl. Now, it would decide the Pac 12 South leader, and the winner would go to the conference championship game. UCLA entered the game with a three-game winning streak over its arch enemy, but now the Bruins were without Hundley. It was Rosen's turn to taste the rivalry. At the end of the first quarter, the Bruins led, 7–3, but things quickly turned sour. In the second quarter, Rosen passed to Duarte for a touchdown, but the Bruins gave up a touchdown run by USC quarterback Cody Kessler and allowed punt returner Adoree Jackson to take one in from 42 yards out. USC kicker Alex Wood knocked in his second field goal of the game, and at halftime the Trojans led, 20–14. The Bruins struck first in the second half on a Perkins touchdown, but USC stormed back and took a commanding lead that the Bruins could not overcome. When the clock ticked down to :00, the Trojans had won, 40–21. It was UCLA's first loss to USC in the Jim Mora era, and while USC was off to the Pac 12 title game, the Bruins went home. On December 26, the Bruins took on the Nebraska Cornhuskers in the Foster Farms Bowl, but the game was nothing if not a letdown. Nebraska physically dominated UCLA and won by the score of 37–29. In what was once a promising season, the Bruins finished with disappointment. Their record was 8–5, and they would again lose a slew of players to the NFL. In 2016, the Bruins would have question marks at a number of positions, but Josh Rosen would not be one of them. He finished his freshman season as one of the best quarterbacks in America, and expectations for him would only keep rising. Overall, the team had to make some changes. Offensive coordinator Noel Mazzone was gone. Running backs coach Kennedy Polamalu was promoted to OC. Coach Mora had no plans of seeing his team take the field again physically weaker than their opponents. The 2016 season couldn't come soon enough.

The Heisman Trust named Derrick Henry from the University of Alabama the 2015 Heisman Trophy Winner.

The University of Alabama beat Clemson University, 45–40, in the CFP National Championship game.

## 2016

2016 was an interesting year for both the United States of America and the UCLA football program. After a long, sometimes frustrating political season, Donald Trump and Hillary Clinton were named the presidential nominees of the two main political parties in the United States. Neither was particularly

UCLA Spirit Squad, 2016 (Erkki Corpuz Collection)

popular, and many Americans were forced to decide between two candidates whom they disliked. In November, Donald Trump was elected president, winning the Electoral College vote despite losing the popular vote. It was a major political upset. For Coach Jim Mora and the UCLA football staff, they had to deal with an upset of a different kind. Despite the often breathtaking true freshman season of Josh Rosen one year earlier, the Bruins had tumbled in the win total, and fans didn't like it. After winning nine games, and then 10, in back-to-back seasons, UCLA had won only eight in 2015 and had lost to USC for the first time in the Jim Mora era. That called for changes in 2016. Gone was Noel Mazzone. Kennedy Polamalu was promoted to offensive coordinator. UCLA would have a new style on offense. After repeatedly seeing Stanford run the ball directly at UCLA and punish the Bruins physically, Coach Mora wanted his squad to be more like the men from Palo Alto, or at least that's what many fans thought. Though some liked the idea, skepticism was still high. Did UCLA have the personnel to run a pro-style offense? Could they run the ball from under center? Did they have the offensive line to protect Rosen on a deep drop back? The season would certainly tell the story, and for the Bruins it would be a story not of joy, but of horror.

The Bruins began their season in one of the most hostile environments in college football. The Aggies fans in College Station, Texas, love their team and are typically nice, inviting guests. It's a dream road trip for college football junkies, as there is more to the game experience at Texas A&M than at practically anywhere else in the country. Over 50,000 fans showed up at Midnight Yell the night before the game, and 100,443 were at Kyle Field to see the season opener. Prior to the game, Josh Rosen made some innocent comments about crowd noise, stating that he believed there is not much difference in the impact on a quarterback between playing in front of a huge crowd or simply a large crowd. He stated that if he couldn't hear on the field when there are 50,000 people roaring, then 100,000 wouldn't be much different. The Aggies fans hardly needed motivation to cheer loud, but Rosen's comments surely fired them up even more. The game would be a classic. UCLA got off to a solid start, with freshman kicker J.J. Molson knocking in two field goals to grab a 6–0 lead, but UCLA would pay for settling for three points at a time. At the half, the score was 10–9, TAMU, with UCLA's only other points coming on another Molson field goal. The third quarter was all Aggies, as quarterback Trevor Knight ran for a touchdown and threw for another. Entering the fourth quarter, the score was 24–9, and the Bruins were paying for their mistakes. Poor offensive line play, coupled with dropped and forced passes, killed the Bruins for much of the game. With four minutes to play, however, UCLA found the end zone on a Bolu Olorunfunmi 9-yard run, and less three minutes later, the Bruins scored again. Josh Rosen heaved the ball up for Kenny Walker, who made a miraculous catch to take the ball in for a 62-yard score. Rosen found Austin Roberts for the two-point conversion, and the game was tied. In overtime, UCLA's luck ran out. Trevor Knight ran for a touchdown, and the Aggies, aided by a key dropped pass in the end zone, stopped the Bruins and won the game. It was a heartbreaking loss for UCLA.

As the season went on, the offense continued to be a problem. UCLA beat UNLV and BYU but then lost to No. 7 Stanford despite a fine performance by Takkarist McKinley, Jayon Brown, and the stellar Bruin defense. UCLA beat the University of Arizona on October 1 to move to 3–2, but the season would soon fall apart. One week after the win over the Wildcats, the Bruins were once again taking on a team from the state of Arizona, but the matchup with the Arizona State Sun Devils wouldn't go as well. The Bruins lost, 23–20, in a frustrating game, but the bigger issue was the status of their quarterback. Rosen injured his shoulder, and his season was over.

There would be no John Barnes fairy-tale story when walk-on Mike Fafaul took the quarterback reins the rest of the season. Fafaul showed his strong arm, but accuracy problems and inexperience haunted him and the Bruins. Replacing Rosen was a difficult enough task, but the porous play of the receivers, as well as that of the offensive line, made the job even more difficult. UCLA lost to Washington State, Utah, and Colorado before finally winning another game, this one over the Pac 12's bottom-dweller, the Oregon State Beavers.

There would be no bowl game in 2016, as UCLA was crushed by USC at the Bruins' home field Rose Bowl and then finished the season with a dispirited showing at Cal, losing, 36–10. The Bruins finished with a 4–8 record, the worst season of Jim Mora's career. UCLA would make badly needed changes to its coaching staff for 2017, but questions arose about whether Head Coach Mora was still the right man to head the program. Many fans wondered openly if Coach Mora was still as passionate about the program as before. They questioned his ability to hire quality assistant coaches, as he had done in 2012. Many questioned if he even cared, if he was distracted by personal issues, and if he had become overly content. Whether right or wrong, fair or unfair, the questions would last the entire offseason. Coach Mora was on the hot seat.

The Heisman Trust named Lamar Jackson from the University of Louisville the 2016 Heisman Trophy Winner.

Clemson University beat the University of Alabama, 35–31, in the CFP National Championship game.

## 2017

For the third consecutive year, Josh Rosen and the UCLA offense would run a system different from the one they had executed the previous season. Rosen, who just two years earlier was a freshman sensation from local St. John Bosco High School, had yet to prove himself convincingly on the field. In 2016, the UCLA offense had struggled. When Rosen missed much of the season due to injury, many pundits believed that he took a step back. As a junior, he would now have to regain his top form in order for the Bruins to take a step forward as a team. Fortunately, with the arrival of another new offensive coordinator, things did change for the Bruins offense.

Jedd Fisch took the reins of the Bruins offense and guided his unit to a spectacular turnaround

UCLA flags pregame (Danielle Alvari Collection)

season. Rosen was truly brilliant, everything that Bruins fans hoped he would be on the field. Fisch brought a sophisticated passing attack, and Rosen was a true field general. On defense, however, the 2017 season is memorable for a different reason. Under the guidance of Defensive Coordinator Tom Bradley and Head Coach Jim Mora, UCLA had one of the worst defenses in the country and one of the worst in school history. The Bruins gave up an average of 36.6 points per game, 117th in the country out of 130. They gave up 287.4 yards per game on the ground, 129th in the nation. UCLA had hit rock bottom on the defensive side of the ball. It would be up to Rosen and the offense to salvage a solid season.

While UCLA improved in one way and regressed in another, one thing remained true throughout the entire season: Head Coach Jim Mora was on the hot seat. UCLA was trending in the wrong direction, and in 2017, Coach Mora was fighting for his job.

The season began on Sunday, September 3. It had been exactly one year since the Bruins lost to the Texas A&M Aggies in heartbreaking fashion in College Station. The two teams would meet again, this time at the Rose Bowl. Four minutes into the game, J.J. Molson knocked in a short field goal, and the Bruins were ahead. All was well. It was early, but the Bruins were leading. No one could have guessed what would happen next. With 6:41 remaining in the first quarter, TAMU running back Keith Ford scored from five yards out. A minute and a half later, Daniel LaCamera added three points on a short field goal, and just over one minute later, Trayveon Williams added another touchdown for the Aggies. It was 17–3 at the end of one, and it would only get worse for the Bruins. Keith Ford added two more touchdowns in the second quarter to run the score to 31–3 Aggies. Jalen Starks scored the first Bruins touchdown of the year with three minutes to play in the half, but just 20 seconds later, Williams raced for 61 yards and another touchdown. As the two teams headed to the locker rooms at halftime, the score was 38–10. Fans booed the Bruins loudly as many headed to their cars and went home.

With the Bruins trailing by 28 points at halftime, even the most optimistic of fans had to be feeling down. When LaCamera added two more field goals to run the score to 44–10 with fewer than 20 minutes to play, nearly all had to believe the game was basically over. Soso Jamabo scored the second Bruins touchdown of the game before the end of the third quarter, however, and at the end of three, the score was 44–17. The final 15 minutes of the game would be both memorable and magical. Though logic would have it that the Bruins were all but dead, nothing is ever predictable in sports; miracles sometimes do happen. It helps when you have the best quarterback in America. With 13:22 to play, Rosen passed to Darren Andrews for a 9-yard score. Five minutes later, the two connected again, this time from 42 yards out when the ball went right through a waiting defender's hands and found Andrews in the end zone. The score was now 44–31, and though the Bruins defense had stiffened in the second half, they needed to play a perfect final quarter to give the team a shot at a win. With 6:44 to play, however, any hope of a comeback was once again seemingly lost. TAMU quarterback Kellen Mond, in for injured starter Nick Starkel, raced down the right sideline for what appeared to be the game-clinching touchdown. Mond was unable to stay inbounds, however, and the ball was spotted at the Bruins 22-yard line. On the ensuing first down, Mond rushed for seven yards. On second-and-3, the Bruins stuffed Williams for a loss of one yard. On third-and-4, Keisean Lucier-South broke through the Aggies front line and sacked Mond for a loss of nine. With the sack, the Aggies' field goal attempt would be longer, but the Bruins were still in need of a break. On the 43-yard field goal attempt by LaCamera, the Bruins got the break they needed. The kick was partially blocked by Adarius Pickett. UCLA was still down 13 but had life. Rosen again drove the Bruins down the field, hitting tight end Caleb Wilson and receivers Darren Andrews and Jordan Lasley, over and over. With 3:10 to play, the Bruins found the end zone, and the touchdown again came in spectacular fashion. Facing pressure up the middle, Rosen was flushed to his left, and just before being hit, he fired across his body to the end zone. Theo Howard was well covered, but his eyes saw the ball first. He quickly cut across the front of the end zone, in front of two defenders, and dived for the ball. He landed just in back of the goal line, and the Bruins had scored again. After the extra point, the score was 44–38. The game was not over, but the Bruins would be forced to rely on their shaky defense.

After UCLA held TAMU to just two yards on

their first two plays, the clock showed 2:53 when the Aggies faced third-and-8 at their own 26-yard line. Mond took the shotgun snap, but the UCLA rush came quick. Senior Jacob Tuioti-Mariner and freshman Jaelen Phillips converged on the quarterback for the biggest defensive play of the game. The remaining crowd erupted. The ball would soon be in the hands of Josh Rosen, and everyone had a rising sense of what that meant: The Bruins could win, and few doubted it anymore. UCLA quickly drove the ball downfield, but with just 54 seconds remaining it was fourth-and-6. The ball sat at the TAMU 20-yard line. The Aggies brought six on the rush. Rosen saw the blitz and lobbed a pass over the defense to Jamabo, who ran a swing route to the left. The pass had incredible touch and landed perfectly in Jamabo's hands. He made the catch and raced to the first-down marker, where he spun to gain four additional yards. Jamabo got the first down and skipped out of bounds, but with no timeouts, the clock would wind on the officials' ready-for-play signal, and UCLA hurried to the line of scrimmage to spike the ball. With :48 left to play, Rosen took the snap, but instead of spiking the ball, he faked a spike and threw a quick fade route to Jordan Lasley in the left corner of the end zone. The throw was perfect, just over Lasley's outside shoulder. He turned, caught the ball, got a foot in bounds, and the referee signaled touchdown! The Bruins had done it! They had been down, 44–10 and came all the way back. TAMU's last-ditch effort would come up short, and UCLA was 1–0. Josh Rosen's performance was the stuff of legends. He had thrown for 491 yards, 292 of which came in the fourth quarter alone. He threw for four touchdowns, all coming in the final quarter. The Bruins were down, 44–10, and then shocked the college football world. Wilson finished with 208 receiving yards on 15 catches. Andrews added 142, and Lasley hauled in 100. The 34-point comeback was the largest in college football in 11 years and the second largest in major college football history.

While the memory of the 2017 season opener will live on for those who attended and all who watched on TV, the season in totality was not one of joy, but rather one of immense frustration. UCLA was able to win at home but never able to win on the road. They followed up their win over TAMU with a victory over Hawaii but then lost consecutive games away from Pasadena, one to Memphis and one to Stanford. UCLA would beat Colorado in a close game but then lose to Arizona in embarrassing fashion. They beat Oregon convincingly but were blown out by Washington and Utah. The Bruins beat Arizona State on November 11, but their next test would be against the USC Trojans, a team with another well-known, talented quarterback.

The matchup between UCLA and USC on November 18 at the Los Angeles Memorial Coliseum was not quite like those matchups had been between the two rivals in '87 and '88, when Rodney Peete and Troy Aikman squared off. The Bruins were just 5–5, with an 0–5 record on the road. USC was on its way to the Pac 12 Championship and a berth in the Fiesta Bowl. The game itself had significant intrigue for another reason. It was not just UCLA vs. USC, it was Josh Rosen vs. Sam Darnold. One year earlier, Darnold had posted an incredible season for the Trojans, while Rosen's season ended with him watching on the sideline, injured. All the hype that followed Rosen in his first year had left and landed on Darnold. Many thought Darnold the best quarterback in the country heading into the 2017 season, but by November 18, it was clear that Darnold was not even the best in Los Angeles. Though USC was a heavy favorite, the Bruins outplayed the Trojans for much of the game. Mistakes in the red zone and atrocious play by its special teams unit haunted UCLA, however, despite Rosen outplaying Darnold in every way. USC won the game, and although UCLA would end its regular season with one final game, fans had an entirely different subject on their minds.

One day after losing to USC, Jim Mora was fired. Many saw this coming, though there was doubt whether UCLA's athletic administration could justify paying a substantial buyout to fire their once-popular coach. Many were skeptical about UCLA's ability to allure a top coach, as few had confidence after two decades of mediocrity. Rumors would swirl all week, but the Bruins still had a game to play. Coach Jedd Fisch was named the interim head coach, and the Bruins took on the California Golden Bears on Black Friday, the day after Thanksgiving. UCLA beat their old rival, 30–27, to finish undefeated at home, despite losing every game away from the Rose Bowl. The Bruins then headed to a bowl game, the Cactus Bowl, on December 26 and would do what they had done all year. They lost, 35–17, as the Wildcats ran the ball down the Bruins' throats all game. UCLA finished 0–7 on the road. Though the season was very much a failure in nearly every way for UCLA, 2017 proved to be a success in another way. One day after the team lost to Cal, Chip Kelly was named the next head coach of the UCLA Bruins. At the time of his arrival, Kelly was the most accomplished coach ever to be hired by UCLA. Heading into the 2018 season, he will be without Josh Rosen, who declared for the NFL Draft, and Bruins fans will be left to feel that the career of a brilliant player was wasted. Even without Rosen, there is much to look forward to in the immediate future. The 2018 season marks the 100th football season in school history—one in which, appropriately, they will be led by one of the greatest coaches in America. Welcome to the Chip Kelly era.

The Heisman Trust named Baker Mayfield from the University of Oklahoma the 2017 Heisman Trophy Winner.

The University of Alabama beat the University of Georgia, 26–23, in the CFP National Championship game.

# CHAPTER 17
# Chip Kelly (2018–present)

When Chip Kelly was hired to be the seventeenth head coach in UCLA history, he brought with him something that no coach in the school's history ever had. His résumé was loaded with success. While other coaches, including Red Sanders and Terry Donahue, found great success while at UCLA and others, such as Tommy Prothro, Rick Neuheisel, and Dick Vermeil, would be remembered for not just their time at UCLA, none had the résumé to match Chip Kelly's at the time of his hiring.

Chip Kelly is an intensely private man. He is a walking paradox. His coaching style is flashy and in your face. His private life is quiet and, well, private. He is an intellectual man, firm in his beliefs, yet he is flexible. He is an innovator, yet he is also a simplifier. He is best known for his time coaching on the West Coast, yet he is an East Coaster, with an East Coast personality. He has coached at the highest level, yet he believes that there are no rivalries, are no games bigger than the next. Every game is his Super Bowl, his National Championship. He doesn't believe in pressure, only preparation. He believes in emotion, but more so he believes in logic. He believes in players, not positions, and the simple idea that big people beat up small people. He has been called "Big Balls Chip," yet he looks to stay out of the limelight. He believes in letting his players play, and letting the players get the credit, for they are the ones achieving on the field, and he is just putting them in the right place. He doesn't like to be called a "genius," and he doesn't believe his offense is magical, yet he is this generation's single greatest force for change in offensive football. Chip Kelly is a lot of things, many seemingly contradictory. He is a science-based thinker. He is a micromanager. He is a CEO. He is a football lifer, a student, a teacher, and a philosopher. He is a winner, and more than anything he is a coach, a man so thorough in his understanding of the game that he has built a reputation as one of America's great football minds. He is also now a UCLA Bruin. Every step along the way, every stop on the map, every game ever won or lost has brought Chip Kelly to Westwood.

Chip Kelly, 17th football coach in UCLA history

Charles Edward "Chip" Kelly was born on November

25, 1963, in Dover, New Hampshire. He was, and is, a prototypical jock. This is not to say he doesn't have other interests, or that he isn't intelligent. He is, in fact, one of the most intelligent coaches in America. He had an affinity for sports at a young age, however, that was unmatched by most. He attended Manchester Central High School, where he played both offense and defense on the football team, as well as basketball and ice hockey. In college, he would follow the same plan on the football field, contributing as both a safety and a quarterback for the home-town University of New Hampshire under legendary coach Bill Bowes. Coach Bowes would say of Kelly, "He wasn't very big, and he didn't possess the outstanding speed that you'd like to see with a guy of his limited height." Despite his physical limitations, Kelly was a valuable member of the team. In his freshman year, the Wildcats finished with seven wins and three losses. Over the next three years, UNH would win four games, then seven, then nine. It is not the on-field record, however, that had a long-lasting impact on Chip's life. It was his connection to coach Bowes. Chip would never start a game at UNH, but he was trusted by his coach, and eventually that trust would earn him his first big break.

There are many mysteries in Chip Kelly's life. After his final year of eligibility in 1984, Chip's story goes dark. Little is known about his life for the following six years. He reportedly took up coaching during this time, returning to Manchester Central High School and beginning his career on the sidelines. In 1990, things changed. Chip has always valued players who graduate, as it shows a commitment to following through on a task, but he was not initially a college graduate himself when he left UNH. It would take additional time, but in 1990, he completed his task. He graduated with a Bachelor's of Science degree in physical education and then took his coaching career to the next level. It was time to try his hand at the college game.

Over the ensuing years, Coach Kelly would take his beliefs, refine them, change them, and build a philosophy that was uniquely his. He spent time coaching multiple positions. He coached linebackers, defensive backs, and special teams at Columbia at both the freshman and varsity levels. He coached running backs at his alma mater, UNH, in 1992, and then was the defensive coordinator at Johns Hopkins in 1993. In 1994, he returned to UNH, and this time he was there for the long haul. From 1994 to 1996, he coached running backs, helping Jerry Azumah rush for over 6,000 career yards, the FCS record at the time. From 1997 to 1998, he coached the offensive line, in the process helping to fine tune his zone rushing scheme. In 1999, Coach Kelly received his second big break as a coach. After his former coach, Bill Bowes, had helped Kelly begin his college coaching career, he was retiring, and though this could have brought great anxiety to coach Kelly concerning his future, it instead created an opening. Offensive Coordinator Sean McDonnell was promoted to head coach, and Kelly was promoted to OC.

It was not at UNH that Chip Kelly became a household name, but it was at UNH that he was able to put his offensive philosophy to the test. In his first 33 games as an OC, his teams averaged 28.6 points per game despite losing Azumah to graduation following the 1998 season. He and the Wildcats would only get better. Suddenly school records began to fall, and Kelly's name began to rise. In 2004, 29 school records went down, and in 2005 the offense was even better, averaging nearly 500 yards per game and finishing in the top five in nearly every statistical category. Coach McDonnell knew that Coach Kelly would not be at UNH forever, but Kelly was reluctant to leave a place where he was happy. McDonnell would say of Kelly, "Someday he's going to be gone." Coach Kelly, however, saw things differently. "I've been offered jobs," said Coach Kelly in 2002, "but every time I get offered a job I talk to Sean and other people I have respect for and ask, is it a better job than I'm in right now?"

In 2007, the answer to Coach Kelly's question was finally "Yes." Coach Mike Bellotti at Oregon had already begun implementing spread offensive principals, but his success was mixed. He wanted a change, and Coach Kelly offered the change he wanted. Reaction to the hiring of Coach Kelly as the new offensive coordinator at the University of Oregon was mostly that of dismay. Who was this new guy? Could the small college coach really do as well in the Pac 10 Conference? Soon they would find out, and soon everyone knew who Coach Chip Kelly was. In 2007, Oregon finished with a 9–4 record and a No. 23 position in the final Associated Press rankings. That does not tell the entire story, however. The offense averaged 38.2 points per game, good for twelfth in the country, up from 29.5 ppg the previous season (twenty-fifth). At one point, the Ducks reached as high as No. 2 in the rankings after starting 8–1, but a devastating injury to Heisman Trophy favorite Dennis Dixon derailed the end of the season, and the Ducks lost three of the final four. One year later, the offense was even better. With Jeremiah Masoli now at quarterback, the Ducks averaged 41.9 points per game, seventh best in the country, and finished with a 10–3 record and a No. 14 final ranking. They would only get better, and now it was time for Coach Kelly to run the show.

On March 31, 2009, Oregon Head Coach Mike Bellotti was promoted to athletic director and retired from coaching the football team. Chip Kelly, the man whom very few people had known two years earlier, became the Oregon head football coach. He would do things his way, and things would forever be different in college football. At the 2011 Nike Coach of the Year Clinic, Chip Kelly reflected on his having taken over the program two years earlier. He explained that the first thing he had to do was identify what the Ducks stood for as a program. The three things that came to mind were **1. Fast. 2. Play Hard. 3. Finish.** Let's look at each and see how Coach Kelly implemented his style at Oregon.

1. **Fast-** From a strategic standpoint, when most fans think of Coach Kelly, they think of speed. They think of the breathtaking speed of the Oregon players, the pace at which the offense operated, and the way the "no huddle" at Oregon changed the game. Speed, however, is not just about electronically timing someone's 40-yard dash. In Coach Kelly's offense, the most important thing is comfort. Players must be comfortable with what they are tasked with doing, so they are able to play as fast as they can. They must process things quickly, make split-second decisions, and utilize their speed effectively.
2. **Play Hard-** The idea of playing hard is simple. It's the goal of every coach to get his team to play hard. Getting his team to respond is more challenging. Chip Kelly has mastered the difficult task of getting his players to play hard for the entirety of games. His teams trust in the game plans, as they have executed every play repeatedly in practice. Quick, simple tasks completed perfectly each time make it easier for players to play hard in games.
3. **Finish-** The word *finish* is integral to Kelly's coaching philosophy. Much like "The Process" at Alabama under Nick Saban, finishing each task is about being in the moment and doing one thing correctly, and then the next, and then the next. Players must finish stretching correctly. They must finish eating correctly, sleeping correctly, practicing correctly, winning correctly.

Coach Kelly's changes were not entirely macro-level philosophical, however. He looks at football readiness from a scientific perspective, as well. Coach Kelly was at the forefront of medical tracking technology, an increased attention to sleep and nutrition, urine and health tests, and strength and conditioning overhaul. When Chip Kelly became a head coach for the first time in 2009, he did things his way. Oregon was his program, and he was able to take the Ducks to sights unprecedented in the school's history.

In Coach Kelly's first season, Oregon got off to an inauspicious start. On September 3, Oregon took on the Boise State Broncos on a Thursday night nationally televised game. Oregon lost, 19–8, and worse than the loss itself was the embarrassment that came after the game. Running back LeGarrette Blount punched an opposing player and then tried to get into the stands while being escorted out. The punch played seemingly on a loop on ESPN-TV, and Coach Kelly had his first major problem to deal with. He subsequently suspended Blount for the season and moved on without the player many saw as the best on the team. LaMichael James took over as the starting running back and proceeded to have a brilliant season, finishing with 1,546 yards and 14 touchdowns on the ground. The Ducks finished with the eighth-best scoring offense in the country and won 10 games. One year later, the Ducks were even better. Darron Thomas took over at quarterback, James had another incredible season, rushing for 1,731 yards, and the Ducks' offense was a juggernaut. Oregon averaged 47.0 points per game, best in the nation, and finished 12–0 on the regular season, reaching the BCS National Championship game.

Oregon would lose, 22–19, to Auburn, in part due to a fluky play in the final minutes, and though they would not bring home the crystal ball trophy, they did enjoy the greatest season in school history. Over the next two years, Oregon would compile a 24–3 record, finishing in the top three in scoring offense each year. After four years, Coach Kelly had accumulated a 46–7 record, won three Pac 10/12 titles, gone to the Rose Bowl twice, Fiesta Bowl once, and the BCS National Championship game. He had proven to be a godsend to the Oregon program, but his time was ticking down. He had aspirations to coach in the NFL, and in 2013, he made the jump.

Chip Kelly coached the Philadelphia Eagles for three years. Prior to his arrival, the Eagles had finished with a 4–12 record in 2012. In his first year, the Eagles went 10–6, won the NFC East, and made a trip to the playoffs. The next year, they again finished 10–6, then followed that up with a disappointing 6–9 record in 2015, before Coach Kelly was fired with one game remaining. Just sixteen days after being fired by the Eagles, Chip Kelly was announced as the next head coach of the San Francisco 49ers, a team that had experienced success under Jim Harbaugh, but that had been spiraling out of control since his departure following the 2014 season. Under Jim Tomsula, the 49ers finished 5–11 and were trending the wrong way. Coach Kelly was with the 49ers for only one year, finishing with a 2–14 record. In 2017, Coach Kelly was out of coaching for the first time in almost 30 years. He spent one season with ESPN as a college football analyst.

On November 25, 2017, Chip Kelly was hired as the seventeenth head coach in UCLA football history. He brings with him an impressive résumé, and a mindset for continual improvement. He has spent his entire coaching career speaking with others, picking the minds of the greatest coaches at every level. He has, in time, become a man whom others seek out, hoping to learn the game from a football innovator. He will bring his style to Westwood, and with him will come great anticipation. We are in the era of Chip Kelly, and we are in a time of great hope. While UCLA fans dream of one day reaching the mountain top, and standing at the pinnacle of the college football world, it is Chip Kelly who is tasked with making that dream come true. Whether in New Hampshire, Oregon, Pennsylvania, or California, Coach Kelly has always done things his way. He has refined his style through decades of learning and will undoubtedly continue to grow as a coach at UCLA. For Bruins fans not old enough to have seen the Red Sanders teams of the '50s, the Prothro teams of the '60s, Vermeil's magical 1975 team, the great success of the early '80s under Donahue, or the incredible Toledo teams in 1997 and 1998, there is hope that Chip Kelly will bring us back to glory, forever with eyes to the future. Only one thing is certain going forward: Chip Kelly is coming, and he's coming fast. Look out, college football world.

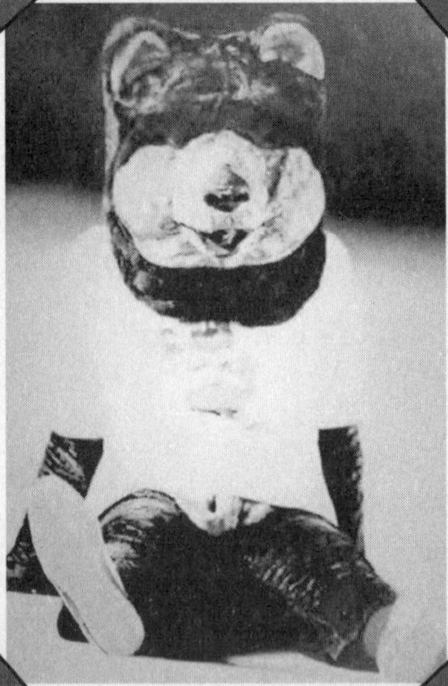

(clockwise from top left) The UCLA band performs at halftime of 1936 UCLA-USC game (Southern Campus Collection); UCLA vs. USC, 1965 (Southern Campus Collection); UCLA fans celebrate thrilling victory over USC, 1965 (Southern Campus Collection); UCLA Cheerleaders, 1965 (Southern Campus Collection); UCLA Coaches Dick Vermeil and Terry Donahue (Southern Campus Collection); Joe Bruin, 1975 (Southern Campus Collection); Everyone loves Joe Bruin (Danielle Alvari Collection)

(clockwise from top left) Geof Strand leads the cheers in 1983 (Southern Campus Collection); Even NBA Superstar Russell Westbrook loves football (Erkki Corpuz Collection); Few places have tailgating as great as the Rose Bowl (Erkki Corpuz Collection); Jackie Robinson's infuence is seen everywhere you go on the UCLA campus (Erkki Corpuz Collection); Legendary UCLA Yell Leader Frank Foellmer in 2012 (Erkki Corpuz Collection); UCLA Spirit Squad 2012 (Erkki Corpuz Campus Collection)

(top to bottom) Legendary UCLA Yell Leader Geof Strand in 2013 (Southern Campus Collection); UCLA Cheerleaders leading the way through Bruin Walk in 2013 (Erkki Corpuz Collection); The Yell Crew plays a major role in making sure the crowd is consistently loud (Erkki Corpuz Collection)

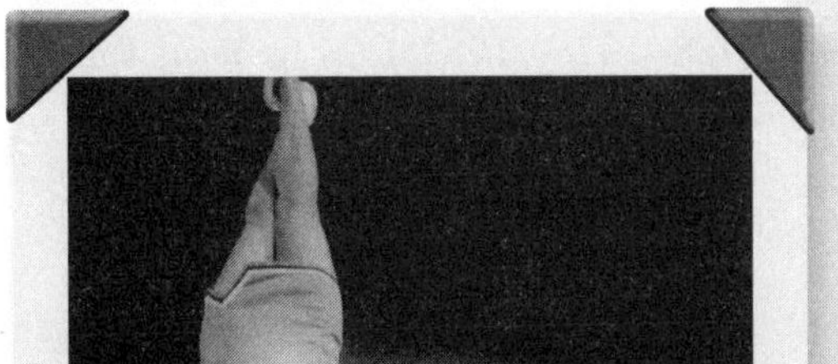

(clockwise from top left) The UCLA Spirit Squad during the playing of the National Anthem, 2015 (Erkki Corpuz Collection); The UCLA Spirit Squad performs a rountine in Lot H prior to game (Erkki Corpuz Collection); UCLA Cheerleaders perform at the Rose Bowl (Danielle Alvari Collection); The UCLA Spirit Squad has been flying high for nearly 100 years (Danielle Alvari Collection)

# CHAPTER 18
# Assistant Coaches

**A-** Nick Aliotti (1998), Sal Alosi (2012–2017), Foster Anderson (1977), Norm Anderson (1982–1986, 1994–1995), Steve Axman (1987–1988, 2003)

**B-** Dino Babers (2004–2007), Mike Balistaras (1949), Pete Barber (1938), William Barnes (1950–1958), John Becker (1970), Tink Bell (1924), Bob Bergdahl (1958–1964), Gary Bernardi (1994–2003), Eric Bieniemy (2003–2005), Gary Blackney (1978–1979), Ken Blair (1971–1973), Carrol Blakemore (1922), Jim Blewett (1939–1940), Sam Boghosian (1957–1964), Alan Borges (1996–2000), Deke Bracket (1950–1963), Tom Bradley (2015–2017), Inoke Breckterfield (2011), M.M. Brockway (1919), Rich Brooks (1970, 1976), Jim Buchanon (1951), Charles Bullough (2006–2010), Jacob Burney (1990–1992)

**C-** Tom Cable (2004–2005), Shelby Calhoun (1945–1948), Jim Camp (1967–1969), Ron Caragher (1996–2002), Norm Chow (2008–2010), A.J. Christoff (1990–1994), James Cline (1922), Jim Colletto (1967–1968, 1980–1981, 2006), Bob Connelly (2007), Gibson Cooper (1929), John Cooper (1965–1966), Larry Coyer (1987–1989), Jim Criner (1973–1975), Dave Currey (1989)

**D-** Jim Dawson (1959–1962), Gary DeLoach (2003), George Dickerson (1946–1957), Terry Donahue (1971–1975), Jimmie Dougherty (2017), Marc Dove (1996–2002), Norman Dow (1968–1969), Ron Dowhower (1974–1975), Norman Duncan (1934–1938), Earnel Durden (1969–1970)

**E-** Ed Eaton (1951), Jon Embree (2003–2005)

**F-** John Farrell (1967–1968), William Fehring (1948), Bob Field (1978–1979, 1981–2000), Jedd Fisch (2017), Deshaun Foster (2017), Hank Fraley (2017), Paul Frampton (1924–1931), Jethro Franklin (1999), Johnny Frawley (1940)

**G-** Frank Gansz Jr. (2008–2010), Frank Gansz Sr. (1976–1977), Joe Guion (1923–1924)

**H-** Tommy Harrison (1949–1950), Tom Hayes (1980–1988), Johnny Hermann (1958–1964), Cece Hollingsworth (1931–1946), Edwin Horrell (1930–1938), Todd Howard (2006–2010), Ron Hudson (1979–1981), Jed Hughes (1976–1981), Tim Hundley (1990–1995, 2009–2011)

**I-**

**J-** Milt Jackson (1979), John Jardine (1965–1969), Don Johnson (2000–2003), Johnny Johnson (1950–1964), Mike Johnson (2011)

**K-** Doug Kay (1977–1979), Larry Kerr (1989, 2003–2005), Ed Kezerian (1982–1992), Adrian Klemm (2012–2016), Tony Kopay (1965–1972), Doc Kreis (2003–2008)

**L-** Carnell Lake (2009), Clark Lea (2010–2011), Mike Linn (2008–2011), R. Todd Littlejohn (2001–2002), Jerry Long (1965–1975), Rocky Long (1996–1997)

**M-** Don Malmberg (1943), Dick Mansperger (1963–1964), Mike Marienthal (1948), Larry Marmie (1995), Steve Marshall (1996), Demetrice Martin (2012–2017), Jim Mastro (2011), Tony Matheson (1971), Bill Matthews (1971–1978), Ned Matthews (1948), Noel Mazzone (2012–2015), Taylor Mazzone (2013–2015), D.J. McCarthy (2006), Angus McClure (2007–2017), Hugh McDonald (1925–1932), Bob McKittrick (1965–1970), Bill McPherson (1975–1977), Mike Mikolayunas (1979), Jack Montgomery (1944–1945), Reggie Moore (2008–2010), Jim Mora (1974), Wayne Moses (1990–1995, 2008–2011), Carl Musendorf (1920), Jim Myers (1949–1956)

**N-** Ray Nagel (1951–1952, 1955–1957), Ron Nay (1971), Rick Neuheisel (1988–1993), Jay Norvell (2007), Wayne Nunnely (1993–1994)

**O-** Fred Oster (1925–1940)

**P-** Dwain Painter (1976–1978), Bob Palcic (1993, 2008–2011), Keith Parke (1921), Marcus Patton (2011), John Pearce (1999–2002), Skip Peete (1996–1997), Carl Peterson (1973–1975), Dan Peterson (1958–1964), Kennedy Polamalu (2014–2016), Tommy Prothro (1949–1954)

**Q-**

**R-** Steven Radicevic (2007), Bill Rees (1979–1993), Art Reichle (1947), Ray Richards (1938–1947), Don Riley (1976–1987, 1995), Greg Robinson (1982–1989), Pepper Rodgers (1965–1966)

**S-** Al Sandahl (1979), Phil Savage (1990), Rip Scherer (2016–2017), Brian Schneider (2003–2005), Mike Sherman (1994), Danny Shoemaker (1920), Ron Siegrist (1965–1968), Cliff Simpson (1930–1938), Kelly Skipper (1998–2002), Homer Smith (1972–1973, 1980–1986, 1990–1993), Phil Snow (2001–2002), Lou Spanos (2012–2013), Lynn Stiles (1971–1975), Lew Stueck (1963–1969), AJ Sturtzenegger (1925–1938, 1946–1948)

**T-** Howard Tippett (1980), Bob Toledo (1994–1995), Dick Tomey (1971–1976), Joe Tresey (2011), Harry Trotter (1923), Marques Tuiasosopo (2012, 2016), Mike Tuiasosopo (2014), Terry Tumey (1995–1998)

**U-** Jeff Ulbrich (2012–2014)

**V-** Muggs Van Sant (1924), Dick Vermeil (1970), Fred Von Appen (1970)

**W-** Dewayne Walker (2006–2008), Kenny Washington (1940), Mike Waufle (1989), Doug Weaver (1971–1972), Larry Weaver (1969–1970), Mark Weber (1997–2003), Scott White (2015–2017), Tom Whitley (1949), Ted Williams (1980–1989), John Wristen (2006).

**X-**

**Y-** Eric Yarber (2012–2016)

**Z-**

# CHAPTER 19
# Players by Jersey Number

**1-** Efren Herrera, Herschel Ramsey, Severn Reece, Ronnie DeBose, Gifford Irvine, Keith Brown, Tab Perry, Junior Lemau'u, Brandon Breazell, Alterraun Verner, Randall Carroll, Shaquelle Evans, Dietrich Riley, Ishmael Adams, Soso Jamabo, Darnay Holmes

**2-** Izzy Cantor, Leo Cantor, Don Malmberg, Dean Strawn, Alton McSween, Harold Hardin, Phil Hubbard, Walter Lang, Herb Welch, Darryl Henley, Scott Miller, Bryan Adams, Scott Miller, Teddy Lawrence, Chris Sailer, Tyler Ebell, Eric McNeal, Ryan Graves, Brandon Sermons, Milton Knox, Anthony Barr, Devin Fuller, Jaleel Wadood, Jordan Lasley, Josh Woods

**3-** John Zaby, George Phillips, Bert West, James McConnaughy, Bill Stamper, Steve Monahan, Steve Monahan, James Owens, Anthony Edgar, Kevin Nelson, James Washington, Carlton Gray, Jason Lesley, Javelin Guidry, Bob Ioja, Freddie Mitchell, Keith Short, Tab Perry, Rodney Van, Ben Olson, Kevin Craft, Rahim Moore, Josh Smith, Darius Bell, Randall Goforth, Jordan Lasley, Josh Rosen, Brandon Burton

**4-** Don Hesse, Noah Curti, Robert Leonard, Dave Anderson, John Sullivan, James Sarpy, David Brown, Ken Potter, Scott Stevenson, Reggie Moore, Kevin Jordan, Vito Clemente, Thaddeus Massey, Jason Stephens, Jason Harrison, Jarrad Page, Brian Callahan, Terrence Austin, Kevin Prince, Stan McKay, Darren Andrews, Cameron Judge, Craig Myers, Bolu Olorunfunmi, Jaleel Wadood

**5-** Bill Overlin, Lawrence Nicolich, Edward Breeding, Jim Brown, Kenny Easley

**6-** Martin Matheson, Milton Shedd, Bert Schneider, Harold Braly, John Sullivan, Johnny Gibbs, Ralph Ochoa, Lyndon Crawford, Dennis Price, Jim Bonds, Bryan Adams, Scott Fitterer, Avery Anderson, Eric Whitfield, Matt Clark, Josh Roenicke, Jamil Turner, Jeremy McGee, Tony Dye, Antwon Moutra, Jordon James, Eric Kendricks, Stephen Johnson, Adarius Pickett, Nick Juels

**7-** Bob Waterfield, Alan Hoisch, Zenon Andrusyshyn, Mark Harmon, Rick Walker, Bobby Hosea, Jay Schroeder, Don Rogers, Chance Johnson, Jim Bonds, Ryan Fien, Marques Anderson, Matt Moore, Justin Medlock, David Koral, Ben Olson, Courtney Viney, Morrell Presley, Josh Smith, Ricky Marvray, Devin Fuller, John Johnson, Darren Andrews, Mo Osling III

**8-** Eugene Alder, Dan Nelson, Lelon Nelson, Wally Henry, Brian Baggott, Norm Johnson, Karl Dorrell, Troy Aikman, Tommy Maddox, Aaron Anderson, Tommy Bennett, Lee Rodney, Scott McEwan, Robert Thomas, Junior Taylor, Brian Callahan, Shawn Oatis, Chris Forcier, Clayton Tunney, Joseph Fauria, Anthony Jefferson, Deon Hollins

**9-** Sherm Phinny, Ernie Case, Cliff Schroeder, Bill Delaney, Steve Bukich, Avon Riley, David Norrie, Mike Farr, Othello Henderson, Aaron Hanes, Abdul McCullough, Durrell Price, Junior Taylor, Ricky Manning Jr., Justin London, Marcus Everett, Donovan Carter, Jerry Johnson, Marcus Rios, Jordan Payton, Soso Jamabo, Dymond Lee, Elijah Gates

**10-** Ernest Hill, Charles Fears, Leon McLaughlin, Edison Griffin, Tim Jackert, Steve Sindell, Clay Gallagher, Pete Boermeester, Rick Neuheisel, Gifford Irvine, Travis Collier, Kusanti Abdul-Salaam, Andy Colbert, Cory Paus, Mil'Von James, Eddie Miller, Brett Mitchell, Gavin Ketchum, Akeem Ayers, Brendan Cross, Nick Crissman, Ryan Sublett, Sam Tai, Jordan Payton, Brendan Cross, Fabian Moreau, Kenneth Walker III, Jake Hall, Aaron Sharp, Jeremiah Martin, Demetric Felton, Colin Samuel

**11-** Jack Sommers, John Obidine, Jack Myers, Chuck Kendall, Mike Haffner, Mike Flores, Clay Gallagher, Rick Bashore, Matt Stevens, Reggie Moore, Bret Johnson, Jeff Clark, Steve Buck, Drew Bennett, Brandon Chillar, Dennis Keyes, Ossar Rasshan, Sean Westgate, Brendan Cross, Ricky Marvray, Darius Bell, Anthony Barr, Jerry Neuheisel, Keisean Lucier-South, Natie Iese, Audie Omotosho

**12-** John Frawley, Hoxie Griswold, Taylor Lewis, Doug Bradley, Dean Moore, Mike Haffner, Don Ghormley, Kip A Puiia, Lee Smith, Bernard Quarles, Steve Bono, Brendan McCracken, Robert Loigu, Al Jordan, Paul Guidry, Jason Bell, Nick Carey, Idris Moss, John Hale, Rodney Van, Patrick Cowan, Jamie Graham, Richard Brehaut, Tevin McDonald, Aaron Wallace, Mike Fafaul, Jayon Brown, Austin Burton, Rahyme Johnson

**13-** Kenny Washington, Kent Pearce

**14-** Eugene Alder, Art Spielman, Don Long, Larry Cox, Mike Molina, Tom Ramsey, Kirk Alexander, Michael Williams, Brent Brennan, Eric Scott, Chris Griffith, Drew Olson, Chris Horton, Drew Olson, McLeod Bethel-Thompson, Clayton Tunney, Kevin Prince, Aramide Olaniyan, TJ Millweard, Jake Hall, Mossi Johnson, Krys Barnes, Theo Howard

**15-** Dell Lyman, Bert DeVries, Phil Tinsley, Sam Brown, Keith Jensen, Larry Zeno, Jim Nader, John Sciarra, Michael Brant, Terry Moore, Danny Thompson, Jon Kelly, Wayne Cook, Jim McElroy, Ed Stansbury, John Sciarra, Marcus Cassell, Tyler Holland, Ryan Moya, Kai Forbath, Alex Masceranas, Justin Posthuma, Ryan Sublett, Ka'imi Fairnairn, Nate Iese, Devin Lucien, Aaron Sharp, Andrew Strauch, Matt Lynch, Jaelan Phillips

**16-** Edward Tyler, Cal Rossi, Alan Raffee, Joe Marvin, Gerry McDougall, Rob Smith, Norman Dow, Gary Beban

**17-** Jack Finlay, Ernie Johnson, Ted Narleski, Billy Kilmer, Larry Thomas, Kevin Buenafe, Mike Farr, Bobby San Jose, Ken Shelton, Rob Walker, Ryan Roques, Ryan Wilkins, Jason Zdenek, Matthew Ware, Justin Hickman, Aaron Perez, Chinonso Anyanwu, Ted Landers, David Allen, Kip Smith, Brett Hundley, Justin Moreno, Dwight Williams, DeChaun Holiday, Nick Nezami, Matt Lynch, JJ Molson, Jackson Gibbs

**18-** Merle Harris, Art Anderson, Bill Huffy, Ronnie Knox, Norman Dow, Bill Bolden, Homer Butler, William Curran, Mike Young, Harold Barkate, J.J. Stokes, Darren Schager, Quentin Givens, Cade McNown, Mike Seidman, Matthew Slater, William Snead, Xavier Burgess, Andrew Baumgartner, Nick Crissman, Jeff Locke, Todd Golper, Mike Fafaul, Charles Dawson, Thomas Duarte, Adarius Pickett, Ben Kreitenberg, Octavius Spencer, Devon Modster

**19-** Joe Brown, Jack Lescoulie, Art Steffen, Primo Villanueva, Bobby Smith, Ken Lopez, Dennis Dummit, Jeff Dankworth, Toa Saipale, David Clinton, Mark McGill, Michael Moore, John Barnes, Greg Andrasick, Michael Desmarais, Zak Haselmo, Nate Fikse, Marcedes Lewis, Trey Brown, Robert Kibble, Dominique Johnson, Dalton Hilliard, Shaquelle Evans, Maxwell Schuh, Zach Hernandez, Jayon Brown, Matt Mengel, Craig Myers, Josh Woods

**20-** Warren Haslem, James Dougherty, Robert Mike, John Smith, Ron Wenz, Ezell Singleton, Andy Herrera, Danny Graham, Ed Couppee, Danny Graham, Bruce Barnes, Herschel Ramsey, Jeff Knapple, Eric Taylor, Anthony Edgar, Larry Thomas, Bob Garibaldi, Kevin Williams, Skip Hicks, Damian Allen, Ryan Wikert, Nmandi Ohaeri, Steve Melton, Brian Malette,

Charlie Schuh, Daniel Al-Gattis, Raymond Carter, Glenn Love, Justin Combs, Melvin Emesibe, Stefan Flintoft, Leni Toailoa

**21-** Bill Chambers, Roy Jenson, Joe Sabol, Ray Smith, Carl Jones, Sandy Green, Reynaud Moore, Rob Scribner, Phil Kimble, Oscar Edwards, Lupe Sanchez, Eric Ball, Deon Wilks, Carl Greenwood, Glenn Thompkins, Lovell Houston, Maurice Jones-Drew, Jebiaus Brown, Craig Sheppard, Wendell Mathis, Christian Ramirez, Ben Bruneau, Aaron Hester, Craig Sheppard, Joe Roberts, Tahaan Goodman, Mossi Johnson

**22-** Everett Riddle, Joe Viger, Dave Dobrow, Bill Huffy, Ike Jones, George Martin, Stu Farber, Mitch Dimkick, Mel Farr, Harold Busby, Greg Davenport, Mike Fryer, Wendell Tyler, Fred Brockington, Jairo Penaranda, Bryan Wiley, Mel Farr Jr., Marvin Goodwin, Eric Holcomb, Joe Hunter, Dennis Keyes, Michael Norris, Justin Fareed, Matt Willis, Sheldon Price, Allen Aguilar, Roosevelt Davis, Kenneth Walker III, Demetric Felton, Nate Meadors

**23-** Ernie Case, Jerry Fields, Tom Bush, Burt Tibbs, Kermit Alexander, Bob Richardson, Gary Bernstein, Lynn Hinshaw, Ron Carver, Bill Little, Kent Pearce, Johnnie Lynn, Chester Goynes, James Primus, Kevin Smith, Jason Arnold, Donnie Edwards, Jermaine Lewis, Ron Allen, Jibril Raymo, Antwaun Smith, Trey Brown, Mark Mangelsdorf, Justin Sieber, Justin Fareed, Johnathan Franklin, Anthony Thompson, Marlon Pollard, Kenny Orjioke, Anthony Jefferson, Nate Starks, Will Lockett

**24-** Mladin Zarubica, Stuart McKenzie, Ken Kiefer, Charles Page, Bill Halopoff, John Sende, Bill Stits, Almose Thompson, Tom Bennett, Frank Jones, Russel Charles, Ernie Saenz, Freeman McNeil, Danny Andrews, Marcus Turner, Robert Gamble, Thaddeus Massey, Duval Hicks, Paul Nelson, Ben Emmanuel II, Bryon Velega, Christian Ramirez, Ryan Carew, Jeff Dickman, Ishmael Adams, Paul Perkins, Charles Dawson, Damian Alloway, Jay Shaw

**25-** Dale Gilmore, Gene Rowland, Billy Greenberg, Burt Tibbs, Dewey Dunaway, Barry Billington, Cornell Champion, Paul Goodrich, Paul Moyneur, Greg Williams, Wilbur Harden, Scot Tiesing, John Lee, Alfredo Velasco, Louis Perez, Derek Ayers, Cody Joyce, Ryan Smith, Bryon Velega, Bret Lockett, Craig Sheppard, Kai Forbath, Damien Thigpen, Isiaiah Bowens, Brandon Sermons, Denzel Fisher, Drew Huusfeldt, Antonio Brown

**26-** Gerald Grubb, Xavier Mena, Harry Thompson, Werner Escher, Doug Peters, Kirk Wilson, Kurt Altenberg, Mark Gustafson, Jerry Jaso, Carl Zaby, Ron Gueringer, Jojo Townsell, Paco Craig, Dion Lambert, Donovan Gallatin, Kevin Walker, Larry Clements, Deshaun Foster, Joe Cowan, Mike Angelo, Robert Kibble, Andrew Abbott, Charles Soon, Ahmaad Harris, Jason Baker, Alvoid Bennett, Leni Toailoa

**27-** Woody Strode, Mike Dimitro, Malcolm Ellis, Luther Keyes, Bob Davenport, John Pierovich, Bill Hauck, Tim McAteer, Steve Durbin, Dennis Spurling, Alan Lemmerman, Dave Cargo, Mike Boyd, Theotis Brown, Blanchard Montgomery, Alan Dial, Maury Toy, Tommy Bennett, Ted Nwoke, Sharmon Shah, Tod McBride, Akil Harris, Erdolo Eromo, John Hall, Chris Markey, Aaron Ware, Joseph Angelo, Ryal Jagd, Tyler Gonzalez, Jeff Dickman, Andrew Roth, Aaron Wallace, Ryan Hofmeister, Alex Staff, Christian Pablico, Joshua Kelley

**28-** Jackie Robinson, Mark Maurer, Dean Ninteman, Julie Weisstein, Don Shinnick, Bert Frescura, Nathan Smith, Joe Zeno, Bob Stiles, Gary Bernstein, Galen Pavelko, Doug Huff, John Nanoski, Michael Coulter, Cliff Thomas, Joe Gasser, Darren Schager, Micah Denison, Devon Reese, Jason Harrison, Joe Garcia, Chris Markey, Matt Caldwell, Jason Harrison, Josh Smith, Malcolm Jones, Taylor Lagace, Khalil Muhammad, Keyon Riley, Cole Kinder

**29-** Don Hunt, John Florence, Willie Collins, Fred Gillett, Allan Ellis, Wendell Tyler, Jim Brown, Michael Person, Mike Durden, Randy Beverly, Eric Turner, Chad LaRose, Aaron Roques, Julius Williams, Manual White Jr., Olukayode Oredugba, Bobby Whithorne, Terry O'Neal, Robert McCurdy, EJ Turner, Alex Levy, Jake Hall, Erick Zumwalt, Brad Sochowski, Ryan Parks

**30-** Louis Kyzivat, Herb Weiner, Bob Wilkinson, Don Stalwick, Jim Decker, Dave Peterson, Joe Rosenkrans,

Mickey Cureton, Bobby Ferrell, Eddie Ayers, Brian Baggott, Dave Gomer, Dokie Williams, Craig Rutledge, Brian Brown, Daron Washington, Akil Davis, Chris Larocca, Derrick Williams, Bradley Johnson, Chris Meadows, Demetrius Papadakis, Eric Kendricks, Erick Zumwalt, Myles Jack, Eli Snyder, Colin Samuel, Sebastian Sharpe, Zachary Byrge, Johnny Den Bleyker

**31-** Lester Sutherland, Nate DeFrancisco, Sherwood Simpson, Jim Buchanon, Pete Dailey, Chuck Hollaway, John Davis, Carmen DiPoalo, Gary Campbell, Eddie Ayers, Kenny Lee, Freeman McNeil, Doug West, Doug Donatelli, Carnell Lake, Mark McGill, Ricky Davis, Morgan Janger, Jarvis Watson, Matt Stanley, Benjamin Lorier, J.D. Groves, Garrett Rubio, Trevor Theriot, Jamal Greer, Librado Barocio, Justin Fareed, Grayson Mazzone, Fabian Moreau, Colin Samuel, Will McClure

**32-** Cecil Dye, Vic Smith, Johnny Roesch, Jim Thomas, Bill Ingles, Bruce Ballard, Lou Elias, Tom Bennett, Vic Lepisto, James McAlister, Bobby Ferrell, Levi Armstrong, Eric Brown, Tom Sullivan, Josh Shinnick, Randy Beverly, Kevin Dickey, Shaun Williams, Mark Reynosa, J.D. Groves, Kevin Brant, Michael Pitre, Michael Ciaccio, Josh Barut, Robert Franco, Sam Handler, Nate Iese, Ron Robinson, Mique Juarez, Jalen Starks

**33-** Hal Hirshon, Johnny Johnson, Al Izmirian, Jerry Whitney, Larry Lampkin, Whitney Arceneaux, Johnny Hermann, Gene Gaines, Marv Luster, Kermit Alexander, Rick Purdy, Randy Tyler, Kenny Lee, Glenn Cannon, Greg Francois, Eugene Leoni, Mark McGill, Kelton Alexander, Carlton Gray, Chris Alexander, Karim Abdul-Jabbar, Ryan Roques, Ken Pritchett, Tim Warfield, Christian Taylor, Kristopher Kiley, Derrick Coleman, Ryan Hofmeister, Steven Manfro, Dylan Luther, Chase Ault

**34-** Douglas Schwartz, Lynn Compton, Robert Keefer, Howard Hansen, Paul Cameron, Warren Jackson, John Champlin, Marv Kendricks, Jimmie Jones, Brett White

**35-** Robin Williams, Bill Kitchen, Harold Beardsley, Roy Vujovich, Dain Laidman, Myron Berliner, Don Duncan, Fred Gillett, Bill Mason, Bill Hauck, Jack Blaine, Clayton Record, Matt Fahl, Scott Stauch, Jimmy Turner, Billy Ray, Bradley Craig, Eric Reidt, Mike Vanis, Larry Atkins, Asi Faoa, Steve Seigel, Ryen Carew, Jonathon Torres, Matt Culver, David Martini, Andy Magee, Lowell Rose, Jordan Zumwalt, Ryan Davis, Ainuu Taua, Kahlil Muhammad, Michael Mapes

**36-** John Ryland, Al Solari, Edward Eaton, Bob Moore, Don Duncan, Jim Colletto, Mike Garratt, Charlie Schuhmann, Tony Paopao, Ricky Coffman, Ted Henderson, Jeff Damron, Shawn Wills, Damion Lyons, James Milliner, Keith Robinson, Eric McNeil, Ramogi Huma, Kahlil Bell, Mark Cordell, Jayson Allmond, Nick Pasquale

**37-** Jack Montgomery, Ray Nagel, Herb Lane, Jimmy Johnson, Kurt Zimmerman, Kermit Johnson, Jewerl Thomas, Matt McFarland, Burness Scott, Chuckie Miller, Shawn Wills, Bjorn Merten, Greg Cass, Joey Strycula, Tommy Bright, Andrew Baumgartner, Jimmy Rotstein, Lucas Barbosa, Christian Wehrly, Zachary Byrge, Quentin Lake

**38-** Don MacPherson, Burr Baldwin, Bob Wilcox, Phil Parslow, Steve Stanley, Dom Mancini, Jim Bright, Jimmy Allen

**39-** George Pfeiffer, Rex Olford, Russ Vlack, Dick Short, Milt Davis, Paul Horgan, Jim Sayre, Bob Manning, Phil Hubbard, Arthur Akers, Michael Wade, Neal Dellocono, Kelton Alexander, Kevin Smith, George Paton, Mike Merrill, Justin Sogoian, Craig Walendy, Chris Kluwe, David Shipp, Kenneth Lombard, Trey Shelton, Trason Bragg, Danny Rees, Dylan Price, Adam Searl, Ethan Fernea, Michael Mapes

**40-** Frank Carroll, Ray Pierson, Tom Asher, Henry Ennen, Lynn Hale, Frank Munoz, Jim Corpora, Terry Debay, Dave Boze, Manu Tuiasosopo, Karl Morgan, Terry Tumey, Roman Phifer, Rod Smalley, Ryan Neufeld, Terry Tumey, Ryan Neufeld, Nikola Dragovic, Wesley Walker, Ben Idemundia, Akeem Ayers, Patrick Jarin, Keenan Graham, Dylan Price, Cameron Griffin, Josh Chambers, Justin Rittman

**41-** Jim Mitchell, Dean Strawn, Dean Witt, Sam

Miller, Bob Watson, Dean Kirby, Ken Perry, Steve Gertsman, Bob Stevens, Eddie Hutt, Willie Campbell, Art Fry, Frank Stephens, Larry Hall, Doug West, Ken Norton, Stacy Argo, Theo Anderson, Jason Nevadomsky, Adam Geitner, Spencer Havner, Ryan Chisholm, Dylan Rush, David Allen, Mike Schmitt, Robert Franco, Willie Green, Blake Backer, Aramide Olaniyan, Zach Whitley, Barrett Redell, Trae Smith, Alex Michaelson, Jayce Smalley

**42-** Carl Olson, Conkling L. Wai, Roy Kurrasch, Don Cogswell, Dave Owen, Bruce Ballard, Ivory Jones, Mike Cochran, Jeff Smith, Ken Walker, Frank Bruno, Greg Langston, Tommy Taylor, Anthony Schexnayder, Andrew McClave, Skip Hicks, Dennis Link, Aaron Whittington, Chane Moline, Chad Moline, Patrick Larimore, Kenny Young

**43-** Clarence Mackey, Ignatius Polizzi, Jim Chadwick, Bob Zelinka, Bob Heydenfeldt, Steve Palmer, Bob Enger, Bob Mackey, Jim Bergman, Chuck Peterson, Len Dodson, John White, Ray Armstrong, Greg Jones, Ken Gruedynke, Frank Corral, Dave Gomer, Danny Lauter, David Franey, Craig Davis, Matt Darby, Travis Shipman, Jevone Moore, Billy Pieper, Dave Ball, Danny Nelson, Steve Sloan, Damien Holmes, Willie Green

**44-** Robert Simpson, Arnold Leckman, Harold Braly, Lewis Williams, Bob Bergdahl, John White, Keith Monty Harrison, Bruce Barnes, Lou Mascola, Scott Stauch, Terry Morehead, Gaston Green, Pat McPherson, Brian Tighe, Thaddeus Massey, Greg Ford, Mark Verti, Marcus Reese, Mark Mangelsdorf, Bruce Davis, David Skara, Phillip Ruhl, Isaako Savaiinaea, Martin Andrus

**45-** Charles Ferenbock, Joe Ruettgers, Jack Watts, Bill Woods, Darrell Riggs, Don Foster, Steve Durbin, Tim McAteer, Paul Derflinger, Arthur Sims, Jimmie Jones, Pat Marty, Darryl Green, Marcus Greenwood, Randy Austin, Jim Wagner, Aaron Anderson, Ali Arriz, Jeff Ruckman, John Hall, Ray Cassaday, Patrick Pierre-Louis, Jimmy Stephens, Charlie Schuh, Tobi Umodu, Nate Chandler, Alex Cusick, Peter Hajimihais, Cameron Judge, Giovanni Gentosi

**46-** Jerry Shipkey, Guy Way, Bill Cope, Gerry Okuneff, Dave Duncan, Byron Nelson, Mike Bergdahl, George Farmer, Rod Stensrud, Marvin Morris, Dan Lei, Frank Cephous, Eugene McGaugh, Jeff Damron, Kirk Maggio, Garrett Greedy, Deron McElroy, Jeff Puffer, Byron Carnes, Garrett Lepisto, Christian Taylor, Chad Moline, Frank Guzman, Peter Hajimihalis, Kene Orjioke, Donovan Williams

**47-** Gordon Mollett, Mario Russo, Rod O'Meara, Cliff Livingston, Art Phillips, Duane Wills, Dom Mancini, Sam Taylor, Brian Graham, Ron Pitts, Brad Bryson, Carrick O'Quinn, Craig Walendy, Ryan Nece, Aaron Whittington, Pat Norton, Chinonso Anyanwu, Ryan Medina, Max Ratkovich, Eddie Vanderdoes, Shea Pitts

**48-** John Baida, Milt Smith, Bob Russell, Gayle Pace, Dave Owen, Pete O'Garro, Don Birren, Don Shinnick, Ken Goodman, John Tautolo, Chuckie Miller, Doug Kline, Kaleaph Carter, Justin London, William Snead, Jimmy Stephens, Ali Abdul Azziz, Mike Schmitt, Kevin McDermott, Jarad Koster, Tre Hale, Parker Chase, Winston Anawalt, Connor Beadles

**49-** Francis Wai, Ken Snelling, Bill Clements, Oran Breeland, Joe Zeno, Vernon Brock, Rob Lipscomb, Norm Johnson, Tony Phillips, Robert Loigu, Marvcus Patton, Courtney Keyler, Bruce Walker, Jeff Ruckman, Cheyane Caldwell, Mat Ball, Fred Holmes, Luke Gane, Eric Chalifour, Derrick Bryant, Christian Pankey

**50-** Ed Irwin, West Matthews, Ernie Stockert, Donn Moomaw, John Peterson, Ron Hull, Don Manning, Dave Dalby, Dan Gilbert, Bill Baggott, Mark Ferguson, Lance Zeno, Jason Arnold, Justin Marshall, Nmaemeka Okoye, Brendon Ayanbadejo, Adam Craven, Troy Danoff, Edward Douglas, Chase Moline, Aaron Meyer, Robert Franco, Kevin McReynolds

**51-** Morris Harrison, Jack Brown, Jack Thornton, Jim Matheny, Andy Von Sonn, Erwin Dutcher, Zenon Andrusyshyn, Greg Snyder, Randy Cross, Tom Murphy, Dave Otey, Tom Whitenight, Emmanuel Onwutuebe, Chris Sanchez, Ramogi Huma, Tony White, Nathaniel Skaggs, Ryan Schon, Reggie Carter, Kai Maiava, Nathaniel Skaggs, Aaron Wallace, Tre Hale, Alex Redmond, Markus Boyer

**52-** Ray Sturtevant, Breck Stroschein, Jim Thomas, Jack McKay, Dennis Dressel, Larry Frankel, Steve Klosterman, Steve Tetrick, Russell Rowell, Terry Theodore, Randy Cole, Shawn Stuart, Chris Johnson, Steve Seigel, Jess Ward, Christian Yount, Phillip Ruhl, Carl Hulick, Scott Quessenberry, Lokeni Toailoa

**53-** Sam Storey, Walter Versen, Francis Mandula, Bob Zelinka, Steve Palmer, Harry Baldwin, Mike Roof, Mike Evans, Mike Martinez, Mike Herrera, Joe Gary, David Simpson, Meech Shaw, Brian Willmer, Kevin Stromsborg, Leo Reed, Marko Dragovic, Joshua Edwards, David Allen, Uche Amajoyi, Christopher Longo, Ryan Hofmeister, Xan Cuevas, Jax Wacasar

**54-** Brewster Broadwell, Ray Terry, Vic Schwenk, Joe Marvin, Bill Smith, Dick Butler, Greg McLandrich, Phil Hendricks, Greg Titsensor, Ron Wollard, Paul Bombolis, Craig Davis, Nkosi Littleton, Michael Wiley, Luke Krall, Robert Chai, Kyle Bosworth, Jake Brendel, Isaiah Bowens

**55-** Ned Matthews, Edward Breeding, Tom Fears, George Kauffman, Leo Hershman, Dan Laidman, Dan Peterson, Steve Truesdell, Roger Anderson, Dallas Grider, Don Widmer, Marv Knupper, Steve Kelly, Rick Baska, Willie Beamon, Martin Moss, Tony Pankopf, Rocen Keeton, Sale Isaia, Tim Wattleton, Shane Lehmann, David Tautofi, Jamal Greer, Korey Bosworth, Sonny Tevaga, Isaiah Bowens, Todd Golper, Ben Wysocki, Sean Burd, Michael Alves, Breland Brandt

**56-** Norman Padgett, Leslie Steiner, Alan Raffee, Prentice O'Leary, John Erquiaga, Greg McLandrich, Rob Scriber, Jim Swick, Terry Tautolo, Rick Obbema, Mark Mannon, John Winnek, Brent Guyton, Travor Turner, Stephen Sua, Tom Blake, Nicky Rodriguez, Jerzy Siewersi, Matt Amundson, Tom Blake, Datone Jones, Xavier Su'a-Filo, Josh Wariboko-Alili

**57-** William Shubin, Walter Marlett, Don Paul, Gayle Pace, Leon Evans, Jim Reynolds, Morris Freedman, Paul Mayfield, Mike Ballou, Vince Mok, Mike Jacoby, Keith Eck, Scott Reid, Jeff Diamond, Randy Dickerson, Rex Gray, Paul Pernecky, Danjuan Magee, Kory Lombard, John Ream, Bruce Davis, Riley Jondle, Jake Dean, Jordan Woolbright, Wesley Flowers, Carl Hulick

**58-** Robert Cress, Al Sparlis, Ben Reiges, Nick Giovinazzo, Joe Horta, Roy Benstead, Tom Bergman, Jim Miller, Ron Tretter, Jim Oliver, Bob Pifferini, Pat Kealey, Mike Martinez, Howard Kipnis, Jeff Glasser, James Malone, Mike Flanagan, Mike Grieb, Nick Amendola, Jeff Grau, Micah Reed, Isaiah Bowens, Sam Saultz, Colby Cyburt, Deon Hollins, Preston Awedisean, Gyo Shojima, Koby Walsh

**59-** Robert Nash, Don Capp, Bob Boyd, Bill Smith, Ira Pauly, Bob Heckman, Chuck Ferrero, Lorry Frankel, Gene Settles, Pete Pele, John Helm, Dan Dufour, Melvin Jackson, John Zilinskas, George Kase, Oscar Cabrera, Mike McCloskey, Michael Lutu, Keenan Graham, Jay Weneta, Christopher Longo, Giovanni Gentosi, Zach Bateman

**60-** Clestine Wyrick, Bill Armstrong, Carl Benton, Don Johnson, George Morgan, Hardiman Cureton, Ken Arndt, Walt Dathe, Rick Deakers, Bruce Jorgenson, Steve Williams, Bruce Adkins, Al Vernon, Mitch Johnson, Scott Spalding, Mitch Miller, Pete Holland, Brian Polak, Chris Joseph, Jeff Baca, Zach Sweeney

**61-** Joe Naar, Lyman Ehrlich, Terry Heselius, Don Birren, Bob King, Dave Stout, Erwin Dutcher, Mike Roof, Vince Bischof, Brian Goodman, Dan Gilbert, Art Kuehn, Steve Shoemaker, Gregg Christiansen, Rex Gray, Duval Love, Eric Rogers, Jeff Bailey, Brian Reemsten, Grady Stretz, Mitch Miller, Sean Gully, Dusan Militech, Brian Ruziecki, Jason Nitz, Andy Keane, Sam Tai, Gyo Shojima, Bryan Weitzman

**62-** Rex Murphy, Ed Flynn, Bob Dutcher, Tom Thaxter, George Cunning, Rod Cochran, Jim Finstad, Jim Sykes, Alan Claman, Tony Furtado, Mike Pavich, Steve Klosterman, Mitch Kahn, Mike Mason, Don Mahlstedt, Kevin Cronin, Steve Davis, James Christensen, Brian Rubinstein, David Dreisbach, Doug Cummings, PJ Tobayansen, Eddie Williams

**63-** Bill Hoyt, Sherwood Simpson, Rudy Feldman, Jim Brown, Joe Harper, Frank Macari, Frank Patrick, Barry Leventhal, Ken Bajerma, Doug Diebolt, Zeno

Veal, Greg Norfleet, Brad Vassar, Vic Mayer, Mark Hartmeier, Paul Kennedy, Matt Pentecost, Aaron Meyer, Blake Worley, Kody Innes, Jake Tourville, Sean Seawards

**64-** Henry Sheller, Bruce MacLachian, Jim Salsbury, Clint Whitfield, John Walker, Terry Donahue, Dan Johnston, Scott Steele, Tom Daniels, Rick Baska, Eugene Clark, Dave Morton, Bobby Leggins, David Randle, Jon Pryor, Chris Rubio, Steve Morgan, Eyoseph Efseaff, Brian Rubinstein, Greg Capella, Sam Marrazzo

**65-** Ray Lewand, Dave Levy, Wilbert Anderson, Duane Lemon, Kurt Lewin, Jack Metcalf, Paul Chavira, Roger Anderson, Mike Arnold, Harold Griffin, Randy Gaschler, Myke Horton, Steve Sosnowski, Kevin Cronin, Dave Hallstrom, Brian Kelly, Mike Rohme, Chris Anderson, Mike Saffer, Charles Thompson, Mike Harris, Paco Perez

**66-** John Nikcevich, Ed Miller, Charles Nance, Mike Riskas, Bob Dutcher, Dave Dabov, Dick Peterson, Tom Ware, Ron Tretter, Bob Barlett, Dan Rice, Bill Sandifer, Jim Williams, John Tautolo, Chris Yelich, Jim Wahler, Siitupe Tuala, London Woodfin, Kevin Jacobs, Jason Rempel, Ed Anderson, PJ Irvin, Nathaniel Skaggs, Scott Glicksberg, Ryan Taylor, Sunny Odogwu

**67-** Orville Hatcher, Clarence Cabell, Cliff Schroeder, Sam Boghosian, Esker Harris, Mike Riskas, Dick Allen, Russ Banducci, Dan Johnston, Dennis Alumbaugh, Russ Leal, Pat Sweetland, Bob Mihihauser, Luis Sharpe, Duval Love, Bobby Menifield, Aron Gideon, Craig Taylor, Kory Lombard, PJ Irvin, Andrew Curtis, Casey Griffiths

**68-** George Brown, Larry Britten, Dave Levy, Don Shinnick, Bob Dinaberg, Jack Roznos, Tom Paton, John LoCurto, Dennis Murphy, Ron Tretter, Gerald Peeke, Gus Coppens, Tim Tennigkeit, Ron Davis, Blake Wingle, Vaughn Parker, Matt Phelan, Brian Abraham, Nik Abele, Jay Barlow, Conor McDermott, Clayton Demski

**69-** George Pastre, George Kroeber, Bill Smith, Dick Braunbeck, Mel Allan, Mike Mahoney, Chuck Davis, Rick Pertulla, Joseph Hembrick, Frank Manumaleuna, Jim Main, Ron Wollard, Joe Goebel, Marc Wilder, Brian Richards, Tyson Clayton, Scott Glicksberg, Chad Overhauser, Brandon Bennett, Blake Bentz, Najee Toran, Preston Awedisean

**70-** Leon McLaughlin, Bob Walters, Wilbert Anderson, Bob Dinaberg, Tony Longo, Steve Butler, Tory Matheson, Lee McElroy, Steve Tamborski, Al Oliver, Mike Jacoby, Gus Coppins, Greg Christiansen, Jeff Chaffin, John Kidder, Rick Fuller, Kris Farris, Matt Mosebar, Scott Kearney, Tony Lee, Connor Bradford, Simon Goines, Jaypal Bedi, Stephan Zabie

**71-** Bob Howard, Gil Moreno, Jim Wallace, Tony Albany, Bob Schoner, Dick Donald, Wayne King, Greg Pearman, Daryl Steen, Bruce Davis, Steve Jones, Dave Baran, Rick Meyer, Craig Novitsky, Mark Weisman, Kris Farris, Alex Potasi, Shannon Tevaga, Wade Yandall, Zach Vinci, Cassius Marsh, Poasi Moala, Nahemia Abera

**72-** Dean Kirby, Fred Andrews, Russ Hampton, Jack McKay, Bill Leeka, Kent Francisco, Larry Agajanian, Mike Pavich, Craig Campbell, Tom Waddell, Brent Boyd, Scott Gordon, Robert Cox, Roy Villalobos, Brian Jacobs, Ron Nielson, Darren McClure, Josh Webb, Jamaal Rhodes, Sean Sheller, Alberto Cid, Jake Jones, Christian Garcia, Zach Cochrun

**73-** Roy Jenson, Terry Debay, Les Cates, Dave Smith, Joe Bauwens, Eric Taylor, Roger Trinchero, Tony Steponovich, Ed Galigher, Rich Gunther, Phil McKinnely, Randy Grounds, Mike Mason, Jim Alexander, Matt Soensen, Tony Ippolito, Ed Blanton, Micah Kia, Will Oliver, Christian Garcia, Tevita Halalilo, Jake Burton

**74-** Xavier Mena, Preston Dills, Foster Anderson, Randy Schwartz, Floyd Reese, Bruce Walton, Bob Reyes, Cliff Frazier, Ron White, Steve Gemza, Russ Warnick, Andre Farr, John Soltis, Karl Schroller, Chad Sauter, Paul Mociler, Noah Sutherland, Nathaniel Skaggs, Stanley Hasiak, Caleb Benenoch, Alex Akingbulu

**75-** Dave Williams, Warner Benjamin, Tom Avery, Gil McCutchan, Don Brooks, Jack Reed, Ken McIntire,

John Richardson, Mike Arnold, Steve Freitas, Earl Peterson, Jake DeMartinis, Max Montoya, Irv Eatman, Doug Wassel, Ramon Washington, Mike Linn, Mike Rohme, Pete Holland, Ryan Boschetti, Kevin Brown, Robert Cleary, Nick Ekbatani, Chris Ward, Andre James, Boss Tagaloa

**76-** Hal Mitchell, Chuck Doud, Chuck Gelfand, Gary Yurosek, Tony Fiorentino, Dave Noyes, Doug Bagby, Willie Smith, Pete Kranske, Steve Preston, Zeno Veal, Ed Kezirian, Cliff Frazier, Glen Titensor, Mike Jolly, Chris Cox, Bill Paige, Derek Stevens, Gene Waters, David Wilford, Steve Vieira, Justin Brown, Austin Hill, Alexandru Ceachir, Kenny Lacy, Alex Rassool, Justin Rittman, Chiemeka Ochi

**77-** Chuck Fraychineaud, Jack Ellena, Bob Lang, Bob Weeden, Phil Oram, Gerald Johns, Larry Stagle, Steve Freitas, Jim Berg, Rick Kukulica, Don Woolley, Larry Lee, Jim McCullough, Heston Silbert, Grady Stretz, Micah Webb, Rodney Leisle, Kenneth Lombard, Darius Savage, Torian White, Kolton Miller

**78-** Jerry Fields, Joe Ray, Roger White, Jim Dawson, Steve Bauwens, John Pentecost, Willie Smith, Kent Roberts, Tim Oesterling, Gene Clark, Rob Kezerian, Dan Dufour, Chris Block, Steve Mehr, Kim Lawhorn, Karl Schroller, Andy Meyers, Bryce Bohlander, Marc Villafuerte, Travis Martin, Aleksey Lanis, Brett Downey, Malcolm Bunche, Justin Rittman, Clayton Demski, Graham Valentine

**79-** John Peterson, Larry Britten, Gerald Penner, Paul Oglesby, Marshall Shirk, Mitch Johnson, Rick Paul, Gordon Bosserman, Chuck Suter, Mark Harris, Greg Taylor, Curt Mohl, Onno Zwaneveld, Lance Zeno, Jonathan Ogden

**80-** Donn Moomaw, Tom Gutman, Bill Tiedemann, John Champlin, Vic Lepisto

**81-** Bob Long, Tom Adams, John Brown, Gordon Hess, Bob Weeden, Gary Callies, Warren Wetzel, Pat O'Neil, Bruce Bergey, Mark Wright, Gene Blaymaier, Jeff Muro, Gene Mewborn, Derek Tennell, Mark McGill, Charles Arbuckle, Mike Nyugen, Tod McBride, Bryan Fletcher, J.J. Hair, Glenn Rauscher, Kyle Slowey, Tyler Scott, Caleb Wilson

**82-** John Stea, Rommie Loudd, Dick Wallen, Don Vena, Don Francis, Wade Pearson, Brad Lyman, Jim Swick, Homer Butler, Scott Tiesing, Larry Oats, Mike Young, Mike Sherrard, Brad Daluiso, Avery Anderson, Brian Poli-Dixon, Will Peddie, Taylor Embree, Eldridge Massington

**83-** Bob Haydenfeldt, Johnny Hermann, Spence Mitchell, John Pierovich, Jim Arens, Bill Tiedemann, Gwen Cooper, Terry Vernoy, Dale Curry, Ronnie DeBose, Cormac Carney, Willie Anderson, John Soltis, Kim Lawhorn, Brad Melsby, Jerry Owens, Jacques Lazarus, Marcus Everett, Adam Heater, Nelson Rosario, Grayson Mazzone, Daniel Eaton, Alex Van Dyke

**84-** Roger White, Larry Monnett, Chuck Kendall, Spence Mitchell, Marv Luster, Mel Profit, Harold Busby, Rick Wilkes, Oscar Roan, Russell Ball, Jerry Robinson

**85-** Myron Berliner, Russ Hampton, Hal Smith, Glen Almquist, Jim Stanley, Jerry Klein, George Farmer, Jim Berg, Mike Clayton, Don Pederson, Rick Walker, Tom Sheffield, Lee Knowles, Rick Daly, Troy Aldrich, Jason Bendinelli, Jon Dubravac, Alex Ghebreselassie, David Carter, Jerry Johnson, John Young, Colby Cyburt, Alex Rassool, Moses Robinson-Carr

**86-** John Smith, Jim Steffen, Craig Chudy, Kurt Altenberg, Ron Ludington, Glen Cooper, Jack Lassner, Gerry Roberts, Raymond Bell, Michael Coulter, Mark Tuinei, Ron Butler, Brian Allen, Langston Woodberry, Stephen Sua, Dennix Fox, Chris Steck, Logan Paulsen, Raymond Nelson, Eric Hurd, Logan Sweet, Audie Omotosho, Devin Asiasi

**87-** John Farhood, Craig Chudy, Dave Gibbs, Rich Spindler, Mike Garratt, Reggie Echols, Raymond Burks, Glenn Windom, Chris Block, Scott Franklin, Paul Richardson, Eric Holcomb, Robert Arthur, Danny Farmer, Craig Bragg, Tyler Holland, Cory Harkey, Ian Taubler, Jordan Wilson

**88-** Pete O'Garro, Trusse Norris, Chuck Hicks, Ken McIntire, Dick Witcher, Mike McGaffrey, Ron Copeland, Drew Sones, Bob Christiansen, Eugene Jones, Pat Schmidt, Billy Don Jackson, Karl Dorrell,

Al Wilson, Anthony Schexnayder, Sean LaChapelle, Mike Grieb, Blane Kezirian, Keith Carter, Matt Willis, Alex Pearlstone, Jerry Rice Jr., Aramide Olaniyan, Daniel Eaton, Austin Roberts

**89-** Pat Pinkston, Earl Smith, Gale Hickman, Ted Bashore, Mickey Erlich, Dave Nuttall, Wes Grant, Jack Lightsy, Norm Anderson, Mike Barbee, Jeff Nowinski, Brian Lockwood, Arnold Ale, Gary Walton, Tyler Scott, Keith Carter, Gabe Crecion, Matt Raney, Tom Blake, Nate Chandler, Jordan Berrett, Thomas Schwab, Zach Bornstein, Will McClure, Jimmy Jaggers

**90-** Clarence Norris, Al Geverink, Lee McElroy, Cal Peterson, Bob Crawford, James Forge, Jim Mastera, Corwin Anthony, Shane Jasper, Vae Tata, Adam Peters, Noah Sutherland, Jerzy Siewerski, Michael Ghobrial, Donovan Carter, Austin Hill, Ellis McCarthy, Rick Wade

**91-** Gary Callies, Kim Griffith, Craig Campbell, Pat Kealey, Glenn Windom, Tim Wrightman, Greg Bolin, Brian Lockwood, Jason Green, Jayson Brown, Tony Thompson, Chris Jackson, Billy Pieper, Matt Kocher, Kevin Harbour, Reginald Stokes, Sam Tai, Jacob Tuioti-Mariner

**92-** Gary Bickers, Steve Smalley, Jim Ford, Rick Basca, Fred McNeill, Eugene Jones, John Fowler, Ike Gordon, Frank Batchkoff, Matt Werner, Josh Eby, Randy Hakes, Kevin Brown, Steve Morgan, Travis Martin, Brian Price, Tre Hale, Brandon Willis, Austin Kent, Osawaru Odighizuwa

**93-** Gale Hickman, Dick Davidson, Bob Geddes, Steve Hookano, Fulton Kuykenhall, Rick Senteno, Joe Pickert, Bryan Wilcox, Steve Blinn, Courtney Keyler, Weldon Forde, Scott Heckman, Saia Makakaufaki, Robert Garcia, Brigham Harwell, Madison Poole, Greg Casciaro, Tre Hale, Ellis McCarthy, Chogozie Nnoruka

**94-** Bob Dietrich, Jim Berg, Eugene Jones, Dale Curry, Kent Brisbin, Paul Bergmann, Mike Lodish, Steve Blinn, Darren Cline, Rusty Williams, Chris Johnson, Kevin Gamarnik, Andy Keane, Joseph Fauria, Justin Mann, Owamagbe Odighizuwa, Najee Toran, Nick Terry

**95-** Max Knupper, Scott Westering, Raymond Robinson, Mark Walen, Randy Austin, Jim Wagner, Jamir Miller, Santi Hall, Phillip Rauscher, Steven Urrutia, Brian Price, Ryan Shott, Brandon Tuliaupupu, Marcus Moore

**96-** Don Hoopwood, Kenny Page, Earl Smith, Jamal Clark, Anthony Fletcher, Shane Gates, Nikola Dragovic, Iuta Tepa, Eli Ankou, Andrew Strauch

**97-** Rich Gray, Harper Howell, Marcus Hudspeth, Arnold Ale, Phillip Ward, Ken Kocher, CJ Niusulu, Darius Savage, Damien Holmes, Luke Gane, Kenny Clark, Jake Burton, Odua Isibor

**98-** Chris Elias, Mike Mahan, Eric Smith, Mike Chalenski, Travis Kirschke, Sean Phillips, Kyle Morgan, Charles Thompson, Kyle Morgan, Jeff Miller, Seali'i Epinesa, Mitch Johnson, Takkarist McKinley

**99-** Brad Plemmons, Steve Jarecki, Ron Evans, Cory Wayland, Brian Richards, Kenyon Coleman, Thomas Patton, Brigham Harwell, Vache Sevajian, Scott Glicksberg, Justin Edison, Andrew Yelich, Cassius Marsh, Matt Dickerson, Jake Jones, Crawford Pierson

**No Regular Number or Unknown Number** (*alphabetical*)- Leslie Abrams, James Adkins, Robert Allington, James Agnew, Bob Andrews, Robert Angle, James Armstrong, Edward Austin, Clarence Baldwin, Ed Ballie, Wayne Banning, Pete Barber, Gordon Barnhill, Robert Barr, Charles Barta, Ray Bartlett, Julius Beck, William Beling, Lenny Bergdahl, Joe Berry, Brooks Biddle, John Binney, Scrib Birlenbach, George Bishop, Harold Bishop, Albert Blower, Jack Boyd, Verdi Boyer, Angel Breiniman, Carl Brown, Dave Brown, Don Brown, Jefferson Brown, Horace Bruce, Jack Bryan, Elmer Bussell, Mark Campbell, William Campbell, Charles Cashon, Sherman Chavoor, Chuck Cheshire, Marion Childers, Kenneth Clark, Walter Clark, Jack Cohen, Dick Coleman, Donald Collins, Vernon Collins, Frank Cory, Elvin Davis, Richard Davis, Robert Decker, Joe Denis, Ted Dennis, Thomas Devlin, George

Dickerson, Ralph Diehl, Mike Dimas, Tom Duddleston, Ted Duffy, John Duncan, Norm Duncan, Tom English, Herman Epstein, Bill Fade, Donvel Ferguson, Earl Fields, Charles Finn, Joe Fleming, John Fletcher, George Forster, Lee Frankovich, Mike Frankovich, Marion French, Wallace Frost, Stuart Frye, Fred Funk, Sigfried Funke, Ed Fyson, Earle Gardner, Richard Gary, Dave Gaston, Alfred Gibson, Maurice Goodstein, Stanley Gould, Doug Graham, Aubrey Grossman, Leslie Haight, Kerns Hampton, Bob Hanson, Howard Haradon, Burnett Haralson, Earl Harris, Morrie Harrison, Clarence Harvey, Fred Haslam, Edgar Hassler, Charles Hastings, John Hastings, Bob Henderson, Robert Hendry, Mason Hohl, Cece Hollingsworth, H.R. Holman, Troy Horton, Jack Howard, James Hudson, Robert Huff, Russell Huse, John Jackson, Abe Jacobson, Don Jacobson, Steward James, William Jarvis, Charles Jennings, Morris Jessup, Arthur Jones, Dick Jones, Gordon Jones, Ted Jones, Joseph Keeble, Paul Keirn, George Kibbe, Nelson King, Jack Kinney, R.F. Key, Laddie Knudson, Don Krehbiel, Frank Kroener, Ben Kvitky, Bert LaBrucherie, Eugene Lee, Bert Lembeck, Clifford Lightner, Rodney Lilyquist, Melville Lippman, Ranson Livesay, Glenwood Lloyd, Freeman Long, Sinclair Lott, Art Mankel, Mike Marienthal, Dean Markham, Charles Marston, Dwight Matheny, William Maxwell, Mike McCabe, Bob McChesney, Lawrence McConnell, Thomas McDougall, Delbert McGue, Leonard McKenzie, Lloyd McMillan, Louis McNairy, Frank Mefferd, Raymond Meigs, William Merrill, Howard Michel, Jim Millet, Edward Milum, Ron Molrine, Charles Mugler, Richard Mulhaupt, Walter Muller, Jack Munro, Lawrence Murdock, William Murphy, Richard Neighbor, Glenn Nelson, Harvey Nelson, Eugene Noble, Phil Nordli, Haughton Norfleet, Jack Northup, Beverly Ogden, Homer Oliver, Remington Olmstead, Carl Olson, Harold Olson, Milo Olson, Earl Painter, Don Pardi, Tillie Parisi, Maury Parker, Ernest Patterson, Loran Peak, Will Peddie, Tom Pedrini, Ray Peers, Elwin Peterson, Marion Peterson, George Phillips, Ray Pierson, Charles Pike, Arthur Piver, Jack Porter, William Putnam, Roy Quinby, Thomas Rafferty, Jack Raney, Bob Rasmus, George Ray, Stanley Reel, Art Reichle, Robert Reinhard, John Remsberg, Glen Rile, Dick Roberts, Howard Roberts, George Robinson, G.H. Robinson, George Robotham, Robert Rohrer, Ben Ross, Don Ross, Eddie Rossell, Bob Rosskopt, Lorenzo Ruddy, Jerry Russom, Earl Sargent, Joe Sarver, Walt Schell, Robert Schroeder, Jack Sergel, John Shubin, John Simons, Clifton Simpson, Jake Singler, Arthur Smith, Chester Smith, Frank Smith, Julian Smith, Martin Smith, Ken Solid, Edward Soloman, Bill Stamper, Charles Stanley, Sam Stawisky, William Stevens, Walter Stickel, William Stiers, Howard Stoeffen, Dean Strawn, Iva Svensguard, Norman Taber, John Tandy, Russell Tauscheck, John Terry, Reuben Thoe, Scott Thursby, George Timmons, Don Toland, Bill Tritt, Harry Trotter, William Troxel, Grayson Turney, Chuck Vannatta, Louis Velasco, Charlie Walter, Cyril Walton, Herb Weiner, Leonard Wellendorf, Donald Wentzel, Walt Wescott, Duke Westland, Bob Wheeler, Gordon White, Milt Whitebook, Tom Wilcox, Billy Bob Williams, Howard Willoughby, Wilton Wilton, Rod Woefle, Wendell Womble, John Wood, Bill Woods, Doc Wright, Harold Wyatt, Clayton Yearick, Chuck Young, H.M. Young, Martin Yturralde, Meyer Zimmerman

# CHAPTER 20
# Year-by-Year Schedules and Results

*All UCLA Schedules from UCLABruins.com**

### 1919: FRED W. COZENS
10/3 L 0 at Manual Arts HS 74
10/10 L 6 at Hollywood HS 19
10/17 L 12 at Bakersfield HS 27
10/24 W 7 Occidental Frosh 2
10/30 W 7 Los Angeles JC 0
11/7 L 0 USS Idaho 20
11/14 L 7 Los Angeles JC 21
11/21 L 13 at Occidental Frosh 30
*W—2, L—6, T—0*

### 1920: HARRY TROTTER
10/2 L 0 at Pomona 41
10/9 L 0 Occidental 21
10/30 L 21 at Redlands 27
11/13 L 0 Caltech 32
11/20 L 0 at Whittier 103
*W—0, L—5, T—0*

### 1921: HARRY TROTTER
10/8 L 7 Redlands 35
10/15 L 7 Pomona 55
10/29 L 0 at Occidental 35
11/5 L 0 Whittier 62
11/11 L 0 at Caltech 27
*W—0, L—5, T—0*

### 1922: HARRY TROTTER
10/7 W 24 at San Diego State 6
10/14 W 34 at Redlands 9
10/21 L 7 Occidental 14
11/4 T 6 at Whittier 6
11/18 L 6 at Pomona 20
11/25 L 6 Caltech 7
*W—2, L—3, T—1*

### 1923: JAMES CLINE
10/13 W 12 San Diego State 0
10/20 W 6 Loyola 0
10/27 L 12 Whittier 14
11/3 L 6 Pomona 27
11/12 L 6 Redlands 12
11/17 L 6 at Occidental 20
11/24 L 6 Caltech (Rose Bowl) 59
*W—2, L—5, T—0*

### 1924: JAMES CLINE
10/4 T 0 Loyola 0
10/11 L 13 La Verne 14
10/18 L 0 at Whittier 6
10/25 L 7 Occidental 20
11/1 L 7 at Pomona 50
11/11 T 0 at Redlands 0
11/15 T 13 at San Diego State 13
11/22 L 0 Caltech 6
*W—0, L—5, T—3*

### 1925: WILLIAM H. SPAULDING
9/26 W 7 San Diego State 0
10/3 W 16 La Verne 3
10/10 W 26 Pomona 0
10/16 L 0 Whittier 7
10/24 W 9 at Occidental 0
10/31 L 0 at St. Mary's 28

11/7 W 23 Redlands 0
11/14 L 0 at Stanford 82
11/21 T 10 at Caltech 10
*W—5, L—3, T—1*

### 1926: WILLIAM H. SPAULDING

9/25 W 25 Santa Barbara St. 0
10/9 W 42 San Diego State 7
10/16 L 6 at Whittier 16
10/23 W 27 at Pomona 7
11/6 W 24 Occidental 7
11/13 W 26 at Redlands 3
11/20 L 3 Caltech 7
11/27 L 0 Iowa State 20
*W—5, L—3, T—0*

### 1927: WILLIAM H. SPAULDING

9/24 W 33 Santa Barbara St. 0
10/1 W 7 Fresno State 0
10/8 W 25 Whittier 6
10/15 W 8 Occidental 0
10/28 W 32 Redlands 0
11/5 T 7 Pomona 7
11/12 W 13 at Caltech 0
11/19 L 13 at Arizona 16
11/26 L 6 Drake 25
*W—6, L—2, T—1*

### 1928: WILLIAM H. SPAULDING

9/22 W 19 Santa Barbara St. 0
9/29 T 7 Arizona 7
10/6 W 32 at Caltech 0
10/13 L 7 at Stanford 45
10/20 W 29 Pomona 0
10/27 L 6 at Idaho 20
11/10 L 0 at Washington St. 38
11/17 W 65 La Verne 0
11/29 L 6 Oregon 26
*W—4, L—4, T—1 (9th in PCC)*

### 1929: WILLIAM H. SPAULDING

9/28 L 0 USC 76
10/5 W 56 Fresno State 6
10/12 L 0 Stanford 57
10/19 W 31 at Caltech 0
10/26 W 20 Pomona 0
11/2 L 0 at Oregon 27
11/16 L 0 St. Mary's 24
11/28 W 14 Montana 0
*W—4, L—4, T—0 (6th in PCC)*

### 1930: WILLIAM H. SPAULDING

9/27 L 0 USC 52
10/11 W 21 Pomona 0
10/17 L 6 St. Mary's 21
10/24 W 30 Caltech 0
10/31 L 0 Stanford 20
11/8 L 0 at Oregon 7
11/21 L 0 Oregon State 19
11/29 W 20 Idaho 6
*W—3, L—5, T—0 (T-8th in PCC)*

### 1931: WILLIAM H. SPAULDING

9/25 T 0 Occidental 0
10/3 L 0 at Washington St. 13
10/17 L 0 at Northwestern 19
10/24 W 46 Pomona 0
10/31 L 6 at Stanford 12
11/11 W 12 St. Mary's 0
11/21 L 6 Oregon 13
11/26 W 13 Florida 0
*W—3, L—4, T—1 (9th in PCC)*

### 1932: WILLIAM H. SPAULDING

9/23 W 26 Calif. Aggies 0
9/30 W 6 Idaho 0
10/15 W 12 at Oregon 7
10/22 W 51 Caltech 0
10/29 W 13 Stanford 6
11/11 L 7 St. Mary's 14
11/19 W 32 Montana 0
11/24 L 0 Washington State 3
12/3 L 0 Washington 19
12/17 L 2 at Florida 12
*W—6, L—4, T—0 (3rd in PCC)*

### 1933: WILLIAM H. SPAULDING

9/23 W 34 Los Angeles JC 0
9/23 W 13 San Diego State 0
9/30 L 0 at Stanford 3
10/6 W 22 Utah 0
10/21 W 20 Loyola 7
10/28 L 0 Oregon 7
11/4 T 0 California 0
11/11 W 14 at San Diego Marines 13
11/18 L 0 at Washington 10

11/25 L 14 St. Mary's 22
11/30 W 7 Washington State 0
*W—6, L—4, T—1 (5th in PCC)*

### 1934: WILLIAM H. SPAULDING
9/22 W 14 Pomona 0
9/22 W 20 San Diego State 0
9/29 L 3 at Oregon 26
10/13 W 16 Montana 0
10/20 L 0 at California 3
10/27 W 49 California Aggies 0
11/3 L 0 Stanford 27
11/12 W 6 St. Mary's 0
11/24 W 25 Oregon State 7
11/29 W 13 Loyola 6
*W—7, L—3, T—0 (6th in PCC)*

### 1935: WILLIAM H. SPAULDING
9/28 W 39 Utah State 0
10/5 W 20 at Oregon State 7
10/19 W 7 at Stanford 6
10/26 W 33 Oregon 6
11/2 L 2 California 14
11/9 L 0 SMU 21
11/15 W 19 Hawaii 6
11/23 W 14 Loyola 6
12/7 W 13 Idaho 6
12/14 W 13 at St. Mary's 7
*W—8, L—2, T—0 (T-1st in PCC)*

### 1936: WILLIAM H. SPAULDING
9/26 W 21 Occidental 0
9/26 W 26 Pomona 0
10/2 W 30 Montana 0
10/10 L 0 Washington 14
10/17 W 17 at California 6
10/24 W 22 Oregon State 13
10/31 L 6 Stanford 19
11/7 W 7 at Oregon 0
11/14 L 7 Washington State 32
11/26 T 7 at USC 7
*W—6, L—3, T—1 (5th in PCC)*

### 1937: WILLIAM H. SPAULDING
9/24 W 26 Oregon 13
10/9 L 7 at Stanford 12
10/16 T 7 at Oregon State 7
10/23 L 0 Washington State 3
10/30 L 14 California 27
11/13 L 0 at Washington 26
11/20 L 13 SMU 26
11/27 W 13 Missouri 0
12/4 L 13 USC 19
*W—2, L—6, T—1 (8th in PCC)*

### 1938: WILLIAM H. SPAULDING
9/23 W 27 Iowa 3
10/1 L 12 at Oregon 14
10/8 W 13 Washington 0
10/15 L 7 at California 20
10/22 W 33 Idaho 0
10/29 W 6 Stanford 0
11/5 W 21 at Washington St. 0
11/12 L 7 Wisconsin (15) 14
11/24 L 7 at USC (14) 42
12/10 T 6 Oregon State 6
12/26 W 46 at Honolulu Town 0
1/2 W 32 at Hawaii 7
*W—7, L—4, T—1 (4th in PCC)*

### 1939: EDWIN C. HORRELL
9/29 W 6 Texas Christian 2
10/7 W 14 at Washington 7
10/14 T 14 at Stanford 14
10/21 W 20 Montana 6
10/28 W 16 Oregon 6
11/4 W 20 (19) California 7
11/18 T 0 (11) Santa Clara (14) 0
11/25 T 13 (13)Oregon State 13
11/30 W 24 (13) Washington State 7
12/9 T 0 (9) at USC (3) 0
W—6, L—0, T—4 (2nd in PCC)
*Ranked 7th by AP*

### 1940: EDWIN C. HORRELL
9/27 L 6 SMU 9
10/4 L 6 Santa Clara 9
10/12 L 0 Texas A&M 7
10/19 L 7 at California 9
10/26 L 0 Oregon State 7
11/2 L 14 Stanford (6) 20
11/9 L 0 at Oregon 18
11/16 W 34 Washington State 26
11/23 L 0 Washington (13) 41
11/30 L 12 at USC 28
*W—1, L—9, T—0 (8th in PCC)*

### 1941: EDWIN C. HORRELL

9/26 W 7 Washington State 6
10/4 L 0 at Stanford 33
10/10 W 14 Montana 7
10/18 L 7 at Washington 14
10/25 W 14 Oregon (16) 7
11/1 L 7 California 27
11/8 L 0 at Oregon State 19
11/15 W 29 Camp Haan 0
11/22 L 13 Santa Clara 31
12/6 T 7 USC 7
12/20 W 30 at Florida 27
*W—5, L—5, T—1 (T-5th in PCC)*

### 1942: EDWIN C. HORRELL

9/25 L 6 Texas Christian 7
10/3 L 7 St. Mary's Pre-Flight 18
10/10 W 30 Oregon State 7
10/17 W 21 at California 0
10/24 W 14 (14)Santa Clara (9) 6
10/31 W 20 (11)Stanford 7
11/7 L 7 (10)at Oregon 14
11/21 W 14 (18) Washington 10
12/5 W 40 (13)Idaho 13
12/12 W 14 (13)USC 7
1/1 L 0 (13)Georgia (Rose Bowl) 9
*W—7, L—4, T—0 (1st in PCC) Ranked 13th by AP*

### 1943: EDWIN C. HORRELL

9/25 L 0 USC 20
10/2 L 7 College of Pacifi c 19
10/9 L 7 at March Field 47
10/16 L 0 California 13
10/30 L 0 at San Diego Navy 28
11/6 L 7 Del Monte Pre-Flight 26
11/13 L 6 at California 13
11/20 W 19 St. Mary's 7
11/27 L 13 at USC 26
*W—1, L—8, T—0 (4th in PCC)*

### 1944: EDWIN C. HORRELL

9/23 T 13 at USC 13
9/30 L 0 at California 6
10/7 L 12 at San Diego Navy 14
10/14 W 39 St. Mary's 0
10/21 L 12 St. Mary's Pre-Flight 21
10/27 W 26 Alameda Co. Guard 13
11/4 L 13 at March Field 35
11/11 W 7 California 0
11/18 W 54 College of Pacifi c 7
11/25 L 13 USC (8) 40
*W—4, L—5, T—1 (3rd in PCC)*

### 1945: BERT LaBRUCHERIE

9/21 L 6 USC 13
9/29 W 20 San Diego Navy 14
10/5 W 50 College of Pacifi c 0
10/13 W 13 California 0
10/19 L 6 St. Mary's Pre-Flight 13
10/26 W 12 Oregon 0
11/17 W 13 St. Mary's (5) 7
11/24 L 0 (12)at California 6
12/1 L 15 at USC (16) 26
*W—5, L—4, T—0 (5th in PCC)*

### 1946: BERT LaBRUCHERIE

9/28 W 50 Oregon State 7
10/5 W 39 at Washington 13
10/12 W 26 (5)Stanford (17) 6
10/19 W 13 (4)at California 6
10/26 W 33 (5)Santa Clara 7
11/1 W 46 (4)St. Mary's 20
11/9 W 14 (4)at Oregon 0
11/16 W 61 (4)Montana 7
11/23 W 13 (4)USC (10) 6
11/30 W 18 (4)Nebraska 0
1/1 L 14 (4) Illinois (Rose Bowl) 45
*W—10, L—1, T—0; (1st in PCC)*
*Ranked 4th by AP*

### 1947: BERT LaBRUCHERIE

9/26 W 22 Iowa 7
10/4 L 26 at Northwestern 27
10/11 W 24 Oregon 7
10/18 W 39 (19)at Stanford 6
10/25 L 0 (16)SMU (12) 7
11/1 L 0 (19)California (14) 6
11/8 W 27 at Oregon State 7
11/15 W 34 Washington 7
11/22 L 0 (18)at USC (4) 6
*W—5, L—4, T—0 (4th in PCC)*

### 1948: BERT LaBRUCHERIE

9/18 W 48 Washington State 26
9/25 L 0 Northwestern 19
10/2 W 28 Idaho 12

10/9 L 6 at Washington 27
10/16 L 14 Stanford 34
10/23 L 0 Oregon State 28
10/30 W 27 at Nebraska 15
11/6 L 13 at California (5) 28
11/12 L 7 Oregon (15) 26
11/20 L 13 USC 20
*W—3, L—7, T—0 (8th in PCC)*

### 1949: RED SANDERS

9/16 W 35 Oregon State 13
9/24 W 41 at Iowa 25
9/30 W 35 at Oregon 27
10/8 W 14 (18)at Stanford 7
10/15 L 0 (13)Santa Clara 14
10/22 W 27 at Washington St. 20
10/29 L 21 (20)California 35
11/12 W 47 Washington 26
11/19 L 7 at USC 21
*W—6, L—3, T—0 (2nd in PCC)*

### 1950: RED SANDERS

9/23 W 28 Oregon 0
9/30 W 42 Washington State 0
10/7 L 20 (13)at Washington (10) 21
10/13 L 6 Illinois 14
10/21 W 21 Stanford (6) 7
10/28 W 20 (18) at Purdue 6
11/4 W 20 (19)Oregon State 13
11/11 L 0 (19)at California (6) 35
11/25 W 39 USC 0
*W—6, L—3, T—0 (3rd in PCC)*

### 1951: RED SANDERS

9/21 L 14 Texas A&M (6) 21
9/29 L 13 at Illinois (10) 27
10/6 W 44 Santa Clara 17
10/13 L 7 at Stanford (19) 21
10/20 W 41 Oregon 0
11/3 W 21 California (9) 7
11/10 W 7 at Oregon State 0
11/17 T 20 (18)Washington 20
11/24 W 21 (18)at USC (11) 7
*W—5, L—3, T—1 (2nd in PCC)*
*Ranked 17th by AP, T-17 by UPI*

### 1952: RED SANDERS

9/20 W 13 (18) Oregon 6
9/27 W 14 (18)Texas Christian (9) 0
10/4 W 32 (14)at Washington 7
10/11 W 20 (11)Rice 0
10/18 W 24 (10)Stanford (13) 14
10/25 W 20 (8)at Wisconsin (10) 7
11/1 W 28 (7)at California (11) 7
11/8 W 57 (5)Oregon State 0
11/22 L 12 (3)USC (4) 14
*W—8, L—1, T—0 (2nd in PCC) / # 6th by AP, UPI*

### 1953: RED SANDERS

9/18 W 41 (4)Oregon State 0
9/25 W 19 (4)Kansas 7
10/3 W 12 (5)at Oregon 0
10/9 W 13 (6)Wisconsin 0
10/17 L 20 (4)at Stanford 21
10/24 W 44 (12)Washington State 7
10/31 W 20 (10)California 7
11/14 W 22 (7)Washington 6
11/21 W 13 (5)at USC (9) 0
1/1 L 20 (5) Michigan State (8) 28
(Rose Bowl)
*W—8, L—2, T—0 (1st in PCC)*
*Ranked 4th by UPI, 5th by AP*

### 1954: RED SANDERS

9/18 W 67 (8)San Diego NTC 0
9/25 W 32 (8)at Kansas 7
10/1 W 12 (4)Maryland (6) 7
10/9 W 21 (2)at Washington 20
10/16 W 72 (3)Stanford 0
10/23 W 61 (3)at Oregon State 0
10/30 W 27 (3)at California 6
11/6 W 41 (1)Oregon 0
11/20 W 34 (2) USC (7) 0
*W—9, L—0, T—0 (1st in PCC)*
*NATIONAL CHAMPIONS (UPI)*
*Ranked 1st by UPI, 2nd by AP*

### 1955: RED SANDERS

9/16 W 21 (1)Texas A&M 0
9/24 L 0 (1)at Maryland (5) 7
10/1 W 55 (7)at Washington St. 0
10/7 W 38 (7)Oregon State 0
10/15 W 21 (9)at Stanford 13
10/21 W 33 (7) Iowa 13
10/29 W 47 (6)California 0
11/5 W 34 (5)at College of Pacific 0

11/12 W 19 (4)Washington 17
11/19 W 17 (5)at USC 7
1/2 L 14 (4)Michigan State (Rose Bowl) 17
*W—9, L—2, T—0 (1st in PCC)*
*Ranked 4th by AP, UPI*

### 1956: RED SANDERS

9/21 W 13 (17)Utah 7
9/29 L 13 at Michigan (13) 42
10/5 W 6 Oregon 0
10/13 W 28 Washington State 0
10/20 W 34 at California 20
10/27 L 7 at Oregon State 21
11/3 W 14 Stanford (10) 13
11/10 W 13 (19)at Washington 9
11/17 W 13 Kansas 0
11/24 L 7 USC 10
*W—7, L—3, T—0 (T-2nd in PCC)*

### 1957: RED SANDERS

9/20 W 47 Air Force 0
9/27 W 16 Illinois 6
10/5 L 0 at Oregon 21
10/12 W 19 Washington 0
10/19 W 26 Oregon State (7) 7
10/26 L 6 (15)at Stanford 20
11/2 W 16 California 14
11/9 W 19 at Washington St. 13
11/16 W 21 at College of Pacifi c 0
11/23 W 20 at USC 9
*W—8, L—2, T—0 (3rd in PCC)*
*Ranked T-18th by UPI*

### 1958: GEORGE DICKERSON

9/20 L 6 Pittsburgh (19) 27
9/27 W 18 at Illinois 14
10/4 L 0 at Oregon State 14
BILL BARNES, ACTING COACH
10/10 L 14 Florida 21
10/18 W 20 at Washington 0
10/25 L 19 Stanford 21
11/1 L 20 Washington State 38
11/8 L 17 at California 20
11/15 W 7 Oregon 3
11/22 T 15 USC 15
*W—3, L—6, T—1 (6th in PCC)*

### 1959: BILL BARNES

9/18 T 0 Purdue (11) 0
10/3 L 21 at Pittsburgh 25
10/17 W 19 California 12
10/23 L 7 Air Force 20
10/31 L 7 Washington (17) 23
11/7 W 55 at Stanford 13
11/13 W 21 North Carolina State 12
11/21 W 10 at USC (4) 3
11/28 W 21 (20)Utah 6
12/5 L 8 (17)Syracuse (1) 36
*W—5, L—4, T—1 (T-1st in AAWU)*

### 1960: BILL BARNES

9/17 W 8 Pittsburgh (7) 7
9/24 T 27 (8)at Purdue 27
10/15 L 8 (15)at Washington (13) 10
10/22 W 26 (19)Stanford 8
10/29 W 7 North Carolina State 0
11/5 W 28 (15)at California 0
11/12 W 22 (11)Air Force 0
11/19 L 6 (11)USC 17
11/26 W 16 at Utah 9
12/3 W 27 Duke (10) 6
*W—7, L—2, T—1 (3rd in AAWU)*

### 1961: BILL BARNES

9/23 W 19 at Air Force 6
9/30 L 6 (9)at Michigan 29
10/7 L 3 at Ohio State (8) 13
10/14 W 28 Vanderbilt 21
10/21 W 20 Pittsburgh 6
10/28 W 20 at Stanford 0
11/4 W 35 California 15
11/10 W 28 Texas Christian 7
11/18 L 13 Washington 17
11/25 W 10 at USC 7
1/1 L 3 Minnesota (Rose Bowl) 21
*W—7, L—4, T—0 (1st in AAWU)*
*Ranked 16th by AP*

### 1962: BILL BARNES

10/6 W 9 Ohio State (1) 7
10/12 W 35 Colorado State 7
10/20 L 6 at Pittsburgh 8
10/27 L 7 Stanford 17
11/3 W 26 at California 16
11/10 L 11 Air Force 17

11/17 L 0 at Washington 30
11/24 L 3 USC (1) 14
12/1 W 14 at Utah 11
12/8 L 7 Syracuse 12
*W—4, L—6, T—0 (5th in AAWU)*

### 1963: BILL BARNES
9/20 L 0 Pittsburgh 20
9/28 L 14 at Penn State 17
10/5 W 10 at Stanford 9
10/11 L 7 Syracuse 29
10/19 L 12 at Notre Dame 27
10/25 L 12 Illinois (4) 18
11/2 L 0 California 25
11/9 L 21 at Air Force 48
11/16 W 14 Washington 0
11/30 L 6 at USC 26
*W—2, L—8, T—0 (3rd in AAWU)*

### 1964: BILL BARNES
9/12 W 17 at Pittsburgh 12
9/26 W 21 Penn State 14
10/3 W 27 Stanford 20
10/10 L 0 at Syracuse 39
10/17 L 0 at Notre Dame (4) 24
10/24 L 7 at Illinois 26
10/31 W 25 at California 21
11/7 L 15 Air Force 24
11/14 L 20 at Washington 22
11/21 L 13 USC 34
*W—4, L—6, T—0 (4th in AAWU)*

### 1965: TOMMY PROTHRO
9/18 L 3 at Michigan State 13
10/2 W 24 at Penn State 22
10/9 W 24 Syracuse 14
10/16 T 14 at Missouri 14
10/23 W 56 California 3
10/30 W 10 at Air Force Academy 0
11/6 W 28 (8)Washington 24
11/13 W 30 (7)at Stanford 13
11/20 W 20 (7)at USC (6) 16
12/4 L 34 (5)at Tennessee (7) 37
1/1 W 14 (5)Michigan State (1) 12
(Rose Bowl)
*W—8, L—2, T—1 (1st in AAWU)*
*Ranked 4th by AP, 5th by UPI*

### 1966: TOMMY PROTHRO
9/17 W 57 (4)Pittsburgh 14
9/24 W 31 (2)at Syracuse 12
10/1 W 24 (2)Missouri 15
10/8 W 27 (2)at Rice 24
10/15 W 49 (4)Penn State 11
10/22 W 28 (3)at California 15
10/29 W 38 (3)Air Force Academy 13
11/5 L 3 (3)at Washington 16
11/12 W 10 (8)Stanford 0
11/19 W 14 (8)USC (7) 7
*W—9, L—1, T—0 (T-2nd in AAWU)*
*Ranked 5th by AP, UPI*

### 1967: TOMMY PROTHRO
9/16 W 20 (8)Tennessee (9) 16
9/23 W 40 (6)at Pittsburgh 8
9/30 W 51 (4)at Washington State 23
10/7 W 17 (3)at Penn State 15
10/14 W 37 (4)California 14
10/21 W 21 (3)at Stanford 16
11/4 T 16 (2)Oregon State 16
11/11 W 48 (4)Washington 0
11/18 L 20 (1)at USC (4) 21
11/25 L 14 (4)Syracuse 32
*W—7, L—2, T—1 (T-2nd in AAWU)*
*Ranked 10th by UPI / Joined Pac-8 Conf.*

### 1968: TOMMY PROTHRO
9/21 W 63 (16)Pittsburgh 7
9/28 W 31 (8)Washington State 21
10/5 L 7 (9)at Syracuse 20
10/12 L 6 Penn State (3) 21
10/19 L 15 at California 39
10/26 W 20 Stanford 17
11/2 L 18 at Tennessee (5) 42
11/9 L 21 at Oregon State (15) 45
11/16 L 0 at Washington 6
11/23 L 16 USC (1) 28
*W—3, L—7, T—0 (T-5th in Pacific-8)*

### 1969: TOMMY PROTHRO
9/13 W 37 (17)Oregon State 0
9/20 W 42 (17)Pittsburgh 8
9/27 W 34 (14)at Wisconsin 23
10/4 W 36 (11)at Northwestern 0
10/11 W 46 (11)at Washington State 14
10/18 W 32 (8)California 0

10/25 T 20 (6)at Stanford (19) 20
11/1 W 57 (9)Washington 14
11/15 W 13 (7)at Oregon 10
11/22 L 12 (6)at USC (5) 14
*W—8, L—1, T—1 (T-2nd in Pacific-8)*
*Ranked 10th by UPI, 13th by AP*

## 1970: TOMMY PROTHRO

9/12 W 14 (18)at Oregon State 9
9/19 W 24 (16)at Pittsburgh 15
9/26 W 12 (15)Northwestern 7
10/3 L 17 (13)at Texas (2) 20
10/10 L 40 (15)Oregon 41
10/17 W 24 (19)at California 21
10/24 L 7 (16)Stanford (8) 9
10/30 W 54 (19)Washington State 9
11/14 L 20 (17)at Washington 61
11/21 W 45 USC 20
12/5 L 17 at Tennessee (5) 28
*W—6, L—5, T—0 (T-2nd in Pacific-8)*

## 1971: PEPPER RODGERS

9/11 L 25 (15) Pittsburgh 29
9/18 L 10 Texas (3) 28
9/25 L 0 at Michigan (4) 38
10/2 L 17 Oregon State 34
10/9 W 34 at Washington State 21
10/16 W 28 at Arizona 12
10/23 L 24 California 31
10/30 L 12 Washington 23
11/6 L 9 at Stanford (12) 20
11/20 T 7 at USC (15) 7
*W—2, L—7, T—1 (8th in Pacific-8)*

## 1972: PEPPER RODGERS

9/9 W 20 Nebraska (1) 17
9/16 W 38 (8)at Pittsburgh 28
9/23 L 9 (6)Michigan (12) 26
9/29 W 65 (15)Oregon 20
10/7 W 42 (14)Arizona 31
10/14 W 37 (14)at Oregon State 7
10/21 W 49 (11)at California 13
10/28 W 35 (9)Washington State 20
11/4 W 28 (8)Stanford 23
11/11 L 21 (8)at Washington 30
11/18 L 7 (14)USC (1) 24
*W—8, L—3, T—0 (2nd in Pacific-8)*
*Ranked 15th by AP, T-17 by UPI*

## 1973: PEPPER RODGERS

9/8 L 13 (10)at Nebraska (4) 40
9/22 W 55 (18)Iowa 18
9/29 W 34 (17)at Michigan State 21
10/6 W 66 (16)Utah 16
10/13 W 59 (15)at Stanford 13
10/20 W 24 (13)at Washington St. 13
10/27 W 61 (13) California 21
11/3 W 62 (10)Washington 13
11/10 W 27 (9)at Oregon 7
11/17 W 56 (8)Oregon State 14
11/24 L 13 (8)at USC (9) 23
*W—9, L—2, T—0 (2nd in Pacific-8)*
*Ranked 9th by UPI, 12th by AP*

## 1974: DICK VERMEIL

9/7 T 17 (12) at Tennessee (16) 17
9/21 L 10 (12)at Iowa 21
9/28 W 56 Michigan State 14
10/5 W 27 at Utah 14
10/12 T 13 Stanford 13
10/19 W 17 Washington State 13
10/26 W 28 at California (20) 3
11/2 L 9 (18)at Washington 31
11/9 W 21 Oregon 0
11/16 W 33 at Oregon State 14
11/23 L 9 USC (8) 34
*W—6, L—3, T—2 (Tied for 3rd in Pacific-8)*

## 1975: DICK VERMEIL

9/13 W 37 (16) Iowa State 21
9/20 W 34 (12)Tennessee (10) 28
9/27 T 20 (10)at Air Force 20
10/4 L 20 (13) Ohio State (2) 41
10/11 W 31 at Stanford 21
10/18 W 37 (18)at Washington State 23
10/25 W 28 (19) California 14
11/1 L 13 (13) Washington 17
11/8 W 50 at Oregon 17
11/15 W 31 (19) Oregon State 9
11/28 W 25 (14) at USC 22
1/1 W 23 (11)Ohio State (1) 10
(Rose Bowl)
*W—9, L—2, T—1; Pct. .792 (T-1st in Pacific-8)*
*Ranked 5th by AP, UPI*

## 1976: TERRY DONAHUE

9/9 W 28 (17) at Arizona State (3) 10

9/18 W 37 (5) Arizona 9
9/25 W 40 (5) Air Force 7
10/2 T 10 (4) at Ohio State (8) 10
10/9 W 38 (5) Stanford 20
10/16 W 62 (4)Washington State 3
10/23 W 35 (4) at California 19
10/30 W 30 (3)at Washington 21
11/6 W 46 (3)Oregon 0
11/13 W 45 (2)at Oregon State 14
11/20 L 14 (2)USC (3) 24
12/20 L 6 (7)Alabama (16) 36
(Liberty Bowl)
*W—9, L—2, T—1 (2nd in Pacific-8)*
*Ranked 15th by AP, UPI*

## 1977: TERRY DONAHUE

9/12 L 13 (11) at Houston (14) 17
9/17 W 17 (14)Kansas 7
9/24 L 13 (18)at Minnesota 27
10/1 W 34 Iowa 16
10/8 L 28 at Stanford 32
10/15 W 27 at Washington State 16
10/22 W 21 California (15) 19
10/29 W 20 Washington 12
11/5 W 21 at Oregon 3
11/12 W 48 Oregon State 18
11/25 L 27 (17)at USC 29
*W—7, L—4, T—0 (T-2nd in Pacific-8)*

## 1978: TERRY DONAHUE

9/9 W 10 (12) at Washington (11) 7
9/16 W 13 (9) at Tennessee 0
9/23 L 24 (8) at Kansas 28
9/30 W 17 (18)Minnesota 3
10/7 W 27 (16) Stanford (17) 26
10/14 W 45 (14)Washington State 31
10/21 W 45 (10)at California 0
10/27 W 24 (10)Arizona 14
11/4 W 23 (9)Oregon 21
11/11 L 13 (9)at Oregon State 15
11/18 L 10 (14)USC (5) 17
12/25 T 10 (15)Arkansas (8) 10
(Fiesta Bowl)
*W—8, L—3, T—1 (2nd in Pacific-10)*
*Ranked 12th by UPI, 14th by AP*

## 1979: TERRY DONAHUE

9/8 L 16 Houston (16) 24
9/15 W 31 Purdue (5) 21
9/22 W 37 (20)at Wisconsin 12
9/29 L 13 (17) Ohio State (14) 17
10/6 L 24 at Stanford 27
10/13 L 14 at Washington State 17
10/20 W 28 California 27
10/27 L 14 Washington (20) 34
11/10 W 31 Arizona State 28
11/17 W 35 at Oregon 0
11/24 L 14 at USC (4) 49
*W—5, L—6, T—0 (7th in Pacific-10)*

## 1980: TERRY DONAHUE

9/13 W 56 Colorado 14
9/20 W 23 at Purdue 14
9/27 W 35 (16) Wisconsin 0
10/4 W 17 (11) at Ohio State (2) 0
10/11 W 35 (5) Stanford (16) 21
10/25 W 32 (3)at California 9
11/1 L 17 (2)at Arizona 23
11/8 L 14 (8)Oregon 20
11/15 W 23 (17)at Arizona State 14
11/22 W 20 (18)USC (12) 17
11/30 W 34 (14)Oregon State (Tokyo) 3
*W—9, L—2, T—0 (2nd in Pacific-10)*
*Ranked 13th by AP, 14th by UPI*

## 1981: TERRY DONAHUE

9/12 W 35 (12) at Arizona 18
9/19 W 31 (9) at Wisconsin (20) 13
9/26 L 7 (6)at Iowa 20
10/3 W 27 (16) Colorado 7
10/10 L 23 (17) at Stanford 26
10/17 T 17 at Washington St.(18) 17
10/24 W 34 California 6
10/31 W 28 at Oregon 11
11/7 W 31 Washington (16) 0
11/14 W 34 (18) Arizona State (9) 24
11/21 L 21 (15)at USC (10) 22
12/31 L 14 (19)Michigan (16) 33
(Bluebonnet Bowl)
*W—7, L—4, T—1 (T-4th in Pacific-10)*

## 1982: TERRY DONAHUE

9/11 W 41 (18)Long Beach State 10
9/18 W 51 (14)at Wisconsin 26
9/25 W 31 (12) at Michigan (20) 27
10/2 W 34 (9)at Colorado 6

10/9 T 24 (8)Arizona 24
10/16 W 42 (12)Washington State 17
10/23 W 47 (11)at California 31
10/30 W 40 (11)Oregon 12
11/6 L 7 (9) at Washington (10) 10
11/13 W 38 (12)Stanford 35
11/20 W 20 (11)USC (15) 19
1/1 W 24 (5) Michigan (19) 14
(Rose Bowl)
*W—10, L—1, T—1 (1st in Pacific-10)*
*Ranked 5th by AP, UPI*

## 1983: TERRY DONAHUE

9/3 L 8 (20)at Georgia (15) 19
9/17 T 26 Arizona State 26
9/24 L 10 at Nebraska (1) 42
10/1 L 35 Brigham Young 37
10/8 W 39 at Stanford 21
10/15 W 24 at Washington State 14
10/22 W 20 California 16
10/29 W 27 Washington (11) 24
11/5 W 24 at Oregon 13
11/12 L 24 at Arizona 27
11/19 W 27 at USC 17
1/2 W 45 Illinois (4) 9
(Rose Bowl)
*W—7, L—4, T—1 (1st in Pacific-10)*
*Ranked 13th by UPI, 17th by AP*

## 1984: TERRY DONAHUE

9/8 W 18 (4) at San Diego State 15
9/15 W 23 (7) Long Beach State 17
9/22 L 3 (8)Nebraska (1) 42
9/29 W 33 (17) at Colorado 16
10/6 L 21 (17)Stanford 23
10/13 W 27 Washington State 24
10/20 W 17 at California 14
10/27 W 21 at Arizona State 13
11/3 L 18 Oregon 20
11/10 W 26 Oregon State 17
11/17 W 29 USC (7) 10
1/1 W 39 (14)Miami (13) 37
(Fiesta Bowl)
*W—9, L—3, T—0 (T-3rd in Pacific-10)*
*Ranked 9th by AP, 10th by UPI*

## 1985: TERRY DONAHUE

9/7 W 27 (20)at BYU (8) 24
9/14 T 26 (10)at Tennessee 26
9/21 W 34 (12)San Diego State 16
9/28 L 14 (13)at Washington 21
10/5 W 40 Arizona State 17
10/12 W 34 at Stanford 9
10/19 W 31 (18)at Washington State 30
10/26 W 34 (17)California 7
11/9 W 24 (14)at Arizona 19
11/16 W 41 (13)Oregon State 0
11/23 L 13 (8)at USC 17
1/1 W 45 (13) Iowa (4) 28
(Rose Bowl)
*W—9, L—2, T—1 (1st in Pacific-10)*
*Ranked 6th by UPI, 7th by AP*

## 1986: TERRY DONAHUE

9/6 L 3 (4)at Oklahoma (1) 38
9/20 W 45 (19)at San Diego State 14
9/27 W 41 (16)Long Beach State 23
10/4 L 9 (15)Arizona State (16) 16
10/11 W 32 Arizona (11) 25
10/18 W 36 (19)at California 10
10/25 W 54 (17)Washington State 16
11/1 W 49 (15)at Oregon State 0
11/8 L 23 (12)Stanford 28
11/15 T 17 (19)at Washington (10) 17
11/22 W 45 (18)USC (10) 25
12/30 W 31 (15)BYU (Freedom Bowl) 10
*W—8, L—3, T—1 (T-2nd in Pacific-10)*
*Ranked 14th by AP, UPI*

## 1987: TERRY DONAHUE

9/5 W 47 (3)San Diego State 14
9/12 L 33 (3)at Nebraska (2) 42
9/19 W 17 (13)Fresno State 0
9/26 W 34 (13)Arizona 24
10/3 W 49 (11)at Stanford 0
10/17 W 41 (9)Oregon (16) 10
10/24 W 42 (8)California 18
10/31 W 31 (7)at Arizona State 23
11/7 W 52 (7) at Oregon State 17
11/14 W 47 (5)Washington 14
11/21 L 13 (5)at USC 17
12/25 W 20 (10)Florida (Aloha Bowl) 16
*W—10, L—2, T—0 (T-1st in Pacific-10)*
*Ranked 9th by AP, 11th by UPI*

## 1988: TERRY DONAHUE

9/3 W 59 (5) San Diego State 6
9/10 W 41 (5) Nebraska (2) 28
9/17 W 56 (2) Long Beach State 3
10/1 W 24 (2)at Washington(16) 17
10/8 W 38 (2)Oregon State 21
10/15 W 38 (2)at California 21
10/22 W 24 (1)at Arizona 3
10/29 L 30 (1)Washington State 34
11/5 W 16 (6)at Oregon 6
11/12 W 27 (6)Stanford 17
11/19 L 22 (6)USC (2) 31
1/2 W 17 (9)Arkansas (8) Cotton Bowl 3
*W—10, L—2, T—0 (2nd in Pacifi c-10)*
*Ranked 6th by AP, UPI*

## 1989: TERRY DONAHUE

9/9 L 6 (6)Tennessee 24
9/16 W 28 (20) at San Diego State 25
9/23 L 23 (24)Michigan (5) 24
9/30 W 24 California 6
10/7 W 33 (25)Arizona State 14
10/14 L 7 (22)at Arizona 42
10/21 L 17 at Oregon State 18
10/28 L 27 Washington 28
11/4 L 14 at Stanford 17
11/11 L 20 Oregon 38
11/18 T 10 at USC (8) 10
*W—3, L—7, T—1 (9th in Pacific-10)*

## 1990: TERRY DONAHUE

9/8 L 14 (19) Oklahoma (23) 34
9/15 W 32 Stanford 31
9/22 L 15 at Michigan (7) 38
9/29 W 30 at Washington State 20
10/6 L 21 Arizona (25) 28
10/13 W 45 San Diego State 31
10/20 L 31 at California 38
10/27 W 26 Oregon State 17
11/3 L 24 at Oregon (22) 28
11/10 W 25 at Washington (2) 22
11/17 L 42 USC (19) 45
*W—5, L—6, T—0 (T-6th in Pacific-10)*

## 1991: TERRY DONAHUE

9/7 W 27 (23)Brigham Young (25) 23
9/14 L 16 (21)at Tennessee (11) 30
9/26 W 37 at San Diego State 12
10/5 L 24 (24)California (18) 27
10/12 W 54 Arizona 14
10/19 W 44 at Oregon State 7
10/26 W 21 at Arizona State 16
11/2 W 44 (23)Washington State 3
11/9 L 10 (22)at Stanford 27
11/16 W 16 Oregon 7
11/23 W 24 (25)at USC 21
12/31 W 6 (22)Illinois (Hancock Bowl) 3
*W—9, L—3, T—0 (T-2nd in Pacific-10)*
*Ranked 18th by USA Today, 19th by AP*

## 1992: TERRY DONAHUE

9/12 W 37 (16)Cal State Fullerton 14
9/19 W 17 (15)at Brigham Young 10
9/26 W 35 (11)San Diego State (21) 7
10/3 L 3 (11)at Arizona 23
10/10 L 7 (19)Stanford (11) 19
10/17 L 17 at Washington St. (22) 30
10/24 L 0 Arizona State 20
10/31 L 12 at California 48
11/7 W 26 Oregon State 14
11/14 W 9 at Oregon 6
11/21 W 38 USC (15) 37
*W—6, L—5, T—0 (8th in Pacific-10)*

## 1993: TERRY DONAHUE

9/4 L 25 California 27
9/18 L 13 Nebraska (8) 14
9/25 W 28 at Stanford (17) 25
9/30 W 52 at San Diego State 13
10/9 W 68 (25)Brigham Young (19) 14
10/16 W 39 (22)Washington (12) 25
10/23 W 20 (19)at Oregon State 17
10/30 W 37 (15)Arizona (7) 17
11/6 W 40 (12)at Washington State 27
11/13 L 3 (10)Arizona State 9
11/20 W 27 (16)at USC (22) 21
1/1 L 16 (14)Wisconsin (9) Rose Bowl 21
*W—8, L—4, T—0 (T-1st in Pacific-10)*
*Ranked 17th by USA Today, 18th by AP*

## 1994: TERRY DONAHUE

9/3 W 25 (14)Tennessee (13) 23
9/10 W 17 (13)SMU 10
9/17 L 21 (13)at Nebraska (2) 49
9/24 L 0 (18)Washington St. (22) 21
10/1 L 10 at Washington (12) 37

10/8 L 7 at California 26
10/15 L 14 Oregon State 23
10/22 L 24 at Arizona (14) 34
10/29 W 31 Stanford 30
11/12 W 59 at Arizona State 23
11/19 W 31 USC (13) 19
*W—5, L—6, T—0 (T-5th in Pacific-10)*

## 1995: TERRY DONAHUE

9/2 W 31 (15)Miami (12) 8
9/9 W 23 (12)at Brigham Young 9
9/16 L 31 (12)Oregon (20) 38
9/23 L 15 (16)at Washington State 24
9/30 W 45 Fresno State 21
10/14 W 17 Arizona 10
10/21 W 42 at Stanford (23) 28
10/28 W 33 (24)California 16
11/4 L 33 (22)at Arizona State 37
11/11 L 14 Washington (23) 38
11/18 W 24 at USC (11) 20
12/25 L 30 Kansas (11) Aloha Bowl 51
*W—7, L—5, T—0 (T-5th in Pacific-10)*

## 1996: BOB TOLEDO

9/7 L 20 at Tennessee (2) 35
9/14 W 44 Northeast Louisiana 0
9/28 L 9 at Michigan (6) 38
10/5 W 41 at Oregon 22
10/12 L 34 Arizona State (4) 42
10/19 L 21 at Washington (25) 41
10/26 W 38 at California 29
11/2 L 20 Stanford 21
11/9 W 38 Washington State 14
11/16 L 17 at Arizona 35
11/23 W 48 USC (2ot) 41
*W—5, L—6, T—0 (4th in Pacific-10)*

## 1997: BOB TOLEDO

8/30 L 34 at Washington St. 37
9/6 L 24 Tennessee (3) 30
9/13 W 66 at Texas (11) 3
9/27 W 40 (24)Arizona 27
10/4 W 66 (22)Houston 10
10/11 W 39 (18)at Oregon 31
10/18 W 34 (17)Oregon State 10
10/25 W 35 (13)California 17
11/1 W 27 (12)at Stanford 7
11/15 W 52 (9)Washington (13) 28
11/22 W 31 (7)at USC 24
1/1 W 29 (5)Texas A&M (19) 23
(Cotton Bowl)
*W—10, L—2, T—0 (T-1st in Pacific-10)*
*Ranked 5th by USA Today, 5th by AP*

## 1998: BOB TOLEDO

9/12 W 49 (6)Texas (23) 31
9/19 W 42 (4)at Houston 24
10/3 W 49 (4)Washington State 17
10/10 W 52 (3)at Arizona (10) 28
10/17 W 41 (2)Oregon (11) (ot) 38
10/24 W 28 (2)at California 16
10/31 W 28 (2)Stanford 24
11/7 W 41 (3)at Oregon State 34
11/14 W 36 (3)at Washington 24
11/21 W 34 (3)USC 17
12/5 L 45 (3)at Miami 49
1/1 L 31 (6)Wisconsin (9) Rose Bowl 38
*W—10, L—2, T—0 (1st in Pacific-10)*
*Ranked 8th by USA Today, 8th by AP*

## 1999: BOB TOLEDO

9/4 W 38 (17)Boise State 7
9/11 L 20 (13)at Ohio State (14) 42
9/18 W 35 (21)Fresno State 21
9/25 L 32 (18)at Stanford 42
10/2 L 27 at Arizona State 28
10/9 W 34 Oregon 29
10/16 L 0 California 17
10/23 L 7 at Oregon State 55
10/30 L 7 Arizona 33
11/13 W 23 Washington(23)(ot) 20
11/20 L 7 at USC 17
*W—4, L—7, T—0 (9th in Pacific-10)*

## 2000: BOB TOLEDO

9/2 W 35 Alabama (3) 24
9/9 W 24 (16)Fresno State 21
9/16 W 23 (14)Michigan (3) 20
9/23 L 10 (6)at Oregon 29
9/30 W 38 (15)Arizona State 31
10/14 L 38 (13)at California (3ot) 46
10/21 L 38 (23)Oregon State (19) 44
10/28 W 27 at Arizona (24) 24
11/4 W 37 Stanford 35
11/11 L 28 at Washington (7) 35
11/18 L 35 USC 38

12/29 L 20 Wisconsin (Sun Bowl) 21
*W—6, L—6, T—0 (T-5th in Pacific-10)*

## 2001: BOB TOLEDO

9/1 W 20 (15)at Alabama (25) 17
9/8 W 41 (14)at Kansas 17
9/22 W 13 (14)Ohio State (21) 6
9/29 W 38 (12)at Oregon State (19) 7
10/13 W 35 (7)Washington (10) 13
10/20 W 56 (4)California 17
10/27 L 28 (4)at Stanford (20) 38
11/3 L 14 (9)at Washington St.(16) 20
11/10 L 20 (17)Oregon (7) 21
11/17 L 0 (20)at USC 27
12/1 W 52 Arizona State 42
*W—7 L—4, T—0 (6th in Pacific-10)*

## 2002: BOB TOLEDO

9/7 W 30 Colorado State (19) 19
9/14 W 38 at Oklahoma State 24
9/21 L 17 (20)Colorado 31
9/28 W 43 at San Diego State 7
10/5 W 43 at Oregon State 35
10/12 L 30 Oregon (7) 31
10/19 L 12 at California 17
10/26 W 28 Stanford 18
11/2 W 34 at Washington 24
11/9 W 37 at Arizona 7
11/23 L 21 (25)USC (7) 52
12/7 L 27 Washington State (7) 48
ED KEZIRIAN, INTERIM COACH
12/25 W 27 New Mexico (Las Vegas Bowl) 13
*W—8, L—5, T—0 (T-4th in Pacific-10)*

## 2003: KARL DORRELL

9/6 L 14 at Colorado (24) 16
9/13 W 6 Illinois 3
9/20 L 24 at Oklahoma (1) 59
9/27 W 20 San Diego State 10
10/4 W 46 Washington (18) 16
10/11 W 24 at Arizona 21
10/18 W 23 California (ot) 20
10/25 W 20 Arizona State 13
11/1 L 14 at Stanford 21
11/8 L 13 at Washington St.(12) 31
11/15 L 13 Oregon 31
11/22 L 22 at USC (2) 47
12/30 L 9 Fresno State 17
(Silicon Valley Football Classic)
*W—6, L—7, T—0 (T-5th in Pacific-10)*

## 2004: KARL DORRELL

9/4 L 20 Oklahoma State 31
9/11 W 35 at Illinois 17
9/18 W 37 at Washington 31
10/2 W 33 San Diego State 10
10/9 W 37 Arizona 17
10/16 L 28 at California (8) 45
10/23 L 42 at Arizona State (21) 48
10/30 W 21 Stanford 0
11/6 L 29 Washington State 31
11/13 W 34 at Oregon 26
12/4 L 24 USC (1) 29
12/23 L 21 Wyoming (Las Vegas Bowl) 24
*W—6, L—6, T—0 (T-5th in Pacific-10)*

## 2005: KARL DORRELL

9/3 W 44 at San Diego State 21
9/10 W 63 Rice 21
9/17 W 41 Oklahoma (21) 24
10/1 W 21 (20)Washington 17
10/8 W 47 (20)California (10) 40
10/15 W 44 (12)at Wash. State(ot) 41
10/22 W 51 (8)Oregon State 28
10/29 W 30 (8)at Stanford (ot) 27
11/5 L 14 (7)at Arizona 52
11/12 W 45 (14)Arizona State 35
12/3 L 19 (11)at USC (1) 66
12/30 W 50 (17)Northwestern (Sun Bowl) 38
*W—10, L—2, T—0 (3rd in Pacific-10)*
*Ranked 13th by USA Today, 16th by AP*

## 2006: KARL DORRELL

9/2 W 31 Utah 10
9/9 W 26 Rice 16
9/23 L 19 at Washington 29
9/30 W 31 Stanford 0
10/7 W 27 Arizona 7
10/14 L 20 at Oregon (18) 30
10/21 L 17 at Notre Dame (10) 20
10/28 L 15 Washington St. 37
11/4 L 24 at California (10) 38
11/11 W 25 Oregon State 7
11/18 W 24 at Arizona State 12
12/2 W 13 USC (2) 9

12/27 L 27 Florida State (Emerald Bowl) 44
*W—7, L—6, T—0 (4th in Pacific-10)*

## 2007: KARL DORRELL

9/1 W 45 (14)at Stanford 17
9/8 W 27 (13)Brigham Young 17
9/15 L 6 (11)at Utah 44
9/22 W 44 Washington 31
9/29 W 40 at Oregon State 14
10/6 L 6 Notre Dame 20
10/20 W 30 California (10) 21
10/27 L 7 at Washington State 27
11/3 L 27 at Arizona 34
11/10 L 20 Arizona State (9) 24
11/24 W 16 Oregon (9) 0
12/1 L 7 at USC (8) 24
DeWAYNE WALKER, INTERIM COACH
12/22 L 16 BYU (19) Las Vegas Bowl 17
*W—6, L—7, T—0 (T-4th in Pacific-10)*

## 2008: RICK NEUHEISEL

9/1 W 27 Tennessee (ot) (18) 24
9/13 L 0 at Brigham Young (18) 59
9/20 L 10 Arizona 31
9/27 L 31 Fresno State (25) 36
10/4 W 28 Washington State 3
10/11 L 24 at Oregon 31
10/18 W 23 Stanford 20
10/25 L 20 at California 41
11/8 L 6 Oregon State 34
11/15 W 27 at Washington 7
11/28 L 9 at Arizona State 34
12/6 L 7 USC (5) 28
*W—4, L—8, T—0 (8th in Pacific-10)*

## 2009: RICK NEUHEISEL

9/5 W 33 San Diego State 14
9/12 W 19 at Tennessee 15
9/19 W 23 Kansas State 9
10/3 L 16 at Stanford 24
10/10 L 10 Oregon (13) 24
10/17 L 26 California 45
10/24 L 13 at Arizona 27
10/31 L 19 at Oregon State 26
11/7 W 24 Washington 23
11/14 W 43 at Washington State 7
11/21 W 23 Arizona State 13
11/28 L 7 at USC (24) 28
12/29 W 30 Temple (Eagle Bank Bowl) 21
*W—7, L—6, T—0 (8th in Pacific-10)*

## 2010: RICK NEUHEISEL

9/4 L 22 at Kansas State 31
9/11 L 0 Stanford (25) 35
9/18 W 31 Houston (23) 13
9/25 W 34 at Texas (7) 12
10/2 W 42 Washington State 28
10/9 L 7 at California 35
10/21 L 13 at Oregon (1) 60
10/30 L 21 Arizona (15) 29
11/6 W 17 Oregon State 14
11/18 L 7 at Washington 24
11/26 L 34 at Arizona State 55
12/4 L 14 USC 28
*W—4, L—8, T—0 (9th in Pacific-10)*

## 2011: RICK NEUHEISEL

9/3 L 34 at Houston 38
9/10 W 27 San Jose State 17
9/17 L 20 Texas (24) 49
9/24 W 27 at Oregon State 19
10/1 L 19 at Stanford (6) 45
10/8 W 28 Washington State 25
10/20 L 12 at Arizona 48
10/29 W 31 California 14
11/5 W 29 Arizona State (20) 28
11/12 L 6 at Utah 31
11/19 W 45 Colorado 6
11/26 L 0 at USC (10) 50
12/2 L 31 at Oregon (8)* 49
12/31 L 14 Illinois (Fight Hunger Bowl) 20
*W—6, L—8, T—0; Pct. .429*
*Pac-12 South Champion*
**Pac-12 Championship Game*

## 2012: JIM MORA

8/30 W 49 at Rice 24
9/8 W 36 Nebraska (17) 30
9/15 W 37 (22)Houston 6
9/22 L 20 (19)Oregon State 27
9/29 W 42 at Colorado 14
10/6 L 17 (25)at California 43
10/13 W 21 Utah 14
10/27 W 45 at Arizona State 43
11/3 W 66 (25)Arizona (24) 10
11/10 W 44 (17)at Washington State 36

11/17 W 38 (17)USC (21) 28
11/24 L 17 (15)Stanford (11) 35
11/30 L 24 (17)at Stanford(8)* 27
12/27 L 26 (17)Baylor (Holiday Bowl) 49
*W—9, L—5 T—0; Pct. .643*
*Pac-12 South Champion*
**Pac-12 Championship Game*

## 2013: JIM MORA

8/31 W 58 (21) Nevada 20
9/14 W 41 (16)at Nebraska (23) 21
9/21 W 59 (13) New Mexico State 13
10/3 W 34 (12) at Utah 27
10/12 W 37 (11) California 10
10/19 L 10 (9) at Stanford (13) 24
10/26 L 14 (12) at Oregon (2) 42
11/2 W 45 (17) Colorado 23
11/9 31 (16) at Arizona 26
11/15 41 (13) Washington 31
11/23 L (14) 33 Arizona State (19) 38
11/30 W 35 (22) at USC 14
12/31 W 42 (17) Virginia Tech (Sun Bowl) 12
*W—10, L—3, T—0*
*Ranked 16 by BCS*

## 2014: JIM MORA

8/30 W 28 (7) at Virginia 20
9/6 W 42 (11) Memphis 35
9/1 W 20 (12) Texas 17
9/25 W 62 (11) at Arizona State (15) 27
10/4 L 28 (8) Utah 30
10/11 L 30 (18) Oregon 42
10/18 W 36 at Cal 34
10/25 W 40 (25) at Colorado 37
11/1 W 17(25) Arizona (14) 7
11/8 W 44 (18) at Washington 30
11/22 W 38 (11) USC (24) 20
11/28 L 10 (9) Stanford 31
1/2 W 40 (14) Kansas State (11) (Alamo Bowl) 35
*W—10, L—3, T—0*
*Ranked 14 by College Football Playoff Committee*

## 2015: JIM MORA

9/5 W 34 (13) Virginia 16
9/12 W 37 (13) at UNLV 3
9/19 W 24 (10) BYU (19) 23
9/26 W 56 (9) at Arizona (16) 30
10/3 L 23 (7) Arizona State 38
10/15 L 35 (18) at Stanford (15) 56
10/22 W 40 California (20) 24
10/31 W 35 (24) Colorado 31
11/7 W 41(22) at Oregon State 0
11/14 L 27(18) Washington State 31
11/21 W 17 at Utah (18) 9
11/28 L 21 (22) USC 40
12/26 L 29 Nebraska (Foster Farms Bowl) 37
*W—8, L—5, T—0*

## 2016: JIM MORA

9/3 L 24 (16)at Texas A&M (ot) 31
9/10 W 42 UNLV 21
9/17 W 17 at Brigham Young 14
9/24 L 13 Stanford (7) 22
10/1 W 45 Arizona 24
10/8 L 20 at Arizona State 23
10/15 L 21 at Washington State 27
10/22 L 45 Utah (19) 52
11/3 L 10 at Colorado (21) 20
11/12 W 38 Oregon State 24
11/19 L 14 USC (15) 36
11/26 L 10 at Cal 36
*W—4, L—8 T—0*

## 2017: JIM MORA

9/3 W 45 Texas A&M 44
9/9 W 56 Hawaii 23
9/16 L 45 (25) at Memphis 48
9/23 L 34 at Stanford 58
9/30 W 27 Colorado 23
10/14 L 30 at Arizona 47
10/21 W 31 Oregon 14
10/28 L at 23 Washington 44
11/3 L at 17 Utah 48
11/11 W 44 Arizona State 37
11/18 L at 23 USC 28
11/24 W 30 Cal 27
12/26 L 17 Kansas State 35
*W—6, L—7 T—0*

# CHAPTER 21
# This Day in UCLA Football History

**January 1-** On this day in 1976, UCLA defeated top-ranked Ohio State University, 23–10, in the Rose Bowl game.

**January 2-** On this day in 1954, UCLA Football's first coach, Fred Cozens, died.

**January 3-** On this day in 2014, former UCLA kicker Chris Kluwe retired from the NFL.

**January 4-** On this day in 1941, UCLA defensive back Kermit Alexander was born.

**January 5-** On this day in 2014, UCLA offensive lineman Xavier Su'a-Filo announced he was forgoing his senior season and entered the NFL Draft.

**January 6-** On this day in 1983, UCLA cornerback Marcus Cassel was born.

**January 7-** On this day in 1987, UCLA receiver Jamil Turner was born.

**January 8-** On this day in 2006, UCLA running back Maurice Jones-Drew announced he was forgoing his senior season to enter the NFL draft.

**January 9-** On this day in 1939, UCLA offensive lineman Paul Oglesby was born.

**January 10-** On this day in 1965, UCLA safety James Washington was born.

**January 11-** On this day in 2004, former UCLA receiver Freddie Mitchell caught a pass on fourth-and-26 in the NFC Championship for the Philadelphia Eagles that resulted in a first down. The Eagles went on to win the game and Mitchell earned himself a nickname "Fourth-down Freddie."

**January 12-** On this day in 1977, Hall of Fame UCLA quarterback Cade McNown was born.

**January 13-** On this day in 2016, UCLA announced that Running Backs Coach Kennedy Polamalu had been promoted to offensive coordinator.

**January 14-** On this day in 1946, UCLA Hall of Fame halfback Cal Rossi became the first UCLA Bruin drafted in the first round of the NFL Draft. He was selected by the Washington Redskins with the ninth overall pick.

**January 15-** On this day in 1959, Hall of Fame UCLA safety Kenny Easley was born.

**January 16-** On this day in 1990, UCLA tight end Joseph Fauria was born.

**January 17-** On this day in 1985, UCLA fullback Jimmy Stephens was born.

**January 18-** On this day in 1976, former UCLA offensive lineman Bruce Walton played in Super Bowl X. Along with his brother, Bill, the Waltons became the only brothers to ever play in the Super Bowl and NBA Finals.

**January 19-** On this day in 1905, UCLA Football Coach Bert LaBrucherie was born.

**January 20-** On this day in 1981, Hall of Fame UCLA linebacker Donn Moomaw led a public prayer at the inauguration of President Ronald Reagan.

**January 21-** On this day in 2010, Loyola High School linebacker Anthony Barr verbally committed to UCLA.

**January 22-** On this date in 1953, UCLA Hall of Fame center Donn Moomaw was drafted with the ninth overall pick by the Los Angeles Rams.

**January 23-** On this day in 2006, UCLA Head Coach Karl Dorrell announced the hiring of D.J. McCarthy to coach the receivers, and the transition from receivers coach to running backs coach for Dino Babers.

**January 24-** On this day in 1959, former UCLA Assistant Coach (1990–1992) Jacob Burney was born.

**January 25-** On this day in 2016, former UCLA linebacker Anthony Barr was named to his first Pro Bowl as a member of the Minnesota Vikings.

**January 26-** On this day in 1976, UCLA cornerback Tod McBride was born.

**January 27-** On this day in 1967, UCLA split end Tom Fears was named the head coach of the expansion New Orleans Saints. He was the first Hispanic head coach in NFL history.

**January 28-** On this day in 1970, UCLA defensive lineman Michael Chalenski was born.

**January 29-** On this day in 1974, UCLA defensive lineman Bill Sandifer was drafted with the tenth overall pick by the San Francisco 49ers.

**January 30-** On this day in 1968, UCLA Hall of Fame quarterback and Heisman Trophy winner Gary Beban was drafted with the thirtieth overall pick by the Los Angeles Rams.

**January 31-** On this day in 1919, former UCLA four-sport star Jackie Robinson was born in Cairo, Georgia.

**February 1-** On this day in 2004, former UCLA running back Deshaun Foster scored a 33-yard touchdown for the Carolina Panthers in Super Bowl XXXVIII.

**February 2-** On this day in 1965, UCLA receiver Paco Craig was born.

**February 3-** On this day in 2010, Huntington Beach Edison High School linebacker Jordan Zumwalt was named Pac 5 Defensive Player of the Year. He signed a scholarship to attend UCLA on the same day.

**February 4-** On this day in 1998, UCLA Football signed a recruiting class of 24 players, including running back Deshaun Foster.

**February 5-** On this day in 1981, UCLA defensive lineman Rodney Leisle was born.

**February 6-** On this day in 2015, UCLA Hall of Fame linebacker Ken Norton Jr. was named the Oakland Raiders' defensive coordinator.

**February 7-** On this day in 1961, UCLA Football Coach Rick Neuheisel was born.

**February 8-** On this day in 1936, Chuck Cheshire became the first UCLA player drafted into the National Football League. He was taken with the 17th overall pick by the Detroit Lions.

**February 9-** On this day in 2009, Hall of Fame UCLA Quarterback Troy Aikman became a member of the National Football Foundation Board of Directors.

**February 10-** On this day in 1997, UCLA quarterback Josh Rosen was born.

**February 11-** On this day in 2011, UCLA safety Rahim Moore was born.

**February 12-** On this day in 1964, UCLA tight end Derek Tennell was born.

**February 13-** On this day in 1942, former UCLA Assistant Coach (1976–78) Dwain Painter was born.

**February 14-** On this day in 1935, UCLA quarterback Ronnie Knox was born.

**February 15-** On this day in 2010, *People Magazine* reported that UCLA running back Kermit Alexander had adopted five children from Haiti following the devastating 7.0 earthquake.

**February 16-** On this day in 1981, UCLA receiver Jerry Owens was born.

**February 17-** On this day in 1961, UCLA linebacker Blanchard Montgomery III was born.

**February 18-** On this day in 2014, UCLA quarterback and baseball outfielder Christoph Bono helped the Bruins baseball team defeat Cal State Northridge, 7–1.

**February 19-** On this day in 2005, UCLA announced the hiring of Defensive Line Coach Thurmond Moore.

**February 20-** On this day in 2003, UCLA tight end and basketball power forward Marcedes Lewis helped Bruins basketball to a 76–75 victory over California Berkeley.

**February 21-** On this day in 1962, UCLA receiver Mike Young was born.

**February 22-** On this day in 1952, UCLA running back Kermit Johnson was born.

**February 23-** On this day in 1961, UCLA defensive lineman Karl Morgan was born.

**February 24-** On this day in 1979, UCLA linebacker Ryan Nece was born.

**February 25-** On this day in 1947, UCLA kicker Zenon Andrusyshyn was born.

**February 26-** On this day in 1987, UCLA tight end Logan Paulsen was born.

**February 27-** On this day in 1990, UCLA linebacker Patrick Larimore was born.

**February 28-** On this day in 1919, Hall of Fame UCLA halfback Leo Cantor was born.

**February 29-** On this day in 1992, UCLA Linebacker Eric Kendricks was born.

**March 1-** On this day in 1990, UCLA cornerback Aaron Hester was born.

**March 2-** On this day in 1899, UCLA Football Coach James Cline was born.

**March 3-** On this day in 1997, UCLA defensive back Carlton Gray signed a four-year contract with the Indianapolis Colts.

**March 4-** On this day in 1946, UCLA Football Coach Bob Toledo was born.

**March 5-** On this day in 2015, UCLA running back Maurice Jones-Drew announced his retirement from the National Football League.

**March 6-** On this day in 1982, UCLA receiver Jacques Lazarus was born.

**March 7-** On this day in 1965, UCLA receiver Willie "Flipper" Anderson was born.

**March 8-** On this day in 1982, UCLA receiver Junior Taylor was born.

**March 9-** On this day in 2016, former UCLA offensive lineman Michael Harris signed a one-year extension with the Minnesota Vikings.

**March 10-** On this day in 2007, Dorsey High School safety Rahim Moore verbally committed to UCLA.

**March 11-** On this day in 2016, former UCLA tight end Logan Paulsen signed a one-year extension with the Washington Redskins.

**March 12-** On this day in 1999, UCLA announced the hiring of Interior Defensive Line Coach Jethro Franklin.

**March 13-** On this day in 1992, UCLA quarterback and pitcher for the baseball team Max Schuh was born.

**March 14-** On this day in 1967, UCLA Hall of Fame running back Mel Farr was drafted with the seventh overall pick by the Detroit Lions.

**March 15-** On this day in 2000, former UCLA Assistant Coach (1965–1970) Bobb McKittrick died of cholangiocarcinoma.

**March 16-** On this day in 1999, UCLA receiver and outfielder for the baseball team Freddie Mitchell helped the Bruins baseball team defeat Long Beach State, 9–7.

**March 17-** On this day in 2016, UCLA safety Rahim Moore signed a one-year contract with the Cleveland Browns.

**March 18-** On this day in 1992, UCLA linebacker Anthony Barr was born.

**March 19-** On this day in 1992, UCLA kicker Justin Moreno was born.

**March 20-** On this day in 2014, St. John Bosco quarterback Josh Rosen verbally committed to UCLA.

**March 21-** On this day in 1946, the Los Angeles Rams signed Kenny Washington. He would break the NFL color barrier.

**March 22-** On this day in 1979, UCLA Assistant Coach (2011–12, 2016) Marques Tuiasosopo was born.

**March 23-** On this day in 1985, UCLA running back Maurice Jones-Drew was born.

**March 24-** On this day in 2006, UCLA offensive lineman Mike Flanagan signed with the Houston Texans.

**March 25-** On this day in 1983, Hall of Fame UCLA quarterback Bob Waterfield died.

**March 26-** On this day in 1991, UCLA cornerback Sheldon Price was born.

**March 27-** On this day in 1977, UCLA offensive lineman Kris Farris was born.

**March 28-** On this day in 1963, former UCLA Assistant Coach (2007) Jay Norvell was born.

**March 29-** On this day in 2002, UCLA offensive lineman Jim Salsbury died at the age of 69.

**March 30-** On this day in 1990, UCLA defensive back James Washington signed a contract with the Dallas Cowboys.

**March 31-** On this day in 2015, UCLA football began spring practice, marking the first practice for quarterback Josh Rosen in a Bruins uniform.

**April 1-** On this day in 1992, UCLA defensive lineman Owamagbe Odighizuwa was born.

**April 2-** On this day in 2011, UCLA receiver and track and field sprinter Randall Carroll helped the UCLA track and field team beat the University of Tennessee in a dual meet.

**April 3-** On this day in 2015, former UCLA long snapper Kevin McDermott signed a two-year contract with the Minnesota Vikings.

**April 4-** On this day in 2009, a trio of multisports freshmen competed in the UCLA Track and Field Invitational. Sheldon Price, Damien Thigpen, and Randall Carroll all ran sprints for the Bruins.

**April 5-** On this day in 2008, Mission Viejo High School Athlete Alex Mascarenas verbally committed to UCLA.

**April 6-** On this day in 1973, UCLA linebacker Donnie Edwards was born.

**April 7-** On this day in 1993, UCLA offensive lineman Carl Hulick was born.

**April 8-** On this day in 1999, UCLA receiver and volleyball player Danny Farmer led the Bruins volleyball team to a 3–2 victory over Pepperdine.

**April 9-** On this day in 1951, UCLA running back Rob Scribner was born.

**April 10-** On this day in 1979, UCLA defensive lineman Kenyon Coleman was born.

**April 11-** On this day in 1989, UCLA running back Raymond Carter was born.

**April 12-** On this day in 1941, former UCLA Assistant Coach (1972–1975) Lynn Stiles was born.

**April 13-** On this day in 1984, UCLA receiver Matt Willis was born.

**April 14-** On this day in 1917, UCLA football player Francis Wai was born. He would lose his life in World War II.

**April 15-** On this day in 1947, Jackie Robinson made his Major League Baseball debut with the Brooklyn Dodgers.

**April 16-** On this day in 2009, former UCLA running back Maurice Jones-Drew signed a five-year, $31M contract extension with the Jacksonville Jaguars.

**April 17-** On this day in 1999, Hall of Fame UCLA quarterback Cade McNown was drafted twelfth overall by the Chicago Bears.

**April 18-** On this day in 1998, UCLA defensive back Shaun Williams was drafted with the 24th overall pick by the New York Giants.

**April 19-** On this day in 1944, UCLA Hall of Fame quarterback Bob Waterfield was drafted in the fifth round of the NFL draft by the Cleveland Rams.

**April 20-** On this day in 1996, UCLA Hall of Fame offensive lineman Jonathan Ogden was drafted with the fourth overall pick by the Baltimore Ravens.

**April 21-** On this day in 1991, UCLA defensive back Eric Turner was drafted with the second overall pick by the Cleveland Browns.

**April 22-** On this day in 1995, UCLA Hall of Fame receiver J.J. Stokes was drafted with the 10th overall pick by the San Francisco 49ers.

**April 23-** On this day in 1989, UCLA Hall of Fame quarterback Troy Aikman was drafted with the number one overall pick in the NFL Draft by the Dallas Cowboys.

**April 24-** On this day in 1988, UCLA running back Gaston Green was drafted with the 14th overall pick by the Los Angeles Rams.

**April 25-** On this day in 2013, UCLA defensive lineman Datone Jones was drafted with the 26th overall pick by the Green Bay Packers.

**April 26-** On this day in 1992, UCLA quarterback tommy Maddox was drafted with the 25th pick by the Denver Broncos.

**April 27-** On this day in 1982, UCLA offensive tackle Luis Sharpe was drafted with the 16th overall pick by the St. Louis Cardinals.

**April 28-** On this day in 1981, UCLA running back Freeman NcNeil was drafted with the third overall pick by the New York Jets.

**April 29-** On this day in 2006, UCLA tight end Marcedes Lewis was drafted with the 28th overall pick by the Jacksonville Jaguars.

**April 30-** On this day in 2007, UCLA kicker Justin Medlock was drafted in the fifth round by the Kansas City Chiefs.

**May 1-** On this day in 1984, UCLA tight end Paul Bergmann was drafted with the eighth overall pick by the Indianapolis Colts.

**May 2-** On this day in 1967, former UCLA Assistant Coach (2011) Mike Johnson was born.

**May 3-** On this day in 1979, UCLA defensive tackle Manu Tuiasasopo was drafted with the 18th overall pick by the Seattle Seahawks.

**May 4-** On this day in 1880, UCLA Football Coach William Spaulding was born.

**May 5-** On this day in 1993, UCLA running back Roosevelt Davis was born.

**May 6-** On this day in 1952, UCLA linebacker Fred McNeill was born.

**May 7-** On this day in 1905, UCLA Football Coach Red Sanders was born.

**May 8-** On this day in 2014, UCLA linebacker Anthony Barr was drafted with the ninth overall pick by the Minnesota Vikings.

**May 9-** On this day in 1998, UCLA linebacker/tight end Robbie Loudd died. Loudd became the first black coach in American Football League history in 1966. In 1974, Loudd became the owner of the Florida Blazers of the World Football League. He was the first black owner of the WFL.

**May 10-** On this day in 2014, UCLA wide receiver Shaquelle Evans was drafted by the New York Jets in the fourth round.

**May 11-** On this day in 1962, UCLA quarterback Steve Bono was born.

**May 12-** On this day in 1956, UCLA offensive lineman Max Montoya was born.

**May 13-** On this day in 1954, former UCLA Assistant Coach (1989) Dave Currey was born.

**May 14-** On this day in 1995, UCLA Football Coach Tommy Prothro died.

**May 15-** On this day in 1935, UCLA linebacker Don Shinnick was born.

**May 16-** On this day in 1993, UCLA receiver Tyler Scott was born.

**May 17-** On this day in 1988, UCLA punter Danny Rees was born.

**May 18-** On this day in 1927, UCLA quarterback and Assistant Coach Ray Nagel was born.

**May 19-** On this day in 1964, UCLA Hall of Fame placekicker John Lee was born in Seoul, South Korea.

**May 20-** On this day in 1955, UCLA running back Wendell Tyler was born.

**May 21-** On this day in 1977, UCLA wide receiver Danny Farmer was born.

**May 22-** On this day in 1977, UCLA offensive lineman James Ghezzi was born.

**May 23-** On this day in 1990, UCLA defensive back Andrew Abbott was born.

**May 24-** On this day in 1935, former UCLA Assistant Coach (1974) Jim E. Mora was born.

**May 25-** On this day in 1945, UCLA defensive lineman John Richardson was born.

**May 26-** On this day in 1979, UCLA safety Marques Anderson was born.

**May 27-** On this day in 1987, UCLA fullback Dylan Rush was born.

**May 28-** On this day in 2000, UCLA defensive back Erin Turner died at the age of 31 from intestinal cancer.

**May 29-** On this day in 1954, former UCLA Assistant Coach (1998) Nick Aliotti was born.

**May 30-** On this day in 1925, UCLA offensive lineman Leon McLaughlin was born.

**May 31-** On this day in 1960, UCLA placekicker Norm Johnson was born.

**June 1-** On this day in 2006, the NCAA announced it was allowing coaches one challenge per game.

**June 2-** On this day in 1985, UCLA offensive lineman Phillip Rauscher was born.

**June 3-** On this day in 1989, UCLA offensive Lineman Kai Maiava was born.

**June 4-** On this day in 1983, UCLA running back Tyler Ebell was born.

**June 5-** On this day in 1971, UCLA offensive lineman Vaughn Parker was born.

**June 6-** On this day in 2007, UCLA offensive lineman and shotputter for the track and field team Darius Savage placed 13th in the NCAA Championships, just missing out on the NCAA finals.

**June 7-** On this day in 2013, UCLA receiver and baseball outfielder Tyler Scott helped the Bruins baseball team defeat Cal State Fullerton, 5–3, in 10 innings.

**June 8-** On this day in 2007, it was announced that UCLA quarterback Osaar Rasshan would be moving to wide receiver.

**June 9-** On this day in 1981, the Chicago Bulls of the National Basketball Association drafted Hall of Fame UCLA safety Kenny Easley in the 10th round.

**June 10-** On this day in 1947, former UCLA Assistant Coach (1987–88, 2003) Steve Axman was born.

**June 11-** On this day in 1988, UCLA offensive lineman Micah Kia was born.

**June 12-** On this day in 2008, Hall of Fame UCLA offensive lineman Jonathan Ogden announced he was retiring from the NFL.

**June 13-** On this day in 1922, Hall of Fame UCLA end Burr Baldwin was born.

**June 14-** On this day in 1951, UCLA offensive lineman Bruce Walton, brother of UCLA basketball legend Bill Walton, was born.

**June 15-** On this day in 1993, UCLA quarterback Brett Hundley was born.

**June 16-** On this day in 1955, UCLA kicker Frank Corral was born.

**June 17-** On this day in 1990, UCLA tight end Cory Harkey was born.

**June 18-** On this day in 2014, UCLA defensive lineman Nate Chandler signed a three-year contract extension with the Carolina Panthers.

**June 19-** On this day in 2014, former UCLA running back Johnathan Franklin announced his retirement from the NFL following a serious neck injury.

**June 20-** On this day in 2000, President Bill Clinton awarded the Medal of Honor to 22 Asian Americans who fought in World War II. UCLA Football player Francis Wai was posthumously awarded.

**June 21-** On this day in 1963, UCLA wide receiver Mike Sherrard was born.

**June 22-** On this day in 1954, UCLA Assistant Coach (2003–2007) Gary DeLoach was born.

**June 23-** On this day in 1960, former UCLA Assistant Coach (2004–06) Jim Svoboda was born.

**June 24-** On this day in 1971, Hall of Fame UCLA Halfback Kenny Washington died of polyarteritis nodosa at the age of 52.

**June 25-** On this day in 2010, the latest batch of UCLA freshman football players moved into their dorms.

**June 26-** On this day in 1920, Hall of Fame UCLA quarterback Bob Waterfield was born.

**June 27-** On this day in 1986, Hall of Fame UCLA safety Don Rogers died of a heart attack one day before he was scheduled to be married.

**June 28-** On this day in 1974, UCLA running back Karim Abdul-Jabbar was born.

**June 29-** On this day in 1999, UCLA was honored by the American Football Coaches Association for having one of the highest graduation rates in the country.

**June 30-** On this day in 1984, UCLA linebacker Wesley Walker was born.

**July 1-** On this day in 1966, UCLA running back Eric Ball was born.

**July 2-** On this day in 1930, UCLA linebacker Cliff Livingston was born.

**July 3-** On this day in 2009, it was announced that tight end Joseph Fauria from Notre Dame would transfer to UCLA.

**July 4-** On this day in 2011, La Habra High School linebacker Aaron Porter verbally committed to UCLA.

**July 5-** On this day in 1955, former UCLA running back and Olympic sprinter James Owens was born.

**July 6-** On this day in 2011, UCLA announced that running back Theotis Brown (1976–1978) and quarterback Ernie Case (1940–41, 1945–1946) would be inducted into the UCLA Athletics Hall of Fame.

**July 7-** On this day in 1992, UCLA defensive lineman Cassius Marsh was born.

**July 8-** On this day in 2014, San Leandro High School Athlete Stephen Johnson verbally committed to UCLA.

**July 9-** On this day in 1961, Hall of Fame UCLA quarterback Tom Ramsey was born.

**July 10-** On this day in 1989, UCLA linebacker Akeem Ayers was born.

**July 11-** On this day in 2015, UCLA end Ray Kurrasch died at the age of 92.

**July 12-** On this day in 2012, Memphis East High School offensive lineman Christian Morris committed to UCLA. He would enroll at UCLA but transfer to Ole Miss after one year.

**July 13-** On this day in 1994, UCLA defensive lineman Ellis McCarthy was born.

**July 14-** On this day in 1967, UCLA Athletic Director Wilbur Johns died.

**July 15-** On this day in 1967, UCLA defensive back Carnell Lake was born.

**July 16-** On this day in 1992, UCLA linebacker Ryan Hofmeister was born.

**July 17-** On this day in 1991, UCLA linebacker Roman Phifer signed a three-year contract with the Los Angeles Rams.

**July 18-** On this day in 1972, UCLA Defensive Lineman Bruce Walker was born.

**July 19-** On this day in 1961, former UCLA Assistant Coach (2004-07) Dino Babers was born.

**July 20-** On this day in 1920, UCLA Football Coach Tommy Prothro was born.

**July 21-** On this day in 1999, UCLA Head Coach Bob Toledo announced that quarterback J.P. Losman was transferring. Losman would go on to an eight-year NFL career.

**July 22-** On this day in 2002, UCLA linebacker Robert Thomas signed a five-year contract with the St. Louis Rams.

**July 23-** On this day in 1976, UCLA cornerback Wasswa Serwanga was born.

**July 24-** On this day in 1990, UCLA defensive lineman Datone Jones was born.

**July 25-** On this day in 1914, UCLA Hall of Fame end Woody Strode was born.

**July 26-** On this day in 2004, UCLA linebacker Brandon Chillar signed a four-year contract with the St. Louis Rams, making him just the second NFL player of Indian descent.

**July 27-** On this day in 1985, Hall of Fame UCLA kicker John Lee signed a four-year, $900,000 contract with the team that drafted him, the St. Louis Cardinals. The contract made Lee the highest-paid kicker in the league and the first East Asian-born player to sign an NFL contract.

**July 28-** On this day in 2010, Rancho Bernardo High School linebacker Aaron Wallace verbally committed to UCLA.

**July 29-** On this day in 1970, UCLA wide receiver Sean LaChapelle was born.

**July 30-** On this day in 1951, UCLA placekicker Efren Herrera was born.

**July 31-** On this day in 1974, Hall of Fame UCLA offensive lineman Jonathan Ogden was born.

**August 1-** On this day in 1966, UCLA running back Gaston Green was born.

**August 2-** On this day in 2011, UCLA kicker Kai Forbath signed with the Dallas Cowboys.

**August 3-** On this day in 2015, Hall of Fame UCLA running back Mel Farr died.

**August 4-** On this day in 1952, former UCLA Assistant Coach Ed Kezirian (1976–77, 1982–92) was born.

**August 5-** On this day in 1946, UCLA Hall of Fame quarterback and Heisman Trophy winner Gary Beban was born.

**August 6-** On this day in 2013, UCLA long snapper Christian Yount signed a five-year contract with the Cleveland Browns.

**August 7-** On this day in 1902, UCLA Chancellor Raymond Allen was born.

**August 8-** On this day in 1948, UCLA defensive lineman Floyd Reese was born.

**August 9-** On this day in 1984, former UCLA quarterback Matt Moore was born.

**August 10-** On this day in 1998, UCLA running back Chuck Fenenbock died.

**August 11-** On this day in 1967, UCLA defensive lineman Mike Lodish was born.

**August 12-** On this day in 1952, UCLA Hall of Fame offensive end Woody Strode began a brief full-time wrestling tour.

**August 13-** On this day in 1988, UCLA linebacker Steve Sloan was born.

**August 14-** On this day in 1958, UCLA Football Coach Red Sanders died of a heart attack.

**August 15-** On this day in 1969, former UCLA Assistant Coach (2003–2005) Eric Bieniemy was born.

**August 16-** On this day in 2012, UCLA Linebacker Bruce Davis played his first career game in the Canadian Football League with the Hamilton Tiger-Cats.

**August 17-** On this day in 1932, Hall of Fame UCLA end Paul Cameron was born.

**August 18-** On this day in 2014, UCLA quarterback Brett Hundley appeared on the cover of *Sports Illustrated.*

**August 19-** On this day in 1951, UCLA cornerback Allan Ellis was born.

**August 20-** On this day in 2007, Hall of Fame UCLA end Burr Baldwin died of cancer.

**August 21-** On this day in 1993, UCLA tight end Ian Taubler was born.

**August 22-** On this day in 2008, UCLA offensive lineman Frank Cornish died of a heart attack.

**August 23-** On this day in 1999, UCLA Head Coach Bob Toledo announced Drew Bennett would start the season at quarterback.

**August 24-** On this day in 1983, UCLA safety/ receiver Jibril Raymo was born.

**August 25-** On this day in 1988, UCLA Wide Receiver Terrence Austin was born.

**August 26-** On this day in 1978, UCLA quarterback/ wide receiver Drew Bennett was born.

**August 27-** On this day in 2015, UCLA held a ground-breaking ceremony for the Wasserman Football Center and Mo Ostin Basketball Center.

**August 28-** On this day in 1917, UCLA running back Chuck Fenenbock was born.

**August 29-** On this day in 1909, UCLA halfback Joe Keeble was born.

**August 30-** On this day in 1997, UCLA played the first game in school history in the month of August, losing, 37–34, to Washington State University.

**August 31-** On this day in 1918, Hall of Fame UCLA running back Kenny Washington was born.

**September 1-** On this day in 2001, the No. 17-ranked Bruins beat the University of Alabama, 20–17, at Bryant-Denny Stadium.

**September 2-** On this day in 1995, the No. 15-ranked Bruins beat Ray Lewis and the No. 12 Miami Hurricanes in the season opener, 31–8.

**September 3-** On this day in 2017, UCLA overcame a 34-point deficit to defeat Texas A&M, 45–44. It is the second largest comeback in college football history.

**September 4-** On this day in 1993, UCLA lost to University of California Berkeley, 27–25, in the season opener. UCLA would go on to finish the regular season with an 8–3 record and win the Pacific 10 Conference.

**September 5-** On this day in 1939, UCLA quarterback Billy Kilmer was born.

**September 6-** On this day in 1986, the No. 4-ranked Bruins took on the top-ranked defending National Champion Oklahoma Sooners in the season opener. Oklahoma beat the Bruins, 38–3.

**September 7-** On this day in 1974, Head Coach Dick Vermeil made his UCLA debut. The No. 12 Bruins tied the No. 16 Tennessee Volunteers, 17–17.

**September 8-** On this day in 2013, UCLA receiver Nick Pasquale was killed when he was struck by a car. He was 20 years old.

**September 9-** On this day in 1976, the No. 17 UCLA Bruins beat the No. 3 Arizona State Sun Devils, 28–10, in Head Coach Terry Donahue's first game.

**September 10-** On this day in 1994, Donnie Edwards tied a UCLA single-game record with 4.5 sacks.

**September 11-** On this day in 1971, No. 15 UCLA lost to the Pittsburgh Panthers, 29–25, in Pepper Rodgers's first game as the UCLA head coach.

**September 12-** On this day in 1987, the No. 3 UCLA Bruins took on the No. 2 Nebraska Cornhuskers. In front of a record 150th consecutive sellout crowd at Memorial Stadium, the Bruins fell by a score of 42–33.

**September 13-** On this day in 1997, the unranked Bruins beat the No. 11 Texas Longhorns, 66–3, in Austin, Texas. The game is known as "Rout 66" and would be the first win in the Bruins' twenty-game winning streak.

**September 14-** On this day in 1985, the No. 10-ranked Bruins rallied from 16 points down in the fourth quarter to tie the Tennessee Volunteers, 26–26.

**September 15-** On this day in 1979, UCLA upset the No. 5 Purdue Boilermakers, 31–21.

**September 16-** On this day in 1949, new Head Coach Red Sanders and the Bruins won their season opener against the Oregon State University Beavers, 35–13.

**September 17-** On this day in 1960, the Bruins

kicked off their season by defeating the Pittsburgh Panthers by a score of 8–7.

**September 18-** On this day in 1954, UCLA football kicked off what would be a National Championship season by defeating the San Diego Navy, 67–0.

**September 19-** On this day in 1981, the No. 9-ranked Bruins defeated the No. 20 Wisconsin Badgers, 31–13.

**September 20-** On this day in 1958, the Bruins would play their first game since the death of Head Coach Red Sanders. George Dickerson and the Bruins lost, 27–6, to the University of Pittsburgh Panthers. Dickerson resigned after three games due to health reasons.

**September 21-** On this day in 1945, UCLA lost to USC, 13–6. It was Head Coach Bert LaBrucherie's first game for the Bruins.

**September 22-** On this day in 1984, the No. 8.-ranked Bruins lost, 41–3, to the No. 1 Nebraska Cornhuskers.

**September 23-** On this day in 1944, UCLA took on USC in the season opener. The two teams tied, 13–13.

**September 24-** On this day in 1955, the top-ranked Bruins lost to the No. 5 Maryland Terrapins, 7–0.

**September 25-** On this day in 1976, UCLA linebacker Jerry Robinson set a school record with 28 tackles against Air Force Academy.

**September 26-** On this day in 1925, UCLA, led by new Head Coach William Spaulding, beat San Diego State, 7–0, in the first game of the season. UCLA would finish with a 5–3–1 record, the first winning season in UCLA history.

**September 27-** On this day in 2008, Terrence Austin set a UCLA record with 206 kickoff return yards against Fresno State.

**September 28-** On this day in 1929, UCLA took on the USC Trojans for the first time in school history, losing, 76–0.

**September 29-** On this day in 1902, UCLA Football Coach Edwin Horrell was born.

**September 30-** On this day in 1989, UCLA beat the University of California Berkeley, 24–6. The victory was the 18th consecutive win for the Bruins over the Bears.

**October 1-** On this day in 1954, the No. 4 Bruins beat the No. 6 Maryland Terrapins, 12–7.

**October 2-** On this day in 1920, UCLA played the first game of the Harry Trotter era, losing 41–0 to Pomona College.

**October 3-** On this day in 1919, UCLA played the first football game in school history, losing 74–0 to Manual Arts High School.

**October 4-** On this day in 1975, No. 13 UCLA lost to No. 2 Ohio State by a score of 41–20. The two teams would meet again in the Rose Bowl three months later, and the Bruins would pull off the "Upset of the Century."

**October 5-** On this day in 1985, UCLA beat Arizona State University, 40–17.

**October 6-** On this day in 1933, Mike Frankovich set the UCLA record for longest drop kick. His 33-yard drop kick is still a school record.

**October 7-** On this day in 1922, UCLA defeated San Diego State University, 24–6. The season-opening win gave the Bruins a winning record (albeit temporarily) for the first time in school history.

**October 8-** On this day in 1931, UCLA Football Coach Pepper Rodgers was born.

**October 9-** On this day in 1954, the Bruins had their toughest game of the season, barely escaping with a 21–20 victory over the University of Washington Huskies.

**October 10-** On this day in 1958, Bill Barnes coached

his first game as the head coach of the Bruins. After the sudden death of Red Sanders and the resignation of George Dickerson after three games due to health reasons, Barnes was forced to coach the team against the University of Florida on short notice. The Bruins lost, 21–14.

**October 11-** On this day in 1980, UCLA Hall of Fame running back Freeman McNeil scored four second-half touchdowns to erase a 14-point halftime deficit and beat Stanford University by a score of 35–21.

**October 12-** On this day in 1966, UCLA Football Coach William Spaulding died.

**October 13-** On this day in 1923, James Cline coached his first game as the head coach of the UCLA Bruins football team, defeating San Diego State University by a score of 12–0.

**October 14-** On this day in 2000, the No. 13-ranked UCLA Bruins lost, 46–38, to the University of California Berkeley in three overtimes.

**October 15-** On this day in 1977, UCLA beat Washington State, 27–16. The win over the Cougars was the first of a five-game winning streak that would get the Bruins to within one game of winning the Pac 8 Conference.

**October 16-** On this day in 1993, UCLA quarterback Wayne Cook connected with J.J. Stokes for a 95-yard touchdown. It remains the longest passing play in school history.

**October 17-** On this day in 1970, the No. 19 Bruins beat the University of California Berkeley, 24–21, in a thriller.

**October 18-** On this day in 1986, UCLA beat Cal by a score of 36–10. It was the fifteenth consecutive win for UCLA over the Bears.

**October 19-** On this day in 1957, UCLA beat the No, 7 Oregon State Beavers, 26–7.

**October 20-** On this day in 1917, UCLA Football Coach William Barnes was born.

**October 21-** On this day in 1978, Brian Baggott became the first and only UCLA player to return two interceptions for touchdowns in the same game.

**October 22-** On this day in 2005, UCLA Quarterback Drew Olson threw for a school-record six touchdown passes against Oregon State University. UCLA won, 51–28.

**October 23-** On this day in 1965, UCLA beat the California Golden Bears, 56–3. The Bruins would go on to win the Athletic Association of Western Universities and the Rose Bowl.

**October 24-** On this day in 1919, UCLA defeated the Occidental College Freshman Team, the first win in school history.

**October 25-** On this day in 1941, UCLA beat the No. 16 University of Oregon, 14–7.

**October 26-** On this day in 1974, the unranked Bruins beat No. 20 California, 28–3.

**October 27-** On this day in 1973, the No. 13 Bruins beat the University of California Berkeley, 61–21. It was one of three games in 1973 in which the Bruins scored over 60 points.

**October 28-** On this day in 1995, UCLA Head Coach Terry Donahue became the Pac 10's all-time leader in wins after UCLA beat the University of California Berkeley, 33–16.

**October 29-** On this day in 1983, UCLA quarterback Rick Neuheisel completed an NCAA-record 92.6 percent of his passes as the Bruins beat the Washington Huskies, 20–12.

**October 30-** On this day in 1936, UCLA Football Coach Dick Vermeil was born.

**October 31-** On this day in 1987, the No. 7-ranked Bruins beat Arizona State University, 31–23.

**November 1-** On this day in 1969, the No. 9 UCLA

Bruins beat the University of Washington, 57–14.

**November 2-** On this day in 1991, the No. 23 Bruins beat Washington State, 44–3.

**November 3-** On this day in 1951, UCLA beat the No. 9 Oregon Webfeet, 21–7.

**November 4-** On this day in 1944, Bob Waterfield set the UCLA record for longest punt. His 91-yard punt is still the school record today.

**November 5-** On this day in 1966, the No. 3-ranked Bruins lost to unranked University of Washington. The Bruins would finish the season with a 9–1 record and a win over USC. The Trojans would finish with a 7–4 record. However, the Trojans played one more conference game than the Bruins, finishing 4–1 in conference, while the Bruins finished 3–1. After a vote, USC was selected to participate in the Rose Bowl.

**November 6-** On this day in 1954, the top-ranked Bruins beat the University of Oregon, 41–0. UCLA would enter the final game against USC undefeated.

**November 7-** On this day in 1992, UCLA beat Oregon State, 26–14, to snap a five-game losing streak.

**November 8-** On this day in 1952, No. 5 UCLA beat Oregon State University, 57–0, moving its record to 8–0.

**November 9-** On this day in 2013, UCLA freshman linebacker Myles Jack made his debut on offense. He rushed for 120 yards on six carries.

**November 10-** On this day in 1990, UCLA beat the No. 2 Washington Huskies, 25–22, on a last-second field goal by Kicker Brad Daluiso.

**November 11-** On this day in 1978, the No. 9 Bruins were stunned by 2–5–1 Oregon State. The Beavers upset the Bruins, 15–13.

**November 12-** On this day in 1983, UCLA lost to the University of Arizona, 27–24, snapping the Bruins' five-game winning streak. One week later, UCLA would clinch the Pac 10 Conference title against USC.

**November 13-** On this day in 1943, UCLA lost to the University of California Berkeley, 13–7, dropping the Bruins to 0–7 for the season.

**November 14-** On this day in 1981, UCLA defeated the No. 16 Washington Huskies, 31–0.

**November 15-** On this day in 1980, the No. 17-ranked UCLA Bruins beat the Arizona State Sun Devils, 23–14.

**November 16-** On this day in 1946, UCLA defeated the University of Montana, 61–7. The Bruins would finish the 1946 regular season undefeated before losing to the University of Illinois in the Rose Bowl.

**November 17-** On this day in 1890, UCLA Football Coach Fred Cozens was born.

**November 18-** On this day in 1967, top-ranked UCLA lost to No. 4 USC in what is considered by many the greatest game in the history of the rivalry.

**November 19-** On this day in 1961, UCLA Football Coach Jim Mora was born.

**November 20-** On this day in 1954, UCLA beat USC, 34–0, and completed an undefeated season. Because of the Rose Bowl's "no-repeat rule," the Bruins were not allowed to participate in the 1955 Rose Bowl.

**November 21-** On this day in 1953, the No. 5 UCLA Bruins beat the No. 9 USC Trojans and clinched a berth in the Rose Bowl.

**November 22-** On this day in 1997, UCLA played in its first-ever overtime game, beating USC by a score of 31–24.

**November 23-** On this day in 1920, Hall of Fame UCLA quarterback Ernie Case was born.

**November 24-** On this day in 1951, UCLA beat the No. 11-ranked USC Trojans, 21–7.

**November 25-** On this day in 2017, Chip Kelly

was named the seventeenth head coach in UCLA history. November 25 is also Chip Kelly's birthday (born 1963).

**November 26-** On this day in 1936, UCLA took on the USC Trojans. After having taken a five-year hiatus from the rivalry, the two teams tied, 7–7.

**November 27-** On this day in 1982, UCLA quarterback David Koral was born.

**November 28-** On this day in 1929, UCLA defeated the University of Montana, 14–0, the first Pacific Coast Conference win in school history.

**November 29-** On this day in 1928, UCLA lost to Oregon State, 26–6.

**November 30-** On this day in 1940, Jackie Robinson played his last football game at UCLA, losing, 28–12, to USC.

**December 1-** On this day in 2001, UCLA beat Arizona State, 52–41. The game was originally scheduled to be played on September 15, but following the 9/11 terror attacks, the game was moved to December 1.

**December 2-** On this day in 2006, UCLA beat the No. 2-ranked USC Trojans, 13–9.

**December 3-** On this day in 1960, UCLA beat No. 11-ranked Duke University, 27–6.

**December 4-** On this day in 1937, UCLA lost to USC, 19–13, despite a brilliant fourth-quarter comeback attempt by Kenny Washington, Woody Strode, and the rest of the Bruins.

**December 5-** On this day in 1975, UCLA lost to No. 5-ranked Tennessee Volunteers in Tommy Prothro's final game at UCLA.

**December 6-** On this day in 2010, former UCLA Assistant Coach (2003–2005) Jon Embree was named the head coach at the University of Colorado.

**December 7-** On this day in 1999, Marcus Reese, Nate Fikse, and Ricky Manning Jr. were all named to the *Sporting News* Freshman All-America team.

**December 8-** On this day in 1933, UCLA Hall of Fame offensive lineman Hardiman Cureton was born. Cureton was the first African American captain at UCLA in 1955 and is a member of the UCLA Football All-Century Team.

**December 9-** On this day in 1939, the No. 9-ranked UCLA Bruins tied the No. 3 USC Trojans, 0–0.

**December 10-** On this day in 1986, UCLA Football Coach Bert LaBrucherie died.

**December 11-** On this day in 2004, UCLA linebacker Spencer Havner and running back Maurice Drew were named team MVPs.

**December 12-** On this day in 1942, the No. 11 UCLA Bruins beat the No. 14 USC Trojans, 14–7, and clinched their first trip to the Rose Bowl in the school's history.

**December 13-** On this day in 2011, Jim Mora was formally introduced to the media as UCLA Football's next head coach.

**December 14-** On this day in 2010, UCLA linebacker Akeem Ayers and safety Rahim Moore were named to the Associated Press All-America Third Team.

**December 15-** On this day in 2002, linebacker Marcus Reese and tight end Mike Seldman were named team MVPs.

**December 16-** On this day in 2014, UCLA Football Head Coach Jim Mora was named a semifinalist for the Dodd Trophy, given to the National Coach of the Year.

**December 17-** On this day in 2004, UCLA Football Coach Karl Dorrell signed a two-year contract extension.

**December 18-** On this day in 1963, UCLA Football Coach Karl Dorrell was born.

**December 19-** On this day in 2002, Karl Dorrell was

announced as the next UCLA Football head coach.

**December 20-** On this day in 1976, UCLA lost to the University of Alabama, 36–6, in the Liberty Bowl.

**December 21-** On this day in 2011, UCLA interim Head Coach Mike Johnson announced that four players were suspended for the Kraft Fight Hunger Bowl.

**December 22-** On this day in 2007, UCLA lost, 17–16, to Brigham Young University in the Las Vegas Bowl.

**December 23-** On this day in 2012, Kai Forbath set an NFL record by making his first 17 career field goal attempts.

**December 24-** On this day in 1981, UCLA punter Chris Kluwe was born.

**December 25-** On this day in 1978, UCLA beat the University of Florida, 20–16, in the Aloha Bowl.

**December 26-** On this day in 1938, UCLA played in its first bowl game, beating the Hawaii All-Stars, 46–0.

**December 27-** On this day in 2006, UCLA lost to Florida State University, 44–27, in the Emerald Bowl.

**December 28-** On this day in 1954, UCLA Football Coach Fred Cozens died.

**December 29-** On this day in 2007, Rick Neuheisel was announced as the next UCLA Football head coach.

**December 30-** On this day in 1986, UCLA beat Brigham Young University, 31–10, in the Freedom Bowl.

**December 31-** On this day in 1991, UCLA beat the University of Illinois, 6–3, in the Sun Bowl.

# Sources


"9/11 Interactive Timelines." *9/11 Memorial Timeline.* Web. 20 Apr. 2016.

"1925 UCLA Bruins Football Schedule (UCLA Football)." *1925 UCLA Bruins Football Schedule.* Web. 07 Dec. 2015.

"1925 Pacific Coast Conference Year Summary | College Football at Sports-Reference.com." *College Football at Sports-Reference.com.* Web. 09 Dec. 2015.

"1928 Pacific Coast Conference Year Summary | College Football at Sports-Reference.com." *College Football at Sports-Reference.com.* Web. 09 Dec. 2015.

"1928 UCLA Bruins." *College Football at Sports-Reference.com.* Web. 09 Dec. 2015.

"1929 UCLA Bruins." *College Football at Sports-Reference.com.* Web. 10 Dec. 2015.

"1930 UCLA Bruins." *College Football at Sports-Reference.com.* Web. 14 Dec. 2015.

"1932 Presidential Election." *Presidential Election of 1932.* Web. 15 Dec. 2015.

"1932 UCLA Bruins." *College Football at Sports-Reference.com.* Web. 15 Dec. 2015.

"1933 UCLA Bruins." *College Football at Sports-Reference.com.* Web. 16 Dec. 2015.

"1934 UCLA Bruins." *College Football at Sports-Reference.com.* Web. 16 Dec. 2015.

"1935 California Golden Bears." *College Football at Sports-Reference.com.* Web. 16 Dec. 2015.

"1935 UCLA Bruins." *College Football at Sports-Reference.com.* Web. 16 Dec. 2015.

"1936 Presidential Election." *Presidential Election of 1936.* Web. 17 Dec. 2015.

"1936 UCLA Bruins." *College Football at Sports-Reference.com.* Web. 17 Dec. 2015.

"1937 UCLA Bruins." *College Football at Sports-Reference.com.* Web. 21 Dec. 2015.

"1938 UCLA Bruins." *College Football at Sports-Reference.com.* Web. 22 Dec. 2015.

"1939 Tennessee Volunteers." *College Football at Sports-Reference.com.* Web. 29 Jan. 2016.

"1939 UCLA Bruins." *College Football at Sports-Reference.com.* Web. 24 Dec. 2015.

"1940 UCLA Bruins." *College Football at Sports-Reference.com.* Web. 28 Dec. 2015.

"1941 UCLA Bruins." *College Football at Sports-Reference.com.* Web. 29 Dec. 2015.

"1942 UCLA Bruins." *College Football at Sports-Reference.com.* Web. 30 Dec. 2015.

"1943 March Field." *College Football at Sports-Reference.com.* Web. 5 Jan. 2016.

"1943 UCLA Bruins." *College Football at Sports-Reference.com.* Web. 5 Jan. 2016.

"1944 UCLA Bruins." *College Football at Sports-Reference.com.* Web. 6 Jan. 2016.

"1945 UCLA Bruins." *College Football at Sports-Reference.com.* Web. 12 Jan. 2016.

"1946 Illinois Fighting Illini." *College Football at Sports-Reference.com.* Web. 13 Jan. 2016.

"1946 UCLA Bruins." *College Football at Sports-Reference.com.* Web. 13 Jan. 2016.

"1947 UCLA Bruins." *College Football at Sports-Reference.com.* Web. 13 Jan. 2016.

"1948 UCLA Bruins." *College Football at Sports-Reference.com.* Web. 18 Jan. 2016.

"1949 UCLA Bruins." *College Football at Sports-Reference.com.* Web. 19 Jan. 2016.
"1950 Purdue Boilermakers." *College Football at Sports-Reference.com.* Web. 20 Jan. 2016.
"1950 UCLA Bruins." *College Football at Sports-Reference.com.* Web. 20 Jan. 2016.
"1950 Washington State Cougars." *College Football at Sports-Reference.com.* Web. 20 Jan. 2016.
"1951 Georgia Tech Yellow Jackets." *College Football at Sports-Reference.com.* Web. 15 Feb. 2016.
"1951 UCLA Bruins." *College Football at Sports-Reference.com.* Web. 20 Jan. 2016.
"1952 Final A.P. Poll." *Results.* Web. 21 Jan. 2016.
"1952 Georgia Tech Yellow Jackets." *College Football at Sports-Reference.com.* Web. 15 Feb. 2016.
"1952 Presidential Election." *Presidential Election of 1952.* Web. 21 Jan. 2016.
"1952 UCLA Bruins." *College Football at Sports-Reference.com.* Web. 21 Jan. 2016.
"1952 USC Trojans." *College Football at Sports-Reference.com.* Web. 21 Jan. 2016.
"1953 Final A.P. Poll." *Results.* Web. 21 Jan. 2016.
"1953 Georgia Tech Yellow Jackets." *College Football at Sports-Reference.com.* Web. 15 Feb. 2016.
"1953 Michigan State Spartans." *College Football at Sports-Reference.com.* Web. 21 Jan. 2016.
"1953 Stanford Indians." *College Football at Sports-Reference.com.* Web. 21 Jan. 2016.
"1953 UCLA Bruins." *College Football at Sports-Reference.com.* Web. 21 Jan. 2016.
"1954 Final A.P. Poll." *Results.* Web. 22 Jan. 2016.
"1954 Maryland Terrapins." *College Football at Sports-Reference.com.* Web. 22 Jan. 2016.
"1954 Ohio State Buckeyes." *College Football at Sports-Reference.com.* Web. 22 Jan. 2016.
"1954 UCLA Bruins." *College Football at Sports-Reference.com.* Web. 22 Jan. 2016.
"1954 USC Trojans." *College Football at Sports-Reference.com.* Web. 22 Jan. 2016.
"1954 Washington Huskies." *College Football at Sports-Reference.com.* Web. 22 Jan. 2016.
"1955 Michigan State Spartans." *College Football at Sports-Reference.com.* Web. 25 Jan. 2016.
"1955 Ohio State Buckeyes." *College Football at Sports-Reference.com.* Web. 25 Jan. 2016.
"1955 UCLA Bruins." *College Football at Sports-Reference.com.* Web. 25 Jan. 2016.
"1956 Presidential Election." *Presidential Election of 1956.* Web. 26 Jan. 2016.
"1956 UCLA Bruins." *College Football at Sports-Reference.com.* Web. 26 Jan. 2016.
"1956 USC Trojans." *College Football at Sports-Reference.com.* Web. 26 Jan. 2016.
"1957 UCLA Bruins." *College Football at Sports-Reference.com.* Web. 28 Jan. 2016.
"1958 UCLA Bruins." *College Football at Sports-Reference.com.* Web. 1 Feb. 2016.
"1958 USC Trojans." *College Football at Sports-Reference.com.* Web. 1 Feb. 2016.
"1959 Syracuse Orangemen." *College Football at Sports-Reference.com.* Web. 2 Feb. 2016.
"1959 UCLA Bruins." *College Football at Sports-Reference.com.* Web. 2 Feb. 2016.
"1960 UCLA Bruins." *College Football at Sports-Reference.com.* Web. 3 Feb. 2016.
"1960 USC Trojans." *College Football at Sports-Reference.com.* Web. 3 Feb. 2016.
"1961 Michigan Wolverines." *College Football at Sports-Reference.com.* Web. 4 Feb. 2016.
"1961 UCLA Bruins." *College Football at Sports-Reference.com.* Web. 4 Feb. 2016.
"1962 UCLA Bruins." *College Football at Sports-Reference.com.* Web. 4 Feb. 2016.
"1962 USC Trojans." *College Football at Sports-Reference.com.* Web. 4 Feb. 2016.
"1963 Penn State Nittany Lions." *College Football at Sports-Reference.com.* Web. 5 Feb. 2016.
"1963 UCLA Bruins." *College Football at Sports-Reference.com.* Web. 5 Feb. 2016.
"1963 USC Trojans." *College Football at Sports-Reference.com.* Web. 5 Feb. 2016.
"1964 UCLA Bruins." *College Football at Sports-Reference.com.* Web. 5 Feb. 2016.
"1965 Michigan State Spartans." *College Football at Sports-Reference.com.* Web. 9 Feb. 2016.
"1965 UCLA Bruins." *College Football at Sports-Reference.com.* Web. 9 Feb. 2016.
"1965 USC Trojans." *College Football at Sports-Reference.com.* Web. 9 Feb. 2016.
"1966 UCLA Bruins." *College Football at Sports-Reference.com.* Web. 10 Feb. 2016.

"1967 Heisman Trophy Voting | College Football at Sports-Reference.com." *College Football at Sports-Reference.com.* Web. 10 Feb. 2016.
"1967 Penn State Nittany Lions." *College Football at Sports-Reference.com.* Web. 10 Feb. 2016.
"1967 UCLA Bruins." *College Football at Sports-Reference.com.* Web. 10 Feb. 2016.
"1968 Penn State Nittany Lions." *College Football at Sports-Reference.com.* Web. 11 Feb. 2016.
"1968 Presidential Election." *Presidential Election of 1968.* Web. 11 Feb. 2016.
"1968 UCLA Bruins." *College Football at Sports-Reference.com.* Web. 11 Feb. 2016.
"1968 USC Trojans." *College Football at Sports-Reference.com.* Web. 11 Feb. 2016.
"1969 Stanford Indians." *College Football at Sports-Reference.com.* Web. 12 Feb. 2016.
"1969 UCLA Bruins." *College Football at Sports-Reference.com.* Web. 12 Feb. 2016.
"1969 USC Trojans." *College Football at Sports-Reference.com.* Web. 12 Feb. 2016.
"1970 UCLA Bruins." *College Football at Sports-Reference.com.* Web. 12 Feb. 2016.
"1971 UCLA Bruins." *College Football at Sports-Reference.com.* Web. 16 Feb. 2016.
"1972 UCLA Bruins." *College Football at Sports-Reference.com.* Web. 16 Feb. 2016.
"1972 USC Trojans." *College Football at Sports-Reference.com.* Web. 16 Feb. 2016.
"1973 UCLA Bruins." *College Football at Sports-Reference.com.* Web. 16 Feb. 2016.
"1973 USC Trojans." *College Football at Sports-Reference.com.* Web. 16 Feb. 2016.
"1974 UCLA Bruins." *College Football at Sports-Reference.com.* Web. 22 Feb. 2016.
"1974 | UCLA Bruins Football Statistics and Results | Totalfootballstats.com." *1974 | UCLA Bruins Football Statistics and Results | Totalfootballstats.com.* Web. 22 Feb. 2016.
"1974 USC Trojans." *College Football at Sports-Reference.com.* Web. 22 Feb. 2016.
"1974 Utah Utes." *College Football at Sports-Reference.com.* Web. 22 Feb. 2016.
"1974 Washington Huskies." *College Football at Sports-Reference.com.* Web. 22 Feb. 2016.
"1975 UCLA Bruins." *College Football at Sports-Reference.com.* Web. 23 Feb. 2016.
"1975 UCLA Bruins Football Team." *Project Gutengerg Self-Publishig Press.* Web. <http://www.gutenberg.us/articles/1975_ucla_bruins_football_team>.
"1975 USC Trojans." *College Football at Sports-Reference.com.* Web. 23 Feb. 2016.
"1975 Washington Huskies." *College Football at Sports-Reference.com.* Web. 23 Feb. 2016.
"1976 Presidential Election." *Presidential Election of 1976.* Web. 14 Mar. 2016.
"1976 UCLA Bruins." *College Football at Sports-Reference.com.* Web. 14 Mar. 2016.
"1976 USC Trojans." *College Football at Sports-Reference.com.* Web. 14 Mar. 2016.
"1977 California Golden Bears." *College Football at Sports-Reference.com.* Web. 15 Mar. 2016.
"1977 Iowa Hawkeyes." *College Football at Sports-Reference.com.* Web. 15 Mar. 2016.
"1977 UCLA Bruins." *College Football at Sports-Reference.com.* Web. 15 Mar. 2016.
"1977 USC Trojans." *College Football at Sports-Reference.com.* Web. 15 Mar. 2016.
"1978 Kansas Jayhawks." *College Football at Sports-Reference.com.* Web. 16 Mar. 2016.
"1978 UCLA Bruins." *College Football at Sports-Reference.com.* Web. 16 Mar. 2016.
"1978 USC Trojans." *College Football at Sports-Reference.com.* Web. 16 Mar. 2016.
"1978 Washington Huskies." *College Football at Sports-Reference.com.* Web. 16 Mar. 2016.
"1979 UCLA Bruins." *College Football at Sports-Reference.com.* Web. 17 Mar. 2016.
"1980 Presidential Election." *Presidential Election of 1976.* Web. 18 Mar. 2016.
"1980 Stanford vs. UCLA." *American Football Wiki.* Web. 18 Mar. 2016.
"1980 UCLA Bruins." *College Football at Sports-Reference.com.* Web. 18 Mar. 2016.
"1980 USC Trojans." *College Football at Sports-Reference.com.* Web. 18 Mar. 2016.
"1980 Wisconsin Badgers." *College Football at Sports-Reference.com.* Web. 18 Mar. 2016.
"1981 UCLA Bruins." *College Football at Sports-Reference.com.* Web. 18 Mar. 2016.
"1982 UCLA Bruins." *College Football at Sports-Reference.com.* Web. 18 Mar. 2016.
"1983 Georgia Bulldogs." *College Football at Sports-Reference.com.* Web. 23 Mar. 2016.

"1983 Nebraska Cornhuskers." *College Football at Sports-Reference.com*. Web. 23 Mar. 2016.
"1983 UCLA Bruins." *College Football at Sports-Reference.com*. Web. 23 Mar. 2016.
"1984 Presidential Election." *Presidential Election of 1976*. Web. 28 Mar. 2016.
"1984 UCLA Bruins." *College Football at Sports-Reference.com*. Web. 28 Mar. 2016.
"1985 Oklahoma Sooners." *College Football at Sports-Reference.com*. Web. 8 Mar. 2016.
"1985 UCLA Bruins." *College Football at Sports-Reference.com*. Web. 30 Mar. 2016.
"1986 UCLA Bruins." *College Football at Sports-Reference.com*. Web. 30 Mar. 2016.
"1987 UCLA Bruins." *College Football at Sports-Reference.com*. Web. 1 Apr. 2016.
"1987 USC Trojans." *College Football at Sports-Reference.com*. Web. 1 Apr. 2016.
"1988 Presidential Election." *Presidential Election of 1976*. Web. 1 Apr. 2016.
"1988 UCLA Bruins." *College Football at Sports-Reference.com*. Web. 1 Apr. 2016.
"1989 UCLA Bruins." *College Football at Sports-Reference.com*. Web. 4 Apr. 2016.
"1990 UCLA Bruins." *College Football at Sports-Reference.com*. Web. 5 Apr. 2016.
"1990 Washington Huskies." *College Football at Sports-Reference.com*. Web. 5 Apr. 2016.
"1991 UCLA Bruins." *College Football at Sports-Reference.com*. Web. 5 Apr. 2016.
"1992 Stanford Cardinal." *College Football at Sports-Reference.com*. Web. 6 Apr. 2016.
"1992 UCLA Bruins." *College Football at Sports-Reference.com*. Web. 6 Apr. 2016.
"1992 United States Men's Olympic Basketball | Basketball-Reference.com." *Basketball-Reference.com*. Web. 06 Apr. 2016.
"1992 USC Trojans." *College Football at Sports-Reference.com*. Web. 6 Apr. 2016.
"1993 Nebraska Cornhuskers." *College Football at Sports-Reference.com*. Web. 7 Apr. 2016.
"1993 UCLA Bruins." *College Football at Sports-Reference.com*. Web. 7 Apr. 2016.
"1994 Nebraska Cornhuskers." *College Football at Sports-Reference.com*. Web. 7 Apr. 2016.
"1994 Tennessee Volunteers" *College Football at Sports-Reference.com*. Web. 7 Apr. 2016.
"1994 UCLA Bruins." *College Football at Sports-Reference.com*. Web. 7 Apr. 2016.
"1995 UCLA Bruins." *College Football at Sports-Reference.com*. Web. 8 Apr. 2016.
"1996 Presidential Election." *Presidential Election of 1976*. Web. 12 Apr. 2016.
"1996 UCLA Bruins." *College Football at Sports-Reference.com*. Web. 12 Apr. 2016.
"1996 USC Trojans." *College Football at Sports-Reference.com*. Web. 12 Apr. 2016.
"1997 UCLA Bruins." *College Football at Sports-Reference.com*. Web. 18 Apr. 2016.
"1997 USC Trojans." *College Football at Sports-Reference.com*. Web. 18 Apr. 2016.
"1997 Washington State Cougars." *College Football at Sports-Reference.com*. Web. 18 Apr. 2016.
"1998 BCS Standings." *BCS Guru*. Web.
"1998 UCLA Bruins." *College Football at Sports-Reference.com*. Web. 18 Apr. 2016.
"1999 UCLA Bruins." *College Football at Sports-Reference.com*. Web. 19 Apr. 2016.
"1999 UCLA Football: UCLA 27 - Arizona State 28." *1999 UCLA Football: UCLA 27 - Arizona State 28*. Web. 19 Apr. 2016.
"1999 USC Trojans." *College Football at Sports-Reference.com*. Web. 19 Apr. 2016.
"2000 UCLA Bruins." *College Football at Sports-Reference.com*. Web. 20 Apr. 2016.
"2000 UCLA Bruins Football Roster." *Fox Sports*, March 29 2016 Web.
"2000 USC Trojans." *College Football at Sports-Reference.com*. Web. 20 Apr. 2016.
"2001 UCLA Bruins." *College Football at Sports-Reference.com*. Web. 20 Apr. 2016.
"2001 UCLA Bruins Football Roster." *Fox Sports*, March 29 2016 Web.
"2002 UCLA Bruins." *College Football at Sports-Reference.com*. Web. 21 Apr. 2016.
"2002 UCLA Bruins Football Roster." *Fox Sports*, March 29 2016 Web.
"2003 UCLA Bruins." *College Football at Sports-Reference.com*. Web. 25 Apr. 2016.
"2003 UCLA Bruins Football Roster." *Fox Sports*, March 29 2016 Web.
"2003 USC Trojans." *College Football at Sports-Reference.com*. Web. 25 Apr. 2016.

"2004 UCLA Bruins." *College Football at Sports-Reference.com*. Web. 25 Apr. 2016.
"2004 UCLA Bruins Football Roster." *Fox Sports*, March 29 2016 Web.
"2004 USC Trojans." *College Football at Sports-Reference.com*. Web. 25 Apr. 2016.
"2004 Washington Huskies." *College Football at Sports-Reference.com*. Web. 25 Apr. 2016.
"2004 Wyoming Cowboys." *College Football at Sports-Reference.com*. Web. 25 Apr. 2016.
"2005 Arizona Wildcats." *College Football at Sports-Reference.com*. Web. 26 Apr. 2016.
"2005 UCLA Bruins." *College Football at Sports-Reference.com*. Web. 26 Apr. 2016.
"2005 UCLA Bruins Football Roster." *Fox Sports*, March 29 2016 Web.
"2006 UCLA Bruins." *College Football at Sports-Reference.com*. Web. 28 Apr. 2016.
"2006 UCLA Bruins Football Roster." *Fox Sports*, March 29 2016 Web.
"2006 USC Trojans." *College Football at Sports-Reference.com*. Web. 28 Apr. 2016
"2006 Washington Huskies." *College Football at Sports-Reference.com*. Web. 28 Apr. 2016
"2007 Oregon Ducks." *College Football at Sports-Reference.com*. Web. 12 Jan. 2018.
"2007 UCLA Bruins." *College Football at Sports-Reference.com*. Web. 28 Apr. 2016.
"2007 UCLA Bruins." *College Football at Sports-Reference.com*. Web. 28 Apr. 2016.
"2007 UCLA Bruins Football Roster." *Fox Sports*, March 29 2016 Web.
"2008 Oregon Ducks." *College Football at Sports-Reference.com*. Web. 12 Jan. 2018.
"2008 UCLA Bruins." *College Football at Sports-Reference.com*. Web. 3 May 2016.
"2008 UCLA Bruins Football Roster." *Fox Sports*, March 29 2016 Web.
"2009 Oregon Ducks." *College Football at Sports-Reference.com*. Web. 12 Jan. 2018.
"2009 Tennessee Volunteers." *College Football at Sports-Reference.com*. Web. 4 May 2016.
"2009 UCLA Bruins." *College Football at Sports-Reference.com*. Web. 4 May 2016.
"2009 UCLA Bruins Football Roster." *Fox Sports*, March 29 2016 Web.
"2010 Oregon Ducks." *College Football at Sports-Reference.com*. Web. 12 Jan. 2018.
"2010 UCLA Bruins." *College Football at Sports-Reference.com*. Web. 5 May 2016.
"2010 UCLA Bruins Football Roster." *Fox Sports*, March 29 2016 Web.
"2011 Oregon Ducks." *College Football at Sports-Reference.com*. Web. 12 Jan. 2018.
"2011 Texas Longhorns." *College Football at Sports-Reference.com*. Web. 6 May 2016.
"2011 UCLA Bruins." *College Football at Sports-Reference.com*. Web. 6 May 2016.
"2011 UCLA Bruins Football Roster." *Fox Sports*, March 29 2016 Web.
"2012 Oregon Ducks." *College Football at Sports-Reference.com*. Web. 12 Jan. 2018.
"2012 UCLA Bruins." *College Football at Sports-Reference.com*. Web. 10 May 2016.
"2012 USC Trojans." *College Football at Sports-Reference.com*. Web. 10 May 2016.
"2012 UCLA Bruins Football Roster." *Fox Sports*, March 29 2016 Web.
"2013 UCLA Bruins." *College Football at Sports-Reference.com*. Web. 11 May 2016.
"2013 UCLA Bruins Football Roster." *Fox Sports*, March 29 2016 Web.
"2014 Arizona Wildcats." *College Football at Sports-Reference.com*. Web. 12 May 2016.
"2014 Colorado Buffaloes." *College Football at Sports-Reference.com*. Web. 12 May 2016.
"2014 UCLA Bruins." *College Football at Sports-Reference.com*. Web. 12 May 2016.
"2014 Virginia Cavaliers." *College Football at Sports-Reference.com*. Web. 12 May 2016.
"2014 UCLA Bruins Football Roster." *Fox Sports*, March 29 2016 Web.
"2015 Virginia Cavaliers." *College Football at Sports-Reference.com*. Web. 13 May 2016.
"2015 UCLA Bruins Football Roster." *Fox Sports*, March 29 2016 Web.
"2017 UCLA Bruins." *College Football at Sports-Reference.com*. Web. 4 January 2018.
"A Brief History of UCLA." *About UCLA*. Web. 08 Dec. 2015.
Aikman, Troy. *MIND, BODY & SOUL - AIKMAN*. Chicago, Illinois: Benchmark, 1998. Print.
"A Look Back - 15 Years Ago To 1991." *Calbears.com*, 11 Dec. 2006. Web. 05 Apr. 2016.
"A Personal Look at the 1974 Collegiate Season Opener." *Dr.Ken*. Jan. 2014. Web. 22 Feb. 2016.

"April 15, 1947 Boston Braves at Brooklyn Dodgers Box Score and Play by Play | Baseball-Reference.com." *Baseball-Reference.com.* Web. 25 Feb. 2016.

"April 18, 1958 San Francisco Giants at Los Angeles Dodgers Play by Play and Box Score | Baseball-Reference.com." *Baseball-Reference.com.* Web. 01 Feb. 2016.

"A Quote by Neil Armstrong." *Goodreads.* Web. 12 Feb. 2016.

Arnold, Geoffrey. "Chip Kelly's Ex-Wife Reveals Intriguing Details about a Complicated and Secretive Man." *OregonLive.com*, OregonLive.com, 24 July 2015.

Aubrey, Coult. "Oh, Jerry, How Could You Do It?" *Tribunedigital-mcall*, 22 July 1987. Web. 13 Apr. 2016.

"Bert LaBrucherie." *Fanbase.* Web. 11 Jan. 2016.

"Bill Barnes, Former Head Football Coach, Passes Away." *Uclabruins.com.* Web. 29 Jan. 2016.

"Biography." *Of President Warren G. Harding for Kids.* Web. 23 Nov. 2015.

"Biography." Red Sanders. *IMDb.* IMDb.com, Web. 19 Jan. 2016.

Bodley, Hal. "Retiring No. 42 One of Baseball's Greatest Moments." *Major League Baseball.* MLB, 11 Apr. 2013. Web. 28 Dec. 2015.

Bonk, Thomas. "Missing Memories : '54 Bruins Might Have Been Best Ever, but They Didn't Reach the Rose Bowl." *Los Angeles Times.* Los Angeles Times, 14 Nov. 1994. Web. 25 Jan. 2016.

"Brief Timeline of Events." *Watergateinfo.* Web. 22 Feb. 2016.

"Bring Back the Los Angeles Rams - Official Site." *Bring Back the Los Angeles Rams - Official Site.* Web. 01 Feb. 2016.

"Burr Baldwin, 85; First UCLA Football Star to Be Consensus All-American." *Los Angeles Times.* Los Angeles Times, 23 Aug. 2007. Web. 17 Mar. 2016.

"Burr Baldwin College Football Statistics | Pro-Football-Reference.com." *Pro-Football-Reference.com.* Web. 17 Mar. 2016.

"Burr Baldwin FAQs 2016- Facts, Rumors and the Latest Gossip." *Vipfaq.com.* Web. 17 Mar. 2016.

"Burr Baldwin NFL Football Statistics | Pro-Football-Reference.com." *Pro-Football-Reference.com.* Web. 17 Mar. 2016.

"Burr B. Baldwin's Obituary on Los Angeles Times." *Los Angeles Times.* Web. 17 Mar. 2016.

"Cade McNown Bio." *Cade McNown Page: Bio.* OC Cities, Web. 19 Apr. 2016.

"Cade McNown." *College Football at Sports-Reference.com.* Web. 19 Apr. 2016.

"Cade McNown Page: Bio." *Cade McNown Page: Bio.* Bloomberg, Web. 19 Apr. 2016.

"Cal Downs No. 13 UCLA In Triple Overtime." *Calbears.com*, 14 Oct. 2000. Web. 20 Apr. 2016.

"Charting UCLA Head Coach Babe Horrell's Man-In-Motion Offense In Action Against Washington State." *CLASSIC UCLA BRUINS REDISCOVERED*, 23 Nov. 2014. Web. 23 Dec. 2015.

Chiccoa, Charles. "Red Sanders and a Paradise Lost." *Scout.com*, 26 July 2010. Web. 19 Jan. 2016.

"Classic TV Sports." *The 1974 Debut of the Football Sideline Reporter Role*, 31 Aug. 2014. Web. 22 Feb. 2016.

"College FB Team Opponent Rushing Yards per Game." *College Football Stats - College FB Team Opponent Rushing Yards per Game on TeamRankings.com.* Web. 04 Jan. 2018.

"College Football Belt - 1972 Nebraska at UCLA." *College Football Belt - 1972 Nebraska at UCLA.* Web. 16 Feb. 2016.

"College Football Belt - 1975 Ohio State vs UCLA." *College Football Belt - 1975 Ohio State vs UCLA.* Web. 23 Feb. 2016.

"College Football Belt - 1976 UCLA at Arizona State." *College Football Belt - 1976 UCLA at Arizona State.* Web. 14 Mar. 2016.

"College Football Belt - 1978 Southern Cal at UCLA." *College Football Belt - 1978 Southern Cal at UCLA.* Web. 16 Mar. 2016.

"College Football Belt - 1985 UCLA at Tennessee." *College Football Belt – 1985 UCLA at Tennessee.* Web. 30 Mar. 2016.

"College Football Belt - 1985 UCLA at Washington." *College Football Belt – 1985 UCLA at Washington.* Web. 30 Mar. 2016.
"College Football Belt - 1990 UCLA at Washington." *College Football Belt - 1990 UCLA at Washington.* Web. 05 Apr. 2016.
"College Football Belt - 1993 UCLA at Arizona State." *College Football Belt - 1993 UCLA at Arizona State.* Web. 07 Apr. 2016.
"College Football Belt - 1993 UCLA at Washington." *College Football Belt - 1993 UCLA at Washington.* Web. 07 Apr. 2016.
"College Football Belt - 1995 UCLA at Arizona State." *College Football Belt - 1995 UCLA at Arizona State.* Web. 08 Apr. 2016.
"College Football Playoff Rankings 2014." *College Football Playoff.* Web. 12 May 2016.
"College Football Playoff Rankings 2015." *College Football Playoff.* Web. 13 May 2016.
Corio, Ray. "Question Box." *The New York Times.* The New York Times, 31 Dec. 1989. Web. 23 Dec. 2015.
"CougarStats: BYU Football: BYU vs. UCLA 1985." *CougarStats: BYU Football: BYU vs. UCLA 1985.* Web. 30 Mar. 2016.
"CougarStats: BYU Football: BYU vs. UCLA 1991." *CougarStats: BYU Football: BYU vs. UCLA 1991.* Web. 05 Apr. 2016.
"CougarStats: BYU Football: BYU vs. UCLA 1992." *CougarStats: BYU Football: BYU vs. UCLA 1992.* Web. 06 Apr. 2016.
"CougarStats: BYU Football: BYU vs. UCLA 1993." *CougarStats: BYU Football: BYU vs. UCLA 1993.* Web. 07 Apr. 2016.
"CougarStats: BYU Football: BYU vs. UCLA 1995." *CougarStats: BYU Football: BYU vs. UCLA 1995.* Web. 08 Apr. 2016.
Crowe, Jerry. "LIFE AFTER THE HEISMAN : Beban Remembers Most the Loss to USC." *Los Angeles Times.* Los Angeles Times, 14 Nov. 1988. Web. 12 Apr. 2016.
Crowe, Jerry. "Unpleasant Questions Looming for UCLA." *Los Angeles Times.* Los Angeles Times, 12 Sept. 1989. Web. 04 Apr. 2016.
"Cuban Dictator Batista Falls from Power." *History.com.* A&E Television Networks, Web. 02 Feb. 2016.
"D-Day and the Battle of Normandy: Your Questions Answered." *D-Day Museum and Overlord Embroidery.* Web. 06 Jan. 2016.
"Disneyland Timeline." *Disneyland Timeline.* Web. 26 Jan. 2016.
"Donn Moomaw's Blog." *Contentment in Retirement,* 23 Dec. 2008. Web. 25 Mar. 2016.
"Donn Moomaw." *IMDb.* IMDb.com. Web. 25 Mar. 2016
"Donn Moomaw: National Football Foundation." *Programs College Football Hall of Fame.* Web. 25 Mar. 2016.
"Edwin C. Horrell." *Fanbase.* Web. 23 Dec. 2015.
"EP-72 Log of Apollo 11." *Log.* NASA, Web. 12 Feb. 2016.
"Every Rose Bowl Game Ever Played: A Brief Look at 99 Glorious Games." *Every Rose Bowl Game Ever Played: A Brief Look at 99 Glorious Games.* Pasadena Star News, 1 Jan. 2014. Web. 21 Jan. 2016
Evolution of the Game of Basketball - HoopTactics Basketball Basics." *Evolution of the Game of Basketball - HoopTactics Basketball Basics.* Web. 04 Aug. 2015.
"Falcons Fire Mora After Disappointing 7–9 Season." *ESPN.* ESPN Internet Ventures, 2 Jan. 2007. Web. 09 May 2016.
"Famous People Born in 1960 - 1960 Births | Famous Birthdays." *Famous People Born in 1960 - 1960 Births | Famous Birthdays.* Web. 03 Feb. 2016.
Farnsworth, Clare. "Seahawks/NFL Beat: Easley Unloads after 15-year Estrangement." *Seattlepi.com,* 15 Oct. 2002. Web. 14 Apr. 2016.
"FCA | Hall of Champions | Hall of Honor – Donn Moomaw." *FCA Hall of Champions Hall of Honor.* Web. 25 Mar. 2016.

Fealey, Oscar. "Desert Sun 22 May 1956 —California Digital Newspaper Collection." *Desert Sun 22 May 1956 —California Digital Newspaper Collection*, 22 May 1956. Web. 26 Jan. 2016.

Flaherty, Dan. "The Road To The 1986 Rose Bowl: UCLA & Iowa." *TheSportsNotebook.com*. 31 July 2015. Web. 30 Mar. 2016.

"Football Archives." *Uclabruins.com*. Web. 28 Feb. 2016.

"Football Names Jeff Horton Offensive Coordinator." *Bob Toledo Bio*. Web. 11 Apr. 2016.

"Football Squad Makes Statement Against Alabama." *Uclabruins.com*, 3 Sept. 2000. Web. 20 Apr. 2016.

Forbes, Gordon. *Dick Vermeil: Whistle in His Mouth, Heart on His Sleeve*. Chicago: Triumph, 2009. Print.

"Former UCLA Football Coach Terry Donahue To Be Inducted Into College Hall of Fame." *Uclabruins.com*. Web. 11 Mar. 2016.

Foster, Chris, and Gary Klein. "John McKay and Tommy Prothro Took USC-UCLA Rivalry To New Level In Mid '60's." *Los Angeles Times*. Los Angeles Times, Web. 08 Feb. 2016.

Foster, Chris. "Bill Barnes Dies at 91; UCLA Football Coach Led Bruins to 1962 Rose Bowl." *Los Angeles Times*. Los Angeles Times, 25 Apr. 2009. Web. 29 Jan. 2016.

Foster, Chris. "Bruins Keep Alive Their Memories of Nick Pasquale." *Los Angeles Times*. Los Angeles Times, 3 Sept. 2014. Web. 11 May 2016.

Foster, Chris. "Jim Mora and Myles Jack Took Same Path from Bellevue, Wash., to UCLA." *Los Angeles Times*. Los Angeles Times, 12 Nov. 2013. Web. 09 May 2016.

Foster, Chris. "Sam Dickerson's Game-winning Catch for USC in 1969 Still Cause for Debate." *Los Angeles Times*. Los Angeles Times, 22 Nov. 2009. Web. 12 Feb. 2016.

Foster, Chris. "UCLA Set Football Program in Motion with Upset Win over Nebraska in 1972." *Los Angeles Times*. Los Angeles Times, 05 Sept. 2012. Web. 16 Feb. 2016

Foster, Chris. "UCLA'S Francis Wai Was an American Hero." *Los Angeles Times*. Los Angeles Times, 22 Aug. 2014. Web. 21 Dec. 2015.

Foundation, Black Fives. "Jackie Robinson, Pro Basketball Star." *Blackfives.org*. 31 Jan. 2008. Web. 14 Aug. 2015.

"Former UCLA, Ram Coach Prothro Dies." *Los Angeles Times*. Los Angeles Times, 15 May 1995. Web. 08 Feb. 2016.

"Frederick Warren Cozens, Physical Education: Berkeley and Los Angeles." *University of Califo LostLettermen.com. UCLA Bruins Football 1919 Roster. Web. 11 Aug. 2015. rnia: In Memoriam, [1957]*. Web. 04 Aug. 2015.

"Fresno State at UCLA Box Score, September 9, 2000 | College Football at Sports-Reference.com." *College Football at Sports-Reference.com*. Web. 20 Apr. 2016.

"From the Vault: Best Season in Arizona Football History." *ArizonaWildcats.com*. Web. 18 Apr. 2016.

"George Dickerson, 88; UCLA Coach and Hall of Fame Athlete." *Los Angeles Times*. Los Angeles Times, 31 Jan. 2002. Web. 29 Jan. 2016. <http://articles.latimes.com/2002/jan/31/local/me-passings31.2>.

"Georgia Bulldogs Football on Fanbase." *Georgia Bulldogs Football*. Web. 31 Dec. 2015.

Gill, Bob. *A Coaching Legend: Tommy Prothro*. College Football Historical Society. Web.

Gill, Joe. "Bill Russell Is A Champion By Definition." *Bleacher Report*, 12 June 2010. Web. 26 Jan. 2016.

Gillon, Steven M. *Pearl Harbor: FDR Leads the Nation into War*. New York: Basic, 2011. Print.

Goldstein, Richard. "John Druze, Last of Fordham's Seven Blocks of Granite, Dies at 91." *New York Times*, 31 Dec. 2005. Web. 17 Dec. 2015.

"Hall of Fame 2013: Jonathan Ogden." *NFL.com*. Web. 15 Apr. 2016.

Hall, Spencer. "PROTO-SPURRIER, PART TWO: A CHAT WITH PEPPER RODGERS." *Every Day Should Be Saturday*. SB Nation, 30 Apr. 2013. Web. 15 Feb. 2016.

Hansen, Greg. "Greg Hansen: Pac-10 Expansions in '78, '10 Have Few Similarities." *Arizona Daily Star*. 22 June 2010. Web. 16 Mar. 2016.

"Harry Trotter, U. C. L. A. Track Coach, Resigns (July 13, 1946)." *July 13, 1946. Chicago Daily Tribune*, 14 Aug. 2015.

Hart, Derek. "Crosstown Rivalry: It Was 20 Years Ago (Not Quite) Today – UCLA vs. USC 1993." *LA Sports Hub*. FanSided, 26 Nov. 2013. Web. 07 Apr. 2016.

Hart, Derek. "UCLA Football: The Ten Greatest Wins Over Rival USC." *Bleacher Report*. 2 Dec. 2008. Web. 07 Apr. 2016.

Hawkins, Sean. "The '88 Upset, Revisited." *WSU Football Blog*, 10 Nov. 2009. Web. 01 Apr. 2016.

Helinski, Paul. "Lee Harvey Oswald's Carcano Rifle - Shooting It Today - GunsAmerica Digest." *GunsAmerica Digest*, 11 Nov. 2013. Web. 05 Feb. 2016.

"Henry Russell Sanders: Los Angeles." Web.

Hinnen, Jerry. "The End for Now? A Realignment Timeline." *CBSSports.com*, 24 Apr. 2013. Web. 06 May 2016.

<http://homepages.cae.wisc.edu/~dwilson/rfsc/history/CoachPolls.txt>.

<http://texts.cdlib.org/view?docId=hb7q2nb431;NAAN=13030&doc.view=frames&chunk.id=div00012&toc.depth=1&toc.id=&brand=calisphere.

"Historic California Posts: Camp Haan." *Historic California Posts: Camp Haan*. Web. 29 Dec. 2015.

History.com Staff. "Persian Gulf War." *History.com*. A&E Television Networks, 01 Jan. 2009. Web. 05 Apr. 2016.

"History/Traditon." Web. http://www.uclabruins.com/fls/30500/old_site/pdf/m-track/09-mg-trad-hist.pdf?DB_OEM_ID=30500

Hodges, Jim. "It's Really Howard's End (Zone) as UCLA Game Falls Apart, 38–9." *Los Angeles Times*. Los Angeles Times, 29 Sept. 1996. Web. 12 Apr. 2016.

Holbreich, Curt. "UCLA Catches San Diego State : Bruins Win, 28–25, on Sneak by Johnson With 2:39 Left." *Los Angeles Times*. Los Angeles Times, 17 Sept. 1989. Web. 04 Apr. 2016

Holmes, Baxter. "USC's History of Major NCAA Infractions." *Los Angeles Times*. Los Angeles Times, 10 June 2010. Web. 22 Mar. 2016.

"Houston Tips UCLA (September 13, 1977)." *September 13, 1977*. The Chicago Tribune, 13 Sept. 1977. Web. 15 Mar. 2016.

"Huskies (University of Washington) Football, 1889-2010." *HistoryLink.org- the Free Online Encyclopedia of Washington State History*. Web. 16 Feb. 2016.

"I like Jim L. Mora . . . Do You?" *Jim L. Mora (American Football Player)*. Web. 09 May 2016.

"Inductee Search." *Bob Elias Hall of Fame*. Web. 17 Mar. 2016.

*Infoplease*. Infoplease, Top News Stories- 1956- Web. 26 Jan. 2016.

*Infoplease*. Infoplease, Top News Stories- 1976- Web. 14 Mar. 2016.

*Infoplease*. Infoplease, Top News Stories- 2009- Web. 4 May 2016.

"Injury Woes Strike down UCLA Quarterbacks - USATODAY.com." *Injury Woes Strike down UCLA Quarterbacks - USATODAY.com*. USA Today, 27 Apr. 2008. Web. 03 May 2016.

"In Memoriam: Bill Barnes." *UCLA Newsroom*. Web.

"Illinois Fighting Illini Football on Fanbase- 1946 Roster" Web. 13 Jan. 2016.

ITV Report. "D-Day in Numbers: The Remarkable Statistics behind the Largest Seaborne Invasion in History." *ITV News*, 6 June 2014. Web. 06 Jan. 2016.

"Jackie Robinson Negro League Statistics on Baseball Almanac." *Jackie Robinson Negro League Statistics on Baseball Almanac*. Web. 25 Feb. 2016.

"Jackie Robinson Statistics and History | Baseball-Reference.com." *Baseball-Reference.com*. Web. 25 Feb. 2016.

"Jackie Robinson Timeline." *Los Angeles Dodgers*. Web. 13 Jan. 2016.

"James Earl Ray." *Bio.com*. A&E Networks Television, Web. 11 Feb. 2016.

"Jerry Robinson Given Fine, Probation." *Los Angeles Times*. Los Angeles Times, 11 Nov. 1987. Web. 13 Apr. 2016.

Jim Mora Biography." *Uclabruins.com*. Web. 09 May 2016.

Johnson, Scott M. "Kenny Easley: Giving His All - HeraldNet.com." *The Daily Herald*, 10 Sept. 2011. Web. 14 Apr. 2016.

"John William Chrestman's Obituary on San Diego Union-Tribune." *San Diego Union-Tribune.* Web. 11 Feb. 2016.

"Jonathan Ogden Biography." *The Jonathan Ogden Foundation.* Web. 15 Apr. 2016.

Jones, James R. "Behind L.B.J.'s Decision Not to Run in '68." *The New York Times.* The New York Times, 15 Apr. 1988. Web. 11 Feb. 2016.

"Journey." *CoachWooden.com.* Web. 18 Jan. 2016. <http://www.coachwooden.com/the-journey>.

"J. Thompson Prothro." *Goduke.com.* Web. 08 Feb. 2016.

"Karl Dorrell: Head Football Coach." *The Head Coach* n. pag. *Fans Only.* Web.

Katz, Greg. "Nov. 22 Brings Haunting Memories to Baby Boomer Generation." *ESPN.* ESPN Internet Ventures, 20 Nov. 2014. Web. 05 Feb. 2016.

Kelly, Chip. "2011 Nike Coach of the Year Speech." *Efficient Use of Practice Time.*

"Ken Easley Force 5 DB Skills Training." *Ken Easley Force 5 DB Skills Training.* Web. 14 Apr. 2016.

"Kenny Washington Biography." *Bio.com.* A&E Networks Television, Web. 09 Mar. 2016.

"Kenny Washington - BR Bullpen | Baseball-Reference.com." *Baseball-Reference.com.* Web. 09 Mar. 2016.

"Korean War Timeline." *Korean War Timeline.* Web. 21 Jan. 2016.

"LaBrucherie, Former Coach of UCLA, Dies." *Los Angeles Times.* Los Angeles Times, 11 Dec. 1986. Web. 11 Jan. 2016.

"Let Them Play: Santa Clara University Football." *Let Them Play: Santa Clara University Football.* Web. 30 Dec. 2015.

Lewis, Jason. "Black History: Jackie Robinson Excelled At a Higher Level in Other Sports." Los Angeles Sentinel, 14 July 2011. Web. 25 Feb. 2016.

Linkowski, Jeff. "Oklahoma 38, UCLA 3." *1986 Oklahoma vs. UCLA Game Recap.* Web. 30 Mar. 2016.

Lloyd, Jared. "BYU Classic Football Faceoff: BYU/UCLA 1983 vs BYU/Boston College 1985." *Daily Herald*, 6 July 2013. Web. 23 Mar. 2016.

"Local Football Legend 'Burr' Baldwin Dies." *The Bakersfield Californian*, 22 Aug. 2007. Web. 17 Mar. 2016.

"Lodi News-Sentinel - Google News Archive Search." *Lodi News-Sentinel - Google News Archive Search*, 5 Jan. 1945. Web. 23 Dec. 2015.

"Los-angeles 1932 Summer Olympics | Olympic Videos, Photos, News." *Los-angeles 1932 Summer Olympics | Olympic Videos, Photos, News.* Web. 15 Dec. 2015.

"Los Angeles High School. Sports History." *Sports History.* Web. 11 Jan. 2016.

"LostLettermen.com." *California Golden Bears Football 1934 Roster.* Web. 16 Dec. 2015.

"LostLettermen.com." *Oregon Ducks Football 1932 Roster.* Web. 15 Dec. 2015.

"LostLettermen.com." *Oregon Ducks Football 1933 Roster.* Web. 16 Dec. 2015.

"LostLettermen.com." Stanford *Football 1930 Roster.* Web. 14 Dec. 2015.

"LostLettermen.com." Stanford *Indians Football 1935 Roster.* Web. 16 Dec. 2015.

"LostLettermen.com." *Stanford Indians Football 1936 Roster.* Web. 17 Dec. 2015.

"LostLettermen.com." *UCLA Bruins Football 1920 Roster.* Web. 19 Nov. 2015.

"LostLettermen.com." *UCLA Bruins Football 1927 Schedule.* Web. 08 Dec. 2015.

"LostLettermen.com." *UCLA Bruins Football 1928 Roster.* Web. 09 Dec. 2015

"LostLettermen.com." *UCLA Bruins Football 1929 Roster.* Web. 10 Dec. 2015.

"LostLettermen.com." *UCLA Bruins Football 1930 Roster.* Web. 14 Dec. 2015.

"LostLettermen.com." *UCLA Bruins Football 1931 Roster.* Web. 15 Dec. 2015.

"LostLettermen.com." *UCLA Bruins Football 1932 Roster.* Web. 15 Dec. 2015.

"LostLettermen.com." *UCLA Bruins Football 1933 Roster.* Web. 16 Dec. 2015.

"LostLettermen.com." *UCLA Bruins Football 1934 Roster.* Web. 16 Dec. 2015.

"LostLettermen.com." *UCLA Bruins Football 1935 Roster.* Web. 16 Dec. 2015.

"LostLettermen.com." *UCLA Bruins Football 1936 Roster.* Web. 16 Dec. 2015.

"LostLettermen.com." *UCLA Bruins Football 1937 Roster.* Web. 21 Dec. 2015.

"LostLettermen.com." *UCLA Bruins Football 1938 Roster.* Web. 22 Dec. 2015.
"LostLettermen.com." *UCLA Bruins Football 1939 Roster.* Web. 22 Dec. 2015.
"LostLettermen.com." *UCLA Bruins Football 1940 Roster.* Web. 28 Dec. 2015.
"LostLettermen.com." *USC Trojans Football 1941 Roster.* Web. 24 Dec. 2015.
"LostLettermen.com." *WSU Cougars Football 1941 Roster.* Web. 28 Dec. 2015.
"LostLettermen.com." *UCLA Bruins Football 1942 Roster.* Web. 30 Dec. 2015.
"LostLettermen.com." *UCLA Bruins Football 1943 Roster.* Web. 5 Jan. 2016.
"LostLettermen.com." *UCLA Bruins Football 1944 Roster.* Web. 6 Jan. 2016.
Lucas, Mike. "Lucas Looks Back: 1994 Rose Bowl." *RSS*, 29 Dec. 2010. Web. 07 Apr. 2016.
"Major Battle Erupts in the Ia Drang Valley." *History.com.* A&E Television Networks, Web. 09 Feb. 2016.
"Major King Events Chronology: 1929-1968." *Major King Events Chronology: 1929-1968.* Stanford University, Web. 11 Feb. 2016.
Malamud, Allan. "When the Heat Was On, Bruins Were Off : UCLA: A Field Temperature of 112 and a Crowd of 97,117 Take Their Toll in Loss to Tennessee." *Los Angeles Times.* Los Angeles Times, 15 Sept. 1991. Web. 05 Apr. 2016.
Manheim, James M. "Karl Dorrell Biography - Criticized Father's Study Habits, Guided Careers of Future Pro Players." *- Ucla, Coach, University, and Football.* Web. 22 Apr. 2016.
Maraniss, David. *When Pride Still Mattered: A Life of Vince Lombardi.* New York, NY: Simon & Schuster, 1999. Print.
Mariella, Rudi. "SANTA MONICA MIRROR." *Trojans vs. Bruins: A Los Angeles-Rotary Tradition.* 27 Nov. 2015. Web. 19 Apr. 2016.
Martinez, Michael. "Bruins Bring Faulk Down to Earth." *The New York Times.* The New York Times, 26 Sept. 1992. Web. 06 Apr. 2016.
Marvin, Joe. *The Sanders Era Ends.* pag. *Sports Library.* Web. 25 Jan. 2016.
Marvin, Joe. *The UCLA Bruins of 1954.* pag. *Sports Library.* Web. 22 Jan. 2016.
"Maryland Terrapins Football on Fanbase- 1955 Roster" *UCLA Bruins Football.* Web. 25 Jan. 2016.
"Mcubed.net : NCAAF Football : Series Records : UCLA vs. Illinois." *Mcubed.net : NCAAF Football : Series Records : UCLA vs. Illinois.* Web. 20 Jan. 2016.
Meister, Dick. "The Stanford Daily 21 May 1956 —The Stanford Daily." *The Stanford Daily 21 May 1956 —The Stanford Daily.* The Stanford Daily, 21 May 1965. Web. 26 Jan. 2016.
"Memories of The Catch: Texas vs UCLA 1970." *Barking Carnival.* SB Nation, 22 Sept. 2010. Web. 12 Feb. 2016.
"Miami vs. UCLA: 1998." *Hurricane Sports.* Web.
"Michigan Stadium Story." *Michigan Stadium Story.* Web. 04 Feb. 2016.
"Michigan State Spartans Football on Fanbase- 1965 Roster" *UCLA Bruins Football.* Web. 8 Feb. 2016.
Miller, Scott. "UCLA Simply Exercised Its Option : San Diego State: Bruins, Who Compiled 515 Yards on Offense, Were Surprised at Their Success on the Ground against the Nation's Worst Defense. 'We've Got to Learn to Make Football Plays,' Luginbill Says." *Los Angeles Times.* Los Angeles Times, 15 Oct. 1990. Web. 05 Apr. 2016.
Morales, Javier. "Arizona Wildcats Top 50 Football Games: No. 14 —UA Upsets No. 2 UCLA in 1980 When Bruins Appeared Ready to Be No. 1." *ALLSPORTSTUCSONcom*, 15 Aug. 2014. Web. 18 Mar. 2016.
Mortenson, Chris. "Carroll Likely to Replace Mora." *ESPN.* ESPN Internet Ventures, 9 Jan. 2010. Web. 09 May 2016.
Moura, Pedro. "The Top 10 Moments in the History of the USC-UCLA Rivalry." *ESPN.* ESPN Internet Ventures, 30 Nov. 2010. Web. 10 Feb. 2016.
Murray, James. "Red Sanders." *Red Sanders.* Sports Illustrated, 25 Aug. 1958. Web. 19 Jan. 2016.
Murray, Patrick. "This Week in Vols History: Tennessee vs. UCLA 1997." 14 Sept. 2013. Web. 18 Apr. 2016.

"National Football Foundation." Jerry Robinson. *Programs College Football Hall of Fame SearchDetail.* Web. 13 Apr. 2016.

"NCAA Football - Oregon State vs. Ucla." *NCAA Football - Oregon State vs. Ucla,* Web. 20 Apr. 2016.

"Nebraska vs. UCLA 1973 -- HuskerMax™." *Nebraska vs. UCLA 1973 -- HuskerMax™.* HuskerMax, Web. 16 Feb. 2016.

"Nebraska vs. UCLA 1987 -- HuskerMax™." *Nebraska vs. UCLA 1987 -- HuskerMax™.* 12 Sept. 1987. Web. 01 Apr. 2016.

"Nebraska vs UCLA 1993 -- HuskerMax™." *Nebraska vs UCLA 1993 -- HuskerMax™.* Web. 07 Apr. 2016.

"Neuheisel Says He Feels Vindicated By Settlement." *ESPN.* ESPN Internet Ventures, 8 Mar. 2005. Web. 02 May 2016.

"New Seahawks Coach Jim Mora Felt the Pull to Return Home." *The Seattle Times,* 26 July 2009. Web. 09 May 2016.

Neyer, Bon. "Coliseum's Dimensions Affected Play on the Field." *ESPN.* ESPN Internet Ventures, 29 Mar. 2008. Web. 01 Feb. 2016.

"No. 14 UCLA Football Defeats No. 21 Ohio St., 13–6." *Uclabruins.com.* N.p., 22 Sept. 2001. Web. 20 Apr. 2016.

"No. 17 UCLA 23, No. 3 Michigan 20." *ESPN.* ESPN Internet Ventures, Web. 20 Apr. 2016.

"No. 18 Washington Downed By UCLA." *GoHuskies.com,* 4 Oct. 2003. Web. 25 Apr. 2016.

"Northwestern Wildcats Football on Fanbase- 1947 Roster" Web. 13 Jan. 2016.

*Norwalk.* Hartford, CT: Connecticut Development Commission. *1976 Ohio State Football Roster.* Web.

Nowlin, Bill. "Doc Prothro." *Doc Prothro.* Society for American Baseball Research, Web. 08 Feb. 2016.

"Ohio Stadium | Home." *Ohio Stadium | Home.* Web. 04 Feb. 2016.

Ohio State's Greatest Drives - 1979 UCLA." *Ohio State's Greatest Drives - 1979 UCLA.* Buckeye 50, Web. 16 Mar. 2016.

"On-air Talent." *Maurice Jones-Drew.* NFL Network. Web. 27 Apr. 2016.

"Oregon Ducks Football on Fanbase- 1957 Roster" *UCLA Bruins Football.* Web. 28 Jan. 2016.

Park, Jack. *The Official Ohio State Football Encyclopedia.* Columbus, Ohio: Sports Pub., L.L.C., 2001. Print.

Parnell, W. Tracy. "Interactive Timeline of the Life of Lee Harvey Oswald." *Interactive Timeline of the Life of Lee Harvey Oswald.* Web. 05 Feb. 2016.

Patterson, Chip. "2015 College Football Hall of Fame Class Announced: The Snubs." *CBSSports.com,* 9 Jan. 2015. Web. 19 Apr. 2016.

"Paul Cameron FAQs, Biography And Facts." - *Fantasy Football Challenge.* Web. 31 Mar. 2016.

"Paul Cameron NFL Football Statistics | Pro-Football-Reference.com." *Pro-Football-Reference.com.* Web. 31 Mar. 2016.

"Penn State Football on Fanbase- 1964 Roster" *UCLA Bruins Football.* Web. 5 Feb. 2016.

Peter, Josh. "A Chip off the Granite Block." *Yahoo! Sports,* Yahoo!, 30 June 2009.

"Player Bio: Maurice Drew - UCLA Official Athletic Site." *Uclabruins.com.* Web. 27 Apr. 2016.

Polzin, Jim. "1999 Rose Bowl Replay: Ron Dayne Powers Badgers to Upset of UCLA." *Madison.com,* 29 Dec. 2012. Web.

Price, Brian. "From UCLA to NCIS: Mark Harmon Still the Quarterback." *Football Foundation,* 31 May 2011. Web. 16 Feb. 2016.

"Prothro Rests After Getting Cancer Treatment at UCLA." *Los Angeles Times.* Los Angeles Times, 04 May 1993. Web. 08 Feb. 2016.

Raley, Dan. "Where Are They Now: Bob Schloredt, Huskies QB." *Seattlepi.com.* Seattle Post, 19 July 2005. Web. 02 Feb. 2016.

Rank, Adam. "Forgotten Hero: Washington Broke NFL's Color Barrier in 1946." *NFL.com.* 17 Feb. 2012. Web. 09 Mar. 2016.

"Recaps." *UCLA 6, Illinois 3.* Sun Bowl. Web. 05 Apr. 2016.

"Recaps." *Wisconsin 21, UCLA 20.* Web. 20 Apr. 2016.

"Rev. Donn Moomaw Chastened by His Religion : Faith: Minister at Bel Air Presbyterian Was Still on Church Probation for Prior Sexual Misconduct When He Resigned in 1993." *Los Angeles Times*. Los Angeles Times, 16 Apr. 1995. Web. 25 Mar. 2016.

"Rick Neuheisel Biography." *UCLABruins.com*. Web.

Rifkin, Alan. "Meet Mr. Motivation." *Los Angeles Times*. Los Angeles Times, 11 Oct. 1998. Web. 11 Apr. 2016.

"RLR - Terry Donahue Biography." *RLR - Terry Donahue Biography*. Web. 11 Mar. 2016.

Robinson, Jackie, and Alfred Duckett. *I Never Had It Made*. New York: Putnam, 1972. Print.

Rodgers, Pepper, and Al Thomy. *Pepper!: The Autobiography of an Unconventional Coach*. Garden City, NY: Doubleday, 1976. Print.

"Rome 1960 Summer Olympics | Olympic Videos, Photos, News." *Rome 1960 Summer Olympics | Olympic Videos, Photos, News*. Olympics, Web. 03 Feb. 2016.

"Ronald Reagan: Chronology of the Shooting." *Doctor Zebra*. Web. 21 Mar. 2016.

"Rose Bowl Recall: The Victorious Thunderchickens." - *GoStanford.com*. Stanford Athletics, 31 Dec. 2012. Web. 16 Feb. 2016

Rosen, Daniel. "The Heisman, Lombardi and Real Estate: Gary Beban." *Blueprint Presented by CBRE Gary Beban The Heisman Lombardi and Real Estate Comments*, 15 Oct. 2015. Web. 12 Apr. 2016.

Rosen, Ron. "UCLA, Oklahoma, Houston Rated Big Winners in 1977 Football Recruiting." *Washington Post*. The Washington Post, 20 Apr. 1977. Web. 15 Mar. 2016.

Rosenberg, I.J. "Whatever Happened To . . . Pepper Rodgers." *My AJC*. Atlanta Journal Constitution, 9 May 2015. Web. 15 Feb. 2016.

Rosenberg, Jennifer. "Must-Know Facts About the Japanese Attack on Pearl Harbor." *About.com Education*. Web. 29 Dec. 2015.

Rosenberg, Jennifer. "What Happened During the Tet Offensive?" *About.com Education*. 20 Oct. 2015. Web. 11 Feb. 2016.

Saltveit, Mark. "Chip: Revealing the Man behind the Curtain." *Philadelphia Local News, Sports, Jobs, Cars, Homes - Philly.com*, 24 Sept. 2014.

Saltveit, Mark. *The Tao of Chip Kelly: Lessons from America's Most Innovative Coach*. New York: Diversion Books, 2013.

Sawyer, Tom. "A Brief Look at UCLA's Football Uniforms through the Years —Part 1: 1919-1921 . . ." *Southern Branch University of California Unofficial Notes on the Early Days of UCLA when She Went by a Different Name The Emphasis Here Is on Pre1955 Football*, 03 Mar. 2014. Web. 01 Mar. 2016

Sawyer, Tom. "A Thin Analysis of S.B.U.C.'s (UCLA's) First Football Game, Played October 3, 1919, against Manual Arts High School . . ." *Southern Branch University of California Unofficial Notes on the Early Days of UCLA when She Went by a Different Name The Emphasis Here Is on Pre1955 Football.*, 14 July 2014. Web. 11 Aug. 2015.

Saywyer, Tom. "Fred Cozens: S.B.U.C.'s 1919 Football Coach. He Was an Outstanding Coach, and His 2-and-8 Record during the 1919 Football Season Does Not Tell You Anything . . ." *Southern Branch University of California Unofficial Notes on the Early Days of UCLA when She Went by a Different Name The Emphasis Here Is on Pre1955 Football*, 29 June 2014. Web. 04 Aug. 2015.

Sawyer, Tom. "S.B.U.C.'s First Football Game: Manual Arts High School, Monday, October 3, 1919 -- "A Crowd Expected to Attend Game on Wilson Field" . . ." *Southern Branch University of California Unofficial Notes on the Early Days of UCLA when She Went by a Different Name The Emphasis Here Is on Pre1955 Football.* 14 July 2014. Web. 11 Aug. 2015.

Sawyer, Tom. "S.B.U.C. (UCLA) Football, Second Season (1920), First Game (October 2): S.B.U.C. 0, Pomona 41 . . ." *Southern Branch University of California Unofficial Notes on the Early Days of UCL Awhen She Went by a Different Name The Emphasis Here Is on Pre1955 Football.* 22 July 2014. Web. 19 Nov. 2015.

Sawyer, Tom. "Taking Another Look at S.B.U.C.'s 1920 Football Team . . ." *Southern Branch University of California Unofficial Notes on the Early Days of UCL Awhen She Went by a Different Name The Emphasis Here Is on Pre1955 Football*, 27 May 2014. Web. 19 Nov. 2015.

Schlabach, Mark. "Which Coaches Have the Hottest Seats?" *ESPN*. ESPN Internet Ventures, 11 Aug. 2011. Web. 06 May 2016.

"Sequoia High School Alumni Association." *Sequoia High School Alumni Association*. Web. 12 Apr. 2016.

Simers, T.J. "Brains & Brawn : The Only Dirt on UCLA's Jonathan Ogden Is What He Gets on His Uniform." *Los Angeles Times*. Los Angeles Times, 18 Apr. 1996. Web. 15 Apr. 2016.

Solomon, Jon. "Read It about JFK: How NFL and College Football Reacted to Assassination (links, Poll)." 22 Nov. 2013. Web. 05 Feb. 2016.

"Southern Campus." *Southern Campus*, 1924. Web. 01 Dec. 2015.

"Southern Campus : University of California (1868-1952). Southern Branch: *Archive*, 1925 Yearbook. Web. 01 Dec. 2015.

"Southern Campus : University of California (1868-1952). Southern Branch: *Archive*, 1926 Yearbook. Web. 01 Dec. 2015.

Southern Campus : University of California (1868-1952). Southern Branch: *Archive*. 1927 Yearbook. Web. 07 Dec. 2015.

Southern Campus : University of California (1868-1952). Southern Branch: *Archive*. 1928 Yearbook. Web. 07 Dec. 2015.

Southern Campus : University of California (1868-1952). Southern Branch: *Archive*. 1929 Yearbook. Web. 09 Dec. 2015.

Southern Campus : University of California (1868-1952). Southern Branch: *Archive*. 1930 Yearbook. Web. 10 Dec. 2015.

Southern Campus : University of California (1868-1952). Southern Branch: *Archive*. 1931 Yearbook. Web. 14 Dec. 2015.

Southern Campus : University of California (1868-1952). Southern Branch: *Archive*. 1932 Yearbook. Web. 15 Dec. 2015.

Southern Campus : University of California (1868-1952). Southern Branch: *Archive*. 1933 Yearbook. Web. 15 Dec. 2015.

Southern Campus : University of California (1868-1952). Southern Branch: *Archive*. 1934 Yearbook. Web. 16 Dec. 2015.

Southern Campus : University of California (1868-1952). Southern Branch: *Archive*. 1935 Yearbook. Web. 16 Dec. 2015.

Southern Campus : University of California (1868-1952). Southern Branch: *Archive*. 1936 Yearbook. Web. 16 Dec. 2015.

Southern Campus : University of California (1868-1952). Southern Branch: *Archive*. 1937 Yearbook. Web. 17 Dec. 2015.

Southern Campus : University of California (1868-1952). Southern Branch: *Archive*. 1938 Yearbook. Web. 21 Dec. 2015.

Southern Campus : University of California (1868-1952). Southern Branch: *Archive*. 1939 Yearbook. Web. 22 Dec. 2015.

Southern Campus : University of California (1868-1952). Southern Branch: *Archive*. 1940 Yearbook. Web. 24 Dec. 2015.

Southern Campus : University of California (1868-1952). Southern Branch: *Archive*. 1941 Yearbook. Web. 28 Dec. 2015.

Southern Campus : University of California (1868-1952). Southern Branch: *Archive*. 1942 Yearbook. Web. 29 Dec. 2015.

Southern Campus : University of California (1868-1952). Southern Branch: *Archive*. 1943 Yearbook. Web. 30 Dec. 2015.

Southern Campus : University of California (1868-1952). Southern Branch: *Archive*. 1944 Yearbook. Web. 5 Jan. 2016.

Southern Campus : University of California (1868-1952). Southern Branch: *Archive.* 1945 Yearbook. Web. 6 Jan. 2016.
Southern Campus : University of California (1868-1952). Southern Branch: *Archive.* 1946 Yearbook. Web. 11 Jan. 2016.
Southern Campus : University of California (1868-1952). Southern Branch: *Archive.* 1947 Yearbook. Web. 13 Jan. 2016.
Southern Campus : University of California (1868-1952). Southern Branch: *Archive.* 1948 Yearbook. Web. 13 Jan. 2016.
Southern Campus : University of California (1868-1952). Southern Branch: *Archive.* 1949 Yearbook. Web. 18 Jan. 2016.
Southern Campus : University of California (1868-1952). Southern Branch: *Archive.* 1950 Yearbook. Web. 19 Jan. 2016.
Southern Campus : University of California (1868-1952). Southern Branch: *Archive.* 1951 Yearbook. Web. 20 Jan. 2016.
Southern Campus : University of California (1868-1952). Southern Branch: *Archive.* 1952 Yearbook. Web. 21 Jan. 2016.
Southern Campus : University of California (1868-1952). Southern Branch: *Archive.* 1953 Yearbook. Web. 20 Jan. 2016.
Southern Campus : University of California (1868-1952). Southern Branch: *Archive.* 1954 Yearbook. Web. 21 Jan. 2016.
Southern Campus : University of California (1868-1952). Southern Branch: *Archive.* 1955 Yearbook. Web. 21 Jan. 2016.
Southern Campus : University of California (1868-1952). Southern Branch: *Archive.* 1956 Yearbook. Web. 25 Jan. 2016.
Southern Campus : University of California (1868-1952). Southern Branch: *Archive.* 1957 Yearbook. Web. 26 Jan. 2016.
Southern Campus : University of California (1868-1952). Southern Branch: *Archive.* 1958 Yearbook. Web. 28 Jan. 2016.
Southern Campus : University of California (1868-1952). Southern Branch: *Archive.* 1959 Yearbook. Web. 1 Feb. 2016.
Southern Campus : University of California (1868-1952). Southern Branch: *Archive.* 1960 Yearbook. Web. 2 Feb. 2016.
Southern Campus : University of California (1868-1952). Southern Branch: *Archive.* 1961 Yearbook. Web. 3 Feb. 2016.
Southern Campus : University of California (1868-1952). Southern Branch: *Archive.* 1962 Yearbook. Web. 4 Feb. 2016.
Southern Campus : University of California (1868-1952). Southern Branch: *Archive.* 1963 Yearbook. Web. 4 Feb. 2016.
Southern Campus : University of California (1868-1952). Southern Branch: *Archive.* 1964 Yearbook. Web. 5 Feb. 2016.
Southern Campus : University of California (1868-1952). Southern Branch: *Archive.* 1965 Yearbook. Web. 4 Feb. 2016.
Southern Campus : University of California (1868-1952). Southern Branch: *Archive.* 1966 Yearbook. Web. 9 Feb. 2016.
Southern Campus : University of California (1868-1952). Southern Branch: *Archive.* 1967 Yearbook. Web. 10 Feb. 2016.
Southern Campus : University of California (1868-1952). Southern Branch: *Archive.* 1968 Yearbook. Web. 10 Feb. 2016.

Southern Campus : University of California (1868-1952). Southern Branch: *Archive.* 1969 Yearbook. Web. 11 Feb. 2016.
Southern Campus : University of California (1868-1952). Southern Branch: *Archive.* 1970 Yearbook. Web. 12 Feb. 2016.
Southern Campus : University of California (1868-1952). Southern Branch: *Archive.* 1971 Yearbook. Web. 12 Feb. 2016.
Southern Campus : University of California (1868-1952). Southern Branch: *Archive.* 1972 Yearbook. Web. 16 Feb. 2016.
Southern Campus : University of California (1868-1952). Southern Branch: *Archive.* 1973 Yearbook. Web. 16 Feb. 2016.
Southern Campus : University of California (1868-1952). Southern Branch: *Archive.* 1974 Yearbook. Web. 16 Feb. 2016.
Southern Campus : University of California (1868-1952). Southern Branch: *Archive.* 1976 Yearbook. Web. 16 Feb. 2016.
Southern Campus : University of California (1868-1952). Southern Branch: *Archive.* 1979 Yearbook. Web. 16 Mar. 2016.
Southern Campus : University of California (1868-1952). Southern Branch: *Archive.* 1980 Yearbook. Web. 16 Mar. 2016.
Southern Campus : University of California (1868-1952). Southern Branch: *Archive.* 1982 Yearbook. Web. 21 Mar. 2016.
Southern Campus : University of California (1868-1952). Southern Branch: *Archive.* 1983 Yearbook. Web. 22 Mar. 2016.
Southern Campus : University of California (1868-1952). Southern Branch: *Archive.* 1984 Yearbook. Web. 23 Mar. 2016.
Southern Campus : University of California (1868-1952). Southern Branch: *Archive.* 1985 Yearbook. Web. 28 Mar. 2016.
Southern Campus : University of California (1868-1952). Southern Branch: *Archive.* 1987 Yearbook. Web. 30 Mar. 2016.
Southern Campus : University of California (1868-1952). Southern Branch: *Archive.* 1988 Yearbook. Web. 1 Apr. 2016.
Southern Campus : University of California (1868-1952). Southern Branch: *Archive.* 1990 Yearbook. Web. 4 Apr. 2016.
Southern Campus : University of California (1868-1952). Southern Branch: *Archive.* 1996 Yearbook. Web. 9 Apr. 2016.
Southern Campus : University of California (1868-1952). Southern Branch: *Archive.* 1998 Yearbook. Web. 18 Apr. 2016.
Southern Campus : University of California (1868-1952). Southern Branch: *Archive.* 1999 Yearbook. Web. 18 Apr. 2016.
Springer, Steve, and Michael Arkush. *60 Years of USC-UCLA Football.* Stamford, CT: Longmeadow, 1991. Print.
Springer, Steve. "END OF AN ERA: DONAHUE RESIGNS : Donahue Calls Screen Play : College Football: After 20 Years as UCLA's Head Football Coach, He Resigns to Become an Analyst for CBS." *Los Angeles Times.* Los Angeles Times, 12 Dec. 1995. Web. 11 Mar. 2016.
Springer, Steve. "UCLA Gives Miami a 31–8 Caning : College Football: Bruins Dominate in Almost Every Phase. Abdul-Jabbar Rushes for 180 Yards and Two Touchdowns." *Los Angeles Times.* Los Angeles Times, 03 Sept. 1995. Web. 08 Apr. 2016.
Staff Reports. Los Angeles Times. "Former UCLA Coach Horrell Dead at 89." 14 Mar. 1992. Web. 23 Dec. 2015.
"Stanford Indians Football on Fanbase- 1951 Roster" *UCLA Bruins Football.* Web. 20 Jan. 2016.

"Stanford Indians Football on Fanbase- 1953 Roster" *UCLA Bruins Football.* Web. 21 Jan. 2016.
Stephen, Eric. "USC vs. UCLA Football: Night Game A Rarity In Series History." *SB Nation Los Angeles*, 26 Nov. 2011. Web. 12 Feb. 2016.
"Stock Market Crash of 1929." *History.com.* A&E Television Networks. Web. 10 Dec. 2015.
"St. Petersburg Times - Google News Archive Search." *St. Petersburg Times - Google News Archive Search*, 2 Dec. 1938. Web. 23 Dec. 2015.
"STUNNING D-DAY FACTS." *AwesomeStories.com.* Web. 06 Jan. 2016.
"Syracuse University Athletics- Floyd Little" *RSS.* Web. 05 Feb. 2016.
*Tennessee Athletics HIstorical Rosters.* Web. <http://www.utsports.com/sports/m-footbl/archive/tenn-m-footbl-mtt-1937.html>.
"Tennessee Football Notes - UCLA Game." - *University of Tennessee Official Athletic Site.* Web. 07 Apr. 2016.
"Terry Donahue Coaching Record | College Football at Sports-Reference.com." *College Football at Sports-Reference.com.* Web. 11 Mar. 2016.
"Terry Donahue- Member Biography." *National Football Foundation.* 11 Mar. 2016. Web.
"Texas A&M vs. UCLA - Box Score - September 3, 2017." *ESPN*, ESPN Internet Ventures. Web. 04 Jan. 2018.
"TEXAS vs UCLA Bruins (Sep 12, 1998)." *TEXAS vs UCLA Bruins (Sep 12, 1998).* Web. 18 Apr. 2016.
"Texas vs UCLA (Sep 18, 1971)." *Texas vs UCLA (Sep 18, 1971).* Texas Sports, Web. 16 Feb. 2016.
"The Atomic Bombings of Hiroshima and Nagasaki." *Total Casualties.* Web. 12 Jan. 2016.
"The Biggest Upsets in KU Football History." *Rock Chalk Talk.* SB Nation, 17 Aug. 2015. Web. 16 Mar. 2016.
"The Cold War Museum." *Cold War Museum.* Web. 04 Apr. 2016.
"The Evening Independent - Google News Archive Search." *The Evening Independent.* Evening Independent, 15 Aug. 1958. Web. 19 Jan. 2016.
"The Gun That Killed Hitler: Walther PPK On The . . ." - *The Gun That Killed Hitler: Walther PPK On The . . .* Web. 12 Jan. 2016.
"The History Place - World War II in Europe Timeline." *The History Place - World War II in Europe Timeline.* Web. 17 Dec. 2015.
"The Milwaukee Journal - Google News Archive Search." *The Milwaukee Journal*, 14 Dec. 1948. Web. 11 Jan. 2016.
"The Official Website of Hall of Fame Broadcaster Vin Scully - Biography." *The Official Website of Hall of Fame Broadcaster Vin Scully - Biography.* Web. 20 Jan. 2016.
"The Simpson Trial Timeline." *The Simpson Trial Timeline.* Web. 07 Apr. 2016.
"The Vanderbilt Houses." *The Decorator and Furnisher* 12.2 (1888): 53–56. Web.
Three Bruins Named to All-Time All-Conf. Team." *Uclabruins.com*, 29 June 2011. Web. 13 Apr. 2016.
"Timeline of World War II: 1943." *Timeline of World War II: 1943.* Web. 05 Jan. 2016.
"Timelines." *Timeline of Korean War Events.* Web. 21 Jan. 2016.
"Tommy Prothro, 74, Football Coach." *The New York Times.* The New York Times, 14 May 1995. Web. 08 Feb. 2016.
"Top 5 Professional Football Players in Wall Street." *University Herald RSS.* 17 July 2013. Web. 19 Apr. 2016.
"Top News Stories from 1960." *Infoplease.* Web. 03 Feb. 2016.
"Trophy History and Design." *RSS.* Web. 16 Dec. 2015.
"Troy Aikman College Stats." *Sports-Reference.* Web. 8 Mar. 2016.
"Troy Aikman Had Interest From Mets; Say What?!" *Mets Merized Online*, 23 Jan. 2011. Web. 08 Mar. 2016.
"Troy Aikman NFL Football Statistics | Pro-Football-Reference.com." *Pro-Football-Reference.com.* Web. 08 Mar. 2016.
"TULANEGREENWAVE.COM - THE OFFICIAL ATHLETIC SITE OF TULANE UNIVERSITY." *Bob Toledo Bio.* Web. 11 Apr. 2016.
Tully, Jeff. "Burbank High School Burbank, California Class of 1967." *: BHS Hall of Fame Announced*, 6 July 2008. Web. 31 Mar. 2016.
"UCLA 38, Boise State 7." *Uclabruins.com.* Web. 19 Apr. 2016.

"UCLA's All-Time Olympians." *Uclabruins.com*. Web. 14 Aug. 2015.
"UCLA Athletics Hall of Fame." *Uclabruins.com*. Web. 03 Dec. 2015.
"UCLA Athletics. "UCLA Honors Jackie Robinson by Retiring #42 Across All Sports." *Uclabruins.com*, 22 Nov. 2014. Web. 28 Dec. 2015.
"UCLA Bruins Football on Fanbase- 1919 Roster" *UCLA Bruins Football.* Web. 1 Mar. 2016.
"UCLA Bruins Football on Fanbase- 1920 Roster" *UCLA Bruins Football.* Web. 1 Mar. 2016.
"UCLA Bruins Football on Fanbase- 1921 Roster" *UCLA Bruins Football.* Web. 1 Mar. 2016.
"UCLA Bruins Football on Fanbase- 1922 Roster" *UCLA Bruins Football.* Web. 1 Mar. 2016.
"UCLA Bruins Football on Fanbase- 1923 Roster" *UCLA Bruins Football.* Web. 1 Mar. 2016.
"UCLA Bruins Football on Fanbase- 1924 Roster" *UCLA Bruins Football.* Web. 1 Mar. 2016.
"UCLA Bruins Football on Fanbase- 1925 Roster" *UCLA Bruins Football.* Web. 1 Mar. 2016.
"UCLA Bruins Football on Fanbase- 1926 Roster" *UCLA Bruins Football.* Web. 1 Mar. 2016.
"UCLA Bruins Football on Fanbase- 1927 Roster" *UCLA Bruins Football.* Web. 1 Mar. 2016.
"UCLA Bruins Football on Fanbase- 1928 Roster" *UCLA Bruins Football.* Web. 1 Mar. 2016.
"UCLA Bruins Football on Fanbase- 1929 Roster" *UCLA Bruins Football.* Web. 1 Mar. 2016.
"UCLA Bruins Football on Fanbase- 1930 Roster" *UCLA Bruins Football.* Web. 1 Mar. 2016.
"UCLA Bruins Football on Fanbase- 1931 Roster" *UCLA Bruins Football.* Web. 1 Mar. 2016.
"UCLA Bruins Football on Fanbase- 1932 Roster" *UCLA Bruins Football.* Web. 1 Mar. 2016.
"UCLA Bruins Football on Fanbase- 1933 Roster" *UCLA Bruins Football.* Web. 1 Mar 2016.
"UCLA Bruins Football on Fanbase- 1934 Roster" *UCLA Bruins Football.* Web. 1 Mar 2016.
"UCLA Bruins Football on Fanbase- 1935 Roster" *UCLA Bruins Football.* Web. 1 Mar 2016.
"UCLA Bruins Football on Fanbase- 1936 Roster" *UCLA Bruins Football.* Web. 1 Mar 2016.
"UCLA Bruins Football on Fanbase- 1937 Roster" *UCLA Bruins Football.* Web. 1 Mar 2016.
"UCLA Bruins Football on Fanbase- 1938 Roster" *UCLA Bruins Football.* Web. 1 Mar 2016.
"UCLA Bruins Football on Fanbase- 1939 Roster" *UCLA Bruins Football.* Web. 1 Mar 2016.
"UCLA Bruins Football on Fanbase- 1940 Roster" *UCLA Bruins Football.* Web. 1 Mar 2016.
"UCLA Bruins Football on Fanbase- 1941 Roster" *UCLA Bruins Football.* Web. 1 Mar 2016.
"UCLA Bruins Football on Fanbase- 1942 Roster" *UCLA Bruins Football.* Web. 1 Mar 2016.
"UCLA Bruins Football on Fanbase- 1943 Roster" *UCLA Bruins Football.* Web. 1 Mar 2016.
"UCLA Bruins Football on Fanbase- 1944 Roster" *UCLA Bruins Football.* Web. 1 Mar 2016.
"UCLA Bruins Football on Fanbase- 1945 Roster" *UCLA Bruins Football.* Web. 1 Mar 2016.
"UCLA Bruins Football on Fanbase- 1946 Roster" *UCLA Bruins Football.* Web. 13 Jan. 2016.
"UCLA Bruins Football on Fanbase- 1947 Roster" *UCLA Bruins Football.* Web. 13 Jan. 2016.
"UCLA Bruins Football on Fanbase- 1950 Roster" *UCLA Bruins Football.* Web. 20 Jan. 2016.
"UCLA Bruins Football on Fanbase- 1951 Roster" *UCLA Bruins Football.* Web. 20 Jan. 2016.
"UCLA Bruins Football on Fanbase- 1952 Roster" *UCLA Bruins Football.* Web. 21 Jan. 2016.
"UCLA Bruins Football on Fanbase- 1953 Roster" *UCLA Bruins Football.* Web. 21 Jan. 2016.
"UCLA Bruins Football on Fanbase- 1954 Roster" *UCLA Bruins Football.* Web. 22 Jan. 2016.
"UCLA Bruins Football on Fanbase- 1955 Roster" *UCLA Bruins Football.* Web. 25 Jan. 2016.
"UCLA Bruins Football on Fanbase- 1956 Roster" *UCLA Bruins Football.* Web. 26 Jan. 2016.
"UCLA Bruins Football on Fanbase- 1957 Roster" *UCLA Bruins Football.* Web. 28 Jan. 2016.
"UCLA Bruins Football on Fanbase- 1958 Roster" *UCLA Bruins Football.* Web. 1 Feb. 2016.
"UCLA Bruins Football on Fanbase- 1959 Roster" *UCLA Bruins Football.* Web. 2 Feb. 2016.
"UCLA Bruins Football on Fanbase- 1960 Roster" *UCLA Bruins Football.* Web. 3 Feb. 2016.
"UCLA Bruins Football on Fanbase- 1961 Roster" *UCLA Bruins Football.* Web. 4 Feb. 2016.
"UCLA Bruins Football on Fanbase- 1962 Roster" *UCLA Bruins Football.* Web. 4 Feb. 2016.
"UCLA Bruins Football on Fanbase- 1963 Roster" *UCLA Bruins Football.* Web. 5 Feb. 2016.
"UCLA Bruins Football on Fanbase- 1964 Roster" *UCLA Bruins Football.* Web. 5 Feb. 2016.

"UCLA Bruins Football on Fanbase- 1965 Roster" *UCLA Bruins Football.* Web. 9 Feb. 2016.
"UCLA Bruins Football on Fanbase- 1966 Roster" *UCLA Bruins Football.* Web. 10 Feb. 2016.
"UCLA Bruins Football on Fanbase- 1967 Roster" *UCLA Bruins Football.* Web. 10 Feb. 2016.
"UCLA Bruins Football on Fanbase- 1968 Roster" *UCLA Bruins Football.* Web. 11 Feb. 2016.
"UCLA Bruins Football on Fanbase- 1969 Roster" *UCLA Bruins Football.* Web. 12 Feb. 2016.
"UCLA Bruins Football on Fanbase- 1970 Roster" *UCLA Bruins Football.* Web. 12 Feb. 2016.
"UCLA Bruins Football on Fanbase- 1971 Roster" *UCLA Bruins Football.* Web. 16 Feb. 2016.
"UCLA Bruins Football on Fanbase- 1972 Roster" *UCLA Bruins Football.* Web. 16 Feb. 2016.
"UCLA Bruins Football on Fanbase- 1973 Roster" *UCLA Bruins Football.* Web. 16 Feb. 2016.
"UCLA Bruins Football on Fanbase- 1974 Roster" *UCLA Bruins Football.* Web. 22 Feb. 2016.
"UCLA Bruins Football on Fanbase- 1975 Roster" *UCLA Bruins Football.* Web. 23 Feb. 2016.
"UCLA Bruins Football on Fanbase- 1976 Roster" *UCLA Bruins Football.* Web. Mar. 2016.
"UCLA Bruins Football on Fanbase- 1977 Roster" *UCLA Bruins Football.* Web. Mar. 2016.
"UCLA Bruins Football on Fanbase- 1978 Roster" *UCLA Bruins Football.* Web. Mar. 2016.
"UCLA Bruins Football on Fanbase- 1979 Roster" *UCLA Bruins Football.* Web. 12 Mar. 2016.
"UCLA Bruins Football on Fanbase- 1980 Roster" *UCLA Bruins Football.* Web. Mar. 2016.
"UCLA Bruins Football on Fanbase- 1981 Roster" *UCLA Bruins Football.* Web. Mar. 2016.
"UCLA Bruins Football on Fanbase- 1982 Roster" *UCLA Bruins Football.* Web. Mar. 2016.
"UCLA Bruins Football on Fanbase- 1983 Roster" *UCLA Bruins Football.* Web. Mar. 2016.
"UCLA Bruins Football on Fanbase- 1984 Roster" *UCLA Bruins Football.* Web. Mar. 2016.
"UCLA Bruins Football on Fanbase- 1985 Roster" *UCLA Bruins Football.* Web. Mar. 2016.
"UCLA Bruins Football on Fanbase- 1986 Roster" *UCLA Bruins Football.* Web. 28 Mar. 2016.
"UCLA Bruins Football on Fanbase- 1987 Roster" *UCLA Bruins Football.* Web. 28 Mar. 2016.
"UCLA Bruins Football on Fanbase- 1988 Roster" *UCLA Bruins Football.* Web. 28 Mar. 2016.
"UCLA Bruins Football on Fanbase- 1989 Roster" *UCLA Bruins Football.* Web. 28 Mar. 2016.
"UCLA Bruins Football on Fanbase- 1990 Roster" *UCLA Bruins Football.* Web. 28 Mar. 2016.
"UCLA Bruins Football on Fanbase- 1991 Roster" *UCLA Bruins Football.* Web. 28 Mar. 2016.
"UCLA Bruins Football on Fanbase- 1992 Roster" *UCLA Bruins Football.* Web. 28 Mar. 2016.
"UCLA Bruins Football on Fanbase- 1993 Roster" *UCLA Bruins Football.* Web. 28 Mar. 2016.
"UCLA Bruins Football on Fanbase- 1994 Roster" *UCLA Bruins Football.* Web. 28 Mar. 2016.
"UCLA Bruins Football on Fanbase- 1995 Roster" *UCLA Bruins Football.* Web. 29 Mar. 2016.
"UCLA Bruins Football on Fanbase- 1996 Roster" *UCLA Bruins Football.* Web. 29 Mar. 2016.
"UCLA Bruins Football on Fanbase- 1997 Roster" *UCLA Bruins Football.* Web. 29 Mar. 2016.
"UCLA Bruins Football on Fanbase- 1998 Roster" *UCLA Bruins Football.* Web. 29 Mar. 2016.
"UCLA Bruins Football on Fanbase- 1999 Roster" *UCLA Bruins Football.* Web. 29 Mar. 2016.
"UCLA BRUINS - Traditions." *Uclabruins.com.* Web. 01 Dec. 2015.
"UCLA Bruins vs. Alabama Crimson Tide 2001." *ESPN.* ESPN Internet Ventures, Web. 20 Apr. 2016.
"UCLA Bruins vs. Arizona State Sun Devils 2003." *ESPN.* ESPN Internet Ventures, Web. 25 Apr. 2016.
"UCLA Bruins vs. Arizona State Sun Devils 2004." *ESPN.* ESPN Internet Ventures, Web. 25 Apr. 2016.
"UCLA Bruins vs. Arizona State Sun Devils 2005." *ESPN.* ESPN Internet Ventures, Web. 26 Apr. 2016.
"UCLA Bruins vs. Arizona State Sun Devils 2008." *ESPN.* ESPN Internet Ventures, Web. 3 May. 2016.
"UCLA Bruins vs. Arizona State Sun Devils 2010." *ESPN.* ESPN Internet Ventures, Web. 5 May. 2016.
"UCLA Bruins vs. Arizona State Sun Devils 2011." *ESPN.* ESPN Internet Ventures, Web. 6 May. 2016.
"UCLA Bruins vs. Arizona State Sun Devils 2013." *ESPN.* ESPN Internet Ventures, Web. 11 May. 2016.
"UCLA Bruins vs. Arizona Wildcats 2003." *ESPN.* ESPN Internet Ventures, Web. 25 Apr. 2016.
"UCLA Bruins vs. Arizona Wildcats 2005." *ESPN.* ESPN Internet Ventures, Web. 26 Apr. 2016.
"UCLA Bruins vs. Arizona Wildcats 2008." *ESPN.* ESPN Internet Ventures, Web. 3 May. 2016.
"UCLA Bruins vs. Arizona Wildcats 2011." *ESPN.* ESPN Internet Ventures, Web. 6 May. 2016.

"UCLA Bruins vs. Arizona Wildcats 2012." *ESPN*. ESPN Internet Ventures, Web. 10 May. 2016.
"UCLA Bruins vs. Arizona Wildcats 2013." *ESPN*. ESPN Internet Ventures, Web. 11 May. 2016.
"UCLA Bruins vs. BYU Cougars 2007." *ESPN*. ESPN Internet Ventures, Web. 28 Apr. 2016.
"UCLA Bruins vs. BYU Cougars 2008." *ESPN*. ESPN Internet Ventures, Web. 3 May. 2016.
"UCLA Bruins vs. BYU Cougars 2015." *ESPN*. ESPN Internet Ventures, Web. 13 May. 2016.
"UCLA Bruins vs. California Golden Bears 2004." *ESPN*. ESPN Internet Ventures, Web. 25 Apr. 2016.
"UCLA Bruins vs. California Golden Bears 2005." *ESPN*. ESPN Internet Ventures, Web. 26 Apr. 2016.
"UCLA Bruins vs. California Golden Bears 2007." *ESPN*. ESPN Internet Ventures, Web. 28 Apr. 2016.
"UCLA Bruins vs. California Golden Bears 2010." *ESPN*. ESPN Internet Ventures, Web. 5 May. 2016.
"UCLA Bruins vs. California Golden Bears 2012." *ESPN*. ESPN Internet Ventures, Web. 10 May. 2016.
"UCLA Bruins vs. California Golden Bears 2014." *ESPN*. ESPN Internet Ventures, Web. 12 May. 2016.
"UCLA Bruins vs. Colorado Buffaloes 2003." *ESPN*. ESPN Internet Ventures, Web. 25 Apr. 2016.
"UCLA Bruins vs. Colorado Buffaloes 2003." *ESPN*. ESPN Internet Ventures, Web. 25 Apr. 2016.
"UCLA Bruins vs. Colorado Buffaloes 2012." *ESPN*. ESPN Internet Ventures, Web. 10 May. 2016.
"UCLA Bruins vs. Colorado Buffaloes 2015." *ESPN*. ESPN Internet Ventures, Web. 13 May. 2016.
"UCLA Bruins vs. Colorado State Rams 2002." *ESPN*. ESPN Internet Ventures, Web. 21 Apr. 2016.
"UCLA Bruins vs. Houston Cougars 2011." *ESPN*. ESPN Internet Ventures, Web. 6 May. 2016.
"UCLA Bruins vs. Kansas Jayhawks 2001." *ESPN*. ESPN Internet Ventures, Web. 20 Apr. 2016.
"UCLA Bruins vs. Kansas State Wildcats 2010." *ESPN*. ESPN Internet Ventures, Web. 5 May. 2016.
"UCLA Bruins vs. Memphis Tigers 2014." *ESPN*. ESPN Internet Ventures, Web. 12 May. 2016.
"UCLA Bruins vs. Nebraska Cornhuskers 2013." *ESPN*. ESPN Internet Ventures, Web. 11 May. 2016.
"UCLA Bruins vs. Nevada Wolfpack 2013." *ESPN*. ESPN Internet Ventures, Web. 11 May. 2016.
"UCLA Bruins vs. Northwestern Wildcats 2005." *ESPN*. ESPN Internet Ventures, Web. 26 Apr. 2016.
"UCLA Bruins vs. Notre Dame Fighting Irish 2006." *ESPN*. ESPN Internet Ventures, Web. 26 Apr. 2016.
"UCLA Bruins vs. Notre Dame Fighting Irish 2007." *ESPN*. ESPN Internet Ventures, Web. 28 Apr. 2016.
"UCLA Bruins vs. Oklahoma Sooners 2003." *ESPN*. ESPN Internet Ventures, Web. 25 Apr. 2016.
"UCLA Bruins vs. Oklahoma Sooners 2005." *ESPN*. ESPN Internet Ventures, Web. 26 Apr. 2016.
"UCLA Bruins vs. Oklahoma State Cowboys 2004." *ESPN*. ESPN Internet Ventures, Web. 25 Apr. 2016.
"UCLA Bruins vs. Oregon Ducks 2001." *ESPN*. ESPN Internet Ventures, Web. 20 Apr. 2016.
"UCLA Bruins vs. Oregon Ducks 2002." *ESPN*. ESPN Internet Ventures, Web. 21 Apr. 2016.
"UCLA Bruins vs. Oregon Ducks 2006." *ESPN*. ESPN Internet Ventures, Web. 26 Apr. 2016.
"UCLA Bruins vs. Oregon Ducks 2007." *ESPN*. ESPN Internet Ventures, Web. 26 Apr. 2016.
"UCLA Bruins vs. Oregon Ducks 2008." *ESPN*. ESPN Internet Ventures, Web. 3 May. 2016.
"UCLA Bruins vs. Oregon Ducks 2010." *ESPN*. ESPN Internet Ventures, Web. 5 May. 2016.
"UCLA Bruins vs. Oregon Ducks 2013." *ESPN*. ESPN Internet Ventures, Web. 11 May. 2016.
"UCLA Bruins vs. Oregon Ducks - Box Score - September 23, 2000." *Home*. Web. 20 Apr. 2016.
"UCLA Bruins vs. Oregon State Beavers 2005." *ESPN*. ESPN Internet Ventures, Web. 26 Apr. 2016.
"UCLA Bruins vs. Oregon State Beavers 2011." *ESPN*. ESPN Internet Ventures, Web. 6 May. 2016.
"UCLA Bruins vs. Oregon State Beavers 2012." *ESPN*. ESPN Internet Ventures, Web. 10 May. 2016.
"UCLA Bruins vs. Rice Owls 2005." *ESPN*. ESPN Internet Ventures, Web. 26 Apr. 2016.
"UCLA Bruins vs. San Diego State Aztecs 2005." *ESPN*. ESPN Internet Ventures, Web. 26 Apr. 2016.
"UCLA Bruins vs. San Diego State Aztecs 2009." *ESPN*. ESPN Internet Ventures, Web. 4 May. 2016.
"UCLA Bruins vs. Stanford Cardinal 2001." *ESPN*. ESPN Internet Ventures, Web. 20 Apr. 2016.
"UCLA Bruins vs. Stanford Cardinal 2006." *ESPN*. ESPN Internet Ventures, Web. 26 Apr. 2016.
"UCLA Bruins vs. Stanford Cardinal 2007." *ESPN*. ESPN Internet Ventures, Web. 26 Apr. 2016.
"UCLA Bruins vs. Stanford Cardinal 2009." *ESPN*. ESPN Internet Ventures, Web. 4 May. 2016.
"UCLA Bruins vs. Stanford Cardinal 2010." *ESPN*. ESPN Internet Ventures, Web. 5 May. 2016.
"UCLA Bruins vs. Stanford Cardinal 2011." *ESPN*. ESPN Internet Ventures, Web. 6 May. 2016.

"UCLA Bruins vs. Stanford Cardinal 2013." *ESPN*. ESPN Internet Ventures, Web. 11 May. 2016.
"UCLA Bruins vs. Stanford Cardinal 2014." *ESPN*. ESPN Internet Ventures, Web. 12 May. 2016.
"UCLA Bruins vs. Stanford Cardinal 2015." *ESPN*. ESPN Internet Ventures, Web. 13 May. 2016.
"UCLA Bruins vs. Stanford Cardinal Pac 12 Championship 2012." *ESPN*. ESPN Internet Ventures, Web. 10 May. 2016.
"UCLA Bruins vs. Tennessee Volunteers 2008." *ESPN*. ESPN Internet Ventures, Web. 3 May. 2016.
"UCLA Bruins vs. Tennessee Volunteers 2009." *ESPN*. ESPN Internet Ventures, Web. 4 May. 2016.
"UCLA Bruins vs. Texas Longhorns 2014." *ESPN*. ESPN Internet Ventures, Web. 12 May. 2016.
"UCLA Bruins vs. USC Trojans 2002." *ESPN*. ESPN Internet Ventures, Web. 21 Apr. 2016.
"UCLA Bruins vs. USC Trojans 2004." *ESPN*. ESPN Internet Ventures, Web. 25 Apr. 2016.
"UCLA Bruins vs. USC Trojans 2005." *ESPN*. ESPN Internet Ventures, Web. 26 Apr. 2016.
"UCLA Bruins vs. USC Trojans 2007." *ESPN*. ESPN Internet Ventures, Web. 28 Apr. 2016.
"UCLA Bruins vs. USC Trojans 2008." *ESPN*. ESPN Internet Ventures, Web. 3 May. 2016.
"UCLA Bruins vs. USC Trojans 2011." *ESPN*. ESPN Internet Ventures, Web. 6 May. 2016.
"UCLA Bruins vs. USC Trojans 2012." *ESPN*. ESPN Internet Ventures, Web. 10 May. 2016.
"UCLA Bruins vs. USC Trojans 2013." *ESPN*. ESPN Internet Ventures, Web. 11 May. 2016.
"UCLA Bruins vs. USC Trojans 2014." *ESPN*. ESPN Internet Ventures, Web. 12 May. 2016.
"UCLA Bruins vs. USC Trojans 2015." *ESPN*. ESPN Internet Ventures, Web. 13 May. 2016.
"UCLA Bruins vs. Utah Utes 2006." *ESPN*. ESPN Internet Ventures, Web. 26 Apr. 2016.
"UCLA Bruins vs. Utah Utes 2007." *ESPN*. ESPN Internet Ventures, Web. 28 Apr. 2016.
"UCLA Bruins vs. Utah Utes 2013." *ESPN*. ESPN Internet Ventures, Web. 11 May. 2016.
"UCLA Bruins vs. Utah Utes 2014." *ESPN*. ESPN Internet Ventures, Web. 12 May. 2016.
"UCLA Bruins vs. Virginia Cavaliers 2014." *ESPN*. ESPN Internet Ventures, Web. 12 May. 2016.
"UCLA Bruins vs. Virginia Cavaliers 2015." *ESPN*. ESPN Internet Ventures, Web. 13 May. 2016.
"UCLA Bruins vs. Washington Huskies 2004." *ESPN*. ESPN Internet Ventures, Web. 25 Apr. 2016.
"UCLA Bruins vs. Washington Huskies 2013." *ESPN*. ESPN Internet Ventures, Web. 11 May. 2016.
"UCLA Bruins vs. Washington State Cougars 2011." *ESPN*. ESPN Internet Ventures, Web. 6 May. 2016.
"UCLA Bruins vs. Washington State Cougars 2015." *ESPN*. ESPN Internet Ventures, Web. 13 May. 2016.
"UCLA Celebrates Jackie Robinson Day." *Uclabruins.com*. 15 Apr. 2014. Web. 25 Feb. 2016.
"UCLA Depth Chart 1998." *Uclabruins.com*. Web. 29 Mar. 2016.
"UCLA Depth Chart 1999." *Uclabruins.com*. Web. 29 Mar. 2016.
"UCLA Depth Chart 2002." *Uclabruins.com*. Web. 30 Mar. 2016.
"UCLA Drafted Players/Alumni | Pro-Football-Reference.com." *Pro-Football-Reference.com*. Web. 26 Feb. 2016.
"U.C.L.A. Fires Toledo As Football Coach." *The New York Times*. The New York Times, 09 Dec. 2002. Web. 21 Apr. 2016.
"UCLA Football Roster 2003." *Uclabruins.com*. Web. 30 Mar. 2016.
"UCLA Football Roster 2004." *Uclabruins.com*. Web. 30 Mar. 2016.
"UCLA Football Roster 2005." *Uclabruins.com*. Web. 30 Mar. 2016.
"UCLA Football Roster 2006." *Uclabruins.com*. Web. 30 Mar. 2016.
"UCLA Football Roster 2007." *Uclabruins.com*. Web. 30 Mar. 2016.
"UCLA Football Roster 2008." *Uclabruins.com*. Web. 30 Mar. 2016.
"UCLA Football Roster 2009." *Uclabruins.com*. Web. 30 Mar. 2016.
"UCLA Football Roster 2010." *Uclabruins.com*. Web. 30 Mar. 2016.
"UCLA Football Roster 2011." *Uclabruins.com*. Web. 30 Mar. 2016.
"UCLA Football Roster 2012." *Uclabruins.com*. Web. 30 Mar. 2016.
"UCLA Football Roster 2013." *Uclabruins.com*. Web. 30 Mar. 2016.
"UCLA Football Roster 2014." *Uclabruins.com*. Web. 30 Mar. 2016.
"UCLA Football Roster 2015." *Uclabruins.com*. Web. 30 Mar. 2016.

"UCLA History - UCLA Alumni." *UCLA Alumni*. Web. 10 Dec. 2015.

UCLA Library- Digital Collection, 7 photos. Creative Commons Attribution 4.0, International License. Publisher: Media Guides, 2005, 2011, 2013, 2014.

UCLA Library- Digital Collection, 41 photos. Creative Commons Attribution 4.0, International License. Publisher: UCLA Yearbooks, 1920-2000.

"UCLA Official Athletic Site - Football- Cade McNown 1997." *Uclabruins.com*. Web. 18 Apr. 2016.

"UCLA Players/Alumni | Pro-Football-Reference.com." *Pro-Football-Reference.com*. Web. 22 Apr. 2016.

"UCLA Record Book." UCLA Athletics, Web.

"UCLA: The First Century." *Google Books*. Web. 26 Jan. 2016.

"UCLA vs Pittsburgh Series." *History*. . Web. 05 Feb. 2016.

"UCLA vs Texas (Oct 3, 1970)." *UCLA vs Texas (Oct 3, 1970)*. Texas Sports Stats, Web. 12 Feb. 2016.

"U.C.L.A. TROUNCES STANFORD." *The New York Times*. The New York Times, 03 Oct. 1987. Web. 01 Apr. 2016.

"UCLA-Washington Postgame Notes." *Uclabruins.com*. Web. 20 Apr. 2016.

"UCLA Year by Year Schedules and Results." UCLA Athletics, Web.

"Underdog Kansas Flattens UCLA (September 24, 1978)." *September 24, 1978*. The Chicago Tribune, 24 Sept. 1978. Web. 16 Mar. 2016.

"USC Trojans Football on Fanbase- 1947 Roster" Web. 13 Jan. 2016.

"USC Trojans Football on Fanbase- 1952 Roster" *UCLA Bruins Football*. Web. 21 Jan. 2016.

"USC-UCLA, 10 Years Ago." *Los Angeles Times*. Los Angeles Times, 26 Nov. 2009. Web. 19 Apr. 2016.

"Varsity Days: 1969 Stanford Football." *Pac-12*. Web. 12 Feb. 2016.

Vertuno, Jim. "UCLA's 66–3 Romp over Texas in 1997 Was Staggering." *Washington Times*. The Washington Times, 21 Sept. 2010. Web. 18 Apr. 2016.

"Vietnam War Timeline." *Vietnam War Timeline*. Modern American Poetry, Web. 09 Feb. 2016.

"Wabash Athletics History." *RSS*. Web. 03 Dec. 2015.

Wagoner, Nick. "The Legacy of Kenny Washington." *News RSS*, 15 Feb. 2013. Web. 09 Mar. 2016.

Wang, Jack. "Former UCLA Football Coach Terry Donahue: 'I Quit Too Early.'" *Former UCLA Football Coach Terry Donahue: 'I Quit Too Early.'* Los Angeles Daily News, 25 Nov. 2015. Web. 11 Mar. 2016.

Wesseling, Chris. "Maurice Jones-Drew Trades Family for UCLA Campus Life." *NFL.com*, 22 Mar. 2013. Web. 27 Apr. 2016.

Wharton, David. "Five More Charged in Parking Scandal." *Los Angeles Times*. Los Angeles Times, 14 Sept. 1999. Web. 19 Apr. 2016.

Wharton, David. "In Chip Kelly, UCLA Gets Coach Who 'Revolutionized' College Football." *Los Angeles Times*, Los Angeles Times, 25 Nov. 2017.

Wharton, David. "The Hard Knock on Rick Neuheisel." *Los Angeles Times*. Los Angeles Times, 24 Aug. 2003. Web. 02 May 2016.

"Wheaties' Endorsement Standards Were Much Lower Back in Bert LaBrucherie's Day." *Blog into Mystery*, 25 May 2012. Web. 11 Jan. 2016.

"When Carcajous Attack!: UCLA's 1982 Defense: Big Plays and a Sack of Roses." *When Carcajous Attack!: UCLA's 1982 Defense: Big Plays and a Sack of Roses*, 7 July 2009. Web. 22 Mar. 2016.

Whicker, Mark. "Gary Beban Helped UCLA Make History 50 Years Ago." *Gary Beban Helped UCLA Make History 50 Years Ago*. Daily News, 24 Nov. 2015. Web. 12 Apr. 2016.

White, Lonnie. "THE RIVALRY / UCLA vs. USC." *Los Angeles Times*. Los Angeles Times, 19 Nov. 2003. Web. 22 Feb. 2016.

Willbanks, James H. "Shock and Awe of Tet Offensive Shattered US Illusions." *UW News*, 29 Jan. 2009. Web. 11 Jan. 2016.

"William F. Barnes." *Project Gutenburg Self-Publishing Press*. Web. <http://www.gutenberg.us/articles/Alamo_Scouts>.

"William F. Barnes." *Project Gutenburg Self-Publishing Press.* Web. <http://www.gutenberg.us/articles/william_f._barnes>.
Wilner, Barry. "Ogden 1st of Class of 2013 to Enter Hall of Fame." *Washington Times.* The Washington Times, 3 Aug. 2013. Web. 15 Apr. 2016.
Wojciechowski, Gene. "COLLEGE FOOTBALL : Bruins' Run Didn't Surprise Anyone : UCLA: Oregon Defenders Were Waiting for Abdul-Jabbar behind Ogden on Final Play, and They Stopped Him." *Los Angeles Times.* Los Angeles Times, 17 Sept. 1995. Web. 08 Apr. 2016.
"World War II: Timeline." *United States Holocaust Memorial Museum.* United States Holocaust Memorial Council, 18 Aug. 2015. Web. 29 Dec. 2015.
Yoon, Peter. "10 Suspended After UCLA-Arizona Brawl." *ESPN.* ESPN Internet Ventures, 22 Oct. 2011. Web. 06 May 2016.
Yoon, Peter. "UCLA Bruins to Hire Jim L. Mora." *ESPN.* ESPN Internet Ventures, 13 Dec. 2011. Web. 09 May 2016.
Yoon, Peter. "UCLA Rivalry Moment No. 2: Hicks Works Double Overtime." *ESPN.* ESPN Internet Ventures, 30 Nov. 2010. Web. 12 Apr. 2016.
Yoon, Peter. "UCLA Rivalry Moment Number 3: Barnes Walks Into History." *ESPN.* ESPN Internet Ventures, 10 Nov. 2010. Web. 06 Apr. 2016.
Yoon, Peter. "UCLA Rivalry Moment Number 5: The Streak." *ESPN.* ESPN Internet Ventures, 3 Dec. 2010. Web. 08 Apr. 2016.
Zhe, Mike. "Kelly Is Mastermind Behind UNH Football's Potent Offensive Attack."*Seacoastonline.com*, Seacoastonline.com, 16 Dec. 2010.
Zylius, Steve. "A UCLA 'Fairy Tale' That Came True." *The Orange County Register*, 2 Dec. 2008. Web. 06 Apr. 2016.